Professional PHP5

Professional PHP5

Ed Lecky-Thompson
Heow Eide-Goodman
Steven D. Nowicki
Alec Cove

Wiley Publishing, Inc.

Professional PHP5

Published by
Wiley Publishing, Inc.
10475 Crosspoint Boulevard
Indianapolis, IN 46256
www.wiley.com

Published simultaneously in Canada

For general information on our other products and services please contact our Customer Care Department within the United States at (800) 762-2974, outside the United States at (317) 572-3993 or fax (317) 572-4002.

Wiley also publishes its books in a variety of electronic formats. Some content that appears in print may not be available in electronic books.

ISBN: 0-7645-7282-2

Printed in the United States of America

10 9 8 7 6 5 4 3 2 1

About the Authors

Ed Lecky-Thompson

Ed Lecky-Thompson is the founder of Ashridge New Media, a professional new media technology consultancy based just outside London, England. Not content with the daily thrill of tax forms and payroll, he still gets involved at a hands-on level with all the company's projects and describes himself as "utterly obsessed with PHP," an obsession that shines through in the business, which works almost exclusively in the language. Ed has more than six years' experience in commercial software development and enterprise-level systems architecture across a myriad of platforms, with particularly strong exposure to open source technologies such as PHP and PERL on the languages front, and Linux and BSD on the systems front. Ed usually spends his spare time driving far too quickly through the English countryside.

Heow Eide-Goodman

Heow Eide-Goodman is a member of NYPHP and LispNYC who uses PHP in his day job to do Web sites, services, and back-office transformations among SQL Server, Interbase/Firebird, and MySQL.

Steven D. Nowicki

Steven D. Nowicki is Director of Software development at The Content Project, a Santa Monica, California–based consulting firm currently developing a massive enterprise resource planning and contact management system comprising more than 300,000 lines of OO PHP code. He has a decade of experience in large-scale software development and system architecture on all major platforms.

Alec Cove

Alec Cove has more than 10 years of software engineering and Web development experience. Before starting his own consulting practice, Alec was senior software architect at <kpe> in New York City, where he designed enterprise software and Web services for Fortune 100 companies. His interests include object-oriented design and architecture, design patterns, and genetic programming. When he's not programming he likes to play guitar, write music, and explore New York City on bicycle. For more information go to `www.cove.org`.

Credits

Acquisitions Editor
Debra Williams Cauley

Development Editor
Sharon Nash

Technical Editor
Michael Southwell

Copy Editor
Susan Christophersen

Editorial Manager
Kathryn Malm Bourgoine

Vice President & Executive Group Publisher
Richard Swadley

Vice President and Publisher
Joseph B. Wikert

Indexer
Johnna VanHoose Dinse

Contents

Introduction xix

Part I: Object-Oriented Software Development Concepts 1

Chapter 1: Introduction to Object-Oriented Programming 3

What Is Object-Oriented Programming? 3
OOP advantages 4
A real-world example 4
Understanding OOP Concepts 5
Classes 6
Objects 6
Inheritance 15
Interfaces 24
Encapsulation 27
Changes to OO in PHP5 28
Summary 29

Chapter 2: Unified Modeling Language (UML) 31

Requirements Gathering 31
Interviewing the Client 32
Use Case Diagrams 32
Class Diagrams 35
Modeling the Domain 35
Relationships 36
Implementation 39
Activity Diagrams 42
Sequence Diagrams 42
State Diagrams 45
Component and Deployment Diagrams 46
Summary 47

Chapter 3: Putting Objects to Work 49

Creating the Contact Manager 49
The Contact Manager UML Diagrams 50
The PropertyObject Class 54
The Contact Type Classes 56
The DataManager Class 60
The Entity, Individual, and Organization Classes 62
Making Use of the System 70
Summary 72

Chapter 4: Design Patterns 73

The Composite Pattern 73
Implementation 75
Considerations 79
The Observer Pattern 80
Widgets 80
Considerations 86
The Decorator Pattern 86
Implementation 88
Using the Decorator 89
Considerations 91
The Facade Pattern 92
The Builder Pattern 93
Implementation 94
Considerations 97
Summary 97

Part II: Creating a Reusable Object Toolkit I: Simple Utility Classes and Interfaces 99

Chapter 5: Collection Class 101

Purpose of the Collection Class 101
Designing the Collection Class 102
Collection Class Basics 103
The addItem Method 104
The getItem and removeItem Methods 105
Other Methods 105
Using the Collection Class 106

Implementing Lazy Instantiation **107**
Callbacks 108
The setLoadCallback Method in the Collection Class 112
Using the Collection Class **116**
Improving the Collection Class **122**
Summary **123**

Chapter 6: CollectionIterator Class **125**

The Iterator Interface **125**
The CollectionIterator Class 127
The IteratorAggregate Interface **129**
Protecting the Iterator's Contents by Using the clone Operator **130**
Summary **132**

Chapter 7: GenericObject Class **133**

The GenericObject Class **133**
When to Use GenericObject 134
What GenericObject Allows You to Do 134
Assessing Suitability for Implementation 135
Typical GenericObject Implementation 136
Meet the Parent 138
GenericObject Database Connectivity 141
GenericObject Methods and Properties 143
Benefits of GenericObject 146
The GenericObjectCollection Class **146**
Traditional Implementation 147
Where the Traditional Implementation Fails 148
Principles behind GenericObjectCollection 149
Meet the Code 149
Typical GenericObjectCollection Implementation 152
Try It 153
How It Works 153
GenericObjectCollection Summary 155
Summary **156**

Chapter 8: Database Abstraction Layers **157**

What Is a Database Abstraction Layer? **158**
A Simple Implementation **158**
The Configuration File 158
Establishing a Connection 159

Selecting Information 159
Altering Information 160
Using the Database class 162
Introducing PEAR DB **164**
Connecting to a Database Using DB 165
Retrieving Information 166
Other Useful Functions 168
Getting More Information 170
The Complete Database Abstraction Layer **170**
Transaction Support 174
The Singleton Design Pattern 175
Summary **178**

Chapter 9: Factory Interface **179**

Factory Method Design Pattern **179**
Factory Interface Example **180**
The Old School Approach 180
The Factory Interface Approach 181
Using the Factory Interface in Database Abstraction 182
Multiple Factories **184**
Leveraging Existing Classes **185**
Summary **186**

Chapter 10: Event-Driven Programming **187**

What Are Events? **187**
Using OOP to Handle Events **188**
Designing an event-driven solution 189
Implementing the solution 191
Implementing security 195
Pause for Thought 198
Summary **198**

Chapter 11: Logging and Debugging **201**

Creating a Logging Mechanism **201**
Simple File Logging 201
Example File System Layout 202
The Logger Class 203
Extending the Logger Class 207
Creating a Debugging Mechanism **217**
Summary **221**

Chapter 12: SOAP **223**

SOAP and PHP5 **223**
The PHP5 SOAP Extension 224
Making a SOAP Client **227**
Under the Hood 230
Exception Handling in the SOAP Client 234
Making a SOAP Server **235**
Summary **237**

Part III: Creating a Reusable Object Toolkit II: Complex (Though Not Complicated) Utilities **239**

Chapter 13: Model, View, Controller (MVC) **241**

Introducing MVC **241**
The Model 242
The View 242
The Controller 243
The Infrastructure 243
MVC in Web Applications 243
MVC in PHP 243
The MVC Mini Toolkit **245**
Introducing the Toolkit 246
Using the Toolkit 258
The Toolkit in the Wild 265
True Templating **265**
Recapping Native PHP Templating 266
The Pitfalls of Native Templating 266
True Templating with Smarty Templates 266
Installing Smarty 267
Using Smarty 268
Advanced Smarty 273
When to Use Smarty vs. Traditional Templating 275
Summary **275**

Chapter 14: Communicating with Users **277**

Why Communicate? **277**
Reasons to Communicate with Users 278
Think Outside the Web Browser 280

Types of Communication **280**
All communications have . . . 280
Not all communications have . . . 280
What about Recipients? 281
Communication As a Class Hierarchy **281**
The Recipient Class: A quick Test of OOP-Like Thinking 281
The Communication Class 285
E-mailing Your Users **286**
Building a Test Version 287
Getting the Message Across 290
Being Smart with Templates 296
Using MIME 298
Other Communication Subclasses **298**
SMS Text Messaging 298
Fax 299
Summary **299**

Chapter 15: Sessions and Authentication **301**

Introduction to Sessions **301**
A Brief Recap on How HTTP Works 302
Definition of a Session 304
Perpetuation of a Session 304
Session Security 307
How PHP Implements Sessions **312**
Basic PHP Sessions 312
Limitations of Basic PHP Sessions 315
Creating an Authentication Class **316**
Connecting PHP Session Management to a Database 316
Introducing the UserSession Class 317
Database Schema 317
The Code: usersession.phpm 318
The Code: Testing the UserSession Class 322
How It Works: The UserSession Class 326
Putting It All Together 328
Summary **328**

Chapter 16: Unit Testing Framework **329**

Methodology and Terminology **329**
Designing the Interface of Your Class 330
Creating a Test Suite for Your Class 331

Writing the Implementation of Your Class 332
The Second Run 332
Introduction to PHPUnit 332
Installing PHPUnit 333
Using PHPUnit 333
Test Cases 333
The Test Suite 336
Why Bother? 337
Regression Testing 337
Framework Usability 337
Demonstrable Quality Assurance 338
Reducing the Burden of Functional Testing 338
A Real-World Example 338
Summary 343

Chapter 17: Finite State Machine and Custom Configuration Files 345

Introducing the Finite State Machine 346
A Simple FSM: The RPN Calculator 346
Theoretical Implementation of FSMs 348
Implementing FSMs in PHP 348
Disassembling the RPN Calculator Example 350
Real-World Examples of FSMs 353
Custom Configuration Files 354
Using PHP 354
Using XML 355
Using INI Files 355
The Config PEAR Class 357
Configuration File Best Practice 358
Summary 359

Part IV: Test Case: Sales Force Automation 361

Chapter 18: Project Overview 363

Widget World 363
The Widget World Landscape 364
The Technical Layer 365
The Financial Layer 366
The Political Layer 366
You 366
Is It Really about Technology? 366

The Development Approach **367**
What Does This Mean to Me? 368
The Technology 370
Summary **370**

Chapter 19: Project Management Methodologies **371**

Do Your Homework **371**
Why Is the Project Happening? 372
Who Is the Project For? 372
What Is the History of the Project? 373
What Are the Anticipated Prerequisites of the Project? 374
Receiving the Formal Brief **374**
Business Requirements 375
Scope 376
Timelines 377
Budget 378
Commercial Terms 380
Future Plans 380
Look and Feel 381
Technology 381
Support 381
What Now? 382
Constructing the Pitch **382**
Pitches versus Quotes 382
Pitches versus Specifications 383
Who to Involve When Pitching 383
When to Go the Extra Mile 384
When to Say No 384
Structuring the Pitch 385
Choosing Your People **386**
Project Manager 386
Account Manager 387
Lead Architect 387
Software Architects and Engineers 388
Client Side Developers 388
Senior Designers 388
Studio Artists 388
Doubling Up of Roles 389
Working Practices 389
Your Client's Role 389
Summary **389**

Chapter 20: Planning the System 391

Choosing a Process 391
The Waterfall Process 391
The Spiral Process 392
Making the Decision 393
Common Process Practices 394
Specification Phase 394
Design Phase 396
Build Phase 398
Testing Phase 398
Handover 399
Programming Methodologies and Practices 399
Test-Driven Development 399
eXtreme Programming 400
Change Management 402
Specification Revisions 402
Specification Changes That Arise after Sign-Off 403
Disputes Arising from Differences in Interpretation 403
Bugs Reported by the Client 403
Summary 404

Chapter 21: Systems Architecture 405

What Is Systems Architecture? 405
Why Is It Important? 405
What Needs Doing? 406
Effectively Translating Requirements 407
Hosting, Connectivity, Servers, and Network 407
Redundancy and Resilience 408
Maintenance 408
Security 408
Designing the Environment 409
Hosting and Connectivity 409
Calculating CIR 409
Servers 411
Network 413
Redundant Storage 414
Maintenance 414
Security 414
Summary 415

Chapter 22: Assembling the Sales Force Automation Toolkit 417

Starting the Project: Monday 417
Getting an Earful 418
Story Weight Estimation 420
Release Planning 426
Starting the Work 427
Outlining Details of Story 9 427
Writing Tests 428
PhpUnit 429
Creating the login screen 436
The Next Story 440
Re-Estimation 450
Cleaning Up 451
Refactoring Code 452
Finishing the Iteration 459
Story 14: Changing the Week Recalls a Previous Week 459
Story 15: Per-Week Items on the Customer Contact Report 460
Travel Expense Report 468
Travel Expense Item 471
Travel Expense Week 473
The Spike 476
More Travel Expense Week Tests 477
Satisifying the Travel Expense Week Tests 480
The Finalized Travel Expense Report 492
Mock Objects 506
Summary 511

Chapter 23: Quality Assurance 513

Introduction to QA 513
Why You Should Aim High 514
What Is Quality? 515
Measurable and Quantifiable Quality 515
Testing 518
Unit Testing 518
Functional Testing 519
Load Testing 520
Usability Testing 520
Fault Tracking 521
Effective Fault Management Using Mantis 522
Getting the Most Out of Mantis 529
Summary 529

Chapter 24: Deployment **531**

Devising Development Environments **531**
The Studio Development Environment 531
The Studio Staging Environment 532
The Live Staging Environment 533
The Live Production Environment 534
Development Databases 534
The Deployment Workflow **536**
Automated Version Control Repository Extraction 537
Using rsync 538
Keeping Servers in Sync with rsync 540
Summary **541**

Chapter 25: Designing and Developing a Robust Reporting Platform **1**

Introduction to Working Data **1**
Understanding Your Client's Needs 2
Managing Your Client 2
Report Deliverables 3
Designing a Report 4
Report Generation Architecture **7**
The Offline Approach 9
The Reports Interface 10
The New Report Interface 11
The Report Processor Script 15
The Process 16
The Report Handler Scripts 17
The My Reports Page 18
The Report Translator Scripts 19
Example Usage of the Reports Engine 21
Visualizations 21
Summary **22**

Chapter 26: Where Do You Go from Here? **565**

Motivation **565**
Your Career As a Developer **566**
More Than Web Development Skills 566
Soft Skills 566
Academic Skills 567
Community Skills 567
Summary **567**

Appendix A: Why Version Control Is a Good Thing 569
Appendix B: PHP IDEs 583
Appendix C: Performance Tuning PHP 599
Appendix D: Best Practice PHP Installation 609
Index 621

Introduction

Professional PHP5 was written for PHP developers who are interested in expanding and leveraging their development skills by utilizing the features of PHP5. This demographic is not set in stone, of course, because professional-level C++ and Java developers should catch on quickly. However, inexperienced PHP developers are highly encouraged to start with *Beginning PHP5* by Wrox.

What Does This Book Cover?

This book aims to go beyond mere syntax and the how's of PHP software development and is designed to help you deliver better quality software in a shorter amount of time. Much of what you'll learn, although written with PHP5 in mind, is not limited to the PHP language. Many of the development techniques are directly translatable into other traditional high-level languages, and the skills you'll learn will follow you the rest of your career.

PHP5 is also a very dynamic language—in terms of utility, that is—and suited for much more than Web development. Here you'll learn about using PHP5 as a Web service, general-purpose development language, and command-line scripting tool.

Who Is This Book For?

This book covers some advanced techniques in PHP, so we assume that you have a solid grounding in the basics of PHP application development. You don't necessarily have to be familiar with PHP5 to get started, however. If you've been working in PHP4 until the recent launch of version 5, you'll be fine. Throughout the book, we've made sure that the differences between PHP5 and PHP4 are highlighted prominently.

To sum it up in two words, we assume that you have what might be called a working knowledge of PHP. If you have that and are eager to learn how you can take PHP to the next level in your Web projects, this book is for you.

You might be a professional Web developer for a big software company. Your company may have been working in PHP for years, but maybe it's eager to take the first steps away from ASP, Java, and other Web development platforms in an effort to discover the benefits of PHP.

You may be a lone (or almost lone) Web professional in an otherwise nontechnical company, assigned the task of implementing some huge project—perhaps a staff intranet or new corporate Web presence—who is looking for an appropriate development platform.

You may just be curious. Perhaps you're a student in university or college who's eager to supplement what you're learning in school with some professional code and project-management techniques plucked straight from the world of commercial Web development.

You might have a background in C++ or Java and have heard good things about PHP5 and how its new OOP support takes it one step closer to being a truly credible professional Web development environment. Perhaps you're skeptical and want to see whether what you've heard is true.

Whoever you are, as long as you know the basics of PHP and are eager to learn a whole lot more from people who not only know PHP inside and out but also love using it, then this book is for you.

What You Need to Use This Book

Here's the minimum that you'll need to get the most from this book:

- A development workstation, running either Windows or Linux with a basic text editor or development environment of your choice, and a Web browser to try the examples.
- A development server running PHP, which needs to be configured roughly in line with the setup detailed in Appendix D.
- A network connection between the two.

Ideally, you should try to secure the following:

- An Internet connection—there are lots of URLs scattered throughout this book, and you'll need an Internet connection to go see them.
- Lots of free time!

How Is This Book Structured?

This section outlines the structure of the book. Check the table of contents for more detail. Although you should feel free to dip in and out of the chapters to get information on a topic as and when you need it, if you're not familiar with object-oriented development, or, more important, how it is implemented in PHP5, you should definitely start by reading Part I. The rest of the book makes use of these techniques from cover to cover, so it's vital for you to have the basic grounding in OOP before trying to press on with the trickier stuff.

Part I: Object-Oriented Software Development Concepts

The first part of *Professional PHP5* is devoted to enlightening the PHP developer in the art of object-oriented development, which is greatly improved in PHP5. You'll learn basic object-oriented concepts and how to read, express, and document your code using UML. You'll also get a short introduction to reusing standard development techniques through the use of design patterns.

After completing the first part, you should be ready to develop in PHP5 in a syntactic capacity. World-wizened PHP4 developers should expect to experience at least one "Ah-ha" moment, and although you'll want to test drive the new PHP features right away, you're encouraged to continue with Part II or Part III.

Part II: Creating a Reusable Object Toolkit I: Simple Utility Classes and Interfaces

The second part, although titled "Simple Utility Classes and Interfaces," is much more than just some random collection of code.

You'll learn about high-level abstractions and see how they are directly used. Collections, iterators, object-persistence, and creational design-patterns are used to create some of the building blocks and are utilized in later chapters.

There are also some core development skills, such as event-driven programs as well as a sample SOAP utility.

Part III: Creating a Reusable Object Toolkit II: Complex (Though Not Complicated) Utilities

Part III is essentially about building up your development skills in PHP 5. This is where you'll learn about the model-view-controller abstraction and how it is used in PHP. An entire chapter is devoted to the technical specifics and process of unit testing, and another covers utilizing the abstraction of finite-state machines.

This part also discusses more high-level utility functionality such as authentication and sessions.

Part IV: Test Case: Sales Force Automation

Programming abstractions are wonderful, but a developer still needs to work with a team in order to deliver substantial software. This is where project management methodologies, planning, and systems architecture collide to help you meet those deadlines.

This part also has an extensive case study that combines many of the tools, development skills, and methodologies to help you experience firsthand how software is developed and shipped in the real world.

Appendices

The appendices are home to some important topics we couldn't neatly fit into any of the previous four sections.

You'll learn about version control—why it's important and how to implement it on a large project using CVS or SourceSafe. You'll also meet a number of PHP development IDEs, allowing you to cast aside your rusty old text editor in favor of a slicker, PHP-tailored solution.

There's also a discussion of how to performance tune your PHP applications to get the most out of them, even on slower server hardware, as well as a simple cheat sheet for setting up PHP and Apache on Linux.

The Bigger Picture

We sincerely hope that you'll help us, the authors, in raising the bar concerning the quality of software found in both professional production environments and in projects found on the Internet.

Professionally and philosophically, none of us codes alone, so maybe together we can help to make our existence just a little bit better.

Conventions

To help you get the most from the text and keep track of what's happening, we've used a number of conventions throughout the book.

> **Boxes like this one hold important, not-to-be forgotten information that is directly relevant to the surrounding text.**

Tips, hints, tricks, and asides to the current discussion are offset and placed in italics like this.

As for styles in the text:

- We *italicize* important words when we introduce them.
- We show keyboard strokes like this: Ctrl+A.
- We show filenames, URLs, and code within the text like so: `persistence.properties`
- We present code in two different ways:

```
In code examples we highlight new and important code with a gray background.
```

```
The gray highlighting is absent from code that's less important in the present
context, or has been shown before.
```

Source Code

As you work through the examples in this book, you may choose to enter all the code manually or use the source code files that accompany the book. All the source code used in this book is available for download at `www.wrox.com`. When you're at the site, locate the book's title (either by using the Search box or by using one of the title lists) and click the Download Code link on the book's detail page to obtain all the source code for the book.

Because many books have similar titles, you may find it easiest to search by ISBN; this book's ISBN is 0-7645-7282-2.

After you download the code, just decompress it with your favorite compression tool. Alternatively, go to the main Wrox code download page at `www.wrox.com/dynamic/books/download.aspx` to see the code available for this book and all other Wrox books.

Errata

We make every effort to ensure that there are no errors in the text or in the code. However, no one is perfect and mistakes do occur. If you find an error in one of our books, such as a spelling mistake or faulty piece of code, we would be very grateful for your feedback. By sending in errata you may save another reader hours of frustration and at the same time you will be helping us provide even higher-quality information.

To find the errata page for this book, go to `www.wrox.com` and locate the title using the Search box or one of the title lists. Then, on the book details page, click the Book Errata link. On this page you can view all errata that has been submitted for this book and posted by Wrox editors. A complete book list including links to each book's errata is also available at `www.wrox.com/misc-pages/booklist.shtml`.

If you don't spot "your" error on the Book Errata page, go to `www.wrox.com/contact/techsupport.shtml` and complete the form there to send us the error you have found. We'll check the information and, if appropriate, post a message to the book's errata page and fix the problem in subsequent editions of the book.

p2p.wrox.com

For author and peer discussion, join the P2P forums at `p2p.wrox.com`. The forums are a Web-based system for you to post messages relating to Wrox books and related technologies and to interact with other readers and technology users. The forums offer a subscription feature to e-mail you topics of interest of your choosing when new posts are made to the forums. Wrox authors, editors, other industry experts, and your fellow readers are present on these forums.

At `http://p2p.wrox.com` you will find a number of different forums that will help you not only as you read this book but also as you develop your own applications. To join the forums, just follow these steps:

1. Go to `p2p.wrox.com` and click the Register link.
2. Read the terms of use and click Agree.
3. Complete the required information to join as well as any optional information you want to provide and click Submit.
4. You will receive an e-mail with information describing how to verify your account and complete the joining process.

You can read messages in the forums without joining P2P, but in order to post your own messages you must join.

After you join, you can post new messages and respond to messages that other users post. You can read messages at any time on the Web. If you would like to have new messages from a particular forum e-mailed to you, click the Subscribe to this Forum icon by the forum name in the forum listing.

For more information about how to use the Wrox P2P, be sure to read the P2P FAQs for answers to questions about how the forum software works, as well as many common questions specific to P2P and Wrox books. To read the FAQs, click the FAQ link on any P2P page.

Professional PHP5

Part I: Object-Oriented Software Development Concepts

Chapter 1: Introduction to Object-Oriented Programming

Chapter 2: Unified Modeling Language (UML)

Chapter 3: Putting Objects to Work

Chapter 4: Design Patterns

Introduction to Object-Oriented Programming

Object-Oriented (OO) software development can be a confusing topic for developers who create primarily procedural code. But it doesn't need to be. In this chapter, you'll explore some of the basic theory behind OO and cover its (sometimes daunting) multisyllabic terminology. You'll learn why you should be interested in OO techniques, how they can really improve the speed with which you develop complex applications, and the ease with which you can modify those applications.

In the next couple of chapters, we'll expand on the ideas and learn some slightly more advanced topics. If you have already had exposure to OO development outside PHP5, you can probably skip this chapter and the next. However, this material will serve as a good review, so we recommend that you read it through.

What Is Object-Oriented Programming?

Object-Oriented Programming (OOP) requires a different way of thinking about how you construct your applications. Objects enable you to more closely model in code the real-world tasks, processes, and ideas that your application is designed to handle. Instead of thinking about an application as a thread of control that passes chunks of data from one function to the next, an OOP approach allows you to model the application as a set of collaborating objects that independently handle certain activities.

As an analogy, when a house is being constructed, the plumbers deal with the pipes, and the electricians deal with the wires. The plumbers don't need to know whether the circuit in the bedroom is 10 amps or 20. They need concern themselves only with their own activities. A general contractor ensures that each subcontractor is completing the work that needs to be accomplished but isn't necessarily interested in the particulars of each task. An OO approach is similar in that each object hides from the others the details of its implementation. How it does its job is irrelevant to the other components of the system. All that matters is the service that the object is able to provide.

The concepts of classes and objects, and the ways in which you can leverage these ideas in the development of software, are the fundamental ideas behind object-oriented programming. This is, in a sense, the opposite of procedural programming, which is programming using functions and global data structures. As you'll see, an object-oriented approach gives you some big benefits over procedural programming and, with the new implementation of OO support in PHP5, some large performance boosts, as well.

OOP advantages

One of the main benefits of OOP is the ease with which you can translate individual business requirements into individual modules of code. Because an OOP approach enables you to model your application based on the idea of real-world objects, you can often identify a direct correlation between people, things, and concepts and equivalent classes. These classes have the same properties and behaviors as the real-world concepts they represent, which helps you to quickly identify what code needs to be written and how different parts of the application need to interact.

A second benefit of OOP is that of code reuse. You frequently need the same types of data in different places in the same application. For example, an application that enables a hospital to manage its patient records would definitely need a class called `Person`. A number of people are involved in patient care—the patient, the doctors, the nurses, hospital administrators, insurance claims people, and so on. At each step in the care of the patient, that patient's record requires a note about which person was performing a given action (such as prescribing medicine, cleaning wounds, or sending a bill to an insurance carrier) and verifying that the person is allowed to perform that action. By defining a generic class called `Person` that encompasses all the properties and methods common to all these people, you get an enormous amount of code reuse that isn't always possible in a procedural approach to programming.

What about other applications? How many applications can you think of that at some point handle information about individuals? Probably quite a few. A well-written `Person` class could easily be copied from one project to another with little or no change, instantly giving you all the rich functionality for dealing with information about people that you developed previously. This is one of the biggest benefits of an OO approach—the opportunities for code reuse within a given application as well as across different projects.

Another OOP advantage comes from the modularity of classes. If you discover a bug in your `Person` class or you want to add to or change the way that class functions, you have only one place to go. All the functionality of that class is contained in a single file. Any processes of the application that rely on the `Person` class are immediately affected by changes to it. This feature can vastly simplify the search for bugs and makes the addition of features a relatively painless task.

A real-world example

They might seem trivial in a smaller application, but in a more complex software architecture the benefits of modularity can be enormous. One of the authors once worked on a project involving more than 200,000 lines of procedural PHP code. Easily 65 percent of the time spent fixing bugs was devoted to uncovering where certain functions were located and determining which data interacted with which functions. A subsequent rewrite of that software in an OO architecture resulted in dramatically less code. Had the application been implemented in such a manner in the first place, it would have resulted in not only less development time from the outset but also the discovery of fewer bugs (the smaller the amount of code, the fewer the opportunities for problems) and a faster turnaround time on bug fixes.

Because an OO approach forces you to think about how the code is organized, learning the structure of an existing application is much easier when you are new to the development team. In addition, you have a framework to aid you in determining the appropriate location for new functionality you might develop.

Larger projects often have a multimember software development team, usually composed of programmers with varying degrees of ability. Here, too, an OO approach has significant benefits over a procedural approach. Objects hide the details of their implementation from the users of those objects. Instead of needing to understand complex data structures and all the quirks of the business logic, junior members of the team can, with just a little documentation, begin using objects created by senior members of the team. The objects themselves are responsible for triggering changes to data or the state of the system.

When the large application mentioned previously was still written using procedural code, new members of the software development team could often take up to two months to learn enough about the application to be productive. After the software was rebuilt using objects, new members of the team usually took no more than a couple of days to begin making substantial additions to the code base. They were able to use even the most complex objects quickly because they did not need to fully understand the particulars of how the functionality contained within those objects was implemented.

Now that you have a good idea about why you should consider using an OO paradigm as your programming method of choice, you should read the next few sections to gain a better understanding of the fundamental concepts behind OO. If all goes well, through the course of the next two chapters you will come to see the benefits of this approach for yourself.

Understanding OOP Concepts

This section introduces the primary concepts of object-oriented programming and explores how they interact. Chapter 3, "Putting Objects to Work," looks at the specifics of implementing them in PHP5. You'll learn about:

- *classes*: the "blueprints" for an object and the actual code that defines the properties and methods
- *objects*: running instances of a class that contain all the internal data and state information needed for your application to function
- *inheritance*: the ability to define a class of one kind as being a subtype of a different kind of class (much the same way a square is a kind of rectangle)
- *polymorphism*: allows a class to be defined as being a member of more than one category of classes (just as a car is "a thing with an engine" and "a thing with wheels")
- *interfaces*: defines a contract specifying that an object is capable of implementing a method without actually defining how it is to be done
- *encapsulation*: the ability of an object to protect access to its internal data

If any of these terms seem difficult to understand, don't worry. The material that follows will clarify everything. Your newfound knowledge may even completely change the way you approach your software development projects.

Classes

In the real world, objects have characteristics and behaviors. A car has a color, a weight, a manufacturer, and a gas tank of a certain volume. Those are its characteristics. A car can accelerate, stop, signal for a turn, and sound the horn. Those are its behaviors. Those characteristics and behaviors are common to all cars. Although different cars may have different colors, all cars have a color. Using a construct known as a *class*, OOP enables you to establish the idea of a car as being something with all those characteristics. A class is a unit of code, composed of variables and functions, which describes the characteristics and behaviors of all the members of a set. A class called `Car` would describe the properties and methods common to all cars.

In OO terminology, the characteristics of a class are known as its *properties*. Properties have a name and a value. Some allow their value to be changed; others do not. For example, in the `Car` class, you would probably have such properties as `color` and `weight`. Although the color of the car can be changed by giving it a new paint job, the weight of the car (without cargo or passengers) is a fixed value.

Some properties represent the state of the object. State refers to those characteristics that change because of certain events but are not necessarily directly modifiable on their own. In an application that simulates vehicle performance, the `Car` class might have a property called `velocity`. The velocity of the car is not a value that can be changed on its own, but rather is a byproduct of the amount of fuel being sent to the engine, the performance characteristics of that engine, and the terrain over which the car is traveling.

The behaviors of a class are known as its *methods*. Methods of classes are syntactically equivalent to functions found in traditional procedural code. Just like functions, methods can accept any number of parameters, each of any valid data type. Some methods act on external data passed to them as parameters, but they can also act on the properties of their object, either using those properties to inform actions made by the method—such as when a method called `accelerate` examines the remaining amount of fuel to determine whether the car is capable of accelerating—or to change the state of the object by modifying values such as the velocity of the car.

Objects

To begin with, you can think of a class as a blueprint for constructing an object. In much the same way that many houses can be built from the same blueprint, you can build multiple instances of an object from its class. But the blueprint doesn't specify details such as the color of the walls or type of flooring. It merely specifies that those things will exist. Classes work much the same way. The class specifies the behaviors and characteristics the object will have, but not necessarily the values of those characteristics. An object is a concrete entity constructed using the blueprint provided by a class. The idea of *a* house is analogous to a class. *Your* house (a specific instance of the idea of a house) is analogous to an object.

With a blueprint in hand and some building materials, you can construct a house. In OOP, you use the class to build an object, this process is known as *instantiation*. Instantiating an object requires two things:

- A memory location into which to load the object. This is automatically handled for you by PHP.
- The data that will populate the values of the properties. This data can come from a database, a flat text file, another object, or some other source.

A class can never have property values or state. Only objects can. You have to use the blueprint to build the house before you can give it wallpaper or vinyl siding. Similarly, you have to instantiate an object from the class before you can interact with its properties or invoke its methods. Classes are manipulated at design time when you make changes to the methods or properties. Objects are manipulated at runtime when values are assigned to their properties and their methods are invoked. The problem of when to use the word *class* and when to use the word *object* is something that often confuses those new to OOP.

After an object is instantiated, it can be put to work implementing the business requirements of the application. Let's look at exactly how to do that in PHP.

Creating a Class

Start with a simple example. Save the following in a file called `class.Demo.php`:

```
<?php

  class Demo {

  }

?>
```

And there you have it—the `Demo` class. Not terribly exciting just yet, but this is the basic syntax for declaring a new class in PHP. Use the keyword `class` to let PHP know you're about to define a new class. Follow that with the name of the class and braces to indicate the start and end of the code for that class.

It's important to have a clearly defined convention for organizing your source code files. A good rule to follow is to put each class into its own file and to name that file class.[ClassName].php.

You can instantiate an object of type `Demo` like this:

```
<?php

  require_once('class.Demo.php');

  $objDemo = new Demo();

?>
```

To instantiate an object, first make sure that PHP knows where to find the class declaration by including the file containing your class (`class.Demo.php` in this example), then invoke the `new` operator and supply the name of the class and opening and closing parentheses. The return value of this statement is assigned to a new variable, `$objDemo` in this example. Now you can invoke the `$objDemo`, object's methods and examine or set the value of its properties—if it actually has any.

Even though the class you've created doesn't do much of anything just yet, it's still a valid class definition.

Adding a Method

The `Demo` class isn't particularly useful if it isn't able to do anything, so let's look at how you can create a method. Remember, a method of a class is basically just a function. By coding a function inside the braces of your class, you're adding a method to that class. Here's an example:

```
<?php

  class Demo {
    function sayHello($name) {
      print "Hello $name!";
    }

  }

?>
```

An object derived from your class is now capable of printing a greeting to anyone who invokes the `sayHello` method. To invoke the method on your `$objDemo` object, you need to use the operator `->` to access the newly created function:

```
<?php

  require_once('class.Demo.php');

  $objDemo = new Demo();

  $objDemo->sayHello('Steve');

?>
```

The object is now capable of printing a friendly greeting. The `->` operator is used to access all methods and properties of your objects.

For those who have had exposure to OOP in other programming languages, note that the -> operator is always used to access the methods and properties of an object. PHP does not use the dot operator (.) in its OO syntax at all.

Adding a Property

Adding a property to your class is just as easy as adding a method. You simply declare a variable inside the class to hold the value of the property. In procedural code, when you want to store some value, you assign that value to a variable. In OOP, when you want to store the value of a property, you also use a variable. This variable is declared at the top of the class declaration, inside the braces that bracket the class's code. The name of the variable is the name of the property. If the variable is called `$color`, you will have a property called `color`.

Open the `class.Demo.php` file and add the highlighted code:

```
<?php

  class Demo {

    public $name;

    function sayHello() {
```

```
        print "Hello $this->name!";
    }
  }
?>
```

This new variable, called `$name`, is all you have to do to create a property of the `Demo` class called `name`. To access this property, you use the same `->` operator as that of the previous example, along with the name of the property. The rewritten `sayHello` method shows how to access the value of this property.

Create a new file called `testdemo.php` and add the following:

```
<?php

  require_once('class.Demo.php');

  $objDemo = new Demo();
  $objDemo->name = 'Steve';

  $objAnotherDemo = new Demo();
  $objAnotherDemo->name = 'Ed';

  $objDemo->sayHello();
  $objAnotherDemo->sayHello();

?>
```

Save the file and then open it in your Web browser. The strings "Hello Steve!" and "Hello Ed!" print to the screen.

The keyword `public` is used to let the class know that you want to have access to the following variable from outside the class. Some member variables of the class exist only for use by the class itself and should not be accessible to external code. In this example, you want to be able to set and retrieve the value of the property `name`. Note that the way the `sayHello` method works has changed. Instead of taking a parameter, it now fetches the `name` value from the property.

You use the variable `$this` so that an object can get information about itself. You might have multiple objects of a class, for instance, and because you don't know in advance what the name of an object variable will be, the `$this` variable enables you to refer to the current instance.

In the previous example, the first call to `sayHello` prints `"Steve"` and the second call prints `"Ed"`. This is because the `$this` variable allows each object to access its own properties and methods without having to know the name of the variable which represents it in the exterior application. Previously, we said that some properties influence the action of certain methods, such as the example in which the `accelerate` method of the `Car` class needs to examine the amount of fuel remaining. The code inside `accelerate` would use code such as `$this->amountOfFuel` to access this property.

> *When accessing properties, you need only one $. The syntax is `$obj->property`, not `$obj->$property`. This fact often causes confusion for those new to PHP. The property variable is declared as public `$property` and accessed using `$obj->property`.*

In addition to the variables that store the values for the properties of the class, other variables may be declared for use by the internal operations of the class. Both kinds of data are collectively referred to as the class's *internal member variables*. Some of these are accessible to code outside the class in the form of properties. Others are not accessible and are strictly for internal housekeeping. For example, if the `Car` class needed to get information from a database for whatever reason, it might keep a database connection handle in an internal member variable. This database connection handle is obviously not a property of the car, but rather is something the class needs to carry out certain operations.

Protecting Access to Member Variables

As the previous example shows, you can set the value of the `name` property to just about anything you want—including an object, an array of integers, a file handle, or any other nonsensical value. However, you don't get an opportunity to do any sort of data validation or update any other values when the `name` property is set.

To work around this problem, always implement your properties in the form of functions called `get[`*`property name`*`]` and `set[`*`property name`*`]`. Such functions are known as *accessor methods,* and are demonstrated in the following example.

Make the changes highlighted in the following to `class.Demo.php`:

```
<?php

  class Demo {

    private $_name;

    public function sayHello() {
      print "Hello {$this->getName()}!";
    }

    public function getName() {
      return $this->_name;
    }

    public function setName($name) {
      if(!is_string($name) || strlen($name) == 0) {
        throw new Exception("Invalid name value");
      }

      $this->_name = $name;

    }
  }
?>
```

Edit `testdemo.php` as shown here:

```
<?php

  require_once('class.Demo.php');

  $objDemo = new Demo();
  $objDemo->setName('Steve');
```

```
  $objDemo->sayHello();

  $objDemo->setName(37); //would trigger an error

?>
```

As you can see, the member access level of name has changed from public to private and has been prefixed with an underscore. The underscore is a recommended naming convention to indicate private member variables and functions; however, it is merely a convention—PHP does not require it. The keyword private protects code outside the object from modifying this value. Private internal member variables are not accessible from outside the class. Because you can't access these variables directly, you're forced to use the getName() and setName() accessor methods to access this information, ensuring that your class can examine the value before allowing it to be set. In this example, an exception is thrown if an invalid value is supplied for the name property. Additionally, the public access specifier for the functions has been added. Public is the default visibility level for any member variables or functions that do not explicitly set one, but it is good practice to always explicitly state the visibility of all the members of the class.

A member variable or method can have three different levels of visibility: public, private, and protected. Public members are accessible to any and all code. Private members are accessible only to the class itself. These are typically items used for internal housekeeping and might include such things as a database connection handle or configuration information. Protected members are available to the class itself and to classes that inherit from it. (Inheritance is defined and discussed in detail later in this chapter.)

By creating accessor methods for all your properties, you make it much easier to add data validation, new business logic, or other changes to your objects in the future. Even if the current business requirements for your application involve no data validation of a given property, you should still implement that property with get and set functions so that you can add validation or business logic functionality in the future.

Always use accessor methods for your properties. Changes to business logic and data validation requirements in the future will be much easier to implement.

Initializing Objects

For many of the classes you will create, you will need to do some special set-up when an object of that class is first instantiated. You might need to fetch some information from a database, or initialize some property values, for example. By creating a special method called a *constructor*, implemented in PHP using a function called __construct(), you can perform any activities required to instantiate the object. PHP will automatically call this special function when instantiating the object.

For example, you could rewrite the Demo class in the following way:

```
<?php

  class Demo {

    private $name;

    public function __construct($name) {
      $this->name = $name;
    }
```

```
    function sayHello() {
      print "Hello $this->name!";
    }
  }
?>
```

The __construct function will be automatically invoked when you instantiate a new object of class Demo.

Note for PHP4 users: In PHP4, object constructors were functions with the same name as the class. PHP5 changed this to use a unified constructor scheme. For backward compatibility, PHP first looks for a function called `__construct`, but if none is found it will still look for a function with the same name as the class (`public function Demo()` in the preceding example).

If you have a class that does not require any special initialization code to be run, you don't need to create a constructor. As you saw in the first version of the Demo class, PHP automatically does what it needs to do to create that object. Create a constructor function only when you need one.

Destroying Objects

The object variables that you create are removed from system memory when the requested page has completed running, when the variable falls out of scope, or when it is explicitly set to null. In PHP5 you can trap the destruction of the object and take actions when that happens. To do so, create a function called __destruct with no parameters. Before the object is destroyed, this function is called automatically, if it exists.

Calling this function gives you the opportunity to perform any last-minute clean-up, such as closing file handles or database connections that might have been opened by the class, or any other last-minute housekeeping that might be needed before the object is destroyed.

The following example writes information to a log file when the object is destroyed that notes how long the object existed. If you have objects that are particularly memory or CPU intensive, a technique like this can be used to allow you to analyze system performance and look for ways to reduce overhead.

As with most of the database examples in this book, this one uses PostgreSQL as its platform. The authors firmly believe that the advanced features, transaction support, and robust stored procedure mechanism of PostgreSQL make it a superior alternative to MySQL and other open-source RDBMSs for large-scale enterprise software development. If you don't have a PostgreSQL environment at your disposal, feel free to make the appropriate modifications for the database platform you use.

Create a table called "widget" using the following SQL statement:

```
CREATE TABLE "widget" (
  "widgetid" SERIAL PRIMARY KEY NOT NULL,
  "name" varchar(255) NOT NULL,
  "description" text
);
```

Insert some data:

```
INSERT INTO "widget" ("name", "description")
VALUES('Foo', 'This is a footacular widget!');
```

Create a file called `class.Widget.php` and enter the following code:

```
<?php

class Widget {

    private $id;
    private $name;
    private $description; private $hDB;
    private $needsUpdating = false;

    public function __construct($widgetID) {
      //The widgetID parameter is the primary key of a
      //record in the database containing the information
      //for this object

      //Create a connection handle and store it in a private member variable
      $this->hDB = pg_connect('dbname=parts user=postgres');
      if(! is_resource($this->hDB)) {
        throw new Exception('Unable to connect to the database.');
      }

      $sql = "SELECT \"name\", \"description\" FROM widget WHERE widgetid =
             $widgetID";
      $rs = pg_query($this->hDB, $sql);
      if(! is_resource($rs)) {
        throw new Exception("An error occurred selecting from the database.");
      }

      if(! pg_num_rows($rs)) {
        throw new Exception('The specified widget does not exist!');
      }

      $data = pg_fetch_array($rs);
      $this->id = $widgetID;
      $this->name = $data['name'];
      $this->description = $data['description'];

    }

    public function getName() {
      return $this->name;
    }

    public function getDescription() {
      return $this->description;
    }

    public function setName($name) {
      $this->name = $name;
      $this->needsUpdating = true;
```

```
    }
    public function setDescription($description) {
      $this->description = $description;
      $this->needsUpdating = true;
    }

  public function __destruct() {
    if(! $this->needsUpdating) {
      return;
    }

    $sql = 'UPDATE "widget" SET ';
    $sql .= "\"name\" = '" . pg_escape_string($this->name) . "', ";
    $sql .= "\"description\" = '" . pg_escape_string
    ($this->description) . "' ";
    $sql .= "WHERE widgetID = " . $this->id;

    $rs = pg_query($this->hDB, $sql);
    if(! is_resource($rs)) {
      throw new Exception('An error occurred updating the database');
    }

    //You're done with the database. Close the connection handle.
    pg_close($this->hDB);
  }
}
?>
```

The constructor to this object opens a connection to a database called `parts` using the default super-user account `postgres`. This connection handle is preserved in a private member variable for use later on. The ID value passed as a parameter to the constructor is used to construct a SQL statement that fetches the information for the widget with the specified primary key in the database. The data from the database is then assigned to private member variables for use with the `get` and `set` functions. Note that if anything should go wrong, the constructor throws exceptions, so be sure to wrap any attempts to construct a `Widget` object in `try...catch` blocks.

The two accessor methods `getName()` and `getDescription()` allow you to fetch the values of the private member variables. Similarly, the `setName()` and `setDescription()` methods allows you to assign a new value to those variables. Note that when a new value is assigned, the `needsUpdating` value is set to true. If nothing changes, then nothing needs to be updated.

To test this, create a file called `testWidget.php` with the following content:

```
<?php

require_once('class.Widget.php');

  try {
    $objWidget = new Widget(1);

    print "Widget Name: " . $objWidget->getName() . "<br>\n";
    print "Widget Description: " . $objWidget->getDescription() . "<br>\n";
```

```
        $objWidget->setName('Bar');
        $objWidget->setDescription('This is a bartacular widget!');
    } catch (Exception $e) {
        die("There was a problem: " . $e->getMessage());
    }

?>
```

Access this file in your Web browser. The first time it runs, the output should be something like:

```
Widget Name: Foo
Widget Description: This is a footacular widget!
```

Any subsequent call should display:

```
Widget Name: Bar
Widget Description: This is a bartacular widget!
```

Look at how powerful this technique can be. You can fetch an object from the database, change a property of that object, and automagically write the changed information back to the database with just a few lines of code in `testWidget.php`. If nothing changes, you don't need to go back to the database, so you save load on the database server and improve the performance of the application.

Users of the object do not necessarily need to understand its internals. If a senior member of the software development team wrote the `Widget` class, she could give this object to a junior member, who perhaps doesn't understand SQL as well, and the junior member of the team could put this object to use without any knowledge whatsoever of where the data comes from or how to save changes to it. In fact, you could change the data source from a PostgreSQL database to a MySQL database or even an XML file without the junior team member ever knowing or having to touch any of the code that uses this class.

This powerful concept is taken a step further in Chapter 7, when you will meet a generic version of the above class called `GenericObject`, which you can use out-of-the-box in virtually any project without modification.

Inheritance

If you were creating an application to handle inventory at a car dealership, you would probably need classes like `Sedan`, `PickupTruck`, and `MiniVan` that would correspond to the same types of automobiles in the dealer's inventory. Your application would need not only to show how many of these items you have in stock but also to report on the characteristics of these vehicles so that the salespeople could give the information to customers.

A sedan is a four-door car, and you would probably want to record the back-seat space and the trunk capacity. A pickup truck doesn't have a trunk but does have a cargo bed with a certain capacity, and the truck itself has a towing capacity (the maximum weight of any cargo that can be safely carried). For a minivan, you would probably need to list the number of sliding doors (either one or two) and the number of seats inside.

But each of these vehicles is really just a different type of automobile and as such would share a number of characteristics in your application, such as color, manufacturer, model, year, vehicle identification number, and so on. To ensure that each of the classes has these same properties, you could just copy the code that creates those properties into each of the files containing your class definitions. As mentioned earlier in this chapter, one of the benefits of an OOP approach is code reuse, so of course you don't need to copy code but instead can reuse the properties and methods of these classes through a process called *inheritance*. Inheritance is the ability for one class to assume the methods and properties of a parent class.

Inheritance enables you to define a base class, in this case `Automobile`, and say that other classes are a type of `Automobile` and as such have all the same properties and methods that all `Automobiles` have. You can say that a `Sedan` is an `Automobile` and therefore automatically inherits everything defined by the `Automobile` class without your having to copy any code. Then you need to write only the additional properties and methods of the `Sedan` class that are not shared by all automobiles. The only work left for you to do is define the differences; the similarities between the classes are inherited from the base class.

The ability to reuse code is one benefit, but there's a second major advantage to using inheritance. Say that you have a class called `Customer` with a method `buyAutomobile`. This method would take one parameter, an object of class `Automobile`, and its internal operations would print the paperwork needed to document the sale and would decrement the car in question from the inventory system. Because all `Sedans`, `PickupTrucks`, and `MiniVans` are `Automobiles`, you can pass objects of these classes to a function expecting an `Automobile`. Because the three specific types inherit from the more generic parent class, you know that they will all have the same base set of properties and methods. As long as you need only the methods and properties common to all `Automobiles`, you can accept objects of any class that inherits from `Automobile`.

Consider the example of cats. All cats share some properties. They eat, sleep, purr, and hunt. They also have shared properties—weight, fur color, whisker length, and running speed. However, lions have a mane of a certain length (at least, the male lions do), and they growl. Cheetahs have spots. Domesticated cats have neither of these things, yet all three animals are cats.

In PHP you specify that a class is a subset of another by using the keyword `extends`, which tells PHP that the class you are declaring should inherit all the properties and methods from its parent class, and that you are adding functionality or providing some additional specialization to that class.

If you had to design an application to handle zoo animals, you'd probably need to have classes `Cat`, `Lion`, and `Cheetah`. Before writing any code, plan your class hierarchy in UML diagrams so you have something to work from when you write the code and the documentation of those classes. (We take a closer look at UML in Chapter 2, so don't worry if you don't completely understand what's shown here.) Your class diagram should indicate a parent class `Cat` with subclasses `Lion` and `Cheetah` inheriting from it. Figure 1-1 shows that diagram.

Both the `Lion` and `Cheetah` classes inherit from `Cat`, but the `Lion` class also implements the property `maneLength` and the method `roar()`, whereas `Cheetah` adds the property `numberOfSpots`.

The `Cat` class, `class.Cat.php`, should be implemented as follows:

```
<?php

  class Cat {
    public $weight;          //in kg
    public $furColor;
    public $whiskerLength;
    public $maxSpeed;        //in km/hr
```

```
    public function eat() {
      //code for eating...
    }

    public function sleep() {
      //code for sleeping...
    }

    public function hunt(Prey $objPrey) {
      //code for hunting objects of type Prey
      //which we will not define...
    }

    public function purr() {
      print "purrrrrrr..." . "\n";
    }
  }
?>
```

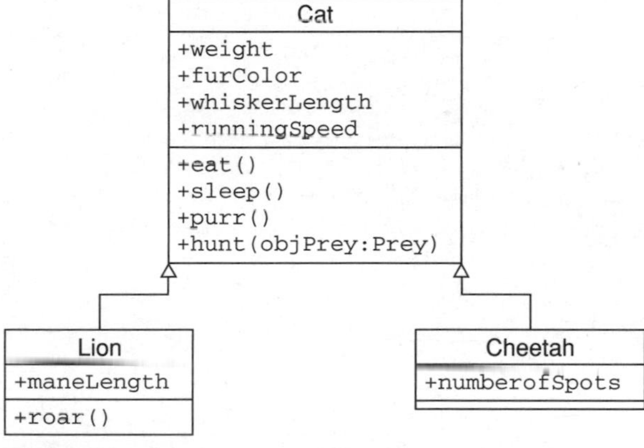

Figure 1-1

This simple class sets up all the properties and methods common to all cats. To create the `Lion` and `Cheetah` classes, you could copy all the code from the `Cat` class to classes called `Lion` and `Cheetah`. However, this generates two problems. First, if you find a bug in the `Cat` class, you have to know to fix it in the `Lion` and `Cheetah` classes, as well. This creates more work for you, not less (and creating less work is supposed to be one of the primary advantages of an OO approach).

Second, imagine that you had a method of some other object that looked like this:

```
public function petTheKitty(Cat $objCat) {
  $objCat->purr();
}
```

Although petting a lion or cheetah may not be a terribly safe idea, they will purr if they let you get close enough to do so. You should be able to pass an object of class `Lion` or `Cheetah` to the `petTheKitty()` function.

So you need to take the other route to creating the `Lion` and `Cheetah` classes, and that's to use inheritance. By using the keyword `extends` and specifying the name of the class that is extended, you can easily create two new classes that have all the same properties as a regular cat but provide some additional features. For example:

```
<?php
  require_once('class.Cat.php');

  class Lion extends Cat {
    public $maneLength; //in cm

    public function roar() {
      print "Roarrrrrrrrr!";
    }
  }
?>
```

And that's it! With the `Lion` class extending `Cat` you can now do something like the following:

```
<?php
  include('class.Lion.php');

  $objLion = new Lion();
  $objLion->weight = 200;    //kg = ~450 lbs.
  $objLion->furColor = 'brown';
  $objLion->maneLength = 36; //cm = ~14 inches
  $objLion->eat();
  $objLion->roar();
  $objLion->sleep();
?>
```

So you can invoke the properties and methods of the parent class `Cat` without having to rewrite all that code. Remember that the `extends` keyword tells PHP to automatically include all the functionality of a `Cat` along with any `Lion`-specific properties or methods. It also tells PHP that a `Lion` object is also a `Cat` object, and you can now call the `petTheKitty()` function with an object of class `Lion` even though the function declaration uses `Cat` as the parameter hint:

```
<?php
  include('class.Lion.php');
  $objLion = new Lion();

  $objPetter = new Cat();
  $objPetter->petTheKitty($objLion);
?>
```

In this way, any changes you make to the `Cat` class are automatically inherited by the `Lion` class. Bug fixes, changes to function internals, or new methods and properties are all passed along to the subclasses of a parent class. In a large, well-designed object hierarchy this can make bug fixing and the addition of enhancements very easy. A small change to one parent class can have a large effect on the entire application.

In this example, you'll see how a custom constructor can be used to extend and specialize a class.

Create a new file called `class.Cheetah.php` and enter the following:

```
<?php
  require_once('class.Cat.php');

  class Cheetah extends Cat {
    public $numberOfSpots;

    public function __construct() {
      $this->maxSpeed = 100;
    }
  }
?>
```

Enter the following code into `testcats.php`:

```
<?php
require_once('class.Cheetah.php');

  function petTheKitty(Cat $objCat) {
    if($objCat->maxSpeed < 5) {
      $objCat->purr();
    } else {
       print "Can't pet the kitty - it's moving at " .
              $objCat->maxSpeed . " kilometers per hour!";
    }
  }

  $objCheetah = new Cheetah();
  petTheKitty($objCheetah);

  $objCat = new Cat();
  petTheKitty($objCat);
?>
```

The `Cheetah` class adds a new public member variable called `numberOfSpots` and a constructor that did not exist in the parent `Cat` class. Now, when you create a new `Cheetah`, the `maxSpeed` property (inherited from `Cat`) is initialized to 100 kilometers per hour (roughly 60 miles per hour), which is the approximate maximum speed of a cheetah over short distances. Note that because a default value for the `Cat` class isn't specified, the `maxSpeed` evaluates as 0 (actually, null) in the `petTheKitty()` function. As those who have ever had a house cat know, the amount of time they spend sleeping means that their maximum speed probably is approaching 0!

By adding new functions, properties, or even constructors and destructors, the subclasses of a parent class can easily extend their functionality and with a minimum amount of code add new features and capabilities to your application.

When you can say that one class is a special type of some other class, use inheritance to maximize the potential for code reuse and increase the flexibility of your application.

Overriding Methods

Just because a child class inherits from a parent doesn't mean that the child class necessarily needs to use the parent class's implementation of a function. For example, if you were designing an application that needed to calculate the area of different geometric shapes, you might have classes called `Rectangle` and `Triangle`. Both of these shapes are polygons, and as such these classes will inherit from a parent class called `Polygon`.

The `Polygon` class will have a property called `numberOfSides` and a method called `getArea`. All polygons have a calculable area; however, the methods for calculating that area can be different for different types of polygons. (A generic equation exists for the area of any polygon; however, it is often less efficient than the shape-specific equations for the simple polygons we're using here.) The formula for the area of a rectangle is `w * h`, where w is the width of the rectangle and h is the height. The area of a triangle is calculated as `0.5 * h * b`, where h is the height of a triangle with base `b`. Figure 1-2 shows some examples of the areas of different types of polygons.

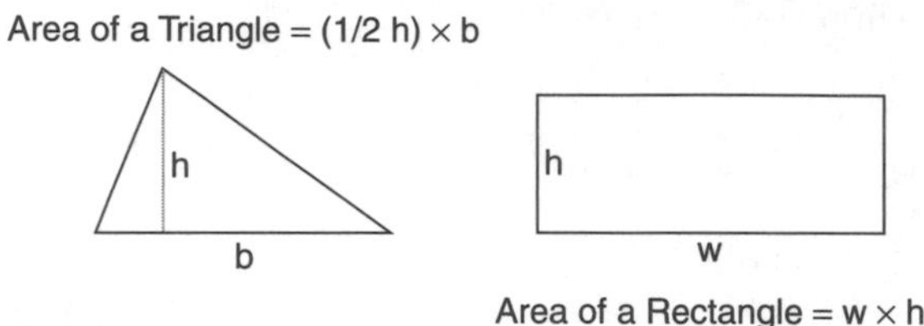

Figure 1-2

For each subclass of `Polygon` that you create, you will probably want to use an equation different than the default implementation of the area method with one specific to the type of polygon class. By redefining that method for the class, you can provide your own implementation.

In the case of the `Rectangle` class, you would create two new properties, `height` and `width`, and override the `Polygon` class's implementation of the `getArea()` method. For the `Triangle` class, you would probably add properties to store information about the three angles, the height, and the length of the base segment and override the `getArea()` method. By using inheritance and overriding methods of the parent class, you can allow the subclasses to specialize their implementations of those methods.

A function that takes a `Polygon` as a parameter and needs to print the area of that polygon will then automatically call the `getArea()` method of the subclass of `Polygon` that was passed to it (that is, `Rectangle` or `Triangle`). This capability for an OO programming language to automatically determine at runtime which `getArea()` method to call is known as *polymorphism*. Polymorphism is the ability of an application to do different things based on the particular object it is acting on. In this case, that means invoking a different `getArea()` method.

> *Override a method in a subclass when the parent class's implementation is different from that required by the subclass. This allows you to specialize the activities of that subclass.*

Sometimes you want to retain the implementation provided by the parent class but also perform some additional activities in the method of the subclass. For example, if you have an application that manages a nonprofit organization, you would probably have a class called `Volunteer` that would have a method called `signUp()`; this method would allow the volunteer to sign up for a community service project and add the user to the list of volunteers for that activity.

You might, however, have some users with restrictions, such as a criminal background, that should prevent them from signing up for certain projects. In this case, polymorphism enables you to create a class called `RestrictedUser` with an overridden `signUp()` method that first checks the restrictions on the user account against the properties of the project and prevents users from signing up if their restrictions do not allow them to volunteer for a particular activity. If their restrictions do not prohibit them from participating, you should invoke the actions of the parent class to complete their registration.

When you override methods of the parent class, you do not necessarily need to completely rewrite the method. You can continue to use the implementation provided by the parent but add additional specialization for your subclass. In this way, you can reuse code and also provide customizations as required by the business rules.

The capability of one class to inherit the methods and properties of another class is one of the most compelling features of an object-oriented system and allows you to gain an incredible level of efficiency and flexibility in your applications.

In this example, you'll create two classes—`Rectangle` and `Square`. A square is a special kind of rectangle. Anything you can do with a rectangle you can do with a square; however, because a rectangle has two different side lengths and a square has only one, you need to do some things differently.

Create a file called `class.Rectangle.php` and add the following code:

```
<?php

  class Rectangle {
    public $height;
    public $width;

    public function __construct($width, $height) {
      $this->width = $width;
      $this->height = $height;
    }

     public function getArea() {
     return $this->height * $this->width;
     }
  }
?>
```

This is a fairly straightforward implementation of a class to model a rectangle. The constructor takes parameters for the width and height, and the area function calculates the area of the rectangle by multiplying them together.

Now take a look at `class.Square.php`, shown next:

```
<?php
  require_once('class.Rectangle.php');

  class Square extends Rectangle {
    public function __construct($size) {
      $this->height = $size;
```

```
        $this->width = $size;
      }

      public function getArea() {
        return pow($this->height, 2);
      }

    }
?>
```

This code overrides both the constructor and the getArea() method. For a square to be a square, both sides must be of the same length. As a result, you need only one parameter for the constructor. If more than one parameter is passed to the function, any values after the first are ignored.

PHP does not raise an error if the number of parameters passed to a user-defined function is greater than the number of parameters established in the function declaration. In a few cases, this is actually desired behavior. If you'd like to learn more, see the documentation of the built-in `func_get_args()` function.

The getArea() function also was overridden. The implementation in the Rectangle class would have returned a perfectly correct result for the Square objects. The method was overridden to improve application performance (although in this case the performance benefit is minuscule). It is faster for PHP to fetch one property and compute its square than to fetch two properties and multiply them together.

By overriding constructors, destructors, and methods, you can alter aspects of how subclasses operate.

Preserving the Functionality of the Parent

Sometimes you want to preserve the functionality provided by the parent. You don't need to completely override the function; you just need to add something to it. You could copy all the code from the parent method into the subclass's method, but as you've already seen, OOP offers you better ways of doing this than just copying lines of code.

To call the functionality provided by the parent, use the syntax parent::[function name]. When you just want to add additional behavior to a method, first you call parent::[function name] and then add your additional code. When extending a function in this way, always call the method on the parent before doing anything else. Doing so ensures that any changes to the operation of the parent won't break your code.

Because the parent class may be expecting the object to be in a certain state, or may alter the state of the object, overwrite property values, or manipulate the object's internal data, always invoke the parent method before adding your own code when extending an inherited method.

The example has two classes: Customer and SweepstakesCustomer. A supermarket has an application that from time to time switches which class is being used in the cash register application when certain promotions are run. Each customer who comes in has his or her own ID value (which comes from a database) as well as a customer number, which indicates how many customers have come to the supermarket before him or her. For this sweepstakes, the millionth customer wins a prize.

Create a file called class.Customer.php and add the following:

```
<?php

  class Customer {
    public $id;
    public $customerNumber;
    public $name;

    public function __construct($customerID) {
      //fetch customer infomation from the database
      //
      //We're hard coding these values here, but in a real application
      //these values would come from a database
      $data = array();
      $data['customerNumber'] = 1000000;
      $data['name'] = 'Jane Johnson';

      //Assign the values from the database to this object
      $this->id = $customerID;
      $this->name = $data['name'];
      $this->customerNumber = $data['customerNumber'];
    }
  }
?>
```

Create a file called `class.SweepstakesCustomer.php` and type this code:

```
<?php
  require_once('class.Customer.php');

  class SweepstakesCustomer extends Customer {
    public function __construct($customerID) {
        parent::__construct($customerID);

        if($this->customerNumber == 1000000) {
          print "Congratulations $this->name! You're our
                 millionth customer! " .
                 "You win a year's supply of frozen fish sticks! ";
        }
    }
  }

?>
```

How Inheritance Works

The `Customer` class initializes values from the database based on the customer ID. You would most likely retrieve the customer ID from a loyalty program swipe card like the type available at most larger grocery store chains. With the customer ID, you can fetch the customer's personal data from the database (just hard-coded in this example) along with an integer value representing how many customers have entered the store before that customer. Store all this information in public member variables.

The `SweepstakesCustomer` class adds a bit of extra functionality to the constructor. You first invoke the parent class's constructor functionality by calling `parent::_construct` and passing to it the parameters it expects. You then look at the `customerNumber` property. If this customer is the millionth, you inform this customer that he or she has won a prize.

To see how to use this class, create a file called `testCustomer.php` and enter the following code:

```
<?php

  require_once('class.SweepstakesCustomer.php');
  //since this file already includes class.Customer.php, there's
  //no need to pull that file in, as well.

  function greetCustomer(Customer $objCust) {
    print "Welcome back to the store $objCust->name!";
  }

  //Change this value to change the class used to create this customer object
  $promotionCurrentlyRunning = true;

  if ($promotionCurrentlyRunning) {
    $objCust = new SweepstakesCustomer(12345);
  } else {
    $objCust = new Customer(12345);
  }

  greetCustomer($objCust);

?>
```

Run `testCustomer.php` in your browser with the `$promotionCurrentlyRunning` variable set first to false and then to true. When the value is true, the prize message is displayed.

Interfaces

Sometimes you have a group of classes that are not necessarily related through an inheritance-type relationship. You may have totally different classes that just happen to share some behaviors in common. For example, both a jar and a door can be opened and closed, however, they are in no other way related. No matter the kind of jar or the kind of door, they both can carry out these activities, but there is no other common thread between them.

What Interfaces Do

You see this same concept in OOP as well. An *interface* enables you to specify that an object is capable of performing a certain function, but it does not necessarily tell you how the object does so. An interface is a contract between unrelated objects to perform a common function. An object that implements this interface is guaranteeing to its users that it is capable of performing all the functions defined by the interface specification. Bicycles and footballs are totally different things; however, objects representing those items in a sporting goods store inventory system must be capable of interacting with that system.

By declaring an interface and then implementing it in your objects, you can hand completely different classes to common functions. The following example shows the rather prosaic door-and-jar analogy.

Create a file called `interface.Opener.php`:

```
<?php

  interface Openable {
    abstract function open();
    abstract function close();
  }

?>
```

Just as you name your class files `class.[class name].php`, you should use the same convention with interfaces and call them `interface.[interface name].php`.

You declare the interface `Openable` using a syntax similar to that of a class, except that you substitute the word `interface` for the word `class`. An interface does not have member variables. It does not specify an implementation of any of its member functions.

Because no implementation is specified, you declare these functions to be `abstract`. Doing so tells PHP that any class implementing this interface is responsible for providing an implementation of the functions. If you fail to provide an implementation of *all* the abstract methods of an interface, PHP will raise a runtime error. You may not selectively choose some of the abstract methods to implement. You must provide implementations of them all.

How Interfaces Work

The `Openable` interface is a contract with other parts of the application that says any class implementing this interface will provide two methods, called `open()` and `close()`, that take no parameters. With this agreed-upon set of methods, you can allow very different objects to pass into the same function without the need for an inherited relationship to exist between them.

Create the following files, beginning with `class.Door.php`:

```
<?php

require_once('interface.Openable.php');

class Door implements Openable {

    private $_locked = false;

    public function open() {
      if($this->_locked) {
        print "Can't open the door. It's locked.";
      } else {
        print "creak...<br>";
      }
    }

    public function close() {
      print "Slam!!<br>";
    }

    public function lockDoor() {
      $this->_locked = true;
```

```
    }

    public function unlockDoor() {
      $this->_locked = false;
    }

  }

?>
```

and then `class.Jar.php`:

```
<?
require_once('interface.Openable.php');

class Jar implements Openable {
  private $contents;

  public function __construct($contents) {
    $this->contents = $contents;
  }

  public function open() {
    print "the jar is now open<br>";
  }

  public function close() {
    print "the jar is now closed<br>";
  }
}
?>
```

To use these files, create a new file called `testOpenable.php` in the same directory.

```
<?php
  require_once('class.Door.php');
  require_once('class.Jar.php);

  function openSomething(Openable $obj) {
    $obj->open();
  }

  $objDoor = new Door();
  $objJar = new Jar("jelly");

  openSomething($objDoor);
  openSomething($objJar);
?>
```

Because both the `Door` class and the `Jar` class implement the `Openable` interface, you can pass both to the `openSomething()` function. Because that function accepts only something that implements the `Openable` interface, you know that you can call the functions `open()` and `close()` within it. However, you should not attempt to access the `contents` property of the `Jar` class or utilize the `lock()` or `unlock()` functions of the `Door` class within the `openSomething()` function, because that property and those methods are not part of the interface. The interface contract guarantees that you have `open()` and `close()` and nothing else.

By using interfaces in your application, you can allow completely different and unrelated objects to talk to each other with a guarantee that they will be able to interact on the terms specified in the interface. The interface is a contract to provide certain methods.

Encapsulation

As mentioned earlier in this chapter, objects enable you to hide the details of their implementation from users of the object. You do not need to know whether the `Volunteer` class mentioned earlier stores information in a database, a flat text file, an XML document, or other data storage mechanism to be able to invoke the `signUp()` method. Similarly, you do not need to know whether the information about the volunteer contained within the object is implemented as single variables, an array, or even other objects. This ability to hide the details of implementation is known as encapsulation. Generally speaking, encapsulation refers to two concepts: protecting a class's internal data from code outside that class, and hiding the details of implementation.

The word *encapsulate* literally means to place in a capsule, or outer container. A well-designed class provides a complete outer shell around its internals and presents an interface to code outside the class that is wholly separated from the particulars of those internals. By doing so, you gain two advantages: you can change the implementation details at any time without affecting code that uses your class, and, because you know that nothing outside your class can inadvertently modify the state or property values of an object built from your class without your knowledge, you can trust the state of the object and the value of its properties to be valid and to make sense.

The member variables of a class and its functions have a visibility. *Visibility* refers to what can be seen by code outside the class. *Private* member variables and functions are not accessible to code outside the class and are used for the class's internal implementation. *Protected* member variables and functions are visible only to the subclasses of the class. *Public* member variables and functions are usable by any code, inside or outside the class.

Generally speaking, all internal member variables of a class should be declared private. Any access needed to those variables by code outside the class should be done through an accessor method. You don't let someone who wants you to try a new food blindfold and force-feed you; you need to be able to examine the item and determine whether you want to allow it into your body. Similarly, when an object wants to allow code outside it to change properties or in some other way affect its internal data, by encapsulating access to that data in a public function (and by keeping the internal data private), you have the opportunity to validate the changes and accept or reject them.

For example, if you are building an application for a bank that handles details of customer accounts, you might have an `Account` object with a property called `totalBalance` and methods called `makeDeposit()` and `makeWithdrawal()`. The total balance property should be read-only. The only way to affect the balance is to make a withdrawal or a deposit. If the `totalBalance` property were to be implemented as a public member variable, you could write code that would increase the value of that variable without having to actually make a deposit. This approach would, obviously, be bad for the bank. Instead, you should implement this property as a private member variable and provide a public method called `getTotalBalance()`, which returns the value of that private member variable. Because the variable storing the value of the account balance is private, you can't manipulate it directly. Because the only public methods that affect the account balance are `makeWithdrawal()` and `makeDeposit()`, you will have to actually make a deposit if you want to increase the value of your account.

By allowing you to hide the details of implementation and protect access to internal member variables, an object-oriented software development approach gives you a flexible, stable application.

> *Encapsulation of internal data and method implementations allows an object-oriented software system to protect and control access to data and hide the details of implementation.*

Changes to OO in PHP5

Support for objects in PHP goes all the way back to PHP3. There was never any intention of supporting the idea of classes or objects, but some limited support was added, almost as an afterthought, to provide "syntactic sugar" (to use Zeev Suraski's phrase) for associative arrays. Object support in PHP was originally designed as a convenient way of grouping data and functions, but only a small subset of the features traditionally associated with a full-blown object-oriented programming language was included. As PHP grew in popularity, the use of an OO approach became increasingly common in large applications. However, the poor internal implementation became limiting.

Most notably, there was no support for real encapsulation. You could not specify member variables or methods to be private or protected. Everything was public—which, as you've seen, can be problematic.

Additionally, there was no support for abstract interfaces or methods. Methods and member variables could not be declared static. There were no destructors. All these concepts are familiar to anyone with a background in another object-oriented programming language, and the lack of these features in PHP's object model could make the transition from a language such as Java (which does support all these ideas) to PHP difficult. For those who have previous experience with PHP4, the following table lists some of the new features in the PHP5 object model.

New Feature	Benefit
Private, protected member variables and methods	Real encapsulation and data protection are now possible in PHP.
Improved dereferencing support	Statements like `$obj->getSomething()->doSomething()` are now possible.
Static member variables and methods	Methods that can be called statically are now clearly identifiable. Class-level constants help control pollution of the global namespace.
Unified constructors	All class constructors are now called `__construct()`. This helps with encapsulation of overridden subclass constructors and makes it easier to alter inheritance when multiple classes are involved in a tree of inheritance.

New Feature	Benefit
Destructor support	Through the `__destruct()` method, classes in PHP can now have destructors. This feature allows actions to be carried out when the object is destroyed.
Support for abstract classes and interfaces	You can define required methods in a parent class while deferring implementation to a subclass. Abstract classes can't be instantiated; only their nonabstract subclasses can.
Parameter type hints	You can specify the class for function parameters that are expecting an object. `function foo(Bar $objBar) { ...` allows you to be sure that the data type of the parameter is what we expect.

Summary

In this chapter you explored the concept of object-oriented programming. A class was seen as a blueprint for creating objects. Objects are runtime bundles of data and functions created from a class definition. Objects have characteristics, called *properties*, and behaviors, called *methods*. Properties can be thought of as variables and methods as functions.

Some classes share a common parent type. Squares are rectangles. When you declare a class to be a subtype of a parent class, it inherits the methods and properties of the parent. You have the option to override inherited methods. You can completely reimplement the method, if you so choose, or continue to use the parent's implementation but also add specializations particular to the subclass (or not override the method at all).

Encapsulation is an important concept to object-oriented programming. It refers to the ability of a class to protect access to its internal member variables and shield users of that class from the particulars of its implementation. Member methods and properties have three levels of visibility; private, protected and public. Private members can be used only by the class's internal operations. Protected members are visible to subclasses. Public members can be used by code outside the class.

Object-oriented support in PHP received a major overhaul with the introduction of PHP5 and the Zend Engine 2. New features and significant performance improvements make PHP a real OO programming language.

Unified Modeling Language (UML)

If you're the only programmer working on a small project, drawing a small sketch of the application on paper or keeping the design completely in your mind is often sufficient. A solo programmer can usually complete a project without any problems this way.

Say that you were to get a larger project requiring two developers. You're the one who's responsible for designing the system, and the second developer is there to help you write the code. How would you communicate the design of this system to the other person? You could describe in words what classes were necessary and provide a description of how the system functions both for the end user and internally. After a while, you might end up with a lot of text describing the system. If you imagine a larger project, it quickly becomes clear that describing a large software system purely in words is not practical. If you created diagrams of your own design, you'd have the added task of explaining your system of notation to the other members of the team.

Another language exists, the Unified Modeling Language (UML), which was designed to solve this problem. UML is primarily a language of standardized diagrams, each of which lends itself to describing a particular area of software design. UML gives everyone the same way of "speaking" about a system and provides a powerful method of visualizing it.

Requirements Gathering

In this chapter you'll work through the design and development of a hypothetical band-tracking system called BandSpy. In the process you'll learn about UML diagrams and where they fit into the process.

A client from a record company has contacted you to develop a Web-based system to track the bands that client represents. During the initial phone conversation, the client explains that BandSpy should allow Web users to view details about the different bands the company represents, and check out upcoming concerts. Someone from the record company should be able to add new bands to the system, edit existing band information, and book new concert performances for the bands. Although your conversation with the client is informal, it begins a key part of the software design—the *requirements-gathering* phase. In this phase you'll want to determine exactly what the software needs to do to satisfy its users.

Interviewing the Client

Speaking on the phone, you arrange to meet with the client. After some quality get-to-know-you time, the meeting progresses to a further discussion of the system. The attendees of the meeting are Bill, the owner of the company; Jane, the operations manager; and Tom, the company "computer guy."

During your initial interviews, getting a feel for the roles of the people who are involved is important. You can infer that the people attending the meeting have some interest in how the software works. That interest, however, may or may not always be beneficial to the outcome of the project.

The key person to identify during requirements gathering is the person who has detailed knowledge of the *domain*—the area that the software will model. That could include someone who previously did manually what the software will now automate, or it could be someone who knows how the business works and what the software needs to do to correctly model it. This person is often referred to as a *domain expert*.

Over the course of the interview, Jane does most of the talking. She describes what they're hoping the system can accomplish and how the company currently handles this process. It's a good bet that Jane is your domain expert. During further interviews, speaking to her directly will be useful. Bill stays quiet most of the time; he probably has other matters to attend to. Tom mentions that he'll be the one actually entering the data into the system. You note that you may have to devote a little time to explaining the use of the administration tools to him.

During the course of the meeting you take notes on what Jane says the system needs to do, and you come out with the following list:

1. Users can visit the BandSpy Web site and browse information about bands. Band information includes the type of band, musicians in the band, and what instruments they play.
2. Users can view information about upcoming performances that might include one or multiple bands.
3. Site administrator can add new information about bands.
4. Site administrator can edit existing band information.
5. Site administrator can add a new performance. Adding a new performance includes booking a venue and generating tickets. Separate third-party companies handle both the venue booking and the tickets. These companies have reservation systems that you will need to notify via the BandSpy software.

Now that you have a list of requirements, it's time to start putting the UML diagrams to work.

Use Case Diagrams

Use case diagrams show the system from the task-oriented perspective of a user. One use case represents a task the user is trying to accomplish with the system. Figure 2-1 shows a simple use case diagram for users visiting the BandSpy site and browsing band information.

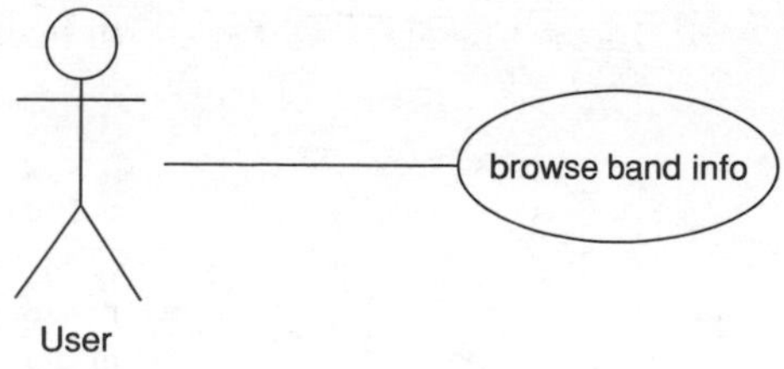

Figure 2-1

The stick figure is called an *actor* and the bubble is the use case. The line indicates that this actor can perform the connected use case. In use case diagrams the actor is usually a role associated with a person, although it can represent an external system that acts upon ours.

Notice that the use case "browse band info" is rather general. A high level of detail isn't necessary here. You just want to be able to cover all the use cases the system should be capable of. If necessary, use cases can be broken down into their separate *scenarios*. A scenario is the sequence of steps comprising the use case. For example, the scenario for the previous use case is as follows:

1. User goes to BandSpy Web site.
2. User navigates site using menu.
3. User examines band/musician/concert information.

The use case diagram for the administrative tasks is shown in Figure 2-2.

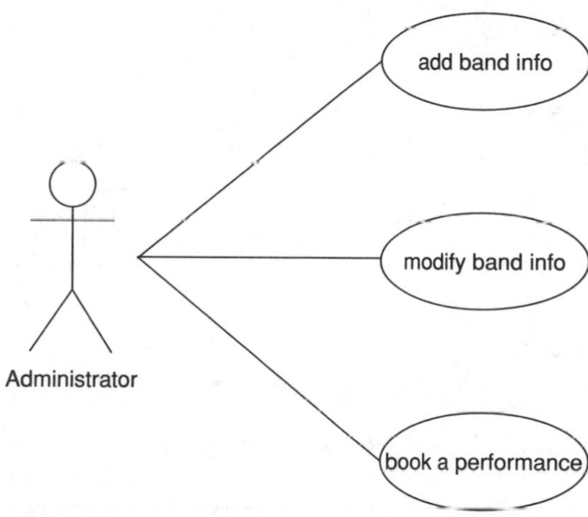

Figure 2-2

The administrative use cases are the separate tasks that the administrator might attempt when using the BandSpy system. The client has mentioned that he would like the administrative section of the site to require a password-protected login. Because the logging into the system can be thought of as a task itself, you can use an `include` to show that this use case is part of all three other use cases. Figure 2-3 shows the use of an `include`, indicated by a dashed line.

Multiple actors may appear within a use case diagram. Often, different actors may share a use case. Figure 2-4 shows the completed use case diagram for the BandSpy system. Because both the

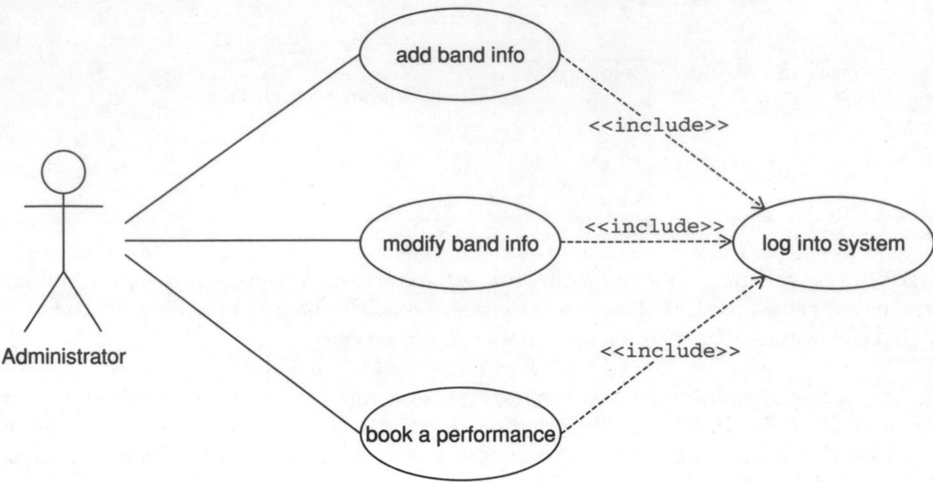

Figure 2-3

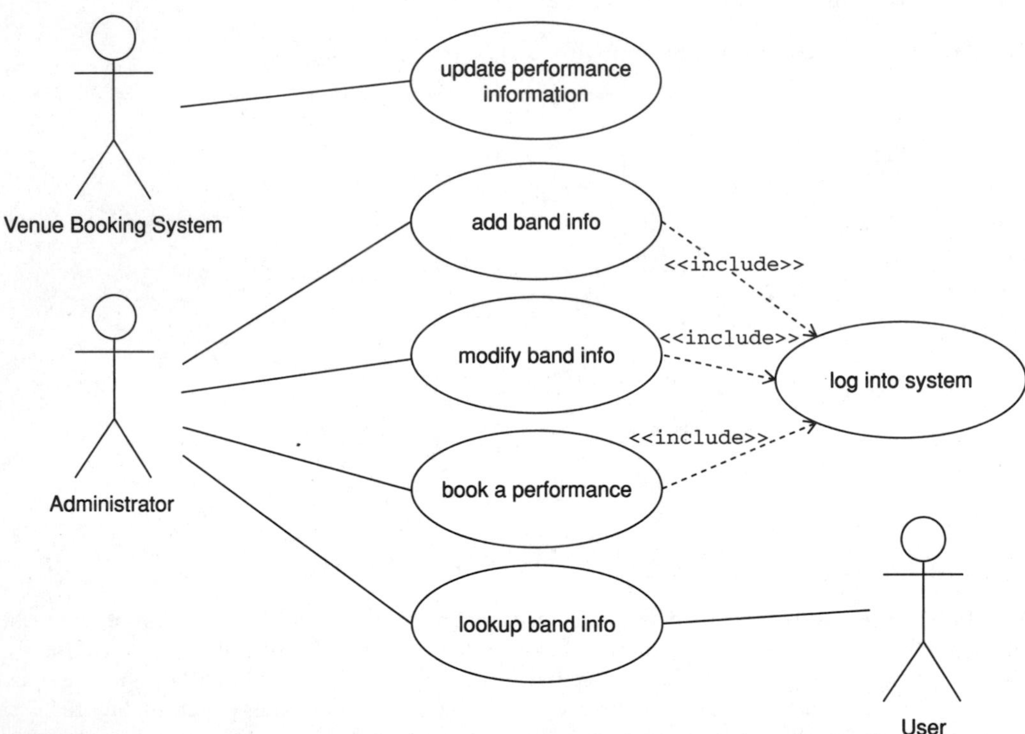

Figure 2-4

administrator and the regular users can look up band information, they share that use case. Additionally, the use case shows the nonhuman actor—the venue booking system—performing the task of updating information about an upcoming performance.

Class Diagrams

Although the use case diagrams provide a useful way to express what capabilities the system will have for various actors, they do little to explain the inner workings of the software. This is the point at which you can start using the other UML diagrams, and your knowledge of objects, to define those inner workings in more detail.

Modeling the Domain

After the interviews with the client are complete and the use cases have been finalized, you can move on to the process of designing the software to model the domain. One thing that means is developing the system so that its classes are closely modeled after what they represent in real life. For example, in our application, users can see information about different types of musicians, so it's probably a good idea to have a Musician class, or even better, a Musician interface that all different types of musicians can implement.

Class diagrams are probably the most important diagrams to use and understand. They provide a good balance of detail and flexibility. They provide a description of the domain you're modeling, and allow a varying level of detail from very high level to very specific about the exact methods and properties of a class. In addition, they're useful to describe interesting object-oriented concepts such as design patterns, which are covered in Chapter 4.

The basics of a class diagram are shown in Figure 2-5. The top box in the rectangle shows the name of the class. The middle box shows its *attributes* and the bottom box shows its *operations.* In PHP, the terms "attributes" and "operations" translate to member variables and methods, respectively, in our Musician class.

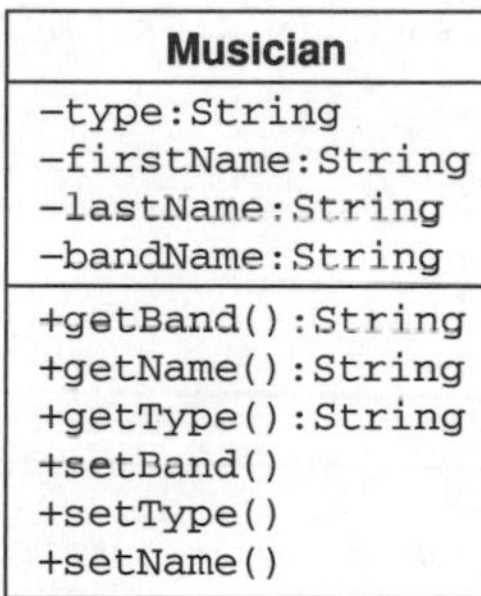

Figure 2-5

The attribute types are indicated after the colon. In this simple example, all our attribute types are strings. The minus sign says that the attributes are private members of the class. The plus sign in front of the operations indicates that they are public. If an operation returns a value, its type is shown after the colon. Again, in this example they are all strings.

The following is the PHP code for `Musician` shown in the class diagram:

```
class Musician {

  private $last;
  private $first;
  private $bandName;
  private $type;

  function __construct($last, $first, $musicianType) {
         $this->last = $last;
         $this->first = $first;
         $this->mtype = $musicianType;
  }

  public function getName() {
         echo $this->first . $this->last;
  }

  public function getBand() {
         echo $this->bandName;
  }

  public function getMusicanType() {
         echo $this->type;
  }

  public function setName($first, $last) {
         $this->first = $first;
         $this->last = $last;
  }

  public function setBand($bandName) {
         $this->bandName = $bandName;
  }

  public function setMusicanType($musicianType) {
         $this->type = $musicianType;
  }
}
```

Relationships

If your application had only one class, it might not be particularly helpful to draw diagrams. Because the BandSpy system will require more than one, you need to think about how the objects will interact with each other. In the previous example, we used strings as the data type for all our member variables. Generally, this is not a good idea. If a musician were a part of a band, it would make sense that you would want more than just the name of the band. You might want, for instance, the other members of the band, what genre of music they play, and so on. This type of thinking will guide you during the design phase of your software. Certain member variables will require a higher degree of complexity and therefore need to be broken out into their own classes.

Associations

Taking a look at Figure 2-6, you can see the `bandName` attribute moved over into an attribute of the `Band` class. Also note that we're not showing every attribute and method in the classes.

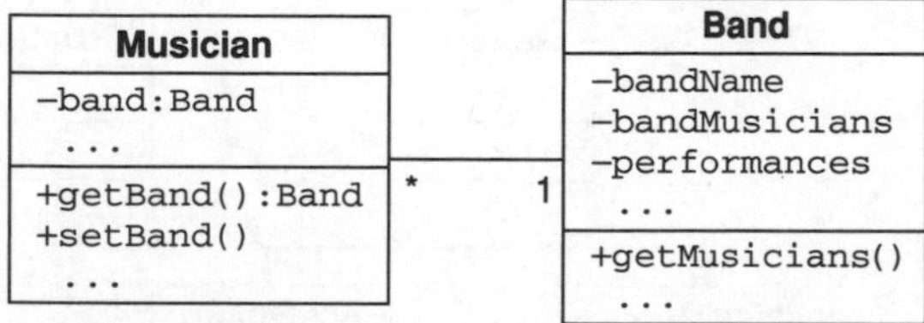

Figure 2-6

When using class diagrams, you need to show only what is important in the context of the diagram. Simple accessor methods for private member variables are assumed and hence left out. When a class diagram is incomplete, you can use an ellipsis (...) to show that certain information is intentionally left out.

The line connecting the two classes is a type of relationship known as an *association*. For this example, the association is one-to-many—one `Band` may have many `Musicians`, or conversely, many `Musicians` can be in one `Band`, as denoted by the * and 1 beneath the association.

The association line can also show *navigability*. In our example, the line without any arrowheads shows that you can move in both directions, also known as *bi-directional navigability*. In other words, each class has an internal reference to the other one. If the association allows you to navigate in only one direction, it is referred to as *unidirectional navigability*. Figure 2-7 shows the relationship between the `Musician` class and the `Instrument` class. The `Musician` class has access to any `Instruments` in its internal collection, but the `Instrument` is not aware of which `Musician` possesses it.

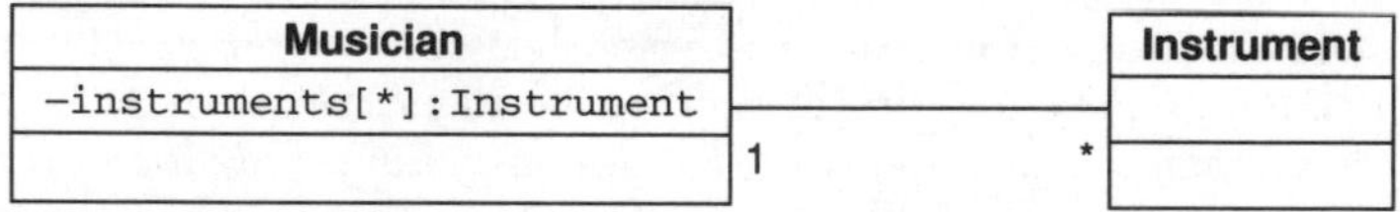

Figure 2-7

Realizations and Generalizations

We mentioned previously that creating a `Musician` interface that all other musician type classes could implement would be a better idea. This way you can derive other classes, such as `Guitarist` and `Drummer`, that follow the rules of how `Musician` behaves in your system. As long as you follow the contract of the `Musician` interface, you can have confidence that your derived classes will play along correctly.

When you want to indicate an interface and the classes that implement it, you show a relationship between them called a *realization*. A dashed line shows a realization with a hollow arrowhead at the end point to the interface. Interfaces in UML diagrams are similar to standard class diagrams but are shown using the word *interface* in guillemots above the interface name. Figure 2-8 displays two classes, and `Guitarist`, implementing the `Musician` interface.

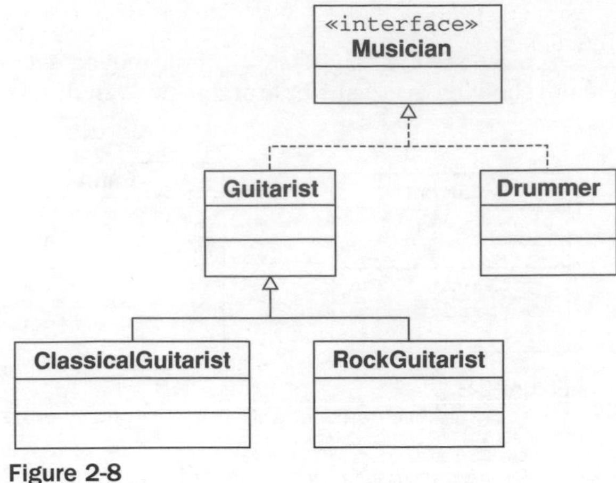

Figure 2-8

When you want to indicate inheritance from either an abstract class or from another concrete one, you can use a generalization. A *generalization* is identical to a realization except that the line is not dashed. The diagram shows the subclassing of `Guitarist` to create the `RockGuitarist` and `ClassicalGuitarist` classes.

Composites

Often, the useful relationships of classes are not based on associations or inheritance but rather on the way classes are grouped. Consider the example of a drum set. In our application, the `Instrument` interface is implemented in a concrete class such as `Guitar` or `Piano`, as shown in Figure 2-9. In addition, the `DrumSet`, `Drum`, and `Cymbal` classes implement it as well. The new notation of the lines with the black diamonds indicates that the `DrumSet` is a *composite* of `Drum` and `Cymbal` classes. One instance of `DrumSet` will contain instances of the `Drum` and `Cymbal` classes. A composite is a strict relationship characterized by two things. First, the parts of a composite may not be shared elsewhere. In other words, an instance of `Drum` belonging to an instance of `DrumSet` may not belong to any other `DrumSet`. The second rule is that when an instance of `DrumSet` is deleted, its composite parts should also be deleted.

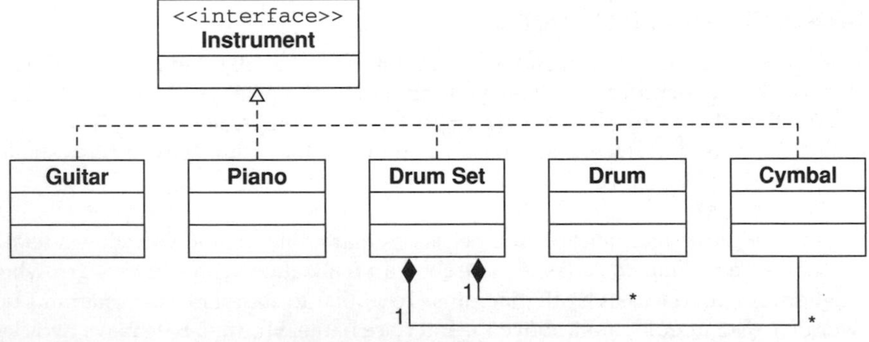

Figure 2-9

A more general type of composite is called an *aggregate*. The notation for an aggregate is the same as a composite, except that the diamond is hollow. Aggregates are allowed to share instances of other classes and therefore are not required to delete them when they themselves are deleted.

Implementation

Now that you've covered the basics of class diagrams, take a look at a bit of sample code based on some of the concepts you just read about:

```
<?php

  interface Band {
     public function getName();
     public function getGenre();
     public function addMusician();
     public function getMusicians();
  }

  interface Musician {
     public function addInstrument();
     public function getInstruments();

     public function assignToBand();
     public function getMusicianType();
  }

  interface Instrument {
     public function getName();
     public function getCategory();
  }

  class Guitarist implements Musician {

    private $last;
    private $first;
    private $musicianType;

    private $instruments;
    private $bandReference;

    function __construct($first, $last) {
       $this->last = $last;
       $this->first = $first;
       $this->instruments = array();
       $this->musicianType = "guitarist";
    }

    public function getName() {
      return $this->first . " " . $this->last;
    }

    public function addInstrument(Instrument $instrument) {
       array_push($this->instruments, $instrument);
    }
```

```
    public function getInstruments() {
        return $this->instruments;
    }

    public function getBand() {
        return $this->$bandReference;
    }

    public function assignToBand(Band $band) {
      $this->$bandReference = $band;
    }

    public function getMusicianType() {
        return $this->musicianType;
    }

    public function setMusicianType($musicianType) {
      $this->musicianType = $musicianType;
    }

}

class LeadGuitarist extends Guitarist {
    function __construct($last, $first) {
            parent::__construct($last, $first);
            $this->setMusicianType("lead guitarist");
    }
}

class RockBand implements Band {

    private $bandName;
    private $bandGenre;
    private $musicians;

    function __construct($bandName) {
        $this->bandName = $bandName;
        $this->musicians = array();
        $this->bandGenre = "rock";
    }

    public function getName() {
        return $this->bandName;
    }

    public function getGenre(){
        return $this->bandGenre;
    }

    public function addMusician(Musician $musician){
        array_push($this->musicians, $musician);
        $musician->assignToBand($this);
    }
```

```
    public function getMusicians() {
        return $this->musicians;
    }
  }

  class Guitar implements Instrument {

    private $name;
    private $category;

    function __construct($name) {
        $this->name = $name;
        $this->category = "guitar";
    }

    public function getName() {
        return $this->name;
    }

    public function getCategory() {
        return $this->category;
    }
  }

  // Test Objects
  $band = new RockBand("The Variables");
  $bandMemberA = new Guitarist("Jack", "Float");
  $bandMemberB = new LeadGuitarist("Jim", "Integer");

  $bandMemberA->addInstrument(new Guitar("Gibson Les Paul"));
  $bandMemberB->addInstrument(new Guitar("Fender Stratocaster"));
  $bandMemberB->addInstrument(new Guitar("Hondo H-77"));

  $band->addMusician($bandMemberA);
  $band->addMusician($bandMemberB);

  foreach($band->getMusicians() as $musician) {
    echo "Musician ".$musician->getName() . "<br>";
    echo "is the " . $musician->getMusicianType() . "<br>";
    echo "in the " . $musician->getBand()->getGenre() . " band <br>";
    echo "called " . $musician->getBand()->getName() . "<br>";

    foreach($musician->getInstruments() as $instrument) {
        echo "And plays the " . $instrument->getName() . " ";
        echo $instrument->getCategory() . "<br>";
    }
    echo "<p>";
  }
?>
```

Although this example is fairly simple, it illustrates one of the important aspects of object-oriented programming. Notice how no conditional branching occurs when the objects are tested at the end. You don't need to find out what type of `Musician` or `Instrument` you're dealing with before calling its methods. Because the rules of the interface were followed, you can trust that the objects will all respond appropriately, and uniquely to their implementation. As discussed in the previous chapter, this is what's referred to as polymorphism. Anytime you need to add another type of `Musician`, you can just write the new class, defining its behavior behind the standard `Musician` interface.

Activity Diagrams

Jane mentioned in an earlier meeting that the BandSpy application will need to hook into two other third-party systems—the ticketing system and the venue reservation system—when a new performance is added. To understand the order of events necessary to accomplish this task, you can draw an *activity diagram.* Activity diagrams are good in any situation when you need to understand the flow of activities going on within a use case. In this example, the use case is the BandSpy administrator booking a performance.

Further conversations with Jane reveal that the BandSpy system will not only have to send a message to the venue reservation system, but will need to receive information back from both systems. The venue system will send a confirmation that the venue is available, and the ticking system will transmit ticking information such as pricing. If the administrator attempts to book a venue on a date or time that is not available, the venue system will indicate that fact to BandSpy, and the administrator will be notified and may try to book another date.

Figure 2-10 shows the activity diagram for the process described previously. Activity diagrams begin with a solid black circle called the *starting point.* From there the flow of the process follows the arrows, known as *transitions,* into rounded rectangles representing *activities.*

A black hollow diamond indicates a *decision point.* As the name suggests, the flow of transitions is split, based on some decision or condition. In the diagram, the decision is whether the venue is available on the requested date.

After the decision, a large black bar called a *fork* splits the flow to two different activities. In the venue system, a confirmation is generated and will be sent back to the BandSpy system, where the ticket system is fired up to start generating tickets for the event. Both the ticket and venue systems information are sent back to BandSpy where they meet up in another black bar called a *join.* The join indicates that both external systems messages must reach the join for the activity diagram to proceed to its final step, storing and updating information about the new performance.

The three large rectangles dividing the activities particular to each system are called *swimlanes.* Although swimlanes are not mandatory, they often help to clarify the diagram when multiple systems are involved.

Sequence Diagrams

You may have noticed that the BandSpy application has a hierarchy of classes. `Bands` contain `Musicians` that have `Instruments` that may be composites of other `Instruments`. During the use of the application, messages get relayed through the object relationships. You can think of method calls as a kind of message that one object might call on another. For example, if an instance of `Band` needed to know what `Instruments` its `Musicians` were playing, it would send a message to called `getInstruments()` to all its `Musicians`. Another way of saying that is `Band` is calling the `getInstruments()` method on all its `Musicians`.

It's useful to visualize how messages move between different objects, and the UML provides another diagram that's designed to represent that movement. This diagram is called the *sequence diagram.*

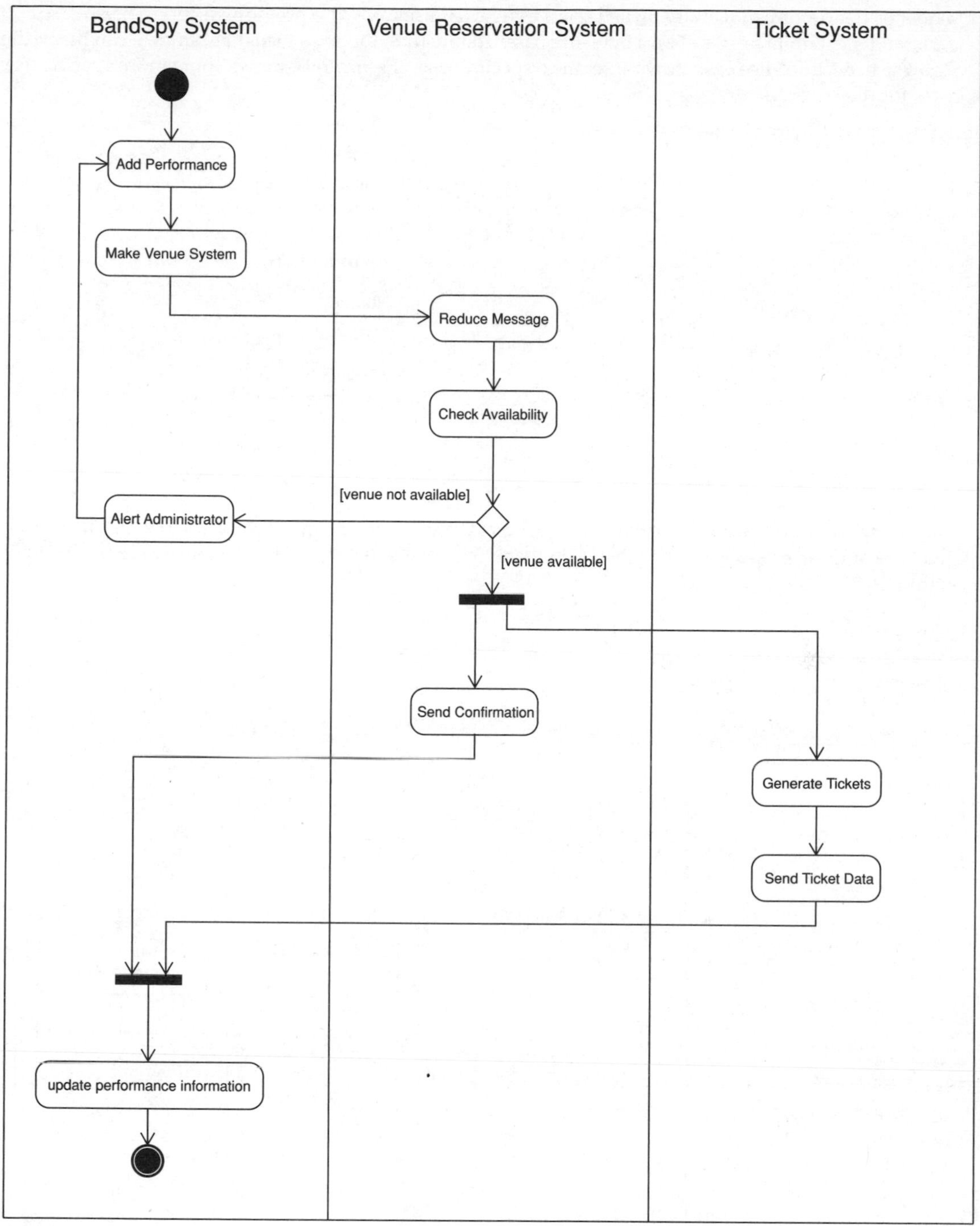
BandSpy System
Venue Reservation System
Ticket System
Add Performance
Make Venue System
Reduce Message
Check Availability
[venue not available]
Alert Administrator
[venue available]
Send Confirmation
Generate Tickets
Send Ticket Data
update performance information

Figure 2-10

Sequence diagrams can usually be tied to an individual use case. The previous section on use cases contained a general "browse band info" use case. To illustrate the sequence diagram, we can break the "browse band info" use case down into more specific cases. Figure 2-11 shows some more specific use cases for the "user" actor.

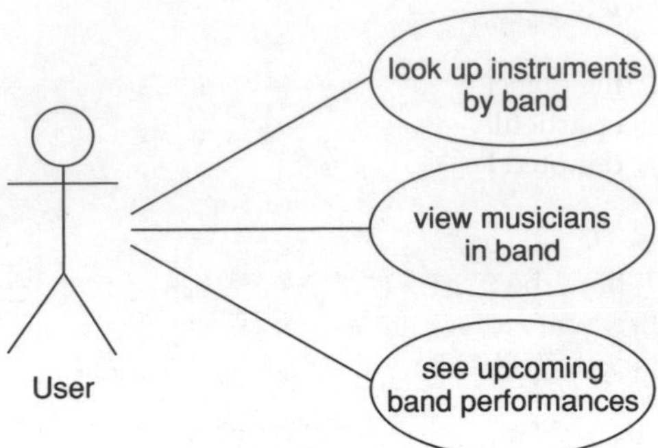

Figure 2-11

Taking the "lookup instruments by band" use case, the sequence diagram should show all the objects involved and the messages passed between them to complete the task. The sequence diagram is shown in Figure 2-12.

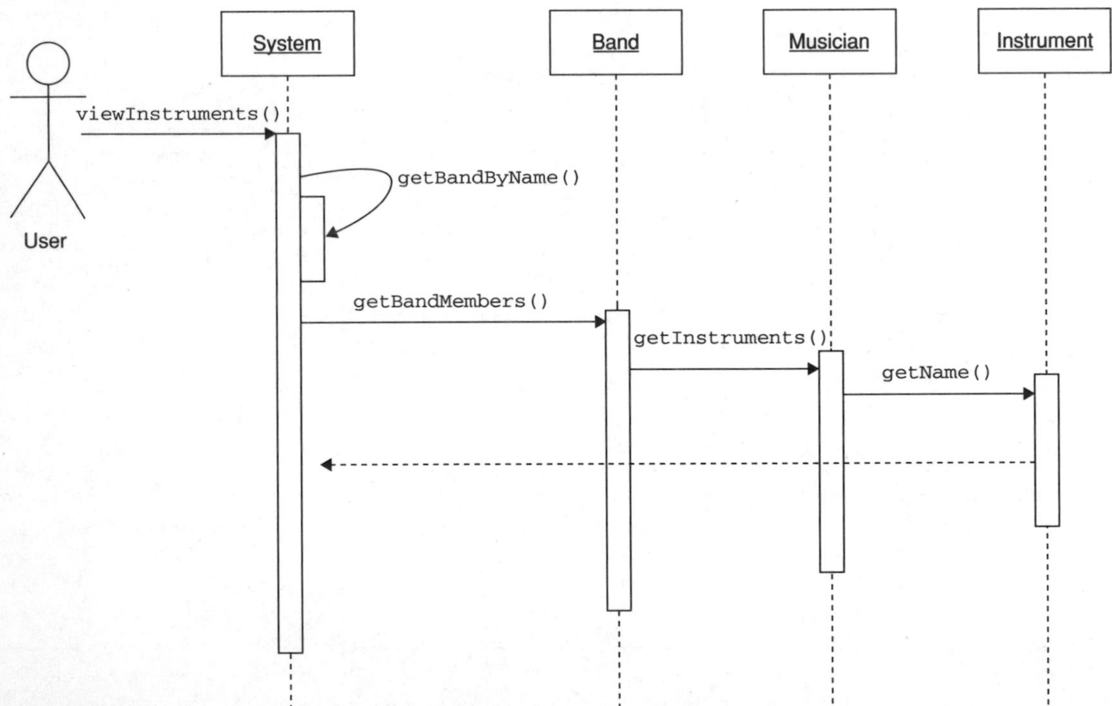

Figure 2-12

The boxes at the top show the instances of objects involved in the sequence. In general, a box with an underlined name denotes an instance as opposed to a class. The dashed line descending from the object is the object's *lifeline*. In this case, the lifeline doesn't indicate the creation or deletion of any of your objects—before this use case was acted upon, all the objects were already there. However, it is possible to indicate the instantiation of an object by using a "create" message and a large X at the bottom of the object's lifeline to show its deletion.

The vertical rectangle shows the object's *activation*, that is, the time during which the object is involved in the execution of a particular operation. Time in this case is represented vertically, so the longer an object's activation (denoted by the length of the rectangle that represents it), the longer it is involved in the operation.

Another object in the application, the `System` object, is introduced in this diagram. In the BandSpy application, the `System` object will receive all messages from the Web GUI, rather than allow it to interact directly with your other objects. This way, the application has a single point of entry.

Arrows indicate messages. They're named with the corresponding method names of the objects, but it's okay to be less formal about it and just use a non method-like name for the message. Taking the messages step by step, the sequence is as follows:

1. A user requests to see all instruments of a particular band by typing in its name.
2. The system object looks up the band reference by performing a *self-call* on its own utility method.
3. The system object uses the found band reference and calls the `getBandMembers` method on it.
4. The band object calls the `getInstruments` method of its assigned musicians.
5. The musician object calls the `getName` method on each of its assigned instruments.
6. The instrument names are returned to the system object for display to the user.

State Diagrams

State diagrams are handy when you want to show the changes to a single object's state during its lifecycle. State changes can be simple differences in member variables or more complex things such as polling for a response from an external source.

In BandSpy, the `Performance` class has a lifecycle that's worth documenting with a state diagram. When a new `Performance` object is created, it must contact the venue reservation system and await a confirmation. If the response from the venue system says the reservation is good, the performance must be permanently stored. If the reservation is not accepted, the `Performance` object should inform the System and then be destroyed. In Figure 2-13 a state diagram shows the various states for the object.

The solid circle shows the start of the object's lifecycle, and arrows indicate transitions from one state to another. After the new `Performance` is initialized and dispatches a message to the venue system, the awaiting confirmation state polls until it receives a message back from the venue system.

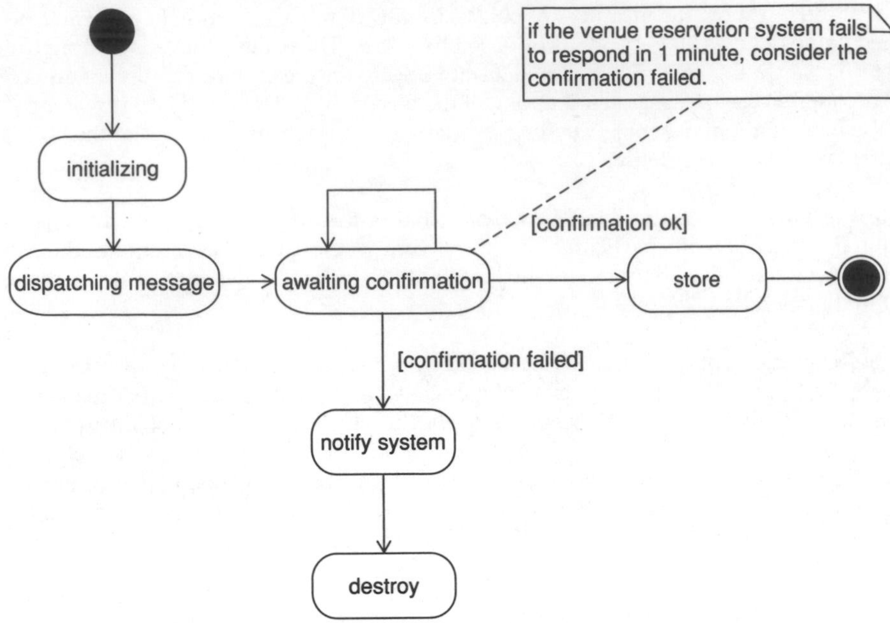

Figure 2-13

One new symbol in Figure 2-13 is a *note* indicating that the awaiting confirmation state should wait one minute to receive a reply from the venue system. A note can be used in any UML diagram where you want to add extra information such as this.

Component and Deployment Diagrams

The last diagram discussed in this chapter is the component diagram. Component diagrams give a high-level, abstract view of your software. For the BandSpy component diagram, the majority of the code is reduced to a single component on the Web server. Technically elements such as the Web server are parts of another UML diagram called *deployment diagrams.* Deployment diagrams show some of the physical elements of your applications' infrastructure, such as the different servers your application runs on.

In Figure 2-14, the large cube-shaped boxes are called *nodes.* Think of a node as a separate piece of physical hardware, or, in a more conceptual sense, as a defined, separate system of software such as a Web browser.

The components are the smaller rectangles within the nodes. Dashed arrows are *dependencies.* The BandSpy Web GUI is dependent upon the BandSpy application on the Web server. The reverse is not true; however, another client could access the system. Solid lines show a connection between nodes—for example, the Web browser communicating over HTTP.

The small circles are a kind of shorthand to show an interface. As mentioned earlier, our application has a single `System` interface that all clients have to use. Another interface is shown within the venue reservation

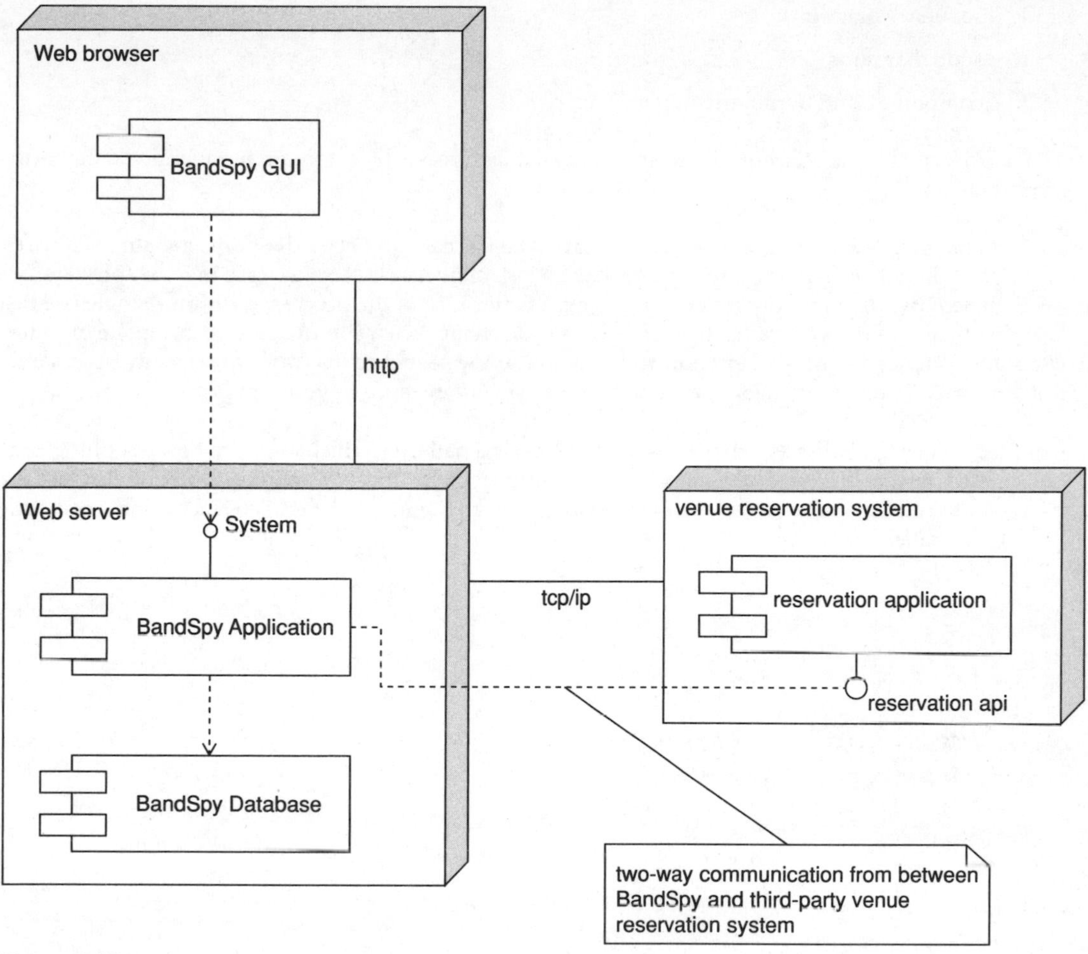

Figure 2-14

system node. The company that manages the system has provided you with a list of the public methods you can use. You don't need to know any of the inner workings of the venue system; you just need to know the methods of the Application Programming Interface (API) used in the reservation system.

Summary

UML gives you a standardized, flexible language to design and model your software. This chapter covered the following UML diagrams:

- use case diagrams
- class diagrams
- activity diagrams

- sequence diagrams
- state diagrams
- component and deployment diagrams

You also learned some concepts about software architecture, such as domain modeling and gathering requirements.

Remember, using every diagram is not necessary. The use case and class diagrams are almost always useful, but the other diagrams are not worth drawing for every class or use case in your software. You need an activity diagram only if you want to get a better idea of the processes within a single use case. Use a state diagram if you have an object whose state changes in a complex way during one or more use cases and you need to make clear how it will work. A few sequence diagrams are usually necessary, but don't try to diagram every message passed between every instance in your application.

Chapter 4, "Design Patterns," discusses software design patterns, which are a way of describing reusable object relationships that you can use to solve various problems in software development. Because each design pattern is described with a UML class diagram, you're in good shape to learn about them when you get to that chapter.

Putting Objects to Work

Now that you have gained a good grounding in object-oriented basics from first two chapters, we'll push on with a slightly more complex look at how you can build a real application using object-oriented techniques.

Our chosen application is a contact manager that is intended to manage data about individuals and organizations and to enable users to look up and edit contact information associated with them. The discussion in this chapter is designed to present you with a good grounding in the issues behind creating working object-oriented applications. Along the way, it will also demonstrate how the major principles behind the object-oriented paradigm, such as code reuse, encapsulation, inheritance, and of course, abstraction, can be applied.

Creating the Contact Manager

A contact management application enables the user to track individuals and organizations, their contact information (such as address, e-mail, and phone number), and the relationships between them. This is basically what Microsoft Outlook's address book does.

Here's a quick, high-level description of what you might expect from this sort of program:

- ❑ The application will track information about individuals and organizations in a database and display it on a Web page.
- ❑ Contacts can have zero or more addresses, e-mail addresses, and phone numbers.
- ❑ An individual has just one employer (an organization).
- ❑ An organization has zero or more employees (individuals).

You can now take a look at how to begin putting together this solution using UML. One caveat, however, should be made clear before you begin: This chapter intends to demonstrate how your thinking while designing an application might evolve as you discover new and better ways of implementing the solution. As a result, this chapter should be read more as a progressive evolution and development of the sample application rather than as a straightforward listing of its code. A concrete example such as this can help you gain a better understanding of how the principles of object-oriented programming work.

The Contact Manager UML Diagrams

Fire up the UML diagramming application of your choice and create a new file called `ContactManager.[extension]`, where `[extension]` is the default file extension for your application (for example, `.dia` for diagrams created using Dia, and so on).

First, create classes for the three different kinds of contact information that you want to represent. In this case, these are address, e-mail address, and phone number classes, but you could create classes for whatever type of contact information you require. Their properties are shown in the following table.

Class	Properties

`Address`	`street1`
	`street2`
	`city`
	`state`
	`zip` (ZIP Code)
	`type` (Home, Work, and so on)

`EmailAddress`	`email` `type`

`PhoneNumber`	`number`
	`extension`
	`type`

These classes just store and display data, so you don't need to define any methods at this time, and the third sections of the class symbols are empty. The properties are all public, so they're prefixed with a plus sign. Figure 3-1 shows the UML representation of these classes as they are at the moment.

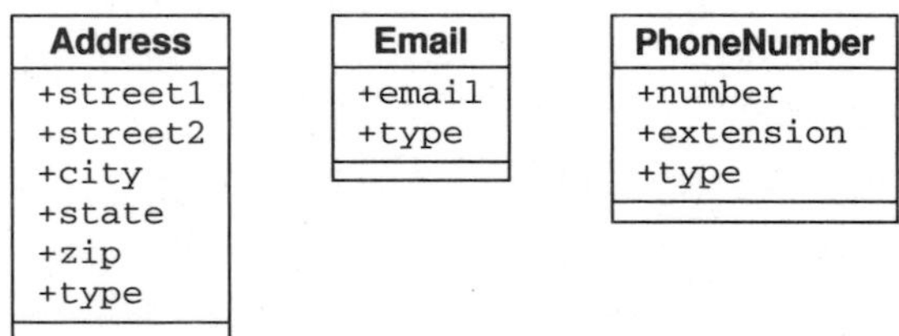

Figure 3-1

Next, you should map out the `Individual` and `Organization` classes. An individual has a first name, a last name, a unique identifier (the id field from the database), a collection (of e-mails, addresses, and phone numbers), an employer, and a job title. You also need to be able to add contact types. Figure 3-2 shows the UML diagram with the `Individual` class.

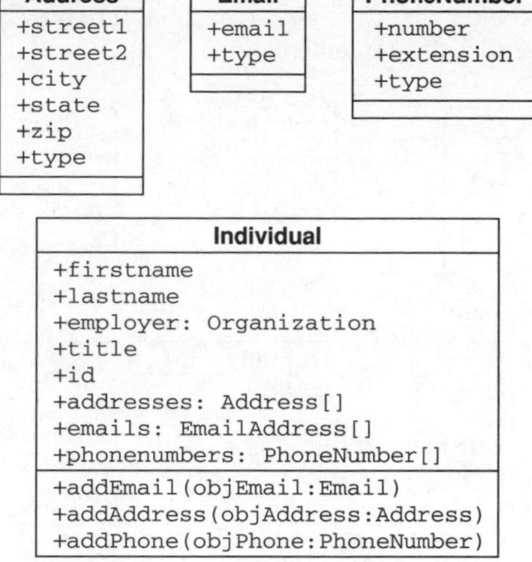

Figure 3-2

An organization has a name, a unique identifier, collections of contact types (much as an individual does), methods to add them, and a collection of employees. Figure 3-3 shows the UML diagram with the `Organization` class.

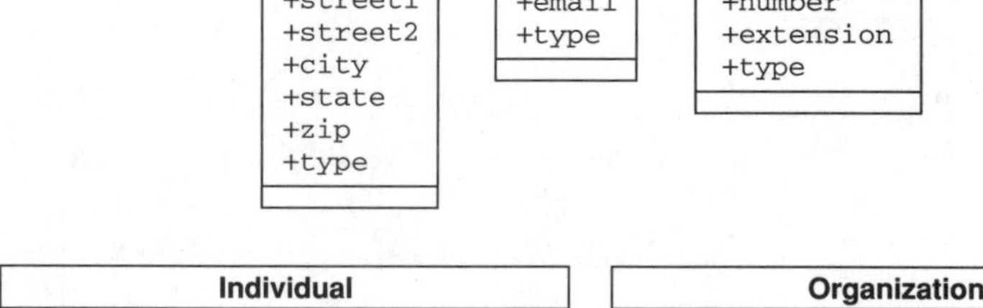

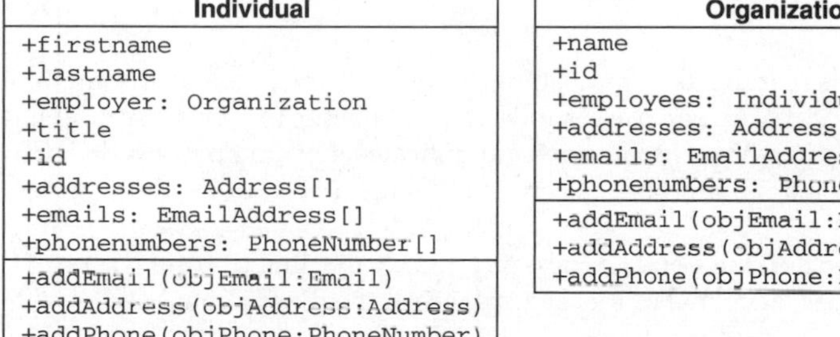

Figure 3-3

The diagram shows the `Individual` and `Organization` classes sharing a lot of the same properties and methods. This is generally an indication that you could save yourself a lot of work and improve the flexibility of your application by using inheritance. You can create another class (`Entity`, in this example) in which you combine the features common to the `Individual` and `Organization` classes and allow them to share the same code. In a UML diagram, you indicate properties and methods only on the class that actually implements them. In this case, you need to move all the common properties and methods of the `Individual` and `Organization` classes to the symbol representing the `Entity` class (see Figure 3-4). You repeat them in the child class (child classes inherit members from their parent classes) only if the child overrides the implementation.

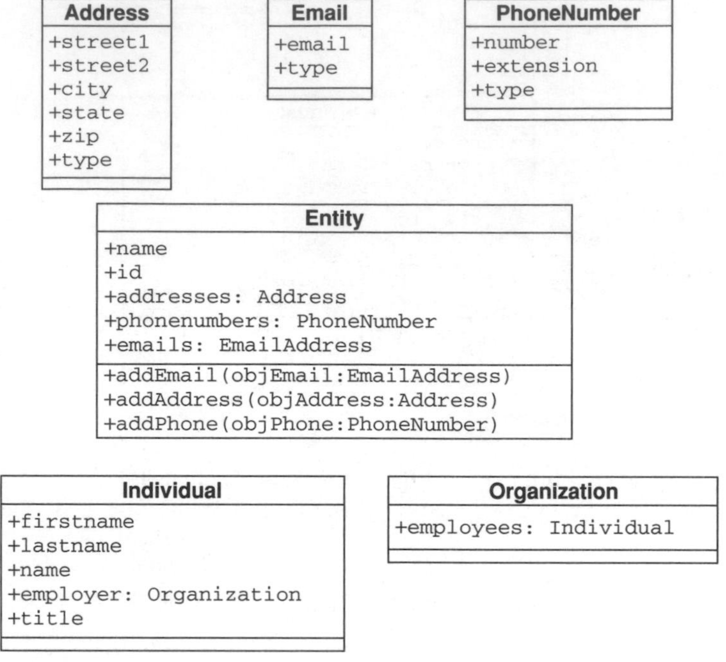

Figure 3-4

In this case, the `name` property of the `Entity` class is overridden in the `Individual` class. When you retrieve the `name` property of an Individual, you'll return "`lastname, firstname`". This way, you can hand the `Organization` or `Individual` classes to a function that will just print a name without having to use separate functions.

UML also defines symbols to indicate relationships. In this example, you need something to show that the `Individual` and `Organization` classes inherit from the `Entity` class. As you have seen, the UML specification calls this relationship *generalization* and indicates it by an open-headed arrow that points from the child class(es) to the parent class, as shown in Figure 3-5.

Now it's clear that the `Individual` and `Organization` classes inherit from the `Entity` class. Using connectors to indicate inheritance makes it easy to glance at the diagram and see how the classes relate to one another.

There's another type of connection you need to show—the `Entity` class, which uses the `Address`, `Email`, and `PhoneNumber` classes. The UML specification calls this relationship a *composite*, and you indicate it by using a black diamond on the end of the line attached to the user of the class (see Figure 3-6). The classes being used also have a property called `multiplicity`, that is, how many of them are used. In this example, an entity may have zero, one, or more of any of the contact types, so you write `0..*` on the connector line closest to the item being used to indicate that a class may have 0 or more of the class to which it points. Figure 3-6 also shows that notation. By revealing this relationship in the

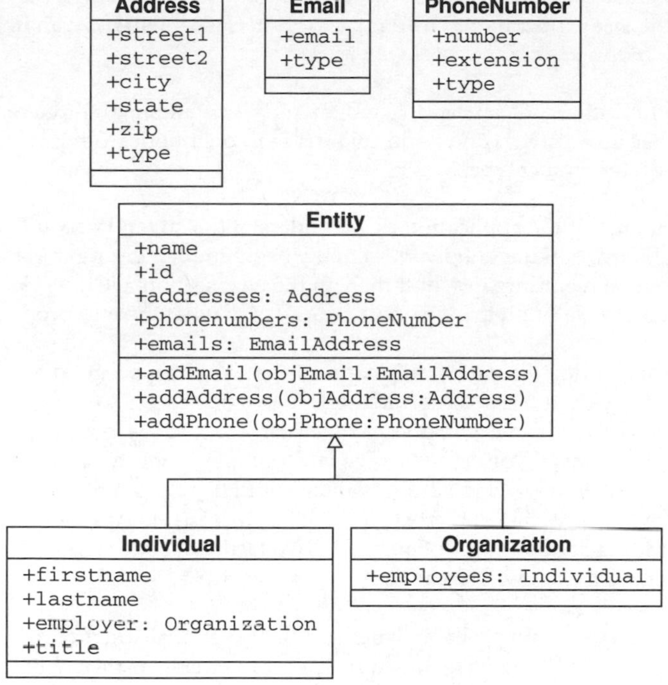

Figure 3-5

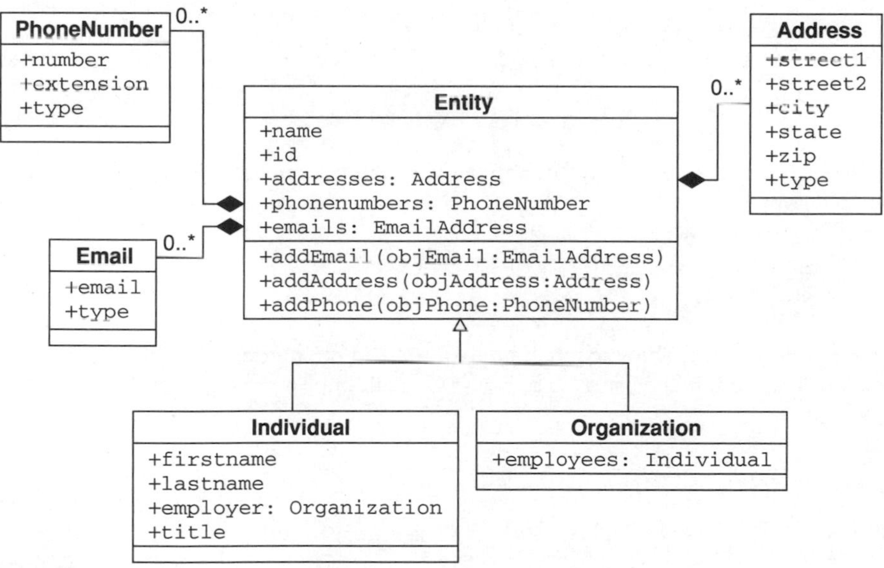

Figure 3-6

diagram, you can clearly see which parts of the application will be affected by a change to another part. Here, a change to the `Email`, `Address`, or `PhoneNumber` classes will have an impact on the `Entity`, `Individual`, and `Organization` classes.

An `Entity` has a `PhoneNumber`, an `Email`, and an `Address`, and in all three cases it may have zero or more of that item. Because `Individual` and `Organization` inherit from `Entity`, both of these also have zero or more of the contact types.

This is the basic structure of the application as we understand it so far. We could, of course, make plenty of improvements to it by thinking of how we actually begin implementing it in real life, there are a few important points to note regarding this, and then, in the next section, we'll work on the application. We present more UML a little later on to give you a clear idea of what the end product looks like.

Recall from the encapsulation discussion in Chapter 1 that it's always a good idea to protect your data in private member variables and use accessor methods to provide access to those properties. Also recall using `__get` and `__set` to make this process a bit easier. You can see just by looking at the class diagrams shown earlier that all your classes have fairly simple property requirements. Because you know about inheritance and how to use it to your advantage in PHP, you can remove the functionality from being tied to just the `Entity` class and create a class that will enable you to reuse its code in other classes—in effect, adding another layer of abstraction to facilitate better use of the functions common to all the classes. This parent class will be called `PropertyObject`.

In the real world, you also would probably want to add a layer of abstraction when dealing with data as a matter of good practice. To this end, creating a `DataManager` class is probably a good idea. One more thing to consider is that at present you have no unified facility for data validation, so you need an interface for anything that can be validated. Quickly, here's the code for the interface:

```
<?php
  interface Validator {
    abstract function validate();
  }
?>
```

Name the file `interface.Validator.php`. Now put it to some use with the new `PropertyObject` class, shown below.

The PropertyObject Class

The code that follows shows how to integrate the `Validator` interface with the `PropertyObject` class. Enter the code in a file called `class.PropertyObject.php`.

```
<?php
  require_once('interface.Validator.php');

  abstract class PropertyObject implements Validator {

    protected $propertyTable = array();      //stores name/value pairs
                                             //that hook properties to
                                             //database field names
```

```
    protected $changedProperties = array(); //List of properties that
                                            //have been modified

    protected $data;                        //Actual data from
                                            //the database

    protected $errors = array();            //Any validation errors
                                            //that might have occurred

    public function __construct($arData) {
      $this->data = $arData;
    }

    function __get($propertyName) {
    if(!array_key_exists($propertyName, $this->propertyTable))
      throw new Exception("Invalid property \"$propertyName\"!");

    if(method_exists($this, 'get' . $propertyName)) {
      return call_user_func(array($this, 'get' . $propertyName));
    } else {
      return $this->data[$this->propertyTable[$propertyName]];
    }
  }

  function __set($propertyName, $value) {
    if(!array_key_exists($propertyName, $this->propertyTable))
      throw new Exception("Invalid property \"$propertyName\"!");

    if(method_exists($this, 'set' . $propertyName)) {
      return call_user_func(
                              array($this, 'set' . $propertyName),
                              $value
                             );
    } else {

      //If the value of the property really has changed
      //and it's not already in the changedProperties array,
      //add it.
      if($this->propertyTable[$propertyName] != $value &&
          !in_array($propertyName, $this->changedProperties)) {
        $this->changedProperties[] = $propertyName;
      }

      //Now set the new value
      $this->data[$this->propertyTable[$propertyName]] = $value;

      }
    }

    function validate() {

    }

  }
?>
```

Take a closer look at what's happening here. You've created four protected member variables. Protected member variables are visible only to subclasses of a class; they aren't visible to the code that uses those objects.

`$propertyTable` will contain a map of human-readable property names to field names in your database. Often the names of database fields have been prefixed with a naming convention to indicate their data type. For example, `entities.sname1` might be a field in the table entities of type `string`, containing the first name. However, `sname1` isn't a terribly friendly name for an object property, so it's worthwhile providing a mechanism to translate database field naming conventions to friendly property names.

`$changedProperties` is an array that stores a list of the names of the properties that have been modified.

`$data` will be an associative array of database field names and values. The array will be supplied to the constructor with the data structure coming directly from `pgsql_fetch_assoc()`. This approach makes constructing a useful object directly from a database query a lot easier, as you'll see shortly.

The last member variable, `$errors`, will contain an array of field names and error messages in the event that the `validate` method (required by the `Validate` interface) should fail.

The class is declared `abstract` for two reasons. The first is that the `PropertyObject` class on its own is not very useful. The classes that extend `PropertyObject` still have some work to do before you can use its methods. The second is that you have not provided an implementation of the required method `validate()`. Because you are still labeling that method `abstract` in `PropertyObject`, you must also label the class itself `abstract`, forcing all inheriting classes to implement that function. Anything that attempts to use classes that extend `PropertyObject` but not implement the function will cause a runtime error.

Next, you see the greatly simplified constructor. The constructor merely accepts the associative array that will most likely be populated from a database query and assigns it to the protected member variable `$data`. Most subclasses of `PropertyObject` will need to override the constructor and do something a little more interesting.

Finally, note the internals of the `__get()` and `__set()` accessor methods. Because you are storing data in the `$data` member, you need to be able to map property names to the actual field names in the database. The lines that contain the code `$this->data[$this->propertyTable [$propertyName]]` are doing just that. By fetching and assigning values to the `$data` member using their database field names rather than their property names, you are implementing a form of data persistence.

If the workings of the `$data` and `$propertyTable` members aren't clear to you yet, don't worry. They will be as soon as you see an example.

The Contact Type Classes

Now that you have the `PropertyObject` class, you can start putting it to some use. The files that follow are for the `Address`, `EmailAddress`, and `PhoneNumber` classes.

In the code you'll see a reference to a class called `DataManager`, which will be a wrapper class for all the database functions you need to use. This wrapper enables you to have one central place for all your data-interaction code. You'll examine that class very soon.

Enter the code that follows (the `Address` class) into a file called `class.Address.php`:

```
<?php
  require_once('class.PropertyObject.php');

  class Address extends PropertyObject {

    function __construct($addressid) {
      $arData = DataManager::getAddressData($addressid);

      parent::__construct($arData);

      $this->propertyTable['addressid'] = 'addressid';
      $this->propertyTable['id'] = 'addressid';
      $this->propertyTable['entityid'] = 'entityid';
      $this->propertyTable['address1'] = 'saddress1';
      $this->propertyTable['address2'] = 'saddress2';
      $this->propertyTable['city'] = 'scity';
      $this->propertyTable['state'] = 'cstate';
      $this->propertyTable['zipcode'] = 'spostalcode';
      $this->propertyTable['type'] = 'stype';
  }

  function validate() {
    if(strlen($this->state) != 2) {
      $this->errors['state'] = 'Please choose a valid state.';
    }

    if(strlen($this->zipcode) != 5 &&
       strlen($this->zipcode) != 10) {
        $this->errors['zipcode'] = 'Please enter a 5- or 9-digit zip code';
    }


    if(!$this->address1) {
         $this->errors['address1'] = 'Address 1 is a required field.';
    }

    if(!$this->city) {
         $this->errors['city'] = 'City is a required field.';
    }

    if(sizeof($this->errors)) {
      return false;
      } else {
        return true;
      }
    }
```

```
        function __toString() {
          return $this->address1 . ', ' .
                 $this->address2 . ', ' .
                 $this->city . ', ' .
                 $this->state . ' ' . $this->zipcode;
        }
      }
    ?>
```

Because the `PropertyObject` class took care of so much of the work, only two methods in the `Address` class needed to be implemented (a `__toString()` implementation was thrown in just for fun). In the constructor, you see for the first time how the `$propertyTable` array works. The list of properties required in the class was specified in the `Address` class UML diagram created during the initial architecture of the application (in the beginning of this chapter). Based on the properties this object has, you can also make some decisions about the structure of the database table. Generally, you need one field for each property and, because this class has to relate back to the `Entity` class, you need to store some reference to the parent `Entity`. Use the following SQL statement to create the `Address` table:

```
CREATE TABLE "entityaddress" (
  "addressid" SERIAL PRIMARY KEY NOT NULL,
  "entityid" int,
  "saddress1" varchar(255),
  "saddress2" varchar(255),
  "scity" varchar(255),
  "cstate" char(2),
  "spostalcode" varchar(10),
  "stype" varchar(50),
  CONSTRAINT "fk_entityaddress_entityid"
    FOREIGN KEY ("entityid") REFERENCES "entity"("entityid")
);
```

A properly named database field indicates its data type by using a one-character prefix, letting you know what kind of data goes in the field. Having naming conventions is just as important for database design as it is for your code.

The `propertyTable` array is set up in the `Address` class to map friendly property names (such as city, state, and zip code) to the less friendly database field names (such as `scity`, `cstate`, and `spostalcode`). Note that you can map multiple property names to the same database field name in `propertyTable`. This mapping enables you to refer to the primary key of the address by either `$objAddress->addressid` or `$objAddress->id`.

What's incredibly exciting about the `Address` class is that the overwhelming majority of the code is spent implementing business logic and data validation. There's almost no extraneous code here. Its sole responsibility is to populate itself and validate its own contents. Everything else is left up to the `DataManager` class (which you'll see in detail shortly) and the `PropertyObject`.

The code for the `Email` class, which looks very similar, follows. Enter it into a file called `class.EmailAddress.php`.

```
<?php
  require_once('class.PropertyObject.php');

  class EmailAddress extends PropertyObject {
```

```
      function __construct($emailid) {
        $arData = DataManager::getEmailData($emailid);

        parent::__construct($arData);

        $this->propertyTable['emailid'] = 'emailid';
        $this->propertyTable['id'] = 'emailid';
        $this->propertyTable['entityid'] = 'entityid';
        $this->propertyTable['email'] = 'semail';
        $this->propertyTable['type'] = 'stype';
      }

      function validate() {
      if(!$this->email) {
            $this->errors['email'] = 'You must set an email address.';
      }

      if(sizeof($this->errors)) {
        return false;
      } else {
        return true;
      }
    }

    function __toString() {
      return $this->email;
    }
      }
?>
```

This file has very little ancillary code; it's just fetching the code from the database and setting up the `propertyTable`. Everything else is data validation. Again, the UML diagram was the guide to deciding on the properties of the `Email` class and the structure of the corresponding database table.

The database table for the `entityemail` table looks like this:

```
CREATE TABLE "entityemail" (
  "emailid" SERIAL PRIMARY KEY NOT NULL,
  "entityid" int,
  "semail" varchar(255),
  "stype" varchar(50),
  CONSTRAINT "fk_entityemail_entityid"
    FOREIGN KEY ("entityid") REFERENCES "entity"("entityid")
);
```

The `PhoneNumber` class works very much like `Address` and `Email`. Here's the code to enter the code into `class.PhoneNumber.php`:

```
<?php
  require_once('class.PropertyObject.php');

  class PhoneNumber extends PropertyObject {
```

```
    function __construct($phoneid) {
      $arData = DataManager::getPhoneNumberData($phoneid);

      parent::__construct($arData);

      $this->propertyTable['phoneid'] = 'phoneid';
      $this->propertyTable['id'] = 'phoneid';
      $this->propertyTable['entityid'] = 'entityid';
      $this->propertyTable['number'] = 'snumber';
      $this->propertyTable['extension'] = 'sextension';
      $this->propertyTable['type'] = 'stype';
    }

    function validate() {
      if(!$this->number) {
            $this->errors['number'] = 'You must supply a phone number.';
      }

      if(sizeof($this->errors)) {
        return false;
      } else {
        return true;
      }
    }

    function __toString() {
      return $this->number .
             ($this->extension ? ' x' . $this->extension : '');
    }
  }
?>
```

And here's the SQL statement to create the `entityphone` table:

```
CREATE TABLE "entityphone" (
  "phoneid" int SERIAL PRIMARY KEY NOT NULL,
  "entityid" int,
  "snumber" varchar(20),
  "sextension" varchar(20),
  "stype" varchar(50),
  CONSTRAINT "fk_entityemail_entityid"
    FOREIGN KEY ("entityid") REFERENCES "entity"("entityid")
);
```

The DataManager Class

You can now take a look at that `DataManager` class. It and the other database code samples in this chapter have been using PostgreSQL, although a class like this would work just as well with MySQL, Oracle, or any other RDBMS.

The primary responsibility of the `DataManager` class is to put all the data access code into a single location, making it much easier to change the database type or connection parameters later on. All the class's methods have been declared static because the class doesn't rely on any member variables. Note the use of the static function variable in `getConnection()`. This is used to ensure that only one database connection is open during a single page request. Much overhead is associated with establishing a database connection, so eliminating unnecessary connections helps to improve performance. Create a file called `class.DataManager.php` and enter the following class code:

```
<?php
require_once('class.Entity.php'); //this will be needed later
require_once('class.Individual.php');
require_once('class.Organization.php');

class DataManager
{
   private static function _getConnection() {
      static $hDB;

      if(isset($hDB)) {
         return $hDB;
      }

      $hDB = pg_connect("host=localhost port=5432 dbname=sample_db user=phpuser
                         password=phppass");
         or die("Failure connecting to the database!");
      return $hDB;
  }

  public static function getAddressData($addressID) {
     $sql = "SELECT * FROM \"entityaddress\" WHERE\"addressid\" =
             $addressID";
     $res = pg_query(DataManager::_getConnection(), $sql);
     if(! ($res && pg_num_rows($res))) {
        die("Failed getting address data for address $addressID");
     }
     return pg_fetch_assoc($res);
  }

  public static function getEmailData($emailID) {
     $sql = "SELECT * FROM \"entityemail\" WHERE\"emailid\" =
             $emailID";
     $res = pg_query(DataManager::_getConnection(), $sql);

     if(! ($res && pg_num_rows($res))) {
        die("Failed getting email data for email $emailID");
     }

     return pg_fetch_assoc($res);
  }

  public static function getPhoneNumberData($phoneID) {

     $sql = "SELECT * FROM \"entityphone\" WHERE \"phoneid\" = $phoneID";
     $res = pg_query(DataManager::_getConnection(), $sql);
     if(! ($res && pg_num_rows($res))) {
        die("Failed getting phone number data for phone $phoneID");
     }
```

```
        return pg_fetch_assoc($res);
    }
}
?>
```

The DataManager class provides the data structures used to populate the $data member of your PropertyObject subclasses. Separate functions return the data for each of the types. You'll be adding a few new functions to this class a bit later.

All the methods of this class are declared to be *static*. Remember, static methods are those requiring all member variables to be static, too. You don't need to instantiate static classes to use their methods. There are several cases in which this makes sense. Consider a class called Math that exposes methods such as squareRoot(), power(), and cosine() and has properties including the mathematical constants e and pi. All instances of this class perform the same math. The square root of 2 doesn't change; 4 raised to the 3rd power will always be 64; and the two constants are, well, constant. There's no need to create separate instances of this class because its state and properties never change. A class called Math implemented in this manner should allow for all its functions to be called statically.

The DataManager class is much the same. All the functions are self-contained. No nonstatic member variables are present for the functions to interact with. The class exposes no properties. You can invoke the methods of the class using the static method operator :: as a result. Because all the methods you've created are static, you need never instantiate the object with $obj = new DataManager() and then call methods using syntax such as $obj->getEmail(). Instead, you can use the simple syntax DataManager::getEmail().

The Entity, Individual, and Organization Classes

With all the supporting classes in place, you can move on to the core of the application: the Entity class and its subclasses.

First, make sure that you're updating your UML diagram as you make changes to the object hierarchy so that you keep track of what you, or the development team, are doing. You've created the PropertyObject class and made all your classes subclasses of it, with one exception—the new DataManager class, which does not inherit from anything but merely provides data abstraction functionality. The PropertyObject implements an abstract interface called Validator. Figure 3-7 shows the updated diagram.

Now you can begin to develop the Entity, Individual, and Organization classes. The following code shows the fully implemented Entity class, class.Entity.php:

```
<?php

  require_once('class.PropertyObject.php');
  require_once('class.PhoneNumber.php');
  require_once('class.Address.php');
  require_once('class.EmailAddress.php');

  abstract class Entity extends PropertyObject {
```

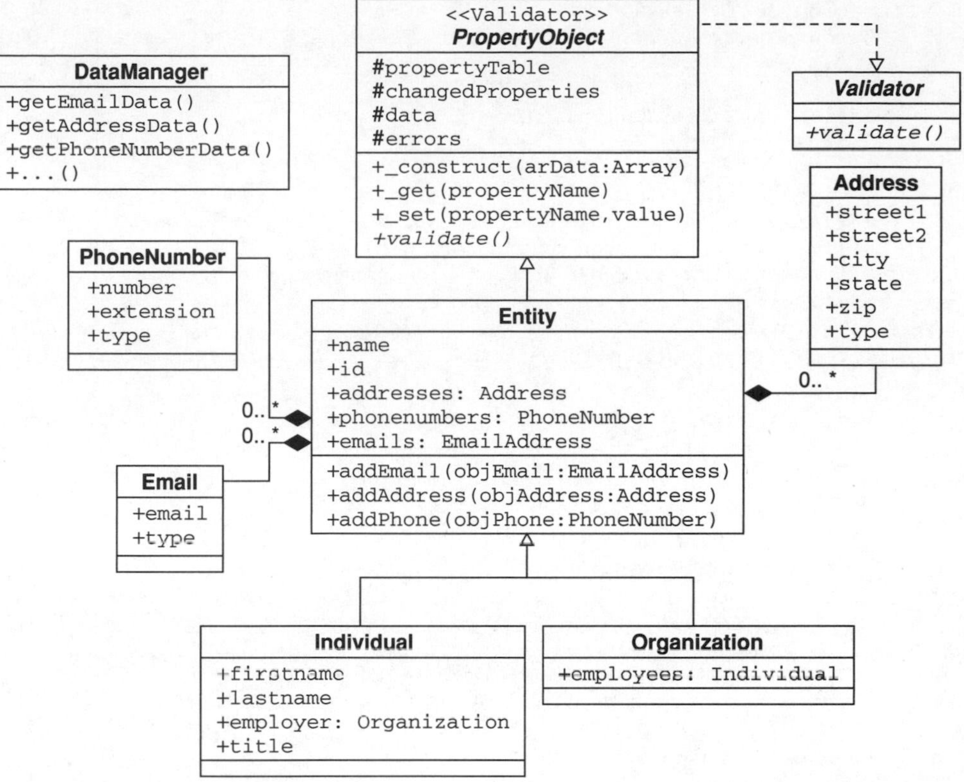

Figure 3-7

```
    private $_emails;
    private $_addresses;
    private $_phonenumbers;

    public function __construct($entityID) {
      $arData = DataManager::getEntityData($entityID);

      parent::__construct($arData);

      $this->propertyTable['entityid'] = 'entityid';
      $this->propertyTable['id'] = 'entityid';
      $this->propertyTable['name1'] = 'sname1';
      $this->propertyTable['name2'] = 'sname2';
      $this->propertyTable['type'] = 'ctype';

      $this->_emails = DataManager::getEmailObjectsForEntity($entityID);
      $this->_addresses = DataManager::getAddressObjectsForEntity($entityID);
      $this->_phonenumbers =
                DataManager::getPhoneNumberObjectsForEntity($entityID);

    }
```

```
    function setID($val) {
      throw new Exception('You may not alter the value of the ID field!');
    }

    function setEntityID($val) {
      $this->setID($val);
    }

    function phonenumbers($index) {
      if(!isset($this->_phonenumbers[$index])) {
        throw new Exception('Invalid phone number specified!');
      } else {
         return $this->_phonenumbers[$index];
      }
    }

    function getNumberOfPhoneNumbers() {
      return sizeof($this->_phonenumbers);
    }

    function addPhoneNumber(PhoneNumber $phone) {
      $this->_phonenumbers[] = $phone;
    }

    function addresses($index) {
      if(!isset($this->_addresses[$index])) {
        throw new Exception('Invalid address specified!');
      } else {
        return $this->_addresses[$index];
      }
    }

    function getNumberOfAddresses() {
      return sizeof($this->_addresses);
    }

    function addAddress(Address $address) {
      $this->_addresses[] = $address;
    }

    function emails($index) {
      if(!isset($this->_emails[$index])) {
        throw new Exception('Invalid email specified!');
      } else {
          return $this->_emails[$index];
      }
    }

    function getNumberOfEmails() {
      return sizeof($this->_emails);
    }

    function addEmail(Email $email) {
```

```
        $this->_emails[] = $email;
      }

      public function validate() {
        //Add common validation routines
      }

    }
?>
```

By moving all the accessor method functionality to the parent `PropertyObject` class, you simplify the `Entity` class and ensure that it is focused only on the code required to implement an entity.

The `Entity` class is declared abstract because it isn't useful on its own. All entities are either `Individuals` or `Organizations`. You do not want to be able to instantiate objects of class `Entity`. Declaring it abstract prevents the class from being instantiable.

To create the PostgreSQL table `entities`, run the following SQL statement:

```
CREATE TABLE "entities" (
  "entityid" SERIAL PRIMARY KEY NOT NULL,
  "name1" varchar(100) NOT NULL,
  "name2" varchar(100) NOT NULL,
  "type" char(1) NOT NULL
);
```

You've added requests to a few new functions of the `DataManager`: `getEntityData()` and `get[x]ObjectsForEntity`. `getEntityData()` returns the data required to instantiate an entity, just as functions you've already seen do for the contact types. The following shows the code for the new functions in `class.DataManager.php`:

```
// top of file omitted for brevity
   . . .
        die("Failed getting phone number data for phone $phoneID");
      }

      return pg_fetch_assoc($res);
    }

    public static function getEntityData($entityID) {
      $sql = "SELECT * FROM \"entities\" WHERE\"entityid\" =$entityID";
      $res = pg_query(DataManager::_getConnection(),$sql);
      if(! ($res && pg_num_rows($res))) {
        die("Failed getting entity $entityID");
      }
      return pg_fetch_assoc($res);
    }

?>
```

To add the `get[x]ObjectsForEntity` functions, place the following code at the end of `class.DataManager.php`, just after the `getEntityData` function:

```
public static function getAddressObjectsForEntity($entityID) {
  $sql = "SELECT \"addressid\" from \"entityaddress\" WHERE \"entityid\" =
          $entityID";
  $res = pg_query(DataManager::_getConnection(), $sql);

  if(!$res) {
    die("Failed getting address data for entity $entityID");
  }

  if(pg_num_rows($res)) {
    $objs = array();
    while($rec = pg_fetch_assoc($res)) {
      $objs[] = new Address($rec['addressid']);
    }
    return $objs;
  } else {
    return array();
  }
}

public static function getEmailObjectsForEntity($entityID) {

  $sql = "SELECT \"emailid\" from \"entityemail\"
          WHERE \"entityid\" = $entityID";
  $res = pg_query(DataManager::_getConnection(), $sql);
  if(!$res) {
    die("Failed getting email data for entity $entityID");
  }

  if(pg_num_rows($res)) {
    $objs = array();
    while($rec = pg_fetch_assoc($res)) {
      $objs[] = new EmailAddress($rec['emailid']);
    }
    return $objs;
  } else {
    return array();
  }
}

public static function getPhoneNumberObjectsForEntity($entityID) {
  $sql = "SELECT \"phoneid\" from \"entityphone\"
          WHERE \"entityid\" = $entityID";
  $res = pg_query(DataManager::_getConnection(), $sql);

  if(!$res) {
    die("Failed getting phone data for entity $entityID");
  }

  if(pg_num_rows($res)) {
    $objs = array();
```

```
      while($rec = pg_fetch_assoc($res)) {
        $objs[] = new PhoneNumber($rec['phoneid']);
      }
      return $objs;
    } else {
      return array();
    }
  }
```

These functions take an entity ID value. They query the database to determine whether any e-mails, addresses, or phone numbers exist for the entity in question. If they do, the functions build an array of `EmailAddress`, `Address`, or `PhoneNumber` objects by passing each id to the constructor for the appropriate object type. This array is then passed back to the `Entity` object, where it is stored in the appropriate private member variable.

With the `Entity` class doing all the heavy lifting, the remaining work is fairly simple: You just need to implement the `Individual` and `Organization` classes. Create a file called `class.Individual.php` and enter the following:

```
<?php
  require_once('class.Entity.php');
  require_once('class.Organization.php');

  class Individual extends Entity {

    public function __construct($userID) {
      parent::__construct($userID);

      $this->propertyTable['firstname'] = 'name1';
      $this->propertyTable['lastname'] = 'name2';

    }

    public function __toString() {
      return $this->firstname . ' ' . $this->lastname;
    }

    public function getEmployer() {
      return DataManager::getEmployer($this->id);
    }

    public function validate() {
      parent::validate();

      //add individual-specific validation

    }

  }
?>
```

Short and sweet. Inheritance makes this easy. The `Individual` class sets up a few new properties that make accessing the first and last name of the individual easier, instead of having to use the rather ugly `name1` and `name2` properties defined in the `Entity` class. It also defines a new method, `getEmployer()`, which requires a new function in the `DataManager`. You get to that function as soon as you have your `Organization` class, which is shown in the following code. Create a file called `class.Organization.php` and enter this code into it:

```
<?php
  require_once('class.Entity.php');
  require_once('class.Individual.php');

  class Organization extends Entity {

    public function __construct($userID) {
      parent::__construct($userID);

      $this->propertyTable['name'] = 'name1';

    }

    public function __toString() {
      return $this->name;
    }

    public function getEmployees() {
      return DataManager::getEmployees($this->id);
    }

    public function validate() {
      parent::validate();
      //do organization-specific validation
    }

  }
?>
```

Again, this is a fairly simple class, thanks to the power of inheritance. You declare a property called `name` that makes it easier to obtain the one and only name that an organization has (the `sname2` property goes unused for organizations).

To add the functions `getEmployer()` and `getEmployee()` to the `DataManager` class, append the following code to the end of `class.DataManager.php`:

```
public static function getEmployer($individualID) {
    $sql = "SELECT \"organizationid\" FROM \"entityemployee\" " .
           "WHERE \"individualid\" = $individualID";
    $res = pg_query(DataManager::_getConnection(),$sql);
    if(! ($res && pgsql_num_rows($res))) {
      die("Failed getting employer info for individual $individualID");
    }

    $row = pgsql_fetch_assoc($res);

    if($row) {
      return new Organization($row['organizationid']);
    } else {
```

```
        return null;
      }
    }

    public static function getEmployees($orgID) {
      $sql = "SELECT \"individualid FROM \"entityemployee\" " .
             "WHERE \"organizationid\" = $orgID";
      $res = pgsql_query(DataManager::_getConnection(), $sql);
      if(! ($res && pgsql_num_rows($res))) {
        die("Failed getting employee info for org $orgID");
      }

      if(pgsql_num_rows($res)) {
        $objs = array();
        while($row = pgsql_fetch_assoc($res)) {
          $objs[] = new Individual($row['individualid']);
        }
        return $objs;
      } else {
        return array();
      }
  }
```

These two functions rely on the presence of a table called `entityemployee`, shown following. This table relates individuals to the organizations by which they are employed. For example, employees of the same company would have different individual ids but the same organization ids:

```
CREATE TABLE "entityemployee" (
  "individualid" int NOT NULL,
  "organizationid" int NOT NULL,
  CONSTRAINT "fk_entityemployee_individualid"
    FOREIGN KEY ("individualid") REFERENCES "entity"("entityid"),
  CONSTRAINT "fk_entityemployee_organizationid"
    FOREIGN KEY ("organizationid") REFERENCES "entity"("entityid")
);
```

One last function is needed to make the entire system work—the `DataManager` method for listing all the entities in the database. It's called `getAllEntitiesAsObjects()` and it finishes all the work you need to do on your objects:

```
public static function getAllEntitiesAsObjects() {
    $sql = "SELECT \"entityid\", \"type\" from \"entities\"";
    $res = pgsql_query(DataManager::_getConnection(), $sql);

    if(!$res) {
      die("Failed getting all entities");
    }

    if(pgsql_num_rows($res)) {
      $objs = array();
      while($row = pgsql_fetch_assoc($res)) {
        if($row['type'] == 'I') {
          $objs[] = new Individual($row['entityid']);
```

```
        } elseif ($row['type'] == 'O') {
          $objs[] = new Organization($row['entityid']);
        } else {
          die("Unknown entity type {$row['type']} encountered!");
        }
      }
      return $objs;
    } else {
      return array();
    }
  }
```

`DataManager` enables you to enumerate over all the contacts in your system. It examines the value of the `ctype` field in the `entity` table to determine whether the entry is an `Individual` or an `Organization` and then instantiates an object of the appropriate type and adds it to the array that the function returns.

Making Use of the System

By now you can see the real power of an OOP approach. The following code, called `test.php`, will display a view of all the contacts in your database with all their contact details:

```
<?php
  require_once('class.DataManager.php'); //everything gets included by it

  function println($data) {
    print $data . "<br>\n";
  }

  $arContacts = DataManager::getAllEntitiesAsObjects();
  foreach($arContacts as $objEntity) {

    if(get_class($objEntity) == 'individual') {
      print "<h1>Individual - {$objEntity->__toString()}</h1>";
    } else {
      print "<h1>Organization - {$objEntity->__toString()}</h1>";
    }

    if($objEntity->getNumberOfEmails()) {
      //We have emails! Print a header
      print "<h2>Emails</h2>";

      for($x=0; $x < $objEntity->getNumberOfEmails(); $x++) {
        println($objEntity->emails($x)->__toString());
      }
    }

    if($objEntity->getNumberOfAddresses()) {
      //We have addresses!
      print "<h2>Addresses</h2>";

      for($x=0; $x < $objEntity->getNumberOfAddresses(); $x++) {
        println($objEntity->addresses($x)->__toString());
      }
    }
```

```
    if($objEntity->getNumberOfPhoneNumbers()) {
      //We have phone numbers!
      print "<h2>Phones</h2>";

      for($x=0; $x < $objEntity->getNumberOfPhoneNumbers(); $x++) {
        println($objEntity->phonenumbers($x)->__toString());
      }
    }

    print "<hr>\n";
  }
?>
```

We leave the job of entering data into your tables to you, because it will help you to figure out how everything goes together. You may want to try to imitate the results shown (by navigating to `test.php` in your browser) in Figure 3-8.

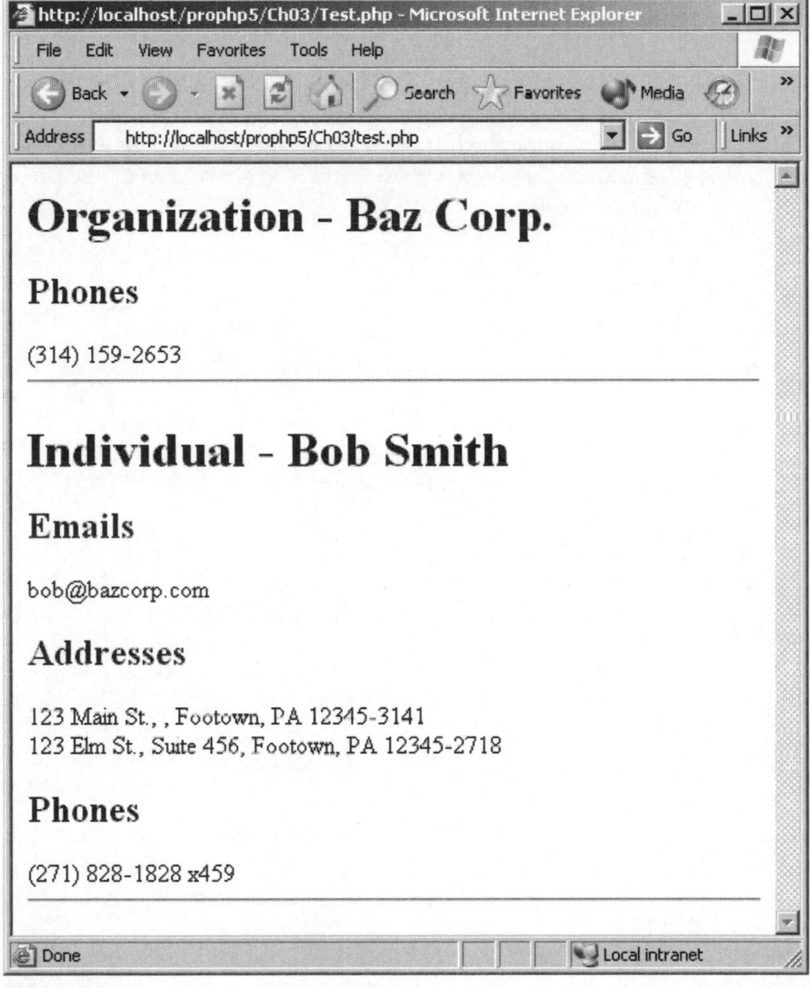

Figure 3-8

In only 36 lines of code you can display nearly everything there is to show about the entities in your system. Employer and employees aren't shown here; again, we leave that as an exercise for you to try. The line that calls the `get_class` function in `test.php` will give you some ideas for figuring out which class you're dealing with so that you'll know whether to call `getEmployer()` on an `Individual`, or `getEmployees()` on an `Organization`.

Summary

UML diagrams are an essential tool for planning complex (and even not-so-complex) applications. Properly designed diagrams enable you to document intricate systems in a clearer way than text alone allows. When you use class diagrams as part of your routine software development process, seeing how your classes and database tables should be designed is much easier.

Take full advantage of the OO features in PHP5 to help you rapidly develop applications and establish a code base that's easier to maintain, offers a greater degree of flexibility and extensibility, and reduces the total volume of code required to implement the business requirements.

By separating the software architecture into a business logic layer, like the `Individual` class, and a data access layer, like the `DataManager` class, you make it easy to change the underlying data source, table structure, or queries without disrupting the rest of the application. Objects that are responsible for implementing business logic aren't cluttered with the data access mechanism, the presence of which can confuse and obscure the business rules.

Design Patterns

In the previous chapters you learned that objects can descend from parent objects via inheritance. You've also seen how objects can contain references to other objects, such as a `DrumSet` object holding `Drum` objects. In general, the technique of composing an object from other objects is referred to as *object composition.*

Both inheritance and object composition are powerful tools in designing object-oriented software and allow for a wide variety of design choices. Of course, having many choices does not always make decisions easier. How would you design your application so that it's easy to maintain and extend? How would you write a component that the other members of your team could use through a simple interface? When writing software, you can solve certain problems on your own using your experience, intelligence, luck, large doses of soda, or any combination of the above.

You've probably reused existing code of your own to solve a problem. Perhaps you have a standard script for connecting to a database. Design patterns are a bit different in that they are not simply about reusing code; they are more abstract and generalized than that. The same design pattern can show up in completely different types of software. Design patterns are about reusing ideas. After you know a pattern, you should be able to recognize where it would be useful. Then you can go ahead and implement it—knowing that it's an accepted solution.

A design pattern is a specific way of solving a particular problem. In our case it represents the way an object or set of objects is structured, how they collaborate and communicate with other objects in the pattern. Each pattern has a descriptive name, such as `Observer` or `Observable`, and each pattern has a specific design that can be shown in a class diagram.

Patterns can be confusing at first. If this initial description doesn't seem clear, don't be concerned: You'll be working through five different patterns in this chapter, building on some of the code you saw in the last few chapters.

The Composite Pattern

You've already had a little experience with one pattern—the composite—from the `Instrument` interface in Chapter 2, "Unified Modeling Language (UML)." Take a look at the class diagram again in Figure 4-1.

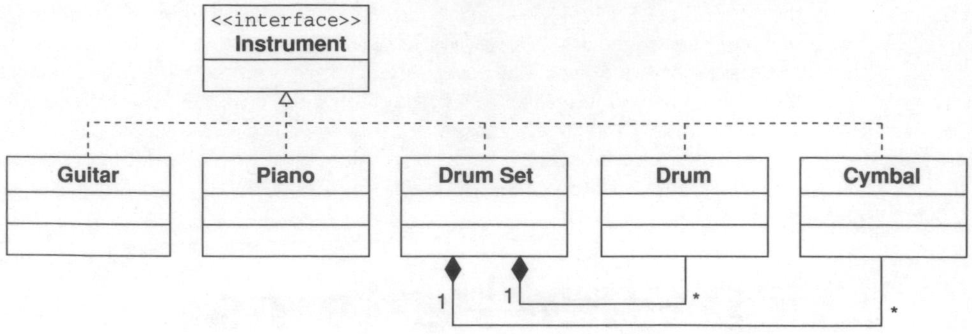

Figure 4-1

Figure 4-1 shows that a `DrumSet` object can be composed of both `Drum` and `Cymbal` objects. `Drum` and `Cymbal` can be thought of as *children* of the `DrumSet` object. A `DrumSet` can be composed of any number of `Drums` and `Cymbals`. Notice, though, that both `DrumSet` and its children are all of the same type, namely `Instrument`. When a client object interacts with `DrumSet`, it does so through the same interface as it would to interact with its children. This relationship is known as the composite pattern.

Figure 4-2 shows the general case for the composite.

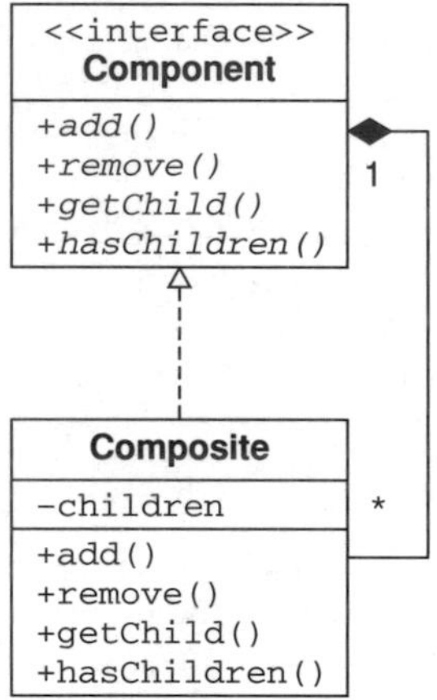

Figure 4-2

The composite pattern has two parts: the `Component` abstract class and the `Composite`, which is a concrete implementation of the `Component` class. All `Composite` objects descend from the abstract `Component` class. Any `Component` can contain other `Components`. A `Component` containing other components can be thought of as a `Composite`. A `Component` with no children can be thought of as an empty `Composite`.

Some implementations of `Composite` make a distinction between `Composite` objects and `Leaf` objects. `Leaf` objects are `Components` that can't contain children. For this example, all `Components` have the ability to be `Composites`.

Moving back from the general case, it will be necessary to make a change in the design and switch the `Instrument` interface to an abstract class. Interfaces and abstract classes are similar because neither one can be used directly to instantiate an object. The key difference is that an abstract class can have some fully implemented methods, whereas interfaces just have method declarations. Use abstract classes when you want to maintain the same methods in all your subclasses but have some general functionality that can be shared by the subclasses. Use interfaces when the implementations will differ across most or all the methods in subclasses. Figure 4-3 shows the new class diagram. Note that abstract class diagrams are indicated with italics.

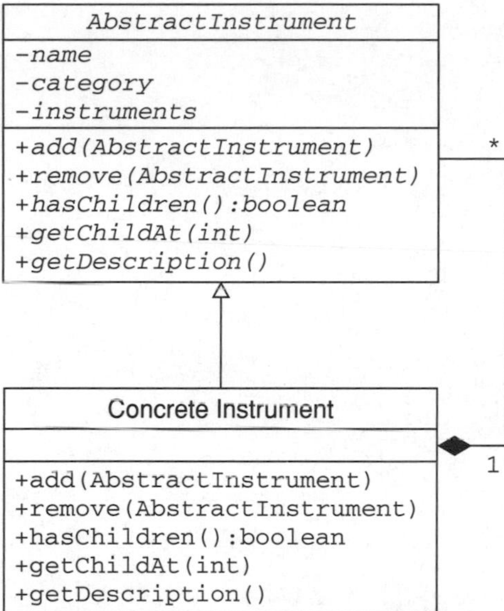

Figure 4-3

The association line indicates that each concrete instance of `AbstractInstrument` may contain any number—including zero—of other instances of `AbstractInstrument`.

Implementation

The following PHP code shows the implementation of the composite pattern.

```
<html>
<body>
<head>
<style>
body {font : 12px verdana; font-weight:bold}
td {font : 11px verdana;}
</style>
</head>

<?php
```

```
abstract class AbstractInstrument {

   private $name;
   private $category;
   private $instruments = array();

   public function add(AbstractInstrument $instrument) {
      array_push($this->instruments, $instrument);
   }

   public function remove(AbstractInstrument $instrument) {
      array_pop($this->instruments);
   }

   public function hasChildren() {
     return (bool)(count($this->instruments) > 0);
   }

   public function getChild($i) {
     return $instruments[i];
   }

   public function getDescription() {
     echo "- one " . $this->getName();
     if ($this->hasChildren()) {
       echo " which includes:<br>";
       foreach($this->instruments as $instrument) {
          echo "<table cellspacing=5 border=0><tr><td>   
                </td><td>-";
          $instrument->getDescription();
          echo "</td></tr></table>";
       }
     }
   }

   public function setName($name) {
     $this->name = $name;
   }

   public function getName() {
     return $this->name;
   }

   public function setCategory($category) {
     $this->category = $category;
   }

   public function getCategory() {
     return $this->category;
    }
}
```

```
class Guitar extends AbstractInstrument {
  function __construct($name) {
    parent::setName($name);
    parent::setCategory("guitars");
  }
}

class DrumSet extends AbstractInstrument {
  function __construct($name) {
   parent::setName($name);
   parent::setCategory("drums");
  }
}

class SnareDrum extends AbstractInstrument {
  function __construct($name) {
    parent::setName($name);
    parent::setCategory("snare drums");
  }
}

class BaseDrum extends AbstractInstrument {
  function __construct($name) {
    parent::setName($name);
    parent::setCategory("base drums");
  }
}

class Cymbal extends AbstractInstrument {
  function __construct($name) {
    parent::setName($name);
    parent::setCategory("cymbals");
  }
}

$drums = new DrumSet("tama maple set");
$drums->add(new SnareDrum("snare drum"));
$drums->add(new BaseDrum("large bass drum"));

$cymbals = new Cymbal("zildjian cymbal set");
$cymbals->add(new Cymbal("small crash"));
$cymbals->add(new Cymbal("large high hat"));
$drums->add($cymbals);

$guitar = new Guitar("gibson les paul");

echo "List of Instruments: <p>";
$drums->getDescription();
$guitar->getDescription();

?>

</body>
</html>
```

Notice that all the concrete instruments, such as `DrumSet` and `Guitar`, descend from the `AbstractInstrument` class. Also notice that all the subclasses inherit the implemented methods in the abstract class. To implement the `getDescription()`, the current instrument is checked to see whether it has children. If it does, the method is called recursively until it travels through the entire tree.

Historically (in PHP4), the `&` symbol caused the object, in this case of type `AbstractInstrument`, to be passed by reference:

```
public function add(AbstractInstrument & $instrument) {
```

This is important because otherwise an entirely new local copy would be used within the function. However, because PHP5 automatically passes objects by reference, the `&` is not required. For our purposes this behavior is desired because we actually want to work on the original object rather than on a copy of it. Figure 4-4 shows the *object diagram* for the previous code after the instruments and their child instruments have been assembled. Object diagrams are similar to class diagrams except that they show instances of objects indicated with their names underlined. Also, they represent the object relationships in the system at a point in time.

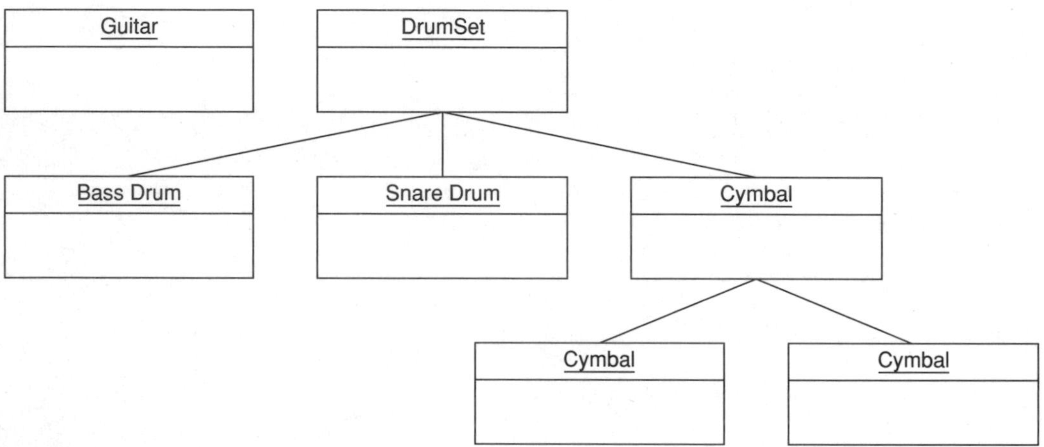

Figure 4-4

In this example, the concrete instrument classes don't really differ in great detail except for overriding the `getDescription()` method in the `Guitar` class. Consider, though, if you needed to add methods to contact a manufacturer to get stocking information. If each manufacturer had a favored way to receive contact from the system, you could specify that in a `contact()` method. First you would add an abstract method to `AbstractInstrument` and then you would implement it in each subclass. Adding the abstract method ensures that you won't forget to implement it in the subclasses. If you don't, you'll get an error.

If you were certain that no additional functionality needed be added to your instruments, you could just create a `GenericInstrument` class that inherited from `AbstractInstrument`. This way when you created, say, a cymbal, you would say:

```
$cymbals = new GenericInstrument("zildjian cymbal set");
```

The key here is that anyone accessing the `Instrument` interface—be it you, another programmer, or another part of the application—doesn't need to know how it was implemented. Calling `getDescription()` returns a description of the tree structure of an `Instrument` whether it has children or not, or its children have children, and so on. The caller of the method doesn't need to know whether it has children.

Because the interface is the same for all instrument objects but they do not respond in the same way, the instrument objects can be thought of as *polymorphic.* The basic description of polymorphism is *same interface, different implementation* or, more generally, *same interface, different behavior.*

Considerations

The composite pattern described here is very flexible; there are no constraints on which instrument may have children. Consider adding the following line:

```
$cymbals->add(new Cymbal("large high hat"));
$drums->add($cymbals);
$cymbals->add($drums);
$guitar = new Guitar("gibson les paul");
```

Adding the drums to the cymbals that already belong to drums creates a circular reference. When calling `getDescription()` a line like this can crash a Web server. You might want to safeguard against such mistakes. One strategy would be to check during the `add()` method to see whether the instrument being added already contains a reference to the one calling the method. If so, you could report an error.

You also might want to experiment with group of instruments that cannot have things added to them. One option is to individually go to each class definition and override the `add()` method so that it does nothing. Another option is to create a new abstract class from which all single instruments descend. This abstract class could have an `add()` method that either does nothing or reports an error. This is more in keeping with the composite pattern discussed previously, in which two classes decend from `Component`. One is a `Leaf` that cannot have children and the other is a `Composite` that can. The class diagram for this is shown in Figure 4-5.

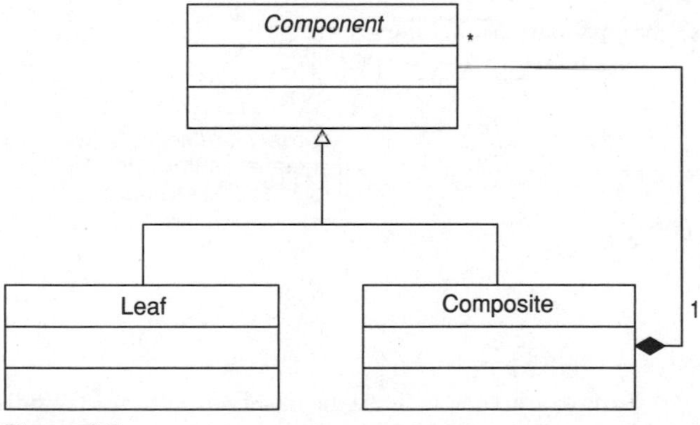

Figure 4-5

One other consideration is constraining certain instruments from being added to composites. Perhaps you don't want to allow a `Guitar` object to be added to a `DrumSet`. In that case you could define certain legal types based on the `category` attribute. Implementing these features are all worthwhile exercises to try on your own.

The Observer Pattern

Often, you'll have data in your application that changes over time. Say that you have some GUI components that are required to show this data and update it when it changes. How would you handle it? One solution might be to pass the newly updated data to a method of the GUI component so that it could redraw the information. A problem with this approach is remembering to do that each time the data is updated. What if it's not clear how often the data will be updated, and whether you want the GUI to update automatically when it does?

The observer pattern solves this problem by using two interfaces, `Observer` and `Observable`. As the name suggests, the `Observer` "watches" the `Observable` to see whether it changes.

Keeping with the theme of human senses, an `Observer` is sometimes called a `Listener`, but for this chapter we stick with the former name.

In its most basic implementation, the `Observable` can add `Observers`. `Observable` then is responsible for notifying them if anything about its state has changed, and the `Observer` is responsible for reacting to the change. In this example, our data is the `Observable` and the GUI components are the `Observers`. If the data changes, those changes will automatically be reflected in any GUI component that is an `Observer` of the data. Figure 4-6 demonstrates the observer pattern.

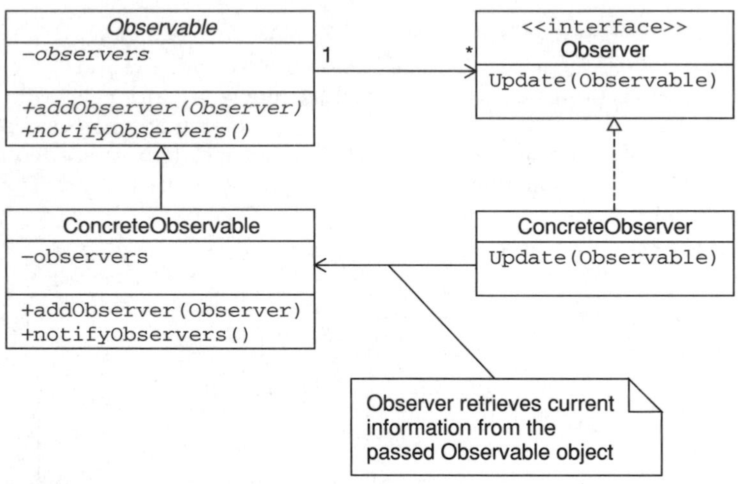

Figure 4-6

Widgets

Continuing with the previous example, you'll use the observer pattern to handle displaying price information for some of the instruments within graphical elements on a Web page. First, you'll need to define some simple graphical components. These components will be basic HTML table structures whose functionality will be contained within an object. Such components often go under the all-purpose term of *widgets*.

The widgets need to display the same instrument information. For this example, that information is just the instrument's and price.

Designing the Widgets

A graphical widget will have two responsibilities. It will need to draw its own HTML so that it can be seen on a Web page, and it will need to update the data it displays. You may have noticed (from Figure 4-6) that an `update` method is defined in the Observer interface.

Each widget is an `Observer`. The item being observed is the data representing the instrument name and price information. The data source is `Observable`.

All widgets, then, should implement the `Observer` interface. In addition, each one should descend from an abstract class that defines some shared functionality between widget objects. This is an example of using interfaces and abstract classes together. Because the `update()` method is the same for all widgets, it can be implemented in the `abstract` class. The class diagram is shown in Figure 4-7.

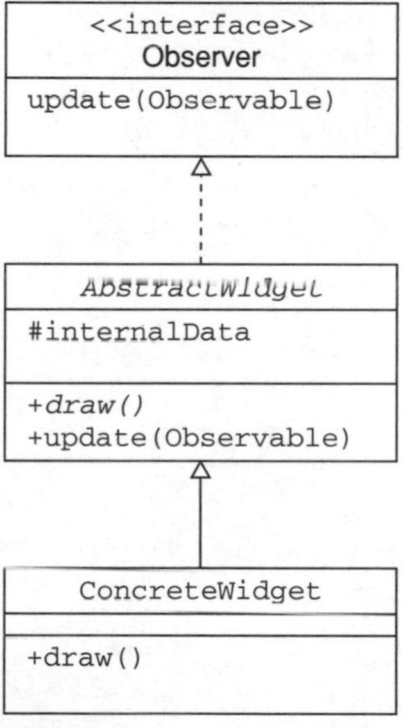

Figure 4-7

Now all concrete implementations of widgets will descend from the `AbstractWidget` class. The `AbstractWidget` class in turn implements the `Observer` interface. Notice the `update()` method in the class diagram for `AbstractWidget` is not shown in italics. This means that the method is actually implemented at that point. The # symbol indicates that the `internalData` property is protected. That means subclasses of `AbstractWidget` have access to it. If it were private, subclasses would not be able to access it.

Take a look at the following `Widget` code, in a file called `abstract_widget.php`:

```
<?php

interface Observer {
  public function update();
}


abstract class Widget implements Observer {

  protected $internalData = array();

  abstract public function draw();

  public function update(Observable $subject) {
        $this->internalData = $subject->getData();
  }
}


class BasicWidget extends Widget {

  function __construct() {
  }

  public function draw() {
        $html = "<table border=1 width=130>";
        $html .= "<tr><td colspan=3 bgcolor=#cccccc>
                      <b>Instrument Info<b></td></tr>";

        $numRecords = count($this->internalData[0]);
        for($i = 0; $i < $numRecords; $i++) {
               $instms = $this->internalData[0];
               $prices = $this->internalData[1];
               $years = $this->internalData[2];
               $html .= "<tr><td>$instms[$i]</td><td> $prices[$i]</td>
                         <td>$years[$i]</td></tr>";
               }
       $html .= "</table><br>";
       echo $html;
  }
}

class FancyWidget extends Widget {

  function __construct() {
  }

  public function draw() {
        $html =
        "<table border=0 cellpadding=5 width=270 bgcolor=#6699BB>
                 <tr><td colspan=3 bgcolor=#cccccc>
```

```
                <b><span class=blue>Our Latest Prices<span><b>
                </td></tr>
                <tr><td><b>instrument</b></td>
                <td><b>price</b></td><td><b>date issued</b>
                </td></tr>";

        $numRecords = count($this->internalData[0]);
        for($i = 0; $i < $numRecords; $i++) {
               $instms = $this->internalData[0];
               $prices = $this->internalData[1];
               $years = $this->internalData[2];

                $html .=
                "<tr><td>$instms[$i]</td><td>
                        $prices[$i]</td><td>$years[$i]
                        </td></tr>";
                }
         $html .= "</table><br>";
         echo $html;
    }
  }

  ?>
```

There are two concrete `Widget` implementations, `FancyWidget` and `BasicWidget`. Both implement the `draw()` method required from the `abstract` parent class they extend, yet the implementations are different. Both also inherit the `update()` method from the parent class.

You might be wondering about the benefit of using the `Observer` interface when you could just put the single method in the subclasses anyway. Earlier PHP versions provided no direct way to ensure that a method parameter was of a certain type. A new feature in PHP5 called *class type hints* serves as a way of guaranteeing that the correct type of object is passed as an argument. In the following function declaration, the reference passed as an argument must be of type `Observer` or you get an error.

```
  public function addObserver(Observer $observer) {
```

If a particular method takes an `Observer` as an argument—as is the case with the `Observable` `addObserver()` method—you know it's safe to pass a `Widget` to it. That's because all `Widget` objects are of type `Observer`. All widgets descend from the `AbstractWidget`, which implements `Observer`, thus the widgets themselves are also that type.

Another question arises: Why not just require the method `addObserver()` to take a `Widget`? That way, you could also do away with the `Observer` interface. Suppose, however, that you wanted to create another type of `Observer` that wasn't a `Widget`. Then the class type hint would prevent you from passing any other type of object to the `addObserver()` method.

The DataSource

The `DataSource` object encapsulates the name, price, and date of issue for a group of musical instruments. It's also our `Observable` object. The key methods in `Observer` are `addObserver()`

and notifyObservers(). Any Observer (in this case, any Widget) that needs to "watch" the DataSource can be added to it using addObserver(). The following code comprises observable.php:

```
<?php
abstract class Observable {

  private $observers = array();

  public function addObserver(Observer $observer) {
         array_push($this->observers, $observer);
  }

  public function notifyObservers() {
         for ($i = 0; $i < count($this->observers); $i++) {
                 $widget = $this->observers[$i];
                 $widget->update($this);
         }
    }

}

class DataSource extends Observable {

  private $names;
  private $prices;
  private $years;

  function __construct() {
         $this->names = array();
         $this->prices = array();
         $this->years = array();
  }

  public function addRecord($name, $price, $year) {
         array_push($this->names, $name);
         array_push($this->prices, $price);
         array_push($this->years, $year);
         $this->notifyObservers();
  }

  public function getData() {
         return array($this->names, $this->prices, $this->years);
  }
}
?>
```

The addRecord() method lets you add a new instrument to the internal storage of the DataSource object. Notice though, that the addRecord() method does one more thing.

```
$this->notifyObservers();
```

Any time the `DataSource` object has its internal data altered, it notifies all its observers. Observers are added using the previously mentioned `addObserver()` method. After an observer is added, it's stored in the internal `$observers` array. When `notifyObservers()` is called, the method iterates through the `$observers` array, calling the `update()` method for each `Observer` stored in the array.

The sole parameter of the `update` method is a copy of the `Observable` object itself:

```
$widget->update($this);
```

This allows the `Widget` (the `Observer`) to get a copy of the most current state of the `DataSource` (the `Observable`). Note that the `Widget` is passed by value—a copy of `DataSource` rather than the actual reference. This way, the `DataSource`'s internal information is not shared.

Connecting Observer and Observable

Now that you've done all the hard work up front, the payoff is an easy-to-use and flexible system for connecting an `Observer` `Widget` to the `Observable` `DataSource`. Take a look at the following example, in a file called `widget.php`:

```
<?php
require_once("observable.php");
require_once("abstract_widget.php");

$dat = new DataSource();
$widgetA = new BasicWidget();
$widgetB = new FancyWidget();

$dat->addObserver($widgetA);
$dat->addObserver($widgetB);

$dat->addRecord("drum", "$12.95", 1955);
$dat->addRecord("guitar", "$13.95", 2003);
$dat->addRecord("banjo", "$100.95", 1945);
$dat->addRecord("piano", "$120.95", 1999);

$widgetA->draw();
$widgetB->draw();

?>
```

All you have to do is create your `DataSource` and `Widget` objects. Then have the `Widget` objects added as observers of the `DataSource`. Now you're free to add as many records as needed to the `DataSource` object, not concerning yourself about updating the widgets—it all happens automatically. Finally, when you call `draw()` on the widgets, they will display themselves with the correct data.

If you were designing a desktop application, you could include a `redraw()` function in the `update()` method of the `Observer`. This way you wouldn't need to call `draw()` explicitly, but instead have the component redraw itself automatically in response to the `DataSource`'s being updated. In a purely server-side Web application, there's no way to redraw a component unless you reload the page.

Another cool feature of the pattern is that you can define multiple DataSources. You just tell the DataSource which widget you want listening to it, and you can reuse the same widget for different DataSources. Figure 4-8 shows the result of running the previous code.

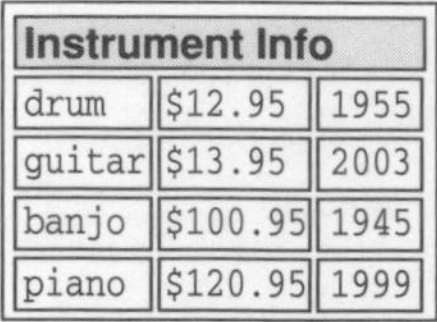

Instrument Info		
drum	$12.95	1955
guitar	$13.95	2003
banjo	$100.95	1945
piano	$120.95	1999

Our Latest Prices

instrument	price	date issued
drum	$12.95	1955
guitar	$13.95	2003
banjo	$100.95	1945
piano	$120.95	1999

Figure 4-8

Considerations

The observer pattern is useful when you have a source of data that you would like to connect to different representations. In this chapter we've used a simple DataSource object, but you can create more complex data sources, such as ones that retrieve data from a database or an XML file. You could design a Widget that could observe either an XML DataSource or a DB DataSource. As long as the DataSource object had the same interface, it wouldn't matter how it retrieved its data.

The Widgets in this example are coded to display a table with three columns, but they could be more flexible. If you want to get creative, try redesigning them so that they can display an arbitrary number of columns. You could also try using a little helper object instead of the arrays to transfer the information between Observable and Observer.

The Decorator Pattern

The two concrete widgets created for the observer pattern have a different appearance. If you needed to add a new style of widget, you would subclass Widget and implement the draw() method to write the HTML. Say that needed to add a feature to all existing widgets, such as a border. You could go into each draw() method and add some more HTML to each, but then the border would be hard-coded and all widgets would be forced to have a border. You could create a new set of subclasses of existing concrete widgets that implemented the border in the draw() method. If you had only two widgets, as in the Observer example, this might be an option—you would end up with four widgets. However, if you had five widgets to start with, it might not seem so appealing. Suddenly you have a lot of widget classes to worry about.

There is another way to handle situations like this, one that doesn't require you to create a new subclass for every widget you want to add a border to. Using the decorator pattern allows you to add features or functionality to existing objects without using inheritance. Figure 4-9 shows the class diagram for the decorator pattern.

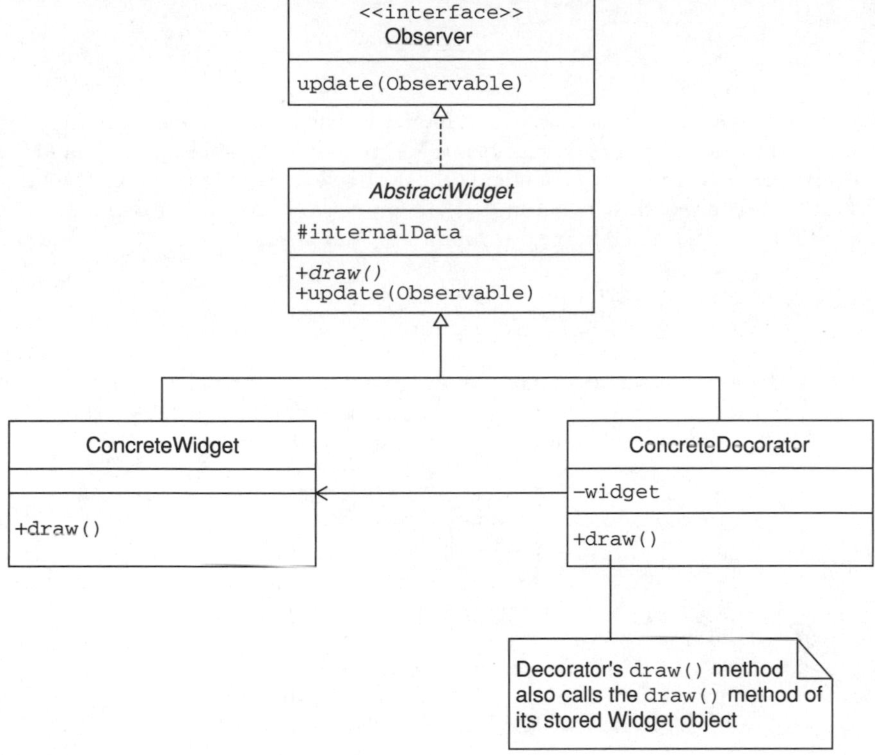

Figure 4-9

The class diagram indicates that `Decorators` are a type of `Widget`, too. This is good because we don't want to change the way we access a `Widget`, whether it's decorated or not. Take a look at the code of the following `Decorator`, saved as `border_decorator.php`, that draws a border around a `Widget`.

```
<?php

require_once("abstract_widget.php");

class BorderDecorator extends Widget {

  private $widget;

  function __construct(Widget $widget) {
         $this->widget = $widget;
  }

  public function draw() {

         $this->widget->update($this->getSubject());
```

```
            echo "<table border=0 cellpadding=1 bgcolor=#3366ff>";
            echo "<tr bgcolor=#ffffff><td>";
            $this->widget->draw();
            echo "</td></tr></table>";
        }
    }
?>
```

In this example we've moved all the classes and interfaces into their own files and used `require_once` to import them. The draw method generates some HTML to draw a table. Notice that in the middle of drawing this border table, the `draw()` method calls the `draw()` method of the `Widget` that was passed in the constructor. Because of this, the `Widget` gets some extra "decoration" around it, namely, the border. An example of how you use the `Decorator` follows:

```
$widgetA = new BasicWidget();
$widgetA = new BorderDecorator($widgetA);
```

After the decorator pattern is set up, you need only to pass it a `Widget` object. Then you can use the decorated `Widget` exactly the same way as you would a regular one. Figure 4-10 shows the `BasicWidget` object with and without the `BorderDecorator` applied to it.

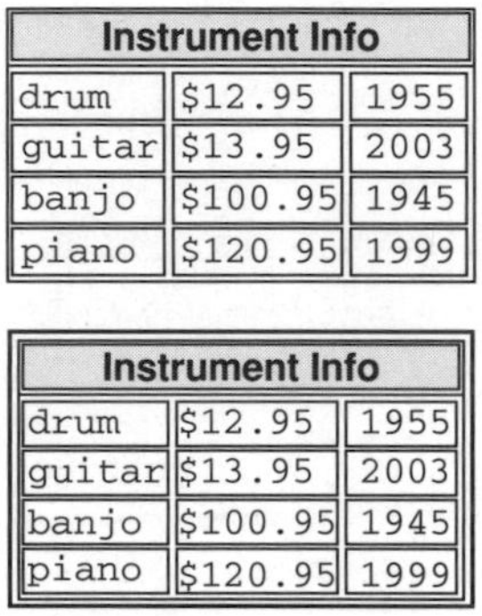

Instrument Info		
drum	$12.95	1955
guitar	$13.95	2003
banjo	$100.95	1945
piano	$120.95	1999

Instrument Info		
drum	$12.95	1955
guitar	$13.95	2003
banjo	$100.95	1945
piano	$120.95	1999

Figure 4-10

Implementation

There are some small but important changes in the implementation of the `Widget` objects to accommodate the decorator pattern. First, the protected `InternalData` array in the abstract `Widget` class has been changed to a private reference to the `DataSource` object stored in the `$subject` variable.

```
abstract class Widget implements Observer {

  private $subject;

  abstract public function draw();

  public function update(Observable $subject) {
        $this->subject = $subject;
  }
```

```
    public function getSubject() {
            return $this->subject;
    }
}
```

Next, during the implemented `draw()` methods in each concrete `Widget` class, the `Widget` accesses its subject by calling its inherited `getSubject()` method.

```
public function draw() {
        $data = $this->getSubject()->getData();
        $numRecords = count($data[0]);

        $html = "<table border=1 width=130>";
        $html .= "<tr><td colspan=3 bgcolor=#cccccc>
                        <b>Instrument Info<b></td></tr>";
        for($i = 0; $i < $numRecords; $i++) {
                $instms = $data[0];
                $prices = $data[1];
                $years = $data[2];
                $html .= "<tr><td>$instms[$i]</td><td> $prices[$i]
                                </td><td>$years[$i]</td></tr>";
                }
        $html .= "</table>";
        echo $html;
}
}
```

Finally, because the `Decorator` class is what is actually assigned as an observer of the `DataSource` object, it must in turn pass the `DataSource` down to its Widget object when the `Decorator's draw()` method is called. This allows the `Widget` object to have access to the data.

```
public function draw() {

        $this->widget->update($this->getSubject());

        echo "<table border=0 cellpadding=1 bgcolor=#3366ff>";
        echo "<tr bgcolor=#ffffff><td>";
        $this->widget->draw();
        echo "</td></tr></table>";
  }
```

Using the Decorator

After you've done the work developing the `Decorator` classes, you'll find that it is a very flexible and powerful pattern. Not only is it easy to use, but different `Decorators` can be combined to give multiple effects to the same widget. `Decorators` can even be applied in different order. Another decorator class follows. Save the file as `closebox_decorator.php`:

```
<?php
require_once("abstract_widget.php");

class CloseBoxDecorator extends Widget {
```

```
    private $widget;

    function __construct(Widget $widget) {
           $this->widget = $widget;
    }

    public function draw() {

           $this->widget->update($this->getSubject());

           print "<table border=0 cellspacing=1 bgcolor=#666666>";
           print "<tr bgcolor=#666666>";
           print "<td align=right>";
           print "        <table width=10 height=10 bgcolor="cccccc">";
           print "        <tr><td><b>x</b></td></tr>";
           print "        </table>";
           print "</td>";
           print "</tr>";
           print "<tr bgcolor=#ffffff>";
           print "<td>";

           $this->widget->draw();

           print "</td>";
           print "</tr>";
           print "</table>";
   }

  }
```

The preceding `Decorator` applies a simple menu bar with a close box on it. Combining the two `Widgets` with the two `Decorators` is easy. Save this file as `decorator.php`:

```
<?php
require_once ("abstract_widget.php");
require_once ("closebox_decorator.php");
require_once ("border_decorator.php");
require_once ("observable.php");

$dat = new DataSource();
$widgetA = new BasicWidget();
$widgetB = new FancyWidget();

$widgetB = new BorderDecorator($widgetB);
$widgetB = new CloseBoxDecorator($widgetB);

$widgetA = new CloseBoxDecorator($widgetA);
$widgetA = new BorderDecorator($widgetA);

$dat->addObserver($widgetA);
$dat->addObserver($widgetB);

$dat->addRecord("drum", "$12.95", 1955);
$dat->addRecord("guitar", "$13.95", 2003);
```

```
$dat->addRecord("banjo", "$100.95", 1945);
$dat->addRecord("piano", "$120.95", 1999);

$widgetB->draw();
echo "<br>";
$widgetA->draw();
?>
```

Notice that the first `Widget` has its `Decorators` applied in one order, and the second has then applied in the opposite order. Figure 4-11 shows the result of this code.

X

Our Latest Prices

instrument	price	date issued
drum	$12.95	1955
guitar	$13.95	2003
banjo	$100.95	1945
piano	$120.95	1999

X

Instrument Info

drum	$12.95	1955
guitar	$13.95	2003
banjo	$100.95	1945
piano	$120.95	1999

Figure 4-11

Considerations

The Decorators in this section all have hard-coded color values. There's no reason that you can't alter them to be more flexible. The `BorderDecorator` class can be changed to allow for a specified border width and color. You can use some DHTML to make the `CloseBoxDecorator` actually hide itself when the close box is clicked.

Remember that the decorator pattern need not be limited to purely graphical elements. In the case of the `Widgets`, the decorator pattern generated additional HTML to alter their look. You could instead have a data structure of some kind and use a `Decorator` to add additional information to it. For example, if you had a fragment of XML, you could use a `Decorator` to embed it in a larger XML structure.

To test your understanding of object-oriented programming, you might want to refine the way the `DataSource` is passed down to the `Widget` object from the `Decorator` object. There are several different ways to handle this. How could the `Widget` get a copy of the `DataSource` object without requiring the `Decorator` to pass it down in the `draw()` method?

The Facade Pattern

The best way to understand the facade pattern is to look at a component diagram of a system before and after using a facade.

Figure 4-12 shows the front end of a Web site communicating with an application on the Web server. In the right side of the diagram, the front end code is accessing various objects in the application. On the left, showing the facade, the front end communicates only with the facade object, which in turn delegates responsibilities to the internal objects.

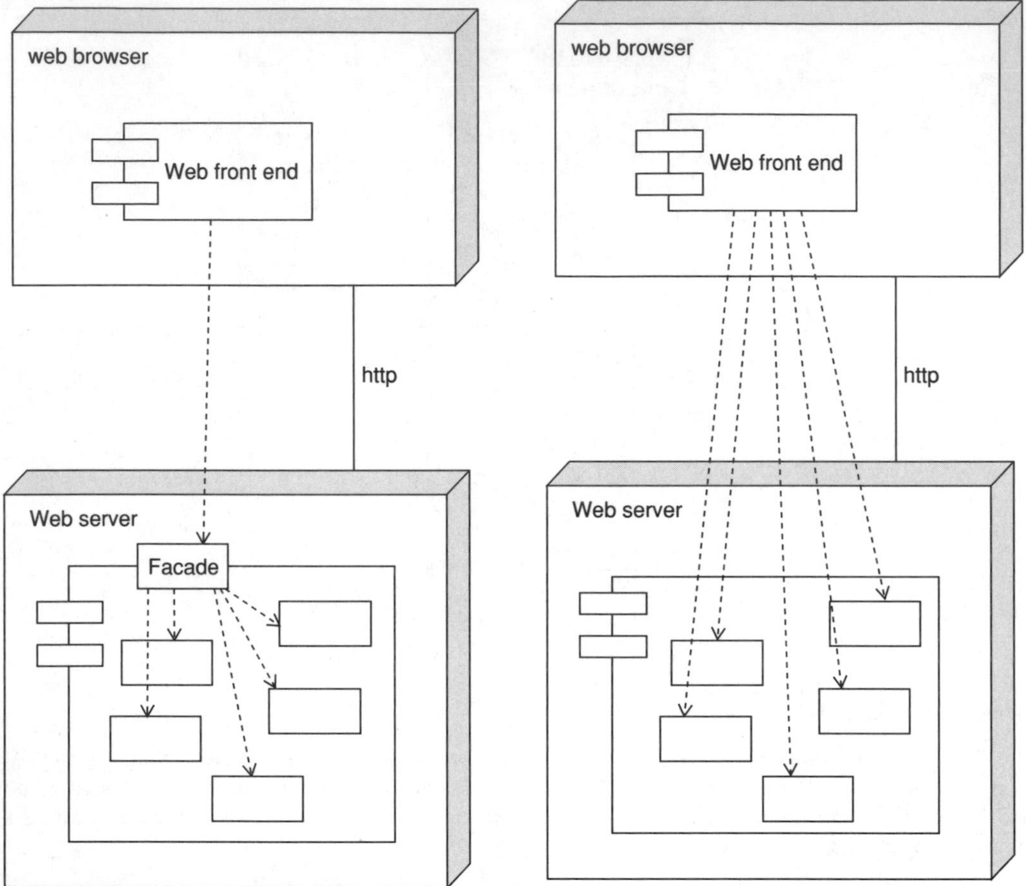

Figure 4-12

Say that you designed a small Web application. Over time, your client kept adding new features to it, and gradually the number of classes in the application increased. Certain pages on your Web site started building up many calls to the various objects. Such pages might resemble the following example.

```
$dbManager = new DBManager();
$userArray = $dbManager.getNewUsers();
```

```
$emailer = new Emailer();
$stats = new StatLog();

for ($i = 0; $i < count($userArray[$i]; $i++) {

  $user = $userArray[$i];
  $userPref = $user->getMailPreference();
  $userMail = $user->getEmail();

  if ($userPref == true) {
         $emailer->sendMailToUser($userMail);
  } else {
         $stats->storeUnmailedUser($user->getID());
  }
}
```

The preceding hypothetical code would send an e-mail to new users who indicated they want to receive mail. If they don't want to receive mail, their `userID` would be sent to a part of the application that manages statistics about users. Although this code isn't too ugly, if you had to mix in large amounts of HTML and get information back to report to the user, it might become unwieldy. Another version of using the Facade pattern follows.

```
Application::mailNewUsers();
```

Now, anytime this functionality is required, the front end just requests it from the facade, in this case the `Application` class. All messages from the front end of the site go through the `Application` class and never interact directly with the other objects in the system. The `Application` object's methods can be static because you don't even need an instance of the `Application` class.

Notice that the client of the `Application` class doesn't need to know how it works internally. One good result of this, in addition to cleaner code, is that it will allow a separation of front-end presentation and backend functionality. The less your application is tied up in a particular presentation of HTML, the more likely it is to be reusable elsewhere. There's more discussion of this good design practice in Chapter 13, "Model View Controller."

The Builder Pattern

If you look back at the composite pattern, you'll notice that the objects that made up the composite were manually created, as shown in the following example:

```
$drums = new DrumSet("tama maple set");
$drums->add(new SnareDrum("snare drum"));
$drums->add(new BaseDrum("large bass drum"));

$cymbals = new Cymbal("zildjian cymbal set");
$cymbals->add(new Cymbal("small crash"));
$cymbals->add(new Cymbal("large high hat"));
$drums->add($cymbals);
```

The code creating this `DrumSet` composite is not particularly complex, but what if you needed to create `Instrument` or `Instrument` composite objects for many different `Musician` objects, and those `Musician` objects in turn were composites of a `Band` object?

It wouldn't be impossible to write out the code that created the new objects and then added them, although it might start to get tedious if you had several bands with several musicians in them, each with their own set of instruments. If you needed to create bands in response to the actions of a user, perhaps through a GUI, then it might start to get difficult—especially if you had to hard code each type of band, with the required musicians and instruments.

Implementation

Say that you were required to create a wizard that generated a `Band` for an end user. The user would choose from a list of genres (for example, rock, country, salsa, heavy metal, and so on), and the resulting `Band` would be returned, assembled with its musicians and their instruments. Figure 4-13 shows the class diagram for the builder pattern.

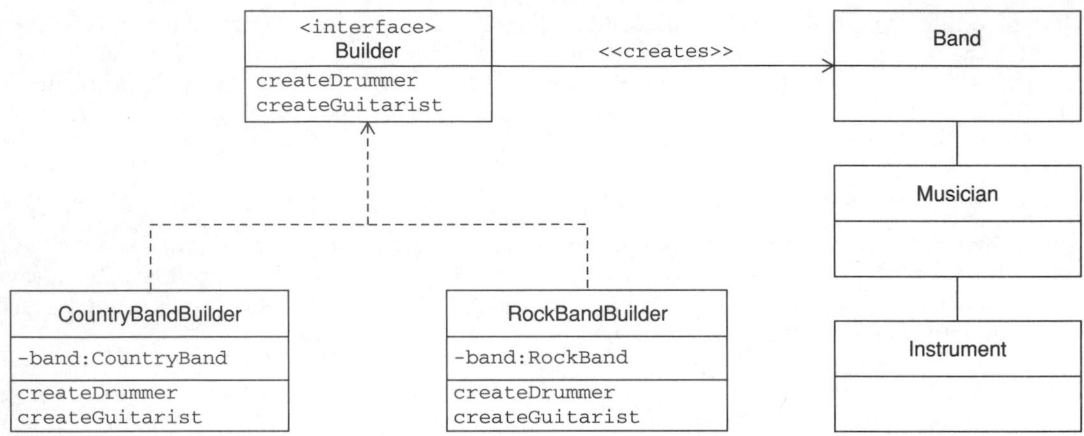

Figure 4-13

For this example, the Builder pattern creates `Band`s that have only two types of `Musicians`, guitarists and drummers.

```
<?php

interface Builder {
    public function buildDrummer();
    public function buildGuitarist();
}
?>
```

Each time a concrete builder class is instantiated, it creates a `Band` object. Take a look at the code for the `RockBandBuilder` class that follows.

```
<?php

require_once("interface_builder.php");
require_once("class_rockband.php");
require_once("class_musician.php");
```

```
require_once("class_instrument.php");

class RockBandBuilder implements Builder {

  private $band;

  function __construct($name) {
         $this->band = new RockBand($name);
  }

  public function getBand() {
         return $this->band;
  }

  public function buildDrummer() {

         $musician = new Musician("rock drummer");

         $drumset = new Instrument("rock drum kit");
         $drumset->add(new Instrument("cymbal"));
         $drumset->add(new Instrument("bass drum"));
         $drumset->add(new Instrument("snare drum"));

         $musician->addInstrument($drumset);
         $this->band->addMusician($musician);
  }

  public function buildGuitarist() {

         $musician = new Musician("rock guitarist");

         $guitar = new Instrument("electric guitar");

         $musician->addInstrument($guitar);
         $this->band->addMusician($musician);

  }

}
?>
```

See how the implementation of the constructor in `RockBandBuilder` creates a `RockBand`? Similarly, the constructor of `CountryBandBuilder` creates a `CountryBand`, shown next, in the file `countryband_builder.php`.

```
<?php
require_once("interface_builder.php");
require_once("class_musician.php");
require_once("class_countryband.php");
require_once("class_instrument.php");

class CountryBandBuilder implements Builder {
```

```
    rivate $band;

    function __construct() {
            $this->band = new CountryBand();
    }

    public function getBand() {
            return $this->band;
    }

    public function buildDrummer() {

            $musician = new Musician("washboard player");

            $drumset = new Instrument("washboard");

            $musician->addInstrument($drumset);
            $this->band->addMusician($musician);
    }

    public function buildGuitarist() {

            $musician = new Musician("country guitarist");

            $guitar = new Instrument("acoustic guitar");

            $musician->addInstrument($guitar);
            $this->band->addMusician($musician);
    }
}
?>
```

Check out the `buildDrummer()` method from `RockBandBuilder`. Now compare it to the one from `CountryBandBuilder`. Notice how each method creates not only the `Musician` object but also the instruments for that musician. Because of the `Builder` interface, both `Builders` are required to implement the `buildDrummer()` and `buildGuitarist()` methods, but they each construct a `Musician` in a completely different way, including the `Instrument` objects belonging to that musician.

You may have noticed that the `Musician` and `Instrument` classes are no longer subclassed into specific subtypes such as `Guitarist`. We did this to demonstrate that `Builders` can be implemented to create different objects—as in the constructor—or the same objects with different parameters and operations, as in the `buildDrummer()` method.

The Director

Builder patterns have one final important aspect, called the `Director`. The `Director` is responsible for calling the methods of the `Builder` to create the finished product, which in this case is a `Band` object. In this example, the `Director` will be the `Application` object similar to the one described in the facade pattern. The `Application` class follows in a file called `application.php`:

```
<?php

class Application {
```

```
    public static function createBand(Builder $builder) {

            $builder->buildGuitarist();
            $builder->buildDrummer();

            return $builder->getBand();
    }
  }
  ?>
```

The Application class has one method, createBand, which takes a Builder as its argument. The Application then calls the create methods of the passed Builder object. You should note two important points here. First, the Application decides which methods of the Builder it wants to call; second, it doesn't care which type of Builder is passed to it.

Finally, here is how you would use the Application (a.k.a. the Director) and Builder together. Simply create an instance of the appropriate Builder object and pass it to the createBand method of the Application.

```
  $builder = new RockBandBuilder();
  $band = Application::createBand($builder);
```

The Application object and Builder work together to build the correct Band object step by step. The Band object is manipulated and stored in the Builder until it's requested by the getBand method.

Considerations

The builder pattern is useful for assembling composites and hierarchical object structures like the Band->Musician->Instrument one. Although having the Builder return a completed object is useful, don't forget that the Band object returned by the Builder is still the same as any Band object you might have created by hand. That means that it can still be altered after its construction.

The Director class can be modified to allow for more than one creation method. In the case of the Application object, you had only one method, createBand, but having methods that called different configurations using the same builder is possible. For example, you could have methods such as createTrio. By passing different Builder objects, the same method would assemble either a rock trio or a country trio.

Summary

In this chapter you've seen five different design patterns:

- The composite
- The observer
- The decorator
- The facade
- The builder

Although each pattern handles a different design issue, one feature is common to them all. After the work to develop and implement the pattern is finished, the code to actually use it is very simple and flexible. Patterns allow developers and software designers to share complex ideas with just a single term. They're also reusable ideas. The same design pattern can be a solution in very different types of software. Often you'll see design patterns incorporated into a language or framework—so if you know about them, you'll understand how they are supposed to work within that language.

The five patterns presented here are just a small subset of the design patterns that exist. You should continue to explore design patterns on your own—they're a great tool for a serious developer.

Part II: Creating a Reusable Object Toolkit I: Simple Utility Classes and Interfaces

Chapter 5: Collection Class

Chapter 6: CollectionIterator Class

Chapter 7: GenericObject Class

Chapter 8: Database Abstraction Layers

Chapter 9: Factory Interface

Chapter 10: Event-Driven Programming

Chapter 11: Logging and Debugging

Chapter 12: SOAP

Collection Class

Now that you've learned the ins and outs of object-oriented application design in PHP, you might be tempted to dive in and start coding your application. With your new-found knowledge, you're certainly ready to do just that, but you will almost certainly be taking the longest route to get there. There are a number of shortcuts you can take along the way, in the form of a series of utilities and reusable classes that together will comprise an immensely powerful, easy-to-use development toolkit. In this part of the book, we'll be introducing you to the toolkit piece by piece, and showing you with real-world examples just how useful it can be. The first class in your toolkit is called `Collection`, and that's what you'll meet in this chapter.

The `Collection` class is an object-oriented replacement for the traditional `array` data type. Much as an array does, it contains member variables, although those variables tend to be other objects, rather than simpler data types like strings, integers, and so forth. The class then provides simple methods to allow you to add member variables, remove them, and fetch them for use in applications. As you'll see in this chapter, it has numerous advantages over using a simple array for storing a series of instantiated objects.

As with all chapters in this section of the book, you will not only utilize the code for the class itself, but will also see exactly how it is put together, based on original design requirements which we will determine together. Along the way, topics such as lazy instantiation using callbacks are discussed, as well as how to put the `Collection` class to use and what possible improvements could be made to it in the future.

In conjunction with the `CollectionIterator` class, covered in the next chapter, the `Collection` class provides a sophisticated but easy-to-implement mechanism for handling groups of objects in your application.

Purpose of the Collection Class

Applications frequently have objects that contain a group of other objects. For example, if you were building an application for a university's registrar's office, you would need to have a `Student` class and a `Course` class. A `Student` object would probably have more than one `Course` object associated with it. The most obvious way to construct this would be to have an array of `Course` objects as a member variable of the `Student` object.

```
/* student class */
class Student {
  public $courses = array();

  // ... other methods/properties
}

/* using the student class */
$objStudent = new Student(1234); //constructor not shown above
foreach($objStudent->courses as $objCourse) {
  print $objCourse->name;
}
```

Of course, if the most obvious approach were the best possible approach, we wouldn't have needed to write this chapter.

The above method has a few problems. First, exposing the array of `Course` objects as a public member variable breaks encapsulation. There is no opportunity to validate changes to the array or change the state of the `Student` object, should that be necessary. Second, it's not obvious from this implementation how the courses will be indexed in the array and how to traverse that array to find a specific `Course` object in which you might be interested. Third, and most important, to ensure that the courses array is available to any code that might want to use the `Student` object, you need to pull up all the course information from the database at the same time as the student information. This means that even if you want to print only the student's name, you have to fetch all the information about courses, unnecessarily increasing load on the database server and bogging down the entire application.

The `Collection` class is designed to solve all these problems. It provides an OO wrapper around an array and implements a mechanism that allows *lazy instantiation*. Lazy instantiation defers creation of the members of the collection until such time as they are actually needed. It's called "lazy" because the application will determine on its own when to instantiate the objects. When you create a `Student` object, the `Course` objects should not be created at the same time. Only when you first attempt to access the courses should they be created, and this should happen automagically without requiring you to do anything special.

The functional requirements of the `Collection` class are as follows:

1. Establish a wrapper around an array of objects.
2. Provide methods to add, remove, and fetch the member objects in a predictable, obvious way.
3. Allow you to easily determine how many member objects exist in the collection.
4. Enable you to use lazy instantiation to save system resources.

Designing the Collection Class

Before writing any code, you should make sure that you've carefully planned the classes you'll create. Based on the written functional requirements in items 1, 2, and 3 from the previous list, you can establish a class diagram that looks something like Figure 5-1.

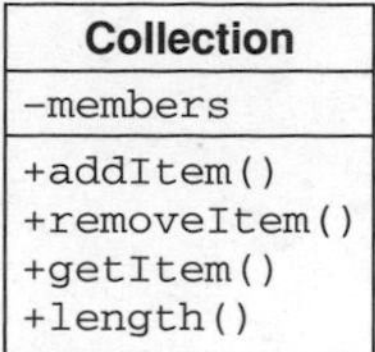

Figure 5-1

To handle the operations to add, remove, and get members "in a predictable, obvious way," users of this object need to be allowed to specify a useful key name when adding the objects. The key will work just like a string index in an associative array, specifying the location in the collection into which the member object of the collection will be stored. This key can then be used for retrieving or removing the object later. To use our previous example of the registrar's office application, the key for each course might be the course code (for example, CS101 for a beginning computer science class). In some cases, you won't have a meaningful key value to use. In this situation, the collection should be able to determine a valid key on its own. The updated UML diagram is shown in Figure 5-2.

Collection
-members
+addItem(obj:mixed, key:String=null)
+removeItem(key:String)
+getItem(key:String)
+length()

Figure 5-2

The `obj` parameter to `addItem()` is the item being added to the collection. This item is usually an object but can be any valid data type. The `key` parameter to `addItem()`, `removeItem()`, and `getItem()` is a string (optional in `addItem()`) representing the key.

After the basic code for manipulating the collection's contents has been established, we'll return to this diagram to explain how the lazy instantiation code will work. One final thing to note here is that `length()` simply returns the number of items currently in the collection.

Collection Class Basics

Based on the UML diagram in Figure 5-2, the code skeleton for the `Collection` class looks like this:

```
<?php
class Collection {

  private $_members = array();

  public function addItem($obj, $key = null) {

  }
```

```
    public function removeItem($key) {

    }

    public function getItem($key) {

    }

    public function length() {

    }

  }
  ?>
```

The $_members variable provides a location in which to store the objects that are members of the collection. addItem() allows you to add a new object to the collection. removeItem() removes an object. getItem() returns the object, and, of course, we already know that length() returns the number of items in the collection. The Collection class does not require a constructor.

The addItem Method

When adding a new object to the collection, that object is inserted into the $_members array, at the location specified by $key. If no key is provided, you'll allow PHP to pick one. If an attempt is made to add an object to the collection using a key that already exists, an exception should be thrown to prevent inadvertent overwriting of information.

```
class Collection {

  private $_members = array();

  public function addItem($obj, $key = null) {
    if($key) {
      if(isset($this->_members[$key])) {
        throw new KeyInUseException("Key \"$key\" already in use!");
      } else {
        $this->_members[$key] = $obj;
      }
    } else {
      $this->_members[] = $obj;
    }
}
```

As with most of the subclasses of Exception used in this book, KeyInUseException has no body, and instead inherits everything from the default Exception class that ships with PHP5.

```
class KeyInUseException extends Exception { }
```

The KeyInUseException class gives you a means of letting users of the object know when they might be overwriting information by specifying the same key more than once. The value of the key is used as the index in the $_members array. If no key is specified, PHP picks a numeric index for this element. In either case, the object is inserted into the array at that location.

Subclasses of `Collection` can override the `addItem()` method with a type hint that will ensure that the items being added are of the correct type for the desired collection. Here's an example:

```
<?php
class CourseCollection extends Collection {

  public addItem(Course $obj, $key = null) {
    parent::addItem($obj, $key);
  }
}
?>
```

Using this technique, with very little code you can create subclasses that enforce a data type for the members of the collection.

The getItem and removeItem Methods

The `removeItem()` and `getItem()` methods take a key as a parameter to allow you to know which items are being removed or fetched. An exception should be thrown if an invalid key is supplied.

```
public function removeItem($key) {
  if(isset($this->_members[$key])) {
    unset($this->_members[$key]);
  } else {
     throw new KeyInvalidException("Invalid key \"$key\"!");
  }
}

public function getItem($key) {
  if(isset($this->_members[$key])) {
    return $this->_members[$key];
  } else {
    throw new KeyInvalidException("Invalid key \"$key\"!");
  }
}
```

The `InvalidKeyException` class is just as simple as the `KeyInUseException` class.

```
class KeyInvalidException extends Exception { }
```

Other Methods

Because the `$key` parameter to the `addItem()` method is optional, you won't necessarily know the key used for each item in the collection. A function called `keys()` will allow you to provide a listing of those keys to any external code that might need it. The keys will be returned as an array.

```
public function keys() {
  return array_keys($this->_members);
}
```

You might want to know how many items are in the collection. The `sizeof` PHP function returns the number of elements in an array, so you'll use that to implement your `length()` method.

```
public function length() {
  return sizeof($this->_members);
}
```

Because `getItem()` throws an exception if an invalid key is passed, you need to have a means of determining whether a given key exists in the collection. The `exists()` method will allow you to check before calling `getItem()`.

```
public function exists($key) {
  return (isset($this->_members[$key]));
}
```

This approach allows you to either use a `try...catch` block to trap for invalid keys or to call the `exists()` method before calling `getItem()`, depending on which method is more convenient for a given chunk of code.

Now that you've added all the basic methods to the class, you can move on to see how the `Collection` class is used.

Using the Collection Class

To use the `Collection` class as it stands now, create a file called `class.Collection.php` and save the code for the `Collection` class into it. Create files for the `KeyInvalidException` and `KeyInUseException` classes. Make sure to add `require_once` statements to the top of `class.Collection.php` to pull in those exception classes. Save the following code into `testCollection.php`.

```
<?php
/* a silly class for testing */
class Foo {
  private $_name;
  private $_number;

  public function __construct($name, $number) {
    $this->_name = $name;
    $this->_number = $number;
  }

  public function __toString() {
    return $this->_name . ' is number ' . $this->_number;
  }
}

$colFoo = new Collection();
$colFoo->addItem(new Foo("Steve", 14), "steve");
$colFoo->addItem(new Foo("Ed", 37), "ed");
$colFoo->addItem(new Foo("Bob", 49));

$objSteve = $colFoo->getItem("steve");
print $objSteve; //prints "Steve is number 14"
```

```
$colFoo->removeItem("steve"); //deletes the 'steve' object

try {
  $colFoo->getItem("steve"); //throws KeyInvalidException
} catch (KeyInvalidException $kie) {
  print "The collection doesn't contain anything called 'steve'";
}
?>
```

Okay, so this example isn't particularly interesting yet, but it should give you some idea of how the `Collection` class is used. The next section discusses how to handle lazy instantiation, which is one of the primary benefits of this class.

Implementing Lazy Instantiation

Lazy instantiation refers to the ability of the `Collection` class to defer creation of its members until such time as they are needed. In the registrar's application discussed at the beginning of the chapter, a `Student` object has multiple `Course` objects associated with it. When you want to use a `Student` object to display the name of a student, you do not need any of the information about that student's courses. However, for the sake of a consistent interface, the course objects should be available as member variables of the student object.

To keep things simple when displaying a list of courses for a given student, the software interface should allow you to write code like this:

```
<?php

  $objStudent = StudentFactory::getStudent(12345); //12345 is the student ID
  print "Name: " . $objStudent->name . "<br>\n";
  print "Courses: <br>\n";
  foreach($objStudent->courses as $objCourse) {
    print $objCourse->coursecode . " - " . $objCourse->name . "<br>\n";
  }
?>
```

For now, it's enough to know that the `StudentFactory` is a class with a static method `getStudent` that returns a new student object, given the ID as a parameter. It does all the heavy lifting in the database. Factory classes are discussed in detail in Chapter 9.

You should assume that the `Student` class constructor takes care of populating the list of courses. But if you just have a listing of students by name, as in the next example, you shouldn't have to incur the overhead of fetching the unwanted courses. Again, assume the `StudentFactory` is a class that creates student objects by interrogating the database for us. In this case, we retrieve a collection of students by searching by their last names:

```
<?php

  $colStudents = StudentFactory::getByLastName("Smith");
  print "<h1>Students With the Last Name 'Smith'</h1>";
```

```
    foreach($colStudents as $objStudent) {
      print $objStudent->name . "<br>\n";
  }
  ?>
```

In this case, getting the course information would be totally unnecessary because you're merely displaying the name. But how can you keep the simple interface of the `Student` class without forcing the database activity? You could add methods such as `$objStudent->loadCourses()` that would populate the collection and have to be called before interacting with the `courses` collection, but that isn't terribly intuitive and clutters the interface. You could do something like `CourseFactory::getCoursesForStudent($objStudent)`, which would return a collection of courses for a given student, but again, it's not obvious to someone who just joined your development team that such a function needs to be called to get the `Course` objects for a given student. There is a better way, and it involves using callbacks.

Callbacks

If you've ever done any JavaScript programming and assigned some activity to happen in the `onclick` event for some object, you've used a callback. A callback is a nifty programming trick for which you tell the application to perform a function when some event happens. That event is out of your control—you don't necessarily know when it will happen. You tell the computer to take care of performing that function if and when the event takes place. Many times in JavaScript an `onSubmit` event handler is created for a form that allows client-side data validation to happen if the user tries to submit that form. You don't know when the user is going to submit the form, or even whether the user will do it at all. After the event handler is specified, the JavaScript engine takes care of the rest. You can also use this technique in server-side application development.

When you're designing the `Student` class for the registrar's application, you don't know whether or when the `course` collection will be accessed by the code that uses the class. Because fairly significant overhead is associated with getting the `Course` objects, this is a great time to take advantage of a callback. You need to be able to tell the `course` collection, "If someone tries to talk to you, you need to populate yourself first."

However, because the `Collection` class is a generic member of the reusable toolkit, you don't want to hard code the name of a function inside the class (this obviously limits the reusability of the class), and you don't want to have to create a new subclass of `Collection` every time you want to use it (because this is creating more work for you, not less). Instead, you should be able to supply the name of a procedural function, or supply a reference to an object and specify the method on that object that you want to call to populate the collection. To do so, you need to understand a special built-in PHP function.

Using call_user_func

When you want to call a function, you usually invoke the literal name of the function. However, PHP also allows you to call functions (and methods on objects) using string variables. The following is perfectly valid PHP:

```
<?php
  $myFunc = "pow";
  print $myFunc(4, 2); //prints 16, or pow(4, 2)
?>
```

PHP evaluates the variable name and executes the function with that name. This works for compiled-in core functions as well as user-defined functions. You can perform the same trick with a method of an object.

```
<?php
  $myMethod = 'sayHello';
  $obj = new Person();
  $obj->$myMethod();
?>
```

Assuming that you have a class called `Person` with a method called `sayHello()`, this would work just fine (you can also invoke static methods that way—that is, `Person::$myMethod()`).

The only problem with this trick is that it's not at all obvious that `$obj->$myMethod()` is calling `$obj->sayHello()`. This would be even more confusing if the value of `$myMethod` was passed in as a parameter to some wrapper function. PHP provides a built-in method for doing the same thing, in a manner a little less confusing and far more transparent.

The function `call_user_func()` takes one mandatory parameter, to define the function to be called, and zero or more additional parameters to be passed as parameters to the user-defined function. The function definition is as follows:

```
mixed call_user_func ( callback function [, mixed parameter [, mixed ...]])
```

The value of the `callback function` parameter takes one of three forms:

- `string $functionName`—a string corresponding to the name of the procedural function to be called
- `array(object $object, string $functionName)`—an array consisting of an instantiated object and a string corresponding to the name of the method to be called on that object
- `array(string $className, string $functionName)`—an array consisting of the name of a class and a string corresponding to the name of a *static* method of that class

Here are a few examples of using this function:

```
<?php
class Bar {
  private $_foo;

  public function __construct($fooVal) {
    $this->_foo = $fooVal;
  }

  public function printFoo() {
    print $this->_foo;
  }

  public static function sayHello($name) {
    print "Hello there, $name!";
  }
}
```

```
//procedural function - not part of the Bar class
function printCount($start, $end) {
  for($x = $start; $x <= $end; $x++) {
    print "$x ";
  }
}

//prints 1 2 3 4 5 6 7 8 9 10
call_user_func('printCount', 1, 10);                    /* ex. 1 */

//calls $objBar->printFoo()
$objBar = new Bar('elephant');
call_user_func(array($objBar, 'printFoo'));             /* ex. 2 */

//calls Bar::sayHello('Steve')
call_user_func(array('Bar', 'sayHello'), 'Steve');      /* ex. 3 */

//This throws a fatal error "Using $this when not
//in object context" because the function call
//is Bar::printFoo, which is not a static method
call_user_func(array('Bar', 'printFoo'));               /* ex. 4 */
?>
```

The first example of calling `call_user_func` is straightforward. You pass the name of the procedural function as a string and supply the two parameters it expects. In the second example, you pass an array as the first parameter. Because the first element of that array is an object, the method `printFoo()` is invoked on that object. In the third and fourth example, the first element in the array is a string. Therefore, PHP attempts to statically invoke the method on the specified class. If the method doesn't exist or relies on nonstatic class variables (that is, `$this`), you will encounter a fatal runtime error. This is what happens in the last line when you try to statically invoke `printFoo()`.

> **Terminology Reminder: Static methods are those that do not rely on nonstatic class member variables and can be invoked without first instantiating an object of that class. The invocation syntax is `ClassName::methodName()`. The keyword `$this` is not available to statically invoked methods.**

Implementing a Callback

You can use `call_user_func` to create a callback in one of your classes. By creating a method that allows the same types of parameters as `call_user_func`, you can allow code outside your class to specify a function or method to be invoked when certain events in your class happen.

To create a callback in one of your classes, take the following steps:

1. Determine which events will be raised by your class.
2. For each of those events, create an `on[EventName]` method that takes two parameters:
    - The name of the function
    - Optionally, an object or class name. The object parameter should be an instantiated object variable. The class name should be a string.

3. For each event, create a private member variable in your class that will store those parameters as a string (if no object or class name was provided), or as an array (if the second parameter had a value).

4. At each point in the class where these callbacks should be triggered, query the private member variable created in step 3 to see whether it has been set. If so, call `call_user_func()`, passing in the value of that variable.

The following example shows how to create an `onspeak()` event in a class called `Dog`. Create a function called `onspeak()` that takes a function name as a string and, optionally, an object or class name. Construct the string or array that should be passed to `call_user_func()`, and test the value to make sure that it's callable. If it is, store the value in a private member variable for later use. Have a look at the `bark()` method to see how this value is used.

```
<?php
class Dog {
  private $_onspeak;

  public function __construct($name) {
    $this->_name = $name;
  }

  public function bark() {
    if(isset($this->_onspeak)) {
      if(! call_user_func($this->_onspeak)) {
        return false;
      }
    }

    print "Woof, woof!";
  }

  public function onspeak($functionName, $objOrClass = null) {
    if($objOrClass) {
      $callback = array($objOrClass, $functionName);
    } else {
      $callback = $functionName;
    }

    //make sure this stuff is valid
    if(!is_callable($callback, false, $callableName)) {
      throw new Exception("$callableName is not callable " .
                          "as a parameter to onspeak");
      return false;
    }

    $this->_onspeak = $callback;
  }
} //end class Dog

//procedural function
function isEveryoneAwake() {
  if(time() < strtotime("today 8:30am") ||
```

```
        time() > strtotime("today 10:30pm")) {
      return false;
    } else {
      return true;
    }
  }

  $objDog = new Dog('Fido');
  $objDog->onspeak('isEveryoneAwake');
  $objDog->bark(); //polite dog

  $objDog2 = new Dog('Cujo');
  $objDog2->bark(); //always barks!

  //Throws exception when onspeak is called.
  $objDog3 = new Dog('Lassie');
  $objDog3->onspeak('nonExistentFunction', 'NonExistentClass');
  $objDog3->bark();
  ?>
```

The `isEveryoneAwake()` function checks to see that the current time is between 8:30 a.m. and 10:30 p.m. If so, return true, allowing the dog to bark. If not, return false, keeping the dog silent. If only real dogs could be programmed with callbacks! This approach works only for `$objDog` because `$objDog2` did not have the callback set.

Note the use of the `is_callable()` function in `onspeak()`. This is another built-in PHP function, as is `call_user_func()`. It's basically a sanity check on the parameters passed to the `onspeak()` method. When you pass in the parameters to `$objDog3->onspeak()`, the nonexistent function and class will cause an exception to be thrown.

The setLoadCallback Method in the Collection Class

Now that you've seen how callbacks can work, you need to understand how to put them to work in the `Collection` class to give it one of its more important advantages—lazy instantiation.

Consider the `Student` class from the registrar's application. You want to be able to keep the very simple interface you saw at the beginning of the chapter, in which the courses are a member variable of the `Student` object. But you shouldn't have to suffer the overhead of fetching the course list every time you fetch a student object. Instead, you need to enable a callback on the `Collection` class that will tell it to call some function before allowing any external code to interact with it.

Each call to `addItem()`, `getItem()`, `length()`, `exists()`, and `keys()` should first make sure that the collection has been loaded and, if not, invoke any callback functions that might be specified. The function specified in the callback is responsible for populating the collection. You will also need some sort of flag to indicate whether the callback has been invoked. This flag will prevent unnecessarily repeated attempts to load a collection that has already been loaded because that could have a detrimental impact on performance.

The code that follows shows the complete `Collection` class with the modifications necessary to implement the lazy instantiation capabilities of this class (shown in gray screen).

```
<?php
class Collection {

  private $_members = array();     //collection members

  private $_onload;                //holder for callback function

  private $_isLoaded = false;      //flag that indicates whether the callback
                                   //has been invoked

  public function addItem($obj, $key = null) {
    $this->_checkCallback();       //_checkCallback is defined a little later

    if($key) {
      if(isset($this->_members[$key])) {
        throw new KeyInUseException("Key \"$key\" already in use!");
      } else {
         $this->_members[$key] = $obj;
      }
    } else {
       $this->_members[] = $obj;
    }
  }

  public function removeItem($key) {
    $this->_checkCallback();

    if(isset($this->_members[$key])) {
      unset($this->_members[$key]);
    } else {
       throw new KeyInvalidException("Invalid key \"$key\"!");
    }
  }

  public function getItem($key) {
    $this->_checkCallback();

    if(isset($this->_members[$key])) {
       return $this->_members[$key];
    } else {
       throw new KeyInvalidException("Invalid key \"$key\"!");
    }
  }

  public function keys() {
    $this->_checkCallback();
    return array_keys($this->_members);
  }

  public function length() {
    $this->_checkCallback();
    return sizeof($this->_members);
  }
```

```
    public function exists($key) {
      $this->_checkCallback();
      return (isset($this->_members[$key]));
    }

    /**
     * Use this method to define a function to be
     * invoked prior to accessing the collection.
     * The function should take a collection as a
     * its sole parameter.
     */
    public function setLoadCallback($functionName, $objOrClass = null) {
      if($objOrClass) {
        $callback = array($objOrClass, $functionName);
      } else {
        $callback = $functionName;
      }

      //make sure the function/method is valid
      if(!is_callable($callback, false, $callableName)) {
        throw new Exception("$callableName is not callable " .
                            "as a parameter to onload");
        return false;
      }

      $this->_onload = $callback;
    }

    /**
     * Check to see if a callback has been defined and if so,
     * whether or not it has already been called. If not,
     * invoke the callback function.
     */
    private function _checkCallback() {
      if(isset($this->_onload) && !$this->_isLoaded) {
        $this->_isLoaded = true;
        call_user_func($this->_onload, $this);
      }
    }
  }
  ?>
```

The `setLoadCallback()` function allows you to supply the name of a function and, optionally, the name of a class or an object variable that will be invoked to populate this collection. If a callback is supplied to the collection, the `$_onload` private member variable is populated with the string or array to be passed to `call_user_func`. Note that just as in the example using the `Dog` class previously, there's a bit of sanity checking to make sure that the callback is callable.

All the other methods of the `Collection` class have had the line `$this->_checkLoadCallback()` added as the first line in the function declaration. Adding this line forces the collection to check for the existence of an as-yet uninvoked callback and will cause that function to be called. Before calling the callback function, we set a flag to make sure that we call that function only once. Note the check for `$this->_isLoaded`. Any function used as a load callback with the `Collection` class should expect exactly one parameter, which will be of type `Collection`. A reference to the current collection (using the `$this` variable) is passed to the callback function with the line:

```
call_user_func($this->_onload, $this)
```

This allows the callback function to operate directly on the collection object that caused the function to be invoked. The example that follows shows how this would work in a real situation.

Create a class called `NightClub`. This class has a `name` property and a collection of `Singer` objects. Sometimes we just need to display the name of the club. Sometimes we want to do something with the collection of singers. As a result, we're using the `setLoadCallback()` method of the collection object to ensure that we don't execute any unnecessary code.

Here are the `NightClub` and `Singer` classes. Name the file `club_singer.php`:

```
<?php
require_once("class.Collection.php");

class Singer {
  public $name;

  public function __construct($name) {
    $this->name = $name;
  }
}

class NightClub {
  public $name;
  public $singers;

  public function __construct($name) {
    $this->name = $name;
    $this->singers = new Collection();
    $this->singers->setLoadCallback('_loadSingers', $this);
  }

  private function _loadSingers(Collection $col) {
    print "(We're loading the singers!)<br>\n";

    //these would normally come from a database
    $col->addItem(new Singer('Frank Sinatra'));
    $col->addItem(new Singer('Dean Martin'));
    $col->addItem(new Singer('Sammy Davis, Jr.'));
    }
  }
}
?>
```

Note the `print` statement in the `_loadSingers()` method. Having this here is just for demonstration purposes. Run the following code (you can add it to the bottom of the previous code, if you wish), and you'll see that the `print` statement does not appear on the screen.

```
<?php
  $objNightClub = new NightClub('The Sands');
  print "Welcome to " . $objNightClub->name . ".<br>\n";
?>
```

Now try it again, this time doing something with the `$singers` collection.

```
<?php
  $objNightClub = new NightClub('The Sands');
  print "Welcome to " . $objNightClub->name . ".<br>\n";
  print "We have " . $objNightClub->singers->length() . " singers " .
        "for your listening pleasure this evening.";
?>
```

Running this should give the following output:

```
Welcome to The Sands.
(We're loading the singers!)
We have 3 singers for your listening pleasure this evening.
```

As you can see, this makes using the `singers` collection really easy. If you were to create the `NightClub` class, you could hand that class off to a more junior member of your software development team who could then use that class to display the screen shown in the example without any knowledge of how or when that collection was loaded. And you can be sure that the application isn't taking up any more system resources than are absolutely necessary.

In the next section, we return to the registrar's office example and show how to put all this to good use in a real-world application.

Using the Collection Class

As we've already mentioned several times in this chapter, our registrar's office application involves a class called `Student` that contains a collection of `Course` objects. Both classes are fairly simple. The UML class diagram is shown in Figure 5-3.

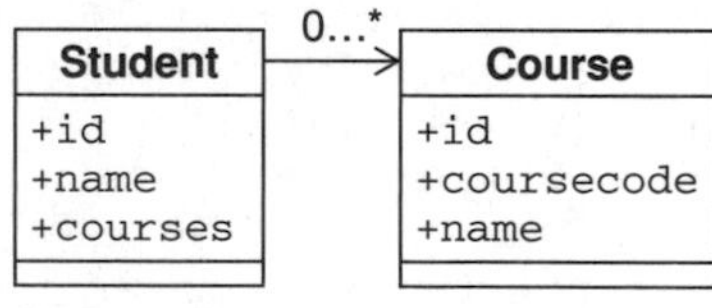

Figure 5-3

Of course, a `Course` should also have a collection of `students`, but the code will be quite similar, so after you've seen how we implement the `courses` collection for the `Student` class, it we'll leave it as an exercise for you to update the UML diagram and add the necessary code to support the `students` collection on the `Course` class.

For the `Collection` class, we're using the code exactly as it appears in the example with the `NightClub` object previously, so if you've already created that class you don't need to make any changes. If you haven't already created a file containing that class, and you want to try the example out for yourself, do so now.

From the UML diagram (Figure 5-3) you can see that the course class is quite simple, having only a name, a course code, and an ID. The course code is the course identifier, such as CS101 for a beginning computer science class. The name is the full name of the course. The ID is the numeric primary key from the database. In a real application, you would probably want to have access to a list of prerequisites (another collection), a syllabus outline, information about the instructor, and so on. Again, these are left as an exercise for you to complete on your own.

Have a look at the code:

```
<?php
class Course {
  private $_id;
  private $_courseCode;
  private $_name;

  function __construct($id, $courseCode, $name) {
    $this->_id = $id;
    $this->_courseCode = $courseCode;
    $this->_name = $name;
  }

  public function getName() {
    return $this->_name;
  }

  public function getID() {
    return $this->_id;
  }

  public function getCourseCode() {
    return $this->_courseCode;
  }

  public function __toString() {
    return $this->_name;
  }
}
?>
```

According to the class diagram, a course has two properties, `$id` and `$name`. Because this part of the application should not allow the name or ID of the class to be modified, we've used private member variables to store those values, and we provided `getID()` and `getName()` methods for retrieving them.When you build the parts of the application that do allow these values to be modified (the course administration tools), you can add `setID()` and `setName()` methods. These methods should probably utilize some sort of security mechanism to ensure that no unauthorized individuals are modifying properties of a course.

We've also provided a __toString() method. This "magic" method can be defined by any objects in PHP5. It allows you to write code like this:

```
print "This course is called " . $objCourse . "<br>";
```

$objCourse is obviously not a string, but because the special __toString() method has been defined, PHP will use the return value of that method when attempting to coerce the variable from an object to a string.

Because the courses collection should only ever consist of Course objects, create a subclass of Collection called CourseCollection. Override the addItem() method to include a type hint that will allow only Course objects to be added to the collection.

```
<?php
class CourseCollection extends Collection {
  public function addItem(Course $obj, $key = null) {
    parent::addItem($obj, $key);
  }
}
?>
```

This will allow PHP to do some type checking to ensure that everything in the $courses collection is exactly what you expect it to be—a Course object.

The Student class has the properties $id and $name, which represent the unique identifier and name of that student. It also needs to have a property called $courses, which is a collection of the courses for which the student is currently registered.

```
<?php
class Student {
  private $_id;
  private $_name;

  public $courses;

  public function __construct($id, $name) {
    $this->_id = $id;
    $this->_name = $name;

    $this->courses = new CourseCollection();
    $this->courses->setLoadCallback('_loadCourses', $this);
  }

  public function getName() {
    return $this->_name;
  }

  public function getID() {
    return $this->_id;
  }
```

```
    private function _loadCourses(Collection $col) {
      $arCourses = StudentFactory::getCoursesForStudent($this->_id, $col);
    }

    public function __toString() {
      return $this->_name;
    }
  }
  ?>
```

Just as in the Course class, implement the $id and $name properties as private member variables and provide getID() and getName() functions. For now, leave the $courses member as a public member variable. Note the creation of a __toString() method for this class, as well. This makes it a little bit easier to display the most common string representation of any object, in this case the name of the student.

In the constructor, call setLoadCallback() and pass in the name of the loading method _loadCourses() and a reference to the object where that method exists, namely, $this.

The _loadCourses() method takes a Collection as its only parameter, as required by the setLoadCallback() function, and uses a static method of the StudentFactory class (which we haven't discussed yet). This method requires the ID of the student and is passed a Collection object into which to load the courses.

The StudentFactory class contains two static methods that do all the work in the database of loading the student and course information. For this application, three tables need to be created in your database: student, course, and studentcourse. The purpose of the first two tables should be fairly obvious— to store the basic information about the students and the courses. The third table has two fields, studentid and courseid. It creates the association between students and courses.

The SQL statements that follow are for PostgreSQL (our preferred database server), but with minor modifications it would also work for most RDBMSes.

```
CREATE TABLE "student" (
  "studentid" SERIAL NOT NULL PRIMARY KEY,
  "name" varchar(255)
);

CREATE TABLE "course" (
  "courseid" SERIAL NOT NULL PRIMARY KEY,
  "coursecode" varchar(10),
  "name" varchar(255)
);

CREATE TABLE "studentcourse" (
  "studentid" integer,
  "courseid" integer,
  CONSTRAINT "fk_studentcourse_studentid"
    FOREIGN KEY ("studentid")
    REFERENCES "student"("studentid"),
  CONSTRAINT "fk_studentcourse_courseid"
    FOREIGN KEY ("courseid")
```

```
    REFERENCES "course"("courseid")
);

CREATE UNIQUE INDEX "idx_studentcourse_unique"
    ON "studentcourse"("studentid", "courseid");
```

Be sure that the foreign keys are created and don't overlook the unique constraint of the `studentcourse` table. A student should not be able to register twice for the same course, and this constraint enforces this fact at database-level.

Insert some sample data into each of the three tables. Statements like the following should work for the purposes of this exercise:

```
INSERT INTO "student"(name) VALUES('Bob Smith');      -- studentid 1
INSERT INTO "student"(name) VALUES('John Doe');       -- studentid 2
INSERT INTO "student"(name) VALUES('Jane Baker');     -- studentid 3

INSERT INTO "course"("coursecode", "name")
    VALUES('CS101', 'Intro to Computer Science');     -- courseid 1
INSERT INTO "course"("coursecode", "name")
    VALUES('HIST369', 'British History 1945-1990'); -- courseid 2
INSERT INTO "course"("coursecode", "name")
    VALUES('BIO546', 'Advanced Genetics');            -- courseid 3

INSERT INTO "studentcourse"("studentid", "courseid") VALUES(1, 1);
INSERT INTO "studentcourse"("studentid", "courseid") VALUES(1, 2);
INSERT INTO "studentcourse"("studentid", "courseid") VALUES(1, 3);
INSERT INTO "studentcourse"("studentid", "courseid") VALUES(2, 1);
INSERT INTO "studentcourse"("studentid", "courseid") VALUES(2, 3);
INSERT INTO "studentcourse"("studentid", "courseid") VALUES(3, 2);
```

The last six statements should be adjusted depending on the `studentid` and `courseid` values that result from the `insert` statements into `student` and `course`.

With the database tables created and populated with sample data, you can write and test the `StudentFactory` class. This class has two static methods: `getStudent()` and `getCoursesForStudent()`. The former is responsible for creating a `Student` object given a student ID. The latter populates the courses collection for a given student. In the code shown next, we're not demonstrating the use of any particular database functions, so some pseudo code is standing in for the calls to actual database functions. In Chapter 8, "Database Abstraction Layers," we show you how to use the PEAR::DB database abstraction functions, but for now you should feel free to substitute the explicit calls to `pg_connect`, `pg_query`, and so on (or whatever the appropriate PHP functions are for your database type).

```
<?php
class StudentFactory {

  public static function getStudent($id) {
    $sql = "SELECT * from \"student\" WHERE \"studentid\" = $id";
```

```
    $data = $db->select($sql); //pseudo code. Assume it returns an
                               //array containing all rows returned
                               //by the query.

    if(is_array($data) && sizeof($data)) {
      return new Student($data[0]['studentid'], $data[0]['name']);
    } else {
      throw new Exception("Student $id does not exist.");
    }
  }

  public static function getCoursesForStudent($id, $col) {
    $sql = "SELECT \"course\".\"courseid\",
                   \"course\".\"coursecode\",
                   \"course\".\"name\"
            FROM \"course\", \"studentcourse\" WHERE
                   \"course\".\"id\" =
                   \"studentcourse\".\"courseid\" AND
                   \"studentcourse\".\"studentid\" = $id";

    $data = $db->select($sql);  //same pseudo code in getStudent()

    if(is_array($data) && sizeof($data)) {
      foreach($data as $datum) {
        $objCourse = new Course($datum['courseid'], $datum['coursecode'],
                                $datum['name']);
        $col->addItem($objCourse, $objCourse->getCourseCode());
      }
    }

  }
}
?>
```

The `getStudent()` method returns a new `Student` object populated with the appropriate data. If no student exists in the database with that ID, an exception is thrown. All calls to `StudentFactory::getStudent()` should be wrapped in a `try...catch` statement.

The `getCoursesForStudent()` method is passed the `$courses` collection from within `_loadCourses()`. The database query selects all the data from the `course` table, employing an implicit JOIN to the `studentcourse` table to get the courses associated with the specified student.

Based on the data returned from the database (if any), new `Course` objects are added to the collection. Note that we're using the `coursecode` value as the key when adding the `Course` to the `courses` collection.

Because all objects in PHP5 are passed by reference, we are able to alter the contents of the collection from within `getCoursesForStudent()` and see those changes manifest in the `$courses` variable of the `Student` object. If the phrase "passed by reference" doesn't mean much to you, see the discussion in Chapter 4, "Design Patterns," on the difference between function parameters passed by value versus those passed by reference.

To finally put all this good stuff to some use, try the following code:

```
<?php
$studentID = 1; //use a valid studentid value from your student table

try {
  $objStudent = StudentFactory::getStudent($studentID);
} catch (Exception e) {
  die("Student #$studentID doesn't exist in the database!");
}

print $objStudent .
      ($objStudent->courses->exists('CS101') ? ' is ' : ' is not ') .
      'currently enrolled in CS101';
//displays: "Bob Smith is enrolled in CS101"
?>
```

In a deployed application, you should do something a bit more graceful than an abrupt termination of the application if the specified student isn't found, but we hope you get the idea of why that `try...catch` statement needs to be used.

After getting `$objStudent`, this code displays a simple message letting you know whether this student is enrolled in CS101. Upon invoking the `exists()` method, the courses collection is populated from the database, courtesy of the `StudentFactory`. Because the course code was used as the key when adding `Course` objects to the collection, you can use the course code ('CS101') as the parameter to `exists()`.

Improving the Collection Class

"Improve the `Collection` class? Impossible! How could it possibly be more powerful, useful, or exciting?" you ask. Well, the problem is that you don't yet have a simple way to iterate over the entire collection, displaying a list of the courses, for example. Right now, you can jump directly only to those items that you already know are in the collection. Obviously, you don't always know what the contents of the collection are before you set out to use it, so you need a way to write code like this:

```
<?php
$objStudent = StudentFactory::getStudent(1);
foreach($objStudent->courses as $objCourse) {
  print $objStudent . ' is currently enrolled in ' . $objCourse . '<br>\n";
}
?>
```

If you were to try to run that code now, you would either get an error or see nothing at all (depending on the `error_reporting` level) because `$objStudent->courses` is not an array, it's a `Collection`. In PHP4, the only data type that could be used as the operand of a `foreach` statement was an array. In PHP5 you have two new built-in interfaces, called `Iterator` and `IteratorAggregate`, that allow you to use `foreach` on objects, so long as they implement those interfaces.

These two interfaces are the topic of the next chapter, so read on and learn how to make the `Collection` class even more useful!

Summary

The `Collection` class is a very useful object-oriented alternative to the traditional array and one that you could usefully employ in virtually any application you might build. It provides careful management of its members and a consistent API that makes writing code that uses the class easy.

Subclassing `Collection` and overriding the `addItem()` method to include a type hint on the first parameter allows you to control the type of objects that are added to the collection. Although not strictly necessary, this approach provides an extra level of error checking.

By wrapping all calls to `addItem()`, `getItem()`, and `removeItem()` in `try...catch` blocks, you have complete control over any errors that may occur in those methods. Be sure to handle these errors with something a bit more graceful than the call to `die()` shown in the examples.

Callbacks are an incredibly powerful technique that you can use to implement lazy instantiation, which conserves system resources and ensures that you're manipulating only the data that it is absolutely necessary to manipulate. When you have a complex hierarchy of objects, you can use callbacks to automatically handle the instantiation of child objects and defer the creation of those not absolutely necessary for the current application activity. Make sure that you understand how this works and see whether you can find other uses for this technique.

6

CollectionIterator Class

The previous chapter gave you a look at the `Collection` class, an object-oriented (OO) wrapper for managing an array of objects that's a powerful and flexible part of the utility toolkit. On its own, however, it is missing some functionality. Namely, it does not provide an easy way to iterate over all its members. In the example application we saw in the previous chapter (a university registrar's office), there existed a `Student` class that has a member variable called `courses`, which is a `Collection`. In this application, you would likely need a view that displays a list of all the courses for which a student is registered. To keep the syntax as simple as possible, ideally you should be able to do something like the following:

```
<?php
  $objStudent = new Student(12345);
  foreach($objStudent->classes as $objClass) {
    print $objClass . "\n";
  }
?>
```

If you have some experience with PHP4, you'll recognize the `foreach` statement as a construct that allows you to easily traverse the elements of an array. In PHP4, the only valid operand to `foreach` was an array. Any other data type caused a runtime error.

PHP5 has a way to allow `foreach` to work on objects, too. The built-in interfaces `Iterator` and `IteratorAggregate` work together to allow you to traverse the elements of an object that contains other objects, such as our `Collection` class.

In this short chapter, you'll learn how to use these interfaces to enable your classes in exactly this manner, so that the `foreach` iteration method becomes just as useful for traversing collections of objects as it has always been for traversing regular arrays.

The Iterator Interface

PHP5's built-in abstract interface `Iterator` defines five methods that allow `foreach` to understand how to interact with a non-array parameter. Here's the interface definition:

```
<?php
/**
 * Traversable is an empty interface
```

```
  */
interface Traversable {}

interface Iterator implements Traversable {
  /**
   * Rewind the Iterator to the first element.
   */
  function rewind();

  /**
   * Return the current element.
   */
  function current();

  /**
   * Return the key of the current element.
   */
  function key();

  /**
   * Move forward to next element.
   */
  function next();

  /**
   * Check if there is a current element after
   * calls to rewind() or next().
   */
  function hasMore();
}
?>
```

The first interface defined is `Traversable`. This interface is an empty abstract interface that cannot be implemented alone by your code. It is used by PHP's internals to determine which constructs can be used with `foreach`. When you implement classes that will be usable by `foreach`, you must implement the `Iterator` interface, which itself implements `Traversable`.

> **Both these interfaces, `Traversable` and `Iterator`, are built in to PHP. You should not redeclare these interface definitions in your own code; doing so gives you this error: "Fatal error: Cannot redeclare class."**

Note that most of the methods defined in the `Iterator` interface share a name with built-in procedural functions used for manipulating arrays. The function `rewind()` sets PHP's internal array pointer to the first element in an array. `current()` returns the item in the array to which the pointer currently points. `key()` returns the key of the current item. `next()` advances the pointer to the next item. When iterating over an `Iterator` object, PHP expects these methods to serve the same purpose. This implies that when extending `Iterator`, you will need to have a private member variable that tracks the current location of the pointer. The `hasMore()` should return true or false to indicate whether the current item is the last item in the list.

The following code demonstrates what is happening internally when you use `foreach` with a class implementing `Iterator`:

```
<?php

/* equivalent to foreach($objIt as $key => $member)
$objIt = new MyIterator();
for($objIt->rewind(); $objIt->hasMore(); $objIt->next()) {
  $key = $objIt->key();
  $member = $objIt->current();
}
?>
```

Now that you understand what this interface does, it's time to put it to work. The `CollectionIterator` class will be used to iterate over a `Collection` object.

The CollectionIterator Class

Recall that as does an array, our `Collection` class stores members in a position using either a string key or an automatically assigned integer. In the previous chapter you created a method called `keys()` but never really did much with it. Recall that the `keys()` method returns an array representing all the keys in the `Collection`. The `CollectionIterator` class will use this method to get a list of the items in the `Collection` and provide a means for iterating over them.

The code for `class.collectioniterator.php` is straightforward and is shown in the following sample.

```
<?
class CollectionIterator implements Iterator {

   private $_collection;
   private $_currIndex = 0;
   private $_keys;

   function __construct(Collection $objCol) {
     $this->_collection = $objCol;
     $this->_keys = $this->_collection->keys();
   }

   function rewind() {
     $this->_currIndex = 0;
   }

   function hasMore() {
     return $this->_currIndex < $this->_collection->length();
   }

   function key() {
     return $this->_keys[$this->_currIndex];
   }
```

```
    function current() {
      return $this->_collection->getItem($this->_keys[$this->_currIndex]);
    }

    function next() {
      $this->_currIndex++;
    }
}
?>
```

By stating that the class implements `Iterator`, you are required to declare all the methods defined in the `Iterator` interface. The member variable `$_collection` holds a reference to the `Collection` over which you are iterating. `$_currIndex` is the internal variable that allows the class to maintain a pointer into the `Collection` that will be used by the methods. Actually, it maintains a pointer into the `$_keys` array.

The `$_keys` array holds the return value of `Collection::keys()` and will be used to fetch the requested member of the `Collection`. Each call to `next()` increments `$_currIndex` by one. Calls to `current()` and `key()` use the value of `$_currIndex` to determine the key of the item to be fetched. Because the actual keys of the `Collection` may or may not be numeric, you need to have some sort of numerically ordered list to use when iterating. To solve this, you can use `Collection::keys()` to get a numerically indexed array of the items in the `Collection`, and reference the value of that array to get the actual key used in the `Collection`. The following example might make this a little clearer:

```
<?php
require_once ("class.collectioniterator.php");
require_once ("class.collection.php");
/* Add some items to the Collection */
$objCol = new Collection();
$objCol->addItem(new Foo(), "foo1");  //key = "foo1"
$objCol->addItem(new Bar(), "bar1");  //key = "bar1"
$objCol->addItem(new FooBar());       //key = 0
$objCol->addItem(new FooBar());       //key = 1

/* Instantiate a CollectionIterator */
$objIt = new CollectionIterator($objCol);

/* $objIt->_keys now looks like this:
 * $objIt->_keys[0] = "foo1";
 * $objIt->_keys[1] = "bar1";
 * $objIt->_keys[2] = 0;
 * $objIt->_keys[3] = 1;
 */

$objIt->rewind();                 //$_currIndex = 0;

$objFoo = $objIt->current();      //$_currIndex = 0, current key = "foo1"
                                  //$objFoo = the first Foo object

$objIt->next();                   //$_currIndex = 1;

$objBar = $objIt->current();      //$_currIndex = 1, current key = "bar1"
                                  //$objBar = the Bar object
```

```
$objIt->next();                        //$_currIndex = 2;


$objFooBar = $objIt->current();        //$_currIndex = 2, current key = 0,
                                       //so $objFooBar is the first FooBar object
?>
```

From this example, you can see how the `$_keys` array and the `$_currIndex` variable work to enable the methods to keep track of what's going on.

The code you've written so far still doesn't allow you to use `foreach` on a `Collection`, but just on a `CollectionIterator`. To get to this final step, you'll need to learn one more built-in abstract interface.

The IteratorAggregate Interface

PHP5 allows `foreach` to work on implementers of `Iterator` or another interface called `IteratorAggregate`. A class that implements `IteratorAggregate` is a class that contains child elements that can be traversed by an `Iterator`. In this case, we have a `Collection` class containing elements that can be iterated by a `CollectionIterator`. To be able to use `foreach` on the `Collection` class, you'll need to modify `Collection` to implement this very simple interface, the definition for which follows.

```
<?php
/**
 * Interface to create an external Iterator.
 */
interface IteratorAggregate implements Traversable
{
  /**
   * Return an Iterator for the implementing object.
   */
  function getIterator();
}
?>
```

Just as with the `Iterator` and `Traversable` interfaces, the `IteratorAggregate` interface is built in to PHP and you should not redeclare it in your own files.

`IteratorAggregate` requires only one method, `getIterator()`. For a class that implements this interface, this function returns an `Iterator` that is capable of traversing its elements. By modifying `Collection` to implement this interface, you'll be able to use `foreach` on it directly.

Modify the class declaration and include an implementation of the one method required by the `IteratorAggregate` interface:

```
<?php
class Collection implements IteratorAggregate {

  //...[snip] the original parts of the Collection class
  //removed for brevity
```

```
    public function getIterator() {
      $this->_checkCallback();
      return new CollectionIterator($this);
    }
}
?>
```

Remember that the `Collection` class implements the idea of lazy instantiation. Don't forget to check for a load callback before returning the `CollectionIterator`. You need to make sure that the data has been populated before you can iterate over it.

With the `CollectionIterator` class created and the `Collection` class modified to implement `IteratorAggregate`, you can now legitimately run the block of code shown at the end of the previous chapter:

```
<?php
$objStudent = StudentFactory::getStudent(12345); //get student #12345
foreach($objStudent->courses as $key => $objCourse){
  print $objStudent . ' is currently enrolled in ' . $objCourse . "<br>\ n";
}
?>
```

Behind the scenes internally in PHP, the functions are invoked like this:

```
<?php

$objStudent = StudentFactory::getStudent(12345);
$itCourses = $objStudent->courses->getIterator();

for($itCourses->rewind(); $itCourses->hasMore(); $itCourses->next()) {
  $key = $itCourses->key();
  $objCourse = $itCourses->current();
  print $objStudent . ' is currently enrolled in ' . $objCourse . "<br>\n";
}
?>
```

If you need to create iterators for other classes you might create, it's important to understand how the methods of the `Iterator` and `IteratorAggregate` interfaces are invoked. When the operand of the `foreach` statement is an `IteratorAggregate`, PHP invokes the `getIterator()` method. The `Iterator`'s internal pointer is reset using `rewind()`. Although there are still more elements to be seen (`hasMore()`), variables are created to hold both the current key and the current member element, and the rest of the `foreach` code block is then executed. The pointer is advanced (`next()`) and execution continues until we hit the end of the content (when `hasMore()` returns false).

Protecting the Iterator's Contents by Using the clone Operator

The code as it stands now could be considered complete if all it would ever be used for is the display of the contents of the `Collection`. But what if you need to alter the `Collection`'s contents on the fly while inside the `foreach` loop? In the code that follows, you loop through the list of courses for a given student looking for courses that require a special fee (a laboratory supplies fee). If the student is not currently in good financial standing, you need to remove the student from the course and display an error message.

```
<?php
function checkCourseFees(Student $objStudent) {
  foreach($objStudent->courses as $key => $objCourse) {
    if( $objCourse->hasSpecialFee && !$objStudent->inGoodStanding() ) {
      $objStudent->courses->removeItem($key);
      print("Sorry, because of your financial standing we " .
            "had to remove you from $objCourse");
    }
  }
}
?>
```

This code looks perfectly safe and reasonable. On the surface, nothing appears wrong with removing an element of the collection while iterating over its contents. But this code is in fact a big no-no and has the potential to cause strange bugs. You have to look under the hood to see why.

Assume that this `Student` has three `Courses` associated with it, two regular and one with a fee.

```
$objStudent->courses->addCourse(new Course(123)); //no fee, key is 0
$objStudent->courses->addCourse(new Course(987)); //_has_ fee, key is 1
$objStudent->courses->addCourse(new Course(456)); //no fee, key is 2
```

When you pass `$objStudent->courses` into the `foreach` statement, the `getIterator()` method is invoked. The `CollectionIterator`, in its constructor, creates the internal `$_keys` array by calling `$_collection->getKeys()`. When you iterate to the first element, `$_currIndex` is 0. You fetch the first course. No problems yet. On the second iteration, `$_currIndex` is 1. This course has a fee, so you remove it from the collection. Now you have a problem.

Because the collection held internally in the `Iterator` was passed by reference, the call to `$objStudent->courses->removeItem()` affects the collection held in the `Iterator`. Now the `$_collection` member variable has only two items, with keys 0 and 1. The attempt to fetch the third key, value of 2, will fail unexpectedly. To counter this problem, you need to do two things.

First, don't modify the collection while iterating through its members. Additions and deletions should be done after the `foreach` loop. Second, to reinforce the idea that the `Iterator` is acting on the `Collection` as it was at the time of the creation of the `Iterator`, you need to pass in a copy of the `Collection`, rather than a reference to it.

The `clone` operator should be used when passing the argument to the `Iterator` constructor in the `getIterator()` method of the `Collection` class. The `clone` operator creates a copy of the operand and is the opposite of the `&` function parameter modifier. Modify `Collection::getIterator()` as follows:

```
public function getIterator() {
  $this->_checkCallback();
  return new CollectionIterator(clone $this);
}
```

This creates a copy of the current object and passes that copy to the `Iterator`. PHP creates this copy by instantiating a new `Collection` (without invoking the constructor) and copying all the private and public member variables from the original to this copy. If you have some sort of special activities that need to happen when one of your objects is cloned, you can define a private method called `__clone()` that will take the place of PHP's default action. Note that the `__clone()` function is `private` and an error will be thrown if you try to invoke it directly. Always use the `clone` operator when you need a copy of an object.

Summary

The `Iterator` and `IteratorAggregate` interfaces make it easy for you to provide `foreach` support over an object that contains child elements. Although you could have implemented the `Iterator` interface directly in the `Collection` class, doing so would have unnecessarily cluttered that class's API. By separating the iteration capabilities into a separate class, you maintain a cleaner code base.

Use the `clone` operator when you need to make a copy of an object. Early release versions of the PHP5 documentation showed example code that directly invoked the `__clone()` method. This is no longer supported. Use the `clone` operator instead. If you have special needs for the copying of your objects, you can implement your own `__clone()` method.

The `Collection` and `CollectionIterator` classes provide a powerful OO mechanism for handling groups of objects. Although there is a fair amount of code between these two classes, you need to write it only once. You'll be able to reuse it verbatim in all your applications.

GenericObject Class

By now, you should be quite comfortable with the idea of object-oriented programming, as well as truly sold on all its benefits. Indeed, OOP allows you to develop highly maintainable, clear, logical code that conforms more closely to a humanized version of your application. Yes, it adds some development overhead, but the benefits will be enormously clear should you, or anybody else in your organization, ever need to look at that project again.

One of the downfalls of this approach, however, is that you may sometimes have to sacrifice raw efficiency to achieve true compliance. For example, so many Web applications have simple pages that allow a user to edit an entity—be it a user, a product, an order, a customer, or whatever. The non-OOP approach is quite straightforward—an HTML form with a single `UPDATE SQL` statement to make the amendments. The OOP approach, by contrast, can seem frightening—a class called `Customer`, with goodness knows how many methods just to update its own properties in the database. The real downer is that huge chunks of the code you'll have in each entity class—that is, in the classes representing users, products, orders and customers—will be replicated time and time again.

Thankfully, there is another way; it's called `GenericObject`. In this chapter, you'll be introduced to it and its sister class, `GenericObjectCollection`, and see how together they can cut your coding time in half while still allowing you to achieve true OOP compliance and all the benefits that brings.

The GenericObject Class

The `GenericObject` class is what is known as an abstract superclass. It is so called because it will never be instantiated directly from within your code. Rather, it will always be instantiated through an extension or subclass that inherits its properties and methods.

If object inheritance doesn't ring a bell, you may want to refer to Chapter 3, "Putting Objects to Work," where they were examined in more detail.

The purpose of `GenericObject` is to allow you to neatly and concisely represent as a class a single row (or tuple) of a single table in your database, where that table describes a single entity, and therefore manage that row in an object-oriented manner.

When to Use GenericObject

Prime examples of tables you may have in your application that are just perfect for class implementation using `GenericObject` are `user`, `customer`, `product`, `order`, and so forth.

The tables you should avoid attempting to represent are those that simply link two entities in some way. For example, you may have a table called `order_product` with columns `order_id`, `product_id`, and `quantity`. You would be very much applauded for doing so. This is, after all, an excellent example of the third normal form of database normalization at work (see `http://databases.about.com/library/glossary/bldef-3nf.htm` for more information).

However, such tables are not representative of entities in their own right because they have no properties that can be read or set, even though they may have qualifiers, such as the `quantity` field in the previous example.

What GenericObject Allows You to Do

The functionality of `GenericObject` is not purely symbolic, nor is it merely a component of some toolkit for ensuring fastidious and unerring OOP-compliance. It is a genuinely useful tool.

For any given row (say, the 314th row) in any given table (say, the `order` table), you can represent that row as an object that extends the `GenericObject` class. This allows you to quickly and effectively:

- Read any given property (column) of that object (row)
- Set any given property (column) of that object (row)
- Save your changes to that object (row)

Crucially, you can also create brand-new instances of your particular entity, set its properties, and save your changes in exactly the same way.

Consider the example of a customer object. You would probably have a table in your database schema called `customer` that has columns `id`, `first_name`, `last_name`, `addr_line_1`, and so forth.

Say that you are interested in the first name of the customer, which is represented by an ID of 3139. The following logic would apply:

- Instantiate a customer object (the class of which extends `GenericObject`) with ID 3139.
- Get the `first_name` property of that object.

And that's it.

What about if you wanted to then change the value of that first name from John to Jane. How would you go about doing that?

- Instantiate a customer object (the class of which extends GenericObject) with ID 3139.
- Set the `first_name` property of that object to be Jane.
- Save your changes.

Say that you wanted to create a brand-new customer. The approach would be much the same:

- Instantiate a customer object (the class of which extends GenericObject) with no parameters.
- Set the `first_name` property of that object to be Jane.
- Save your changes.
- Get the ID just allocated to your customer for future reference.

In this last example, you do not pass any identifying parameter when you instantiate the class. This tells `GenericObject` that you are creating a brand new instance of the entity in question.

After you have saved, the ID that has been allocated to this new row by the database will then be a property that you may retrieve for your own use.

It must be admitted that all the above examples could easily be implemented using simple, procedural code with embedded SQL statements. Perhaps that variety of implementation might even be slightly quicker than using `GenericObject`. But this is often true of object-oriented programming, of course, and the value in adopting this approach is the additional human clarity introduced by it. The extra few hours it might take to implement the preceding approach may well save you hundreds of hours in weeks to come, when you may need to maintain or evolve your code.

Assessing Suitability for Implementation

There is just one big prerequisite for using `GenericObject`. Your entities in your database tables must all have a unique ID that is their primary key and that increments automatically.

This is almost always certainly the case. It is good database design to have a primary key, and it almost always makes sense to have a numeric primary key for reasons of speed, even when another column lends itself naturally to being a primary key, too.

A good example (in PostgreSQL) of a database that lends itself well to implementation in your application using `GenericObject` is as follows:

```
CREATE TABLE "user" (
 "id" SERIAL PRIMARY KEY NOT NULL,
 "username" character varying(32),
 "first_name" character varying(64),
 "last_name" character varying(64)
);
```

As you can see, we have an `id` column uniquely representing each user, and properties `username`, `first_name`, and `last_name`, which we can read or write.

Bad examples for `GenericObject` implementation include:

```
CREATE TABLE "airport" (
 "iata_airport_code" character(3) PRIMARY KEY NOT NULL,
 "airport_name" character varying(128),
 "airport_city" character varying(128)
);
```

The preceding is perfectly valid and quite plausible. Airports are often uniquely identified by their three-letter IATA code (LAX for Los Angeles International, JFK for Kennedy Airport, and so forth). This is not, however, suitable for `GenericObject` implementation without the addition of a numeric ID column, which must be the primary key. The reason for this is that `GenericObject` expects new instances to have their unique identifiers produced by the database and does not allow the user to set them explicitly. A three-letter airport code is not something the database knows to generate automatically; a numeric identifier is.

Another bad example is something like the following:

```
CREATE TABLE "user_group" (
 "user_id" int2,
 "group_id" int2,
 PRIMARY KEY (user_id, group_id)
);
```

This is a classic example of an associative table used in the practice of good normalization techniques. It does not, however, readily represent an entity; also, it sports a composite primary key. Using `GenericObject` here is definitely a no-no.

As a rule, if you can happily prefix the name of the table with an article (that is, *the*, *a*, or *an*) and it still makes grammatical sense, you have an entity and, as long as a numeric primary key is in place, using `GenericObject` is feasible.

Typical GenericObject Implementation

Consider the example of the user entity from the previous section, doubtless used to contain user logins to some closed or semiclosed Web application, such as a corporate intranet.

Without the benefit of `GenericObject`, we would probably implement a corresponding class as follows:

```
class User {

 private $user_id;

 public function __construct($id) {
         $this->user_id = $id;
 }

 public function GetField($strFieldName) {
         // ...
 }

 public function SetField($strFieldName, $strValue) {
         // ...
 }
```

```
    public function Save() {
            // ...
    }

    public function Destroy() {
            // ...
    }

    // etc ...
};
```

This approach means, of course, that a huge copy-and-paste job is necessary to implement the basic get and set methodology for each entity. Not only that, but the resulting core functionality for each entity class (such as `AddToGroup` for `user`) is obfuscated from view by the noncore entity management functionality. Your class will be littered with the methods illustrated in the preceding code. All these are important, but they are off-the-shelf routines common to every class, and of little interest to you as a programmer. The important routines will be those that are specific to and tailored for that class. The off-the-shelf and unimportant routines' very existence will make it harder to work with those bespoke, and therefore important, routines.

Using `GenericObject`, we implement our class simply as follows:

```
class User extends GenericObject {
 public function __construct($id) {
         $this->initialize("user", $id);
 }
}
```

We'll introduce the code for `GenericObject` itself shortly. Don't panic.

In practice, after you have defined your basic extension of `GenericObject` as a new class called `User`, you can then put it to use. Before you do that, you might want to populate your `user` table with some data, so here's some test data for you to use. You can paste the following SQL statements directly into a console session with PostgreSQL:

```
COPY "user" (id, username, first_name, last_name) FROM stdin;
1       ed              Ed      Lecky-Thompson
2       steve           Steve   Nowicki
3       alec            Alec    Cove
4       heow            Heow    Eide-Goodman
5       john            John    Doe
6       jane            Jane    Doe
\.
SELECT pg_catalog.setval('user_id_seq', 6, true);
```

With some test data in the database, and using the new version of your `User` class that makes use of `GenericObject`, the following simple code will produce useful output:

```
$objUser = new User(1);
$strUsername = $objUser->GetField("username");
print $strUsername;
```

Using the preceding data set as an example, this would produce `ed` as its output—because that is the value for the `username` column in the row where the `id` is 1.

Using the instantiation parameter 2 would yield `steve`, 3 would yield `alec`, and so on.

Updating properties of an entity using `GenericObject` is just as easy.

```
$objUser = new User(1);
$strUsername = $objUser->GetField("username");
print $strUsername . "<br />\n";
$objUser->SetField("username", "edward");
$strUsername = $objUser->GetField("username");
$objUser->Save();
print $strUsername . "<br />\n";
```

In the previous example, the username is changed from `ed` to `edward`. Calling the `Save()` method generates and executes the necessary SQL statements to make your changes to the object permanent.

Creating brand-new users is also child's play:

```
$objUser = new User();
$objUser->SetField("username", "clive");
$objUser->SetField("first_name", "Clive");
$objUser->SetField("last_name", "Gardner");
$objUser->Save();
$id = $objUser->GetID();
print $id;
```

`GenericObject` is neat in that upon saving changes to a new entity, it takes the time to figure out what ID has been allocated by the database. The database will have looked at the most recent ID used to identify a row in the database, incremented it by one, and given it to your new row. In order to be able to make good use of your new row, `GenericObject` determines the actual value of `id` that has just been allocated. This means that any subsequent changes you make to that object will be recorded with an appropriate `UPDATE` statement completely transparently, by making use of that new `id`.

That's the instruction manual over and done with, but as a PHP professional, you want to know how it works, don't you?

Meet the Parent

Take a look at the source code for the `GenericObject` class. We list the complete code to start with, and then we look at the methods and properties in more detail. Save this class as `genericobject.phpm`.

```
<?
class GenericObject {

   # Member Variables

   private $id;
   private $table_name;

   private $database_fields;
   private $loaded;
```

```
private $modified_fields

# Methods

public function Reload() {
  $sql = new sql(0);
  $id = $this->id;
  $table_name = $this->table_name;
  $sql->query("SELECT * FROM \"$table_name\" WHERE id='$id'");
  $result_fields = $sql->get_row_hash(0);
  $this->database_fields = $result_fields;
  $this->loaded = 1;
  if (sizeof($this->modified_fields) > 0) {
    foreach ($this->modified_fields as $key => $value) {
      $this->modified_fields[$key] = false;
    };
  };
}

private function Load() {
  $this->Reload();
  $this->loaded = 1;
}

public function ForceLoaded() {
  $this->loaded = 1;
}

public function GetField($field) {
  if ($this->loaded == 0) {
    $this->Load();
  };
  return $this->database_fields[$field];
}

public function GetAllFields() {
  if ($this->loaded == 0) {
    $this->Load();
  };
  return($this->database_fields);
}

public function GetID() {
  return $this->id;
}

public function Initialize($table_name, $tuple_id = "") {
  $this->table_name = $table_name;
  $this->id = $tuple_id;
}

public function SetField($field, $value) {
  if ($this->loaded == 0) {
    if ($this->id) {
```

```
        $this->Load();
      };
    };
    $this->database_fields[$field] = $value;
    $this->modified = 1;
    $this->modified_fields[$field] = true;
  }

  public function Destroy() {
    $id = $this->id;
    $table_name = $this->table_name;
    if ($id) {
      $sql = new sql(0);
      $stmt = "DELETE FROM \"" . $table_name . "\" WHERE id='" . $id . "'";
      $sql->query($stmt);
    };
  }

  public function Save() {
    $id = $this->id;
    $table_name = $this->table_name;
    $sql = new sql(0);
    if (!$id) {
      $this->loaded = 0;
    };
    if ($this->loaded == 0) {
      # assume this is a new entity
      $stmt = "INSERT INTO \"" . $table_name ."\"(";
      foreach ($this->database_fields as $key => $value) {
        if (!is_numeric($key)) {
          $key = str_replace("'", "\'", $key);
          if ($value != "") {
            $stmt .= "\"$key\",";
          };
        };
      };
      # Chop last comma
      $stmt = substr($stmt,0,strlen($stmt)-1);
      $stmt .= ") VALUES (";
      foreach ($this->database_fields as $key => $value) {
        if (!is_numeric($key)) {
          if ($value != "") {
            $value = str_replace("'", "\'", $value);
            $stmt .= "'$value',";
          };
        };
      };
      # Chop last comma
      $stmt = substr($stmt,0,strlen($stmt)-1);
      $stmt .= ")";
    } else {
      $stmt = "UPDATE \"" . $table_name ."\" SET ";
      foreach ($this->database_fields as $key => $value) {
        if (!is_numeric($key)) {
```

```
          if ($this->modified_fields[$key] == true) {
            $value = str_replace("'", "\'", $value);
            if ($value == "") {
              $stmt .= "\"$key\" = NULL, ";
            } else {
              $stmt .= "\"$key\" = '$value', ";
            };
          };
        };
      };
      # Chop last comma and space
      $stmt = substr($stmt,0,strlen($stmt)-2);
      $stmt .= " WHERE id='$id'";
    };
    $return_code = $sql->query($stmt, 1);
    if ($this->loaded == 0) {
      # Try to get the ID of the new tuple.
      $stmt = "SELECT MAX(id) AS id FROM \ "$table_name\" WHERE ";
      foreach ($this->database_fields as $key => $value) {
        if (!is_numeric($key)) {
          if ($value) {
            if ($this->modified_fields[$key] == true) {
              $value = str_replace("'", "\'", $value);
              $stmt .= "\"$key\" = '$value' AND ";
            };
          };
        };
      };
      # Chop last " AND " (superfluous)
      $stmt = substr($stmt,0,strlen($stmt)-5);
      $sql->query($stmt);
      $result_rows = $sql->get_table_hash();
      $proposed_id = $result_rows[0]["id"];
      if ($proposed_id > 0) {
        $this->loaded = 1;
        $this->id = $proposed_id;
        return true;
      } else {
        return false;
      };
      };
    return($return_code);
  }
};
```

GenericObject Database Connectivity

The first thing to notice is that this class makes very heavy use of a class called `sql`—an interface to a PostgreSQL database.

In fact, this class can be made to work with virtually any database: Microsoft SQL Server, MySQL, Oracle, anything. Only small amendments are required. For now, however, you can use the following to provide an interface to PostgreSQL. Save this class as `sql.phpm`.

```
class sql {
  private $result_rows; # Result rows hash
  private $query_handle; # db: the query handle
  private $link_ident; # db: the link identifier

  public function __construct() {
    $db_username = "gobjtest";
    $db_password = "";
    $db_host = "db";
    $db_name = "gobjtest";
    $this->link_ident = pg_Connect("user='$db_username'password=
'$db_password' dbname='$db_name' host='$db_host'");
  }

  public function query($sql, $code_return_mode = 0) {
    $q_handle = pg_exec($this->link_ident, $sql);

    for ($i=0; $i<=pg_numrows($q_handle)-1; $i++) {
      $result = pg_fetch_array($q_handle,$i);
      $return_array[$i] = $result;
    };
    if (!$q_handle) {
      error_log("QUERY FAILED: $sql\n");
    };
    $this->result_rows = $return_array;
    if (!$q_handle) {
      return(1);
    } else {
      return(0); # return 0 if it fails
    };
  }

  public function get_result($row_num, $column_name) {
    return ($this->result_rows[$row_num][$column_name]);
  }

  public function get_row_hash($row_num) {
    return ($this->result_rows[$row_num]);
  }

  public function get_table_hash() {
    return $this->result_rows;
  }

  public function done($close_connection = 0) {
    if ($close_connection) {
      pg_Close($this->link_ident);
    };
  }
};
```

Note that we've hard coded the database username, password (none in this case), and name into the class. This is considered bad form in production projects and is the kind of data that should be exported into constants files or, even better, human-readable configuration files. For the purposes of this chapter, however, we keep things simple.

There's nothing particularly clever about the sql class in the preceding code. An example of simple usage is as follows:

```
$sql = new sql();
$sql->query("SELECT id FROM \"user\"");
$result_rows = $sql->get_table_hash();
for ($i=0; $i<=sizeof($result_rows)-1; $i++) {
  print ($result_rows[$i] . "\n");
};
$sql->done(1);
};
```

Calling the done() method with a nonfalse parameter causes the database connection to be closed. If this is not desired, you can omit it.

As you can see, the class as a whole is not exactly rocket science. In the next chapter, we discuss the concept of database abstraction layers, which you can use to truly genericize and insulate your source code from the subtle differences between databases.

GenericObject Methods and Properties

Back now to the GenericObject class. This section discusses how it works in more detail.

Properties

If you examine the code listing in the previous section, you can see that GenericObject has the following member properties:

Property	Details
id	The identifier for the row in question, for example, 6.
table_name	The name of the table in question, for example, user.
database_fields	An associative array with keys representing the names of the columns of the table, and their values being the value of that column for the given row (for example, username => ed).
loaded	Indicates whether this object has been populated with data from the database. It is not necessary to load data unless it will be retrieved. This is set to 0 if no data is loaded, 1 if data is loaded.
modified_fields	A hash identical in key-values to database_fields, but with values true or false to represent whether that particular database field has been modified since the contents from the database was last loaded (for example, username => true, first_name => false).
modified	Has anything at all been modified since the load? 1 if yes, 0 if no.

Methods

If you examine the code listing for `GenericObject`, you'll also see that it has the following member methods available to you:

Method	Parameters	Details
`Initialize`	`table_name`: name of table in database; `tuple_id`: identifier of row in question	Called by the subclass to set the table name and id of the row in question.
`Load`	None	An alias for `Reload`.
`Reload`	None	Populates the `database_fields` member variable with current values from the database.
`ForceLoaded`	None	Makes this instance of the subclass think that it is loaded even if it isn't; useful if values have been set manually by some third-party process because this precludes any automatic loading taking place when `GetField` is called.
`GetID`	None	Gets the current ID of the loaded row. This will either have been set upon instantiation or will have been determined when `Save()` was called if originally a new entity.
`GetField`	field—name of the field to retrieve	Gets the value of the field in question. If not yet loaded, it will automatically call `Reload` first to load values from the database.
`GetAllFields`	None	Same as preceding, but returns a hash of all fields and values rather than just a single field. Again, automatically calls `Reload` if so required.
`SetField`	`field`: the name of the field to set; `value`: the value to set	Updates the internal hash (database_fields) to reflect new value of given field; it then sets `modified` to 1 and the appropriate `modified_fields` key to 1.
`Destroy`	None	Permanently deletes the entity from the database. The object should not be used after this method has been called!
`Save`	None	Saves the contents of the object to the database.

It's worth examining how the `Save` method works in a bit more detail because it is among the more sophisticated methods in the class.

The Save Method

The method first determines whether this is a new entity in the database or an existing entity. It does this quite simply by looking at the `id` property. If it is null, this is a new entity; otherwise, this is an existing entity. This decision is then used to determine whether an `UPDATE` or `INSERT` statement is required of the database. An `UPDATE` is used to update an existing tuple; an `INSERT` is used to insert a new one.

In the event of an `INSERT`, a SQL statement is built up and inserted into the table in question with every field and value pair that has been specified prior to the method's call. The class is not aware of which columns in your table you may have specified as `NOT NULL` and that are optional, so in your code you must ensure that a value has been set for every column upon which the database insists; otherwise, your insertion will fail.

For example, if you specify the fields `first_name` and `last_name` of your user object to have meaningful values (say, John and Doe respectively), then `GenericObject` will in turn produce the following statement:

```
INSERT INTO "user"("first_name", "last_name") VALUES ('John','Doe')
```

Note that the username was never specified, hence it never made it into the insert. It will be left null by the database or, if in a `NOT NULL` column, an error will be returned.

Having successfully made the insert, our extended instance of `GenericObject` suddenly changes shape. We are no longer dealing with a new entity; we are dealing with an existing entity. With this in mind, it must have what all existing entities have—an `id` value. How is this determined?

Both MySQL and PostgreSQL have functionality to determine the last `id` generated automatically as a result of an immediately preceding insertion. Such functionality is not available in all database platforms, however, and its implementation differs massively.

Accordingly, the easiest route is to use a `SELECT` to determine the value. The following approach might work 90 percent of the time:

```
SELECT MAX(id) FROM "user"
```

However, in the split second between `INSERT` and SELECT, it's entirely possible that somebody else has made an insertion, which would incorrectly skew your result.

A safer route is to add a condition to this query. Use the parameters originally specified to find the highest matching record with those results. The chances of another identical record's having been inserted in that split second gap are infinitesimal.

```
SELECT MAX(id) FROM "user" WHERE "first_name"='John' AND "last_name"='Doe'
```

The `id` value retrieved is then applied to the object, and it is set as loaded.

In the event of updating an existing record, there is no need to try to determine the tuple's id value—it is already well known. A simple `UPDATE` statement built in much the same way as the `INSERT` statement shown previously is all that's required. However, rather than simply updating all columns, only those columns that have been modified are changed.

This is important not just as a time saver but also for the purposes of enforcing the integrity of your database. Any `NULL` values from the database will be stored as empty strings in `GenericObject`. The difference may not matter much to you, but if your `UPDATE` statement blithely turned all those `NULL` values into empty strings during an update, and subsequent filter queries that your application performed used a `NOT NULL` clause to filter results, you could get some quite unexpected behavior.

As you can see, the `Save()` method is really very clever and truly at the heart of `GenericObject` and its inner workings.

Benefits of GenericObject

By now, you've met `GenericObject` and seen how it works. We hope that you've had a chance to run through the code and match up each line against the preceding description above. The power of this class is such that it isn't something you should use lightly.

You'll meet a small demo application later in the chapter, but in the meantime, it's worth summarizing what some of the benefits of using `GenericObject` in your application might be.

- Spend far less time writing SQL statements, more time writing code.
- Port the majority of your application from one database to another by tweaking SQL in one file, not hundreds.
- Make your code cleaner and smaller, and easier to maintain.
- Focus on your application's core functionality safe in the knowledge that the simple entity management techniques are complete and bug free out of the box.

Dealing with entities in isolation is all very well, but many times you'll find that you want to deal with them as part of a collection of entities of the same ilk.

It's time to meet the `GenericObjectCollection` class, which allows you to do just that.

The GenericObjectCollection Class

There are two main cases for which you will have code that needs to generate a collection of entity objects, be they user objects, customer objects, order objects, or any object written using the `GenericObject` concept just discussed.

These two cases are the following:

- You are generating a list of matching entities related to some other entity.
- You are generating a list of matching objects by some arbitrary search criterion.

Good examples of each include:

- Generating a collection of user objects that are members of a group administrators.
- Generating a collection of user objects whose first name begins with the letter *A*.

The difference between the two is subtle, but important.

In the first case, a method of a foreign entity is clearly at work. A method called GetAllUsersWhoAreMembers would be appended to the Group class, which would somehow return a collection of users who are members of that group.

In the second case, your criterion is some simple parameter not readily expressed as another class. Sure, you could be intensely pedantic and invent a LetterOfTheAlphabet class, and give it a method called GetAllUsersWhoseFirstNameBeginsWith, but that would be OOP correctness run amok.

Instead, many developers opt for what is known as a Home class. This is a class whose purpose is solely to create other classes. For this reason it is sometimes called a Factory class.

In the previous example, you might well have a class called UserHome, which would have a method called GetAllUsersWithFirstNameBeginningWith that would take a single letter as its parameter. Usage would therefore be something along the lines of:

```
$arUserCollection = Array();
$arUserCollection = UserHome::GetAllUsersWithFirstNameBeginningWith('A');
```

Note the instantiation of UserHome as a static class. There is no difference between any instance of UserHome, hence it is always used as a static class. Refer to Chapter 3, "Putting Objects to Work," if you need further convincing.

Let's look now at how you might be tempted to implement the previous example method. You'll see a bit later why this is not the best solution to the problem.

Traditional Implementation

There is nothing wrong, per se, with the following code:

```
class UserHome {
  public function GetAllUsersWithFirstNameBeginningWith($strLetter) {
    $sql = new sql();
    $strLetter = strtolower($strLetter);
    $sql->query("SELECT id FROM \"user\" WHERE lower(first_name) LIKE
'$strLetter%'");
   $result_rows = $sql->get_table_hash();
   $arUserObjects = Array();
   for ($i=0; $i<=sizeof($result_rows)-1; $i++) {
     $arUserObjects[] = new User($result_rows[$i]["id"]);
   };
   return($arUserObjects);
  }
};
```

Go ahead and try it. Save the file as userhome.phpm and try the following code:

```
require("sql.phpm");
require("genericobject.phpm");
require("user.phpm");
```

```
require("userhome.phpm");
$arUsers = UserHome::GetAllUsersWithFirstNameBeginningWith('j');
print sizeof($arUsers);
```

You should get a 2 on-screen if you used our test data from earlier in the chapter, which featured both John Doe and Jane Doe (hence two *J*s, resulting in the number 2 appearing).

You can use the previous style of method to implement any form of collection-generating requirement, be it as part of a `Home` class as demonstrated previously, or as part of a more complicated method comprising part of a foreign entity.

It does have a failing, however. The next section discusses what that is and how `GenericObjectCollection` may prove to be a more useful alternative.

Where the Traditional Implementation Fails

The way in which the approach described in the previous section fails is in SQL efficiency.

Consider the previous example. All we have done is ask for a collection of user objects to be returned. Say that the total was twenty, not two. Still, only one query would be needed—the query used in our previous method.

However, what if we want to do something useful with the twenty users returned, such as output their full names to a list?

Consider the following code extract:

```
$arUsers = UserHome::GetAllUsersWithFirstNameBeginningWith('j');
for ($i=0; $i<=sizeof($arUsers)-1; $i++) {
  print $arUsers[$i]->GetField("first_name") . " " .
        $arUsers[$i]->GetField("last_name")  . "<br />\n";
};
```

Sure, it works, but think about each iteration of your loop. You are causing `GenericObject` to call its `Load()` method to populate the fields of every single object.

If you had twenty matching users, you'd perform twenty-one queries—one query to find all the matching users and twenty to get their details:

```
SELECT id FROM "user" WHERE first_name LIKE 'j%';
SELECT * FROM "user" WHERE id = 12091;
SELECT * FROM "user" WHERE id = 12092;
SELECT * FROM "user" WHERE id = 12093;
```

Not exactly efficient. As you can surely see, only one query is required:

```
SELECT * FROM "user" WHERE first_name LIKE 'j%';
```

Is there a more efficient way to achieve the data set of the preceding set of queries, minimizing SQL while still allowing you to remain as OO compliant as possible?

There is, and it's called `GenericObjectCollection`.

Principles behind GenericObjectCollection

The reason we were encountering a twenty-one query marathon previously was quite simple. The first query returned a set of empty, unpopulated objects, each with its `id` identifier set but nothing else. By treating them all individually as part of a loop, you must perform individual queries; but what if you treated them as a set and populated them all simultaneously?

Say that your original query informs you that the following ten rows match; those with `id` values as follows:

```
12091, 12092, 12093, 12094, 12095, 12096, 12097, 12098, 12099, 12100
```

It is perfectly feasible to execute a single bulk population query as follows:

```
SELECT * FROM "user" WHERE id IN (12091, 12092, 12093, 12094, 12095,
12096, 12097, 12098, 12099, 12100)
```

Okay, this approach is not quite as efficient as doing it one query because, counting our original filter query, this uses two, but it's a darned sight better than the eleven it would be using the traditional approach described earlier.

`GenericObjectCollection` uses this bulk population query to great effect. It allows you to find the `id` values of matching rows in the same way as the traditional approach but then invites you to push those `id` values onto a stack. By your having told it what class name and database table names these `id` values represent, it will then create an array of instantiated objects for you, and, crucially, populate them for you, too. It will set the values for you and force them to be set as loaded (see earlier in the chapter), hence negating any need for them to repopulate when they are called again.

The following section shows the code.

Meet the Code

Following is the code in the file `genericobjectcollection.phpm`. Shortly, we present a better version of the `UserHome` class that can make practical use of this code.

```
<?
  class GenericObjectCollection {

    # Member Variables
    var $table_name;
    var $class_name;

    var $items_per_page;
    var $item_count = 0;

    var $id_array;

    var $obj_array;

    function __construct($table_name, $class_name) {
      $this->table_name = $table_name;
```

```
      $this->class_name = $class_name;
    }

    function AddTuple($id) {
      if (!$this->id_array) {
        $this->id_array = array();
      };
      array_push($this->id_array, $id);
      $this->item_count = sizeof($this->id_array);
    }

    function SetPageSize($items_per_page) {
      $this->items_per_page = $items_per_page;
    }

    function GetItemCount() {
      return $this->item_count;
    }

    function GetNumPages() {
      return(ceil($this->item_count / $this->items_per_page));
    }

    function _GetCommaSeparatedIDList($start_lim = 0, $end_lim = -1) {
      $s = "";
      if ($end_lim == -1) {
        $end_lim = sizeof($this->id_array)-1;
      };
      for ($i=$start_lim; $i<=$end_lim; $i++) {
        if (is_numeric($this->id_array[$i])) {
          $s = $s . $this->id_array[$i] . ",";
        };
      };
      $s = substr($s, 0, strlen($s) - 1);
      return $s;
    }

    function _GetIndexFromTupleID($tuple_id) {
      $index = -1;
      for ($i=0; $i<=sizeof($this->id_array)-1; $i++) {
        if ($this->id_array[$i] == $tuple_id) {
          $index = $i;
        };
      };
      return $index;
    }

    function PopulateObjectArray($page_num = 0) {
      $items_per_page = $this->items_per_page;
      if ($this->item_count > 0) {
        if ($page_num > 0) {
          $start_lim = ($items_per_page * ($page_num - 1));
          $end_lim = ($start_lim + $items_per_page) - 1;
          if ($end_lim > ($this->item_count-1)) {
            $end_lim = $this->item_count - 1;
```

```
        };
        $stmt = "SELECT * FROM \"" . $this->table_name . "\" WHERE id IN (" .
$this->_GetCommaSeparatedIDList($start_lim, $end_lim). ")";
      } else {
        $stmt = "SELECT * FROM \"" . $this->table_name . "\" WHERE id IN (" .
$this->_GetCommaSeparatedIDList(). ")";
      };
      # Perform SQL query
      $sql = new sql(0);
      $sql->query($stmt);
      $result_rows = $sql->get_table_hash();

      for ($i=0; $i<=sizeof($result_rows)-1; $i++) {
        $this_row = $result_rows[$i];
        $this_db_row_id = $this_row["id"];
        $this_index = $this->_GetIndexFromTupleID($this_db_row_id);
        if ($this_index >= 0) {
          $refObjArrayIndexObj = &$this->obj_array[$this_index];
          $s = "\$refObjArrayIndexObj = new " . $this->class_name . "(" .
$this_db_row_id . ");";
          eval($s);
          $refObjArrayIndexObj->ForceLoaded();
          foreach ($this_row as $key => $value) {
            if (!(is_numeric($key))) {
              $refObjArrayIndexObj->SetField($key, $value);
            };
          };
        };
      };
    };
  }

  function RetrievePopulatedObjects($page_num = 0) {
    if ($page_num > 0) {
      $items_per_page = $this->items_per_page;
      # Calculate start and end limits from page number.
      $start_lim = ($items_per_page * ($page_num - 1));
      $end_lim = ($start_lim + $items_per_page) - 1;
        if ($end_lim > ($this->item_count-1)) {
          $end_lim = $this->item_count - 1;
        };
    } else {
      $start_lim = 0;
      $end_lim = $this->item_count - 1;
    };
    $return_array = array();
    $counter = 0;
    for ($i=$start_lim; $i<=$end_lim; $i++) {
      $return_array[$counter] = $this->obj_array[$i];
      $counter++;
    };
    return($return_array);
  }
}
?>
```

Typical GenericObjectCollection Implementation

Here's the code for the new version of the `UserHome` class (in the file `userhome.phpm`) that makes use of `GenericObjectCollection`. You may notice from the fact that this class has member variables that this particular version cannot be used as a static class. It needs to be instantiated as any other does. This requirement is brought about by the pagination methods introduced; shortly, you'll see why we've introduced them.

```
<?
class UserHome {

  var $items_per_page = 12;
  var $item_count;
  var $page_count;

  public function __construct() {
    return(true); # No useful constructor in a Home Class
  }

  public function SetItemsPerPage($items_per_page) {
    $this->items_per_page = $items_per_page;
  }

  public function GetItemCount() {
    return ($this->item_count);
  }

  public function GetPageCount() {
    return ($this->page_count);
  }

  public function GetAllUsersWithFirstNameBeginningWith($strLetter,$page_
num=1) {
    $dbc = new GenericObjectCollection("user", "User");
    $sql = new sql();
    $strLetter = strtolower($strLetter);
    $sql->query("SELECT id FROM \"user\" WHERE lower(first_name) LIKE
'$strLetter%'");
    $result_rows = $sql->get_table_hash();
    for ($i=0; $i<=sizeof($result_rows)-1; $i++) {
      $dbc->AddTuple($result_rows[$i]["id"]);
    };
    $dbc->SetPageSize($this->items_per_page);
    $dbc->PopulateObjectArray($page_num);
    $objArray = $dbc->RetrievePopulatedObjects($page_num);

    $this->item_count = $dbc->GetItemCount();
    $this->page_count = $dbc->GetNumPages();

    return($objArray);
  }
}
?>
```

Note that the previous class looks quite different from our previous incarnation of `UserHome`, even though it has the same core method—`GetAllUsersWithFirstNameBeginningWith`—and that method appears to return an array of `User` objects, just as before.

It works quite differently, however, as you'll see.

Try It

Use the following snippet of code to try out the new `UserHome` class.

```
$uH = new UserHome();
$arUsers = $uH->GetAllUsersWithFirstNameBeginningWith('j');
for ($i=0; $i<=sizeof($arUsers)-1; $i++) {
  print $arUsers[$i]->GetField("first_name") . " " .
        $arUsers[$i]->GetField("last_name")  . "<br />\n";
};
```

You should see exactly the same output as before, if you're still using our test data from earlier:

```
John Doe
Jane Doe
```

How It Works

The new `UserHome` class does not extend `GenericObjectCollection`. It simply makes use of it as a support class.

The method to get matching users whose name begins with a given letter starts out much the same as with the traditional method discussed earlier. A crucial additional line exists before the query takes place, however:

```
$dbc = new GenericObjectCollection("user", "User");
```

This creates a new instance of `GenericObjectCollection`, mapped to the `user` table and the `User` object. Note that the `User` object must have been declared previously for this to work. The name of the table and the name of the class are both stored as private member variables of `GenericObjectCollection` and retained for later use.

Things get back to their usual self for a little while as we query the database to find matching users and ask only for their `id` values.

```
    $sql = new sql();
    $strLetter = strtolower($strLetter);
    $sql->query("SELECT id FROM \"user\" WHERE lower(first_name) LIKE
'$strLetter%'");
    $result_rows = $sql->get_table_hash();
```

In a similar fashion to earlier, we loop through the resulting data—except that this time, rather than simply instantiate a matching `GenericObject` instance, we add the `id` value to the

GenericObjectCollection class, as follows:

```
$dbc->AddTuple($result_rows[$i]["id"]);
```

The GenericObjectCollection class simply records this data onto a stack for later use.

We then tell the GenericObjectCollection class a vital piece of information: a page size. In the preceding example, this is simply hard coded into the UserHome class. This information is offered because you are unlikely to ever want to retrieve populated versions of the entirety of your matching entities in one fell swoop. Rather, you will want to retrieve a certain slice of them.

You may well have a thousand matching objects; you aren't likely to want to do anything with a thousand simultaneously, so by setting your page size to, say, 12 items per page, you can retrieve a collection of objects equal only to the size of the page you have specified. This is not just neatness. It is pretty much a must to ensure any degree of performance when working with large numbers of matching entities.

This class-level logic closely mirrors the likely logic for the implementation of your particular application.

```
$dbc->SetPageSize($this->items_per_page);
```

All you need to do now is to tell the GenericObjectCollection class to give you that particular slice of objects as an array. This method accepted a page number parameter, defaulting to 1 if not specified. You simply pass this on, here:

```
$dbc->PopulateObjectArray($page_num);
```

In response, the GenericObjectCollection now constructs and executes a query like that shown previously:

```
SELECT * FROM "user" WHERE id IN (12091, 12092, 12093, 12094, 12095,
12096, 12097, 12098, 12099, 12100)
```

This simple list of id values is constructed using the _GetCommaSeparatedIDList() internal method. This takes start and end limits as its parameters, which are derived from the current page number. The list of id values returned corresponds to these limits, so, for example, if 50 and 60 are passed as respective start and end limits, the 50th thru 60th matching id values returned by the original query will be included in the output list of id values.

Before making use of the query results, the class first creates an internal collection of user objects in a loop. It uses the eval method because when you originally instantiated the GenericObjectCollection class, you passed the name of the class you are using as a string. The eval method allows you to build up and then execute PHP code dynamically or on the fly, as shown:

```
$refObjArrayIndexObj = &$this->obj_array[$this_index];
$s = "\$refObjArrayIndexObj = new ".$this->class_name."(".$this_db_row_id.");";
eval($s);
```

The value of $this_index is calculated using the internal _GetIndexFromTupleID() method, which matches the position in the complete array of matching objects to the row id value currently being examined in the query output.

> **You may note that the preceding example doesn't make use of the collection class discussed in Chapter 5. Rather, it simply returns an array of objects. This means you can't do fancy things such as run an iterator over the collection. To keep things simple, though, we've left it as it is. It's not hard to adapt if you feel strongly about it.**

The method then refers to the grid of data generated by the query to repeatedly use the `SetField` property of that `GenericObject` instance to make its various fields match the results returned by the database:

```
$refObjArrayIndexObj->ForceLoaded();
foreach ($this_row as $key => $value) {
  if (!(is_numeric($key))) {
    $refObjArrayIndexObj->SetField($key, $value);
  };
};
```

By using the `ForceLoaded` method, the `GenericObjectCollection` class can trick the `GenericObject` instance in question into "thinking" it has been loaded. This is perfectly okay because all the fields of that class are being set right now—by `GenericObjectCollection`, using the grid of data it has just retrieved from the database.

Finally, back to `UserHome`, where you can now see it retrieving the array of instantiated objects:

```
$objArray = $dbc->RetrievePopulatedObjects($page_num);
```

Again, start and end limits are quickly calculated from the supplied page number and the appropriate slice of objects taken and returned.

You can also see the results of the enforced pagination by getting the total number of matches and, from there, the total number of pages (some fairly simple math is at work here):

```
$this->item_count = $dbc->GetItemCount();
$this->page_count = $dbc->GetNumPages();
```

These values can then be retrieved using the exposed methods of the `UserHome` class.

GenericObjectCollection Summary

The `GenericObjectCollection` class can seem daunting at first; it's certainly a large amount of code to perform a relatively simple task.

In fact, its source code belies the simplicity of its essential premise. It prepopulates an array of instantiated `GenericObject`-extended classes with data so that when they are dealt with as a set rather than in isolation, the number of SQL queries that needs to be performed against your database is kept to a minimum.

Any kind of administration application that needs to display some kind of tabular, paginated view of entities on a system and then allows your user to drill down to view or edit that entity will benefit immensely from using this hierarchy.

Experimentation is the key to understanding. Why not have a go at rewriting some of your existing applications to make use of the `GenericObject` and `GenericObjectCollection` classes? They will be used extensively in the rest of this book, so it's worth getting to know them well now.

Summary

In this chapter, you learned how the `GenericObject` and `GenericObjectCollection` classes can truly revolutionize the way you develop classes to represent entities in your application's database tables.

It's worth pointing out that almost all subclasses of GenericObject will have other methods, too, which cannot be effectively automated, so the requirement for good SQL practice still remains. Still, `GenericObject` provides an excellent means of cutting down on the mundane (and rather dull) programming of `UPDATE`, `INSERT`, and `DELETE` statements that otherwise would form an enormous percentage of your application.

`GenericObjectCollection` demonstrates both that OOP is not flawless and that true compliance can yield to inefficiency at your application's bottom line, but also that there is almost always a workaround to such side effects. By using `GenericObjectCollection` judiciously, you can build an application that is both OOP-compliant to a tee and also highly efficient when it comes to talking to your database.

In the next chapter, we stay on the database theme, with a look at database abstraction layers—an important technique that you can use to keep your application as database-portable as possible.

Database Abstraction Layers

Most of the enterprise-level applications you will build with PHP will at some point need to interact with a relational database such as MySQL, PostgreSQL, Oracle, or Microsoft SQL Server. Many of the components in the toolkit presented in this book have some obvious integration points with a database. Unfortunately, PHP's data interaction functions are very platform specific.

For example, to connect to a MySQL database, the PHP function is called `mysql_connect`. To connect to a PostgreSQL database, the function is `pg_connect`. The Oracle and ODBC APIs have their own names. The various database functions are similar, though not identical, across the different platforms. As a result, any change to the database platform on which your application runs will require changing all the database function calls. To help resolve this problem, a number of different open source and commercial projects have endeavored to create a unified set of data access functions that can work with any database. The main idea behind doing this is to allow applications to easily change the database they run on. In theory, you should be able to easily change from PostgreSQL to MySQL or any other platform.

In reality, because of the differences between the different SQL dialects and the different levels of support for the SQL specification and the proprietary SQL extensions used by most databases, real portability between databases is neither a reality nor a necessity for most large-scale enterprise applications. However, because the components in this toolkit are designed to be generic and completely reusable between different applications, ease of portability between database platforms is a requirement for the components.

To make it easy for toolkit components to be reused between different applications, running on different platforms, this chapter will explore the creation of a database abstraction layer and take a brief look at some of the more popular database abstraction layer projects that exist.

You'll also learn about an important design pattern called Singleton. The Singleton Design Pattern allows you to create exactly one instance of a particular class, and no more than one. This is useful when you have something like a database connection and you don't want to allow the application to be creating lots of these connections during a single page request.

What Is a Database Abstraction Layer?

A database abstraction layer is a set of PHP code that allows you to use a common syntax for interacting with different kinds of databases. Instead of having to learn the vagaries of the various native PHP database functions, you can use the same function names, with the same calling syntax, taking the same kinds of parameters and returning the same types of results and errors, to communicate with any number of different types of databases.

By using a database abstraction layer, you can easily take a component from one application, perhaps designed to work with PostgreSQL, and reuse that component in a different application, designed to work with an Oracle database. Although you might need to tweak the SQL statements used in that component, none of the PHP code would need to be modified.

Abstraction layers also make it very easy to implement logging or debugging functionality for all database interaction because the PHP functions that handle database interactions are centralized. Rather than have calls to `pg_query` or `mysql_query` littered throughout the application, you'll have a single function to which all queries are passed that allows you to intercept those queries and log them to a file, or do some sort of debugging.

A Simple Implementation

The easiest way to implement a basic abstraction layer is to create a class that acts as a wrapper around the native functions of a particular database backend. To reuse this component in a project with a different backend, you would need to rewrite the code in which you use the native functions for that RDBMS. This example happens to use PostgreSQL. Later in this chapter we introduce you to a more sophisticated approach, but this simple example should help illustrate how a database abstraction layer works.

Because most applications don't need to modify the internal structure of the database, we can limit the functionality of this simple abstraction layer to `SELECT`, `INSERT`, `UPDATE`, and `DELETE` statements. The `select()` method should return an associative array that represents the entire recordset. The `insert()`, `update()`, and `delete()` functions should return the number of records affected by the underlying SQL statement. To make life easier, these last three functions should handle any string escaping that needs to happen.

The Configuration File

You're likely to need only to connect to one database concurrently, so create a central configuration file that stores the information needed to connect. We'll use PHP for this configuration file, but you could just as easily use a number of more human-readable formats, as you'll discover in Chapter 17. Save this file as `config.php`:

```
<?php
$cfg['db']['host'] = 'localhost';
$cfg['db']['port'] = 5432; //PostgreSQL default port
$cfg['db']['user'] = 'postgresql';
$cfg['db']['password'] = 'mypass';
$cfg['db']['name'] = 'mydatabase';
?>
```

Establishing a Connection

The class should open a connection to the database in its constructor and close the connection in its destructor. The connection string will come from the `config.php` configuration file. Create a file called `class.Database.php` and enter the following code:

```
<?php
require_once('config.php');

class Database {

  private $hConn;

  public function __construct() {

    global $cfg;  // allow our method to access the $cfg associative array
                  // by making it global

    $connString  = ' host=' . $cfg['db']['host'];
    $connString .= ' user=' . $cfg['db']['user'];
    $connString .= ' password=' . $cfg['db']['password'];
    $connString .= ' port=' . $cfg['db']['port'];
    $connString .= ' dbname=' . $cfg['db']['name'];

    $this->hConn = @pg_connect($connString);

    if(! is_resource($this->hConn)) {
      throw new Exception("Unable to connect to the database " .
                          "using \"$connString\"", E_USER_ERROR);
    }

  }

  public function __destruct() {
    if(is_resource($this->hConn)) {
      @pg_close($this->hConn);
    }
  }

}
```

In the constructor, a connection to the database server is opened and the connection handle is assigned to the private `$hConn` member. If a connection could not be established using the supplied data, an exception is thrown. Be sure to wrap all calls to `new Database()` in a `try...catch` block.

To make this useful, you'll need to create methods that allow `SELECT`, `INSERT`, `UPDATE`, and `DELETE` statements. The code in the next section shows how these might be implemented.

Selecting Information

When selecting information from the database, that information is a lot easier to access if it's stored in an associative array, in which the keys correspond to the field names of the table in question. The `select()` method shows how this works in PostgreSQL.

```
public function select($sql) {

 $hRes = @pg_query($this->hConn, $sql);
  if(! is_resource($hRes)) {
    $err = pg_last_error($this->hConn);
    throw new Exception($err);
  }

  $arReturn = array();
  while( ($row = pg_fetch_assoc($hRes)) ) {
    $arReturn[] = $row;
  }

  return $arReturn;

}
```

For each row of data returned by the query specified in the `$sql` parameter, a two-dimensional array is built. The first dimension is a numeric index representing the row number (starting with 0). The second dimension is the name of the field.

This isn't a great approach for dealing with very large recordsets because every row (or *tuple*) is stored in memory. We look at some alternate ways of implementing a `select()` method later in this chapter that will be far more efficient for dealing with large recordsets.

Altering Information

Now that you can get information out of the database, you'll need to be able to add, modify, and delete records. The following code shows one possible implementation of the `insert()`, `update()`, and `delete()` methods. The first method takes as its parameters the name of a table and an associative array of field names and values. The SQL statement is constructed inside the function, properly escaping string values in the process:

```
public function insert($table, $arFieldValues) {
  $fields = array_keys($arFieldValues);
  $values = array_values($arFieldValues);

  // Create a useful array of values
  // that will be imploded to be the
  // VALUES clause of the insert statement.
  // Run the pg_escape_string function on those
  // values that are something other than numeric.
  $escVals = array();
  foreach($values as $val) {
    if(! is_numeric($val)) {
      //make sure the values are properly escaped
      $val = "'" . pg_escape_string($val) . "'";
    }
    $escVals[] = $val;
  }
```

```
    //generate the SQL statement
    $sql = " INSERT INTO $table (";
    $sql .= join(', ', $fields);
    $sql .= ') VALUES(';
    $sql .= join(', ', $escVals);
    $sql .= ')';

    $hRes = pg_query($sql);
    if(! is_resource($hRes)) {
      $err = pg_last_error($this->hConn) . "\n" . $sql;
      throw new Exception($err);
    }

    return pg_affected_rows($hRes);
  }
```

The `update` method takes as its parameters the name of a table and an associative array of field names and values, where the keys of the array are the fields to be altered and the values are the new values for those fields. The `$arConditions` array is a similarly structured array of fields and values to be used in the `WHERE` clause:

```
  public function update($table, $arFieldValues, $arConditions) {

    // create a useful array for the SET clause
    $arUpdates = array();
    foreach($arFieldValues as $field => $val) {
      if(! is_numeric($val)) {
        //make sure the values are properly escaped
        $val="'" . pg_escape_string($val) . "'";
      }

      $arUpdates[] = "$field = $val";
    }

    // create a useful array for the WHERE clause
    $arWhere = array();
    foreach($arConditions as $field => $val) {
      if(! is_numeric($val)) {
        //make sure the values are properly escaped
        $val = "'" . pg_escape_string($val) . "'";
      }

     $arWhere[] = "$field = $val";
    }

    $sql  = "UPDATE $table SET ";
    $sql .= join(', ', $arUpdates);
    $sql .= ' WHERE ' . join(' AND ', $arWhere);

    $hRes = pg_query($sql);
    if(! is_resource($hRes)) {
      $err = pg_last_error($this->hConn) . NL . $sql;
```

```
      throw new Exception($err);
    }

    return pg_affected_rows($hRes);
  }
```

The `delete` method takes as its parameters the name of the table from which rows are to be deleted, and an associate array of field => value pairs, which are used to generate the `WHERE` clause applicable to this deletion:

```
  function delete($table, $arConditions) {

    //create a useful array for generating the WHERE clause
    $arWhere = array();
    foreach($arConditions as $field => $val) {
      if(! is_numeric($val)) {
        //make sure the values are properly escaped
        $val = "'" . pg_escape_string($val) . "'";
      }

      $arWhere[] = "$field = $val";
    }

    $sql = "DELETE FROM $table WHERE " . join(' AND ', $arWhere);

    $hRes = pg_query($sql);
    if(! is_resource($hRes)) {
      $err = pg_last_error($this->hConn) . NL . $sql;
      throw new Exception($err);
    }

    return pg_affected_rows($hRes);
  }
```

In each of these three functions the SQL statement is constructed by `join`ing members from the `$arFieldValues` and `$arCondition` arrays. The string values of these arrays have been properly escaped to handle awkward characters—in particular, apostrophes.

Having executed the generated SQL statement, each function returns the number of rows affected by the query. Note that a return value of 0 (which will evaluate as false) does not necessarily indicate failure, just that nothing was modified.Especially for `UPDATE` and `DELETE` statements, this may well be what is expected, depending on the input to the function and the contents of the table. Generally, `INSERT` statements should always affect exactly one record, but if the table has triggers that interfere with the `INSERT`, a valid `INSERT` statement may affect zero records, or more than one.

Using the Database class

Using this class in your applications is very straightforward, and far cleaner than directly interacting with the `pg_[x]` functions. Create a simple table called `mytable` in PostgreSQL by using the following SQL statement.

```
CREATE TABLE "mytable" (
  "id" SERIAL PRIMARY KEY NOT NULL,
  "myval" varchar(255)
);
```

Then create a test file, `DB_test.php` that looks like this:

```
<?php

require_once('class.Database.php');

try {
  $objDB = new Database();
} catch (Exception $e) {
  echo $e->getMessage();
  exit(1);
}

try {
  $table = "mytable";
  $objDB->insert($table, array('myval' => 'foo') );
  $objDB->insert($table, array('myval' => 'bar') );
  $objDB->insert($table, array('myval' => 'blah') );
  $objDB->insert($table, array('myval' => 'mu') );
  $objDB->update($table, array('myval' => 'baz'), array('myval' => 'blah'));
  $objDB->delete($table, array('myval' => 'mu'));
  $data = $objDB->select("SELECT * FROM mytable");
  var_dump($data);
} catch (Exception $e) {
  echo "Query failure" . NL;
  echo $e->getMessage();
}
?>
```

In this example, four `insert` statements are issued, creating four rows in `mytable` where `myval` is equal to `'foo'`, `'bar'`, `'blah'`, and `'mu'` respectively. The `update` statement sets `myval` to `'baz'` in any rows where `myval` is currently `'blah'` (which will be just one row, that which we have previously inserted). The `delete` statement removes the record where `'myval'` is equal to `'mu'`.

The `var_dump` statement is used to show the current contents of the table after this flurry of activity and should give you output similar to the following:

```
array(3) {
  [0]=>
  array(2) {
    ["id"]=>
    string(2) "1"
    ["myval"]=>
    string(3) "foo"
  }
  [1]=>
  array(2) {
    ["id"]=>
```

```
        string(2) "2"
        ["myval"]=>
        string(3) "bar"
      }
      [2]=>
      array(2) {
        ["id"]=>
        string(2) "3"
        ["myval"]=>
        string(3) "baz"
      }
    }
```

Note that subsequent runs of this test script will result in further insertions into the database table, as there is no code to empty it before or after use. If you've hit the Refresh button in your browser a few times, your output may well be somewhat longer than the above.

You'll notice from the above output that the `select` statement has returned the entire recordset as a two-dimensional array. The topmost level of the array is numerically indexed with one member for each row. The second level is an associative array in which the field name is the key.

If you ever wanted to use this component in an application that ran on MySQL instead of PostgreSQL, you would need to change all the `pg_[x]` functions to their `mysql_[x]` equivalents. Doing so sometimes requires changing the order of parameters to those functions or changing the way in which the specific parts of the internals of this class work, but the external API can remain the same regardless of the type of database. Other reusable componentry that needs to interact with a SQL backend can either be recycled from application one to application two without modification (if the SQL statements needed by those components can run without modification on the second platform) or will run with minor changes to the SQL statements and no changes to the PHP code.

The example `Database` class shown previously is, however, too simple for most applications. It doesn't handle large recordsets efficiently, lacks support for transactions, and has very rudimentary error handling. You could spend the rest of the chapter inventing a more robust set of database abstraction functions, but much of this work has already been done for you.

Introducing PEAR DB

For a far more sophisticated look at what's possible with database abstraction, have a look at the PEAR DB class that ships with PHP. This database abstraction layer is capable of simultaneously handling connections to more than a dozen databases types natively, and many more through its ODBC capabilities.

It uses the same syntax for all connection strings, unlike the native PHP database functions. To establish a connection using the DB class, the syntax is

```
[database type]://[user]:[password]@[hostname/[database name]
```

This string is called the *data source name* (DSN). Using this common DSN syntax, you can connect to any kind of database supported by DB.

```
// connect to a MySQL server on db01 using the root account
// with the password passw0rd and connect to the database 'dbfoo'
$dsn = 'mysql://root:passw0rd@db01/dbfoo';

// connect to a PostgreSQL server on the local machine using the
// user postgres, no password, and connect to the database 'mydb'
$dsn = 'pgsql://postgres@localhost/mydb';
```

The currently supported database backends and database type strings are as follows:

PEAR DB Type	Database
dbase	dBase
fbsql	FrontBase
ibase	InterBase
ifx	Informix
msql	Mini SQL
mssql	Microsoft SQL Server
mysql	MySQL (for servers running MySQL <= 4.0
mysqli	MySQL (for servers running MySQL >= 4.1
oci8	Oracle 7/8/9
odbc	Open Database Connectivity
pgsql	PostgreSQL
sqlite	SQLite
sybase	Sybase

Note that support for the relevant database must either be compiled into your build of PHP or loaded as a dynamic module for connections to any of the above databases to work. As with the previous example, the DB classes provide a wrapper around the native PHP functions. If those functions aren't available, you can't connect to a database of that type.

Connecting to a Database Using DB

To establish a connection to a database using DB, you need to include the main DB class file and create a valid DSN. In the following example, `DB_connect.php`, a connection is created to a PostgreSQL database, we select some data from a table, and we print that data to the screen with `var_dump`.

```
<?php

require_once('DB.php');
$dsn = 'pgsql://postgres@localhost/mydb';
$conn = DB::connect($dsn);
```

```
if(DB::isError($conn)) {
  //you would probably want to do something a bit more graceful here
  print("Unable to connect to the database using the DSN $dsn");
  die($conn->getMessage());
}

//get all results as an associative array
$conn->setFetchMode(DB_FETCHMODE_ASSOC);

$sql = "SELECT * FROM mytable";
$data =&$conn->getAll($sql); //returns all rows. Only use with small recordsets


// Always check that $data is not an error
if (DB::isError($data)) {
    print("Error trying to run the query $sql");
    die ($data->getMessage());
}

var_dump($data);

$conn->disconnect(); //close the connection
?>
```

Notice that all DB functions could return an object of class `DB_Error`. To check for this, use `DB::isError()` on all return values. In your application, you'll want to do something a bit more graceful than simply calling `die()`. You should also never print sensitive information such as the DSN or details of the query to the screen. It is far better to log this sort of information to an application log file. In Chapter 11 you'll look at creating a robust logging mechanism.

Also note that all the methods of the DB class are static. The DB class itself is a wrapper around lower-level classes that do all the real heavy lifting. It provides only some utility methods, such as `connect()`, `disconnect()`, `isError()` and a few others. None of these methods is dependent on any object state, and, as a result, each is declared static.

Retrieving Information

The DB package provides you with a few different methods for retrieving information from the database, all of which are useful at different times. You've already seen one of them in the `DB_connect.php` code file. The `DB::connect()` method returns a subclass of `DB_common`. The name of that subclass is determined by the first part of the DSN. In this example, you get a `DB_pgsql` object.The `DB_common` class exposes a method called `getAll()`, which returns all the records for the given query in the form specified to the `fetchMode()` method. The previous example specifies `DB_FETCHMODE_ASSOC` as the default. This means that each of the data-fetching methods will, by default, return the results as an associative array in which the keys of the array are the same as the field names in the database.

Other easy-to-use methods include `getOne()`, which returns the first field in the first row of a recordset. This method is especially useful when retrieving single values, such as ID number, from a database. The `getRow()` method returns the first row. If you're looking for an array of the values from a single column, use `getCol()`. The following sample code, which requires the same mydb database and `mytable` table you used in the previous section, shows the use of all these methods and the structure of the values they return.

```
$sql = "SELECT id, myval FROM mytable";

$arData = $conn->getAll($sql);
/*
 * $arData = array (
 *               0 => array('id' => 1, 'myval' => 'foo'),
 *               0 => array('id' => 2, 'myval' => 'bar'),
 *               0 => array('id' => 3, 'myval' => 'baz'),
 *           )
 */

$id = $conn->getOne($sql);
/*
 * $id = 1;
 */

$arData = $conn->getRow($sql);
/*
 * $arData = array('id' => 1, 'myval' => 'foo');
 */

$arData = $conn->getCol($sql);
/*
 * $arData = array(1, 2, 3);
 */
```

Efficient Data Handling

All the `get*()` methods shown previously are utility wrappers around `fetch*()` methods. For most situations, you'll want to use `fetchRow()`. Unlike `getAll()`, which reads the entire recordset into memory, `fetchRow()` grabs only one row at a time. This allows you to iterate through large datasets without having to take up large quantities of memory, as the database is interrogated only one row at a time, as when you request another row from within your code.

The `fetch*()` methods require a `DB_result` object as an argument. This argument is obtained through the use of the `query()` method. To see how these functions work together, have a look at the sample following code.

```
// get all results as an associative array
$conn->setFetchMode(DB_FETCHMODE_ASSOC);

$sql = "SELECT * FROM mytable";
$result =& $conn->query($sql);

// Always check that $result is not an error
if (DB::isError($result)) {
    print("Error trying to run the query $sql");
    die ($result->getMessage());
}
```

```
// call the fetchRow() method to get each row, one at
// a time from the resultset.
while($row = $result->fetchRow()) {
  print $row['myval'] . "<br>\n";
}
```

If you've used the native PHP database functions in the past, you'll recognize this syntax as similar to the `*_fetch_row()` function used by your favorite database extension. Each call to `fetchRow()` increments an internal counter that keeps track of which row should be retrieved next. It returns `null` at the end of the recordset.

Other Useful Functions

The DB package provides a number of other functions that will be of use to you. This is by no means an exhaustive list, just some highlights.

Function query()

The same `query()` method that performed `SELECT` statements will allow you to issue `UPDATE` and `DELETE` statements, as well.

```
$sql = "INSERT INTO mytable (myvalue) VALUES('Foobar')";
$result = $conn->query($sql);
if(DB::isError($result)) {
  print("Unable to perform insert statement.");
  die($result->getMessage());
}

$sql = "UPDATE mytable SET myvalue = 'foobar' WHERE id = 4";
$result = $conn->query($sql);
if(DB::isError($result)) {
  print("Unable to perform update statement.");
  die($result->getMessage());
}
```

As with all methods of the `DB_common` class, the return value of all methods should be checked with `DB::isError()`.

Function nextID()

When you're performing an `INSERT`, finding a platform-independent way to retrieve the value of an auto-incrementing field can be difficult. Many RDBMSes support the concept of a sequence. A sequence is simply a persistent counter that starts at some predefined number (usually 1) and allows you to increment and fetch the new value. PostgreSQL, Oracle, and other RDBMSes that don't have a native auto-increment field use these structures to implement auto-increment field capabilities. MySQL does not have any such concept as a sequence (it supports auto-increment fields natively), but for portability the DB package emulates this capability by using a table with only one `AUTOINCREMENT` field, called `id`.

Here's how this is useful. Assuming that you're using PostgreSQL here, you might well create a table using the following shorthand SQL statements:

```
CREATE TABLE info (
  id SERIAL PRIMARY KEY NOT NULL,
  data varchar(255)
);
```

In fact, behind the scenes, PostgreSQL is actually creating a table using the following syntax:

```
CREATE SEQUENCE info_id_seq;

CREATE TABLE info (
  id integer NOT NULL PRIMARY KEY DEFAULT nextval('info_id_seq'),
  data varchar(255)
);
```

As you can see, PostgreSQL has simulated the implementation of an auto-incrementing primary key by creating a sequence object called `info_id_seq`. This naming convention is used to indicate that this relation is a sequence object used to drive the column named `id` of the table called `info`. The `info` table uses the `nextval()` function to increment the sequence's value by one and return the new value. By using `nextval('info_id_seq')` as the default value of the `id` field, you can issue statements like this:

```
INSERT INTO info(data) VALUES('blah blah blah');
```

However, there is no way for you to reliably get the `id` value for this newly created record because there might be more than one record with `'blah blah blah'` as the value for the `data` field. Oracle uses a pseudo field called ROWID, PostgreSQL has OID, and other RDBMSes use other means for retrieving information about the newly created row. To get around this difference in behavior, you can use the DB package's `nextID()` method to fetch the next value of a given sequence object and use it explicitly in your `INSERT` statements.

```
$newID = $conn->nextID('info_id', true); //uses table name, assumes $name_seq
                                         //The second parameter creates the
                                         //sequence info_id_seq if it doesn't
                                         //already exist.
if(DB::isError($newID)) {
  print("Failed getting the new ID!");
  die($newID->getMessage());
}
$sql = "INSERT INTO info(id, data) VALUES($newID, 'blah blah blah')";
$result = $conn->query($sql);

if(DB::isError($sql)) {
  print("Insert failed for $sql");
  die($result->getMessage());
} else {
  print("Created record with id $newID");
}
```

The `nextID()` method returns the value of the next number in the sequence whose name is the value of the first parameter plus `"_seq"`. The second parameter allows the sequence object to be created if it doesn't already exist in the database. This can be a useful option; however, we strongly recommend that you create the sequence objects outside your code (or, ideally, allow your RDBMS to do it for you) so that you have control over the creation options.

Function quoteSmart()

In the original simple abstraction layer from the beginning of the chapter, you used the pg_quote_string() function when using literal values in the insert(), update(), and delete() methods. This function automatically handles escaping characters such as ' in string values in the query. The DB package provides a similar method, called quoteSmart(), that is portable across RDBMS back ends. It takes a literal value as its sole parameter and spits out a string properly escaped based on the rules of the database to which you are connected.

```
function searchByName($name) {
  global $conn;  //assume the connection was established somewhere else

  $sql = "SELECT * FROM users WHERE name = " . $conn->quoteSmart($name);
  $result = $conn->query($sql);

  //make sure you use DB::isError to check for problems!

  return $result;
}
```

For simplicity's sake, we didn't repeat the error handling code you've already seen several times. In this example, assuming that $name = "O'Malley", $conn->quoteSmart($name) will return "'O\'Malley'" for PostgreSQL (note the single quotation marks around the name, and the escaped apostrophe). The way in which this function escapes that apostrophe may be different depending on the backend to which you are connected. For example, Microsoft SQL Server uses two quotes in a row ('') as part of its TransactSQL syntax.

Getting More Information

You've looked at only a few of the methods provided by the classes of the DB package. The full documentation, including examples, can be found at http://pear.php.net/manual/en/package.database.php.

The Complete Database Abstraction Layer

PEAR's DB package provides a lot of utility functions that you can take advantage of to build a fully customized database abstraction layer for use with any database backend. The class that follows is a complete tool that you can reuse on all your projects.

Create a configuration file called config.php to store the DSN:

```
$cfg['db']['dsn'] = 'pgsql://postgres:password@localhost/mydb';
```

Call your class Database and create a file called class.Database.php. In the constructor, you'll establish a connection, possibly throwing an error if there were any problems.

```
<?php

require_once('config.php');
require_once('DB.php');
```

```
class Database {
  private $conn;

  function __construct($dsn = null) {
    global $conn;

    //If nothing was passed in, use the value from $cfg
    if($dsn == null) {
      $dsn = $cfg['db']['dsn'];
    }

    //Open a connection using the info in $dsn
    $this->conn = DB::connect($dsn);

    if(DB::isError($this->conn)) {
      //We're not connected.  Throw an exception
      throw new Exception($this->conn->getMessage(), $this->conn->getCode());
    }

    //Always fetch data as an associative array
    $this->conn->setFetchMode(DB_FETCHMODE_ASSOC);
  }

  function __destruct() {
    $this->conn->disconnect();
  }
}
?>
```

Under normal circumstances you'll be using the DSN from the configuration information, so you don't need to supply a parameter to the constructor; however, should you need to use some alternate connection string for some reason, the constructor will accept a DSN as its only parameter. Because no significant overhead is involved in fetching information from the database as an associative array rather than as a numerically indexed array, and because an associative array is so much easier to deal with, you should add the line of code found at the end of the constructor that makes all `get*()` and `fetch*()` methods return associative arrays.

Note that the constructor throws an exception if things go wrong. This will be the case for nearly every method of the `Database` class. The arguments to the `Exception` object's constructor are the string message and numeric code from the `DB_error` object returned by the `DB::connect()` method.

You should also create the destructor to ensure that the database connection is closed when this object is no longer needed. This is important, because without closing the connection properly you may well find that each subsequent request of your PHP script ties up yet another spare socket on your database server; it will quickly run out, and could easily fall over as a result.

Now let's add a few methods to your class for selecting chunks of data from the database. You'll provide `select()`, `getAll()`, `getOne()`, and `getCol()` methods. The `select()` method will return a `DB_result` object. This should be used whenever the recordset might be more than just a few records. The other methods will just pass through to the `DB_common` methods with the same name.

```
    //returns a DB_result object
    function select($sql) {
      $result = $this->conn->query($sql);

      if(DB::isError($result)) {
        throw new Exception($result->getMessage(), $result->getCode());
      }

      return $result;
    }

    //returns 2D assoc array
    function getAll($sql) {
      $result = $this->conn->getAll($sql);

      if(DB::isError($result)) {
        throw new Exception($result->getMessage(), $result->getCode());
      }

      return $result;
    }

    //returns single scalar value from the first column, first record
    function getOne($sql) {
      $result = $this->conn->getOne($sql);

      if(DB::isError($result)) {
        throw new Exception($result->getMessage(), $result->getCode());
      }

      return $result;
    }

    //returns numerically indexed 1D array of values from the first column
    function getColumn($sql) {
      $result = $this->conn->getCol($sql);

      if(DB::isError($result)) {
        throw new Exception($result->getMessage(), $result->getCode());
      }

      return $result;
    }
```

All these methods will throw an exception if there are any problems. By throwing exceptions instead of just returning the value of the `DB_common` methods, you're able to properly encapsulate the use of the DB package. If at some point you decide you want to use a different database abstraction (such as the PEAR MDB package), you won't need to change code outside this class.

Now let's look at adding an `update()` method, so we can easily manipulate existing data in the database. The `update()` method takes the name of a table, an associative array of field names (as the key) and values (as the value) to be updated, and a string `WHERE` clause. The reason you don't construct the `WHERE` clause from an array of field names and values is that you will probably want to have the ability to use different operators (=, LIKE, IN, and so on.) and use regular expressions, if supported by your RDBMS. Creating a WHERE parameter that supports this effectively across multiple database backends is difficult, if not impossible, so the WHERE clause strings needs to be manually generated outside the class.

```
function update($tableName, $arUpdates, $sWhere = null) {

  $arSet = array();
  foreach($arUpdates as $name => $value) {
    $arSet[] = $name . ' = ' . $this->conn->quoteSmart($value);
  }
  $sSet = implode(', ', $arSet);

  //make sure the table name is properly escaped
  $tableName = $this->conn->quoteIdentifier($tableName);

  $sql = "UPDATE $tableName SET $sSet";
  if($sWhere) {
    $sql .= " WHERE $sWhere";
  }

  $result = $this->conn->query($sql);

  if(DB::isError($result)) {
    throw new Exception($result->getMessage(), $result->getCode());
  }

  //return the number of rows affected
  return $this->conn->affectedRows();
}
```

Use the quoteSmart() method to ensure that the values you've supplied in the second parameter are properly escaped before executing the SQL statement. The quoteIdentifier() method is used for table names. The return value of update() is the number of records affected.

Be careful! If you don't supply a WHERE clause to this function, every row in the table will be altered.

The insert() method works similarly to update(), except there is no WHERE clause.

A special value token in the insert() method allows you to fetch the id value for newly created records. If any value of the $arValues array is equal to the literal string '#id#', assume that the corresponding column is the primary key value for this table and replace that value with the nextID() from the sequence called $tableName_id_seq. If that token was encountered, the function returns the new ID value. If not, it returns the number of records affected by the insert statement (usually 1).

```
function insert($tableName, $arValues) {
  $id = null;

  $sFieldList = join(', ', array_keys($arValues));

  $arValueList = array();
```

```
        foreach($arValues as $value) {
          if(strtolower($value) == '#id#') {
            //we need to get the next value from this table's sequence
            $value = $id = $this->conn->nextID($tableName . "_id");
          }
          $arValueList[] = $this->conn->quoteSmart($value);
        }
        $sValueList = implode(', ', $arValueList);

        //make sure the table name is properly escaped
        $tableName = $this->conn->quoteIdentifier($tableName);

        $sql = "INSERT INTO $tableName ( $sFieldList) VALUES ( $sValueList )";
        $result = $this->conn->query($sql);

        if(DB::isError($result)) {
          throw new Exception($result->getMessage(), $result->getCode());
        }

        //return the ID, if there was one, or the number of rows affected
        return $id ? $id : $this->conn->affectedRows();
    }
```

If `'#id#'` was found as one of the values, the class returns the value of the new ID; otherwise, it returns the number of affected records. Make sure that you know which flavor of return value you're expecting when calling this function, or you might mistakenly assume that an ID was 1 when that was really the number of affected records.

This class is significantly more robust than the simple abstraction layer created at the beginning of the chapter, but there are still two more features this needs to support to be complete. The first is transactions.

Transaction Support

Transactions are used to allow changes to a database to be grouped and *proposed* before they are *committed*. Such a technique is typically used when the changes to be made are useless in isolation from one another, and hence should one fail for either technical or logistical reasons, any previously proposed changes will be discarded.

With this in mind, when `INSERT`, `UPDATE`, and `DELETE` statements are issued within a transaction context, they aren't actually written to the database until you call `COMMIT`. If something goes wrong, *all* the changes are undone and no other users of the database are aware that anything ever changed. To support transactions in the `Database` class, you need to implement three methods: a method to declare the commencement of a transaction, a method to commit the proposed changes of the transaction, and a method to abort the transaction to date and undo any changes made since the transaction started.

The `startTransaction()` method establishes a transaction context. This means that the database backend is informed that you want to do everything inside a transaction. If your chosen backend does not support transactions, an error will be raised by the `DB_common` class.

```
function startTransaction() {
  //autoCommit returns true/false if the command succeeds
  return $this->conn->autoCommit(false);
}
```

Normally, most RDBMSes ship out of the box with `autoCommit` turned on. This means that all `INSERT`, `UPDATE`, and `DELETE` statements automatically commit to the database. There is no need to explicitly commit all changes in this state. Accordingly, you can effectively enter a transaction context by setting `autoCommit()` to false, which will require all statements to be committed explicitly.

Having issued the series of changes that make up your transaction proposal, you have two choices. You can either `commit()` those changes, which writes them to the database, or you can `abort()` the transaction, which rolls everything back to the state it was before issuing the first statement.

```
function commit() {
  $result = $this->conn->commit();

  if(DB::isError($result)) {
      throw new Exception($result->getMessage(), $result->getCode());
  }

  $this->conn->autoCommit(true);
  return true;
}

function abort() {
  $result = $this->conn->rollback();

  if(DB::isError($result)) {
    throw new Exception($result->getMessage(), $result->getCode());
  }

  return true;
}
```

Recent versions of most of the major database platforms support transactions. This includes PostgreSQL, MySQL, Oracle, Microsoft SQL Server, and several others. Any time your application needs to alter more than one table to accomplish a single function, you should use a transaction to ensure that a problem with one statement will not affect the referential integrity of your database—that is, there are not references to entities in foreign tables which do not actually exist (for example, a column `user_id` with a value 235, when there is no user with `id` 235 in the `user` table). For more information on the transaction support provided by your preferred database, see the documentation provided by its vendor.

Previously, we said there were *two* more features to be implemented in our `Database` class. Transactions were one; the other concerns the way in which database connections are opened. In the next section we introduce you to an important design pattern called Singleton.

The Singleton Design Pattern

The Singleton design pattern provides a mechanism whereby the number of instances of a class is limited to one. You may have either zero instances of the class, or one instance—never more than one.

Typical situations in which you might want to do this include the instantiation of classes that have particularly large overhead, or where having more than one copy is nonsensical. In this case, you have only one database that drives the application (specified in the `config.php` files as `$cfg['db'][dsn']`). Opening a connection to the database usually takes far more resources than all but the most complex queries. Because you have only one database to connect to and PHP is not a multithreaded programming language (the PHP engine itself is multithreaded, but applications written in PHP are not), there is no reason to open more than one database connection for a given page request, unless, for some reason, you are connecting to two separate databases.

As a result, you want to make sure that you suffer the overhead of establishing a database connection only once. Here's how this works.

First, add a static method to the `Database` class called `instance()`. This method will return an instantiated `Database` object. Second, to make sure that nothing can create new instances of the class, declare the constructor to be `private`. The `instance()` method should contain a static variable that holds a reference to an instantiated `Database` object. The first time the `instance()` method is called, this variable will be null. Subsequent calls should return only the object created during the first invocation.

```
private function __construct($dsn = null) {
  global $cfg;

  if($dsn == null) $dsn = $cfg['db']['dsn'];
  println( "DSN: $dsn");

  $this->conn = DB::connect($dsn);

  if(DB::isError($this->conn)) {
    //We're not connected.  Throw an exception
    throw new Exception($this->conn->getMessage(), $this->conn->getCode());
  }

  //Always fetch data as an associative array
  $this->conn->setFetchMode(DB_FETCHMODE_ASSOC);
}
static public function instance() {
  static $objDB;

  if(! isset($objDB)) {
    $objDB = new Database();
  }

  return $objDB;
}
```

You changed the constructor to be private. Any attempts to run the line `$db = new Database()` will now cause a fatal error. To get an instance of a `Database` object, call `$db = Database::instance()`.

Remember: Static function variables retain their value between invocations of that function.

Using the Database Class

The following code provides a good example of how to use the completed `Database` class.

```
<?php

require_once('class.Database.php');

try {
  $db = Database::instance();
} catch (Exception $e) {
  // No point continuing...
  die("Unable to connect to the database.");
}

$sql = "SELECT count(1) FROM mytable";
$count = $db->getOne($sql);
print "There are $count records in mytable!<br>\n";

// start a transaction
$db->startTransaction();

// do an insert and an update
try {
  $arValues = array();
  $arValues['id'] = '#id#';
  $arValues['myval'] = 'blah blah blah';
  $newID = $db->insert('mytable', $arValues);

  print "The new record has the ID $newID<br>\n";

  // update the record we just created
  $arUpdate = array();
  $arUpdate['myval'] = 'foobar baz!';
  $affected = $db->update('mytable', $arUpdate, "id = $newID");

  print "Updated $affected records<br>\n";

  // write the changes to the database
  $db->commit();
} catch (Exception $e) {
  // some sort of error happened - abort the transaction
  // and print the error message
  $db->abort();
  print "An error occurred.<br>\n" . $e->getMessage();
}

?>
```

Be sure to read this example carefully to understand how everything works. Don't forget to wrap your code in `try...catch` blocks to make sure that any connection or query problems that might arise are caught and handled gracefully.

Summary

Because the underlying database abstraction layer is the very flexible and quite powerful PEAR DB package, the `Database` class is one you'll be able to use in nearly every project on which you work. Although not every query you write will be portable across different database backends, the ability to quickly change the database type makes it much easier to reuse data-driven components across different projects.

In Chapter 11, you'll build a robust logging and debugging system that will plug into the `Database` class and provide a means for debugging database problems without printing query details to the screen. Because every query in your applications will go through the `Database` class, you'll have a centralized location to capture the queries and add them to logs or debug output.

Use the Singleton design pattern when you want to ensure that there is no more than one instance of a class. Any time the instantiation of a class has a large overhead, such as establishing a connection to a database, and when it is possible to limit users of that class to only one instance, this technique can reduce system load and improve overall application performance.

Factory Interface

In previous chapters you have learned what a *design pattern* is and how you can make best use of them in your PHP development. In this chapter you'll see once again that design patterns are not just academic exercises but can be frequently and effectively deployed in real-word applications. Sometimes well-known patterns emerge without your even realizing it.

This chapter introduces you to the *factory interface* and sets out not only the situations for which it is most appropriate, but also how you can successfully apply it in your own programs.

To help you get the most out of this chapter, we will introduce some code examples that make use of factory interfaces. We also discuss how those code examples can be improved with the new features of PHP5, taking care to note any important implementation details along the way.

Factory Method Design Pattern

The factory method design pattern (see *Design Patterns,* by Gamma, Helm, Johnson, and Vlissides, Addison-Wesley, 1995) is a *creational* design pattern, which means that it is characteristically charged with the creation (instantiation) of objects. But why might you want to complicate your life by using a design pattern, rather than simply using `new`, as in `$variable = new MyClass()`? There are two main scenarios where it might prove useful:

- **Runtime flexibility:** Sometimes it's impossible to choose ahead of time which specific object should be instantiated. The choice of objects to use may depend on something in the runtime environment such as user input, environmental settings (for example, internationalization), or even hardware/software support.
- **Abstraction:** By using a factory interface, you can delegate the instantiation of your application's classes to subclasses. This means your entire application can be constructed on the assumption that a set of generic, *abstracted* classes will be used as a proxy for real utility classes. This allows you to develop with a view to integrating only with those abstracted classes, rather than directly with the useful classes they represent.

Factory Interface Example

Database access for Web-based applications is not uncommon, so assuming that you require access to a database, how do you decide which query method to use if you are required to support multiple databases? Sometimes, you can't make that decision ahead of time; it's dependent on what the client has or wishes to use. This is frequently the case if you are creating Web-based applications for a large audience, such as an open-source project.

In this case, assume that MySQL, PostgreSQL and Interbase are all feasible options. These are some simplified code snippets that might be used to create each connection.

- MySQL:

```
$query = mysql_query ($sql, $database_handle);
```

- Postgres:

```
$query = pg_query ($database_handle, $sql);
```

- Interbase:

```
$query = ibase_connect ($database_handle, $sql);
```

The Old School Approach

Assuming that you have populated a variable (`$databasetype`) with the required database type, you could use a `switch()` statement, as below, to figure out what method to use:

```
// run query
switch (strtolower($databasetype)) {
    case "mysql":
        $query = mysql_query ($sql, $database_handle);
        break;
    case "postgres":
        $query = pg_query ($database_handle, $sql);
        break;
    case "interbase":
        $query = ibase_query ($database_handle, $sql);
        break;
    default:
        die ("Unknown database type:".$databasetype);
}
```

This code will work, no question about it. But what if somebody later needs you to add support for SQL Server? You would have to go through your code and add these lines wherever you are executing your queries:

```
case "mssql":
    $query = mssql_query ($sql, $database_handle);
```

Imagine then you start getting complaints that your software doesn't work with Interbase. How can that be? Interbase is supported. Looking further into the problem, people are entering *firebird* when they mean *interbase*. Although it's an honest mistake, the Interbase product (by Borland) was also released as open source software called Firebird. Regardless, you have to go back to your code and add the following:

```
case "interbase":
case "firebird":
    $query = ibase_query ($database_handle, $sql);
```

Although making those seemingly trivial changes isn't hard, your switch structure would most likely be replicated throughout your code—and not just for executing queries, either. Closing the database might be accomplished in the following way:

```
// close database
switch (strtolower($databasetype)) {
    case "mysql":
        mysql_close ($database_handle);
        break;
    case "postgres":
        pg_close ($database_handle);
        break;
    case "interbase":
    case "firebird":
        ibase_close ($database_handle);
        break;
    case "mssql":
        mysql_close ($database_handle);
    default:
        die ("Unknown database type:".$databasetype);
}
```

Have you noticed that expanding the functionality even by a little can lead to a whole lot more work—in effect, tracking down every place the changes should be replicated? It gets even more complicated if you throw in the fact that you may not want to close connections, such as when using persistent connections.

The code we have just looked at, although syntactically and technically correct, lead to a wide distribution of required modifications borne out of subsequent support for new database platforms. For instance, if support for SuperCoolDatabase were introduced, changes would have to be made in many different places in the code base. Since developers are human, any dependency upon multiple source-code modifications tends to lead to errors and omissions, which is obviously something best avoided. This situation, or *smell* (as in "something smells not quite right here") can be avoided altogether by using what is known as the Factory Method design pattern.

The Factory Interface Approach

Clearly, in our recurring example, it is impossible for you as a developer to decide ahead of time which databases you'll need to support. How can you plan for future expansion, therefore, whilst ensuring your code remains maintainable and readable?

You might consider using the *factory method* design pattern as one possible solution the problem. It works by abstracting the creation of objects (that is, instantiation) by using inheritance. In the factory method design pattern, an interface is defined that represents a standard by which subclasses can specify the correct class to instantiate.

Figure 9-1 shows an overview of the factory method in UML(Gamma *et al., Design Patterns*).

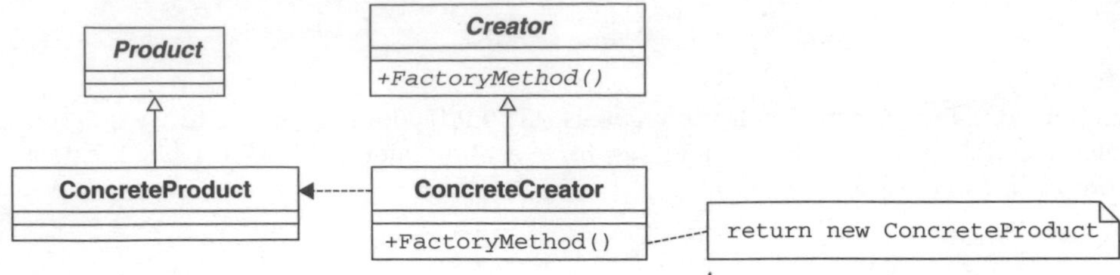

Figure 9-1

The key component here is the Creator class, which defines the factory interface method. Here it is listed as `FactoryMethod`.

The running instance of the `ConcreteCreator` class dutifully offers its unique implementation of the `FactoryMethod`. The `FactoryMethod` relies on the ConcreteCreator (of which there may be many different flavors) to instantiate the correct `Product` class, listed here as `ConcreteProduct`. You are, of course able to have other lifecycle or utility operations in the `ConcreteCreator` class, demonstrated here as `AnOperation`.

Using the Factory Interface in Database Abstraction

First, consider the instance of the class that you are required to create at runtime. That class should always be the center of your programming attention. In the following example, the code requires you to throw a special exception depending on which database you're running. Since you can't determine exactly which database your client is using at their end, the choice of which type of exception to throw will be left up to the Factory Interface.

Here follows an abbreviated example utilizing a PostgreSQL Database (Figure 9-2).

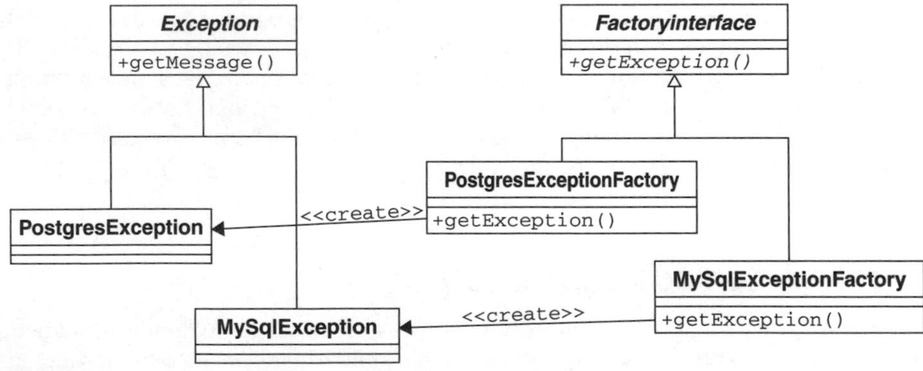

Figure 9-2

```
interface ExceptionFactory {
   public function getException($result=NULL, $message=NULL);
}

class PostgresExceptionFactory implements ExceptionFactory {
    public function getException($result=NULL, $message=NULL) {
        return new PostgresException ($result, $message);
    }
}

class PostgresException extends Exception {

    function __construct($result=NULL, $message=NULL) {
        $code = 0;
        if ($message == NULL) {
            if ($result <> NULL) {
                $mess ge = pg_result_error ($result);
                $code = pg_result_status($result);
            } else {
                $message = pg_last_error();
            }
        }
        parent::__construct ($message, $code);
    }
}

class MySqlExceptionFactory implements ExceptionFactory {
    public function getException($result=NULL, $message=NULL) {

        return new MySqlException ($result, $message);
    }
}

class MySqlException extends Exception {
    function __construct($result=NULL, $message=NULL) {
        if ($message == NULL) {
            $message = mysql_error();
        }
        $code = 0;
        if ($result <> NULL) {
            $code = mysql_errno($resource);
        }
        parent::__construct ($message, $code);
    }
}

/*
 * pseudo-code example usage
 */

// create your required factory
$factory = new PostgresExceptionFactory();
```

```
// getException returns a PostgresException
if ( ... something goes horribly wrong ... ) {
    throw $factory->getException();
}
```

Let's work our way through the example diagram and code above:

1. After your client determines which database will be used to support your application, it can be adapted to make use of the relevant `ExceptionFactory` implementation. If none exists, one can be easily written by following the edicts of the `ExceptionFactory` interface.
2. When your application must throw an exception, it does so by calling the `getException` method of the appropriate `ExceptionFactory` class.
3. The `getException` method represents the *factory interface* in this case. Because it is implemented by a specific instantiated class, it returns the correct type of exception for the database being used.

This example is simple by design. Notice how the `ExceptionFactory` interface relies on its subclasses `PostgresExceptionFactory` and `MysqlExceptionFactory`. They should be the only classes to instantiate your exceptions.

Multiple Factories

Adding another factory interface into the mix is certainly within the spirit of this particular design pattern. For instance, many databases support the concept of *transactions*, which allow blocks of related queries to be treated (and, therefore, executed) as one for the purposes of ensuring the integrity of the underlying database. Interbase happens to be just such a database.

Figure 9-3 shows how transactions can be supported, and makes use of the factory interface to create them.

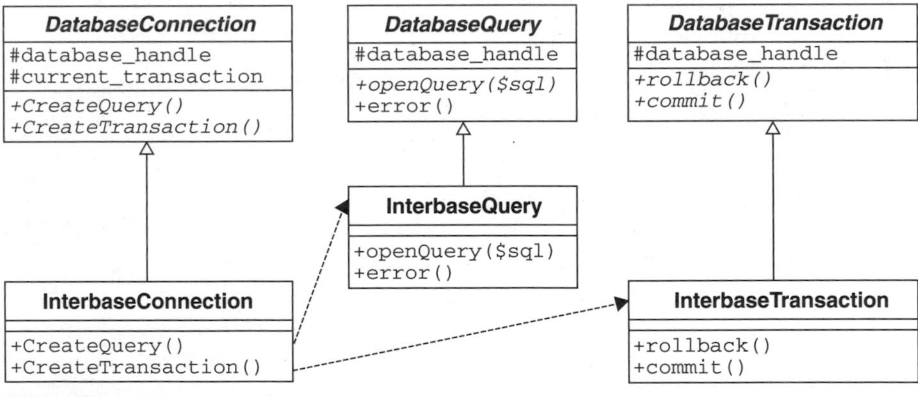

Figure 9-3

The `InterbaseTransaction` appears to work in a very similar fashion to the `InterbaseQuery` in that `InterbaseConnection` instantiates both of them. The lifecycle is somewhat different, however, since transactions typically outlive queries, as shown in the following sample code:

```
$con = new InterbaseConnection();
$trans = $con->CreateTransaction();
$query = $con->query("delete from employee");
if ($query->error()) {
   $trans->rollback();
} else {
  $trans->commit();
}
```

Leveraging Existing Classes

Inheriting from the `InterbaseConnection` class is not only legal but also useful, as shown in Figure 9-4.

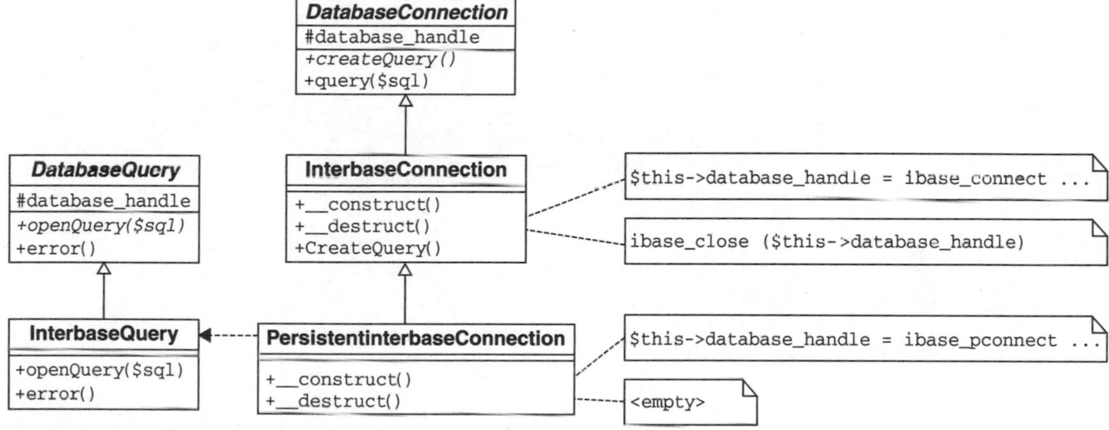

Figure 9-4

Notice the differences between `InterbaseConnection` and `PersistentInterbaseConnection`. First, note the use of `ibase_connect` vs `ibase_pconnect` to actually make the connection to the database server. Second, you'll note that `PersistentInterbaseConnection` has no need to close the physical connection in its destructor, because `pconnect` has assigned the class its `database_handle` from a pool of connections. In practice, this means that `pconnect` doe not require a corresponding `ibase_close()` function call to be made.

But because `PersistentInterbaseConnection` is being forced to make use of a regular `InterbaseQuery` in providing its exposed query method rather than, say, a fictitious `InterbasePersistableQuery`, it is totally reliant upon the generic `InterbaseConnection` factory interface for instantiation of the `InterbaseQuery`.

As a result, `PersistentInterbaseConnection` internally overrides `InterbaseConnection`'s constructor and destructor, replacing the Interbase connections with Interbase persistent connections. This is a great example of adding functionally by extending an existing class structure, which is in turn the classic example of a factory method design pattern.

Summary

In this chapter you've seen how the factory interface design pattern can be implemented, and the various situations in which it works best.

You have seen the power of this design pattern by examining a model for database abstraction which makes use of the factory method. This shows how database-dependent code can live in easy-to-find places in your application, instead of being needlessly scattered about the code base in hard-to-maintain structures.

In the next chapter, you'll look at the theory of event-driven programming, and see how easy it can be to implement event handling using the vastly improved OOP support in PHP5.

Event-Driven Programming

Sometimes it is useful to think of applications in terms of *events* and how best to handle them, rather than look at that application's architectural design from a traditional object-oriented perspective. That's not to say that we must discard an OOP approach altogether to implement event handling, rather that we build classes around the events relevant to the application. This approach is rather radical, but for many applications you may find that it gives you a massively powerful mechanism for approaching the software architecture of the whole project.

Events occur pretty much all the time, and some of the best examples of event-driven programming are the applications we use every day to manage e-mail or write text. For the end-user, Windows-based programs, event handling is of paramount importance. This is because these applications are designed to lurk around until the user does something and then react accordingly. Of course, the same is now true for many Web-based applications. Anything with a GUI is a likely candidate for the event-driven programming paradigm.

Nearly all actions taken by a user, and even those taken by the applications themselves, can be thought of as an event. A rather contrived example of an event not initiated by a user is your machine's clock. If you wanted to create an application that performed various actions depending on the time, you could capture certain changes in time as an event, and bundle it off to a piece of code that deals with it accordingly.

Whatever needs to be done, applications have various ways to implement a solution, and PHP5 is no different in this regard. There is, of course, no new extension or library to deal with events, because the way we deal with them is more about how we "think" about designing an application rather than how we actually implement it. In other words, they need no special underlying technology. Let's take a look at one way to handle events in PHP.

What Are Events?

An event is any occurrence to which your application can react. You will almost certainly have already written applications that have handled events in some capacity or other. When something happens or some condition is suddenly met, deciding what action to take in your code, no matter how trivial, is a form of event handling. For example, imagine that you have implemented a database holding a number of records, and you want your customers to be able to work on those records via a Web interface. You would probably realize that the users would need to at least be able to view and update records, so your likely reaction would be to create functions to view and edit records.

The decision of which function to call depends entirely on the input provided by the user. Accordingly, the interface you develop will need to present the various options and let the users decide which one they want. After the user has decided, the application needs to respond accordingly by calling the correct functions, which will handle the request.

Typically, you might create a home page with two buttons, one offering the option to view the records and another to edit them. The following code snippet might suffice as a mechanism to handle their choice:

```
switch($_GET['action']) {
  case "edit_record":
    edit_record();
  break;
  case "view_record":
    view_record();
  break;
}
```

As you can see, the previous snippet of code is designed to interpret information from `$_GET` (in other words, the user's request) and make a decision about what response to take, based on what the user has requested. That's it—you have handled an event that was fired by the simple action of the user's clicking a button.

This principle stands for pretty much any event you could possibly imagine. For those of you who use Outlook or something similar, system-generated events are commonplace. Warnings about meetings and deadlines pop up all the time based on a specific event firing (for example, the system's clock reaching a certain time).

Of course, how you implement the code to handle events is up to you. Using a `switch` statement is not the only way; any sort of loop could allow you to respond to events. An `if` / `else` block would work just as well in the previous example.

"So what is all the fuss about events?" you may ask. After all, what we've seen so far seems simple enough; why can't we just leave it at that? The problem with what we have discussed so far is that you could easily end up with a big mess if your application changes or grows after your initial development run. What starts off as a nice simple `if` statement could grow to monstrous proportions, rendering any attempts to understand it in the future very difficult indeed. This has obvious implications as your application's needs become more complex. Accordingly, you should use the simple methods alluded to above only for very simple requirements, where you can be sure the code is at no time going to blossom into a full-blown enterprise application.

Using OOP to Handle Events

To implement effective event-driven solutions in your own PHP applications, it is best to take a step back and determine, from a high-level perspective, how these applications should behave. A more sophisticated approach to implementing events would allow you to more easily control their behavior exactly as you wish, should the need ever arise. Creating an object-oriented solution to event-driven programming is the answer.

Not only will using classes and objects help you maintain uncluttered code, it will also allow you to create an easily extensible architecture. Extensibility in application development is all the rage these days, so this has to be a good thing. There are plenty of other benefits, too, which we will explore in some detail later in the chapter. Additionally, considering an OO approach should alert you to the fact that there might well exist a design pattern that could fit the event-driven model quite well.

Let's build a picture of what is needed to implement proper event handling using an object-oriented approach. We can then see whether a pattern, or patterns, exist that will fit this model appropriately.

Designing an event-driven solution

There are three main steps to take when designing any event-driven application.

The first is to determine how you will go about capturing the events the application will need to handle. This is difficult to discuss in an abstract manner, since your approach to capturing these events relies on exactly what type of events you're trying to capture.

Second, you will need a way of deciding how to go about handling the events captured. Depending on the specific application you are considering, there may be a number of questions worth posing at this early stage. For example, it's worth determining how many distinct sources will be sending events to your event handler. Also, you will need to decide whether the application will handle just one class of event or a number of different classes, and, if necessary, how handlers will effectively differentiate between them.

Finally, after you have determined the events applicable to your application and decided how they will be handled, you need to design the handlers necessary to carry out whatever tasks the application requires in response to each event. The types of responses an event could elicit are almost unlimited. Anything from directing a user to a new page, to updating a record, to firing more events—all could be regarded as proper responses.

Effectively, we have just described the use of a reactor, or *dispatcher* class, to take an event and make sure that the correct handler deals with it. Let's explore this idea a little further.

In keeping with our initial example, let's assume that a user of our application will want to edit or view records of some form or another. We could expect a URL such as the following to be requested as a result of a user's input returned from a form:

```
http://myserver/interface.php?event=edit
```

It's fairly clear from the URL that the event being triggered is an `edit` event, whatever that may mean. By passing this event to the dispatcher class, that determines which handlers to call based on what is required from the application. After the dispatcher determines which handler to call (in this case, by checking the values associated with the `$_GET` or `$_POST` array keys), the actual processing of the request is done by the relevant handler, and not by the dispatcher.

The handlers themselves are an exercise in OOP in their own right. Indeed, one effective way to implement individual handlers in your application is to extend a generic parent `handler` class. Using inheritance makes implementing new handlers easy, since the functionality common to all event handlers can be kept hidden away inside the parent class. For example, code to establish database connections can be made available to subclasses of `handler` that may require access to such a connection.

To begin with, we can map the perceived course of actions for this example by drawing the following activity diagram (Figure 10-1).

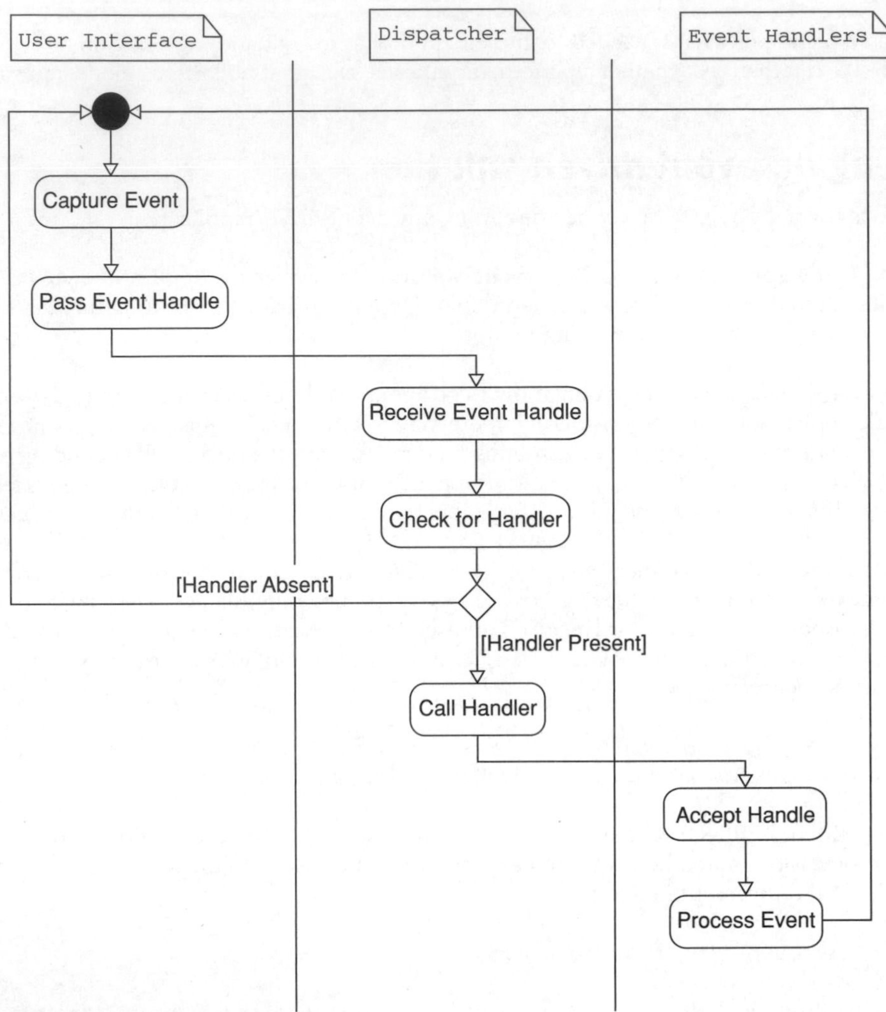

Figure 10-1

This is a pretty simple representation, but for the sake of the example we needn't worry about the niceties behind the implementation. Admittedly, a virtually unlimited number of concerns could well be brought to bear here on the strength of this illustration; security, database, handler registration, and multiple event sources are just some of the valid considerations you might well need to take into account at this stage.

Having said that, you are now equipped with a basic model to work from, so go ahead and look at the class diagram derived from these perceived requirements (Figure 10-2).

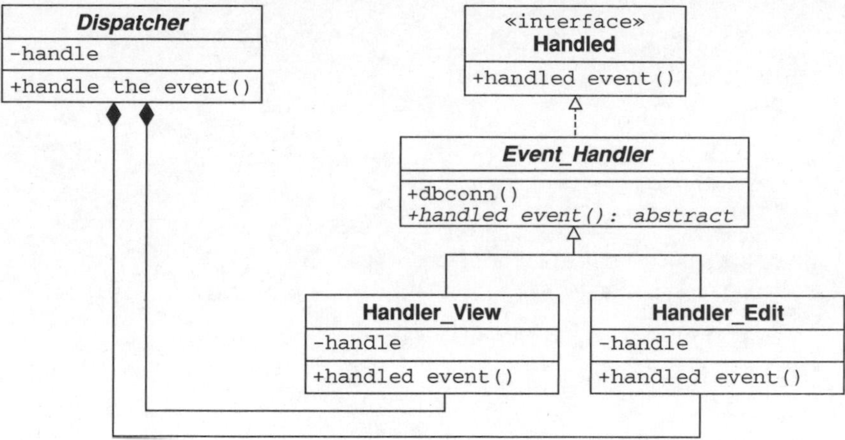

Figure 10-2

There is no need to be too concerned about the code driving the user interface here, because choices concerning such matters are better made by the end-user, not the software architect. Concentrate instead on representing in your class diagram the *dispatcher* and *handlers*. This application provides just the bare bones in terms of functionality; we have concentrated instead on the event-driven paradigm and the advantages derived from using it.

Implementing the solution

Recall from the class diagram that we are making use of an interface to implement each event handler. The use of an interface to enforce the existence of certain methods within each handler is crucial to our example and is good practice in general since it will standardize the way in which your handlers are built. This is important, as your application may grow to the stage at which third-party developers want to add functionality of their own. Having an interface will promote the "plug and play" aspect of your code—or, more simply, make your code more extensible.

Aside from being extensible, there are several other advantages yet to be gained. After presenting the classes in this section, we will look at how easy it is to implement fine-grained security using our model. First, we'll look through the code class by class.

class.Dispatcher.php

To begin with, the code for the `Dispatcher` class looks something like this:

```
<?php
require_once('class.Event_Handler.php');
require_once('class.Handler_View.php');
require_once('class.Handler_Edit.php');
```

```
class Dispatcher
{

    private $handle;

    function __construct($event_handle){
        $this->handle = $event_handle;
    }

    function handle_the_event(){
        $name = "handler_{$this->handle}";
        if (class_exists("$name")){
            $handler_obj = new $name($this->handle);
            $response = $handler_obj->handled_event();
            return $response;
        }else{
            echo "I can't handle this!";
        }
    }
}
?>
```

Crucially, the constructor is responsible for capturing the event handle and retaining it within the class, so that it can be used later to decide what action to take. The event handle may be needed as part of the event handler's processing, so we will pass this value on to any handlers upon which we may call. Of course, the handlers might need additional information, too.

As part of our application, when querying the database for existing records, the user might want to return only records in a certain range. When this crops up, you can simply capture the delimiter parameters as part of the event, as demonstrated in the following URL:

```
http://myserver/interface.php?event=edit&first=2&last=7
```

It is a simple enough job to populate a suitable array (for example, `$event_parameters`) as part of the constructor. These values can then be passed on to the handler, which will use them to return records within only the specified range. We'll stick to simply sending the actual event handle for this example, but you get the picture.

The `handle_the_event()` function relies on you and your development team sticking to a particular naming convention for any new event handler classes. If someone wanted to add functionality to our application, he or she would need to be aware that each handler's name is in the following form:

```
class Handler_(Unique_Event_Handle)
{
    //Handle the event with handle Unique_Event_Handle
}
```

In this case, you have only two event handlers, `Handler_View` and `Handler_Edit`. The `handle_the_event()` method in our dispatcher class checks to see whether the relevant handler exists within the PHP namespace before creating an instance of the pertinent handler object. If not, it confesses:

```
echo "I can't handle this!";
```

Notice that the instantiation of the handler passes the event handle into the constructor, in case it is needed. In the same way, you could pass an array of values here for use in the handler's processing:

```
$handler_obj = new $name($this->handle);
```

We don't want to concern ourselves too much with the action of the handler—we simply want to pass off any information that we collect in the dispatcher to the correct handler without having to worry about what it might actually be doing with that information.

The next step is to call the `handled_event()` method to extract any response from the handler that might have arisen out of its handling of the event:

```
$response = $handler_obj->handled_event();
```

As you have already seen the class diagram, both the existence and precise format of the `handled_event()` function is enforced through the use of an interface. The consequence of this is that the dispatcher can safely call the `handled_event()` method on its instantiated handler to retrieve a response, even if that method simply returns `NULL`. Once the response from the handler, if any, has been returned, the dispatcher's work is done.

We'll now take a look at the handlers' side of things.

interface.Handled.php

The interface ensures that we implement the `handled_event()` function in any handler classes we might developed. As mentioned previously, this is important from the perspective of the dispatcher, but if you do intend to take on larger game, this is where you can enforce the existence of any other important methods which might be relevant to your event handlers. Such methods can then either be implemented in the parent handler and overridden by the children, or simply declared abstract, passing the implementation off to the children handlers directly. As you can see from the interface code below, for our example we've stuck to simply requiring the existence of the `handled_event()` method.

```
<?php
interface Handled
{
   abstract function handled_event();
}
?>
```

The `handled_event()` method itself is implemented either by the parent event handler class for your application, or its children. Let's look first at the parent event handler class.

class.Event_Handler.php

The parent event handler class is really more of a utility class specifying how to handle lower-level events which may occur in your application. In this specific example, it creates a database connection. The `common_db.inc` file contains a `db_connect()` function that creates a database connection—pretty straightforward stuff, and the implementation of such a method is left to you. However, if you are creating an application of any serious magnitude, the best way to approach such a challenge is to make use of a database abstraction layer, as explored in Chapter 8.

Of course, you may consider adding any number of appropriate methods here depending on the nature of the problem you are solving. For now, here's the code for a simple `class.Event_Handler.php`:

```
<?php
require_once ("interface.Handled.php");
require_once('common_db.inc');

abstract class Event_Handler
{
   function dbconn(){
      $link_id = db_connect('sample_db');
      return $link_id;
   }

   abstract function handled_event();
}
?>
```

Since you are unlikely to know what each event is going to do, you declare the `handled_event()` function abstract so that the descendent handler classes can each implement it as they see fit. In order to allow this, you will notice that the whole class has been declared abstract. This has no real bearing on the application itself, because you will never directly instantiate this class—the dispatcher will figure out which descendent event handler to instantiate, and will do so directly.

class.Handler_View.php

This descendent handler gives a quick demonstration of the type of code you can usefully execute within a typical handler. Note how you are forced to give an implementation of `handled_events()`, since this has been declared as an abstract method in the parent handler class. In this case, we have shown how to view a few records pulled straight from a database:

```
<?php
require_once('class.Event_Handler.php');

class handler_View extends Event_Handler
{
   private $handle;

   function __construct($event_handle){
      $this->handle = $event_handle;
   }

   function handled_event(){
      echo "The event, $this->handle, is now handled. <BR>
      It is, I promise!<BR><BR>Your records are as follows: <BR> <BR>";

      $id = parent::dbconn();
      $result = pg_query($id, "SELECT * FROM user");
      while($query_data = pg_fetch_row($result)) {
         echo "'",$query_data[1],"' is a ",$query_data[4],"<br>";
      }
   }
}
?>
```

Of course, the actual data being pulled out of here is irrelevant—this is just an example. If you want to try it out, however, simply hook this up to an example database of your own and query it as you like, changing the SQL statement.

Note that in the constructor, the handler still holds onto the event handle passed to it, by saving it into a local private member variable. It's not actually used in this example, but it does demonstrate that you can get such parameters through to the handlers if necessary.

class.Handler_Edit.php

Let's meet another descendent handler. This demonstration of an edit handler simply returns a message to the user when invoked:

```
<?php
require_once('class.Event_Handler.php');

class handler_Edit extends Event_Handler
{
   private $handle;

   function __construct($event_handle){
      $this->handle = $event_handle;
   }

   function handled_event(){
      echo "This is event $this->handle, which is now handled - no
            kidding! <BR>";
   }
}
?>
```

As usual, you capture the event handle and store it locally. In this case, the handler does actually use it as part of its event processing. Admittedly, the `handled_event()` method implementation is nothing special; it simply returns a message confirming that the event has been dealt with.

That's about it for setting things up. We can now explore how easy it is to modify the application and get great results with little effort.

Implementing security

Assume that you wanted to limit the functionality of the application depending on who was using it—a not uncommon requirement. An application with such a requirement could be something like a wiki, which should allow certain trusted sources to edit whatever they like but limit others to only read, and not change, the content.

First off, have the application create a new session after you have successfully validated the user. You can then populate the session variable with relevant details concerning who the user is; in this case, we have used a session variable containing the user's name. This means that you now have access to the current users' details from virtually anywhere in your application, including from within your event handlers, which your can use this information to determine whether or not to allow the event to take place at all.

Add the following method to each of the descendent event handler classes whose use you wish to restrict. As you can see, the method simply checks the author's name currently held in the session, and if the name being offered isn't acceptable, the method will consider the user unauthorized to perform the requested action:

```
function secure_handler(){
     if ($_SESSION['name'] == "David"){
        $this->handled_event();
     } else {
        echo "Sorry $_SESSION['name'] you are not authorised!";
     }
}
```

To ensure that only the secure method is used when handling the event, you will need to change one line in the dispatcher. Open the file and change this line:

```
$response = $handler_obj->handled_event();
```

to this:

```
$response = $handler_obj->secure_handler();
```

You also need to ensure that you keep to the design principles we first set out by making sure that the the existence of this method in the children handlers is enforced via the use of the interface. This means that the parent handler must at least contain an abstract representation of the `secure_handler()` function.

Add the following line to the interface:

```
abstract function secure_handler();
```

There is no way to know precisely what level of permission each event will require; it may well differ from event to event. Accordingly, the parent event handler does not directly implement the secure handler itself. Instead, much in the same way as the regular handler method we met a few pages ago, it passes responsibility for its implementation to its children, by again declaring the method abstract:

```
abstract function secure_handler();
```

Each descendent event handler is now required to implement both a `handled_event()` and `secure_handler()` method as specified by the interface. To determine whether to allow the event to take place, each event handler's `secure_handler()` method could retrieve its own permission setting from a file held by the administrator. This file would of course be encrypted or at least held somewhere secure, and would most likely be editable by the wiki administrator, such that he or she could change which handlers were available to which users.

Here is a little example user interface that would make use of our secure, event-oriented application:

```
<?php
require_once ('class.Dispatcher.php');
?>
```

```
<HTML>
   <HEAD>
      <TITLE>Secure, Event Driven Record Viewer!</TITLE>
   </HEAD>
   <BODY>
      <FORM method="GET" ACTION="<?=$_SERVER['PHP_SELF']?>">
         <INPUT type="submit" name="event" value="View">
         <INPUT type="submit" name="event" value="Edit">
      </FORM>
   </BODY>
</HTML>

<?php
function handle(){
   $event = $_GET['event'];
   $disp = new dispatcher($event);
   $disp->handle_the_event();
}

session_start();
$_SESSION['name'] = "Horatio";

handle();
?>
```

The session variables would normally be set during the user's login, but for brevity's sake, we will assume that Horatio wants in—hence why we have hard coded this in. By way of example, let's check whether we can allow Horatio to use the edit function. We quite rightly expect the following output if Horatio clicks the `Edit` button: (Figure 10-3).

As you can see, Horatio's attempts to edit records are stopped in their tracks, since only David may edit records.

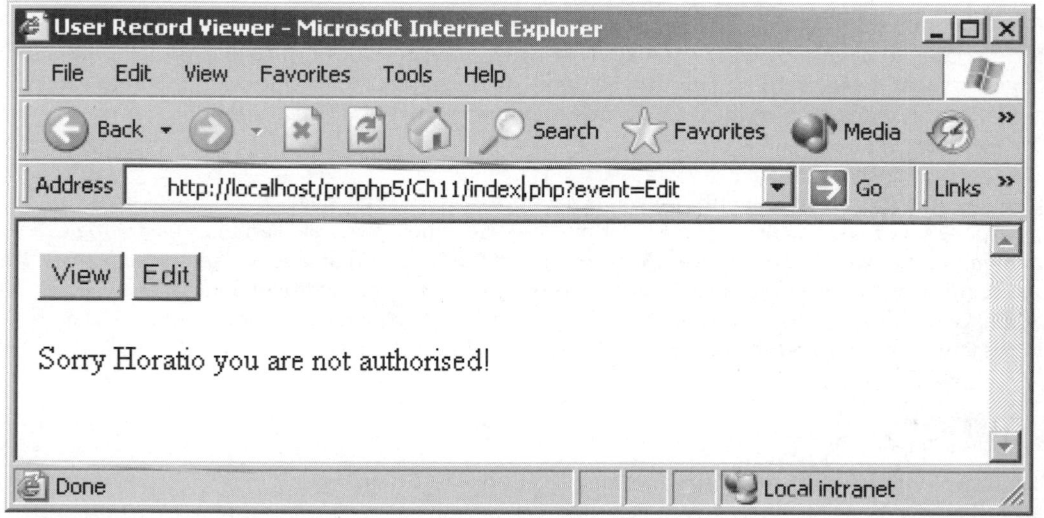

Figure 10-3

The power of this approach should be making itself clearer now. We have looked at security as an example of how easy it is to modify the application, but this approach can apply to any number of new requirements which might come about.

Pause for Thought

Many issues need to be carefully considered when designing a well-architected, enterprise-level, event-driven application. Improvements to our event handling methodology could include some sort of handler registration, for example. This would mean that when a user logs onto a site (logging on, in this case, would be an event captured by the application), the application could automatically check which handlers are available to the user. This is achieved through the use of a default handler, which retrieves a list of the user's permissible handlers from a database and returns that information to the presentation layer.

Armed with this information, the presentation layer would know which buttons to render for the user. The administrator would get many buttons, whereas a visitor might have only one `View` button. If access is restricted to a view button, there is little chance that an untrusted user can maliciously modify anything to which he or she has no access.

A second issue to consider before using this method for your next big contract (albeit closely related to the first) is how to get the dispatcher to include the correct PHP project files in the first place. Because the dispatcher instantiates the event handlers, it needs to have the correct classes included. In our example, we simply included every handler class that we would need. For larger applications this approach would be wasteful because we might be including a hundred classes and using only ever one of them.

One way to rectify this problem is to mark certain handlers as being available by default, with the rest being made available on a per-user basis. Each user stored in the database would have, amongst other properties, a field containing a list of handlers available to that user. This information could be used to automatically include the relevant handlers in the dispatcher at the same time as the relevant buttons are being added to the user interface.

Finally, your various events may be fired by different entities, so you may want to consider adding functionality to determine what entity is invoking that event, and return an appropriate response based largely on that determination. This may be useful, for example, should you want to return some piece of data either in machine-readable XML format or human-readable HTML, depending on which entity has invoked the event.

One design pattern that may interest you is the *reactor pattern*. This deals with multisource enterprise-level event-handling and is definitely worth a look if you are serious about using events. Remember that we mentioned near the beginning of the chapter that a design pattern may exist that fits our requirements? Well, the reactor pattern is very similar to what we have done in this chapter, but has added capabilities to allow your handlers to easily differentiate between event sources. For more information on this, refer to *Pattern-Oriented Software Architecture, Volume 2* (Wiley, ISBN 0-471-60695-2).

Summary

This chapter has served as an introduction to event-driven programming in PHP. You should now have a good idea of how the event-driven paradigm can be implemented using simple object-oriented programming.

Creating an event-driven application is a problem-specific business, and much attention should be paid to the environment in which the intended application is to run. Event-driven programming has applications in many areas of computing, but good candidates are often those programs that have graphical user interfaces.

Finally, we have demonstrated that the power and elegance inherent in object-oriented programming can be effectively complimented by designing applications using an event-driven programming paradigm, such as the one met in this chapter.

In the next chapter, we'll take a look at implementing an effective logging and debugging mechanism in your application, to aid you and your development team during both the development and testing phases of your project.

Logging and Debugging

In every application you build, robust logging and debugging mechanisms can save you hours of effort trying to track down problems that might occur.

Logs can be used to help you analyze historical usage patterns that can't be obtained through the Web server log, such as server load, specific SQL statements that were executed, or application-specific messages that wouldn't otherwise be captured.

A debugging mechanism allows you to examine the values of variables, see which conditional loops are being executed, or otherwise determine the state of the application at runtime without having to litter your code with `print` statements that will need to be deleted before you deploy. After you've worked through the code in this chapter, you'll have a set of classes that should be a part of every project you work on.

Creating a Logging Mechanism

The primary purpose of logging is to allow you to see what the application was doing, or how it was performing, at some time in the past. A properly written log will allow you to do a historical analysis of system behavior to determine whether changes need to be made. Three basic mechanisms exist for capturing this information.

Simple File Logging

The easiest way to handle logging is to write the information to a file. Usually, the user ID from which your Web server process is running does not have the access needed to write to the file system, except for a temporary directory (`/tmp` on most UNIX systems), which isn't necessarily the best location in which to keep important application log files. To allow the Web server user to be able to write to a file, create a dedicated directory in which to store your log files.

Create a folder above the document root of your application called `logs` and ensure that the Web server user has write permissions to this folder (`chmod 744` and `chown nobody` on UNIX systems).

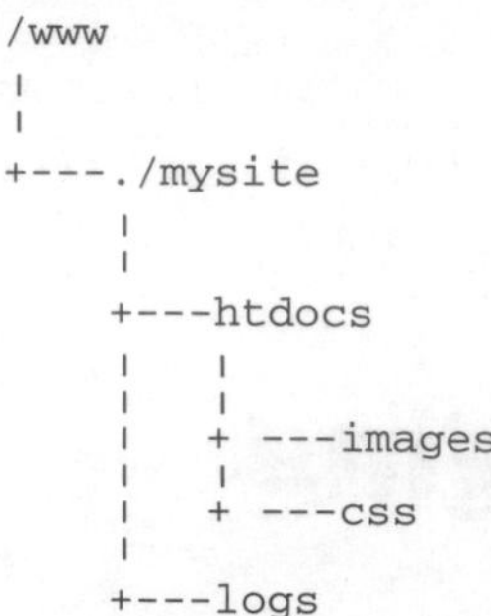

```
/www
|
|
+---./mysite
     |
     |
     +---htdocs
     |    |
     |    |
     |    + ---images
     |    |
     |    + ---css
     |
     +---logs
```

Example File System Layout

To write to a file in PHP, use `fopen()` to get a file handle and specify that you want to open the file for writing. Use `fwrite()` to write data to the file and `fclose()` to close the file. The following code defines and then demonstrates a simple method called `logMessage()`, which uses these basic methods to write to a pre-defined log file.

```
<?php

function logMessage($message) {
  $LOGDIR = '/www/mysite/logs/'; //chmod 744 and chown nobody
  $logFile = $LOGDIR . 'mysite.log';
  $hFile = fopen($logFile, 'a+'); //open for appending, create
                                  //the file if it doesn't exist
  if(! is_resource($hFile)) {
    printf("Unable to open %s for writing. Check file permissions.",
$logFile);
    return false;
  }

  fwrite($hFile, $message);
  fclose($hFile);

  return true;
 }

logMessage("Hello, log!\n");
?>
```

If you run this code and you have all the permissions correctly set on the `$LOGDIR` directory, you should see the message `Hello, log!` in the `mysite.log` file. For the most rudimentary needs, this function might be sufficient, but for a real application, you'll want to track more than just the message. The log should be a machine-parsable file, meaning that you should be able to process the log data using a separate application that analyzes the information held within it. The log should keep track of the date and time of each message, some sense of the severity or importance of the message, and some remark about which module of the application generated the message.

The Logger Class

The class in the following code sample provides an OO mechanism for generating a more detailed log file than that created using the code in the previous section. Create a file called `class.Logger.php`. This file will contain the `Logger` class, which will allow you to write information in a tab-delimited format to a text file on the server, tracking the timestamp, log level (which is the severity of the message), the message itself, and an optional module name. The module name can be any string that helps to identify the part of the application that generated the message. The code for the `Logger` class follows.

```
<?php

 //Log Levels.  The higher the number, the less severe the message
 //Gaps are left in the numbering to allow for other levels
 //to be added later
 define('LOGGER_DEBUG', 100);
 define('LOGGER_INFO', 75);
 define('LOGGER_NOTICE', 50);
 define('LOGGER_WARNING', 25);
 define('LOGGER_ERROR', 10);
 define('LOGGER_CRITICAL', 5);

 class Logger {

   private $hLogFile;
   private $logLevel;

   //Note: private constructor.  Class uses the singleton pattern
   private function __construct() {
     global $cfg;  //system configuration info array from some external file

     $this->logLevel = $cfg['LOGGER_LEVEL'];
     $logFilePath = $cfg['LOGGER_FILE'];

     if(! strlen($logFilePath)) {
       throw new Exception('No log file path was specified ' .
                           'in the system configuration.');
     }

     //Open a handle to the log file.  Suppress PHP error messages.
     //We'll deal with those ourselves by throwing an exception.
     $this->hLogFile = @fopen($logFilePath, 'a+');
     if(! is_resource($this->hLogFile)) {
       throw new Exception("The specified log file $logFilePath " .
                           'could not be opened or created for ' .
                           'writing.  Check file permissions.');
     }

   }

   public function __destruct() {
     if(is_resource($this->hLogFile)) {
       fclose($this->hLogFile);
     }
   }

   public static function getInstance() {
```

```
        static $objLog;

        if(!isset($objLog)) {
          $objLog = new Logger();
        }

        return $objLog;
      }

      public function logMessage($msg, $logLevel = LOGGER_INFO, $module = null) {

        if($logLevel <= $this->logLevel) {
          $time = strftime('%x %X', time());
          $msg = str_replace("\t", '    ', $msg);
          $msg = str_replace("\n", ' ', $msg);

          $strLogLevel = $this->levelToString($logLevel);

          if(isset($module)) {
            $module = str_replace("\t", '    ', $module);
            $module = str_replace("\n", ' ', $module);
          }

          //logs: date/time loglevel message modulename
          //separated by tabs, new line delimited
          $logLine = "$time\t$strLogLevel\t$msg\t$module\n";
          fwrite($this->hLogFile, $logLine);
        }
      }

      public static function levelToString($logLevel) {
        switch ($logLevel) {
          case LOGGER_DEBUG:
            return 'LOGGER_DEBUG';
            break;
          case LOGGER_INFO:
            return 'LOGGER_INFO';
            break;
          case LOGGER_NOTICE:
            return 'LOGGER_NOTICE';
            break;
          case LOGGER_WARNING:
            return 'LOGGER_WARNING';
            break;
          case LOGGER_ERROR:
            return 'LOGGER_ERROR';
            break;
          case LOGGER_CRITICAL:
            return 'LOGGER_CRITICAL';
          default:
            return '[unknown]';
        }
      }
    }

  ?>
```

This class should seem straightforward enough. You'll note you create a private constructor to prevent having to open the file handle several times during the execution of a page request. The `getInstance()` method allows code that will use this class to get an instance of it. This is known as the *singleton* pattern, which you first saw in Chapter 8, "Database Abstraction Layers."

The first few lines of the file establish a number of logging level constants. These constants allow you to control what information gets logged. While developing the first version of an application, for debugging purposes you'll probably want to log quite a bit of information to help you track down bugs. When the application is finally put into production, you'll want to log less information to save on system resources. Logging less information also increases the signal-to-noise ratio, meaning there is more useful information in a given number of lines of log information. When an application is running in a production environment, much of the debugging information you used during development will be of little use when trying to track down problems and will make finding those problems in the log more difficult.

In the constructor, two pieces of information are pulled from a global array of configuration information; the name of the log file, and the current debugging level. For this example, you can assume that there is only one log file per application. Later in this chapter you'll look at ways to extend this class to provide even more functionality and greater flexibility in where information is logged.

Store the logging level in a private member variable that will be used later to determine which information is written to the log file. The log filename is checked to make sure it has a value and that the Web server user can actually open or create the log file for appending. The `a+` parameter to `fopen()` means "open this file for appending and if it doesn't exist, create it." Store the file handle as another private member variable. If for any reason you can't create a valid file handle, the constructor throws an exception.

Any attempt to call `Logger::getInstance()` should be wrapped in a `try...catch` block because of the possibility of failure arising from incorrect permissions on the log file, or lack of disk space on the volume on which it resides. In the event that this happens, the entire application should not cease to work because of the logger. You should catch this exception and take appropriate action, perhaps by sending an e-mail to a systems administrator (see Chapter 14, "Communicating with Users," for a robust e-mailing class you can use).

This class also has a destructor (lines 41–45) that closes the file handle if it is open. If the file path wasn't valid, the file handle will not be a valid resource. Even though the exception was thrown in the constructor, the destructor will still be called when the object is deallocated from memory, so you need to make sure that yet another error isn't generated by trying to close a file handle that was never opened successfully in the first place.

Just as with the `Database` class from Chapter 8, the `getInstance()` method in the `Logger` class has a static variable that will store an instance of the class in between invocations of the `getInstance()` method. The first time the method is called, that variable will be null, resulting in the creation of a new instance of `Logger`. If the log file path is invalid, the exception will bubble up to this method. On subsequent calls to this method, the variable will store the reference created during the first invocation, and that original instance will be returned. Using the singleton pattern here allows you to save the system resources required to open a file handle.

The `logMessage()` method does all the hard work. It takes the message text, the logging level, and an optional module name. If the current system-wide logging level configuration parameter (assigned to the private member variable `$logLevel` in the constructor) is at least as large as the log level specified in the second parameter to this function, an entry in the log file is created. If the current application logging level is less than the level specified in the second parameter, no entry is created. This allows you to control what is or is not entered into the log. For each message sent to the `logMessage()` method, a log level should be supplied indicating the severity of the message. For example, if you're printing just the contents of some variable to the log for debugging purposes, the second parameter to `logMessage()` should be `LOGGER_DEBUG`. Then, when deploying the code to the production server, you should set the `$cfg['LOGGER_LEVEL']` parameter to `LOGGER_WARNING` or higher. This will stop debug messages from being printed to the log, saving CPU cycles and restricting the content in the log to errors of varying severity.

`logMessage()` generates a time stamp on line 60 using PHP's `strftime()` function, which takes a format string as its first parameter and a UNIX timestamp as the second. The format string used in the code sample uses the system default short date representation (`%x`) and the system default time representation (`%X`). On my server, which is located in the United States, an example output from `strftime('%x %X', time())` is "`03/17/2004 03:55:25`" (meaning March 17, 2004, at 3:55:25 in the morning). If your computer is located in other parts of the world, the date representation would be shown appropriately for your location (in this case that would likely mean 17/03/2004). If you want more control over the formatting of the timestamp in the log, see the documentation for the `strftime()` function at `http://www.php.net/strftime`. If your log requires higher time resolution than one second, you can use the `microtime()` function to get milliseconds. Again, see the documentation for more information on how to use this function.

After creating a textual representation of the timestamp, `logMessage()` then needs to do some formatting of the message. Because you want to create a log file that is easily machine readable, separate the fields on each line of the log with a tab (`\t`). Each log entry is separated by a newline character (`\n`). Because of this, you need to remove any tabs or new lines that might exist in the message because these would corrupt the log file and make it difficult to parse with a log analyzer. Replace the tabs with four spaces (the default number of characters occupied by a tab in most text editors) and replace new lines with a space. If the `$module` parameter has a value, the same replacements should be made.

The only other thing of interest that happens here is the conversion of the numeric log level constant to a string. Because PHP sees the constants as their actual numeric value, there is no easy way to convert the name of a constant to a string representation of that constant name. As a result, the string representations are hard-coded into the method `levelToString()`. The `switch` statement loops through the constants and returns the name of the constant. Although the `break` statements are not technically necessary, they are added for clarity's sake. Also not actually necessary is the declaration of this method as static, but because it doesn't depend on any of the member variables and because you may find a need to print the log level in code outside this class, declaring the method static makes it easy to write code like `echo Logger::levelToString($cfg['LOGGER_LEVEL'])`, for example.

The following code sample shows how you might be able to use the `Logger` class in a real application.

```
<?php

require_once('class.Logger.php');

$cfg['LOGGER_FILE'] = '/var/log/myapplication.log';
$cfg['LOGGER_LEVEL'] = LOGGER_INFO;
$log = Logger::getInstance();
```

```
if(isset($_GET['fooid'])) {

  //not written to the log - the log level is too high
  $log->logMessage('A fooid is present', LOGGER_DEBUG);

  //LOG_INFO is the default so this would get printed
  $log->logMessage('The value of fooid is ' .  $_GET['fooid']);

} else {

  //This will also be written, and includes a module name
  $log->logMessage('No fooid passed from ' . $_SERVER['HTTP_REFERER'],
                   LOGGER_CRITICAL,
                   "Foo Module");

  throw new Exception('No foo id!');
}
?>
```

If `$_GET['fooid']` is set, two calls to `logMessage()` are made, but only one message will actually be written to the file because of the configured logging level. The contents of the log will look something like the following:

```
03/17/04 03:58:42      LOGGER_INFO     The value of fooid is 25
```

Here you see the timestamp, the logging level of the message, and the message itself. If `$_GET['fooid']` is not set, you will see the following log entry:

```
03/19/04 05:30:07    LOGGER_CRITICAL  No fooid passed from                ⮐
http://localhost/testLogger.php    Foo Module
```

In this case, the `testLogger.php` page failed to pass `fooid` to the page that invoked the logger, so the `LOGGER_CRITICAL` error was written to the file.

Extending the Logger Class

Logging to a text file is an incredibly useful way to store log data. There are literally thousands of utilities you can use to parse and analyze this data from simple UNIX utilities such as `sed` and `grep` to fancy commercial log analysis software packages costing tens of thousands of dollars. But sometimes a text file isn't the most convenient storage medium. You might want to use a relational database or integrate with your platform's system logger to centralize all your application logs. Additionally, the `Logger` class as developed thus far is capable of writing only to a single file no matter where in the application it is invoked. There are several circumstances in which you might want to keep separate logs for different sections of an application or of different tasks performed. In this section, you'll extend the `Logger` class to be able to integrate with any data storage medium and support multiple logs in a single application.

In Chapter 8, "Database Abstraction Layers," you learned how the `PEAR DB` class can connect to a completely different database backend by a simple change to its connection string. By connecting with `"mysql://root@localhost/mydb"`, you can connect to a MySQL database running on the local machine using the username "root" and connecting to the database called "mydb". To connect to a PostgreSQL database, the connection string looks like "pgsql://postgres@localhost/yourdb", which connects to a PostgreSQL database cluster on the local machine, authenticates as the user postgres, and connects to the database called "yourdb". After a connection has been established using this common connection string syntax, everything else about the use of the DB class is identical, regardless of which RDBMS you're connected to. You can use a very similar construct to allow your Logger class to connect to any kind of storage medium.

The goal of the enhanced Logger class is to use a similar syntax for establishing a connection to a storage medium for log data. Because you'll be able to use different storage media, you should also be able to store different logs for different parts of the application. The new Logger class should support some sort of "registry" of log connections. For example, you should be able to have a log called "errors" and one called "queries," which will store error messages and SQL statements, respectively. The following sample code represents what you should be able to do with the redesigned class:

```
<?php

Logger::register('errors', 'file:///var/log/error.log');
Logger::register('app,
                 'pgsql://postgres@db/errors?table=applog&timestamp=dtlog&' .
                                              'msg=smesg&level=slevel&module
                                                  =smod');

$objQLog = Logger::getInstance('queries');

$sql = "SELECT * FROM foo";
$objQLog->logMessage("Selecting all foos");

try {
  Database->getInstance()->select($sql);
} catch (DBQueryException $e) {
   $objErrLog = Logger::getInstance('errors');
   $objErrLog->logMessage($e->getMessage(), LOGGER_CRITICAL);
}
?>
```

Showing this code before showing the new class that drives it may be a little confusing, but sometimes it's easier to design a class by first knowing how you want to be able to use it. In a real application you would put the first two lines in a globally included file. These two lines establish two different logs, called app and errors. The app log will store its log messages in a PostgreSQL database, in a table called applog using the field names specified for the timestamp, message, logging level, and module. The error log will be a text file located in /var/log/error.log. In the main part of the application, you would store most messages in the app log for later analysis. Any errors that occur will be stored in the errors log, which is a text file. We use a text file for the errors because one of the errors may be an inability to connect to the database.

Parsing the Connection String

The first step toward creating the new Logger class is to be able to parse strings of the form scheme://user:password@host:port/path?query#fragment. Luckily, PHP provides us with an incredibly handy function for doing just that. The parse_url() function takes a string in this general form and returns an array containing the elements from the URL that exist (the array keys are the same as the names used in the previous string). If one or more of the elements do not exist, no item with that key is added to the array (as opposed to having a null entry for that key). For example:

```
$url = "ftp://anonymous@ftp.gnu.org:21/pub/gnu/gcc"
$arParts = parse_url($url);
var_dump($arParts);

//print out:
Array (
    [scheme] => ftp
    [user] => anonymous
    [host] => ftp.gnu.org
    [port] => 21
    [path] => /pub/gnu/gcc
)
```

Note that the password, query, and fragment keys do not appear in the array, because they do not appear in the URL.

Redesigning Logger to Use the Connection String

As does PEAR DB, `Logger` will use the `scheme` part of this array to determine which logging backend to use. The `register()` method will be used to establish a new connection and will take a canonical name and a URL as parameters. Because the `register()` method was statically invoked in the sample code, you'll need to use some sort of intermediate function that will allow both the `register()` and `getInstance()` methods to talk to the same set of information. The following code shows the new `register()` method and the reworked `getInstance()` and constructor. In fact, this code sample represents the entirety of the new `Logger` class. The parts that have changed are highlighted.

```
<?php

//Log Levels.  The higher the number, the less severe the message
//Gaps are left in the numbering to allow for other levels
//to be added later
define('LOGGER_DEBUG', 100);
define('LOGGER_INFO', 75);
define('LOGGER_NOTICE', 50);
define('LOGGER_WARNING', 25);
define('LOGGER_ERROR', 10);
define('LOGGER_CRITICAL', 5);

class Logger {

  private $hLogFile;
  private $logLevel;

  //Note: private constructor.  Class uses the singleton pattern
  private function __construct() {

  }

  public static function register($logName, $connectionString) {
    $urlData = parse_url($connectionString);
```

```
  if(! isset($urlData['scheme'])) {
    throw new Exception("Invalid log connection string $connectionString");
  }

  include_once('Logger/class.' . $urlData['scheme'] . 'LoggerBackend.php');

  $className = $urlData['scheme'] . 'LoggerBackend';
  if(! class_exists($className)) {
    throw new Exception('No logging backend available for ' .
                        $urlData['scheme']);
  }

  $objBack = new $className($urlData);

  Logger::manageBackends($logName, $objBack);
}

public static function getInstance($name) {
  return Logger::manageBackends($name);
}

private static function manageBackends($name, LoggerBackend
   $objBack = null) {static $backEnds;

  if(! isset($backEnds)) {
    $backEnds = array();
  }

  if(! isset($objBack)) {
    //we must be retrieving
    if(isset($backEnds[$name])) {
      return $backEnds[$name];
     } else {
      throw new Exception("The specified backend $name was not " .
                          "registered with Logger.");
     }

   } else {
     //we must be adding
    $backEnds[$name] = $objBack;
   }
}
 public static function levelToString($logLevel) {
  switch ($logLevel) {
    case LOGGER_DEBUG:
      return 'LOGGER_DEBUG';
      break;
    case LOGGER_INFO:
      return 'LOGGER_INFO';
      break;
    case LOGGER_NOTICE:
      return 'LOGGER_NOTICE';
      break;
```

```
                case LOGGER_WARNING:
                  return 'LOGGER_WARNING';
                  break;
                case LOGGER_ERROR:
                  return 'LOGGER_ERROR';
                  break;
                case LOGGER_CRITICAL:
                  return 'LOGGER_CRITICAL';
                default:
                  return '[unknown]';
              }
            }
          }

          ?>
```

In the preceding code, `Logger` pulls in the file that defines an abstract class called `LoggerBackend`, which serves as the base class for the classes that will do the actual work of writing to a given logging mechanism. `Logger`'s constructor is now empty but is still declared to be private to prevent its instantiation outside the `getInstance()` method.

The new static method `register()` is responsible for instantiating a `LoggingBackend` object based on the scheme part of the URL specified in the second parameter. To do so, it makes a call to `parse_url()` to determine the scheme. If no scheme was present in the URL, `register()` throws an exception. If the scheme is present, an attempt is made to `include_once` a filed called `Logger/class.[scheme]LoggerBackend.php`, and the class contained therein is instantiated by passing the `$urlData` array.

If the specified `LoggerBackend` class is properly instantiated, the new instance is passed, along with the canonical name specified in the first parameter to `register()` to the private function `manageBackends()`. This function exists because all public methods of `Logger` are now static. As a result, the class can't use any member variables to store the instantiated backend objects. `manageBackends()` contains a static variable that takes the place of a class member. If the function has two parameters, it stores the `LoggerBackend` object in the `$backEnds` array using the `$name` parameter as a key. If only one parameter is specified (the `$name` parameter), `manageBackends()` returns the `LoggerBackend` object stored in `$name`, if one exists.

The new `getInstance()` method no longer returns a `Logger` object but instead returns an instantiated `LoggerBackend`. It does so by calling `manageBackends()` with only one parameter, the canonical name of the particular log requested. If the named log wasn't previously registered, or was unable to be instantiated during `register()`, `manageBackends()` throws an exception that will bubble up to `getInstance()`.

The LoggerBackend Class

The `manageBackends()`, `register()`, and `getInstance()` methods all interact with `LoggerBackend` objects. This class provides a concrete constructor (a construct that exists and is callable) and an abstract method called `logMesage()`, which you probably remember from the original `Logger` class. The latter method is unchanged in number and type of parameters from the code we saw previously. However, in the `LoggerBackend` class, the `logMessage()` method is abstract—no actual function body exists, just the declaration of a function that must be implemented by classes that inherit from LoggerBackend. The constructor of the class takes the array output from parse_url() and stores it in a protected member variable. No other methods are defined by the LoggerBackend class. Save the following as Logger/class.LoggerBackend.php.

```
<?php
abstract class LoggerBackend {
  protected $urlData;

  public function __construct($urlData) {
    $this->urlData = $urlData;
  }

  abstract function logMessage($message, $logLevel = LOGGER_INFO, $module);
}
?>
```

The class itself should be declared abstract because it contains one abstract method and because there is no practical use for an instance of LoggerBackend. Only the subclasses of LoggerBackend will do any real work.

Subclassing LoggerBackend

To make the new and improved Logger class be able to do anything, you'll need to create at least one subclass of LoggerBackend. Because we already had some code that will log information to a file, this will be the easiest LoggerBackend subclass to create first.

Create a file called class.fileLoggerBackend.php (pay attention to capitalization in the filename) and enter the following code:

```
<?php

require_once('Logger/class.LoggerBackend.php');

class fileLoggerBackend extends LoggerBackend {

  private $logLevel;
  private $hLogFile;

  public function __construct($urlData) {
    global $cfg;  //system configuration info array from some external file

    parent::__construct($urlData);

    $this->logLevel = $cfg['LOGGER_LEVEL'];

    $logFilePath = $this->urlData['path'];
    if(! strlen($logFilePath)) {
      throw new Exception('No log file path was specified ' .
                          'in the connection string.');
    }
```

```
    //Open a handle to the log file.  Suppress PHP error messages.
    //We'll deal with those ourselves by throwing an exception.
    $this->hLogFile = @fopen($logFilePath, 'a+');
    if(! is_resource($this->hLogFile)) {
      throw new Exception("The specified log file $logFilePath " .
                          'could not be opened or created for ' .
                          'writing.  Check file permissions.');
    }

  }

  public function logMessage($msg, $logLevel = LOGGER_INFO, $module = null) {
    if($logLevel <= $this->logLevel) {
      $time = strftime('%x %X', time());
      $msg = str_replace("\t", '    ', $msg);
      $msg = str_replace("\n", ' ', $msg);

      $strLogLevel = Logger::levelToString($logLevel);

      if(isset($module)) {
        $module = str_replace("\t", '    ', $module);
        $module = str_replace("\n", ' ', $module);
      }

      //logs: date/time loglevel message modulename
      //separated by tabs, new line delimited
      $logLine = "$time\t$strLogLevel\t$msg\t$module\n";
      fwrite($this->hLogFile, $logLine);
    }
  }

}
?>
```

Much of this code should look familiar to you. It comes nearly verbatim from the original `Logger` class. The `fileLoggerBackend` class will respond to logs registered with the `file://` scheme. It writes the log to the file specified in the `path` component of the `parse_url()` array. To register a log of this type, the URL should be something like `file:///var/log/app.log`. Note that these components are `file://` (ending in two forward slashes) and `/var/log/app.log` (starting with one forward slash). There are three initial forward slashes in the `file` scheme.

To use this backend, you can write code like the following (just like what you saw at the beginning of this section):

```
<?php
Logger::register('app', 'file:///var/log/applog.log');
$log = Logger::getInstance('app');
$log->logMessage('This is a new log message!', LOGGER_CRITICAL, 'test');
?>
```

This registers a `fileLoggerBackend` with the `Logger` class called 'app', which writes to the file `/var/log/applog.log`.

Logging to a Database Table

We can use this same process of subclassing LoggerBackend to create a mechanism for logging to any conceivable data repository. The following code shows a PostgreSQL backend, but the same principles can be used to log to any database platform.

This class has a significantly longer constructor. The connection parameters and the names of the fields in the database to which the information gets written should all be representable in the connection string with sensible defaults for those items that can be optional. As a result, the code must check to see whether certain values are set before building up connection strings and field names. None of this code is very interesting but we include all of it here to show how to parse the connection string to allow a flexible PostgreSQL logging mechanism. This code should be saved in `Logger/class.pgsqlLoggerBackend.php`.

```
<?php

require_once('Logger/class.LoggerBackend.php');

class pgsqlLoggerBackend extends LoggerBackend {

  private $logLevel;
  private $hConn;

  private $table = 'logdata';
  private $messageField = 'message';
  private $logLevelField = 'loglevel';
  private $timestampField = 'logdate';
  private $moduleField = 'module';

  public function __construct($urlData) {
    global $cfg;  //system configuration info array from some external file

    parent::__construct($urlData);

    $this->logLevel = $cfg['LOGGER_LEVEL'];

    $host = $urlData['host'];
    $port = $urlData['port'];
    $user = $urlData['user'];
    $password = $urlData['password'];
    $arPath = explode('/', $urlData['path']);
    $database = $arPath[1];

    if(!strlen($database)) {
      throw new Exception('pgsqlLoggerBackend: Invalid connection string.' .
                          ' No database name was specified');
    }

    $connStr = '';
    if($host) {
      $connStr .= "host=$host ";
    }

    if($port) {
```

```
      $connStr .= "port=$port ";
    }

    if($user) {
      $connStr .= "user=$user ";
    }

    if($password) {
      $connStr .= "password=$password ";
    }

    $connStr .= "dbname=$database";

    //Suppress native errors.  We'll handle them with an exception
    $this->hConn = pg_connect($connStr);

    if(! is_resource($this->hConn)) {
      throw new Exception("Unable to connect to the database using $connStr");
    }

    //Take the query string in the form var=foo&bar=blah
    //and convert it to an array like
    // array('var' => 'foo', 'bar' => 'blah')
    //Be sure to convert urlencoded values
    $queryData = $urlData['query'];
    if(strlen($queryData)) {
      $arTmpQuery = explode('&',$queryData);

      $arQuery = array();
      foreach($arTmpQuery as $queryItem) {
        $arQueryItem = explode('=', $queryItem);
        $arQuery[urldecode($arQueryItem[0])] = urldecode($arQueryItem[1]);
      }
    }

    //None of these items is mandatory.  The defaults are established in the
    //private member declarations at the top of the class.
    //These variables establish the name of the table and the names of
      the fields
    //within that table that store the various elements of the log entry.
    if(isset($arQuery['table'])) {
      $this->table = $arQuery['table'];
    }

    if(isset($arQuery['messageField'])) {
      $this->messageField = $arQuery['messageField'];
    }

    if(isset($arQuery['logLevelField'])) {
      $this->logLevelField = $arQuery['logLevelField'];
    }

    if(isset($arQuery['timestampField'])) {
      $this->timestampField = $arQuery['timestampField'];
    }
```

```
    if(isset($arQuery['moduleField'])) {
      $this->logLevelField = $arQuery['moduleField'];
    }

  }


  public function logMessage($msg, $logLevel = LOGGER_INFO, $module = null) {

    if($logLevel <= $this->logLevel) {
      $time = strftime('%x %X', time());

      $strLogLevel = Logger::levelToString($logLevel);

      $msg = pg_escape_string($msg);

      if(isset($module)) {
        $module = "'" . pg_escape_string($module) . "'";
      } else {
        $module = 'NULL';
      }

      $arFields = array();
      $arFields[$this->messageField] = "'" . $msg . "'";
      $arFields[$this->logLevelField] = $logLevel;
      $arFields[$this->timestampField] = "'". strftime('%x %X', time()) . "'";
      $arFields[$this->moduleField] = $module;

      $sql = 'INSERT INTO ' . $this->table;
      $sql .= ' (' . join(', ', array_keys($arFields)) . ')';
      $sql .= ' VALUES (' . join(', ', array_values($arFields)) . ')';

      pg_exec($this->hConn, $sql);

    }
  }

}
?>
```

In the constructor, the class parses out the query part of the URL to determine the table name and the names of the fields in which the log information is stored. The assumption is that the table will be created using a SQL statement like the following. The field names don't matter because they're configurable in the connection string, but the data types in your table should be the same (or should be compatible data types).

```
create table logdata (
   message text,
   loglevel smallint,
   logdate timestamp,
   module varchar(255)
 );
```

To use the new PostgreSQL logger, the code should look something like the following:

```
<?php

$cfg['LOGGER_LEVEL'] = LOGGER_INFO;

Logger::register('app', 'pgsql://steve@localhost/mydb?table=logdata');

$log = Logger::getInstance('app');

if(isset($_GET['fooid'])) {

  //not written to the log — the log level is too high
  $log->logMessage('A fooid is present', LOGGER_DEBUG);

  //LOG_INFO is the default, so this would get printed
  $log->logMessage('The value of fooid is ' .  $_GET['fooid']);

} else {

  //This will also be written and includes a module name
  $log->logMessage('No fooid passed from ' . $_SERVER['HTTP_REFERER'],
                   LOGGER_CRITICAL,
                   "Foo Module");

  throw new Exception('No foo id!');
}
?>
```

The connection string passed to `Logger::register()` specifies a log called `app` that connects to a PostgreSQL database running on `localhost`. The `LoggerBackend` connects as the user `steve` to the database called `mydb`. The table into which the log entries are written is called `logdata`. Had we not specified any of these parameters, the defaults declared as the class's private member variables would have been used. Of course, this backend can easily be modified to support any type of database for which there is a PHP module, including MySQL and SQL Server.

Creating a Debugging Mechanism

Although a logging mechanism as robust as the one you just created has nearly infinite possibilities for flexibility and storage, sometimes it's far more convenient to print debugging messages to the browser window rather than have to pore through a big log file. But just as the `Logger` class was meant to prevent having dozens of `print` statements that have to be manually deleted prior to deployment, the debugging mechanism allows the developer to print messages to the screen in such a way that they can easily be removed at deploy time.

The `Debugger` class stores the debug messages in the session, then prints them out at the bottom of a screen at the end of a page request. This centralizes debug output into one location on the screen, making it easier to find the specific output for which you're looking. It also enables you to print large amounts of data without disturbing the structure of the user interface, and makes suppressing the debug output easy.

The reason we store this information in the session is that not every page request generates output. For example, when saving information to the database by posting a form, you should usually issue a 302 redirect to prevent data modification when a user presses the reload button on his or her browser. A 302 redirect refers to the HTTP response code issued by the browser when you issue code like `header('Location: [url]')`.

`Debugger` has two primary functions. The debug function writes code to the debug array in the session with an optional key and debug level. The debug level works just like the logging level in the logger class. The lower the logging level value, the higher its priority. The second function is called `debug_print` and should be invoked at the bottom of every page that generates output. It takes the array from the session and generates an HTML table containing the contents of the array. When it's done printing, it removes the information from the session. In this way, page requests that do not generate output will still have their debugging information preserved.

The code for this class is as follows. Call this `class.Debugger.php`:

```
<?php

define('DEBUG_INFO', 100);
define('DEBUG_SQL', 75);
define('DEBUG_WARNING', 50);
define('DEBUG_ERROR', 25);
define('DEBUG_CRITICAL', 10);

class Debugger {

  public static function debug($data, $key = null, $debugLevel = DEBUG_INFO) {
    global $cfg;

    if(! isset($_SESSION['debugData'])) {
      $_SESSION['debugData'] = array();
    }

    if($debugLevel <= $cfg['DEBUG_LEVEL']) {
      $_SESSION['debugData'][$key] = $data;
    }
  }

  public static function debugPrint() {

    $arDebugData = $_SESSION['debugData'];
    print Debugger::printArray($arDebugData);

    $_SESSION['debugData'] = array();

  }

  function printArray($var, $title = true) {

    $string = '<table border="1">';
    if ($title) {
        $string .= "<tr><td><b>Key</b></td><td><b>Value</b></td></tr>\n";
    }

    if (is_array($var)) {
```

```
        foreach($var as $key => $value) {

            $string .= "<tr>\n" ;
            $string .= "<td><b>$key</b></td><td>";

            if (is_array($value)) {
                $string .= Debugger::printArray($value, false);
            } elseif(gettype($value) == 'object') {
                $string .= "Object of class " . get_class($value);
            } else {
                $string .= "$value" ;
            }

            $string .= "</td></tr>\n";
        }
    }

    $string .= "</table>\n";
    return $string;
  }

}
?>
```

The five constants defined at the top of the file define debugging levels that work in exactly the same way as the logging level constants in `class.Logger.php`. The `debug()` method expects to find an array called `$cfg` in the global namespace that contains an element `DEBUG_LEVEL` which defines the current debug level for the whole application.

By default, the debug level is `DEBUG_INFO`, though the third parameter of `debug()` allows you to set it to any level. In this way, you can display as much or as little debugging information as you want by simply altering `$cfg['DEBUG_LEVEL']`.

The `$key` parameter is an option label for the information in the debugging array. Though it is second in the parameter list, it will appear in the leftmost column of the table that is eventually produced by `debugPrint()`.

The `debugPrint()` function just passes the debug information from the session to the `printArray()` method, which does all the real heavy lifting. After printing the debug information, `debugPrint()` then blows out the session array to clear the debug information for the next page view.

`printArray()` takes an array of at least one dimension and prints an HTML table that shows the contents of that array. Multidimensional arrays are properly handled. Objects have only their class name printed.

The following code shows how this class is used:

```
<?php

  require_once('class.Debugger.php');

  $cfg = array();
```

```
    $cfg['DEBUG_LEVEL'] = DEBUG_INFO;

    $myData = array();
    $myData[] = 'hello';
    $myData[] = array('name' => 'Bob',
                'colors' => array('red', 'green', 'blue'));

    Debugger::debug($myData, 'my data');

    $x = 5 + 8;
    Debugger::debug($x, 'x');

    Debugger::debugPrint();

?>
```

This example is easier to appreciate from Figure 11-1 which shows the output from the `debugPrint()` function as rendered on the screen.

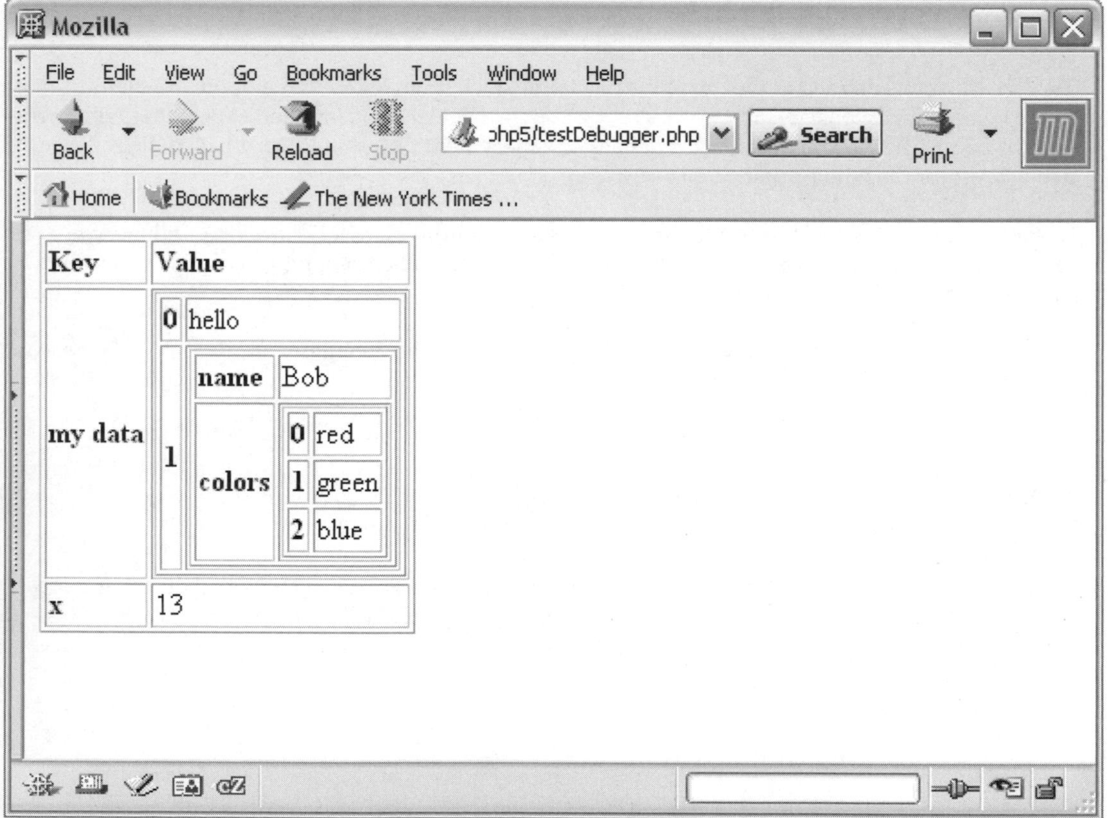

Figure 11-1

Summary

The `Logger` class can be extended to support logging information to virtually any conceivable data repository. Just create and use the backend that best supports your needs. For most uses, the `fileLoggerBackend` class should be the most appropriate, but there are some definite advantages to using a database.

The `Debugger` class gives you functionality similar to the `Logger` class but allows the information to be displayed on the screen and stored in the session for display, even if the original page request contains no output.

In the next chapter, you'll meet SOAP—Simple Object Access Protocol—and learn how PHP5 is just perfect for writing both clients and servers that take advantage of this protocol.

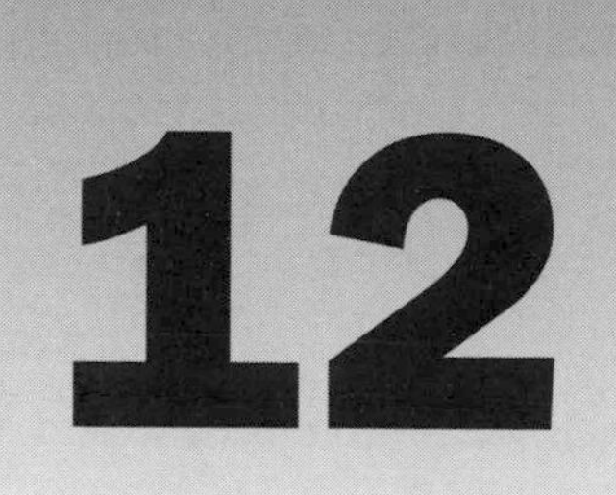

SOAP

It is becoming more apparent these days that applications can no longer live in a vacuum, but are instead required to interact with other systems in some way or another. There isn't one great big chunk of code on a mainframe computer dealing with absolutely everything anyone could need. Phrases like "loosely coupled" and "code-reuse" are winning the day because they make it easy for developers to effectively "piggy-back" a ride on the work of others—or, at the very least, separate and isolate different functionalities, making it easier to modify or maintain their code.

Code reuse implies that once something is done, we don't need to reinvent it. Instead, we ask the inventors nicely if we can incorporate their work into our own project. Looking at this phenomenon from a pragmatic point of view, we can see the results of this decoupling of functionality, and code reuse, evidenced by the multitude of Web Services that are present on the Internet.

Of course, part of not reinventing the wheel each time you need to accomplish something means that communicating with legacy systems is also necessary now and then, and quite a lot of work has and is being done to ensure seamless communication between older systems and the new ones being rolled out.

The upshot of this distributed, loosely coupled architecture and design paradigm is that communication is more important than ever. Whatever the communication needs of modern systems are, it is a safe bet that somewhere along the line XML will come into play as the transport medium of choice—and if that is not quite true now, it will be true soon enough.

XML is a huge topic and we don't cover it in great detail here. We assume that you have a basic knowledge of XML in order to use this chapter. And if you're not familiar with XML but would like a good grounding, you might want to take a look at *Beginning XML, 3rd Edition* (Wiley, ISBN 0-7645-7077-3). However, having already advocated the use of XML as a mechanism for allowing applications to communicate with one another, we spend this chapter looking at how SOAP (Simple Object Access Protocol) can be used to implement XML based communications in PHP5.

SOAP and PHP5

SOAP is a messaging protocol that is platform agnostic and happy to use a variety of Internet protocols such as HTTP, SMTP, and even MIME. We already know that it makes use of XML as part of its information exchange methodology, and the only other thing we need to note here is that WSDL (Web Service Description Language) is also used to make our lives easier by describing how we can use the services that are to be accessed by SOAP. We discuss WSDL, as well as all other aspects of SOAP, in more detail a little later on in the chapter.

But what does SOAP do? The simple answer is that it allows us to pass structured, typed data in a decentralized, distributed environment. Perhaps we should clarify how astounding this is. The second we can pass information from one platform to another at will, we effectively drop the boundaries of communication between heterogeneous platforms and systems—a veritable babel fish (see *The Hitchhiker's Guide to the Galaxy* by Douglas Adams) for computers.

PHP5, not to be left behind, provides several different libraries for implementing SOAP. They are as follows:

- The PHP5 SOAP extension: Bundled with PHP5
- PEAR::SOAP: `http://pear.php.net/package/SOAP`
- ezSOAP: `http://ez.no`
- NuSOAP: `http://dietrich.ganx4.com/nusoap`

Depending on what you feel most comfortable with, you can pick and choose which you would like to go for. However, for the purposes of this chapter we look only at the use of the SOAP extension that comes bundled with PHP5.

The PHP5 SOAP Extension

As of this writing you have to manually write in the SOAP extension to the `php.ini` file, `extension=php_soap.dll`, for Windows, or compile with `--enable-soap` for Linux versions. Please be aware that this may change, so keep an eye on the documentation.

There are a couple of things to note with regards to configuring SOAP in PHP5. One of the biggest drawbacks to using SOAP is that you really end up relying on the speed of your connection because the SOAP client making the request needs to first download the WSDL document in order to know how to make a function call to the target service. Obviously, downloading a file over a slow connection or, perhaps more important, one with a high latency ("ping time"), could present the greatest bottleneck in terms of the time taken for a given task to be executed.

The solution is provided in the form of PHP configuration settings, which allow you to specify whether you want to cache WSDL pages, where you want them to be cached to, and how long you want to use that cached copy of the files. This means that your application's execution time is "charged" only once in order to download the WSDL; from then on, you use the cached version.

If you think that this will significantly enhance the performance of your application, you can go ahead and add the following lines to your `php.ini` file (substituting whatever values you deem necessary):

```
; SOAP

;Boolean paramater to indicate whether caching should occur
soap.wsdl_cache_enabled = "1"

;directory where files are to be cached
soap.wsdl_cache_dir = "/usr/local/php/wsdlcache"

;time, given in seconds, to use the cached copy - ttl = time to live
soap.wsdl_cache_ttl = "1000"
```

The functions provided with PHP5 can nominally be divided into three categories. The main two are `SoapClient` and `SoapServer` functions, with the other category handling miscellaneous functions. We discuss each one briefly in the next few sections, but for more comprehensive coverage, see the documentation at `http://www.php.net/manual/en/ref.soap.php`.

SoapClient Functions

In keeping with all things object oriented, available SOAP functions are exposed through the use of SOAP objects, and you can instantiate a generic `SoapClient` object to work with as follows:

```
$client = new SoapClient (mixed wsdl [, array options]);
```

The first parameter can take either the null value (if you aren't using WSDL), or the Uniform Resource Identifier (URI) of the WSDL document to be used. The `options` parameter that follows should be passed as an array, and can be used to give proxy settings or stipulate the SOAP specification to which the SOAP client should adhere. For example, to create a SOAP client that uses encoded SOAP messages and RPC style, you can say:

```
$client = new SoapClient(null,
   array('location' => "http://localhost/my_soap.php",
   'uri' => "http://my_uri/",
   'style' => SOAP_RPC, 'use' => SOAP_ENCODED));
```

After you have the SOAP client instantiated, you have a number of methods provided by PHP5 that you can call in the resulting client object. They are as follows:

- `__call`: Use this to make a SOAP call directly. Most times you can simply call the SOAP functions as a `SoapClient` method, but this may come in handy for transmitting SOAP headers and footers, for example.
- `__getFunctions`: Exposes the functions provided by a given Web Service.
- `__getLastRequest`: As the name implies, you can retrieve the previous request made by the SOAP client, but only if your `SoapClient` instance was created with the `trace` option set to true in the `options` array parameter.
- `__getLastResponse`: Again, you can use this to determine the previous response received by the SOAP client, again provided that your `SoapClient` has the `trace` option enabled.
- `__getTypes`: This will return a list of SOAP types (i.e., structures and objects defined and implemented by the Web Service) and can be used only if your `SoapClient` was instantiated in WSDL mode (i.e. supplied with a WSDL URI as its first argument).

We discuss how to create and use a SOAP client in some detail a little later but, for the moment, we'll continue to explore the other SOAP functionality provided by PHP5.

SoapServer Functions

Of course, accessing information from a client is not the only way developers use SOAP. Providing the server is high up on the Web Service to-do list, and PHP5 provides some methods to create SOAP servers.

As with the `SoapClient`, you have a constructor that can be used to create the `SoapServer` object as follows:

```
$server = new SoapServer (mixed wsdl [, array options])
```

You can either specify the WSDL document to use in the first parameter, or leave it as null. If the first option is null, you have to set the `uri` option as part of the options array in much the same way as the `SoapClient`. The server methods available are the following:

- `addFunction`: Allows functions to be added to service SOAP requests.
- `getFunctions`: Returns a list of the functions available on the server.
- `handle`: Takes values either from the single `soap_request` parameter or, in its absence, the global variable `$HTTP_RAW_POST_DATA` and deals with the given request, returning a response to the client.
- `setClass`: Allows PHP methods (and entire classes) to be added to the server in order to handle SOAP requests.
- `setPersistence`: Assuming that you have used `setClass` to add the server's functionality, this can be used to perpetuate data between requests in a session.

Miscellaneous Functions

The final few SOAP functions deal with a couple of different issues, the most important of which is exception handling. You can create a `SoapFault` object to return fault responses from the server as follows:

```
$fault = new SoapFault (string faultcode, string faultstring [, string
faultactor [, mixed detail [, string faultname [, mixed headerfault]]]]);
```

If a `SoapClient` has its `exceptions` option set to 0, the requested method will return the `SoapFault` object on any failure. With this in mind, you can use the following function (just a function, not part of any class) to test whether a function call failed:

```
is_soap_fault ($methodresult)
```

This returns true if the result parameter passed in is in fact an instance of the `SoapFault` object.

Apart from these exception-related issues, PHP5's SOAP extension also implements the `SoapVar` object, which can be used to set type properties when not in WSDL mode. It is instantiated like this:

```
$type = new SoapVar ( mixed data, int encoding [, string type_name [, string
type_namespace [, string node_name [, string node_namespace]]]]);
```

SoapHeader, as the name implies, allows you to pass raw SOAP headers between client and server. This can be done from either the `__call()` or `handle()` functions:

```
client->__call("myFunction", null, null,
  new SoapHeader('http://thenamespace.org/mynamespace/', 'myExample',
  'an example'));
```

Finally, you are also given the `SoapParam` object to pass name and value pairs as SOAP parameters from clients that are not in WSDL mode. For example, to supply parameters to a SOAP server's method call, you can say something like:

```
$client->__call ("getSoapMethod", array(new SoapParam($value, "name")));
```

With that, you now have a brief idea of how the first bundled SOAP extension goes about using SOAP. You can use this to create an example SOAP client as well as a simple SOAP server, as discussed near the end of the chapter.

Making a SOAP Client

As luck would have it, several demo Web Service servers exist on the Internet, many of which are free to use. You'll hook the SOAP client up to one of these. You need to know a few things to get things working properly. For a start, the address of Web site hosting the demo servers would be helpful: `http://www.xmethods.com/`. Navigate to this page in your browser and go to the bottom of the page. You should see something like Figure 12-1.

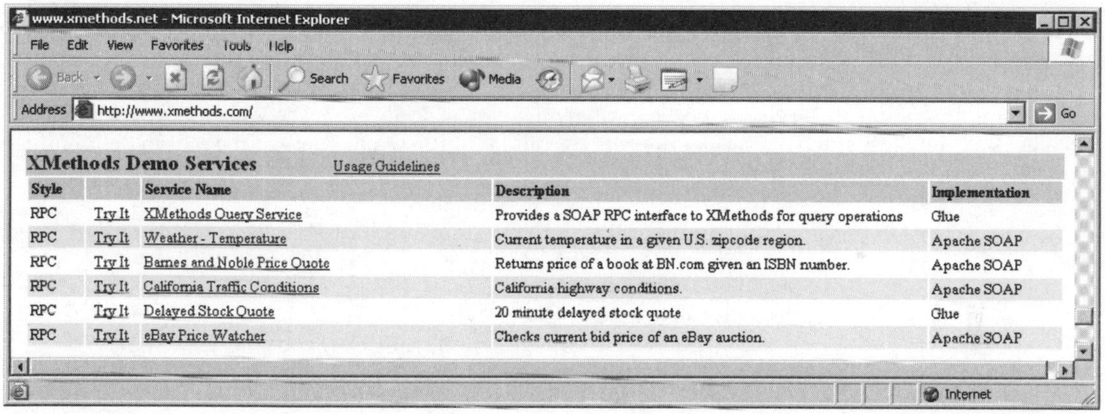
www.xmethods.net - Microsoft Internet Explorer
File Edit View Favorites Tools Help
Back Search Favorites Media
Address http://www.xmethods.com/
Go
XMethods Demo Services
Usage Guidelines
Style
Service Name
Description
Implementation
RPC Try It XMethods Query Service Provides a SOAP RPC interface to XMethods for query operations Glue
RPC Try It Weather - Temperature Current temperature in a given U.S. zipcode region. Apache SOAP
RPC Try It Barnes and Noble Price Quote Returns price of a book at BN.com given an ISBN number. Apache SOAP
RPC Try It California Traffic Conditions California highway conditions. Apache SOAP
RPC Try It Delayed Stock Quote 20 minute delayed stock quote Glue
RPC Try It eBay Price Watcher Checks current bid price of an eBay auction. Apache SOAP
Internet

Figure 12-1

> *Of course, if the demo services have been changed or removed, you will need to make some modifications to the code we present in this chapter, but the important thing is the method by which you interact with the server, not which server you use.*

Before going any further, take a quick look at the conditions of use, copied verbatim from the site, for these demo services:

The "XMethods Demo Services" are sample services provided by XMethods to help developers experiment. There is no charge for their use. However, please take note of the following.

1. *Our machine resources and bandwidth are limited. Please do not abuse these services through excessive invocation. Any such abuse may lead to blocking of your IP address without warning.*
2. *Any of these services may be discontinued at any time without warning.*
3. *While we do our best to keep the services running, there are absolutely no uptime guarantees.*
4. *We do not warrant the accuracy of the information provided by these services. Use at your own risk.*
5. *Because of the points listed above, we strongly discourage the use of these services for "real" production purposes, such as integration into a portal.*

Luckily, our friends at XMethods provide a SOAP-based Web server that allows us to get a book price quote from Barnes & Noble, and we will use this one to return a price for this particular book. Click the Barnes and Noble Price Quote link on the home page. Notice that they have made things quite easy in that they have given us the URI (see the following code snippet) for the appropriate WSDL document, which, as you know, will tell your SOAP client how to use the service.

Recall from earlier in the chapter that you have a choice when creating a new `SoapClient` object: whether to use WSDL mode, or not. Because we have a WSDL link, let's use it:

```
<?php
$client = new SoapClient("http://www.xmethods.net/sd/2001/
BNQuoteService.wsdl");
?>
```

That's pretty much it. If we had chosen not to use WSDL mode, or it were not made available to us, we would have had to add to the array options such as location, URI, style, and so on.

Assuming that the Web Service is working, then our work is done. From the Web site, you can click the Analyze WSDL link to see the service definitions, but let's instead use some of the native PHP5 functions to determine how we can use this service.

The best way to do this is simply dump the output of the `__getFunctions()` function to the screen, like so:

```
<?php
$client = new SoapClient("http://www.xmethods.net/sd/2001/
BNQuoteService.wsdl");
var_dump($client->__getFunctions());
?>
```

Save this code as `soap_functions.php` and navigate to it in your browser. You will see something like Figure 12-2.

From this you can see that you have one method available, `getPrice()`, which takes a string denoting the desired book's ISBN number and returns a floating-point value. That's all you need to know. You can now query the server for the price of *Professional PHP5*:

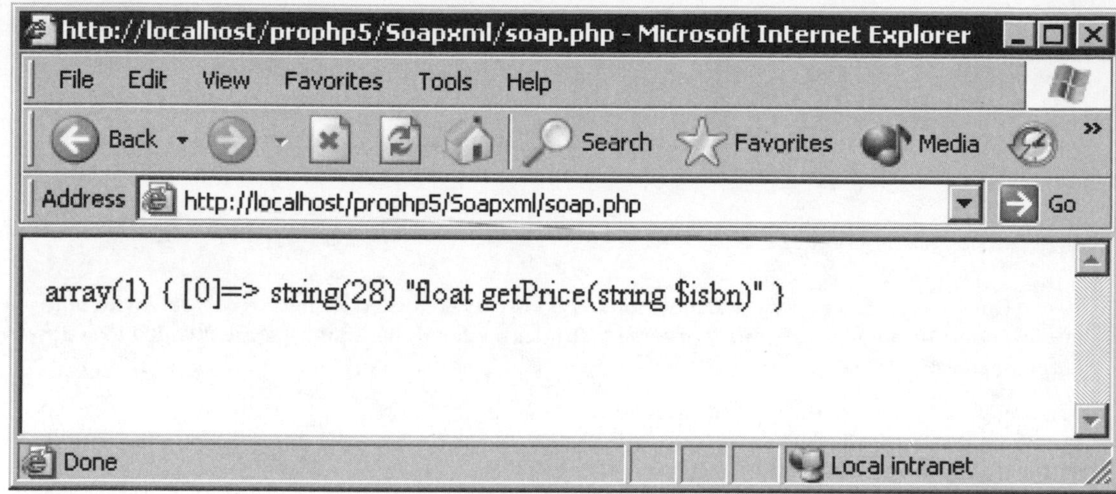

Figure 12-2

```
<?php
$client = new SoapClient("http://www.xmethods.net/sd/2001/
BNQuoteService.wsdl");
echo "The price of the book you requested is: <BR><B>$";
print $client->__call("getPrice", array("0764572822"));
?>
```

Save this code as `BNQuote.php` and navigate to it in your browser. If all is well, you will see something like Figure 12-3.

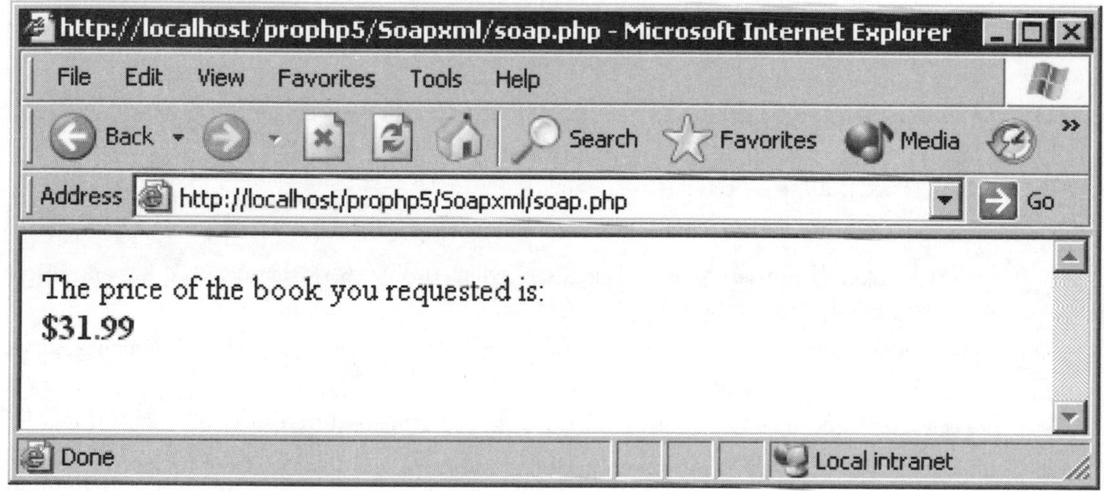

Figure 12-3

Of course, the result shown here may not be the actual price of this particular book. This is simply a demonstration and may not necessarily reflect the actual price given by Barnes & Noble, so don't feel hard done by if you paid more!

Remember that you don't have to use the `__call()` method to access a server method. You can simply call the method directly, like this:

```
print $client->getPrice("0764572822");
```

As you can see, you can easily get a quote for any book that is stocked by Barnes & Noble with only a few lines of code. Of course, a little more is going on under the hood. Let's take a more detailed look at what's happening here.

Under the Hood

Although the programming interface of PHP5's SOAP extension is simple to use, a lot of work goes into ensuring that all communications are carried out correctly. Understanding the WSDL document's role in this is important, because this determines how communication will be carried out between client and server. Basically, you can think of WSDL as an extensible, XML-based means of defining Web Services as a set of *endpoints* that can operate on *messages*.

In this section we discuss the WSDL document that we utilized in the previous example in detail, and we look at the request and response SOAP messages that were passed between the client and server in order to get our book price.

The WSDL Document

A WSDL document is divided into various sections, which together make up the contract by which the clients and servers of this Web Service must communicate. WSDL documents are structured to contain several major components and some slightly less important ones. Not all these elements have to be included at any one time, but here is a list with a short explanation of each:

- **definitions**: The root element. Defines the name and target namespaces.
- **types**: Describes the data types to be used. It is not required and defaults to the W3C XML Schema specification if no types are defined.
- **message**: Describes either a request or response message.
- **portType**: Defines, or describes, an operation, which usually consists of the request and response messages together—a round trip.
- **bindings/operation**: Describes how messages are to be transported. Contains elements such as binding and message coding style.
- **service**: As the name implies, this gives the address for the required service.
- **documentation**: Simply allows the service provider to give a description of its service.
- **import**: Enables you to decouple your WSDL documents into different elements so that they can be stored in different documents to be imported as and when required.

We don't spend much time discussing WSDL, but to take a more in-depth look at it, go to `http://www.w3.org/TR/wsdl`.

As you can see from the first piece of XML that follows, we define which version of XML we are using (1.0), and then declare the `definitions` element. The `definitions` element is always the root element and gives the name of the Web Service (in our case, BNQuoteService) as well as defines target namespaces for use in the document:

```
<?xml version="1.0" ?>
<definitions name="BNQuoteService"
 targetNamespace="http://www.xmethods.net/sd/BNQuoteService.wsdl"
 xmlns:xsd="http://www.w3.org/2001/XMLSchema"
 xmlns:soap="http://schemas.xmlsoap.org/wsdl/soap/"
 xmlns="http://schemas.xmlsoap.org/wsdl/"
 xmlns:tns="http://www.xmethods.net/sd/BNQuoteService.wsdl">
```

Next come the message elements. This section gives the request and response message names and defines the types they will use (refer to the documentation at `http://www.php.net/manual/en/ref.soap.php` for a list of what types are defined for use with the SOAP extension):

```
<message name="getPriceRequest">
  <part name="isbn" type="xsd:string" />
</message>
<message name="getPriceResponse">
  <part name="return" type="xsd:float" />
</message>
```

The `portType` describes a full round-trip operation called `getPrice`, which consists of the input and output messages `getPriceRequest` and `getPriceResponse`:

```
<portType name="BNQuotePortType">
  <operation name="getPrice">
    <input message="tns:getPriceRequest" name="getPrice" />
    <output message="tns:getPriceResponse" name="getPriceResponse" />
  </operation>
</portType>
```

Notice that, in the following code snippet, we give the binding a name and then define its type to be `BNQuotePortType`. What this means is that we are really defining this binding for the `portType` `BNQuotePortType`, which is the `portType` that has just been defined. Further, we define the binding style, in this case RPC, as well as the transport mechanism. Because we are using HTTP, we specify the SOAP HTTP transport. Note that this section also defines the type of encoding to use for the body of the SOAP message—in this case it is encoded, but it could have a document or literal-use attribute, for example:

```
<binding name="BNQuoteBinding" type="tns:BNQuotePortType">
  <soap:binding style="rpc" transport="http://schemas.xmlsoap.org/soap/http" />
  <operation name="getPrice">
    <soap:operation soapAction="" />
    <input name="getPrice">
      <soap:body use="encoded" namespace="urn:xmethods-BNPriceCheck"
```

```
        encodingStyle="http://schemas.xmlsoap.org/soap/encoding/" />
    </input>
    <output name="getPriceResponse">
      <soap:body use="encoded" namespace="urn:xmethods-BNPriceCheck"
        encodingStyle="http://schemas.xmlsoap.org/soap/encoding/" />
    </output>
  </operation>
</binding>
```

Finally, we define a single endpoint with the port element, giving the address of the actual service to use. In this case it is `http://services.xmethods.net:80/soap/servlet/rpcrouter`. Notice also that the creators have snuck in a little documentation element telling us what the service is all about. This doesn't have to be given here but it's as good a place as any:

```
  <service name="BNQuoteService">
    <documentation>
     Returns price of a book at BN.com given an ISBN number
    </documentation>
    <port name="BNQuotePort" binding="tns:BNQuoteBinding">
      <soap:address
        location="http://services.xmethods.net:80/soap/servlet/rpcrouter" />
    </port>
  </service>
</definitions>
```

We hope this has served as a good introduction for you to create your own WSDL documents. As mentioned, you can find plenty more reading on WSDL at `http://www.w3.org/TR/wsdl`, and if you intend to create your own Web Services, this is where you should start for help in creating WSDL documents for your services.

We'll now look at how requests and responses are formed. We already have an idea from the WSDL document, but PHP can help further here.

The Request and Response Envelopes

PHP5, if you recall, provides a couple of functions that can be used to look at the requests and responses from our client. Open the `BNQuote.php` file from earlier and modify it like this:

```
<?php
$client = new SoapClient("http://www.xmethods.net/sd/2001/BNQuoteService.wsdl",
  array("trace" => 1));
echo "The price of the book you requested is: <BR><B>$";
print $client->__call("getPrice", array("0764572822"));
echo "</B><BR> The request envelope result is: <B>";
print "<BR>".($client->__getLastRequest())."</BR>";
echo "</B> The response envelope result is: <B>";
print "<BR>".($client->__getLastResponse())."</B></BR>";
?>
```

This gives you the output shown in Figure 12-4.

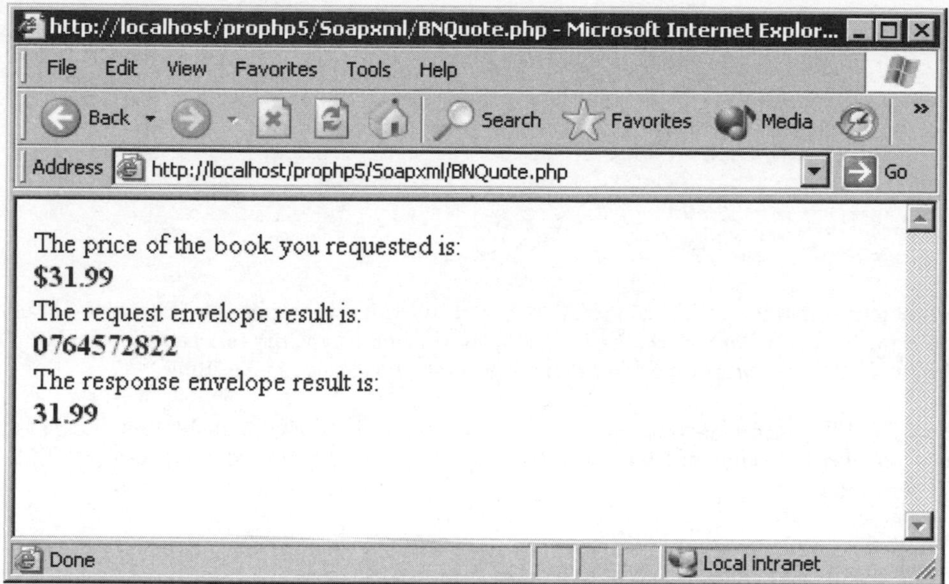

Figure 12-4

Nothing new here. Click View Source to see what we're after. Following is the request envelope, which you can quite easily relate to how message transmission was defined in the WSDL—for example, you can see that the request is sent as a string:

```
<?xml version="1.0" encoding="UTF-8"?>
<SOAP-ENV:Envelope
   xmlns:SOAP-ENV="http://schemas.xmlsoap.org/soap/envelope/"
   xmlns:ns1="urn:xmethods-BNPriceCheck"
   xmlns:xsd="http://www.w3.org/2001/XMLSchema"
   xmlns:xsi="http://www.w3.org/2001/XMLSchema-instance"
   xmlns:SOAP-ENC="http://schemas.xmlsoap.org/soap/encoding/"
   SOAP-ENV:encodingStyle="http://schemas.xmlsoap.org/soap/encoding/">
  <SOAP-ENV:Body>
    <ns1:getPrice>
      <isbn xsi:type="xsd:string">0764572822</isbn>
    </ns1:getPrice>
  </SOAP-ENV:Body>
</SOAP-ENV:Envelope>
```

Next, we have the response envelope that is returned by the Web Service server. Once again, you can relate it to the WSDL document quite easily; among other things, for example, you will notice that the return type is a floating point number as stipulated:

```
<?xml version='1.0' encoding='UTF-8'?>
<SOAP-ENV:Envelope
```

```
    xmlns:SOAP-ENV="http://schemas.xmlsoap.org/soap/envelope/"
    xmlns:xsi="http://www.w3.org/2001/XMLSchema-instance"
    xmlns:xsd="http://www.w3.org/2001/XMLSchema">
  <SOAP-ENV:Body>
    <ns1:getPriceResponse xmlns:ns1="urn:xmethods-BNPriceCheck"
      SOAP-ENV:encodingStyle="http://schemas.xmlsoap.org/soap/encoding/">
      <return xsi:type="xsd:float">31.99</return>
    </ns1:getPriceResponse>
  </SOAP-ENV:Body>
</SOAP-ENV:Envelope>
```

Unfortunately, something has been forgotten. If you substitute an impossible ISBN number into your code and run it, you will notice that we don't throw any helpful messages. In a real-world application, we absolutely need to perform some sort of error checking and exception handling.

Obviously, in the larger context of your application you can decide what the best method is for doing this, but let's look quickly at how we can use PHP5's SOAP implementation to make things slightly more robust here and now.

Exception Handling in the SOAP Client

Recall that earlier we mentioned a `SoapFault` object that's readily available for your use. Open your `soap.php` file and modify it like this (Save it as `soapfaults.php`):

```
<?php
$client = new SoapClient("http://www.xmethods.net/sd/2001/BNQuoteService.wsdl",
array("exceptions" => 0));
echo "The price of the book you requested is: <BR><B>$";
print $client->__call("getPrice", array("0764572822"));
?>
```

Having the exceptions `array` option set to `0` means that the `SoapClient` object will automatically return a `SoapFault` object if something goes wrong. You can catch this in a `try...catch` block, or use the `is_soap_fault` method provided, which checks to see whether if the argument supplied is a `SoapFault` object. For this example, modify `soapfaults.php` to use the PHP `is_soap_fault()` method:

```
<?php
$client = new SoapClient("http://www.xmethods.net/sd/2001/BNQuoteService.wsdl",
array("exceptions" => 0));
$methodresult = $client->__call("getPriceRequest", array("0764572822"));
if (is_soap_fault($methodresult)){
   echo "We have a problem: <BR>";
   var_dump($methodresult);
}
?>
```

You can use `var_export` instead of `var_dump` if you want to see hidden object members, but the important thing is getting a relatively sensible message explaining the problem by simply getting the client to return `SoapFault` objects on error. You should get results similar to Figure 12-5, explaining, quite correctly, that you have requested an invalid method.

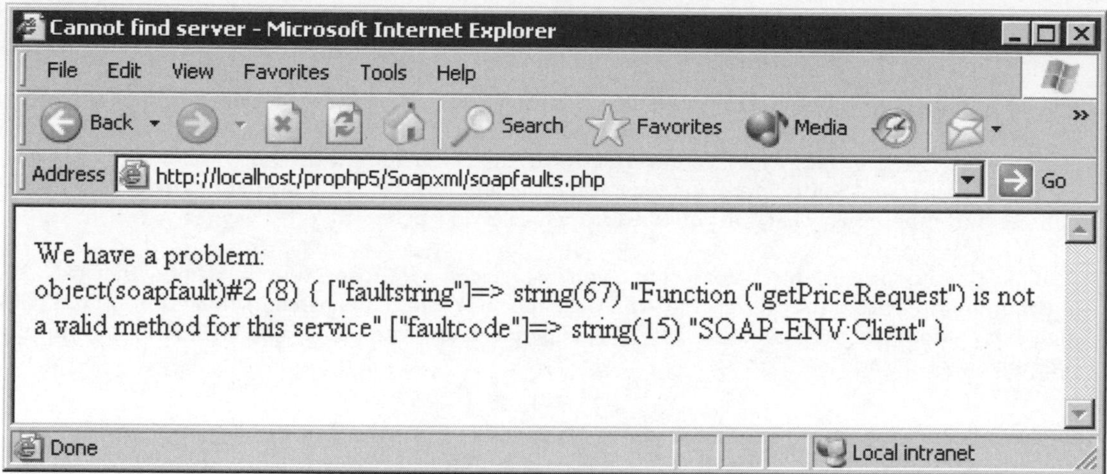

Figure 12-5

Obviously, there are plenty of ways to go about implementing exception handling, and you should pick the method that fits in with your application as a whole. The point of this section was simply to alert you to the available functionality.

Making a SOAP Server

Most often, you'll want to create a server that will provide its clients with a useful service. This can be absolutely anything, ranging from book price quotes to employee information to domain name verification. In this section we create a server that we can connect to with a client to receive a short message. We also use a short WSDL document to describe how the two parts of our SOAP application can communicate. (We have already demonstrated a WSDL document in action, so we won't explain this one again in detail.)

This example receives a `name` string from the client and returns a message to the effect that we should be glad SOAP is so reliable. Open a new code file called `soapserver.php`:

```
<?php
function sayHello($name){
   $salutation = "You, $name, will be delighted to know I am working!";
   return $salutation;
}

$server = new SoapServer ("greetings.wsdl");
$server->addFunction("sayHello");
$server->handle();
?>
```

First, although our example is actually a simple "hello world" example, there is not much further to go in terms of making something really useful. For example, if you wanted to have a Web Service to return results from a database, you would merely need to substitute a couple of functions that returned the relevant results into your SOAP server file, add the functions to the server, modify the WSDL quickly to reflect these changes, and away you go.

The preceding code has a function entitled `sayHello()`, which is the only method our fledgling service provides. The server can then be created referencing the `greetings.wsdl` document (which we define in a moment), the `sayHello()` function added with the PHP5 `addFunction()` method (discussed earlier in the section "Soapserver Functions"), and then `handle()` doing the hard work of processing the request and responding. That's all you need from the server's perspective.

To make the service work nicely for a client, you just need to tell prospective clients how they can expect to communicate with the server via the WSDL document. We don't rehash the whole concept of WDSL here, but the following is a good example of what you can use with our simple Web Service. Naturally, it is entitled `greetings.wsdl`:

```
<?xml version ='1.0' encoding ='UTF-8' ?>
<definitions name='greetings'
  targetNamespace='http://myserver.co.za/sayHello'
  xmlns:tns=' http://myserver.co.za/sayHello '
  xmlns:soap='http://schemas.xmlsoap.org/wsdl/soap/'
  xmlns:xsd='http://www.w3.org/2001/XMLSchema'
  xmlns:soapenc='http://schemas.xmlsoap.org/soap/encoding/'
  xmlns:wsdl='http://schemas.xmlsoap.org/wsdl/'
  xmlns='http://schemas.xmlsoap.org/wsdl/'>

  <message name='sayHelloRequest'>
    <part name='name' type='xsd:string'/>
  </message>
  <message name='sayHelloResponse'>
    <part name='salutation' type='xsd:string'/>
  </message>

  <portType name='sayHelloPortType'>
    <operation name='sayHello'>
      <input message='tns:sayHelloRequest'/>
      <output message='tns:sayHelloResponse'/>
    </operation>
  </portType>

  <binding name='sayHelloBinding' type='tns:sayHelloPortType'>
    <soap:binding style='rpc'
      transport='http://schemas.xmlsoap.org/soap/http'/>
    <operation name='sayHello'>
      <soap:operation soapAction=''/>
      <input>
        <soap:body use='encoded' namespace=''
          encodingStyle='http://schemas.xmlsoap.org/soap/encoding/'/>
      </input>
      <output>
        <soap:body use='encoded' namespace=''
          encodingStyle='http://schemas.xmlsoap.org/soap/encoding/'/>
      </output>
    </operation>
  </binding>
```

```
    <documentation>This is Wiley's SOAP server Example</documentation>
    <service name='sayHelloService'>
      <port name='sayHelloPort' binding='sayHelloBinding'>
        <soap:address location='http://localhost/prophp5/Soapxml/
         soapserver.php'/>
      </port>
    </service>
  </definitions>
```

With that, you're all set. Remember, though, that you need to set the address location URI to the correct value for your setup.

Now, all that remains is to make use of the new server. The following file, called `soapclient.php`, does that:

```
<?php
$client = new SoapClient("greetings.wsdl");
print_r($client->sayHello("David"));
?>
```

Navigating to this file will give you the slightly terse, yet reasonably accurate results displayed in Figure 12-6, depending on which name you have substituted in.

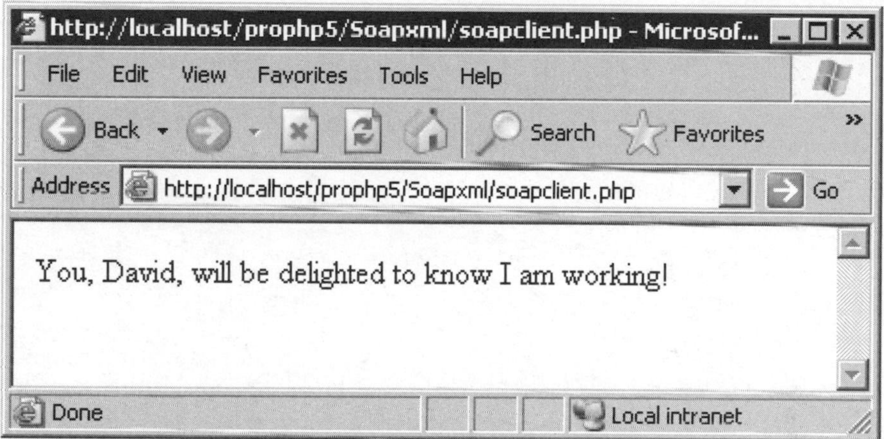

Figure 12-6

Summary

This chapter has served as a platform from which developers can begin to harness the power of SOAP-based applications. SOAP and its associated technologies constitute a huge body of knowledge that we could not possibly hope to cover in the space allotted here. However, knowing how to create and utilize Web Services is a valuable weapon in the PHP developer's armory—especially given the current trend toward distributed programming architectures.

Specifically, we discussed how PHP5 supports the use of SOAP through various open source initiatives. We then focused on the new/experimental PHP5 SOAP extension and briefly covered what it has to offer. Following this, we demonstrated the power of using Web Services by creating an example, in only a couple of lines, that retrieved a quote for book prices based on a supplied ISBN using a third-party Web Service. As part of this discussion we talked about the structure of the WSDL document that presents a contract between the SOAP server and client.

Finally, we demonstrated how to create a simple SOAP server and use it to return a basic query.

Part III: Creating a Reusable Object Toolkit II: Complex (Though Not Complicated) Utilities

Chapter 13: Model, View, Controller (MVC)

Chapter 14: Communicating with Users

Chapter 15: Sessions and Authentication

Chapter 16: Unit Testing Framework

Chapter 17: Finite State Machine and Custom Configuration Files

Model, View, Controller (MVC)

When PHP first arrived on the scene, a minor revolution took place. Interactive Web applications, once the preserve of the development professional, were springing up left, right, and center. Suddenly, some seemingly sophisticated interactive Web content, which went well beyond the traditional guest book CGI script, was appearing in some very surprising places.

The reason for this revolution was the enormous accessibility of PHP. It's not just that the "hello world" program was refreshingly easy to implement. Even traditionally complex procedures such as database integration became possible with just a few lines of code.

The problem, however, is that this accessibility was quickly abused. In some cases, it resulted in complex applications' being built by inexperienced development staff. In others, previously dedicated professionals understandably let their traditional values lapse slightly in the face of enormous temptation to take advantage of the simplicity PHP offered.

The risk associated with such development is obvious. Such abuse has led to unmaintainable applications on a shocking scale along with well-documented cases of instability, unreliability, and even exploitable security holes.

Although many programming languages such as Java and C++ enforce good programming practices through their design, PHP requires self-discipline. The difference between a seasoned PHP professional and a bedroom coder is exactly that—self-discipline. One of the most notable examples of such best-practice methodology is that of the model, view, controller (MVC) pattern.

In this chapter, you'll learn what MVC is all about and why it's a great methodology to use in your own programming. You'll build up a useful toolkit for handling some core parts of the MVC principles and learn how to use them in your applications.

Finally, you'll be introduced to two effective ways to implement the use of templates in your application and how to use templates alongside the MVC toolkit you've just met.

Introducing MVC

The *M* is for model, the *V* is for view, and the *C* is for controller. But what does it all mean?

MVC is best described as what is often known as a design pattern. A *design pattern* is best defined as a description of a reusable solution to a recurring problem given a particular context. Design patterns exist so that the challenges faced when designing large-scale applications may be approached in a consistent manner. Best practice can be achieved by tackling the architecture in a tried-and-tested manner.

In this case, the problem is how to best separate the user control of a program (the controller), its output (the view), and its inner processing and decision-making (the model) into a manner whereby they represent three distinct, separable components. The solution is, as you might have guessed, MVC. But why the need for this approach?

First, separation yields interchangeability. By keeping three components separate, yet having them talk to one other in a consistent manner, you can swap any component out should you need to. For example, if you need to rebuild your Web application to work on PDAs instead of Web browsers, you can swap out your View component for one that renders content especially for the PDA rather than the Web browser. If you need to accept data via voice input rather than mouse clicks, you can swap out your Controller component for one that uses VoiceXML.

Second, debugging to catch hard-to-trace bugs, as well as maintenance programming after release, are made immeasurably simpler if there is a separation of logic in sensible places. The rationale behind using object-oriented programming, detailed in the very first chapter of this book, also applies here. It's much better to have lots of small components that talk to each other than just a handful of huge, unwieldy files filled to the brim with code. A complex software architecture can be made a great deal simpler by separating components in this way.

Finally, you may wish to implement multiple controllers and views for your single-model application. To take our earlier example of PDAs, if you choose an MVC architecture, you can implement the necessary controllers and views to support traditional Web browsers, PDAs, cellular phones, voice, tablet PCs, and even legacy browsers, all of which will use the same model, even if they use different views and controllers. Without MVC, you'll find yourself unable to reuse the code behind the model, and you'll be burdened with all the problems associated with unnecessary duplication.

As you can see, MVC is a great design pattern and one that you should endeavor to use whenever possible. The following sections examine each of the three components in turn, how they interact with one another, and, most important, how MVC sits in the context of Web application architecture in PHP.

The Model

The model is the very heart of your application. Generally speaking, it refers to the suite of classes you have developed to handle the various processes involved in your application's behavior. It concerns itself with retrieving the data behind the output, as well as manipulating data as a result of user input. It also connects directly to both the controller and the view. The controller supplies the model with its instructions; the view manipulates the data retrieved from the controller into a human-usable output.

The View

The view is at the user end of the application. It presents data from the model that the user has requested or information that the model considers that the user needs to know. The view also connects directly to the model. The model supplies data directly to the view for it to display in a manner appropriate to the display device in question. Arguably, the view also connects to the controller, in the sense that it provides the physical rendering of the necessary controls for input to be made to your application in the first place.

The Controller

The controller represents the user's interface to your model. Generally, it offers the necessary input facilities that allow users to get data and requests for data into your application. The controller connects directly to the model, to which it supplies the data or request in question. The model then goes about fulfilling that request or storing that data as appropriate.

The Infrastructure

There is actually a fourth component to MVC—the *infrastructure*. Put simply, the job of the infrastructure is to glue the model, view, and controller together. How this is accomplished varies enormously from language to language, but you'll learn how to handle it in PHP very shortly.

MVC in Web Applications

MVC is not a new concept. Indeed, it is considered by some to be the evolution of IPO (Input, Processing, Output), which was the best-practice model applied to the linear, text-only applications of yesteryear. The application of MVC in a Web context is relatively simple.

The model is represented by your suite of classes, assuming that you have followed an object-oriented approach in your application. In any Web language, these classes perform the core communication with any external data source, make critical application decisions, and perform parsing and processing on both input and output.

The view is represented by the Web browser, or rather what is displayed in it. Upon making a request, be it a simple request for a page or an instruction to update or query a database, the output determined by the model is actually displayed by the Web browser.

Perhaps confusingly, the controller is also represented by the Web browser or rather the user's actions within it. Whether just a series of links or a complex form, the `GET` and `POST` requests made by the user's browser represent the effort to get data into the model in the first place.

MVC in PHP

As discussed earlier, PHP's simplicity and accessibility can easily be abused to the point at which applications become unmaintainable. Specifically, this abuse takes the form of combining model, view, and controller into a single PHP script. In fact, the term *script* is appropriate only in such an approach. In a proper MVC application, there are no scripts, only components.

How Not to Do It

Ask any inexperienced PHP developer to create a guest book application and he or she will probably come up with a single file. The file would be called `guestbook.php` and would handle both displaying existing entries and adding new ones to the database. Stepping through the code, it might look something like this:

- Look at the `GET` parameters passed to it to determine which page of the guest book to show.
- If no page is specified, decide to show page 1.
- See whether a parameter called `NewGuestBookEntry` has been passed. If so, check whether it conforms to various validity constraints (length and content) and enter it into the database. If not, write an error message and quit.
- Get the current guest book entries from the database matching this page number.
- Write them out in an HTML table (embedded right here in the script).
- Write out the HTML form pointing to this same script, allowing the user to add an entry.

This approach has a number of problems, quite apart from using `GET` instead of `POST` to effect a change in a database (strictly speaking, the RFC in question says this is a bad idea).

If you think back to the reasons in favor of MVC, such as interchanging controllers and views, ease of maintenance and initial development, and multiple simultaneous controllers and views, you can see that in all three cases we encounter difficulties.

Instead, take a look at a more mature approach to development that allows you to follow the MVC design pattern.

Getting It Right: An MVC Approach

The first rule of MVC in PHP is to *split up your files*. There are a number of possible approaches, but many favor taking the step of actually using different file extensions to represent different roles in the MVC pattern and then using `require_once` at the appropriate time to link them together.

The documented practice of naming files to be `included` or `required` with an extension `.inc` should not be followed. After all, it tells you nothing about the content of that file and thus encourages role overlap between files.

You may wish to try something like the following:

Extension	Component	Role
`.php`	Infrastructure	Behavioral logic—the communications infrastructure between model, view, and controller
`.phpm`	Model	PHP Classes—the heart of the application
`.phtml`	View/Controller	The rendering of both the results of the user's input and the interface for the user to make further input

It may seem odd that we've combined the view and controller into just one file, but it does more closely match the physical separation we've described earlier. Because the user's Web browser handles both the interface (controller) and the display of data (view), it is not unreasonable for us to use a single file to provide both of these two corners of the MVC square.

If you are unsure as to what code should appear in which modules, you can rely on a few rules to ensure that you're following this methodology:

- `.php` (control page) should never contain SQL queries or HTML.
- `.phpm` (classes) should never contain HTML.
- `.phtml` (templates) should never contain SQL queries, and only very basic PHP (`for/if/while`).

What you are accomplishing in this separation is a very primitive form of templating known as *native templating*. In such a setup, PHP is used to render the output of the application in a separate template file (in this case, the `.phtml` file). That output is decided upon by presentation of the user's input by the logic file (the `.php` file) to the classes (the `.phpm` files).

This is implemented in practice as follows:

- The `.php` file is the actual recipient of the `GET` or `POST` request (hence, there is no need to reconfigure Apache to support these new extensions).
- The `.php` file is home to all `require()` statements needed to import the necessary classes (with each class stored in a `.phpm` file).
- The `.php` file examines the input in `GET` and `POST` parameters and determines a course of action. It passes that data (either in a raw or processed form) into methods of these classes that have been made available to it through inclusion in the previous step.
- The classes in question parse the input data, update and query databases or other data sources as necessary, and return data to the `.php` file.
- The `.php` file then examines the output from those classes. It may make decisions based on that output, deliver the output in some processed state, or simply deliver it as is. The delivery is always, however, performed through the construction of a single supervariable (usually a hash) that contains, unformatted, the output we wish to display to the user.
- The `.php` file then `includes` the appropriate `.phtml` file, which effectively takes over execution.
- The `.phtml` file recurses that supervariable, displaying it in whatever form is appropriate and rendering whatever new user input components are required, such that the user is presented with the finished Web page.

This may sound more complex than it actually is; in fact, it is a remarkably simple process. You'll get to see some examples later in the chapter about how this native templating is best implemented. For now, you'll take a look at a few toolkit classes that can help you in the quest to use an MVC design pattern in PHP by vastly simplifying some of the steps set out previously.

Later, you'll learn how this toolkit integrates neatly with the native templating techniques just discussed.

The MVC Mini Toolkit

The mini toolkit you are about to meet makes sticking to an MVC design pattern a whole lot easier. The toolkit concerns itself only with the infrastructure of the MVC methodology. Later, you'll meet an off-the-shelf PEAR package called Smarty that allows for an effective implementation of the model and view components.

Introducing the Toolkit

The mini toolkit allows you to handle the connection between controller and model in a consistent, clean, and clear manner. The core of this is a request object that seeks to provide a more object-oriented perspective on the user's input into your application. As well as sporting the usual means for interrogating the user's input directly, it supports the concept of applying constraints to each parameter, such that you may easily specify in your code what you are and are not prepared to accept.

Such error-checking practices are almost certainly not new to you, of course. However, the concept of constraints allows you to separate the controller and model. The model may now assume that its input is within expected parameters, allowing you to divorce cleanly such code from methods within the model, safe in the knowledge that it has been vetted by the infrastructure of your MVC design pattern.

This is an entirely appropriate approach. After all, sanity checks are not core to your model's functionality. By leaving responsibility for such checks well outside the model itself, you can also apply different rules for different controllers and different views. This is very much the philosophy behind MVC.

You may want to extend or modify these classes to suit your own needs better; what is provided here is a very basic implementation. For example, you may want to examine the feasibility of adding methods to automatically perpetuate `GET` and `POST` variables using hidden form parameters, without having to turn to session variables. This may prove useful for the purposes of pagination forward and backward through a data set of search results, maintaining those search criteria with each request for a new page. Such functionality could easily be integrated into the request object itself.

In addition, the prepackaged constraint types supplied here are not exhaustive. However, a quick glance at the code should make it quite clear how easily you can add your own, should your application require them.

Constants

You do need to define a number of constants for your classes to work seamlessly together. They define the three types of parameter (`GET`, `POST`, and `Cookies`) as well as the various types of constraint you can apply. As previously mentioned, you should feel free to define additional constraints that may suit your application, as long as you also remember to implement them in the `Request` class.

Examine the following code, in a file called `constants.phpm`:

```
<?php
// Constants

define(VERB_METHOD_COOKIE, 1);
define(VERB_METHOD_GET, 2);
define(VERB_METHOD_POST, 4);
define(CT_MINLENGTH, 1);
define(CT_MAXLENGTH, 2);
```

```
define(CT_PERMITTEDCHARACTERS, 3);
define(CT_NONPERMITTEDCHARACTERS, 4);
define(CT_LESSTHAN, 5);
define(CT_EQUALTO, 6);
define(CT_MORETHAN, 7);
define(CT_NOTEQUALTO, 8);
define(CT_MUSTMATCHREGEXP, 9);
define(CT_MUSTNOTMATCHREGEXP, 10);
?>
```

Note the two numbering schemes as an approach in defining these constants. These are an exponential sequence to define the three verbs of parameters offered in an HTTP request and a purely sequential sequence to define the constraint types.

The reason for the two differing approaches touches briefly on the properties of *bitwise logic*. Because this subject has not been touched upon elsewhere in the book, we touch on it briefly here.

Consider the following piece of code:

```
$var3 = ($var1 && $var2);
```

The conditional statement here clearly requires that `$var1` is true (either literally, or as some nonzero or non-empty value), and that `$var2` is true (employing traditional use of the `&&` operator to express Boolean logic). If both are true, `$var3` will also be true. This if fairly basic, but there is a second form of comparison logic that uses the same basic operators, `AND` and `OR`.

Consider the following:

```
$var3 = ($var1 & $var2);
```

Note the *single* ampersand. This indicates that you wish to perform bitwise rather than Boolean logic to effect the comparison. What then takes place, assuming that `$var1` and `$var2` are integers, is that the corresponding binary bits of each value are subject to the traditional Boolean comparison (with 1 meaning true and 0 meaning false). If `$var1` is 34 and `$var2` is 11, the following applies:

```
34      =    00100010
11      =    00001011
34 & 11 =    00000010     =     2
```

Accordingly, the bitwise logic of 34 and 11 yields 2, because it is only in the 2 column where both bits are 1 in each number.

But what does this have to do with constants?

Put simply, it allows us to combine constants together to form a single value, which consists of the arithmetic sum of its constituent constants, and then easily determine later what those constituent constants are.

If each constant represents the incrementing decimal value of a single bit of a binary number (essentially, a power of two), then when summed together, the resulting binary number will have bits set to 1 representing those constants that have been included in that sum.

```
CONST_A =       1       =       00000001
CONST_B =       2       =       00000010
CONST_C =       4       =       00000100
CONST_D =       8       =       00001000
CONST_E =       16      =       00010000
```

Say that you wish to define a parameter consisting of constants B, D, and E combined (whatever that might mean). Simply add the values 2, 8 and 16 together to get a value of 26. Take a look at what 26 looks like in binary, next to its constituent components:

```
CONST_B =           2       =       00000010
CONST_D =           8       =       00001000
CONST_E =           16      =       00010000
CONST_B+D+E =       26      =       00011010
```

Notice how you can clearly recognize that the constituent constants of the combination are B, D, and E. But how do you test for this in code?

Enter and run the following code from the command line (rather than in a Web browser):

```
define('CONST_A', 1);
define('CONST_B', 2);
define('CONST_C', 4);
define('CONST_D', 8);
define('CONST_E', 16);

$myCombinedConstant = CONST_B + CONST_D + CONST_E;

if ($myCombinedConstant & CONST_A) {
 print "Combined constant contains A\n";
};
if ($myCombinedConstant & CONST_B) {
 print "Combined constant contains B\n";
};
if ($myCombinedConstant & CONST_C) {
 print "Combined constant contains C\n";
};
if ($myCombinedConstant & CONST_D) {
 print "Combined constant contains D\n";
};
if ($myCombinedConstant & CONST_E) {
 print "Combined constant contains E\n";
};
```

You will see output similar to the following:

```
Combined constant contains B
Combined constant contains D
Combined constant contains E
```

As you have probably deduced, the test to determine whether a combined constant contains a particular original constant is simply to perform a bitwise AND against that original constant. This will produce a nonzero (that is, true) value only if the bit in question is set both in the original constant and in the combined constant you are testing.

We have adopted this tactic in our constants for expressing request methods, but not in our constants used to express constraint types. This is because the code might allow the combination of request methods as a parameter for a method at some stage in the future. However, the nature of constraint types means that one constraint object has one constraint type. To combine constraints, therefore, their objects must be combined, not the constants behind them. Accordingly, we have adopted a linear (1, 2, 3, 4, 5) numbering system for these constants, because they will never be added together in the way described in this section.

The Request Class

The `request` object itself represents the request made by the user in order to generate the page. Those of you who have ever worked in ASP are familiar with using a preinstantiated object to access parameters, but this `Request` class is a somewhat more sophisticated.

Unlike ASP, you will have to instantiate the `request` object yourself, but you will notice that the constructor written requires no parameters. It examines the existing `$_REQUEST`, `$_COOKIE`, `$_POST` and `$_GET` hashes itself quite successfully in order to populate its various member variables.

You could start to make use of the `request` object right away. By using the various methods supplied to retrieve parameters, you could get on and build your application. To do this, however, is to disregard the syntax validation methods provided by the `Constraint` class and its sister `ConstraintFailure` class.

Examine the following source code, called `request.phpm`, in detail:

```
<?
require_once("constants.phpm");
require_once("constraint.phpm");
require_once("constraintfailure.phpm");
class request {
  private $_arGetVars;
  private $_arPostVars;
  private $_arCookieVars;
  private $_arRequestVars;
  private $_objOriginalRequestObject;

  private $_blIsRedirectFollowingConstraintFailure;

  private $_blRedirectOnConstraintFailure;
  private $_strConstraintFailureRedirectTargetURL;
  private $_strConstraintFailureDefaultRedirectTargetURL;

  private $_arObjParameterMethodConstraintHash;
  private $_arObjConstraintFailure;
  private $_hasRunConstraintTests;

  function __construct($check_for_cookie = true) {
```

```
    // Import variables
    global $_REQUEST;
    global $_GET;
    global $_POST;
    global $_COOKIE;
    $this->_arGetVars = $_GET;
    $this->_arPostVars = $_POST;
    $this->_arCookieVars = $_COOKIE;
    $this->_arRequestVars = $_REQUEST;
    if ($check_for_cookie) {
      if ($this->_arCookieVars["phprqcOriginalRequestObject"]) {
        $cookieVal = $this->_arRequestVars["phprqcOriginalRequestObject"];
        $this->_blIsRedirectFollowingConstraintFailure = true;
        if (strlen($cookieVal) > 0) {
          $strResult = setcookie ("phprqcOriginalRequestObject", "",
time() - 3600, "/");
          $origObj = unserialize(stripslashes($cookieVal));
          $this->_objOriginalRequestObject = &$origObj;
          $this->_arRequestVars["phprqcOriginalRequestObject"] = "";
          $this->_arGetVars["phprqcOriginalRequestObject"] = "";
          $this->_arPostVars["phprqcOriginalRequestObject"] = "";
        };
        $this->_blIsRedirectOnConstraintFailure  = true;
      } else {
        $this->_blIsRedirectOnConstraintFailure  = false;
      };
    } else {
      $this->_blIsRedirectOnConstraintFailure  = false;
    };
    $this->_arObjParameterMethodConstraintHash = Array();
    $this->_arObjConstraintFailure = Array();
    $this->_blHasRunConstraintTests = false;
  }

  function IsRedirectFollowingConstraintFailure() {
    return($this->_blIsRedirectOnConstraintFailure);
  }

  function GetOriginalRequestObjectFollowingConstraintFailure() {
    if ($this->_blIsRedirectOnConstraintFailure) {
      return($this->_objOriginalRequestObject);
    };
  }

  function SetRedirectOnConstraintFailure($blTrueOrFalse) {
    $this->_blRedirectOnConstraintFailure  = $blTrueOrFalse;
  }

  function SetConstraintFailureRedirectTargetURL($strURL) {
    $this->_strConstraintFailureRedirectTargetURL = $strURL;
  }

  function SetConstraintFailureDefaultRedirectTargetURL($strURL) {
    $this->_strConstraintFailureDefaultRedirectTargetURL = $strURL;
```

```
  }

  function GetParameterValue($strParameter) {
    return($this->_arRequestVars[$strParameter]);
  }

  function GetParameters() {
    return($this->_arRequestVars);
  }

  function GetCookies() {
    return($this->_arCookieVars);
  }

  function GetPostVariables() {
    return($this->_arPostVariables);
  }

  function GetGetVariables() {
    return($this->_arGetVariables);
  }

  function AddConstraint($strParameter, $intMethod, $objConstraint) {
    $newHash["PARAMETER"] = $strParameter;
    $newHash["METHOD"] = $intMethod;
    $newHash["CONSTRAINT"] = $objConstraint;
    $this->_arObjParameterMethodConstraintHash[] = $newHash;
  }

  function TestConstraints() {
    $this->_blHasRunConstraintTests = true;
    $anyFail = false;
    for ($i=0; $i<=sizeof($this->_arObjParameterMethodConstraintHash)
-1; $i++) {
      $strThisParameter = $this-
>_arObjParameterMethodConstraintHash[$i] ["PARAMETER"];
      $intThisMethod = $this->_arObjParameterMethodConstraintHash[$i]
["METHOD"];
      $objThisConstraint = $this-
>_arObjParameterMethodConstraintHash[$i] ["CONSTRAINT"];
      $varActualValue = "";
      if ($intThisMethod == VERB_METHOD_COOKIE) {
        $varActualValue = $this->_arCookieVars[$strThisParameter];
      };
      if ($intThisMethod == VERB_METHOD_GET) {
        $varActualValue = $this->_arGetVars[$strThisParameter];
      };
      if ($intThisMethod == VERB_METHOD_POST) {
        $varActualValue = $this->_arPostVars[$strThisParameter];
      };
      $intConstraintType = $objThisConstraint->GetConstraintType();
      $strConstraintOperand = $objThisConstraint->GetConstraintOperand();
```

```
      $thisFail = false;
      $objFailureObject = new constraintfailure($strThisParameter,
$intThisMethod, $objThisConstraint);
      switch ($intConstraintType) {
        case CT_MINLENGTH:
          if (strlen((string)$varActualValue) < (integer)
$strConstraintOperand) {
            $thisFail = true;
          };
          break;
        case CT_MAXLENGTH:
          if (strlen((string)$varActualValue) > (integer)
$strConstraintOperand) {
            $thisFail = true;
          };
          break;
        case CT_PERMITTEDCHARACTERS:
          for ($j=0; $j<=strlen($varActualValue)-1; $j++) {
              $thisChar = substr($varActualValue, $j, 1);
              if (strpos($strConstraintOperand, $thisChar) === false) {
                $thisFail = true;
              };
            };
          break;
        case CT_NONPERMITTEDCHARACTERS:
          for ($j=0; $j<=strlen($varActualValue)-1; $j++) {
              $thisChar = substr($varActualValue, $j, 1);
              if (!(strpos($strConstraintOperand, $thisChar) === false)) {
                $thisFail = true;
              };
            };
          break;
        case CT_LESSTHAN:
          if ($varActualValue >= $strConstraintOperand) {
            $thisFail = true;
          };
          break;
        case CT_MORETHAN:
          if ($varActualValue <= $strConstraintOperand) {
            $thisFail = true;
          };
          break;
        case CT_EQUALTO:
          if ($varActualValue != $strConstraintOperand) {
            $thisFail = true;
          };
          break;
        case CT_NOTEQUALTO:
          if ($varActualValue == $strConstraintOperand) {
            $thisFail = true;
          };
          break;
```

```
        case CT_MUSTMATCHREGEXP:
          if (!(preg_match($strConstraintOperand, $varActualValue))) {
            $thisFail = true;
          };
          break;
        case CT_MUSTNOTMATCHREGEXP:
          if (preg_match($strConstraintOperand, $varActualValue)) {
            $thisFail = true;
          };
          break;
      };
      if ($thisFail) {
        $anyFail = true;
        $this->_arObjConstraintFailure[] = $objFailureObject;
      };
    };
    if ($anyFail) {
      if ($this->_blRedirectOnConstraintFailure) {
          $targetURL = $_ENV["HTTP_REFERER"];
          if (!$targetURL) {
            $targetURL = $this->_strConstraintFailureDefaultRedirectTargetURL;
          };
          if ($this->_strConstraintFailureRedirectTargetURL) {
            $targetURL = $this->_strConstraintFailureRedirectTargetURL;
          };
          if ($targetURL) {
            $objToSerialize = $this;
            $strSerialization = serialize($objToSerialize);
            $strResult = setcookie ("phprqcOriginalRequestObject",
$strSerialization, time() + 3600, "/");
            header("Location: $targetURL");
            exit(0);
          };
      };
    };
    return(!($anyFail));  // Returns TRUE if all tests passed, otherwise
returns FALSE
  }

  function GetConstraintFailures() {
    if (!$this->_blHasRunConstraintTests) {
      $this->TestConstraints();
    };
    return($this->_arObjConstraintFailure);
  }
}
?>
```

Take a look at each of the member variables. These are all private, and accessor methods are provided to get to or set their useful values. We've continued to use Hungarian notation—that is, we've included a hint at the data type each member variable should contain at the start of the variable's name.

Member Variable	Role
`$_arGetVars`	A copy of `$_GET`, an associative array of HTTP `GET` variables passed in this request.
`$_arPostVars`	A copy of `$_POST`, an associative array of HTTP `POST` variables passed in this request.
`$_arCookieVars`	A copy of `$_COOKIE`, an associative array of pre-existing cookies passed in this request.
`$_arRequestVars`	A copy of `$_REQUEST`, an associative array of `GET` and `POST` variables, as well as cookies, combined into one. Where `GET/POST` variables or cookies of the same names exist, precedence is determined by PHP.INI.
`$_objOriginalRequest Object`	In the event that the user has been redirected back to the original page by the `request` object as a result of passing parameters that failed constraint tests, this will contain a copy of the original `request` object supplied.
`$_blIsRedirectFollowing ConstraintFailure`	A Boolean variable determining whether this `request` has been created as a result of a redirect following a constraint test failure.
`$_blRedirectOnConstraint Failure`	In the event that a constraint test is failed, should the `request` object automatically redirect the browser back to the original page, or to some other URL?
`$_strConstraintFailure RedirectTargetURL`	In the event that a constraint test is failed, and `_blRedirectOnConstraintFailure` is set to true, should the `request` object divert to any URL in particular? If this is left blank, the referring URL shall be used.
`$_strConstraintFailure DefaultRedirectTargetURL`	In the event that `_strConstraintFailure RedirectTargetURL` is not set, and `_blRedirectOnConstraintFailure` is set to true, and no referring URL is available, the URL to which the browser should be redirected.
`$_arObjParameterMethod ConstraintHash`	An array of constraints, the indices of which contain three keyed components in a hash. First, it contains the parameter name on which the constraint applies. Second, it contains the method in which this parameter is expected to be passed (as a constant). Finally, it contains the constraint object expressing the test to be applied.
`$_arObjConstraintFailure`	An array of constraint failure objects, should any constraints have failed, assuming that the tests have been run.
`$_blHasRunConstraintTests`	A Boolean variable expressing whether the constraint tests have yet been run on this request object.

The following table shows the methods provided by the `request` object.

Method	Role
`__construct`	Instantiates the `request` object. Does not take any required parameters. Instead, it consults `$_REQUEST`, `$_POST`, `$_GET` and `$_COOKIE` and populates member variables (see earlier) as appropriate. In addition, the existence of a cookie called `phprqcOriginalRequestObject` is checked for. Should it exist, another `request` object is assumed to be passed back as a result of throwback following constraint test failures. The cookie is nullified at this stage to prevent an infinite loop when the original request object is created. Its contents are then unserialized (via the `stripslashes` PHP function) into a new request object, which is then made available for interrogation through the `GetOriginalRequest ObjectFollowingConstraintFailure` accessor method (detailed in this table).
`IsRedirectFollowing ConstraintFailure`	If the page being displayed has been automatically loaded following a 302 redirect issued as a result of a constraint test failure, this method will return true.
`GetOriginalRequest ObjectFollowing ConstraintFailure`	If the page being displayed has been automatically loaded following a 302 redirect issued as a result of a constraint test failure, this method will return the `Request` object that existed when that page was called, just before the constraint tests were failed.
`SetRedirect OnConstraintFailure`	Accepting true or false as a parameter, this method allows you to tell the `Request` object whether it should perform a 302 redirect upon any constraint tests failing. The target for that redirect is set using the `SetConstraintFailureRedirectTargetURL` and `Set ConstraintFailureDefaultRedirectTargetURL` methods.
`SetConstraintFailure RedirectTargetURL`	Sets the target for a 302 redirect following a constraint failure taking place. If one is not set, either the referring page (which is normally the desired target) is used or, if that is not available, a default URL will be used (which is set using the `SetConstraintFailure DefaultRedirectTargetURL` method).
`SetConstraintFailure DefaultRedirect TargetURL`	In the event that no target URL is set using the preceding accessor method, the referring page will be used should a referral become necessary as a result of a constraint test failing. If no referring page is available, for example as a result of a user visiting from a bookmark, the default URL specified using this method will be used instead.
`GetParameterValue`	Returns the value of the specified parameter. This value is pulled directly from `$_REQUEST`, so the precedence of search for `GET` variables, POST variables and COOKIE variables will be dependent on PHP's overall configuration.

Continued

Method	Role
`GetParameters`	Returns a hash of parameters—essentially, a direct copy of `$_REQUEST`.
`GetCookies`	Returns a hash of cookies —essentially, a direct copy of `$_COOKIE`.
`GetPostVariables`	Returns a hash of POST variables—essentially, a direct copy of `$_POST`.
`GetGetVariables`	Returns a hash of GET variables—essentially, a direct copy of `$_GET`.
`AddConstraint`	Adds a constraint to this request. A constraint is applied to a single parameter and specifies a condition that must be met in order for that constraint to be considered met. This method takes the name of the parameter, the delivery method (VERB_METHOD_GET, VERB_METHOD_POST, or VERB_METHOD_COOKIE as a constant) and a constraint object (discussed shortly) as its parameters. After a constraint is added, it cannot be removed. More than one constraint may be applied to a single parameter.
`TestConstraints`	Tests each constraint in turn. Makes a note of any that fail by populating the member variable `$_arObjConstraintFailure`, accessible using `GetConstraintFailures`. In the event that `$_blRedirectOnConstraintFailure` is set to true, redirects automatically to the appropriate URL, having first issued a temporary cookie that is a serialized representation of the current request object.
`GetConstraintFailures`	Returns an array of `constraintfailure` objects (discussed shortly) such that the conditions that were not met may be evaluated. If a redirect has taken place in `TestConstraints` as a result of a constraint failure, this method will need to be accessed on the original request object, accessed using `GetOriginalRequestObjectFollowingConstraintFailure` (described earlier in this table).

Don't worry if the theory isn't quite clear from the preceding table. Later in this chapter, you'll find a practical example of how to employ this class and the rest of the toolkit in the real world.

Now take a look at the constraint class and its close cousin, the `constraintfailure` class.

The Constraint Class

The constraint class exists only as an object-oriented encapsulator. It does not concern itself with the code necessary to test whether the constraint is passed. As you have just seen, this is handled by the `request` object.

Examine the following code, in a file called `constraint.phpm`:

```
<?php
require_once("constants.phpm");
class constraint {
  private $_intConstraintType;
  private $_strConstraintOperand;

  function __construct($intConstraintType, $strConstraintOperand) {
    $this->_intConstraintType = $intConstraintType;
    $this->_strConstraintOperand = $strConstraintOperand;
  }

  function GetConstraintType() {
    return($this->_intContraintType);
  }

  function GetConstraintOperand() {
    return($this->_strConstraintOperand);
  }
}
?>
```

Note how the constructor takes the constraint type (chosen from one of the constraint types that have been enumerated as constants) as its first parameter and the operand as its second. The meaning of the operand depends on the type of constraint. Its interpretation is up to the request object in its implementation of each type of constraint. For example, for a `CT_MAXLENGTH` constraint, the operand should contain the maximum length of the parameter. For a `CT_PERMITTEDCHARS` constraint, the operand should contain a string containing all permitted characters that may exist in the parameter.

To accommodate this flexibility, the operand is a string. However, it will be cast back to its most appropriate native form when the test takes place.

Note that you do not store the name of the parameter being tested in a constraint object. A constraint is simply a condition and can be applied to any (or even multiple) parameters using the methods in the request object. For that reason, to encapsulate neatly any given failure of a constraint, you also need to store the parameter and delivery method that have provoked the failure. This is done using an instance of the `ConstraintFailure` class.

The ConstraintFailure Class

A constraint failure object is instantiated whenever a particular constraint fails. Its constructor expects the name of the parameter, the delivery method (`VERB_METHOD_GET`, `VERB_METHOD_POST`, or `VERB_METHOD_COOKIE`), and the original constraint object that caused the failure.

In normal use, the `GetFailedConstraintObject` method will be used to determine the nature of the constraint which failed through the use of the native `Constraint` class methods described previously.

Take a look at the following code, in a file called `constraintfailure.phpm`:

```
<?php
require_once("constants.phpm");
require_once("constraint.phpm");
class constraintfailure {
  private $_strParameterName;
  private $_intVerbMethod;
  private $_objFailedConstraintObject;

  function __construct($strParameterName, $intVerbMethod,
$objFailedConstraintObject) {
     $this->_strParameterName = $strParameterName;
     $this->_intVerbMethod = $intVerbMethod;
     $this->_objFailedConstraintObject = $objFailedConstraintObject;
  }

  function GetParameterName() {
    return($this->_strParameterName);
  }

  function GetVerbMethod() {
    return($this->_intVerbMethod);
  }

  function GetFailedConstraintObject() {
    return($this->_objFailedConstraintObject);
  }
}
```

This class neatly encapsulates a failure that has occurred as a result of the user's input to the page not meeting your acceptance criteria.

As you can see in the preceding code, it contains the name of the parameter that has failed, the method (`GET`, `POST`, or `Cookie`) in which the parameter was passed, and the constraint (expressed as a `constraint` object) test that has not been passed.

Instances of this object can be retrieved from the `Request` class using the `GetConstraintFailures` method, provided that the `Request` class has been instantiated in the context of a 302 redirect following redirection caused by constraint failures.

Using the Toolkit

Now that you've learnt a little bit about the basic classes that constitute the toolkit, it's worth looking at how you'd go about implementing this in a real-world application.

You'll also see in this example a practical case of an MVC approach as defined earlier in the chapter—namely, the use of native PHP templating. (The next section goes into further detail on how this works.)

Assume that you have a search engine consisting of two pages: a search page in which the terms are entered, and a search terms page in which the results are displayed.

search.php

The initial search page has the following jobs:

- Require all necessary components.
- Define the template file (`search.phtml`).
- Define an associative array (`$displayHash`) to contain the content to be rendered by the template file.
- Check to see whether this page has been reached as a result of a referral following a constraint failure.
    - If so, set part of the `$displayHash` to indicate this, and retrieve the original failed request object from the current request object (which has been made available through the temporary cookie).
    - Retrieve an array of `constraintfailure` objects from this retrieved request object.
    - Loop through these `constraintfailure` objects, populating a newly formed array in `$displayHash` with the type of failure in each case.
- Require the template file for immediate rendering.

The code is reproduced here:

```
require_once("constants.phpm");
require_once("request.phpm");
require_once("constraint.phpm");
require_once("constraintfailure.phpm");

$strTemplateFile = "search.phtml";

$displayHash = Array();

$objRequest = new request();
$blHadProblems = ($objRequest->IsRedirectFollowingConstraintFailure());

$displayHash["HADPROBLEMS"] = $blHadProblems;

if ($blHadProblems) {
  $objFailingRequest = $objRequest-
>GetOriginalRequestObjectFollowingConstraintFailure();
  $arConstraintFailures = $objFailingRequest->GetConstraintFailures();
  $displayHash["PROBLEMS"] = Array();
  for ($i=0; $i<=sizeof($arConstraintFailures)-1; $i++) {
    $objThisConstraintFailure = &$arConstraintFailures[$i];
    $objThisFailingConstraintObject = $objThisConstraintFailure-
>GetFailedConstraintObject();
    $intTypeOfFailure = $objThisFailingConstraintObject->GetConstraintType();
    switch ($intTypeOfFailure) {
      case CT_MINLENGTH:
        $displayHash["PROBLEMS"][] = "Your search term was too short.";
        break;
```

```
        case CT_MAXLENGTH:
          $displayHash["PROBLEMS"][] = "Your search term was too long.";
          break;
        case CT_PERMITTEDCHARACTERS:
          $displayHash["PROBLEMS"][] = "Your search term contained characters
I didn't understand.";
          break;
      };
    };
};

require_once($strTemplateFile);
exit(0);
```

Note the `exit` statement at the end. It's not strictly necessary but prevents you from accidentally writing code after the template has been handed control.

Now take a look at the template itself.

search.phtml

The template has the sole responsibility of intelligently rendering the contents of `$displayHash` with appropriate surrounding HTML. Note how you do not need to declare `$displayHash` as global. The act of requiring the template glues it to the end of the original script. The interpreter treats it as a single script.

In this particular template, in addition to rendering the straightforward HTML required to create the search form, you must render any error messages generated as a result of a failed search that has just taken place.

```
<html>
<head>
  <title>Ed's Search Page</title>
</head>

<body>
<H1>Ed's Search Page</H1>
<hr>
You can search for types of steak here.
<BR><BR>
<? if ($displayHash["HADPROBLEMS"])  ?>
  <B>Sorry, there <?=((sizeof($displayHash["PROBLEMS"]) > 1) ? "were
problems" : "was a problem")?> with your search!</B>
  <? for ($i=0; $i<=sizeof($displayHash["PROBLEMS"])-1; $i++)  ?>
    <?=$displayHash["PROBLEMS"][$i]?>
  <? ; ?>
<? ; ?>
<FORM METHOD="GET" ACTION="searchresults.php">
  <TABLE BORDER="0">
    <TR>
      <TD>Type of Steak</TD>
      <TD><INPUT TYPE="TEXT" NAME="typeOfSteak"></TD>
    </TR>
  </TABLE><BR>
```

```
    <INPUT TYPE="SUBMIT">
  </FORM>

  </body>
  </html>
```

Note how simple the PHP is including very basic statements such as `if` and `for`. As a rule, if you find yourself writing code of greater complexity in a template file, it is most likely in the wrong place and should be in either the control page (`.php`) or in one of the classes.

In the next part of the chapter, we describe an alternative for using these simple statements in templates, a method that doesn't use PHP at all—*true templating*.

If you fire up `search.php` in your browser, you should see that it successfully renders a standard search form (see Figure 13-1).

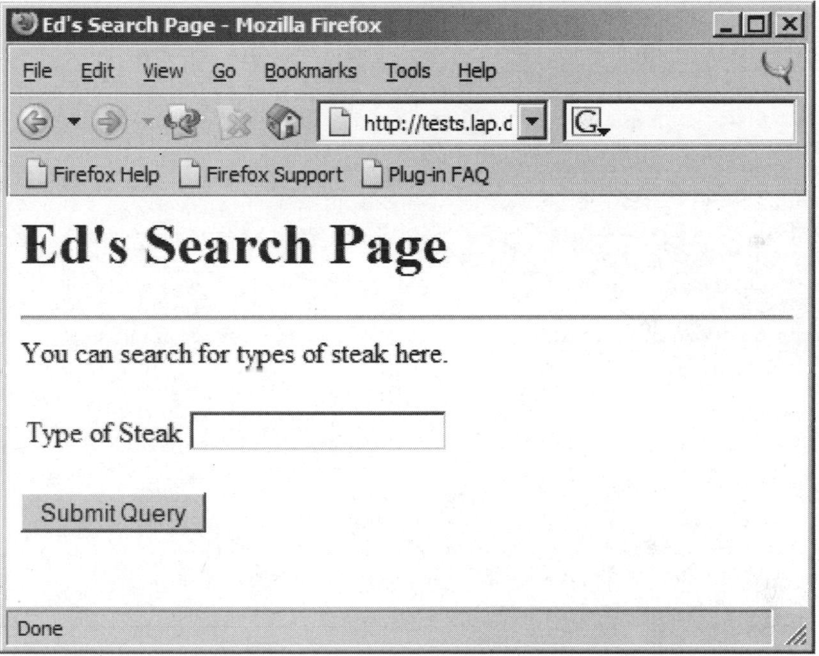

Figure 13-1

Obviously, the search page needs a target. This is provided using two pages—a control page and a template.

searchresults.php

The search results page will be the immediate target of the search page and has the job of determining whether its input is acceptable.

It does *not* have the job of informing the user if the input is not acceptable. Instead, the user will be diverted via a 302 HTTP redirect *back* to the original search page, which then explains the shortcomings.

The conditions that apply in the following example relate to the only search parameter passed to the script—the search string provided by the user. It must contain between 4 and 11 characters, which must be letters, not numbers.

```
<?
require_once("constants.phpm");
require_once("request.phpm");
require_once("constraint.phpm");
require_once("constraintfailure.phpm");


$strTemplateFile = "searchresults.phtml";

$displayHash = Array();

$objRequest = new request();
$objRequest->SetRedirectOnConstraintFailure(true);

$objConstraint = new constraint(CT_MINLENGTH, "3");
$objRequest->AddConstraint("typeOfSteak", VERB_METHOD_GET, $objConstraint);
$objConstraint = new constraint(CT_MAXLENGTH, "12");
$objRequest->AddConstraint("typeOfSteak", VERB_METHOD_GET, $objConstraint);
$objConstraint = new constraint(CT_PERMITTEDCHARACTERS,
"ABCDEFGHIJKLMNOPQRSTUVWXYZabcdefghijklmnopqrstuvwxyz");
$objRequest->AddConstraint("typeOfSteak", VERB_METHOD_GET, $objConstraint);

$objRequest->SetConstraintFailureDefaultRedirectTargetURL("/search.php");
$objRequest->TestConstraints();

# If we've got this far, tests have been passed - perform the search.
$displayHash["RESULTS"] = Array();
$arSteaks = array("fillet", "rump", "sirloin", "burnt");

for ($i=0; $i<=sizeof($arSteaks)-1; $i++) {
  if (!(strpos(trim(strtolower($arSteaks[$i])), strtolower(trim($objRequest-
>GetParameterValue("typeOfSteak")))) === false)) {
    array_push($displayHash["RESULTS"], $arSteaks[$i]);
  };
};

require_once($strTemplateFile);
exit(0);
?>
```

You will notice that the `$displayHash` template content variable is defined again just as the request object is instantiated again.

Each constraint on input is defined as a new instance of a constraint object. It is then added using `AddConstraint`, specifying the delivery method (`GET`, in this case) and parameter name as additional operands.

To negate the need for the referral page to be available, you specify a default URL (the original search page). If you are trying out this example, you will need to adjust the path to this chapter's scripts accordingly.

A single method is then called: `TestConstraints()`. This proceeds to perform the tests necessary to validate whether all the constraints you have expressed have been met. If one has not, it is added to the array of constraint failures contained in this `request` object.

At the end of these tests, if *any* one of them has resulted in failure, the `request` object is authorized to force the user back to the search page, as a result of the use of `SetRedirectOnConstraintFailure()`. First, it serializes a snapshot of the `request` object as it stands on this page and then pushes this as a cookie to the browser. When the user returns to the search page, this cookie will be parsed by the `request` object to work out what went wrong.

If a redirect takes place, the template is not displayed at all. As a result, the user is none the wiser that he or she has hit the second page at all. This improves the user experience; users do not feel as if they have "left" the original search page, hence they instantly recognize that something is wrong.

Assuming that the tests passed, the search can go ahead. In the example, you will notice the search mechanism is pretty simple. In a real-world scenario external classes would undoubtedly be used to execute the search.

After a search results variable has been populated, the template can be displayed.

searchresults.phtml

The search results template is extremely simple. It displays the results of the search. There is no provision in the example for displaying a `your search produced no results` message. However, the implementation of such a message would be relatively straightforward.

```
<html>
<head>
 <title>Ed's Search Page</title>
</head>

<body>
<H1>Search Results</H1>
<hr>
Here are the results of your search.
<UL>
<? for ($i=0; $i<=sizeof($displayHash["RESULTS"])-1; $i++)  ?>
  <LI><?=$displayHash["RESULTS"][$i]?></LI>
<? ; ?>
</UL>
<A HREF="search.php">Go back and search for more steaks!</A>
</body>
</html>
```

Try It!

Assuming that you've entered the code for the previous four files, you can open the search page again, as you did before, and enter some search terms.

First, try an example that should work just fine. Enter **fil** as your search term and click the submit button. This should bring back `fillet` as a search result (see Figure 13-2).

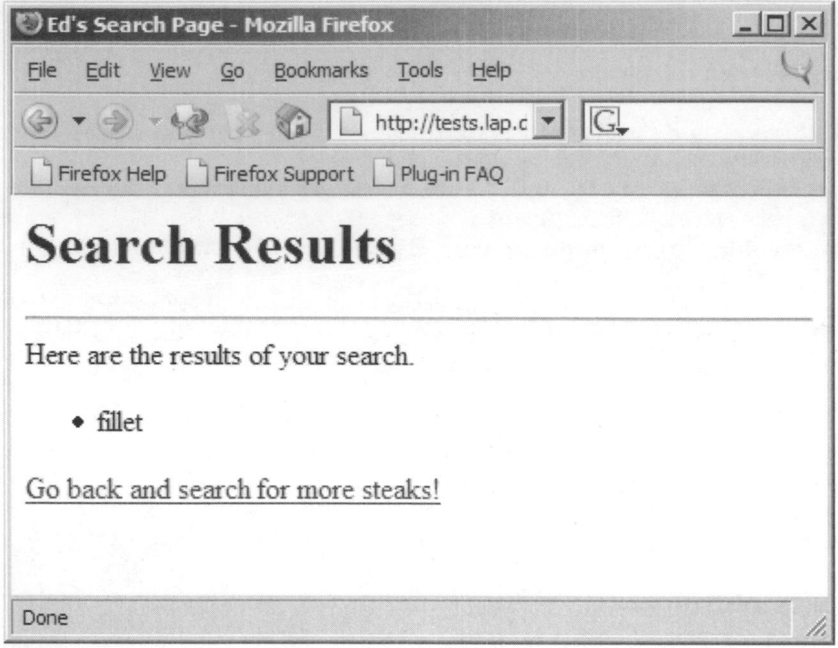

Figure 13-2

Assuming that all looks good, it's time to try out the real purpose of the toolkit: handling things when bad input is supplied.

Try offering **fi**. This is only two characters in length and hence should fail (see Figure 13-3).

As you can see, you are immediately redirected back to the search page and an error message is displayed.

The `searchresults.php` ran three constraint tests against your search parameter and failed on one. That one failure caused a bounce back to the search page, but not before a snapshot serialization of the `request` object you had generated had been taken.

That snapshot was issued to your browser as a cookie immediately before you were redirected back to the original page. The search page then detected the presence of that cookie and knew that you had been referred back to it following a failure as a result. It then proceeded to read the constraint failures that were embedded in that object and display them to you one at a time.

Try issuing a string that is too long ("myfavoritesteak" or a term that contains invalid characters such as "11431") and you will see similar failure messages. Issue something like "my 1st choice." which violates more than one constraint, and you should see that you are chastised twice.

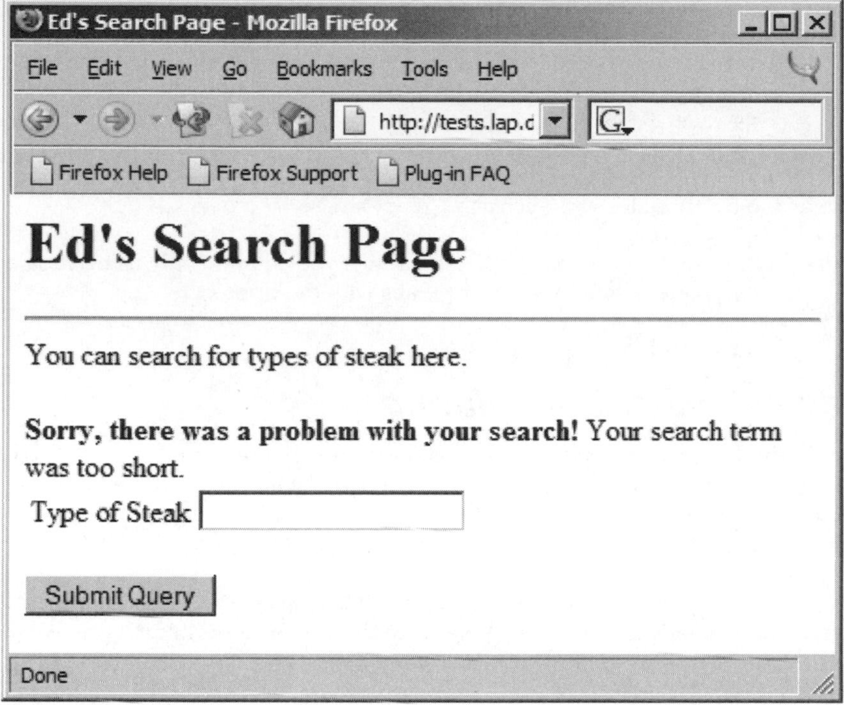

Figure 13-3

The Toolkit in the Wild

By this section of the chapter, you have built up a mini toolkit to allow you to easily handle requests and constraints as part of your use of an MVC design pattern in your projects, as well as learned a simple method for using templates in native PHP.

The built-in constraints in the `request` object you have created here are relatively simple and, admittedly, could be quite easily be implemented in raw PHP within your control page. Constraints really come into their own when they get complex, such as when they need to query a data source to determine validity. On occasions like this, it may make sense to genericize your request object and then extend it to form multiple request objects, perhaps one per page, which handle a different range of constraints in each case.

In the next part of the chapter, you'll learn about Smarty—an entirely different way of doing templating.

True Templating

You've met PHP templating, but what is true templating and how is it different?

Recapping Native PHP Templating

You've been well introduced to the concept of MVC by now, and with luck, it has become clear enough for you to realize that approaching large PHP projects using templating makes sense.

So far, all the templating you've looked at has revolved around the principle of populating a single, multidimensional hash of content and then injecting HTML (or some other markup language) with that content using simple PHP statements such as `if`, `for`, `while`, or others.

However, the very fact that you are required to discipline yourself into only using certain PHP keywords within the templates points to some very clear pitfalls with this approach.

The Pitfalls of Native Templating

The first and most obvious problem is that you are using a very powerful language (PHP) to do a very simple job (spitting out content). The problem is not a performance issue, though. It's simply that by using PHP to take care of the content rendering, you are introducing yet another point in your project where things can go wrong.

Think of the common problems you face when writing big classes—typographical errors, misspelling variable names, accidentally reusing counter variables in heavily nested `for` loops. All these problems are just as constant if you also use PHP for your templating.

The second, and perhaps more serious problem, becomes obvious when you consider larger projects. One of the big advantages of using MVC in PHP projects is that the view and the controller can be delegated to developers skilled in the art of design and HTML, but possibly not so skilled with PHP. This allows the more expensive software architects to work on the heavy-duty PHP driving the model of the project, and the less expensive Web developers to work on the interface.

This is a great use of resources. Not only does it save time and money, it also tends to ensure that the project is as slick on the interface side of things as it is on the back-end code.

However, if you choose to use PHP templating, then the Web developers have no choice but to write in PHP. Admittedly, there's not much PHP they need to know. It's the kind of PHP that could easily go on a cheat sheet. The problem is not so much one of a learning curve but rather one of danger. PHP, after all, does not restrict what these Web developers may or may not use in their templates. Rather, they must restrict themselves. Infinite loops, dangerous system calls, and other potentially critical mistakes are just a tiny typographical error away.

If there were some way to allow Web developers to render the output of a page using flexible tags as part of an arbitrary language, rather than using PHP, this problem could easily be negated. Smarty provides just such a solution.

True Templating with Smarty Templates

Smarty is a package for PHP that allows developers to easily prepare output for a template and then leave the template to display it in whatever way it sees fit.

Smarty is unique in that it provides not just simple 'dump value' methodology, but also allows loops, conditionals, and the traversing of multidimensional arrays. In a nutshell, it replicates all the traditional simple PHP methods used in native PHP templating, without using PHP at all.

Another big advantage of Smarty is its speed. Believe it or not, it actually works by *creating* native PHP from the template. That native PHP is then cached, such that if the template is not changed with subsequent requests, the template itself does not have to be translated into PHP again. It is simply pulled straight from the cache and executed.

Installing Smarty

Installing Smarty is straightforward. Unlike many other template engines, however, it is not a traditional PEAR package, so you have to download and install it manually.

Currently, Smarty resides at `http://smarty.php.net`.

After you have downloaded it, unpack it:

```
root@linuxvm:~# tar -xzvf Smarty-2.6.2.tar.gz
Smarty-2.6.2/
Smarty-2.6.2/COPYING.lib
Smarty-2.6.2/.cvsignore
Smarty-2.6.2/BUGS
Smarty-2.6.2/demo/
...
Smarty-2.6.2/misc/smarty_icon.README
Smarty-2.6.2/misc/smarty_icon.gif
root@linuxvm:~#
```

Next, you need to shift the libraries provided by Smarty to somewhere PHP can see them. Generally, all you need to do is to copy the full contents of the `libs/` subfolder into `/usr/local/lib/php`, like so:

```
root@linuxvm:~/Smarty-2.6.2# cp -r libs/ /usr/local/lib/php
```

Next, you need to hook up your application to use Smarty. Immediately beneath the PHP files that will be using Smarty in your application, you need to create directories called `templates`, `templates_c`, `cache`, and `configs`.

```
root@linuxvm:~# cd public_html/tests/prophp5/mvc/
root@linuxvm:~/public_html/tests/prophp5/mvc# mkdir templates_c
root@linuxvm:~/public_html/tests/prophp5/mvc# mkdir configs
root@linuxvm:~/public_html/tests/prophp5/mvc# mkdir templates
root@linuxvm:~/public_html/tests/prophp5/mvc# mkdir cache
```

Mercifully, Smarty is sympathetic to the needs of real-world projects, for which configuration steps such as these might not always be possible, such as when your PHP scripts reside in multiple directories. You can also manually specify where these folders should exist. You will learn how later in this section.

Next, you need to set some permissions on two of these folders, `template_c` and `cache`. You will need to set the ownership of these folders to be that of the user name of your Web server. In most cases this is the `nobody` user, but it may also be `apache` or various others. If you are unsure, you can check by issuing:

```
ps axuw | grep httpd | grep -v grep | awk '{print $1}' | tail -1
```

The key thing is that this user and the group of which that user is a member are able to read and write to these folders freely. Set permissions as follows:

```
chown nobody.users ./cache
chown nobody.users ./template_c
chmod 770 ./cache
chmod 770 ./template_c
```

The mode 770 means that the owner of these folders may read, write, and execute their contents and that nobody else may. If this bothers you, and you are unable to become root on this machine, you may wish to use 775 instead, which will allow others read and write access. You may, however, rightly deem this to be a security risk.

Using Smarty

A typical Smarty implementation consists of a control file, much as before, ending in .php, and a template file, this time ending in .tpl.

smartytest.php

Take a look at a very simple example:

```
<?
require('Smarty.class.php');

$objSmarty = new Smarty;
$strTemplate = "smartytest.tpl";

$objSmarty->assign("test_variable", "This is the value of my test variable");

$objSmarty->display($strTemplate);
?>
```

You also need to enter the template code for this script. The script needs to reside in the folder called `template` that you have created underneath this one.

smartytest.tpl

Take a look at the following code:

```
<html>
<head>
  <title>Untitled</title>
```

```
</head>

<body>
  This is my template!<BR>
  The value of the variable is: {$test_variable}

</body>
</html>
```

You've probably guessed that the output from running `smartytest.php`, which then invokes the output `template smartytest.tpl`, is something like the following:

```
This is my template!
The value of the variable is: This is the value of my test variable
```

As you can see, we have assigned our Smarty template object a variable called `test_variable`, the output of which we have successfully rendered by using the syntax `{$test_variable}` in the template itself.

Simple enough, but how do you go about expressing arrays, displaying content conditionally, and taking advantage of all the functionality traditionally available in the native PHP templating discussed earlier?

Linear Arrays in Smarty

Pushing a linear array to Smarty and then recursing its contents are relatively simple. Consider the following code in your PHP control script:

```
$objSmarty->assign("FirstName",array("John","Mary","James","Henry"));
```

As you can see, you can assign PHP variables to your Smarty template object in exactly the same way as you would assign a normal garden-variety string. To render it, you would typically use the Smarty equivalent of a `for` loop:

```
{section name=x loop=$FirstName}
   {$FirstName[x]}<BR>
  {/section}
```

The output is predictable enough:

```
John
Mary
James
Henry
```

Associative Arrays in Smarty

You can approach associative arrays (hashes) in a very similar manner to how you approach linear arrays. Consider the following control code to supply the Smarty template:

```
$arHash["Name"] = "Ed";
$arHash["Age"] = 22;
```

```
$arHash["Location"] = "London";
$objSmarty->assign("Writer", $arHash);
```

Again, the approach for assignment appears to be very similar. Take a look at how you can now render the output in your template:

```
The author of this chapter is {$Writer.Name}, {$Writer.Age} years of age,
currently residing in {$Writer.Location}.
```

Notice how we use the simple syntax of {$X.Y}, where X is the name of our Smarty variable and Y is the key from the hash which has been assigned to it. This yields the following output:

```
The author of this chapter is Ed, 22 years of age, currently residing
in London.
```

Conditionals in Smarty

What if you want to display content only if a certain condition is met? This would be of particular interest to you in displaying error messages. You would want to display the error only if an error has definitely occurred.

You would assign variables in your PHP as follows:

```
$objSmarty->assign("isError", 1);
$objSmarty->assign("ErrorText", "You did not specify a search term.");
```

The following template logic can support this:

```
{if $isError == 1}
    The following error occurred: {$ErrorText}
{/if}
```

As you can see, we have used a conditional expression very similar to that which you would use in PHP to perform the test. This will render only the introductory text, and the error itself, if `isError` is set to 1.

```
The following error occurred: You did not specify a search term.
```

To prove this to yourself, change the assignment to `isError` in your PHP to 0, and you will see that the output is not rendered at all.

This is somewhat laborious, though. In native PHP templating you would probably just have checked to see whether an error message has been defined. You can also do this in Smarty:

```
{if $ErrorText}
    The following error occurred: {$ErrorText}
{/if}
```

This completely negates the need to explicitly tell Smarty whether an error exists. It can determine this for itself.

Rewriting search.php with Smarty

Now put these skills into practice with a slightly more complex example. Using Smarty, you can quite easily rewrite the `search.php` and `search.phtml` pair from the first part of the chapter.

Look at the content you are creating in `search.php` so that you know what you have to reproduce using Smarty.

Currently, the `$displayHash` variable may, by the time it reaches `search.phtml`, contain:

- `HADPROBLEMS`: a true/false variable, which again, you can represent as an ordinary variable in Smarty
- `PROBLEMS`: an array of strings, each of which is a problem that has been experienced, only to be echoed if `HADPROBLEMS` is set to true

Quickly modify `search.php` so that it looks like this. The shaded area indicates the code we've modified or added from our original version:

```
require_once("constants.phpm");
require_once("request.phpm");
require_once("constraint.phpm");
require_once("constraintfailure.phpm");

$strTemplateFile = "s_search.tpl";

require('Smarty.class.php');
$objSmarty = new Smarty;

$objRequest = new request();
$blHadProblems = ($objRequest->IsRedirectFollowingConstraintFailure());

if ($blHadProblems) {
  $objSmarty->assign("HADPROBLEMS", "true");
};

if ($blHadProblems) {
  $objFailingRequest = $objRequest-
>GetOriginalRequestObjectFollowingConstraintFailure();
  $arConstraintFailures = $objFailingRequest->GetConstraintFailures();
  $problemArray = Array();
  for ($i=0; $i<=sizeof($arConstraintFailures)-1; $i++) {
    $objThisConstraintFailure = &$arConstraintFailures[$i];
    $objThisFailingConstraintObject = $objThisConstraintFailure-
>GetFailedConstraintObject();
    $intTypeOfFailure = $objThisFailingConstraintObject->GetConstraintType();
    switch ($intTypeOfFailure) {
      case CT_MINLENGTH:
        $problemArray[] = "Your search term was too short.";
        break;
      case CT_MAXLENGTH:
        $problemArray[] = "Your search term was too long.";
        break;
      case CT_PERMITTEDCHARACTERS:
```

```
        $problemArray[] = "Your search term contained characters I didn't
understand.";
        break;
    };
  };
};
if ($problemArray) {
  $objSmarty->assign("PROBLEMS", $problemArray);
};
$objSmarty->display($strTemplateFile);
```

Create a corresponding template file in the `templates` subfolder called `s_search.tpl`:

```
<!DOCTYPE HTML PUBLIC "-//W3C//DTD HTML 4.01 Transitional//EN">

<html>
<head>
 <title>Ed's Search Page</title>
</head>

<body>
<H1>Ed's Search Page</H1>
<hr>
You can search for types of steak here.
<BR><BR>
{if $HADPROBLEMS}
 <B>Sorry, there were problems with your search!</B>
  {section name=x loop=$PROBLEMS}
    {$PROBLEMS[x]}
  {/section}
{/if}
<FORM METHOD="GET" ACTION="searchresults.php">
  <TABLE BORDER="0">
    <TR>
      <TD>Type of Steak</TD>
      <TD><INPUT TYPE="TEXT" NAME="typeOfSteak"></TD>
    </TR>
 </TABLE><BR>
 <INPUT TYPE="SUBMIT">
</FORM>
</body>
</html>
```

Run the revised `search.php` and try to generate errors as you did before. You'll notice that the output upon receiving such errors is almost exactly the same, so the template conversion has been a resounding success.

There is one small problem, however. Generate only one error, and you will still receive a message stating that "there were problems," rather than "there was a problem," with your search.

In the original .PHTML native PHP template, you accounted for this using:

```
<B>Sorry, there <?=((sizeof($displayHash["PROBLEMS"]) > 1) ? "were problems" :
"was a problem")?> with your search!</B>
```

Thankfully, you can account for this in Smarty, too. All you need to do is measure the size of the array and adjust the output accordingly, exactly as you have done in native PHP.

```
<B>Sorry, there {if $PROBLEMS[1]}were problems{else}was a problem{/if}
with your search!</B>
```

There is some slight cheating going on, however. There is no way in Smarty to measure the size of an array without calling upon PHP code, so the code simply checks for the existence of a second element in the array. If it exists, the user sees the plural text. Otherwise, the user sees the singular text.

If you modify your template to use this new code, you should find that the output of the script is exactly the same now as it was when you used native PHP templating in the first half of the chapter.

Advanced Smarty

Now that you've familiarized yourself with basic Smarty use, it's worth looking in a little more detail at some of the more advanced features it offers.

Runtime Configuration

First, as mentioned at the beginning of this section, you may well find yourself confronted with situations in which creating subfolders under every single location where .php files reside is undesirable. Thankfully, Smarty allows you to specify these locations at runtime:

```
$smarty->template_dir = '/web/www.mydomain.com/smarty/guestbook/templates/';
$smarty->compile_dir = '/web/www.mydomain.com/smarty/guestbook/templates_c/';
$smarty->config_dir = '/web/www.mydomain.com/smarty/guestbook/configs/';
$smarty->cache_dir = '/web/www.mydomain.com/smarty/guestbook/cache/';
```

Multidimensional Arrays

Multidimensional arrays may be treated in much the same manner as their single-dimensional counterparts, whether they are associative, linear, or a mixture:

```
$multiArray = Array(Array("x","o","x"),Array("o","x","x"),
Array("o","o","x")); $objSmarty->assign("TicTacToBoard", $multiArray);
```

Tie this to the following template:

```
<TABLE BORDER="1">
  {section name=y loop=$TicTacToBoard}
    <TR>
      {section name=x loop=$TicTacToBoard[y]}
        <TD>{$TicTacToBoard[y][x]}</TD>
      {/section}
    </TR>
  {/section}
</TABLE>
```

This is the expected familiar Tic Tac Toe board with X winning down the left-to-right diagonal.

Variable Modifiers

Variable modifiers may be used by template designers to perform very simple modifications to the variables they have received.

```
$smarty->assign('bookTitle', "Beginning PHP5");
```

Couple this with the template code:

```
{$bookTitle|replace:"Beginning":"Professional"}
```

The output is very much as expected.

Functions

Smarty defines a number of functions in its language. It considers some to be built in—unable to be modified or overwritten. The functions provided in Smarty are really better described as methods, in that they do not generally perform any function on an input, unlike the modifiers you have just met, such as `replace`, which changes its input before rendering it.

One very useful example is the `strip` function, which allows you to neatly lay out HTML properly tabulated and spaced, safe in the knowledge that any extraneous whitespace will be stripped out before it is sent to the browser. This makes the templates very easy to maintain.

```
{strip}
<table border="0">
 <tr>
    <td>
        Here is some content.
    </td>
 </tr>
</table>
{/strip}
```

This is a great deal easier for a human being to read. At the time when the HTML is sent to the browser, however, how it looks behind the scenes is far less important than how it displays to the user. So, the `{strip}` tag removes any whitespace for you that might disturb the output:

```
<table border="0"><tr><td>Here is some content.</td></tr></table>
```

Capturing Output

Sometimes, rather than simply spit parsed template output directly to screen, you may want to capture it into a variable. This can be particularly useful should you, for example, want to render XML content using Smarty and then pass it through an XSL stylesheet to actually render it to the Web browser. Alternatively, you may not want to pass the rendered content at all. For example, you may be sending an HTML e-mail. Here, Smarty is very useful indeed, as you will discover in the next chapter, "Communicating with Users."

```
// capture the output
$strOutput = $objSmarty->fetch("index.tpl");
```

Simply assign the rendered template's output HTML to the variable `$strOutput`, with which you can then do whatever you desire.

Including Other Templates

Smarty even allows you to include other templates, which will be parsed in the normal way. You may use this to add common headers and footers to your pages:

```
{include file="header.tpl"}
```

Further Reading

The functionality of Smarty is enormous and far beyond the scope of this chapter. Having been introduced to some examples of standard usage, however, you should now be well equipped to explore its functionality further.

The obvious starting point is the Smarty reference site at `http://smarty.php.net/manual/en/`. All modifiers, functions, and even obscure configuration parameters are documented here in full. Conveniently, the documentation is split into two sections, targeting programmers and HTML template developers alike.

When to Use Smarty vs. Traditional Templating

The decision to use Smarty over traditional native PHP templating should not be taken lightly. Although Smarty is clearly a great tool for simple templating, its functionality is still only a subset of that which might be needed in large-scale projects.

Although it can be extended with native PHP through the use of the `{php}` and `{/php}` tags, doing so rather defeats the purpose of using safe templates in the first place. Indeed, Smarty's own Web site states: "embedding PHP code into templates is highly discouraged."

The skills and experience of any other developers working with you on the project are likely to be the deciding factor. If you are the sole engineer working on a project, it is almost certainly better to use native templating. However, if the project requires a number of designers and HTML specialists working on the output from your scripts, Smarty templates are a much safer bet because they allow such individuals to manipulate the display logic of your application to their hearts' content, without touching the PHP code behind it.

Summary

In this chapter, you learned about the model, view, controller design pattern and why it is an excellent methodology to follow on complex PHP projects.

As well as learning the theory behind MVC methodology, you were introduced to two very different ways in which that methodology can be followed. First, you met an MVC toolkit that allowed you to implement a `request` and `constraint` object hierarchy in your projects to greater enforce the separation between model, view, and controller.

Second, you were introduced to the concept of templating and how and why it proves to be an excellent example of best-practice MVC compliance.

Last, you met Smarty templates in some detail. You saw just how easily you can convert native PHP templates into Smarty templates in just a few minutes, as well as how some of the advanced features of Smarty mean it can be a valid templating choice for all but the most complex of projects.

In the next chapter, you'll look at the importance of communicating with your users and examine an object model to support such communication.

Communicating with Users

The Web is a simple method of communication when you come right down to it. The end user requests a page, things happens in the background, and the Web server fires back some content in response. Repeat *ad infinitum*. But if you limit yourself simply to talking to users through their Web browsers, you're missing out on a very big part of what makes a truly impressive user interface.

In this chapter, you learn about the building blocks of user communication and how it translates into an extraordinarily natural PHP object hierarchy. You'll see how you can extend and develop this hierarchy to support virtually any form of electronic communication. You'll also see practical examples of implementing some functionality that PHP doesn't provide and that you may find useful in your day-to-day development.

Perhaps most important, you'll learn why you should communicate with your users in the first place.

Why Communicate?

In the early days of the Web, long before PHP came onto the horizon, the user experience—that is, the impact on the user of using your Web site—was largely unimportant. Content was key. In fact, content was all there was. The Web was little more than a magazine with convenient tabs for ease of turning the pages.

No more. The Web is more and more accepted as a superb mechanism for implementing thin client applications, from the simple Webmail facilities of an entertainment portal to the sophisticated multiuser inventory control network of a big corporation. This capacity is, after all, why you learned PHP in the first place.

Unfortunately, the adoption of the Web as a means for implementing thin client solutions has been less than plain sailing. Many authors have omitted (perhaps with the best of intentions) providing modern-day equivalents of the key features that made thin client architectures of yesteryear usable.

One of the biggest of these is the capacity for communicating with users outside the context of the immediate user interface. Consider an abstract example. The immediate user interface of a telephone consists of the mouthpiece and earpiece. Yet, all telephones include ringers so that you know when a call is incoming. This is an example of *notifying* the user of an event.

A second example is the fax machine. Many fax machines print a delivery report when a fax has been sent successfully. This report is auxiliary to the keypad and LCD display, which constitute the immediate user interface, and is an example of keeping the user informed.

One final example. If you have ever applied for a bank loan over the phone, you have doubtless found acquiring debt in a matter of minutes remarkably easy. Still, the bank sends papers for you to sign to your registered home address. Even if you are approved in principle over the phone, the money doesn't go anywhere near your checking account until you sign and return the papers they sent you. This is an example of using communication with the user as a form of security, a form of validation.

There are other examples. But this chapter examines how those mentioned here have an impact on the real world and how you act on them through OOP mechanisms.

Reasons to Communicate with Users

Take these three examples and try applying them to the Web. Examine why you might want your application to notify, inform, or validate your users.

Notification

A number of scenarios can arise in which you may want to notify your users of something through a means other than a Web browser.

This issue is particularly relevant if you remember that HTTP is what is known as a stateless protocol. It is not particularly easy to get the Web browser to sit there and wait for something to happen before informing the user. You can do it in various ways, but none is particularly pretty.

Imagine that your application has a sophisticated reporting system that allows users to request reports on all manner of business details. Particularly if those reports are extremely SQL intensive, a strong argument can be made for generating those reports offline—that is, independently of any Web browser usage. That way, the user is not presented with any excessively long request in order to view the report. It is simply not realistic to guarantee the user will not give up and click Stop halfway through a two-minute wait for a page to be generated. In a real-world-scenario, the user would use the Web browser to order the report, doing so in the understanding that the system would notify him or her when the report is ready.

In another example, imagine that a subscription Web site is set up to bill the user's credit card automatically every month on the first of the month. It wouldn't be terribly good customer service if, because the user's credit card had been declined during that month's billing process, the user were simply unable to log into the Web site. Instead, you would issue what is sometimes known as an *exceptional notification*—a notification that occurs as a result of something out of the ordinary (typically, bad) happening—in the form of an e-mail inviting the user to log on and give details of one of his or her many other valid credit cards.

Notification is not restricted to e-mail, of course. Operators of data centers all over the world have fallen in love with SMS (Short Message Service) notifications to their cellular phones to advise them when vital servers or processes have fallen over, regardless of where they are at the time.

Information

Communicating information to users differs slightly from notification in that it is not necessarily event driven. Instead, it is a fully expected communication issued with the intent of updating the user as to the status of something. Compare the arrival of the morning newspaper on your front porch with a sudden notice from the Emergency Broadcast System during a television show. You expect the newspaper's arrival, but the notice of impending blizzards in Tampa Bay come as a bit of a surprise.

A good example of keeping users informed is that of a weekly newsletter from a subscriber Web site. This could be something automatically generated by tabulating an extract of that week's news stories, or it could be something put together by an editorial team. Either way, you're keeping your users up-to-date.

Another good example is an order update from an online e-tailer. If seven days have expired without the arrival of the books you ordered, you might be getting worried, and you would undoubtedly be reassured by an e-mail explaining that the books are still on order. Again, this is *not* a notification. Nothing's changed. Nothing's new. It's just a quick update.

This means of communication is perfectly adaptable to other information methods—fax, text message, snail mail—you name it. You'll learn shortly that the various communications media you may previously have thought to be completely different are in fact virtually identical (at least from a software architecture perspective).

Validation

Validation is often a means of communicating once for the purpose of communicating again. You validate a destination address of some description so that you may reassure yourself of its accuracy should you need to use it again. Alternatively, you may have some piece of information your user wants, but to be doubly sure of the requesting user's identity, you will send that information only to the user's registered address.

The bank loan example on the previous page represents the more serious side of things. After all, the bank wants to verify your correct address so that it can send the repo men in if your repayments are tardy. Numerous Web sites, however, validate e-mail addresses in this way for later direct marketing usage. The simple way to do this is to send out an activation link (usually presenting some kind of unique key stored against the user's record in the database) to the e-mail address offered by the user. The user must click the link to activate his or her membership.

Similar methods can be used to throw a rope to users who've forgotten their password, although it isn't usually either a good or feasible idea to tell reveal their password via email. You shouldn't be storing their password unencrypted or in any reversible form, or transmitting it in plain text over e-mail. You can certainly provide them with a link (generally of limited-time validity) for the purposes of gaining temporary access to your site so that they may set a new password.

In Europe, where it is increasingly common to communicate with web site visitors via their cell phones as well as via e-mail, some sites send an activation code as a short text message to the cell phone number the user offered at registration. The user must then enter that activation code on the site to prove the validity of the number he or she provided.

As an aside, this SMS code-sending technique can actually be used as a poor man's form of second-layer authentication. Authentication on systems is generally provided by one or more of three keys. These are *something you are* (a fingerprint, iris scan, or even originating IP address), *something you know* (a password), and *something you have* (a key or fob). The accepted wisdom is for any system guarding data of any kind of sensitivity to implement more than one of these mechanisms. By sending a unique code to a registered mobile phone upon entry of a username and password, that extra layer of protection is provided.

Think Outside the Web Browser

By realizing the potential of alternative communication mechanisms (particularly e-mail), you offer users a far more enhanced user experience on your site. Take a look at how you can implement this in PHP (beyond the `mail()` function, of course).

> **It's probably worth stressing that the `mail()` function in PHP is to sending e-mail from your code what a ten-year-old's treehouse phone is to digital telephony. It should never appear in serious production sites.**

Types of Communication

Before you get down and dirty with some communication code, take a step back from the problem for a second. Doing so can give you a better grasp on the obvious outbound communication class hierarchy in front of you, which you will have to write yourself because PHP doesn't provide it. What do all communications have in common?

All communications have . . .

You can quite reasonably say that all communications have the following:

- Recipients—one or more people to receive the communication. This communication can be in the form of e-mail addresses, fax numbers, mobile phone numbers, postal addresses, PO boxes, pigeon holes, and so on.
- A message—the actual body of what you want to send. The message can be transmitted in plain text or HTML (for an e-mail), a letter-sized bitmap (for a fax), 160 characters of text (for a text message), a stream of 11 KHz audio (for an automated phone call), and so on.

Not all communications have . . .

On the flip side, you must also understand the differences between the various types of communication. Not all communications have:

- Subjects—typically, only emails that have subjects.
- Content variants—e-mails these days are often sent with both HTML and plain text versions entwined in one MIME package (more on this later).
- Attachments—these are e-mail and text message specific.
- Revealing of or differentiation between Carbon and Blind Carbon recipients—if you send a fax, text message, or letter to more than one person, nobody will know who else received the message unless you make a list and stick it in the body.

What about Recipients?

A recipient of an e-mail is a totally different kind of recipient from a recipient of a text message. Take a look at the following table.

Type of communication	Recipient Component	Format
E-mail	Name	String
	Address	String following RFC822 specification
SMS Text Message to cell phone	Number	String, consisting of plus sign, country prefix, and local number
Fax	Number	String, consisting of Telco-understood telephone number
Letter	Full Name	String
	House Number	Integer
	Street	String
	Town / City	String
	State	String
	Zip	String matching USPS ZIP format

Communication As a Class Hierarchy

There are many possibilities to consider if you are to construct a class hierarchy. You need to understand that although communications have much in common, fundamental differences exist between one media form and another, as do totally different methods of addressing.

The Recipient Class: A Quick Test of OOP-Like Thinking

All messages have recipients (and often more than one). Given that these recipients are clearly more involved than strings, it would be nice to have a class to represent them with such useful methods as `isValid()` to determine whether the recipient is a valid one.

The difficulty is obvious. How are you to implement such a class effectively when so much variation in the data is required?

You could create a single `Recipient` class covering all possible scenarios, but this isn't particularly OOP-compliant because large numbers of member methods and variables are peculiar to one form of communication and irrelevant to others. The solution must be to have some kind of generic `Recipient` class, with each special case having a class in its own right. But how do you relate these special-case recipients to the master `Recipient` class?

First, reject the use of traditional class inheritance. Although technically feasible, it's still a misuse of OOP design. Superclasses—classes that are extended to form subclasses—must be classes in their own right. Ford is a subclass of superclass Car, but although Ford may contain additional or even overloaded methods or member variables, certain characteristics of Car indicate that it is (or once was) an object of use in its own right. It has its own methods (such as Drive and Shift) and its own member variables (such as Registration and Color), and these are not likely to be overloaded. A recipient of a particular ilk (such as that for an e-mail) could have member variables and methods of its own just like the Ford, but it would not inherit any of them from a parent generic recipient superclass. For reasons that a glance at the table in the previous section should make apparent, a generic recipient cannot have any useful member variables or methods,. Accordingly, we must reject the use of class inheritance.

The answer becomes apparent if you consider the bigger picture. What is your communications framework likely to want from these recipient objects? In fact, you can limit it to just two methods that will be accessed by the communications framework—`isValid()` and `getStringRepresentation()`. These two would return a usable string representation of the framework, dependent on the context. Any other methods (`setHouseNumber`, for example) are for use by your application solely for populating the recipient. You can quite safely say that the communications framework will never touch them.

So the task can be summarized as follows. Create some means for a number of distinct classes representing recipients of different types of communications media to be universally accessed by an external framework of other classes, such that additional distinct classes may be added at a later date without any modification to that external framework.

The solution is to create an *interface* for the generic recipient class (not really a class at all). That interface provides definitions for these two key methods (`isValid()` and `getStringRepresentation()`) that the individual recipient objects must provide exactly as shown.

Consider the following code snippet, which provides just such a generic interface. You may wish to save this code as `recipient.phpm` at this stage:

```
interface Recipient {
   public function isValid();
   public function getStringRepresentation();
}
```

You might be tempted to implement an abstract recipient class to almost exactly the same effect, but this would be bad design rearing its ugly head once more. Again, remember that the recipient as you understand it has no useful properties and no useful methods. It would be fatuous to try to extend it in any way that infers class status when you merely want to provide a common means for other classes to interface with a collection of unrelated classes in some common way. If you have doubts as to the lack of commonality of the various recipient classes, refer to the table earlier in this section.

The EmailRecipient Class

Take a look at how to implement this. You won't reproduce every single type of recipient, so look at a simple one—the `EmailRecipient` class. Start it by declaring a class that implements the `Recipient` interface we declared previously:

```
class EmailRecipient implements Recipient {
```

Add some member variables to use to store important properties of your e-mail recipient. You saw in the table appearing earlier in the chapter that an e-mail recipient has both a recipient name and a recipient address:

```
private $recipient_name;
private $recipient_address;
```

Now you must provide an implementation of every method declared in the `Recipient` interface. In fact, there are just two. The first will validate your recipient after it has been set up by whatever application is using it:

```
  public function isValid() {
    if (preg_match("/[\<\>\r\n]{1,}/", $this->recipient_name)) {
      return(false);
    };
    if (preg_match("/^([A-Z0-9._%-]+)()([A-Z0-9._%-]+)(\.)([A-Z0-9._%-
]{2,4})$/i", $this->recipient_address)) {
      return(true);
    } else {
      return(false);
    };
  }
```

What's going on here is straightforward. A couple of regular expression matches are performed on the recipient. First, the recipient name is validated to ensure that it consists of one or more valid characters. Then, the e-mail address is checked against a regular expression to ensure its conformity to RFC 822 format.

Next you need to provide some means to get an intelligent (that is, readily usable) string representation of your recipient.

```
public function getStringRepresentation() {
  $strMyRepresentation = "";
  if ($this->recipient_name) {
    $strMyRepresentation .= $this->recipient_name . " ";
  };
  $strMyRepresentation .= "<" . $this->recipient_address . ">";

  return($strMyRepresentation);
}
```

As you might be aware, the readily accepted format for e-mail addresses is `First Name Last Name <user@example.com>`, so we stick to that format here.

The remainder of the class is dedicated to accessor methods—that is, methods to get and set the various properties of the e-mail recipient. As you can see, we have provided an easy means to set all these within the constructor. For other recipients, such as with those of a snail mail letter, doing this may be cumbersome.

```
  public function __construct($strRecipientAddress, $strRecipientName = "") {
    $this->recipient_name = $strRecipientName;
    $this->recipient_address = $strRecipientAddress;
  }
```

```
    public function setRecipientName($strRecipientName) {
      $this->recipient_name = $strRecipientName;
    }

    public function setRecipientAddress($strRecipientAddress) {
      $this->recipient_address = $strRecipientAddress;
    }

    public function getRecipientName() {
      return($this->recipient_name);
    }

    public function getRecipientAddress() {
      return($this->recipient_address);
    }

  }
```

That concludes the e-mail recipient class, an implementation of the generic `Recipient` interface. If you wanted to save this as `emailrecipient.phpm` at this stage, nobody would hold it against you.

Even though you haven't reached the communication framework yet, you can test this by using the following snippet of sample code. You need to use `require()` in both the `Recipient` interface and `EmailCommunication` class that you've saved so far.

```
$objEmailRecipient = new EmailRecipient("ed@example.com", "Ed Lecky-
Thompson");
if ($objEmailRecipient->isValid()) {
  print "Recipient is valid! ";
  print "The string representation of this recipient would be: " .
htmlentities($objEmailRecipient->getStringRepresentation());
} else {
  print "Recipient is not valid!";
};
```

This yields the following output:

```
Recipient is valid! The string representation of this recipient would be: Ed
Lecky-Thompson <ed@example.com>
```

If you take a quick look at the `EmailRecipient` class in more detail, you can see just how simple it is. The two private member variables are specific to this class, as are the constructor and the (somewhat superfluous) `setRecipientName` and `setRecipientAddress` accessor methods and their (less superfluous) `get` counterparts.

Because you have declared this class to implement the `Recipient` interface, you are obliged to provide the two methods so described in that interface. If you do not, PHP helpfully yields an error message.

In the `getStringRepresentation` method, you simply glue the pieces together to form a usable RFC822-compliant representation of the recipient's name and e-mail address. This is something you can drop straight into an SMTP session.

In the `isValid` method, you check the recipient's name for any bad characters that might confuse the SMTP server; then you check the e-mail address for basic syntactical validity against a regular expression.

Other Implementations

You have just implemented an EmailRecipient class to encapsulate neatly the concept of e-mail recipients. Other types of communication have their own types of recipient, and each will need an implementation of the Recipient interface, too.

You can follow a very similar procedure to implement such alternative recipient types. First, ensure that sufficient member variables exist to hold every property of that recipient type, and that you have suitable Get and Set accessor methods to read and write to those member variables. Second, implement the mandatory methods required by the Recipient interface: the validator method and the string representation method.

The Communication Class

Even though recipients are different by nature, with streamlined interface access to any and all recipient objects, you can greatly simplify your communication class.

A communication object is literally that—a single communication by whatever method. We don't particularly mind which method, nor do we even allude to which ones are possible.

The communication class will never itself be instantiated. Instead, it will be extended by a class representing the particular form of communication to be used: EmailCommunication, SMSCommunication, and so forth.

Unlike the generic recipient construction, however, it will have useful methods of its own. For this reason, it really will be a genuine class and not just an interface. However, one method—send—will be declared as abstract so that it is implemented only in subclasses.

Subclasses of Communication may, of course, have methods and member variables of their own that supplement those of their superclass. A likely use for this are methods that somehow manipulate the message property of Communication in some way. An example is a method in SMSCommunication in which to load a bitmap (.BMP) file to send as a cellular phone operator logo in place of a standard text message.

Take a look at the following code. Note that it makes use of the Collection and Collection Iterator discussed in Chapters 5 and 6. If you want the following to compile, you'll need to require() that code somewhere along the way.

```
abstract class Communication {

  protected $arRecipientCollection;
  private $strMessage;

  protected $strErrorMessage;
  protected $errorCode;

  abstract public function send();

  public function __construct() {
    $this->strMessage = "";
  }
```

```
    public function addRecipient($objRecipient, $strIdentifier = "") {
      $strRecipient = $objRecipient->getStringRepresentation();
      if (!$strIdentifier) {
        $strIdentifier = $strRecipient;
      };
      $this->arRecipientCollection->addItem($objRecipient, $strIdentifier);
    }
    public function removeRecipient($strIdentifier) {
      $this->arRecipientCollection->removeItem($strIdentifier);
    }

   protected function _setMessage($strMessage) {
      $this->strMessage = $strMessage;
    }

    protected function _getMessage() {
      return($this->strMessage);
    }

    public function getErrorMessage() {
      return($this->strErrorMessage);
    }

    public function getErrorCode() {
      return($this->errorCode);
    }

  }
```

As you can see, you declare the recipient collection as protected. This means that although it cannot be tinkered with from within your application's code, it *can* be tinkered with by subclasses of the `Communication` class—which is a good thing.

You probably have noticed how we are brazenly adding recipient objects passed to `addRecipient` to the recipient collection, even though we have absolutely no idea of what type that object is, and equally no idea of what type of collection `arRecipientCollection` is. You may well think this is a recipe for runtime errors but, in fact, it is the subclass that will initialize the collection, and it will make it a collection of whatever it wants. As long as whatever is passed as a recipient object supports the interface developed earlier and is of the same type as the type required by the subclass, there will be no problems.

Use the string representation of the object as a suitable key for the collection. The message property remains private and can be manipulated using `_setMessage` and `_getMessage`, accessible only from the subclass. Don't worry about the error message and error code member variables yet. You'll meet those a bit later.

So how do you use this in practice? Quite simply, you extend it to form a useful subclass. Take a look at `EmailCommunication`, which, as the name suggests, is used for sending a message to one or more `EmailRecipient` objects.

E-mailing Your Users

Now look at `EmailCommunication` (the subclass to `Communication`) in detail. First, you need some simple way of enforcing the recipient collection of the superclass to contain only `EmailRecipient` objects. You can do this by reworking the `Collection` class slightly to form a subclass called `EmailRecipientCollection`. This may by definition consist only of `EmailRecipient` members.

```
class EmailRecipientCollection extends Collection {
  public function addItem(EmailRecipient $obj, $key = null) {
    parent::addItem($obj, $key);
  }
}
```

Note that this offers no new functionality. It merely offers the enforcement through *Class Type Hints* as to the class type that new members must be.

With this class now understood by PHP, you can implement the `EmailCommunication` class itself.

Building a Test Version

It's a good idea to first build a reduced-functionality implementation to test the OOP interfaces. After all, if you can get that right, the rest should be fairly straightforward. By using some strategic printouts, you can see what's going on and check that the logic works.

After you are certain the logic and, hence, the OOP integration and interfaces work all right, you can concentrate on the implementation; that is, getting the e-mail out the door.

Start class in a fairly standard manner, declaring it and its two properties: one a visible address and one a collection of visible carbon copy addresses. You do not need to worry about blind carbon copy addresses; they are not visible and thus can be handled solely by the parent `Communication` class.

```
class EmailCommunication extends Communication {

 private $objApparentPrimaryRecipient;          // Visible To: address
 private $arObjApparentSecondaryRecipients;     // Visible Cc: address(es)
```

Next, provide a means to set the primary recipient of the e-mail. Note that the class adds to the main recipient collection of the parent class (generic), while also setting the primary visible recipient (specific to the `EmailCommunication` class).

```
  public function setPrimaryRecipient($objRecipient) {
    if (!($this->arRecipientCollection->exists($objRecipient-
>getStringRepresentation()))) {
      parent::addRecipient($objRecipient);
    };
    $this->objApparentPrimaryRecipient = $objRecipient->__clone();
  }
```

The methods for adding and removing carbon copy (Cc:) recipients are much the same. Again, you manipulate both the parent collection and the local apparent recipients array.

```
  public function addCarbonRecipient($objRecipient) {
    if (!($this->arRecipientCollection->exists($objRecipient-
>getStringRepresentation()))) {
```

```
      parent::addRecipient($objRecipient);
    };
    if (!($this->arObjApparentSecondaryRecipients->exists($objRecipient-
>getStringRepresentation()))) {
      $this->arObjApparentSecondaryRecipients->addItem($objRecipient,
$objRecipient->getStringRepresentation());
    };
  }

  public function removeCarbonRecipient($objRecipient) {
    if ($this->arRecipientCollection->exists($objRecipient-
>getStringRepresentation())) {
      parent::removeRecipient($objRecipient);
    };
    if ($this->arObjApparentSecondaryRecipients->exists($objRecipient-
>getStringRepresentation())) {
      $this->arObjApparentSecondaryRecipients->removeItem($objRecipient-
>getStringRepresentation());
    };
  }
```

The same principle applies for adding and removing blind recipients, except that you do not touch the apparent recipients list:

```
  public function addBlindRecipient($objRecipient) {
    if (!($this->arRecipientCollection->exists($objRecipient-
>getStringRepresentation()))) {
      parent::addRecipient($objRecipient);
    };
  }

  public function removeBlindRecipient($objRecipient) {
    if (!($this->arRecipientCollection->exists($objRecipient-
>getStringRepresentation()))) {
      parent::removeRecipient($objRecipient->getStringRepresentation());
    };
  }
```

Now turn your attention to the constructor, which must initialize the superclass collection to be a collection of the appropriate type, and the local collection of apparent recipients to be another collection of the same type (though not necessarily with the same contents). Note that you also call the parent class constructor when you're done.

```
public function __construct() {
  // Superclass collection
  $this->arRecipientCollection = new EmailRecipientCollection();
  // Local collection of visible (CC:) recipients
  $this->arObjApparentSecondaryRecipients = new EmailRecipientCollection();
  parent::__construct();
}
```

Now comes the dummy send method, used to ensure that your class works correctly:

```
    public function send() {
      print "ACTUAL RECIPIENTS<BR><BR>";
      foreach ($this->arRecipientCollection as $strRecipientIdentifier =>
  $objEmailRecipient) {
        print "NAME: " . $objEmailRecipient->getRecipientName() . "<BR>";
        print "EMAIL ADDRESS: " . $objEmailRecipient->getRecipientAddress() .
  "<BR>";
      };

      print "<BR><BR>APPARENTLY TO RECIPIENT<BR><BR>";
      print "NAME: " . $this->objApparentPrimaryRecipient-
  >getRecipientName() . "<BR>";
      print "EMAIL ADDRESS: " . $this->objApparentPrimaryRecipient-
  >getRecipientAddress() . "<BR>";

      print "<BR><BR>APPARENT SECONDARY RECIPIENTS<BR><BR>";
      foreach ($this->arObjApparentSecondaryRecipients as
  $strRecipientIdentifier => $objEmailRecipient) {
        print "NAME: " . $objEmailRecipient->getRecipientName() . "<BR>";
        print "EMAIL ADDRESS: " . $objEmailRecipient->getRecipientAddress() .
  "<BR>";
      };

    }
  }
```

Let's examine the above in a bit more detail. First, notice the member properties:

```
  private $objApparentPrimaryRecipient;          // Visible To: address

  private $arObjApparentSecondaryRecipients; // Visible Cc: address(es)
```

These two member properties exist in addition *to* the master recipient list inherited from the Communication superclass. They represent a single EmailRecipient object representing to whom the e-mail is directly addressed (the "To:" line) and a collection of EmailRecipients representing any Carbon Copy (Cc:) addresses. These two member properties are not, strictly speaking, important in determining who gets the message. That is still handled by the collection in the superclass. However, they exist for the purpose of formatting the e-mail so that the "master" and "Cc:" recipients appear in the right place in the message headers.

The constructor method concerns itself with the setup of these two additional private member variables, as well as calls the superclass constructor for good measure.

The various methods used for adding and removing the master recipient, carbon copy recipients, and blind carbon copy recipients, all work in much the same way. They check to see whether an object of that key (the key being the string representation of the recipient object) exists in the collection before performing the relevant operation. This is achieved using the exists method provided by the collection object.

Take a look at some test addresses just to prove that it works. You can then go back and look at the way we actually send the mail. To execute the following code, you will need to `require()` all the classes developed so far in this chapter.

```
$objEmail = new EmailCommunication;
$objEmailRecipient = new EmailRecipient("ed@example.com", "Ed
Lecky-Thompson");
$objEmailCCRecipient = new EmailRecipient("ted@example.com", "Ted
Lecky-Thompson");
$objEmailBCCRecipient = new EmailRecipient("zed@example.com", "Zed
Lecky-Thompson");
$objEmail->setPrimaryRecipient($objEmailRecipient);
$objEmail->addCarbonRecipient($objEmailCCRecipient);
$objEmail->addBlindRecipient($objEmailBCCRecipient);
$objEmail->send();
```

Run the preceding code, and you get output like that shown in Figure 14-1.

This looks pretty healthy. As you can see from the code, Ed is the main recipient of this e-mail while Ted's been CC'd, and Zed's been BCC'd. When Ed receives the mail, he will be able to see his name on the To: line and Ted's on the Cc: line. Ed won't know Zed got the mail. When Ted receives the mail, he will see much the same. Again, he won't know Zed was BCC'd on this important message. When Zed receives the mail, he won't see his name anywhere, but he'll be able to deduce that he must have been BCC'd on the original message.

The output from our dummy test implementation shows that our code is correct. The list of actual recipients displays all three genuine recipients of the e-mail. The primary recipient is correct, and the CC'd recipient is listed correctly, too.

Getting the Message Across

You need to do a couple of things to make the EmailCommunication class function properly.

First, get the body of the e-mail built up and slotted into the `message` member variable. A simple, plain text e-mail consists of two parts—the header and the body. Conveniently enough, the two are separated by nothing more complex than a blank line. The header contains the sender's address, recipient's address, subject, CC: addresses, and myriad other bits and pieces.

Now add two member variables—one for the subject line and one for the sender. The sender can again be an `EmailRecipient` object because a sender has a name and an address, same as a recipient.

```
private $objApparentSender;  // Visible From: address
private $strSubjectLine;     // Subject line
```

The use of some basic methods will allow users of the class to set these properties.

For the time being, assume that you're dealing with purely plain text e-mails. You add a simple method to allow public setting of the message property. The message property is synonymous with the body of the e-mail, because the headers will be managed separately.

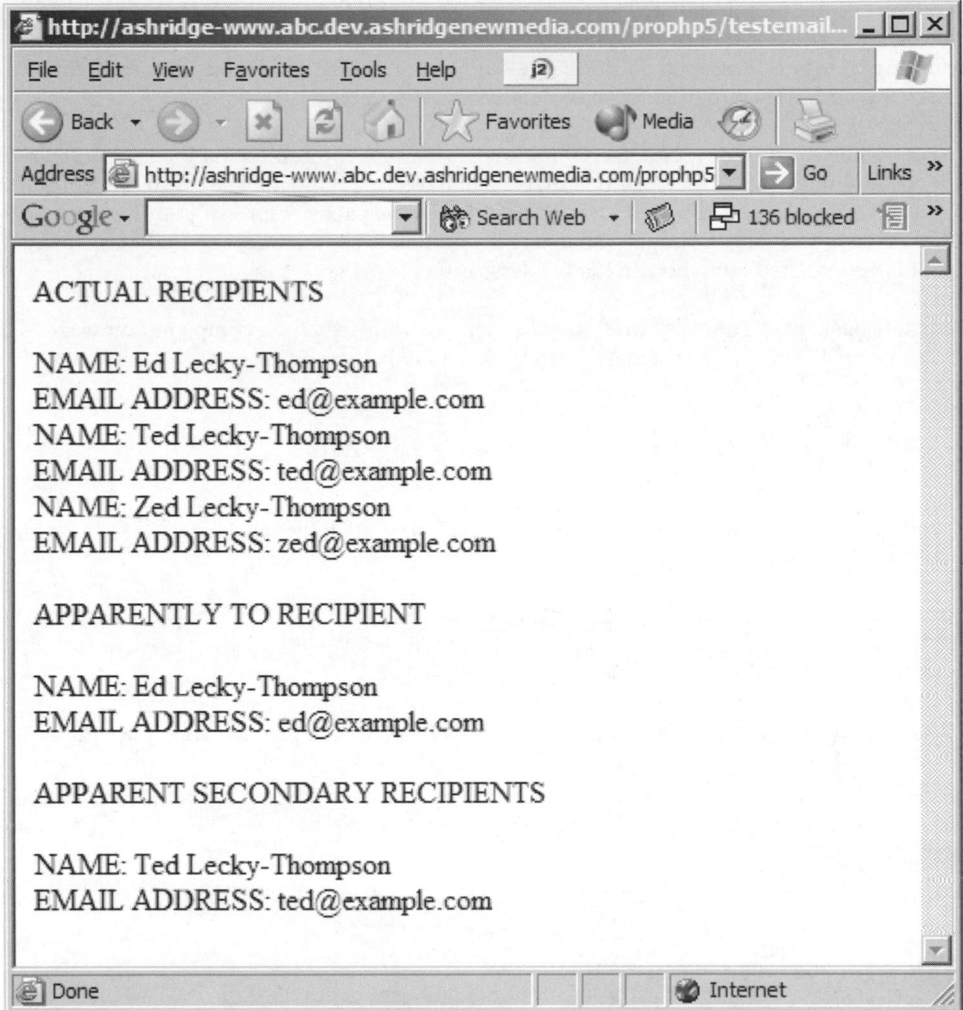

Figure 14-1

```
  public function setSubject($strSubject) {
    $this->strSubjectLine = $strSubject;
  }

  public function setMessageBody($strMessageBody) {
    $this->_setMessage($strMessageBody);
  }

  public function setSender($objSender) {
    $this->objApparentSender = $objSender->__clone();
  }
```

All that remains to do now is to convert the `send()` method into something that assembles a header, assembles a body, glues them together, and spits them out to the Internet.

How do you go about doing that? The easiest way is with PEAR's Net_SMTP package, which gels quite neatly with our setup and once again provides a good example of why PEAR is so useful in avoiding reinventing the wheel in your application development. The Net_SMTP package may already be installed in your PHP setup. If not, install it in the usual way.

The basic syntax for using the Net_SMTP package is simple. You can feed it the assembled message as-is with no changes. Just tell it the operands to use when talking to the mail server. The minimum the mail server requires is a sender and a list of recipients. The server doesn't look at your headers. This is why blind carbon copies work. Although the server is told to deliver the message to that recipient, the recipient is never listed anywhere in the headers.

Here's some basic usage of Net_SMTP, step by step, assuming that the completed message is in `$full_message_content` and that an array of recipients exists in `$rcpt`:

```
if (! ($smtp = new Net_SMTP("mail"))) {
    die("Unable to instantiate Net_SMTP object\n");
}
```

First, you instantiate a new instance of the Net_SMTP class with the name of your SMTP server, and `die` if you are unable to do so for some reason.

```
if (PEAR::isError($e = $smtp->connect())) {
    die($e->getMessage() . "\n");
}
```

Next, you make sure that you can connect to the SMTP server you just specified OK and, if not, you die.

```
if (PEAR::isError($smtp->mailFrom("sender@example.com''))) {
    die("Unable to set sender\n");
}
```

In this case, the sender was set to be `sender@example.com`.

```
foreach($rcpt as $recipient) {
    if (PEAR::isError($res = $smtp->rcptTo($rcpt))) {
        die("Unable to add recipient: " . $res->getMessage() . "\n");
    }
}
```

Next you loop through your array of recipients, adding each into the Net_SMTP class instance and dying if any single recipient proves impossible to add.

```
if (PEAR::isError($smtp->data($full_message_content))) {
    die("Unable to send data\n");
}
$smtp->disconnect();
```

Finally, you send your message and disconnect from the SMTP server.

It's worth noting that this example uses "mail" as the hostname of the remote SMTP server. If you're running on Linux or something similar, you can probably stick a reference to the hostname `mail` in your

/etc/hosts file pointing to 127.0.0.1 and find that everything works fine out of the box. Otherwise, you need to locate the nearest friendly SMTP server to relay for you and use that instead.

Now, take a look at the finished EmailCommunication class, complete with an SMTP send through Net_SMTP:

```
class EmailCommunication extends Communication {

  private $objApparentSender;                        // Visible From: address
  private $strSubjectLine;                          // Subject line
  private $objApparentPrimaryRecipient;              // Visible To: address
  private $arObjApparentSecondaryRecipients;        // Visible Cc: address(es)


  public function __construct() {
    // Superclass collection
    $this->arRecipientCollection = new EmailRecipientCollection();
    // Local collection of visible (CC:) recipients
    $this->arObjApparentSecondaryRecipients = new EmailRecipientCollection();
    parent::__construct();

  }

  public function setPrimaryRecipient($objRecipient) {
    if (!($this->arRecipientCollection->exists(
$objRecipient->getStringRepresentation()))) {
      parent::addRecipient($objRecipient);
    };
    $this->objApparentPrimaryRecipient = $objRecipient->__clone();
  }

  public function addCarbonRecipient($objRecipient) {
    if (!($this->arRecipientCollection->exists(
$objRecipient->getStringRepresentation()))) {
      parent::addRecipient($objRecipient);
    };
    if (!($this->arObjApparentSecondaryRecipients->exists(
$objRecipient->getStringRepresentation()))) {
      $this->arObjApparentSecondaryRecipients->addItem(
$objRecipient, $objRecipient->getStringRepresentation());
    };
  }

  public function removeCarbonRecipient($objRecipient) {
    if ($this->arRecipientCollection->exists(
$objRecipient->getStringRepresentation())) {
      parent::removeRecipient($objRecipient);
    };
    if ($this->arObjApparentSecondaryRecipients->exists(
$objRecipient->getStringRepresentation())) {
      $this->arObjApparentSecondaryRecipients->removeItem(
$objRecipient->getStringRepresentation());
    };
  }
```

```
  public function addBlindRecipient($objRecipient) {
    if (!($this->arRecipientCollection->exists(
$objRecipient->getStringRepresentation()))) {
      parent::addRecipient($objRecipient);
    };
  }

  public function removeBlindRecipient($objRecipient) {
    if (!($this->arRecipientCollection->exists(
$objRecipient->getStringRepresentation()))) {
      parent::removeRecipient($objRecipient->getStringRepresentation());
    };
  }

  public function setSubject($strSubject) {
    $this->strSubjectLine = $strSubject;
  }

  public function setMessageBody($strMessageBody) {
    $this->_setMessage($strMessageBody);
  }

  public function setSender($objSender) {
    $this->objApparentSender = $objSender->__clone();
  }

  public function send() {

    // Establish headers
    $strHeaders .= "From: " . $this->objApparentSender
->getStringRepresentation() . "\n";
    $strHeaders .= "To: " .
$this->objApparentPrimaryRecipient->getStringRepresentation() . "\n";
    foreach ($this->arObjApparentSecondaryRecipients as
$strRecipientIdentifier => $objEmailRecipient) {
      $strHeaders .= "Cc: " . $objEmailRecipient->getStringRepresentation() .
"\n";
    };
    $strHeaders .= "Date: " . date("D, M j H:i:s T Y O")  . "\n";

    // Establish body
    $strBody = $this->_getMessage();

    // Pull together to form complete email, correctly formatted
    $strFullEmail = $strHeaders . "\n" . $strBody;


    if (! ($smtp = new Net_SMTP("mail"))) {
        $this->strErrorMessage = "Unable to instantiate Net_SMTP object";
        $this->errorCode = 1;
        return(false);
    }

    if (PEAR::isError($e = $smtp->connect())) {
```

```
            $this->strErrorMessage = $e->getMessage();
            $this->errorCode = 2;
            $smtp->disconnect();
            return(false);
        }

        if (PEAR::isError($smtp->mailFrom(
    $this->objApparentSender->getStringRepresentation()))) {
            $this->strErrorMessage = "Unable to set sender";
            $this->errorCode = 3;
            $smtp->disconnect();
            return(false);
        }

        // Send to each recipient
        foreach ($this->arRecipientCollection as $strRecipientIdentifier =>
    $objEmailRecipient) {
          $strThisAddress = $objEmailRecipient->getRecipientAddress();
          if (PEAR::isError($res = $smtp->rcptTo($strThisAddress))) {
            $this->strErrorMessage = "Unable to add recipient " . $strThisAddress;
            $this->errorCode = 4;
            $smtp->disconnect();
            return(false);
          };
        };

        if (PEAR::isError($smtp->data($strFullEmail))) {
            $this->strErrorMessage = "Unable to send data to server";
            $this->errorCode = 5;
            $smtp->disconnect();
            return(false);
        }

        $smtp->disconnect();
        return(true);

      }
    };
```

There are a few things to note about our approach here. First, when a recipient is added as primary recipient or a member of the carbon copy (Cc:) list, you can add them to the collection held in the parent superclass and then clone the recipient object before adding to the list of apparent recipients. This step isn't vital but it means you can implement your own `_clone()` method in your `EmailRecipient` class, if you want, to modify the behavior taken when this copy is made.

Second, we've made use of the error code and error message member variables of the `Communication` superclass. These are accessible through public functions. You can use these to debug your applications. E-mail can be an unpredictable phenomenon at times, and failure can occur through any number of scenarios, including a failure to reach the SMTP server, being denied permission to send e-mail to your particular IP address, or having a recipient be rejected outright by the SMTP server.

Third, we've used the code `date("D, M j H:i:s T Y O")` to construct our e-mail header's date property. A quick glance at the PHP documentation reminds us that this produces a timestamp in the format `Tue, Jul 20 22:58:58 BST 2004 +0100`, which is of the format required in e-mail headers.

To test the final working class, you can knock out some code like the following:

```
$objEmail = new EmailCommunication;
$objEmailRecipient = new EmailRecipient("ed@example.com",
"Ed Lecky-Thompson");
$objEmailCCRecipient = new EmailRecipient("cc@example.com",
"Ted Lecky-Thompson");
$objEmailSender = new EmailRecipient("info@example.com", "Test Sender");
$objEmail->setPrimaryRecipient($objEmailRecipient);
$objEmail->setSender($objEmailSender);
$objEmail->setMessageBody("Hello,\n\nThis is a short test email.\n\nGoodbye!");
$objEmail->setSubject("Test Subject");
$objEmail->addCarbonRecipient($objEmailCCRecipient);
$objEmail->addBlindRecipient($objEmailBCCRecipient);

if ($objEmail->send()) {
 print "DONE! All went well! Mail sent successfully.";
} else {
 print "Sorry, didn't send mail successfully.";
};
```

Being Smart with Templates

In Chapter 13 we started talking about how separating application and display logic from each other through the Model View Controller (MVC) philosophy was generally an excellent idea, one well worth pursuing in your own application architecture.

Chapter 13 also covers a package called Smarty, which helps you do just that, and you learned just how useful it could be in traditional Web application implementation. Smarty has another use that is often overlooked. It can produce template-driven e-mail output.

As you know, nine times out of ten the e-mails you send your users will be virtually the same. A few tags, or the first name after "Dear," or an account number might change, but not much else.

Splicing variables into strings is fine for smaller operations. But when those e-mails start to get bigger and more unwieldly, and even contain printed array structures, things will get tough. The solution is to use the `TemplatedEmailCommunication` class.

The `TemplatedEmailCommunication` class makes full use of Smarty. If you haven't read Chapter 13 yet, now would be an excellent time. You need to know how Smarty works in order to pull this off.

The class you're about to create actually extends `EmailCommunication`, so have that up and running first. Have Smarty installed and working, too.

```
class TemplatedEmailCommunication extends EmailCommunication {

  private $path_to_template_file;
  private $objSmarty;

  public function __construct($strPathToTemplateFile) {
```

```
    $this->objSmarty = new Smarty;
    $this->path_to_template_file = $strPathToTemplateFile;
    parent::__construct();
  }

  public function setParameter($strParameter, $strValue) {
    $this->objSmarty->assign($strParameter, $strValue);
  }

  public function parse() {
    $this->setMessageBody($this->objSmarty->fetch($this
->path_to_template_file));
  }
}
```

The preceding code above is simple but effective. Now try the following code. It needs to point to a simple Smarty template, so first create a template file named `test.tpl` as follows:

```
Name: {$name}
Favorite Food: {$favefood}
```

Next, enter the PHP code that follows. Make sure that it resides in the same directory as your Smarty template, or else modify the first line to point to the right path. You'll see it's very similar to the last time we took `EmailCommunication` for a drive, but the differences in the code are highlighted for you:

```
$objEmail = new TemplatedEmailCommunication("test.tpl");
$objEmail->setParameter("name", "Ed");
$objEmail->setParameter("favefood", "Steak");
$objEmail->parse();
$objEmailRecipient = new EmailRecipient("ed@example.com", "Ed
Lecky-Thompson");
$objEmailSender = new EmailRecipient("info@example.com", "Test Sender");
$objEmail->setPrimaryRecipient($objEmailRecipient);
$objEmail->setSender($objEmailSender);
$objEmail->setSubject("Test Subject");

if ($objEmail->send()) {
 print "DONE! All went well! Mail sent successfully.";
} else {
 print "Sorry, didn't send mail successfully.";
};
```

This gives the following output in the body of sent e-mail:

```
Name: Ed
Favorite Food: Steak
```

As you can see, the `parse()` method constructed the body of the e-mail for you. Smarty parsed the template according to the two parameters you gave it. But rather than use the traditional `display()` method, you used `fetch()` to capture its output into a string. You then set the message body to be that string and you're all set to send the e-mail.

Note that by extending the `EmailCommunication` class, you've not only avoided re-inventing the wheel with respect to the recipient management and SMTP connectivity but also kept the `TemplatedEmailCommunication` class down to just a few lines of code, making it much easier to tinker with.

Of course, what's been demonstrated here is but a subset of what is possible with Smarty, but it does go to show just how easy Smarty is to adapt for e-mail.

Using MIME

You've probably noticed that throughout this chapter we've dealt almost exclusively with simple, plain-text e-mails. These are easier to deal with, but inevitably, occasions will for arise for sending HTML e-mail, maybe even templated HTML e-mail. And what about attachments? How do you handle those? MIME is the answer, and it is an enormous topic.

Mercifully, PEAR has it largely covered. See `http://pear.php.net/package/Mail_Mime` for more details. The suggested approach is to extend `EmailCommunication` to form `RichEmailCommunication`, which sports additonal methods such as `setHTMLContent`, `setPlainTextContent`, `addAttachment`, and so forth.

We don't have the space to go into more detail here. However, if you've got the hang of this chapter, you can probably integrate MIME functionality into the classes you've already built without difficulty. Download and install the PEAR package from `http://pear.php.net/package/Mail_Mime` and read the documentation thoroughly. Constructing the relevant new `RichEmailCommunication` class should be straightforward enough.

You can find out more about MIME in the Usenet comp.mail.mime FAQ, the latest version of which is available in the newsgroup and is replicated across the Web, such as at `http://www.uni-giessen.de/faq/archiv/mail.mime-faq.part1-9/`.

Other Communication Subclasses

This chapter sticks firmly to e-mail. That's simply because it's the most common form of communicating with users on the Web. It's free, and everybody knows the basics.

But the whole point of the `Communication` class is that it can be extended to form virtually anything—a fax, an SMS, a voice call. But how would you go about implementing such facilities? Here are a couple of suggestions.

SMS Text Messaging

A number of gateway providers have sprung up in the last year or so who will send messages on your behalf for a small fee. Rather than use physical cellular phones to send the messages, they use direct links straight into the cellular networks. This saves time and money.

The interface is usually via a simple `HTTP POST`. Search the Web for "SMS Gateways" if you're curious.

The more instant alternative is via a serial cable to your cellular phone, if your phone supports it. Again, the Web has more details on the API for communicating with your phone in this way. The trick is to treat it as though it were a modem; a Hayes-compatible AT command set is perfect for such communication. More information can be found at: `http://www.cellular.co.za/sms_at_commands.htm`.

Fax

Rather than physically render a fax page and fire it down a modem, a far simpler solution is to use one of the many e-mail-to-fax gateways in existence today. Most of these will accept a TIFF or similar file e-mailed as an attachment to a special e-mail address, upon which the gateway will send the fax on your behalf. By using PHP's built in graphics functions, you should be able to compose a TIFF on the fly, e-mail it to such a catcher address, and create an instant, dynamically produced fax as a result.

An example of such a service is eFax; see `www.efax.com` for more information.

Summary

In this chapter, you learned about communicating with your users, not just through a Web browser but through that most vital of modern media, electronic mail.

We weaned you off PHP's `mail()` function early on by showing you how communications with users can be represented in an elegant class hierarchy. We took this further by creating `EmailRecipient` and `EmailCommunication` classes as part of that hierarchy, robust and stable enough for everyday use.

We also showed you how Smarty can play a big part in letting you produce template-driven e-mails, and we hinted at some of the more advanced possibilities for the class framework we discussed.

In the next chapter, you meet some of the most important concepts in building enterprise PHP application—sessions and authentication.

Sessions and Authentication

Despite the advancements of PHP in recent years that have brought it to the full-featured, object-oriented Web application development platform it has become today, it still relies, as do all other languages of its ilk, on the basics. That is, it relies on the HTTP protocol and the CGI (Common Gateway Interface, the most basic building block of any kind of interactivity on the Web) functionality that HTTP provides.

When people speak of HTTP they often describe it as *stateless*—meaning that no "memory" is retained from one user's request to the next; the request is made via `GET` or `POST`, data is returned, and the request is completed—and, as far as the Web server is concerned, forgotten.

This characteristic isn't much use if you're trying to build complex Web applications that emulate the functionality of their equivalent desktop counterparts. You need to be able to keep track of users' previous actions, not just what they're doing right at this moment, in order to be able to produce meaningful output. Thankfully, PHP provides a way around this: sessions. This technique allows you to maintain certain stateful information from one request by the user to the next. This leads very neatly to one of the most common and useful applications of session handling—that of authentication and user state persistence.

The first half of this chapter discusses PHP's built-in session-handling features. You'll see that although on the surface the functionality available to you may seem basic, it can be extended and adapted to provide enormous degrees of flexibility, including integrating with third party databases. You'll also learn the ins and outs of session security so that you can devise session architectures that keep hackers at bay.

In the second half of the chapter, you'll learn how to apply this knowledge of session management to develop an essential component of your toolkit: a reusable, database-driven authentication class that can be deployed on almost any Web site that needs users to authenticate at some stage.

Introduction to Sessions

Before we get into how sessions work in PHP and the benefits they can bring your application, we look at the broader concept of sessions in general. What are they, how do they work, and why are they so important?

A Brief Recap on How HTTP Works

Consider how a Web request actually works.

When the user's Web browser makes a request, it presents, among other bits and pieces, the following core information to the Web server:

- Method of request—either `GET` or `POST`—and the protocol version used (1.0 or 1.1)
- The actual document required (for example, `/index.php`)
- The server hostname from which the document is being requested (important because many Web sites are hosted on a single server with a single IP address)
- The request parameters (for example, `foo=bar`, `username=fred`, `password=letmein`) in URL-encoded format
- The browser type (known as the user agent; essentially variant, platform and version)
- Any cookies stored on the client's machine that have been previously issued by the server of which the client is now making a request

If you want to see this in action, telnet to port 80 on the Web server of your choice and issue something that looks like the following:

```
GET /pub/WWW/TheProject.html HTTP/1.1
User-Agent: CERN-LineMode/2.15 libwww/2.17b3
Host: www.w3.org
```

In response to your request, the Web server will spit out an appropriate Web page.

You would not be dense if you struggled to see how this protocol could be anything but stateless—the server, after all, is completely unaware at the time of a given request of what went on during a previous request.

This approach causes problems because although the Web server sees a user's requests as stateless, the user does not. The user remembers perfectly well what was done at the time of the last page requested and expects, rather reasonably, the Web server to do the same. A particularly good example of this is when a username and password are required to access a particular page resource. The user expects to enter this information once and only once. The application should remember the details and not ask for them again should the user need to request a similarly restricted page on the site.

After all, this is generally how computers have worked for decades. Mirroring this functionality in your Web applications is vital for the sake of your users' collective sanity.

In the early days of the Web, this functionality was sometimes provided by the server's checking the remote IP address of the connecting user against a database. When the user first logged in, the IP address was recorded and subsequent requests (within a given time frame) from that IP were assumed to have come from the same user.

This was fine in an Internet with no firewalls, Network Address Translation, proxy servers, or other such pesky intrusions. Today's Internet is quite different, of course. Some consumer ISPs will actually present completely different external proxy server addresses with each request a user makes to your Web site—a side effect of their own proxy load balancing technology.

Another common solution to the problem, which does not depend on a consistent IP address from request to request, is to use HTTP Authentication. If you've ever visited a Web site and been presented with a box that looks something like Figure 15-1, then you've met HTTP Authentication.

Figure 15-1

Provided, again, from the very early days of the Web, HTTP Authentication allows certain files and directories on Web servers to be restricted to a group of users. Traditionally, this user list was a simple plain-text file, but recent advances have allowed Apache to directly consult a MySQL database for this information.

This method works well, and after you have issued a username and password for a given directory on a Web server, any subsequent requests to files in that directory or its subdirectories, whatever they may be, will be automatically presented to the Web server alongside that username and password.

This method is of little use when building PHP applications, however. It is rare to want to protect specific scripts, or even directories; far more likely is needing to restrict functionality delineated in some way that is recognized and understood in PHP but not necessarily in Apache. Even though replicating the HTTP headers required to emulate this functionality from within PHP itself is feasible, it's rarely desirable, for a number of reasons:

- You have almost no control over the appearance of this box, so it's not exactly a user-friendly approach.
- You can't ask for any other information (for example, to pose a security question, as in "What is your mother's maiden name?")
- You can't store any information against the request beyond the identity as which the user has logged.

The list goes on. Thankfully, a third and far more desirable solution is available, and that is to use *sessions*.

Definition of a Session

Strictly speaking, a session is defined as a series of consecutive HTTP requests made at designated time intervals by a single user from a single computer on a single Web application.

The general methodology behind sessions is that the *first* request made by a user will generate a new session, should one not yet exist. Subsequent requests will be considered to be *part* of that session, unless they are made outside some arbitrary time period (the *session timeout* period).

A session is normally used to determine the currently connected user of an application, if any. After a user has successfully logged in for the first time, the application's database should record the user's user ID against that session, such that any subsequent requests proffering that session are understood to have been made by that user and no other.

The real meat of a session is the *session identifier.* This uniquely identifies the session, which may exist concurrently with hundreds of other user sessions. When a session ID is generated and sent to the client for the first time, it is important that the session identifier is both unique and obscure enough so that another, valid session ID could not easily be "invented" by a potentially hostile third party. For example, although issuing session numbers 1, 2, 3, 4, and so on would certainly satisfy the requirement for uniqueness, it fails to satisfy the security side of things, because a user who has been allocated session number 3 could simply suddenly claim to be session number 4 and potentially gain access to another user's account as a result.

Session identifiers are more often than not 32-character strings consisting of numbers and letters. This is how PHP's built-in session handling (discussed later in the chapter) generates session identifiers. The stumbling of one user across a valid session ID of another is unlikely, therefore, except through brute force—and later in this chapter we look at a couple of easy ways to stop that from happening, too.

Perpetuation of a Session

With the first of the user's requests made and a session identifier generated for that request, you are faced with the challenge of ensuring that the session identifier in question is perpetuated with each subsequent request.

There are two ways to do this: URL rewriting and cookies. A good way to begin is to look at the principles of these without getting bogged down just yet in how PHP's own session handling works.

URL Rewriting

This is the simplest form of session perpetuation. It involves ensuring that every single link, form target, and JavaScript relocation is doctored to include the session identifier as a `GET` or `POST` parameter, as appropriate.

Consider the following example. Assume for the sake of argument that PHP has decided upon the following session identifier:

```
abcde1234567890abcde1234567890ab
```

and you want this session identifier to be issued with every subsequent request by the Web browser. Wherever you have anchor links in your HTML, you need to arrange for PHP to doctor them so that

```
<A HREF="mybasket.php">Go to my basket</A>
```

becomes

```
<A HREF="mybasket.php?session_id=abcde1234567890abcde1234567890ab
">Go to my basket</A>
```

Obviously, you would not hard-code this into your HTML; rather, you would work out some clever way to infuse your HTML on the fly with such session identifiers.

It would also be necessary for PHP to doctor form targets, so that

```
<FORM METHOD="POST" ACTION="mybasket.php">
```

becomes

```
<FORM METHOD="POST" ACTION="mybasket.php">
<INPUT TYPE="HIDDEN" NAME="session_id" VALUE="abcde1234567890abcde1234567890ab">
```

Your PHP would even need to update any JavaScript you might have, to make:

```
window.location.replace("index.php")
```

become

```
window.location.replace("index.php?session_id=abcde1234567890abcde1234567890ab")
```

Indeed, there may well be rare cases of URLs being missed and, consequently, the session lost. The really unpleasant part about URL rewriting is that if you lose the session on one request, it's lost forever, so thoroughness is essential. But this is not the only pitfall.

How do you bookmark pages in this way? If you bookmark the page you're on, you'll also record the session identifier, and this won't be valid next time you log in. So, you'll have to manually scrub out the session identifier when you bookmark.

The biggest and most prevalent pitfall comes when people try to copy and paste links to their friends and colleagues. Joe User simply will not think to strip out the session identifier before he e-mails a page on your site to his friends. As a result, when his friend clicks the link, one of two things will happen depending on the level of security you've implemented. Either the friend will gain full access to the user's original login, or the system will freak out at a potential security breach because the user is claiming to be the rightful owner of a valid session without presenting other credentials associated with that session.

There is a better way, but it's not without its share of (largely unwarranted) controversy—using cookies.

Cookies

Although URL rewriting is theoretically speaking the simplest form of session perpetuation, using cookies is even simpler in terms of the amount of code required.

Cookies are little nuggets of information sent by a Web browser along with the HTML output of a page. The Web browser is instructed to record that information and then volunteer it with every subsequent request made to that Web server.

Cookies have, much the same as variables, a name and a value. Some also have a validity (how long it lasts) and a scope (which server or servers should receive it). With each request to the Web server, the user's Web browser offers the name and value of any cookies within the scope of that Web server's domain that have yet to expire. Expired cookies are deleted automatically by the Web browser, but live cookies can also be instantly deleted by the Web server if necessary.

The implementation is simple. As with the previous example, assume that the session identifier is

```
abcde1234567890abcde1234567890ab
```

With the first request made by the user's Web browser in a session, this session identifier needs to be pushed to the user's Web browser so that the Web browser knows to offer it on subsequent requests. Accordingly, a cookie is sent to the user's Web browser instructing it to save the value `abcde1234567890abcde1234567890ab` to an appropriately named identifier.

With each subsequent request made to the Web server, PHP looks for a cookie offering a valid session identifier, with that validity remaining to be checked against some external set of rules and/or a database of valid sessions. If a valid session identifier has been offered as part of the cookies sent by the Web browser, PHP can assume this to be the correct session identifier and proceed with the script as normal. If none is offered, or that which is offered is deemed to be invalid, a new session identifier is generated and in turn sent as a cookie, as in the previous step.

This cycle continues from request to request throughout the remainder of the user's session.

For the name for your cookie, you should stick with something easily identifiable such as `session_id`. The scope should be restricted to your own Web server (or, in a pinch, domain), and the validity equal to the maximum dwell time you think users will need on your site. For example, if you don't think a typical user will ever use the site for more than half an hour, setting a validity period of 30 minutes isn't a bad idea.

The media have generated much controversy about cookies. The bulk of that controversy has arisen from ignorance on the part of the media, some instances of extraordinarily poor site design, and perhaps some commercially unscrupulous site operators.

Despite the controversy, there is absolutely no reason for any user to fear a simple session identifier being issued through a cookie. Do ensure, however, that you restrict the scope of the cookie to your server and your server only so that it is not inadvertently sent to any other sites that may attempt to use it for tracking purposes. In addition, it makes sense to post a clear and concise Privacy Policy on your Web site that explains to your users the purpose of the cookies you use and the steps you have taken to safeguard users' privacy and security.

Some potential pitfalls do exist, as the next section explains.

Session Security

Is a session identifier really secure in itself? There are certainly a few risks associated with using session identifiers as the sole means of identifying logged-in users on your site but, mercifully, there are countermeasures you can take to help minimize those risks.

Guessing at Valid Sessions

If a malicious visitor to your site happens to fashion a valid session identifier, he or she can hijack the session of another visitor. After all, if user A is making request after request using session identifier X, and then malicious user B comes along and uses session identifier X to make a request as well, what is your Web site to think? It will assume that user B is user A, and user B will have access to everything user A has access to, potentially exposing sensitive information.

For this scenario to be realized, the potential hacker needs to guess at a valid session identifier. How feasible is doing so in a real-world situation?

Consider your 32-character hexadecimal string. This could be generated in any number of ways, but assume that it is largely random. With 32 bytes, and 16 possible characters for each byte (a thru f, 0 thru 9), you have 16^{32} possible combinations for your session identifier. It would take an awfully long time for a potential hacker to cycle through all possible session identifiers—00000000000000000000000000000000, 00000000000000000000000000000001, 00000000000000000000000000000002, and so on, all the way up to ffffffffffffffffffffffffffffffff.

But what if the identifier were an MD5 serialization of a 10-digit number? If the hacker actually knew this fact, there would only be 10,000,000,000 combinations to cycle through, given that the MD5 hash of any given number is a constant answer. It would be a very small matter to knock up a script (perhaps even in PHP) to try each session identifier on a loop until it struck one that actually worked.

Consider what would happen if the user requested an "update my details" page (`mydetails.php`). This page behaves in one of two ways, depending on whether a valid session was issued with the request:

- If a valid session is issued and the session is known to be logged in, the page displays the user's details and allows the user to reset his or her password, among other things.
- If a valid session is not issued, the page issues a 302 redirect to a login page.

The mischievous script would have to iterate through these 10 billion combinations while making an HTTP request to `mydetails.php` with each one. If it gets a 302 redirect, ignore it and move on; if it gets the contents of the "my details" page, reset the user's password to 12345 by submitting the form on the page, making a note of the username, and moving on to the next session.

Leave this running for a few weeks, and it can absolutely be guaranteed that the script would have chanced upon a few valid sessions during its run. It may even have alerted the hacker via e-mail or an SMS text message when it struck a user account whose password it managed to reset. Keep in mind that with a fast connection (and the ability to run multiple instances of this script across multiple servers), a really determined hacker can get through many thousands of session identifiers every second.

If the hacker *didn't* know how your session identifiers were formed, you would be fairly safe. Using a random number between two limits is a pretty bad idea, however, even if the hacker didn't know what those limits were. It would be a simple matter to write a script to bombard your site with cookie-less requests, each of which would generate a new session; soon enough, the laws of probability would dictate that your hacker would be furnished with a complete database of all feasible MD5 encoded session identifiers (all 10 billion, in the previous example). The hacker wouldn't be able to reverse-engineer these to work out how they were formed, but doing so isn't necessary. The hacker can simply feed the list of pre-hashed identifiers into his or her brute-force script.

The only way to prevent such analysis is to make sure that sessions are single use. This means that the same session identifier will never be generated twice, or at least not within a considerable time span of its first generation. A good way to do this is to construct your session identifier based on a combination of a random number *and* the current timestamp. That way, any script constructed to fish for a complete database of session identifiers will be practically useless because its database of valid session identifiers will (theoretically) grow to near-infinity.

Obliterating Session Guessing

One simple way to completely obliterate session guessing is to send as a second cookie a supplemental key alongside the session identifier. This key would be completely random and generated at the time the session is formed. The key associated with that session would be stored in the database.

With each request, both the session identifier cookie and the session key cookie would be transmitted. Even if the session offered is valid, PHP would still check that the key transmitted matches the key originally issued and, if not, immediately cancel and invalidate the session. By canceling the session offered, any attempt to force further possible combinations of key against that session would be pointless because the first wrong key issued would invalidate that session anyway. The only downside of this approach is that your legitimately logged-in user would be logged out as the session was cancelled, but it's better to be safe than hacked.

For true randomness when generating such keys, try to avoid using any kind of randomization whose seed is based on the system clock. Using truly random seeds such as processor temperature, PHP process identifiers, and network interface statistics produce a more satisfactory random number.

Discovery of valid sessions

Discovery of valid sessions is a less prominent threat but a harder one to protect against. Essentially, the risk is that a malicious third party can somehow gain access to the cookies on your legitimate user's machine and use them to gain access to the user's session.

Unfortunately, this technique is not immune to the session key methodology discussed previously. If a hacker can gain access to the session cookie, the key cookie is just as easily obtainable.

There are a few scenarios in which this could happen:

- A session cookie is mis-issued by your site so that its scope is broader than it needs to be. A malicious Web site within that overly broad scope then visited by the user would be made privy to that session cookie, too. The operators of that site could then use the cookie to hijack your session on the original site. The user does not even necessarily have to visit a malicious site. Literally millions of pieces of HTML spam e-mail every day are sent out containing images, the purpose of which is simply to cause its recipient to make a Web request, the hope being that session cookies from other poorly constructed sites will be offered accidentally.

- A physical intrusion to the machine could allow access to the cookies stored on it, from which data on valid sessions could be extracted.
- An intrusion to the machine that somehow modifies the HOSTS file could redirect traffic supposedly for your site's hostname to a third-party site. This third-party site may even relay the genuine data from your Web server, such that the user is none the wiser. It would, crucially, collect the session identifier for later use.
- A poorly configured network could allow session identifiers to be sniffed in HTTP traffic by malicious systems administrators on-site.
- A malicious employee of an ISP that employs proxy servers (transparent or otherwise) could easily enable session identifiers transmitted to be logged.

The first of these scenarios is easy to overcome. When issuing cookies from your site, always get the scope right! This most basic of errors is exploited with such frequency only because of the frequency with which it is made in the first place.

A physical intrusion is almost impossible to guard against. Any physical exploitation is attributable more to lackluster physical security of the location from which the site is being accessed than to anything else. Good session practice (see the following section) can help minimize the risk of this kind of occurrence.

Another major problem is the modification of the HOSTS file of a machine allowing nameservers to be overridden transparently. It is remarkable there are not more e-mail worms in circulation that exploit this, but it is only a matter of time. The HOSTS file exists on almost every variant of Windows imaginable, and unless a tight local administration rights policy has been set up, users can modify it themselves. An e-mail worm (distributed as an attachment, as are most modern worms) exploiting this vulnerability would work as follows:

1. The user regularly visits `www.myfictionalbank.com` to use an online checking account management facility. This resolves to 10.123.123.123.
2. An attachment (which might be .vbs, .scr, .pif or any of the other numerous file extensions that still aren't universally blocked by e-mail clients) viral payload creates an entry in your HOSTS file pointing to a malicious foreign IP address, which is actually a server owned by the hacker. The IP address is 192.168.123.123 and is probably located somewhere in Eastern Europe.
3. Next time the user goes to log into his or her online banking account, he or she enters `www.myfictionalbank.com` and appears to get the account login page as normal. In fact, the connection is being made to the malicious Web server. The malicious server in turn makes a real connection to the real bank's Web server and mirrors every request made by the user. It re-transmits all the data returned by the real bank's Web server. The only data not relayed back in this way is that generated when the user's session details (immediately after login) are instantly recorded by the malicious relay server, which then seizes control of the session, denying the real user any further access. In just a few seconds, several thousand dollars of the user's hard-earned cash are on their way to Eastern Europe.

Of course, a scam like this wouldn't last long. The bank would get wind of it pretty quickly and block off the malicious server's IP address (unless the worm actually acted as a relay for other instances of itself on un-firewalled machines and updated some central database of the IP addresses of places where the worm has nested), but it does serve to illustrate just how easily this kind of scam can be pulled off.

On-site exploitation is as big a threat as exploitation from Eastern Europe, particularly in big companies. Many corporate networks may be switched at their most central point, but when floor socket availability starts to get tight, most systems administrators slap in a hub. It's cheap and quick, and the two PCs on that hub can immediately sniff each other's traffic. If a savvy user is on the same hub as a colleague whose session the user wishes to seize, some simple traffic-sniffing software can retrieve those session identifiers.

Finally, keep in mind that many ISPs these days use transparent proxy servers. That is, all HTTP traffic is intercepted and relayed through a standard proxy server without the user's explicit knowledge (and without any kind of configuration required on the user's part). Ostensibly, this is to improve performance by caching commonly requested pages and images at the ISP so that they are only one hop away from the user. The more genuine reason is that ISPs are under increasing pressure in the current climate to maintain very detailed logs on the behavior of their customers on the Web. This is not for commercial reasons, but rather for the purposes of handing over this information to law enforcement agencies should they demand it. The potential for abuse of this facility is quite obvious. If cookies are logged, seizing them is a simple matter for a bored systems administrator.

Good Session Practice

As we have seen, physically obtaining the session identifier (and session key if available) is very difficult to guard against. The most effective barriers to such exploitation are physical, political, or economic in nature. They certainly have nothing to do with PHP.

But there are a few neat things you can do in your code should you wish to minimize the risk of these theoretical exploits being put into practice.

Use Session Timeouts

First and foremost, use session timeouts. These are *not* the same as session expiration times. When issuing a user with a cookie, you will almost certainly give it an expiration time, but this does not guard against the user's walking away from his or her computer and forgetting to log out. Using session timeouts involves recording the timestamp of each request against the session and then, with each subsequent request made against that session, measuring the time elapsed since the last request. If it exceeds five or ten minutes, you would be *strongly* advised to revoke the session and request the user to log in again.

This is a remarkably effective measure. Many of the attacks described earlier rely on being able to make use of a session perhaps only some moments after the user has finished with it. By reducing the window of opportunity to just a few minutes, you reduce the effectiveness of those attacks.

The implementation of session timeouts has nothing to do with cookies; rather, the code you implement to handle sessions has responsibility for measuring the time elapsed between requests and determining when to revoke a session due to a timeout. In the next section of this chapter, you'll find out about the `UserSession` class, which can do just that.

Use Low Expiry Times

Having a low expiration time in your session cookie does make sense. Users don't mind being asked to log in again occasionally, so setting an expiration time of an hour or so is fine. If you do this, be sure to build the rest of your application so that the interruption to the user is minimal. For example, if you are building a Webmail application, don't instruct your code to arbitrarily end a user's session if he or she is in the middle of sending out an e-mail. Try to design sympathetically.

As mentioned previously, you will see how to effectively implement a low cookie expiration time in the next section of this chapter.

Check User Agent Consistency

One simple check you can make involves recording the user's Web browser User Agent against the session. This is the string issued by the Web browser identifying the manufacturer, browser name, version, and platform. It is by no means unique to that computer, but there are so many different browsers and browser versions in use that there is a strong chance that any two computers produce slightly different User Agent strings. By ensuring that subsequent requests against a session carry the same User Agent as the original request, you provide an additional line of defense against session hijacking. Interestingly, the user agent string that Internet Explorer produces can be modified in the Windows registry. System administrators can take advantage of this fact by making their network's workstations have organization-specific user agent strings; this further strengthens the usefulness of this mechanism of security.

Don't Be Afraid to Ask the User to Log in Again

If you're about to let the user place an order, or view and update his or her details, don't be afraid to ask for the username and password again. That way, should a hacker succeed in taking over a session, the damage that can be done will be limited to some degree. Many large commercial sites employ this practice, and the user will not be too irritated at this request if used judiciously.

Watch for Unusual Traffic

If you're feeling particularly brave, you could construct some algorithms to watch for unusual traffic against a particular session in order to determine multiple usage. How you define unusual traffic is open to debate, but you could, for example, raise an alarm if more than one request is made in any one-second period and cancel the session as a result. Alternatively, you could map the physical navigation of your site to likely user paths and ensure that the requests made by the user's session is following one of those paths. For example, on an e-commerce site, should the user request the index of a particular product category with one request, it is exceedingly unlikely that he or she would then immediately select the view product page for a product that falls *outside* that category. To do that he or she would have to have accessed it from a bookmark or third-party link, or have typed the URL in. However, if your algorithms are not rock solid, the false-positives rate could easily start to disgruntle your users.

Watch for Bizarre IP Address Variance

Although it is not legitimate to determine the validity of a session based on the consistency of the IP address, it is still possible to detect some possible break-in attempts by keeping an eye on its variance. Load balancing proxy servers are likely to change IP address with each request, but by how much? It is incredibly unlikely that anything but the last two octets would change. Certainly, the request would most definitely remain within the same net block (that is, the owner of the block would be consistent from request to request). An excellent way to check this is to consult RIPE, ARIN, and so on in real time.

In your application, you would simply devise a low-overhead means of checking the net block owner, utilizing some kind of caching technology if possible. And if requests of the same session seem to be coming from different owners, it's worth raising the alarm and destroying the session.

Avoiding Storing Session Variables on the Client Side

One obvious benefit of sessions is the ability to associate the value of relevant variables to a session. These variables could be the contents of a shopping basket or the population of a search form, for example.

Nevertheless, storing this information on the client side is best avoided. For one thing, this can get privacy activists very upset; for another, the value of those variables is open to modification outside the control of your code (either malicious or accidental).

Pumping that much data upstream with each HTTP request can be quite inefficient. Keep in mind that most broadband connections are asymmetric, meaning that they upload slower than they download. So if you are storing 16K worth of session variables on the client side, that will add a second or so to each request. That may not sound like much but it can quickly drive users crazy, so using cookies in this manner is not good practice.

All you need to store on the client side is the session identifier (and supplemental security key, if used). You should store everything else on the server side somewhere, out of harm's reach, and associate those variables with the session identifier in question.

The lesson of this part of the chapter is that 100 percent security is always just out of reach. However, there are always steps you can take to minimize your own exposure.

How PHP Implements Sessions

PHP allows you to implement a highly effective session management infrastructure in your applications, but you have to do a lot of the hard work yourself.

As you'll see in this section, PHP's built-in session handling isn't really appropriate for enterprise-class applications. Luckily, it has been made extensible enough to give you a head start when you're writing your own more robust solution.

Basic PHP Sessions

Take a look at the following code. Enter it and save it as `firstpage.php`.

```
<?php

 session_start();
 $_SESSION['favorite_artist'] - 'Tori Amos';

?>Currently, my favorite artist is Tori Amos. It may also interest you to
know that my identifer for this browser session, as allocated by PHP, is
<?=session_id()?>.
<BR><BR>
<A HREF="secondpage.php">Go to the second page</A>
?>
```

Now start a brand-new bit of code. Call this `secondpage.php`.

```
<?php

session_start();

?>Having checked, I can tell you that my favorite artist is still
<?=$_SESSION['favorite_artist']?>.
At the moment, my identifier for this browser session, as allocated by PHP, is
<?=session_id()?>.
<BR><BR>
<A HREF="firstpage.php">Go back to the first page</A>
?>
```

Run the first of these and you should get some predictable output. It turns out that my favorite artist is Tori Amos, and PHP has given me a session identifier (see Figure 15-2).

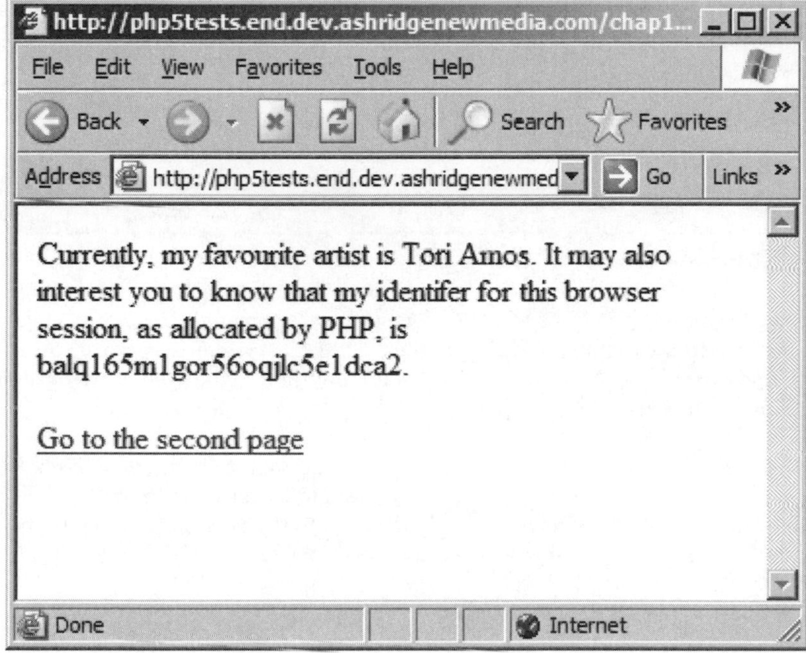

Figure 15-2

You can see that the session identifier is 32 characters in length. PHP actually uses the full alphabet as well as 0–9. This increases the number of possible session identifiers to 36^{32}. If you click the link, you should see something that looks like Figure 15-3.

There are two important things to note. The session identifier is the same, and the second script seems to have remembered my musical preferences.

This result is obtained in a straightforward manner. First, use `session_start()` to tell PHP to enable sessions, well before the first character of HTML of the script. Using `session_start()` is important because the session data sent to the Web browser needs to go in the HTTP headers, and the first use of any HTML (or even whitespace) precludes this from happening.

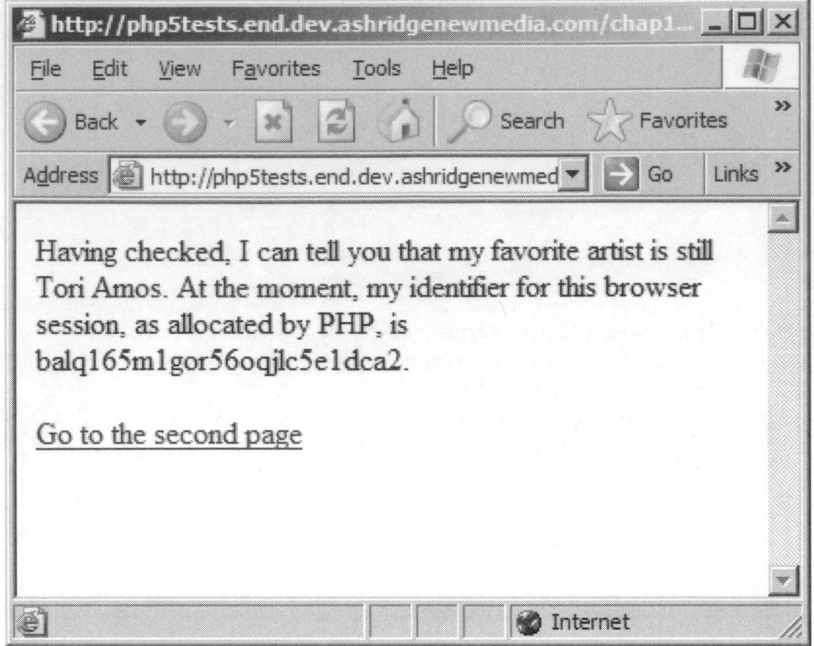

Figure 15-3

Second, register a session variable by adding to the `$_SESSION` global associative array (or *hash*). This can come anywhere in the script because it won't send anything to the Web browser; it just makes a note on the server side, as you will see shortly.

On the second page, call `session_start()` just as you did on the first to enable session management, but now you can read from `$_SESSION` just as you wrote to it on the first page. Lo and behold, the value `Tori Amos` has been successfully retained from one page to the next. This value has been inextricably associated with the session identifier, which explains why the server remembered it.

But how did PHP remember the session identifier from the first page to the second?

Take a look on your server in `/tmp`. Perform a directory listing using `ls` for all files starting with `sess_` (the word *sess* followed by an underscore). Notice a file called `sess_` followed by the session ID you were allocated in the previous example. Open it using the editor of your choice. You should see something that looks like Figure 15-4.

The output there looks quite straightforward. You should see the session variable you created and its contents in plain text:

```
favorite_artist|s:9:"Tori Amos";
```

In fact, its format might look familiar. It's the output from the PHP function `serialize()`, a string representation of a PHP data structure.

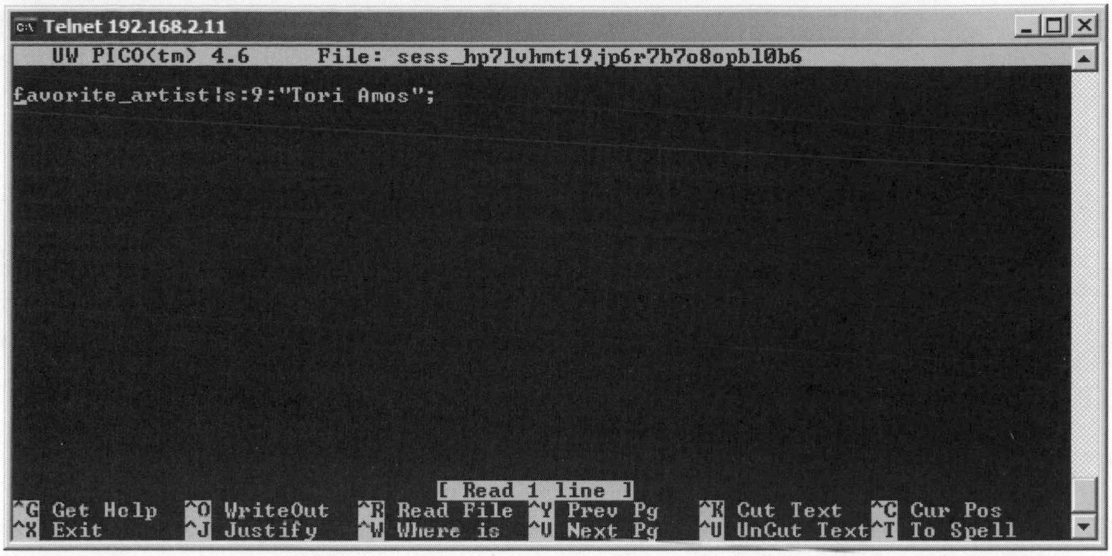

Figure 15-4

Regardless of how complex or large the data structure you create in the `$_SESSION` variable is, PHP will store its contents in this file by default. The location for storing such files, as well as the length of time for which they are stored, are all settings that can be altered in `php.ini`.

That's really all there is to native PHP sessions. Let's look now at some of their limitations to see why they can't be used in an enterprise environment.

Limitations of Basic PHP Sessions

There are a few key problems with implementing sessions in this manner, most of which relate to the manner in which PHP stores its session data on disk.

What if you have multiple Web servers servicing your request with a load balancer appliance round-robin dividing traffic between them? You would have to implement some kind of shared `/tmp` using NFS, and this would be dreadfully slow.

Second, if you're running on a shared Web server (with a hosting company, for example), the directory listing of `/tmp` is readable by all even if the contents of its files aren't. Given that PHP uses the session identifiers as part of the filename, a malicious fellow user on that Web server could quite easily get a full listing of all the session identifiers created as well as when they were created. This would once again open the door for easy session hijacks as discussed earlier.

Third, this implementation of session handling is not very efficient. Not one of the additional measures discussed earlier is employed for additional security, nor is it easily possible to employ them in this state. So as far as a secure environment for a production Web site using sessions is concerned, PHP session handling in its off-the-shelf state isn't really a viable option.

Finally, given that you store the rest of your application's data in a database, you are bound to have times when you need to construct queries that consult both session variables and database tables in tandem. With session data totally exterior to the database, you must first extract that data using PHP and then inject it into an SQL statement. Serious performance implications are associated with this approach when compared to conducting a single SQL query to extract the data you need. On a production server, for example, this could become quite a serious issue. The solution to this problem is to integrate the PHP session management with a database.

Creating an Authentication Class

In the final part of this chapter you'll learn how to adapt PHP's session handling technology to talk to a PostgreSQL database, which will be used to store the session data hitherto stored on disk. At the same time, you'll put together a class to handle user authentication that you should be able to reuse on any project.

Connecting PHP Session Management to a Database

Getting PHP to use a database as opposed to the server's disk to store its data is far easier than you might expect. The following examples use PostgreSQL, but this method can easily be adapted to work with MySQL, XML flat files, or whatever you prefer.

The key to all this is just one PHP function: `session_set_save_handler`. If you take a look at the PHP manual reference entry for the function, you can see its syntax quite clearly:

```
bool session_set_save_handler ( string open, string close, string
read, string write, string destroy, string gc)
```

The idea is simple. You call this function *before* `session_start()` is used on any page that employs sessions. The function instructs PHP which custom functions to call when certain session behavior takes place, such as when a session is started, finished, read to, written from, or destroyed. There are certain requirements regarding the parameters passed into these methods as well as the value they must return. These are outlined in some detail on the PHP manual page for `session_set_save_handler`, but the following sections cover the basics.

The open() Function

The `open()` function is called whenever `session_start()` is called. PHP passes two values, the path in which it thinks the session should be stored if it is to be saved on disk (which we can ignore for our purposes) and the cookie name (for example, `PHPSESSID`) it is using for the session. It needs to return a `true` value for the session to be regarded by PHP as having been successfully created.

The close() Function

The `close()` function (not to be confused with the `destroy()` function) is called at what is effectively the end of the execution of any PHP script that uses session handling. For your purposes, it need do nothing other than return a `true` value although it might be nice to close its database connection if it isn't going to be used any more. In most production environments, you'll be using a globally accessible handle to a database that's already open for other purposes, so you'll no doubt have code in place to close it down again at the end of the script anyway. In practice, therefore, all this function needs to return is a `true` value.

The read() Function

The `read()` function is used whenever an attempt to retrieve a variable from the `$_SESSION` hash is made. It takes the session identifier as its sole operand and expects a serialized representation of `$_SESSION` in its entirety to be returned. You won't actually be using this in your class because you'll be doing your own session variable handling.

The write() Function

The `write()` function is used whenever an attempt to change or add to `$_SESSION` is made. It takes the session identifier, followed by the preserialized representation of `$_SESSION`, as its two parameters. It expects true to be returned if the data is successfully committed. This method is called even if no session variables are registered, and it is the first time the generated session ID is revealed to you.

The `destroy()` function

The `destroy()` function is called whenever the `session_destroy` function is used in code. It must return true upon execution.

The gc() Function

The `gc()` (garbage cleanup) function should be able to accept the "maximum lifetime of session cookies" parameter as its only operand and get rid of any sessions older than that lifetime. It should return true when it's done. This function appears to be called just before `open()` so that PHP rids itself of any expired sessions before they may be used.

Introducing the UserSession Class

The `UserSession` class is a convenient way of implementing an object-oriented approach to session management as well as providing basic authentication methods for your applications. Here, you will implement your own methods to replace those of PHP, using the `session_set_save_handler()` method discussed previously.

It will be an entirely self-contained class that hides all PHP's `session_` functions from your application's main body.

It also provides session variable handling, which bypasses PHP's own. Rather than store multiple variables in a single serialized hash, your methodology will use separate table rows for each variable. This could speed up access immensely. Note, however, that the previous session handling instruction method was not designed to cope with class methods, so you'll have to be rather cunning in your implementation.

Database Schema

The class depends upon three tables existing. The SQL (PostgreSQL flavor) to recreate these tables is in the following code. Create a new database with these tables in them before you go any further.

You can customize the user table to suit your needs. You will probably want to store more than just first and last name. Note that we've included a column called last_impression, too. This is used to store the time and date at which the user last made an impression (that is, requested a page) against his or her session. This is used to calculate session timeouts.

```
CREATE TABLE user_session (
  "id" SERIAL PRIMARY KEY NOT NULL,
  "ascii_session_id" character varying(32),
  "logged_in" bool,
  "user_id" int4,
  "last_impression" timestamp,
  "created" timestamp,
  "user_agent" character varying(256)
);

CREATE TABLE "user" (
  "id" SERIAL PRIMARY KEY NOT NULL,
  "username" character varying(32),
  "md5_pw" character varying(32),
  "first_name" character varying(64),
  "last_name" character varying(64)
);

CREATE TABLE "session_variable" (
  "id" SERIAL PRIMARY KEY NOT NULL,
  "session_id" int4,
  "variable_name" character varying(64),
  "variable_value" text
);
```

As you can see, the sessions are stored as indexed by a standard serial ID rather than by their PHP-generated session ID. This allows for far faster indexing when you look at session variables (numbers always index better than strings).

It's worth creating a test user at this stage (for example, username 'ed', password '12345'). You need to know the MD5 representation of this password to enter it into the database. Of course, in the real world you'd have an application to do this, but for now, here's the SQL you need to make the examples that follow work:

```
INSERT INTO "user"(username,md5_pw,first_name,last_name) VALUES
('ed','827ccb0eea8a706c4c34a16891f84e7b', 'Ed', 'Lecky-Thompson');
```

First, take a look at the complete code for the class usersession.phpm. Don't worry. You'll go through it all, including how to tell session_set_save_handler to use class methods, right after you've tried it.

The Code: usersession.phpm

Remember that you use the .phpm extension to explicitly signify this as a class rather than as a template or an executable script in its own right.

```
<?php
  class UserSession {
    private $php_session_id;
    private $native_session_id;
    private $dbhandle;
    private $logged_in;
    private $user_id;
    private $session_timeout = 600;       # 10 minute inactivity timeout
    private $session_lifespan = 3600;     # 1 hour session duration

    public function __construct() {
      # Connect to database
      $this->dbhandle = pg_connect("host=db dbname=prophp5 user=ed")  or die
("PostgreSQL error: --> " . pg_last_error($this->dbhandle));
      # Set up the handler
      session_set_save_handler(
          array(&$this, '_session_open_method'),
          array(&$this, '_session_close_method'),
          array(&$this, '_session_read_method'),
          array(&$this, '_session_write_method'),
          array(&$this, '_session_destroy_method'),
          array(&$this, '_session_gc_method')
      );
      # Check the cookie passed - if one is - if it looks wrong we'll scrub
it right away
      $strUserAgent = $GLOBALS["HTTP_USER_AGENT"];
      if ($_COOKIE["PHPSESSID"]) {
       # Security and age check
       $this->php_session_id = $_COOKIE["PHPSESSID"];
       $stmt = "select id from \"user_session\" where ascii_session_id = '" .
$this->php_session_id . "' AND ((now() - created) < ' " . $this->session_
lifespan . " seconds') AND user_agent='" . $strUserAgent . "' AND ((now() -
last_impression) <= '".$this->session_timeout." seconds' OR last_impression
IS NULL)";
       $result = pg_query($stmt);
       if (pg_num_rows($result)==0) {
         # Set failed flag
          $failed = 1;
         # Delete from database - we do garbage cleanup at the same time
         $result = pg_query("DELETE FROM \"user_session\" WHERE
(ascii_session_id = '". $this->php_session_id . "') OR (now() - created)
> $maxlifetime)");
         # Clean up stray session variables
         $result = pg_query("DELETE FROM \"session_variable\" WHERE
session_id NOT IN (SELECT id FROM \"user_session\")");
         # Get rid of this one... this will force PHP to give us another
         unset($_COOKIE["PHPSESSID"]);
       };
      };
      # Set the life time for the cookie
      session_set_cookie_params($this->session_lifespan);
      # Call the session_start method to get things started
      session_start();
    }
```

```
    public function Impress() {
      if ($this->native_session_id) {
        $result = pg_query("UPDATE \"user_session\" SET last_impression =
now() WHERE id = " . $this->native_session_id);
      };
    }

    public function IsLoggedIn() {
      return($this->logged_in);
    }

    public function GetUserID() {
      if ($this->logged_in) {
        return($this->user_id);
      } else {
        return(false);
      };
    }

    public function GetUserObject() {
      if ($this->logged_in) {
        if (class_exists("user")) {
          $objUser = new User($this->user_id);
          return($objUser);
        } else {
          return(false);
        };
      };
    }

    public function GetSessionIdentifier() {
      return($this->php_session_id);
    }

    public function Login($strUsername, $strPlainPassword) {
      $strMD5Password = md5($strPlainPassword);
      $stmt = "select id FROM \"user\" WHERE username = '$strUsername'
AND md5_pw = '$strMD5Password'";
      $result = pg_query($stmt);
      if (pg_num_rows($result)>0) {
        $row = pg_fetch_array($result);
        $this->user_id = $row["id"];
        $this->logged_in = true;
        $result = pg_query("UPDATE \"user_session\" SET logged_in = true,
user_id = " . $this->user_id . " WHERE id = " . $this->native_session_id);
        return(true);
      } else {
        return(false);
      };
    }

    public function LogOut() {
      if ($this->logged_in == true) {
        $result = pg_query("UPDATE \"user_session\" SET logged_in = false,
user_id = 0 WHERE id = " . $this->native_session_id);
```

```
        $this->logged_in = false;
        $this->user_id = 0;
        return(true);
      } else {
        return(false);
      };
    }

    public function __get($nm) {
      $result = pg_query("SELECT variable_value FROM session_variable WHERE
session_id = " . $this->native_session_id . " AND variable_name = '" .
$nm . "'");
      if (pg_num_rows($result)>0) {
        $row = pg_fetch_array($result);
        return(unserialize($row["variable_value"]));
      } else {
        return(false);
      };
    }


    public function __set($nm, $val) {
      $strSer = serialize($val);
      $stmt = "INSERT INTO session_variable(session_id, variable_name,
variable_value) VALUES(" . $this->native_session_id . ", '$nm', '$strSer')";
      $result = pg_query($stmt);
    }

    private function _session_open_method($save_path, $session_name) {
      # Do nothing
      return(true);
    }

    private function _session_close_method() {
      pg_close($this->dbhandle);
      return(true);
    }

    private function _session_read_method($id) {
      # We use this to determine whether or not our session actually exists.
      $strUserAgent = $GLOBALS["HTTP_USER_AGENT"];
      $this->php_session_id = $id;
      # Set failed flag to 1 for now
      $failed = 1;
      # See if this exists in the database or not.
      $result = pg_query("select id, logged_in, user_id from \"user_session\"
where ascii_session_id = '$id'");
      if (pg_num_rows($result)>0) {
       $row = pg_fetch_array($result);
       $this->native_session_id = $row["id"];
       if ($row["logged_in"]=="t") {
         $this->logged_in = true;
         $this->user_id = $row["user_id"];
       } else {
```

```
          $this->logged_in = false;
        };
      } else {
        $this->logged_in = false;
        # We need to create an entry in the database
        $result = pg_query("INSERT INTO user_session(ascii_session_id,
logged_in, user_id, created, user_agent) VALUES ('$id','f',0,now(),
'$ strUserAgent')");
        # Now get the true ID
        $result = pg_query("select id from \"user_session\" where
ascii_session_id = '$id'");
        $row = pg_fetch_array($result);
        $this->native_session_id = $row["id"];
      };
      # Just return empty string
      return("");
    }

    private function _session_write_method($id, $sess_data) {
      return(true);
    }

    private function _session_destroy_method($id) {
      $result = pg_query("DELETE FROM \"user_session\" WHERE ascii_session_id =
'$id'");
      return($result);
    }

    private function _session_gc_method($maxlifetime) {
      return(true);
    }


  }
?>
```

The Code: Testing the UserSession Class

Before going through the code, test the class for an imaginary user logging in and out. The following simple script shows the class in action:

```
<?php
require_once("usersession.phpm");

$objSession = new UserSession();
$objSession->Impress();



?>
UserSession Test Page
<HR>
```

```
<B>Current Session ID: </B> <?=$objSession->GetSessionIdentifier();?><BR>
<B>Logged in? </B> <?=(($objSession->IsLoggedIn() == true) ? "Yes" : "No")?><BR>
<BR><BR>
Attempting to log in ...
<?php $objSession->Login("ed","12345"); ?>
<BR><BR>
<B>Logged in? </B> <?=(($objSession->IsLoggedIn() == true) ? "Yes" : "No")?><BR>
<B>User ID of logged in user: </B> <?=$objSession->GetUserID();?><BR>

<BR><BR>
Now logging out...
<?php $objSession->Logout(); ?>

<BR><BR>
<B>Logged in? </B> <?=(($objSession->IsLoggedIn() == true) ? "Yes" : "No")?><BR>
<BR><BR>
```

Run this and you should see output similar to Figure 15-5.

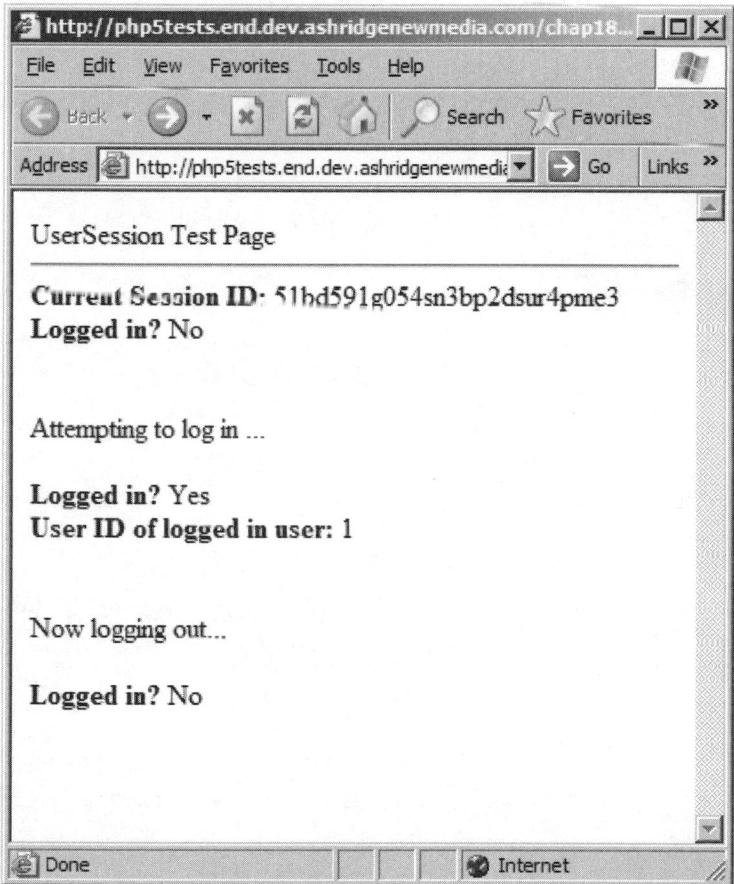

Figure 15-5

If you click Refresh several times, you should see that you get the same output time and time again. The session identifier is perpetuated.

If you want to prove to yourself that the logged-in state of the session really is maintained, try commenting out the Logout line and clicking Refresh. You should see that the Logged in statement at the top of the page repeatedly returns `Yes`.

It's worth looking at the database, too. As soon as the user is logged in successfully, that flag is set against the session in the database table and remains until either the session itself is deleted or the explicit `LogOut` method is called.

```
prophp5=# SELECT * FROM user_session ;
 id  |       ascii_session_id        | logged_in | user_id |        last_impression
     |          created              |                                user_agent

-----+---------------------------+-----------+---------+---------------------
-----+---------------------------+------------------------------------------
-------------------------
 168 | 51bd591g054sn3bp2dsur4pme3 | f          |        0 | 2004-02-23 07:31:04.33
4694 | 2004-02-23 06:54:31.802746 | Mozilla/4.0 (compatible; MSIE 6.0;
Windows NT 5.1; .NET CLR 1.1.4322)
(1 row)
```

Now try the session variable functionality:

```
<?php
require_once("usersession.phpm");

$objSession = new UserSession();
$objSession->Impress();


?>
UserSession Variable Test Page
<HR>
<B>Current Session ID: </B> <?=$objSession->GetSessionIdentifier();?><BR>
<B>Logged in? </B> <?=(($objSession->IsLoggedIn() == true) ? "Yes" : "No")?><BR>
<BR><BR>
<B>Current value of TESTVAR:</B> [<?=$objSession->TESTVAR?>]<BR>
<BR><BR>
Setting TESTVAR to 'foo'
<BR><BR>
<?php
  $objSession->TESTVAR = 'foo';
?>
<B>Current value of TESTVAR:</B> [<?=$objSession->TESTVAR?>]<BR>
<BR><BR>
```

Run this just once and you will see something like Figure 15-6.

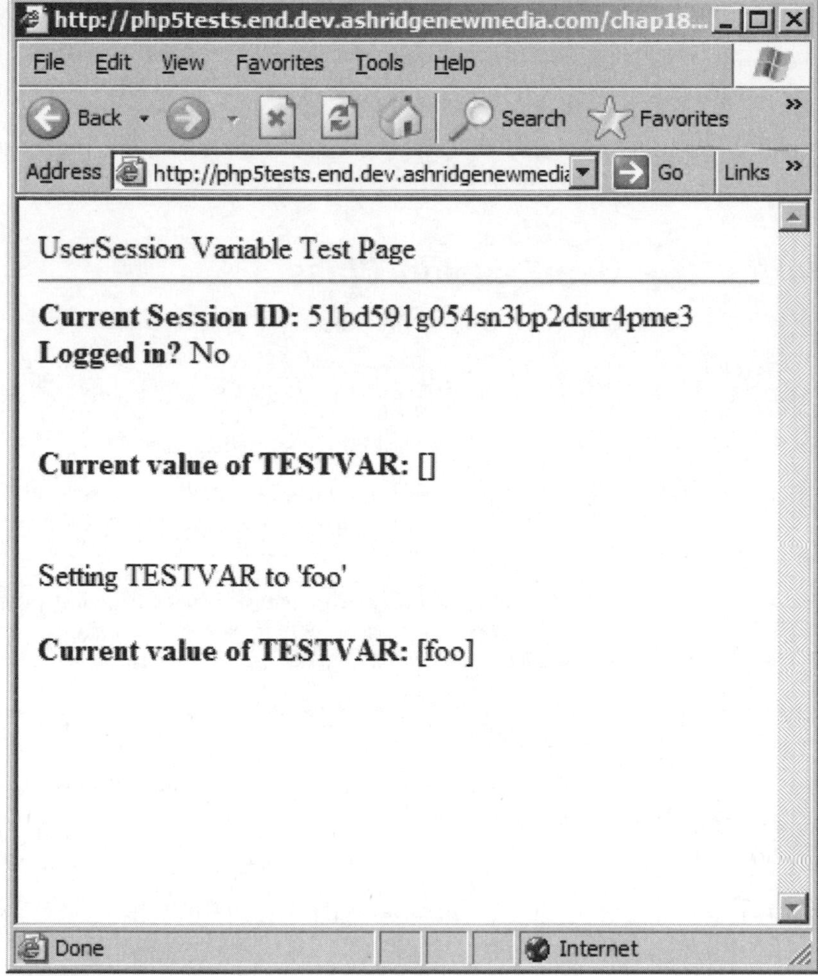

Figure 15-6

Click Refresh and you will see that the value of `TESTVAR` is perpetuated. The top current value statement will read `foo` as well. A quick glance at the `session_variable` table in the database shows what actually gets stored:

```
prophp5=# SELECT * FROM session_variable ;
 id | session_id | variable_name | variable_value
----+------------+---------------+----------------
  6 |        168 | TESTVAR       | s:3:"foo";
(1 row)
```

As you can see, using serialization to store the data follows PHP. However, unlike PHP, we use a new row for each variable. This allows more than one variable to be stored, separately serialized, against an individual session. With PHP's native session variable handling, all variables are lumped together in a single associative array that is then serialized. This can have very serious performance implications; serialization and deserialization have a fair amount of overhead, and PHP is not the quickest language in the world when it comes to string processing—that honor probably goes to PERL! With this in mind, the decision is duly made to go against the grain on this occasion.

Clearly, the `UserSession` class is incredibly easy to use. But take a look at the class itself in more detail, both to understand the logic behind it and be fully equipped to deploy it in production applications.

How It Works: The UserSession Class

Start by looking at the private member variables of the class.

Variable	Purpose
`php_session_id`	The 32 character PHP-generated session ID.
`native_session_id`	The native session ID used to identify the session in the database. Never sent to the Web browser. Used only for the purpose of database entity relationships.
`Dbhandle`	A database connection handle. In production environments this would be declared elsewhere as a global resource, and the `UserSession` class would make use of it the same as any other.
`Logged_in`	Is this session a logged-in session? If this is true, then a user ID will be available.
`user_id`	The ID (from the database table) of the currently logged-in user.
`session_timeout`	An inactivity timeout. If a period of time greater than this elapses between reported impressions, the session is destroyed.
`session_lifespan`	The maximum age of the session. This is given to PHP for the purpose of setting the cookie and is also used in garbage cleaning SQL to keep the database clean of dead sessions.

The Constructor

You want your class to be plug and play. This is so that the programmer can instantiate it once and forget about it.

The constructor:

- Sets up the database connection. This would normally be handled by another class in a production environment.
- Tells PHP how to handle session events in the custom class (discussed in further detail shortly).
- Checks to see whether an existing session identifier is being offered by the client before PHP has a chance to get its hands on it, which would be the case if the user is in the middle of a session

instead of starting a new one. Performs various checks on age, inactivity, and the consistency of the reported HTTP User Agent. If it fails, remove it altogether (and any garbage found) so that PHP believes it has to issue a new session from scratch.

- Sets up the session lifespan parameter, which PHP will obey when issuing the cookie itself.
- Tells PHP to go ahead and start the session in the normal way.

Note the interesting syntax used for `session_set_save_handler`:

```
session_set_save_handler(
  array(&$this, '_session_open_method'),
  array(&$this, '_session_close_method'),
  array(&$this, '_session_read_method'),
  array(&$this, '_session_write_method'),
  array(&$this, '_session_destroy_method'),
  array(&$this, '_session_gc_method')
);
```

Largely undocumented, parameters for this method do not necessarily have to be strings representing procedural function names. Instead you may pass an array of two components. The first is a reference to an instance of a class (in this case, `&$this` refers to this instance of the class). The second is the name of the method of that class.

The _session_read_method() Handler

Because the first method called by PHP's own session management after a valid session ID has been decided upon (through generation of a brand new session or the presentation of a still-valid cookie by the web browser), you use this method to ensure that the session database is kept fully up-to-date.

If the 32 character session identifier supplied by PHP does exist in the database, then the class member variables (`logged_in` and `user_id`) are updated against the database record. If it does not, it is inserted with defaults in place.

The Impress() Function

This method touches the session to indicate that a new page impression has taken place. Generally, this method would be called on any page that uses the session class directly after it has been instantiated.

The last impression column in the database is used for determining session timeouts, and so it is very important to call this method if you want a given page to count against a user's accrued inactivity timeout.

The IsLoggedIn() Function

This method simply reports from the private member variable as to whether this session has undergone a successful login in its lifespan that has not been rescinded by means of a `logout()`.

The GetUserID() and GetUserObject() Functions

If a user is logged in, these two functions return, respectively, the ID of the logged in user (from the user table defined in the database) and, if possible, an instantiated object of the user class should one exist. One has not been defined in this chapter because it is slightly outside the scope of session management, but you will almost certainly wish to develop one for any serious production application because you will almost certainly frequently wish to read and write the properties of your currently logged-in user.

The class is instantiated using the ID as the sole operand of the constructor and works well with the discussion of `GenericObject` in Chapter 7, "GenericObject Class."

The GetSessionIdentifier() Function

This method returns the 32-character PHP session identifier rather than the internal (database) identifier. This is the property more likely to be used in applications because the internal identifier is only really meaningful to postgreSQL, and is never exposed to the application or Web browser.

The _get() and _set() Overload Methods

Taking advantage of PHP5's support for overloading the inspection and assignment of ostensibly public member variables, the overload methods provide their own session variable functionality. Quite simply, a variable for a given session is set by simply assigning it a value. Likewise, it is read by simply reading it, as if it were a publicly declared member variable.

Putting It All Together

The `UserSession` class built in this chapter is a fully reusable, modular component. It easily can be included in virtually any project that has the requirement to maintain session data as well as support the authentication of registered users.

We have provided an object-oriented interface to PHP's own session management and replaced its session variable functionality with a more flexible variant whereby each variable is stored separately for the sake of speed and cleaner code.

Integration with your own applications should be most straightforward. You may find you need to extend its functionality to suit your own needs, but its being a self-contained class makes this significantly easier than extending PHP's session management out of the box.

It's also worth pointing out that the only additional security mechanism incorporated from earlier in the chapter is the User Agent check. Should you require firmer security, you may wish to explore integrating some of the other security functionality such as the IP variance analysis discussed earlier.

Summary

In this chapter, you learned about sessions: why they're useful, how to best implement them in your applications, and how to avoid some of the security pitfalls normally associated with them through some strategic security measures.

You also learned about PHP's traditional implementation of sessions and why it is largely inadequate for professional software architects. You looked at how you can easily extend and adapt it to make it far more functional and scalable.

Finally, you used this knowledge to build a single, modular, self-contained `UserSession` class that can be easily integrated into your future applications.

Unit Testing Framework

One of the main benefits of structured, modular programming in any language is that the components you develop will nearly always be self-contained. They can be cleanly taken away from their mother project and worked on in their own right, and this includes testing.

Making sure that a component does exactly what you want it to do is an essential step in application development. As you will have already learned elsewhere in this book, it is vital that components are tested *before* they are integrated with the bigger picture application. Always write the application around the components. Never write your components around your application.

For slightly more complex classes (or even hierarchies of several classes), devising a suitable test strategy can appear quite tricky. The temptation to resort to spitting out huge chunks of data with `var_dump()` to the error log can be overwhelming, but you should resist it because you can save yourself a great deal of time by using a prewritten Unit Testing Framework. Not only that, but a coherent, thorough, and professional approach to testing is something you can actively demonstrate to your clients (or your boss), whereas having hundreds of `error_log()` statements is not.

There is indeed such a framework available for PHP, a semi-official one called PHPUnit. In this chapter, you'll learn not only how to install and use PHPUnit but also why it's so useful on a day-to-day basis. At the end of the chapter, we cook up a class with some deliberate but hard-to-spot logic errors and use PHPUnit to fix it.

Methodology and Terminology

Before examining the ins and outs of the PHPUnit package, take a closer look at the idea of unit testing in general. First, take a look at a traditional component test workflow. Does the following approach seem familiar?

1. Write the class.
2. Produce a short test script that `require()`s the class, instantiates it, calls some methods, and spits out some output.
3. Run the script.
4. Check the output of the script against what you expected (in your head).

5. If the output looks good, move on; if not, adjust the class and repeat steps 3 and 4 until the output appears to work.
6. Integrate the component into the mother application.

It sounds almost comical, but this kind of process is actually more widespread than you might think.

The problem with approaching your component testing this way is that it's neither thorough nor systematic. In other words, not only are you potentially testing only a small subset of your component, you're also taking longer than you really need to do so. Furthermore, if you do find problems, your short test script won't be much help when it comes to tracking them down. You'll have to make the decision on whether your test is successful or not every time you test.

Thankfully, there is another way. Revise the component test workflow to look more like this:

1. Design the interface (but not the implementation) of the class.
2. Create a test suite for the (empty) class, and check that it tests okay.
3. Write the implementation of the class.
4. Run the test suite again.
5. Fix any errors that are causing unexpected results and then go back to step 4.
6. Integrate the component into the other application.

Now take a look at these steps in more detail and discover exactly what we mean by a test suite. The concept of the test case is covered later in the chapter.

Designing the Interface of Your Class

Let's recap some OOP (Object-Oriented Programming) edicts for a moment. In OOP design, it's often said that the most important part of your object hierarchy is the interface and the least important part is the implementation.

This might sound odd, but think of it as follows. If you're designing a user class, what's actually going through your head?

> **"I'll need to have username, first name, last name, and encrypted password properties. And I'll need methods to tell my application which security groups this user belongs to, and a method to work out how long it's been since their last login, and. . . . "**

You're being smart without even realizing it. You're listing to yourself the methods and member variables of the object. What you're not trying to work out is how you'll go about figuring out how long it's been since the user's last login. In fact, there's probably more than one way to do it. It doesn't really matter. Whichever way you go about it won't affect your interface.

When you consider the interface, you know it's pretty much set in stone as a result of your knowledge of the application's business requirements. It's just not open for discussion. When you consider the implementation, it's safe to say that it's really just detail. As a PHP professional, you might prefer to have a junior software engineer (if you're fortunate enough to have one working under you) handling this detail.

Approaching this in terms of the unit-testing friendly workflow is simple. At first, leave all the methods of the class completely blank. Use nothing but whitespace between opening and closing braces. You'll look at this in more detail later.

Creating a Test Suite for Your Class

With the skeleton class to test, it's not a bad idea to go ahead and create your test suite. Right now, you learn about the theory; the specifics of how to implement this with a particular testing framework are covered in the next section.

The function of a test suite is to provide a simple, black-box solution for testing your class. When invoked, it hooks directly into the important functionality of your class, performs a series of tests, and then states whether those tests were successful. It is truly an appliance.

The nature of these tests is important to understand. You implement a test suite by extending what is known as the test case class. This is provided as part of the Unit Testing framework you choose to use (in this case, PHPUnit, which is covered in much more detail in the next section). You must take care of certain administrative bits and pieces in the extended class (largely relating to instructing the test unit how to instantiate and destroy the test class), but after that it's up to you to provide a test method for every actual method in the test class.

The test methods must be named according to the Unit Testing framework's requirements so that it knows to execute them as part of the test suite's runtime behavior. They are responsible for testing the core functionality of the test class.

Each test method follows the same basic pattern:

1. Decide upon some input parameters for the test class method.
2. Determine what the result expected to be returned from the test class method is based on those input parameters.
3. Call that method, with those input parameters, and trap the result.
4. Assert the result to be equal to what was determined to be the expected result.

You don't need to worry about doing anything else; you should assume that the Test Suite functionality provided by your Unit Testing framework knows what to do when that assertion is or isn't true. This is certainly true of PHPUnit, which you'll meet shortly.

By creating your test case class you have effectively provided the *modus operandi*—that is, the operational inner workings—for your test suite.

At this stage, you would run your black box for the first time and watch it fail spectacularly. It will fail, of course, because you don't have any implementation in your class yet. You should, however, at least be able to get your first idea of what the test results will roughly look like when the implementation has been taken care of.

Writing the Implementation of Your Class

Without altering the interface of your class, go about writing your code to make it work. There's no need to test anything as you go; this is what the test suite is for. However, you may want to do a syntax check as you go to make sure that you haven't made any typos. A test suite is really for rooting out logic errors rather than compilation errors.

In case you've not encountered it before, you can perform a syntax check at the command line by using `php` with the `-l` parameter, followed by the filename of the class or script whose syntax you want to check.

If your class talks to a database, it may not be a bad idea to also check any database SQL queries before you walk away from the implementation. Because PHP isn't closely linked into the database server, rooting out malformed SQL syntax may be easier to do now than after you discover that your test suite fails on one or more methods. In addition, keep in mind that because data in a database can change independently from your code, you'll find it tricky to accurately predict the expected output of methods that do query a database.

Take a look at the following sample query, pulled from a typical user class:

```
$sql = "SELECT group_id FROM user_group WHERE user_id = $user_id";
```

Substitute the `$user_id` for a sensible value and check that the query works in the PostgreSQL (or other) console. If it does, you're in business.

Assuming that your PHP syntax and SQL queries check out okay and you've implemented all your methods, you can go ahead and start testing.

The Second Run

Fire up your test suite black box once more. Now that you've implemented your class, you should have more luck with the test results than last time you ran it.

If your class didn't pass all the tests, it's time to retrace your steps. This is where traditional debugging methods may come in handy. These are covered in some detail in Chapter 23, "Quality Assurance."

After your test suite runs with a 100 percent success rate, you can be fully confident that your class is ready for the production environment, and you can accordingly integrate it into the mother application.

Introduction to PHPUnit

PHPUnit is developed by Sebastian Bergmann and is one of a small number of PHP unit testing frameworks available at the time of writing. You might prefer PHPUnit to some of its competitors because it is freely available, easy to use, and, best of all, is available from PEAR.

Perhaps rather confusingly, two packages are readily available for PHP, both of which are named PHPUnit and both of which perform essentially the same task; indeed, they even share a similar implementation. The implementation examined in this chapter is that by Sebastian Bergmann, which is better suited for PHP5.

The PHPUnit package is effectively a suite of classes rather than a single class. This chapter focuses on its Test Case and Test Suite functionality. There is more to PHPUnit, of course. If you're curious, when you're done with this chapter you may want to take a look at `http://www.sebastian-bergmann.de/PHPUnit/`, which goes into more detail.

Those of you with a Java persuasion may have already drawn comparisons to JUnit (`http://www.junit.org`), and you would be right to do so; PHPUnit is in fact loosely based on JUnit. Much of this chapter's content may therefore already be familiar to you. What you may not be familiar with is just how easily this powerful methodology can be put to use in PHP 5.

Installing PHPUnit

A good starting point is to get your PHP setup equipped with PHPUnit. It is not part of the PEAR Foundation Classes, so you will need to install it yourself. Even if you have previously installed it, it might not be a bad idea now to check on whether you are running the latest version.

Use the standard PEAR syntax to execute an installation of PHPUnit. If you are running the latest version, PEAR will tell you. If not, or you don't have it installed, you will see output similar to the following:

```
root@genesis:~# pear install PHPUnit
downloading PHPUnit-0.6.2
...done: 11,551 bytes
install ok: PHPUnit 0.6.2
root@genesis:~#
```

If you want (or need) to install manually, for example, on a production environment in which you are not blessed with root access to the server, simply visit the PEAR package page at `http://pear.php.net/package/PHPUnit` and download and decompress the archive into an appropriate place. After everything's installed okay, you can continue safely.

Using PHPUnit

This section covers how PHPUnit implements the concepts of test suites and test cases, putting theory into practice.

By first writing a test case for your class, you can then easily develop a test suite to provide a black-box test mechanism that you can be use repeatedly to test your class, even after you've made major changes to the underlying code of that class.

Test Cases

Take a look at how to create a test case using PHPUnit.

We assume that you have a test class saved in a separate file, `testclass.phpm`. Because you're still looking at the theory of PHPUnit, it doesn't matter too much at this stage what's in that class. Something similar to the following will suffice for now:

```
<?php
class TestClass {
 private $testVar;

 function myMethod($strParam) {
  $this->testVar = $strParam;
  return('expected result');
 }

};
```

You can now create the test case in separate PHP file, `testcase.phpm`.

The first two lines of the test case should include both the necessary PHPUnit class and the test class file(s):

```
require_once("testclass.phpm");
require_once("PHPUnit.php");
```

Assuming that you used PEAR to install PHPUnit, it should be able to find `PHPUnit.php` just fine. If not, and you had to install it manually, you may have to help PHP out by pointing it to the correct file, as follows:

```
require_once("/home/ed/myphplibs/PHPUnit.php");
```

In this case, PHPUnit is installed in `/home/ed/myphplibs`.

Now take a look at how to extend the `PHPUnit_TestCase` class to form your very own test case with some pseudocode:

```
class MyTestCase extends PHPUnit_TestCase
{
    var $objMyTestClass;

    function __construct($name) {
       $this->PHPUnit_TestCase($name);
    }

    function setUp() {
        $this->objMyTestClass = new TestClass();
    }

    function tearDown() {
        unset($this->objMyTestClass);
    }

    function testMyMethod() {
        $actualResult = $this->objMyTestClass->myMethod('parameter');
        $expectedResult = 'expected result';
        $this->assertTrue($actualResult == $expectedResult);
    }
}
```

You can now go through this step by step.

```
class MyTestCase extends PHPUnit_TestCase
```

Name the class whatever you want. Make sure that it extends `PHPUnit_TestCase`, however.

```
var $objMyTestClass;
```

The only member variable your extended test case class needs is a single instance of your test class. However, in more complex situations you may want to use multiple instances of the same class, or even more than one class. You should try to keep the number of classes involved in any given test case to a minimum, however, for simplicity's sake. Certainly, you should never group unrelated classes together in a single test case.

```
function __construct($name) {
   $this->PHPUnit_TestCase($name);
}
```

The constructor for your extended test case class falls here. Its only job is to call its parent constructor. Note the non-optional `$name` parameter, however, which is used by the test suite class:

```
function setUp() {
    $this->objMyTestClass = new TestClass();
}

function tearDown() {
    unset($this->objMyTestClass);
}
```

These two methods are best described as virtual constructors and destructors. These are called before and after the various test functions are executed. Usually, their only job is to instantiate a working instance of your test class into the member variable you defined earlier.

```
function testMyMethod() {
    $actualResult = $this->objMyTestClass->myMethod('parameter');
    $expectedResult = 'expected result';
    $this->assertTrue($actualResult == $expectedResult);
}
```

This is where the real meat of your test case is defined. Declare one method for each method of your test class that you want to test. The method must begin with the word `test` for it to be automatically executed by the test suite. You should name the method `test` followed by the name of the real method in your test class. This makes things a great deal clearer if you need to look at the test case again.

The actual functionality of this method is largely up to you. Ultimately, however, you will be doing four things. First, you will be declaring (that is, hard-coding) or determining a test parameter to pass into your test class's method. Second, you will be declaring or determining the *expected* result based on that parameter. Third, you will be calling the method with that parameter and capturing the actual result. Finally, you will be comparing the actual result to your hypothesis.

That comparison should be done using one of a number of assertion methods provided by PHPUnit. It is these assertions that allow the test suite to report test results. Essentially, it is the accuracy of your assertions that will be reported.

Numerous assertion methods are available—`assertEquals`, `assertTrue`, `assertFalse`, `assertNotNull`, `assertNull`, `assertSame`, `assertNotSame`, `assertType`, and `assertRegExp`. They pretty much all do exactly what you'd expect from their name, but if you're curious, check out `/usr/local/lib/php/PHPUnit/Assert.php`, or the file `Assert.php` in the directory in which you installed PHPUnit, for definitive answers.

You may be wondering why having so many assert methods is necessary. Surely all comparisons can be handled using `assertEquals` and making liberal use of appropriate built-in PHP functions? This is true. It's really just a convenience to make your code a little easier to read, and to let you avoid using double negatives and so forth. In later versions of PHPUnit, the assertions actually provide assertion-specific details with any failed test (such as showing the two types in question in `assertType`, and which characters don't actually match when comparing two strings).

The Test Suite

Having developed your test case class, using it in a test suite is actually a relatively simple mechanism. You might name the following `testsuite.php`:

```
<?php
require_once 'testcase.php';
require_once 'PHPUnit.php';

$objSuite = new PHPUnit_TestSuite("MyTestCase");
$strResult = PHPUnit::run($objSuite);

print $strResult->toString();
?>
```

You need to replace `MyTestCase` with the actual name of your test case class. If you run this from the command line (as opposed to using your Web browser), you'll get output that looks something like this if things worked:

```
TestCase objMyTestClass->myMethod() passed
```

It will look like this if things didn't work:

```
TestCase objMyTestClass->myMethod() failed: expected true, actual false
```

Note that if you want to run in a Web browser rather than at the command line, you should use the `toHTML` rather than the `toString` method on the output string so that carriage returns get converted to `<br />` and so forth.

As you can see, constructing a simple test unit is a pretty simple exercise. But why would you bother in the first place, and how do you go about implementing this methodology to test a real-world class? The next section should answer these questions.

Why Bother?

It can at first be difficult to see the immense advantages arising from using this method of testing over a more quick-and-dirty method involving the server error log, such as the one we somewhat contemptuously described earlier.

There are four core benefits. First, the black box that your test suite will become will allow you to effectively regression test your class should you make changes to it later in the project. Second, your test suite will become a jack-of-all-trades hammer that you can use in myriad situations on your project with very little modification. Third, this form of formal testing provides a degree of demonstrable quality assurance that informal use of debug statements cannot ever hope to match. Finally, the inevitable burden of functional testing is lessened when a formal test plan involving frameworks has been followed.

The next sections look at these benefits in more detail.

Regression Testing

The vast majority of code you'll ever work on will, at some stage, need to evolve. It may not necessarily be you who works on it, but you can lay money on its not staying untouched for too long.

You might need to rework an existing method to make it provide exactly the same functionality as it did before but with a big performance increase. The only way to do this is to completely rewrite the method, keeping the interface the same but with an optimized inner algorithm. In this kind of example, your testing suite is immensely useful. Simply run it before and after your new algorithm has been developed, and check that you get the same results both times.

A more likely scenario, however, is that your class needs to be extended with a new method to support some new business requirement. Even then, your testing suite is useful in its unmodified form. You can ensure that your new method does not in any way impact the functionality of any other methods. After verifying this, you can simply extend your test case class to test your new method.

Either way, you can see that using unit test frameworks for this kind of testing, commonly known as regression testing, makes good sense.

Framework Usability

Your test case classes may have wider uses than you think. Other classes you develop with similar or identical interface functionality can be quickly and reliably tested using your existing test suites.

In particular, you may have inherited classes that overwrite the functionality of their parent class. Alternatively, taking advantage of PHP 5's new object model, you may have classes that implement abstract interfaces. A good example of this is objects representing entities stored in a database, which will almost certainly have `getProperty`, `setProperty` methods, and so forth. With little or no adaptation, a standard test suite can be used to provide an instant and reliable commentary on the functionality of such classes.

Demonstrable Quality Assurance

A professional software development environment can often contain a complex hierarchy of individuals involved on any given project; from the project manager right through to the lead architect, the software engineers, the designers, and others.

In this kind of environment, literally tens of thousands of lines of code can be churned out every single day. It is simply impossible for the project's lead architect to test every single component his or her developers produce.

With this kind of structured testing methodology, the management buzzword of *empowerment* becomes an achievable reality. That is to say, engineers can be safely trusted to test their own code, because this methodology encourages a thoroughness that is often absent in other, more haphazard component-testing techniques. Lead architects can easily standardize quality assurance across all component production and have far greater confidence in his or her team's output as a result.

The formal nature of this process is likely to be viewed favorably by nontechnical individuals with a keen interest in the progress of a project, such as project and account managers.

Reducing the Burden of Functional Testing

It's often said that the least sexy part of the project life-cycle is functional testing. Whether this statement is fair or not, it is certainly an additional cost that needs to be borne and budgeted for.

By requiring the development team to take ownership of the functional testing of its own components, the need for exhaustive and extensive functional testing of the completed application can be greatly reduced.It is not eliminated entirely, however, and as you will learn in Chapter 23 it is still vitally important.

A Real-World Example

The following example puts to work your knowledge of PHPUnit and Unit Testing frameworks in general.

The component is called `xDir`. It is a variant of PHP's built-in `Dir` class (see `http://www.php.net/manual/en/class.dir.php`). The only real difference is that `xDir` supports recursion through subdirectories, something that can be immensely useful.

Entirely deliberately, the syntax for `xDir` is virtually identical to that of the PHP `Dir` class, with the exception of an optional parameter to specify whether recursion is required.

Those of you with a strong traditional programming background will be familiar with recursion as a programming concept. It simply refers to a function's or method's calling itself in order to perform some operation recursively across a hierarchy. If you've ever played with generating fractals, this will be more than just a little familiar.

Take a look at the following code. It contains a deliberate mistake that you might find difficult to spot.

```
<?php

class xdir {

  public $path;
  public $entries = array();
  public $counter = 0;
  public $isRecursive;

  public function __construct($path, $recursive = false) {
    if ((substr($path, strlen($path)-1, 1) == "/")  && (strlen($path) != 1)) {
      $path = substr($path, 0, strlen($path)-1);
    };
    $this->path = $path;
    $this->isRecursive = $recursive;
    if ($this->path) {
      $this->_getDirList($this->path);
    };
  }

  public function read() {
    if ($this->counter <= (sizeof($this->entries)-1)) {
      $s = ($this->entries[$this->counter]);
      return($s);
      $this->counter++;
    } else {
      return(false);
    };
  }

  public function isRecursive() {
    return($this->isRecursive);
  }

  public  function rewind() {
    $this->counter = 0;
    return(true);
  }

  public  function close() {
    return(true);
  }


  public  function _getDirList ($dirName) {
    $objDir = dir($dirName);
    if ($objDir) {
      while($strEntry = $objDir->read()) {
        if ($strEntry != "." && $strEntry != "..") {
          if (!(is_dir($dirName."/".$strEntry))) {
            array_push($this->entries, $dirName."/".$strEntry);
          } else {
            if ($this->isRecursive) {
              $this->_getDirList($dirName."/".$strEntry, true);
```

```
                };
              };
            };
          };
          $objDir->close();
        };
      }
    };
    ?>
```

A typical quick-and-dirty test application for this might look like the following:

```
<? require_once("xdir.phpm"); ?>
<html>
 <head><title>Ed's Quick and Dirty xDir Test App</title>
</head>
 <body>
  <?php
    $objXDir = new XDir("/home/ed/public_html/pacha", true);
    while (false !== ($entry = $objXDir->read())) {
      echo $entry."<br>\n";
     }
    $objXDir->close();
  ?>
 </body>
</html>
```

Note that for the purposes of familiarity, this is shamelessly pulled from the example on `php.net`, right down to the slightly unusual ordering in the `while` statement. We ask the class to show us the recursive contents of `/home/ed/public_html/pacha` as the script's output. In fact, this test application would work perfectly if the class actually worked.

Sadly, the class doesn't work, so we get one line of output and then appear to get stuck in an infinite loop. The error log shows nothing because, strictly speaking, as far as PHP's concerned, the script has done nothing wrong.

Where do you go from here? Build a test case. Notice how we've left all our member variables and methods public. This isn't sloppy programming on our part. Rather, it allows us to interrogate our class more easily. After we're satisfied that everything works, we can set what should be private (namely, those three member variables and `_getDirList`) to be private.

```
class MyTestCase extends PHPUnit_TestCase
{
    var $objXDirClass;

    function __construct($name) {
       $this->PHPUnit_TestCase($name);
    }

    function setUp() {
        $this->objXDirClass = new XDir("", "true");
    }
```

```
    function tearDown() {
        unset($this->objXDirClass);
    }

    function testRead() {
        $this->objXDirClass->counter = 1;
        $intCounterBefore = $objXDirClass->counter;
        $this->objXDirClass->entries = array("/home/ed/test1", "/home/ed/test2",
"/home/ed/test3", "/home/ed/test4");
        $strActualResult = $this->objXDirClass->read();
        $intActualCounterAfter = $this->objXDirClass->counter;
        $strExpectedResult = "/home/ed/test2";
        $intExpectedCounterAfter = 2;
        $this->assertTrue(($strActualResult == $strExpectedResult) &&
($intActualCounterAfter == $intExpectedCounterAfter));
    }
}
```

Notice how we're testing only one method here—the `read` method. In practice you should ideally devise a test for every method in the class, including `_getDirList`, but because `_getDirList` talks directly to the file system, it would be virtually impossible in practice to falsify its input in order to test its expected output against actual output. Go ahead and test the first method, anyway, and see whether it's the culprit. If it's not, you can always return to `_getDirList` later.

A quick word on the logic in play here. First, we are setting our array counter to be `1`. This counter variable refers to the class's current position in its list of matching files (starting at 0 – so `1` is the second position). We're then defining a falsified list of matching files—`test1` thru `test4`, for convenience.

What we expect to get back from the method is the second file in the list, which is `test2`. We also expect the counter to tick forward by one, from 1 to 2. We apply these two tests as an assertion. If the assertion fails, we know that one of our two tests is wrong.

Build your test suite. Assume that you saved your test case as `testcase.phpm`. Create the following script and call it `testsuite.php`:

```
<?php
require_once 'xdir.phpm
require_once 'testcase.phpm;
require_once 'PHPUnit.php';

$objSuite = new PHPUnit_TestSuite("MyTestCase");
$strResult = PHPUnit::run($objSuite);

print $strResult->toString();
?>
```

Run this at the command line and you'll see something like the following:

```
TestCase mytestcase->read() failed: expected true, actual false
```

This is clearly both a good and a bad result. You now know that it is in fact the `read()` method that is causing the infinite loop, but you don't yet know why (though you could guess). Just to be sure, modify the last line of the `testRead()` method so that it looks like this:

```
$this->assertTrue($strActualResult == $strExpectedResult);
```

Run it again and you get:

```
TestCase mytestcase->testRead() passed
```

You can deduce from this that the test that is actually failing is the test between the expected value of the counter variable and the actual value of the counter variable after the `read()` method has been called. Modify the last line of the `testRead()` method once more, to read:

```
$this->assertEquals($intActualCounterAfter, $intExpectedCounterAfter);
```

Run it again and you get:

```
TestCase mytestcase->testRead() failed: expected 2, actual 1
```

You can see that the counter variable is not being incremented as you expect it to be. You expect it to be 2 but are in fact getting 1. What's going on? Well, at least now you know where to look. Turn back to the `read()` method of your original code for `xDir`:

```
public function read() {
    if ($this->counter <= (sizeof($this->entries)-1)) {
            $s = ($this->entries[$this->counter]);
            return($s);
            $this->counter++;
    } else {
            return(false);
    };
}
```

Can you see what it is yet?

That's right. The `return()` for the function is being called before the counter is incremented. PHP won't execute any code after the `return()` statement. As a result, the counter increment is never actually executed at all.

Revise the code to swap the position of the `return()` and counter increment statements:

```
public function read() {
        if ($this->counter <= (sizeof($this->entries)-1)) {
                $s = ($this->entries[$this->counter]);
                $this->counter++;
                return($s);
        else {
                return(false);
        };
}
```

And run the test once more:

```
TestCase mytestcase->testRead() passed
```

Go back to the original test—the one that combined the two vital tests with `assertTrue`. Check that this, too, now gives a good result:

```
TestCase mytestcase->testRead() passed
```

Everything now looks good.

In theory, this is all you need to do to be completely sure this method works. But if you need the added psychological reassurance, you can always refer back to the quick-and-dirty script, which should now execute fine without problems. Run it in your Web browser and you'll get something similar to:

```
/home/ed/public_html/pacha/perl/cleanbuf.sh
/home/ed/public_html/pacha/perl/cleandb.pl
/home/ed/public_html/pacha/perl/deploylocaldata.sh
/home/ed/public_html/pacha/perl/mailfwd.pl
/home/ed/public_html/pacha/perl/oldphotouploads.pl
/home/ed/public_html/pacha/perl/pafserver.pl
```

As you can see, you've made it, and your PHPUnit testing framework was vital in helping you track down that hard-to-spot bug. Can you imagine how long it would have taken to fudge through that using `var_dump` and `error_log`?

Summary

In this chapter, you learned about Unit Testing and why it is a subtantial improvement over less formal component-testing methodologies. You learned the principles of any unit-testing framework and met one of the more popular frameworks in the form of PEAR's PHPUnit. You saw how to install it and the basics behind how it works. You then applied it to a useful real-world debugging example to track down an errant bug in a class, thereby proving just how useful it really is.

In the next chapter, you'll meet an incredibly useful concept from the earlier years of computer science—that of the Finite State Machine—and how it can be resurrected in PHP 5 to help solve some of the trickier algorithmic problems you might encounter in application development.

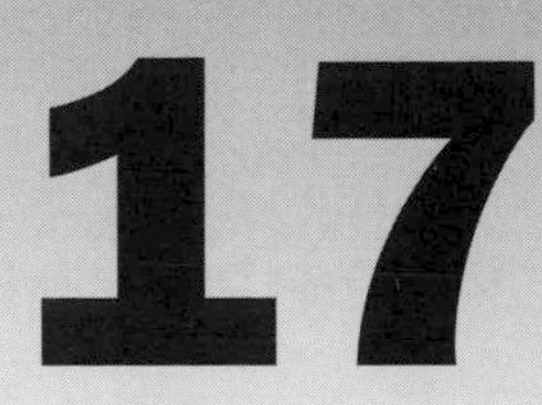

Finite State Machine and Custom Configuration Files

Most people would argue that PHP is a modern language, designed for modern applications. As are almost all modern Web development languages, it is regarded as being high level. It concerns itself more with rapid application development instead of allowing its programmers to fiddle with the underlying system directly for the sake of optimizing performance.

Indeed, languages that are particularly high level, such as PHP, further widen the gap now firmly established between programming in the traditional, computer science college-textbook sense of the word, and application development (using the language as simply a tool designed to solve a problem).

For example, it was not so long ago that games programmers were locked in a battle to determine who could produce the fastest assembly-language `putpixel` routine, to draw a single pixel on the screen. Nowadays, however, few games programmers concern themselves with such low-level matters, preferring instead to make use of Microsoft's DirectX library, which pretty much has it cracked. In much the same way, PHP takes the burden of developing low-level, highly tuned, optimized routines away from the programmer and exposes only useful functionality instead—"tell me what you want me to do, not how you want me to do it."

However, some of the more traditional programming techniques also have a role to play in PHP. We're not suggesting or recommending trying to get PHP to execute register-level CPU instructions, of course, but there is one more elderly concept worth resurrecting—the Finite State Machine.

In this chapter, you'll meet the Finite State Machine in some detail, including learning what it does, how it does it, and how it can prove to be a useful solution to a variety of the more difficult and awkward challenges you might face in your own projects. After learning the basics of the FSM model, you'll meet a PEAR class that enables you to quickly and easily implement a basic FSM in PHP. As a proof of concept, you'll meet a simple programming puzzle solved using the FSM PEAR class and then dissect it piece by piece. In the process, you'll discover why that puzzle lends itself so well to implementation using an FSM, and how you might easily identify similar opportunities yourself. In the second half of this chapter, you'll look at the concept of user-modifiable configuration files, which provide an excellent example of an off-the-shelf Finite State Machine implementation. You'll see why they're important, what the role they play in your applications, and how best to go about implementing them in PHP.

Introducing the Finite State Machine

A Finite State Machine (FSM) is best described as an example of an abstract machine. It's not a machine in the traditional, physical sense, but a logic model implemented entirely in software. In some respects, it is a mini computer in its own right. It has inputs, outputs, and processing in which decisions are made on what its output should be at particular points in time, based on its input.

The true test for any abstract machine is that it could be implemented outside a software environment. For those of you with a background in electronics, the simplest example is an AND gate—two inputs, one output, and the output determined by two inputs. The AND gate can be constructed in the real world using two transistors. In programming it is implemented using the AND operator (`&&` in PHP).

The FSM is an example of a somewhat more sophisticated abstract machine, however.

The traditional textbook definition suggests that a Finite State Machine consists of a set of arbitrary states. These include an initial state, which is applicable as soon as it is first initialized, a set of input events, a set of output events (although the word *events* is somewhat misleading), and a state transition function.

In other words, an FSM is a device for iterating or traversing some collection of inputs in an intelligent manner to produce an answer of some kind. Unlike a simple `foreach` statement, or even an implementation of `Iterator` against a collection class, it is not simply a single action performed against a series of candidates. Rather, an FSM implements an action performed against each candidate that can depend on all the previous candidates encountered before it.

For example, it would not be correct to consider a simple `for` loop passing over each object in an array of objects to be a Finite State Machine, because the `for` loop is simply applying the same logic to each object. Although the logic applied may be determined or influenced in some way by the progress through the loop, it is not affected in any manner by the actions it has performed previously, or by those objects it has encountered earlier in the loop. A real-life example of such iterations is traversing the result tuples returned from a database query in order to instantiate corresponding objects. The act of instantiation is the same regardless of the data in the previous iteration.

A Simple FSM: The RPN Calculator

The simplest known example of an FSM, one frequently demonstrated in textbooks explaining the theory, is that of the Reverse Polish Notation (RPN) Calculator. Those of you with UNIX exposure may be familiar with `bc` and other similar command-line tools. These helpful GNU utilities allow you to easily parse an arithmetic expression, as shown in the following example:

```
ed@genesis:~$ bc
bc 1.05
Copyright 1991, 1992, 1993, 1994, 1997, 1998 Free Software Foundation, Inc.
This is free software with ABSOLUTELY NO WARRANTY.
For details type 'warranty'.
7 * (9 + 1) * 29
2030
```

In this example, bc is used to calculate a simple sum [7 × (9 + 1) × 29].

This is all well and good for modern tools such as bc and sophisticated spreadsheet packages such as Excel, but in the earlier days of computing the concept of the precedence of operators (that is, parentheses, indices, multiplication and division, addition and subtraction) was hugely difficult to implement, especially given that parentheses may be nested. Accordingly, the use of parentheses was out and some other means of expressing precedence was required. This was where Reverse Polish Notation, or RPN, came in.

The concept was simple. Operators were written to the right of the numbers to which they related, with those numbers being written in reverse. In the previous example, you would normally write:

```
7 * (9 + 1) * 29
```

In RPN, you would write the same expression as:

```
1 9 + 29 7 * *
```

Essentially, a stack of numbers is maintained. Moving from left to right, every time a number is encountered it is pushed onto the very top of a stack. Every time an operator is encountered the topmost two numbers are taken from the stack and that single expression evaluated in isolation. The result is added to the top of the stack as a number in its own right.

In the previous example, the numbers 1 and 9 are added to the stack. A plus sign is then encountered, meaning that two numbers must be taken from the stack. The 1 and the 9 are taken, leaving the stack empty. The 1 and the 9 are added together, giving 10. This number 10 is added to the empty stack. Next, the number 29 is encountered, then the number 7. These are all added to the top of the stack, giving us 10, 29, and 7 in the stack. Next, a multiplication sign is encountered. The top two numbers, 7 and 29, are taken and multiplied together, to give 203. This number 203 is then put back on the stack, leaving the numbers 230 and 10 on the stack. Finally, a multiplication sign is encountered again, at which point the final two numbers on the stack, 203 and 10, are taken and multiplied together to give 2030. At the end of the series of inputs, there is no more data, so 2030 is the answer.

This is a very good example of a Finite State Machine. There are two states, either accumulating the number stack or performing a basic operation. For each piece of entry data, which will either be a number or an operator, the FSM determines both what it has been doing last (accumulating the stack or performing an operations) and what it is looking at now (an operator or a digit).

It then has to decide what to do now:

Current State	Current Symbol	Action	New State
Accumulating	Number	Add number to stack	Accumulating
Accumulating	Operator	Take top two numbers off the stack, perform the operation on the two numbers, put the result on the top of the stack	Operating
Operating	Number	Add number to the stack	Accumulating
Operating	Operator	Take top two numbers off the stack, perform the operation on the two numbers, put the result on the top of the stack	Operating

This particular FSM does not really need to decide its next state at any stage, because this is not determined by previous inputs, only by the current input.

This variety of FSM is actually known as a Push Down Automaton, or PDA, because it has a concept of memory in the form of its stack. All PDAs are FSMs. Not all FSMs are PDAs.

Theoretical Implementation of FSMs

At the simplest level, an individual Finite State Machine is defined by building what are known as transition tables.

These tables map combinations of input symbols and current machine states into a combination of an action and a subsequent state. There needs to be one rule for each combination of input and state. For example, if two inputs and two states are conceivable, the following transition table might apply:

$$\{input_1,\ current_1\} \dashrightarrow \{action,\ next\}$$
$$\{input_2,\ current_1\} \dashrightarrow \{action,\ next\}$$
$$\{input_2,\ current_1\} \dashrightarrow \{action,\ next\}$$
$$\{input_2,\ current_2\} \dashrightarrow \{action,\ next\}$$

For any given input symbol, the Finite State Machine uses these tables to decide what action to perform and what the next state will be. Generally, a default transitional rule is also defined, either to avoid verbosity or to trap errors in input.

There are two basic variations on the FSM theme: deterministic FSMs (DFSMs) and nondeterministic FSMs (NDFSMs). In a deterministic FSM, the next state of the machine is determined solely by a single input symbol. By contrast, the next state of a nondeterministic FSM depends on both the current input symbol and one or more subsequent symbols. The RPN calculator is an example of an NDFSM in the respect that its next state is determined from whether the next symbol it encounters is an operator or a numeric, and cannot be determined from only the current symbol.

Implementing FSMs in PHP

FSMs are relatively easy to implement syntactically. Indeed, you may well have unconsciously written code in the past that could easily be classified as an FSM to satisfy some algorithmic requirement. However, PHP has an implementation of FSM of its own in the form of a PEAR class known simply as `FSM`.

Installing the FSM Class

You should install the FSM PEAR class in the normal manner. Use the PEAR package manager to install it from your development server's command prompt:

```
root@genesis:~# pear install FSM
downloading FSM-1.2.1.tgz ...
...done: 3,151 bytes
install ok: FSM 1.2.1
```

You can test your installation by executing the following command-line input, simply by entering code straight into the PHP command-line application:

```
root@genesis:~/public_html/prophp5# php
<?
require_once("FSM.php");
?>
```

Press Control+D on UNIX (Control+Z on Windows systems) to indicate EOF and you should see nothing at all. If PHP throws an error message about not finding the class, double-check that the package installed correctly into `/usr/local/lib/php` (or your setup's equivalent).

The Syntax of the FSM Class

The FSM class is very simple. Unlike other programming frameworks such as `PHPUnit`, it is not extended in everyday use but is implemented like any other class you may have written yourself. For the curious, the full syntax of the FSM class can be found at author Jon Parise's Web site at `http://www.indelible.org/pear/FSM/api/`, but we detail the essential methodology in this section.

This particular implementation of the FSM model is limited to coping with a single string as its input. Accordingly, should you wish it to cope with collections of objects or something more complex, you will need to serialize them in some manner. In addition, symbols are read strictly one character at a time, so you must implement transitions to account for characters that are delineating entities (for example, the string `'53 15 19 * * ='` will be read as characters '5', '3', ' ', '1', '5', ' ', and so on, so your code must be able to rebuild '5' and '3' to '53', and so forth).

Instantiating the Class

The FSM class is instantiated as follows:

```
$stack = array();
$fsm = new FSM('INIT', $stack);
```

The first parameter passed is the initial state of the machine. States in the FSM class are named using simple strings, and these names have no real significance beyond code readability (consider them equivalent to variable names in this respect). Here, the initial state is named `INIT`, which seems a sensible choice.

Note also that we have passed a stack variable (which should be of a simple array type) for the FSM to use as its "memory." The FSM constructor specifies that this is passed "by reference" rather than as a copy, so you do not need to pass it as a reference here, too.

Setting the Default Transition

First, you should endeavor to tell your instantiated Finite State Machine the name of the default method to call if it is unable to match another transition against the input and current state. This may be either an error routine (that is, to handle bad input) or a catch-all method.

```
$fsm->setDefaultTransition('INIT', 'Error');
```

The first parameter passed refers to the machine state that should be adopted when this transition is encountered. The second parameter is the name of the method, which will be called prior to this state's being set. Calling this method in your own FSM implementation is optional but is highly recommended nonetheless.

Setting a Single Transition

You may set a single transition for a given input symbol and given entry state using the `addTransition` method.

```
$fsm->addTransition('=', 'INIT', 'INIT', 'DoEqual');
```

The first parameter is the symbol in question. The second is the entry state that must be matched for this transition to apply. The third is the state that will be set after this transition has completed. The fourth is the method that should be called when this transition occurs. The final action parameter may be null.

Setting a Transition for an Array of Inputs

You may simplify your code by specifying a given transition for a single state and an array of input symbols. This can be very useful, for example, for specifying a single transition that applies for all digits 0 thru 9.

```
    $fsm->addTransitions(range(0,9), 'BUILDING_NUMBER', 'BUILDING_NUMBER',
'BuildNumber');
```

The first parameter is the array of matching symbols in question. The second is the entry state that must be matched for this transition to apply. The third is the state that will be set after this transition has completed. The fourth is the method that should be called when this transition occurs. Again, the final action parameter may be null.

Starting the Machine

After you have defined your transitions, the machine is started by calling the `processList` method as follows:

```
$fsm->processList($symbols);
```

One parameter is allowed: the string containing the symbols to be processed. If this is directly dependent on user input, you may want to perform some sanity checking and cleansing before it is passed to the FSM class.

Disassembling the RPN Calculator Example

An example implementation of the RPN Calculator can be found within the PEAR class API at `http://www.indelible.org/pear/FSM/api/`. Although the source code for the RPN Calculator is listed in full within the API at the preceding URL and works perfectly, no explanation is provided as to its inner workings. Accordingly, it's time to look further through this simple example to discover how it works.

The full source code is available online, so if you haven't done so already, copy and paste the source code into a new file and call it `rpn.php`. Run this script from the command line, not from your Web browser, as shown in the following example:

```
root@genesis:~/public_html/prophp5# php ./rpn.php
Expression:
1 9 + 29 7 * * =
2030
root@genesis:~/public_html/prophp5#
```

The RPN implementation from the FSM API documentation is a command-line application rather than a traditional Web-based PHP script, but it would be a relatively trivial matter to adapt it should you feel any great need to do so.

As you can see, we have supplied our expression `29 × (1 + 9) × 7` and reached the correct answer. But how does it work?

Take a look at the code itself. The entry point is after the function definitions:

```
    $stack = Array();
    $fsm = new FSM('INIT', &$stack);

    $fsm->setDefaultTransition('INIT', 'Error');

    $fsm->addTransitionAny('INIT', 'INIT');
    $fsm->addTransition('=', 'INIT', 'INIT', 'DoEqual');
    $fsm->addTransitions(range(0,9), 'INIT', 'BUILDING_NUMBER',
'BeginBuildNumber');
    $fsm->addTransitions(range(0,9), 'BUILDING_NUMBER', 'BUILDING_NUMBER',
'BuildNumber');
    $fsm->addTransition(' ', 'BUILDING_NUMBER', 'INIT', 'EndBuildNumber');
    $fsm->addTransitions(array('+','-','*','/'), 'INIT', 'INIT', 'DoOperator');
```

As you can see, the first steps are to set up the instance of the FSM class, and set the default and normal-use transitions.

Only two states are defined. The initial state is known as `INIT`, which is active as soon as the class is instantiated, after an operation has been performed, and after a distinct number has been added to the stack. The second is known as `BUILDING_NUMBER`, which is active only while the digits of a number are being glued together.

Note that the `range()` method is used to specify the numerals 0 thru 9 and that the arithmetic operators are specified using a simple, in-line array. Five custom methods are referred to for the transitions: `BeginBuildNumber`, `BuildNumber`, `EndBuildNumber`, `DoOperator`, and `DoEqual`. You can now look at these in more detail.

BeginBuildNumber

This method is called whenever the string contains a numeric and the machine had not previously been building a number; for example, when the previous character was a space and this character is a 5—this 5 must be the beginning of a number, so this method is called.

```
function BeginBuildNumber($symbol, $payload)
{
    array_push($payload, $symbol);
}
```

This method, in common with all methods called as part of a transition, takes two non-optional parameters: a reference to the FSM stack and the symbol being passed.

In the case of this method, the symbol passed is added to the stack and nothing else. Don't concern yourself with changing states; this is handled by the FSM directly.

BuildNumber

This method is called whenever the string contains a numeric and the machine had previously been building a number; for example, when a 1 is encountered, and the last digit encountered was a 5. This is therefore the second digit in a number being built up.

```
function BuildNumber($symbol, $payload)
{
    $n = array_pop($payload);
    $n = $n . $symbol;
    array_push($payload, $n);
}
```

The number may be 51, or it could be 51310—you not know this yet, so you take the number as it previously existed on the stack off the stack, append this new digit, and place it back on the stack. For example, if the number was previously 5 in the stack, this 5 is removed from the stack, 1 is appended to give 51, and the number is placed back on the stack.

EndBuildNumber

This method is called whenever the string contains a blank space and the machine had previously been building a number; for example, when a space is encountered and the last digit encountered was a 1.

```
function EndBuildNumber($symbol, $payload)
{
    $n = array_pop($payload);
    array_push($payload, (int)$n);
}
```

The assembled number is taken from the stack; however, it currently resides there in string form because it has been appended to using the string concatenation operator. Before it is placed back on the stack, it is cast into an integer, ready for arithmetic operations.

DoOperator

This method is called whenever the string contains an operator (plus, minus, multiply by, or divide by) and the state is `INIT`—that is, a number build process is not under way (see the `BuildNumber` method, discussed previously).

```
function DoOperator($symbol, $payload)
{
    $ar = array_pop($payload);
    $al = array_pop($payload);

    if ($symbol == '+') {
        array_push($payload, $al + $ar);
    } elseif ($symbol == '-') {
        array_push($payload, $al - $ar);
```

```
        } elseif ($symbol == '*') {
            array_push($payload, $al * $ar);
        } elseif ($symbol == '/') {
            array_push($payload, $al / $ar);
        }
    }
```

The last two numbers of the stack are recorded and removed. Because they will have both undergone the `EndBuildNumber` process, they will be integers, not strings. A simple `if` construct is then used to determine which operator has been specified, and the two numbers are operated on accordingly. The result of the operation is pushed back onto the stack.

DoEqual

This method is called whenever the string contains an equals sign and the state is `INIT`—that is, a number build process is not under way. This tells the FSM to complete its operation and output the result currently on the stack.

```
    function DoEqual($symbol, $payload)
    {
        echo array_pop($payload) . "\n";
    }
```

One small oversight here is that no checking is done to see whether the stack contains only one value, or more than one. For any valid RPN expression, after all operators have been processed, the stack should be empty but for one final number, which is the evaluated expression.

If you feel strongly about this, it should be straightforward enough to add a further state to allow the FSM to determine whether the stack is ready for exit. Calls to the `DoEqual` method when this state is not true would not be allowed.

Real-World Examples of FSMs

An RPN calculator is a nice textbook example to follow, but it is not likely to be something you would want to implement in your own applications. In PHP in particular, you will find that you can use the `eval()` function to evaluate any numeric expression with relative ease, and certainly without recourse to the slightly obscure Reverse Polish Notation.

There are some real-world examples, however, of when the FSM is a genuinely useful approach.

Many implementations of FSM involve string parsing, and almost all could be solved with either a lethally complex regular expression (as is popular with PERL programmers) or some variety of `while` loop coupled with a series of "flags." Neither of these is a particularly elegant solution, and an FSM approach allows you to construct shorter, simpler, more maintainable code.

Configuration Files

One of the most common uses for a Finite State Machine is that of the configuration file. The file must be human readable in order to be human modifiable, but also computer readable in order to be useful in your application. For all the benefits of XML, it still requires some specialist knowledge to accurately modify, and as such is not a particularly useful format for a configuration file (far more common is that in fact used by PHP—`php.ini`). In the next section of this chapter, you'll look at parsing a configuration file of that very format using PHP's built-in methods.

Lexical Analysis for Artificial Intelligence

You will almost certainly have played with "chat-bots." Early examples such as Eliza have been superseded by extraordinarily sophisticated models that are almost capable of passing the "Turing Test," which dictates that a machine professing to be artificially intelligent will have succeeded only if it can convince a questioner that it is in fact not a machine at all. Chat-bots are a fun implementation of lexical analysis, but real-world implementations are cropping up for "helpdesk" search algorithms that allow users to express their questions in plain English.

FSMs provide an excellent mechanism for parsing language constructs; they can understand characters, words, and sentences and, at a more complex level, verbs, nouns, adverbs, adjectives, and more. Because the FSM is "state-aware," it can be programmed to expect these verbs, nouns, adverbs, and adjectives based on the current "state" of the sentence.

The precise implementation of such an FSM is outside the scope of this book and probably too sophisticated for the FSM class met in this chapter. However, the Web has many excellent resources on the subject, including a white paper by the Universität des Saarlandes at `http://www.coli.uni-sb.de/~kay/motivation.pdf`.

Custom Configuration Files

Many applications, including Web-based applications written in PHP, have "installation variables" that need to be set by the systems administrator. These variables usually switch features on and off, specify limits and ranges, server hostnames, and addresses, and define server paths to features.

The way to allow these values to be changed is to specify one or more configuration files for your installation. These will be modified by the systems administrator at the time of deployment to make your application work correctly. These can be implemented in a number of ways, including using native PHP and external XML and INI files.

Using PHP

In some cases, you will be the systems administrator, in which case it is perfectly acceptable to include a file named `constants.phpm` and specify constant declarations one by one, as in the example following:

```
<?
# Hostname or IP address of the Windows SQL Server
define("DATABASE_HOST", "winsqldb");

# Username and password for database
define("DATABASE_USER", "xyz");
define("DATABASE_PASS", "abc");

# Database name
define("DATABASE_NAME", "def");

?>
```

You can then access these properties directly from your code by referring to the name of the constant, as shown in the following code excerpt, in which a connection is established using those constants if a valid connection handle does not already exist:

```
if (!(array_key_exists("db", $GLOBALS))) {
 $GLOBALS["db"] = mssql_connect(DATABASE_HOST, DATABASE_USER, DATABASE_PASS);
 mssql_select_db(DATABASE_NAME);
};
```

This approach is remarkably simple, but you are exposing yourself to problems if there is a requirement for anybody other than a PHP-literate individual to modify the configuration file. Many systems administrators working for your clients' IS departments will be perfectly able to modify a configuration file but could easily make errors—such as omitting a semicolon—when modifying PHP. In these environments, using PHP as the basis for your configuration files will not be appropriate.

Using XML

Given that PHP5 has excellent support for parsing XML, there is some argument for using it as a configuration file syntax, as shown in the following example, which you might name `config.xml`:

```
<database>
  <hostname>winsqldb</hostname>
  <hostusername>xyz</hostusername>
  <hostpassword>abc</hostpassword>
  <hostdbname>def</hostdbname>
</database>
```

This could be relatively easily parsed using Simple XML:

```
$confFileObject = simplexml_load_file("config.xml");
$strDatabaseHostname = $confFileObject->hostname;
```

This approach has advantages over using straight PHP in that it is immune to accidental invalidation through ignorance of PHP. However, the same problem manifests itself to a lesser extent in that some knowledge of XML is still required, especially when dealing with more complex structures. It is by no means obvious, for example, even to the most seasoned expert, which characters have to be escaped before they can be included in a valid XML document.

Another disadvantage is that it can be relatively difficult to read XML on-screen, especially if your configuration file has large amounts of it. Comments guiding the editor are almost impossible to include in any detail, too.

Using INI Files

The final and preferred approach is to use an .INI file. This is a somewhat arbitrary format that has sprung up over the years but which has been adapted as an informal standard, helped in particular by the popularity of Windows. Windows formerly used INI files in its 16-bit incarnations prior to the invention of the Windows Registry.

INI files are incredibly simple to read and edit, and they allow comments to be easily injected to help with the editing process. The nature of comments means that one can easily comment out an objectionable parameter with a simple keystroke.

The Universal Format for INI Files

There is an accepted format for INI files that looks something like the following. You might name this file `config.ini`:

```
; This is a sample configuration file using INI format

[database]
; Hostname or IP address of the Windows SQL Server
DATABASE_HOST = winsqldb

; Username and password for database
DATABASE_USER = xyz
DATABASE_PASS = abc

# Database name
DATABASE_NAME = def

[server_paths]
installation_path = /home/ed/public_html/application
public_url = "http://www.example.com/application"
```

Note that all parameters are specified using the format

```
NAME = value
```

The name of the parameter should not contain spaces. A space should follow the name of the parameter, followed by the equal sign, followed by another space and then the value. Values may not span more than one line.

Different sections may be specified in the INI file to allow your user tasked with modifying it to find his or her way around more easily. These are delineated using an opening square bracket, the name of the section, and a closing square bracket. Finally, comments may be specified in the INI file using a semicolon to start a line.

Parsing INI files Using PHP's Built-In Methods

Given that PHP's own INI file is written in this format, and that PHP must parse it in order to function correctly, PHP's authors sensibly decided to make this routine available to you, the programmer. These routines are in fact written using the Finite State Machine methodology you met in the first half of this chapter.

The routine is called `parse_ini_file`, and takes two parameters—one showing the path to the INI file (which must be local) and the other establishing whether the names of sections should be included in the output array. If this second parameter is set to true, a multidimensional array is generated that resembles the following:

```
Array
(
    [database] => Array
        (
            [DATABASE_HOST] => winsqldb
            [DATABASE_USER] => xyz
            [DATABASE_PASS] => abc
            [DATABASE_NAME] => def
        )

    [server_paths] => Array
        (
            [installation_path] => /home/ed/public_html/application
            [public_url] => http://www.example.com/application
        )

)
```

If it is set to false, a single-dimensional associative array is created that ignores section headers. In this case, the output resembles the following:

```
Array
(
       [DATABASE_HOST] => winsqldb
       [DATABASE_USER] => xyz
       [DATABASE_PASS] => abc
       [DATABASE_NAME] => def
       [installation_path] => /home/ed/public_html/application
       [public_url] => http://www.example.com/application
)
```

Be aware that if you do instruct PHP to ignore sections, you must ensure that all parameter names are unique across all sections.

In practice, you use this in your code as follows:

```
$confFileArray = parse_ini_file("config.ini");
$strDatabaseHostname = $confFileArray["database"]["DATABASE_HOST"];
```

You may want to pass the parsing of the configuration file into a separate class, which makes native PHP constants available for referral throughout your application.

The Config PEAR Class

Although PHP's built-in routine allows for very simple configuration file parsing, a PEAR class known simply as `Config` allows for far more sophisticated and flexible parsing of various types of files.

The package is installed in the normal way, but keep in mind that the `XML_Util` class is a dependency, which must be installed first.

```
root@genesis:~/scripts# pear install XML_Util
downloading XML_Util-0.5.2.tgz ...
Starting to download XML_Util-0.5.2.tgz (6,540 bytes)
.....done: 6,540 bytes
install ok: XML_Util 0.5.2
root@ genesis:~/scripts# pear install Config
downloading Config-1.10.tgz ...
Starting to download Config-1.10.tgz (17,577 bytes)
......done: 17,577 bytes
install ok: Config 1.10
root@genesis:~/scripts#
```

Full documentation on the package can be found at `http://pear.php.net/manual/en/package.configuration.php`, but it's worth looking briefly at some of the more notable features.

Parsing INI Files Using Config

Parsing a traditional INI file using the `Config` class isn't much harder (or any more useful) than using PHP's built-in routine:

```
$c = new Config();
$root = &$c->parseConfig("config.ini", "IniFile");
$strDatabaseHostname = $root["DATABASE_HOST"];
```

Note that the `parseConfig` method takes two parameters. The first is the path to the configuration file you want to parse. The second of these is a string constant specifying the method to use to parse the configuration file.

Parsing XML Files Using Config

One thing the `Config` class can do that PHP can't is natively parse XML configuration files.

```
$c = new Config();
$root = &$c->parseConfig("config.xml", "XML");
$strDatabaseHostname = $root["DATABASE_HOST"];
```

Writing Configuration Files Using Config

The `Config` class is also able to write the contents of an associative array to a configuration file, in the format of your choice:

```
$myConfig = array("foo" => "bar");
$c = new Config();
$root =& $c->parseConfig($myConfig, "PHPArray");
$c->writeConfig("my.conf", "IniFile");
```

This is an immensely powerful bit of functionality but is arguably open to abuse (discussed in the next section).

Configuration File Best Practice

Configuration files provide an easy way to make your application portable from one deployment to another, without worrying that others may be modifying your PHP code. However, as with all gifts to the PHP programmer, it can be misused.

Don't Write; Just Read

Your own application should concern itself only with reading configuration files, never writing them. If you find that your application has some need to write some piece of data to a configuration file at runtime, you should be using a proper relational database such as PostgreSQL to store that piece of data.

The exception to the rule is if you have provided some form of auto-configuration script for use by your client's IS department. This may legitimately challenge with questions in order to generate a configuration file. This script could quite feasibly be written in PHP, although a shell script might be a better choice.

Cache Me If You Can

Reading a configuration file written in anything other than native PHP has performance implications. Given the stateless nature of HTTP, every single request could quite easily cause this parsing to take place. On a busy site, this could have quite serious implications.

If possible, therefore, you should implement some kind of caching mechanism. The underlying configuration file is not likely to change frequently, so you should consider implementing some means of translating an INI or XML file into native PHP using the `Config` PEAR class, and then simply including that native PHP in your application. You could implement a timestamp check on the native INI file to determine whether it has changed since its last translation and then force a translation only if it has in fact changed.

Keep It Simple

Try to keep the configuration file to an absolute minimum. If a given parameter can be calculated using, for example, the `$_SERVER` object, do so. This is far better than relying on the systems administrator of your deployment platform to get it right. Second, ask yourself whether there is likely to be any commercial desire to ever change any nonserver specific constants, ranges, or limits found in the configuration file. If the answer is no, then don't include them. Hard-code them instead.

Summary

In this two-part chapter, you were introduced to the computer science theory of a Finite State Machine (FSM). You learned how it is defined, what separates it from other abstract machines, and how it is useful. You met the theory of any FSM and saw how it translates into the simple example of a Reverse Polish Notation (RPN) Calculator. You saw the code of a working example of the RPN Calculator dissected in detail, paying close attention to how the PEAR class FSM had been used in its implementation.

You then looked at configuration files. You examined why they are useful in your application, saw the various flavors available, and learned how to best parse them We also covered the do's and don'ts of configuration file implementation.

This concludes Part III of this book. By now, you've built up a complete toolkit of code and techniques to deploy in your own applications. In Part IV, you'll look at how to assemble a useful, real-life application using these tools, and examine the optimal way to manage projects of that nature.

Part IV: Test Case: Sales Force Automation

Chapter 18: Project Overview

Chapter 19: Project Management Methodologies

Chapter 20: Planning the System

Chapter 21: Systems Architecture

Chapter 22: Assembling the Sales Force Automation Toolkit

Chapter 23: Quality Assurance

Chapter 24: Deployment

Chapter 25: Designing and Developing a Robust Reporting Platform

Chapter 26: Where Do You Go from Here?

Project Overview

Writing software is hard. If it were easy, you wouldn't be bothering to read this book and we'd all be enslaved by machines by now, so thank your blessings that it's not a trivial task.

But why should software development be hard? It requires no purchase of paint or canvas, and it binds you by few physical constraints. It should be the ultimate blank slate, yet one of your biggest impediments is that of logically painting yourself into a corner. In essence, your very own mind is one of your biggest enemies.

Another constraint is time. Although few things are technically beyond your means, you are mortal and cannot possibly physically create something as powerful and flexible as the entirety of the GNU/Linux operating system in just two weeks.

And for whom is this software written? Yourself? Your friends? A rather common scenario is writing custom software for a client. The fantasy client used as an example in this chapter is called "Widget World." The type of scenario it presents is very common, because the majority of software is not written for consumers but rather to meet the specifications of businesses, governments, and other groups.

The rest of this chapter assumes that you're an average developer, working on an average project at an average company with average clients. For simplicity's sake, however, we've given this example project some perhaps uncommon traits:

- You are developing a new product. (A much more common scenario would be to modify a currently existing system.)
- You are working alone because you are reading this text alone. (In the real world, you would most likely be working closely with or interfacing with other developers.)

Widget World

Widget World designs, produces, and sells widgets. It has a dedicated, distributed sales staff that scours the globe attending the latest widget conventions, approaching widget-friendly businesses, engages in old-fashioned cold-calling, and creates a grassroots suburban Widget Ware sales-party network.

Widget World is also the victim of its own success. As is true of many businesses, it has not planned for double-digit growth and is failing to keep its sales force supplied with information about sales opportunities and the latest in widget technology, and it's not managing to obtain quick and timely feedback from the sales staff in order to capitalize on trends in widget fashion.

Widget World cannot hire enough summer interns to work the phones and fax to keep the widgets flowing. The Widget Master is well aware that Widget World needs to be more efficient; therefore, after looking at commercial offerings, the Widget Master has decided to commission the writing of specialized software called the Widget World Sales Force Automation Tool, or WW-SFAT for short.

Although the Widget Master holds the purse strings, she utilizes the Widget Marketing department to forecast the latest trends, which in turn helps plan the road map of Widget World.

The Widget Marketers depend upon the Regional Widget Sales Managers (both Eastern and Western) to keep them supplied with up-to-date information. Widget Marketers also let the managers know about the pricing of widgets in reference to their competitors.

The Regional Widget Sales Managers reward and motivate their widget sales personnel by supplying them with timely information regarding widget hot spots. They also set quotas, cut bonus checks, and make sure that all salespeople are doing their best to put a Widget on every desktop.

Widget World Sales Force Automation Tool Manager is a newly created position with input from both Widget Marketing and Regional Widget Managers and is charged with creating a process as well as accompanying software to solve the problem of automating the streamlining of the Widget World sales force's daily operating procedures.. The WW-SFAT Manager is also given significant yet crucial power of "stopping the buck"—whatever the WW-SFAT Manager decides goes. This power is critical to the success of the project because it limits the number of meetings and documentation required. The WW-SFAT Manager is also dedicated to working closely with you on this project. Because you know nothing of widgets or sales and you are charged with streamlining the Widget World sales force's existing paper-based phone and fax system of tracking salespeople and contacts, you have a million questions. Figure 18-1 shows the current tracking form in use.

Here are a few questions that might occur to you:

1. "Do you want to see the time in 12- or 24 hour format?"
2. "Time-zones, do they matter?"
3. "When should X's report be submitted by?"
4. "What happens if X's report is NOT in by the required date?"
5. "How are expenses reimbursed?"
6. "How often does the federal mileage reimbursement change?"
7. "Does the federal mileage reimbursement need to be historical? Retroactive?"

The Widget World Landscape

The following section details the makeup of the Widget World landscape. These include the technical, financial, and political layers as well as your role in them.

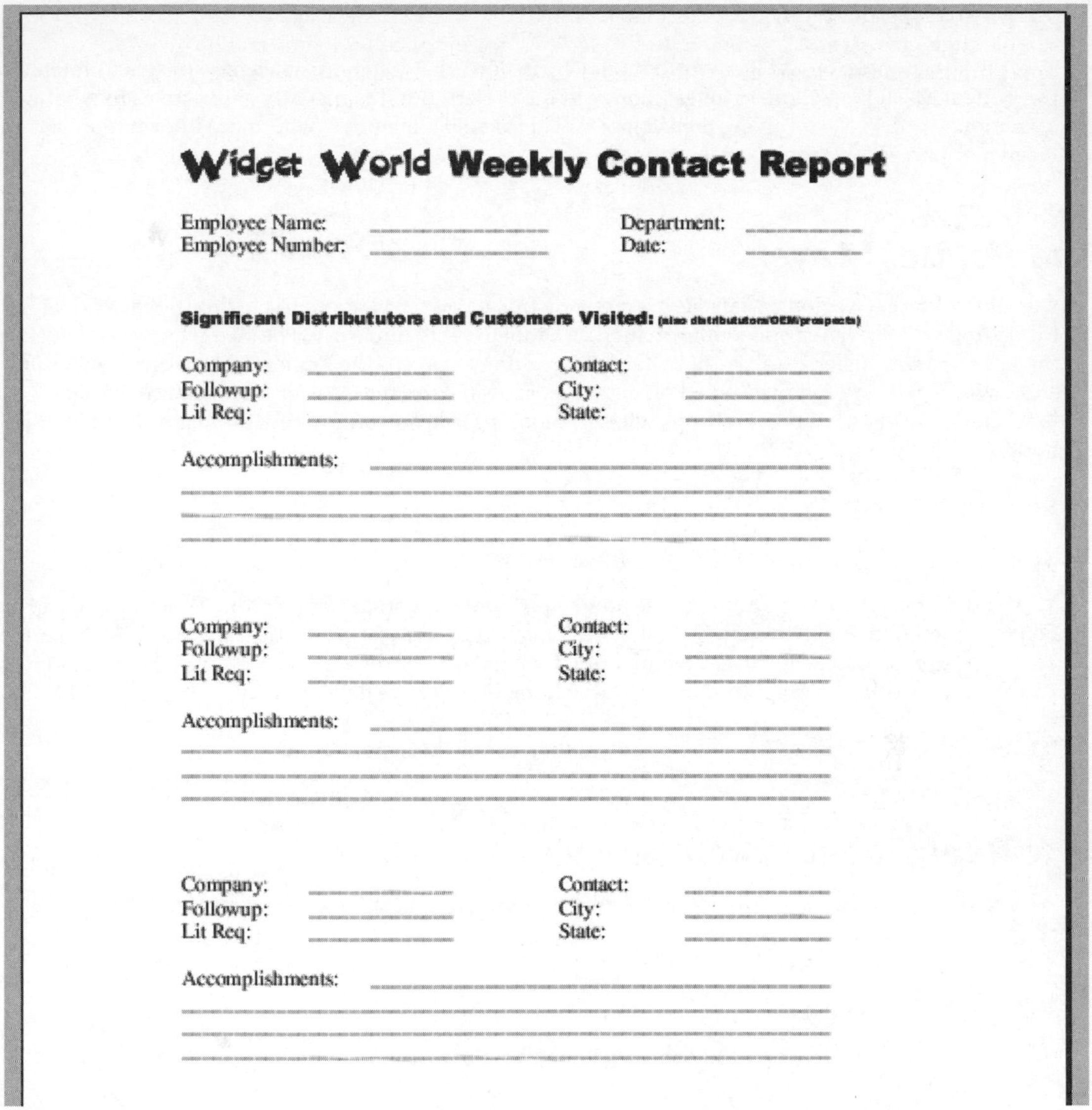

Widget World Weekly Contact Report

Employee Name: __________ Department: __________
Employee Number: __________ Date: __________

Significant Distribututors and Customers Visited: (also distributors/OEM/prospects)

Company: __________ Contact: __________
Followup: __________ City: __________
Lit Req: __________ State: __________

Accomplishments: __________

Company: __________ Contact: __________
Followup: __________ City: __________
Lit Req: __________ State: __________

Accomplishments: __________

Company: __________ Contact: __________
Followup: __________ City: __________
Lit Req: __________ State: __________

Accomplishments: __________

Figure 18-1

The Technical Layer

If you've been paying close attention, you'll notice that information needs to flow from the Widget sales personnel up the chain to the Widget Master and back down again. In this case, information flow is definitely a two-way street.

1. Widget Marketing needs the sales information summarized by region.
2. Widget sales managers need to track various aspects of their personnel.

The Financial Layer

This project should save Widget World money by making the staff more efficient, which is ultimately why the Widget Master is willing to invest money in the project. But it's currently a toss-up as to what would save money quicker—supplying the Widget World sales staff members with more information or receiving more information back from them.

The Political Layer

One of the Widget Regional Managers secretly distrusts Widget Marketing. He thinks that Widget Marketing will use his supplied information as a tool to retire him early. The Widget sales staff welcomes the use of hard numbers to show how hard it's working—it keeps the Regional Managers honest and will show who's getting promoted based on nepotism instead of on the basis of performance. Widget Marketers want to have press releases with nice-looking graphs and to show those graphs to their golf buddies.

You

You landed this job by responding to the ad in your local paper that said, "Widget World Needs a Sales Force Automation Tool Developer." You were contacted by the Widget World Sales Force Automation Tool Manager, passed its technical examination (in part by your dedicated study of *Professional PHP5*), and arrived at your job eager to start your new career in software development.

It happens to be 8:00 a.m. on Monday, and you'll never be this naïve again.

Is It Really about Technology?

Widget World's Sales Force Automation Tool requirements appear to consist vaguely of:

- Sales contact reports
- Sales lead reports
- Sales contact management lists distributed by e-mail, BlackBerry, fax, and Web reports
- Widget Production feed based upon sales performance
- Widget marketing reports and full-color, glossy, ready-to-print graphs
- Widget accounting reports
- Training

However, it's really the embodiment of a common scenario of a common project using best-of-breed development techniques to keep the customer happy. But even though the "customer" may appear to be just like the Widget World Sales Force Automation Tool Manager, he doesn't live in a vacuum; all the actors here have a vested interest in the outcome of their portion of the project.

The Development Approach

You'll begin to utilize some development practices typified by eXtreme Programming (XP). Don't let the name fool you. XP is a collection of agile development methodologies, and the following list of practices were best characterized by Kent Beck in *Extreme Programming Explained* (Addison-Wesley, 2000):

- Planning—Determine the scope of the project by combining business priorities and technical estimates, continually updated.
- Small releases—Get the system used by the people to be using it and release new versions on a very short schedule.
- Simple Design—Keep the design as simple as possible at all times. Complexity is removed continuously.
- Testing—Developers continually write unit tests to ensure that the system runs flawlessly all the time. Customers write tests to demonstrate that features work as required.
- Refactoring—Restructure the code without modifying the behavior to keep it easy to read, to remove duplication, or to simplify.
- On-site customer—The WW-SFAT Manager is half your team and is available at all times to answer business-related questions.

These practices allow you to manage the complexity and scope of both the project and the software that you are developing. A typical system flows similarly to this curve (Figure 18-2).

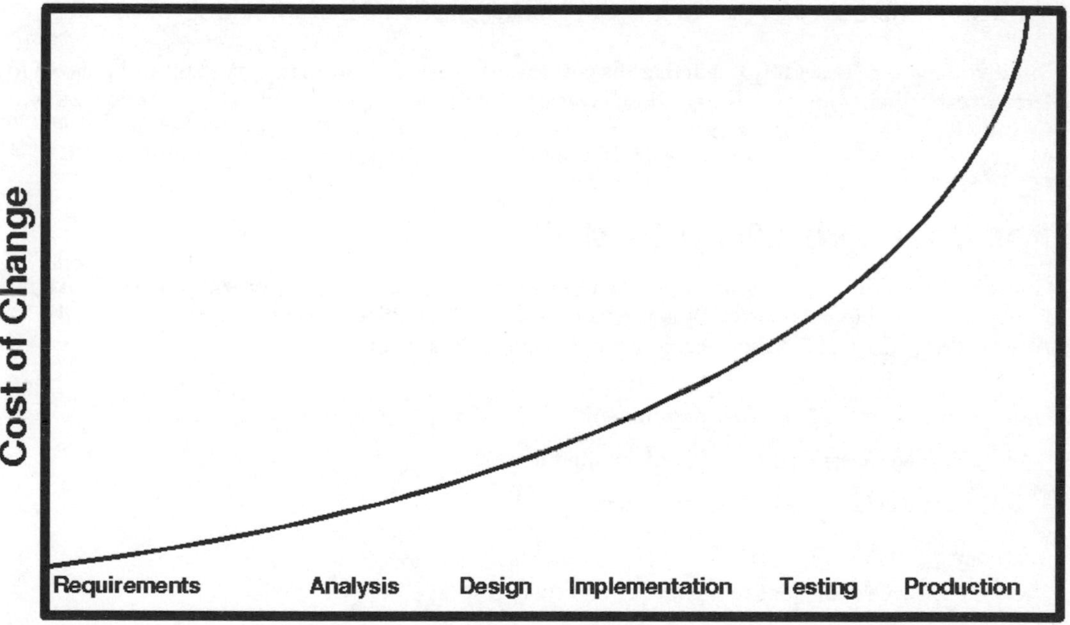

Figure 18-2

By managing complexity from many different angles, we make the curve drastically different (Figure 18-3).

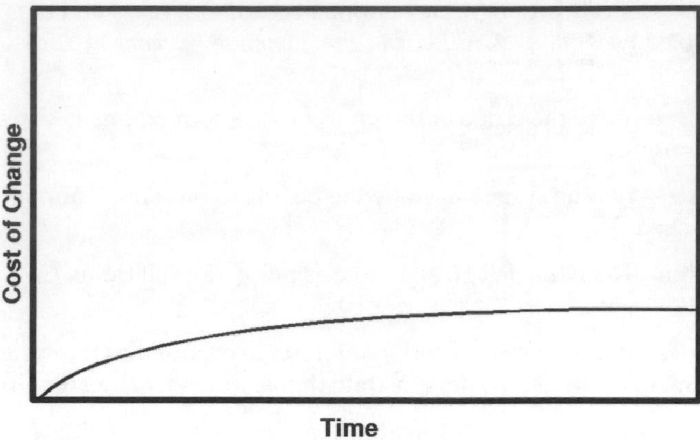

Figure 18-3

Creating features as you need them is a great way to manage the complexity of your system. The cost of adding features later is not significantly higher than it is now (whenever "now" would be in the process), which means that you aren't forced to guess about what you think you'll require in the future and avoid building features that are not used.

Think of it like this: Using the traditional approach to complexity, if the cost to you (in time) is $5.00 to add a feature now, but later that same feature would cost you $100.00, it would be safer to add it now.

But if you manage to set it up such that the cost to add the same feature now is $5.00 and the cost to add it later is $6.00, then you gain little to add it now. Omit it for now; your system stays simpler, and you end up only with features that are used from the outset.

What Does This Mean to Me?

Consider the traditional waterfall approach first documented by Dr. Winston W. Royce ("Managing the Development of Large Software Systems: Concepts and Techniques," Proceedings of IEEE WESCON, August 1970.) Figure 18-4 represents this concept, which calls for:

- Two weeks of gathering requirements
- Two weeks of analyzing and debating them
- Two weeks of designing the system
- Eight weeks of coding it
- Four weeks of Quality Assurance and other testing

Although very regimented in its ways, the waterfall model tends to be implemented as a shotgun approach and has a couple of weaknesses:

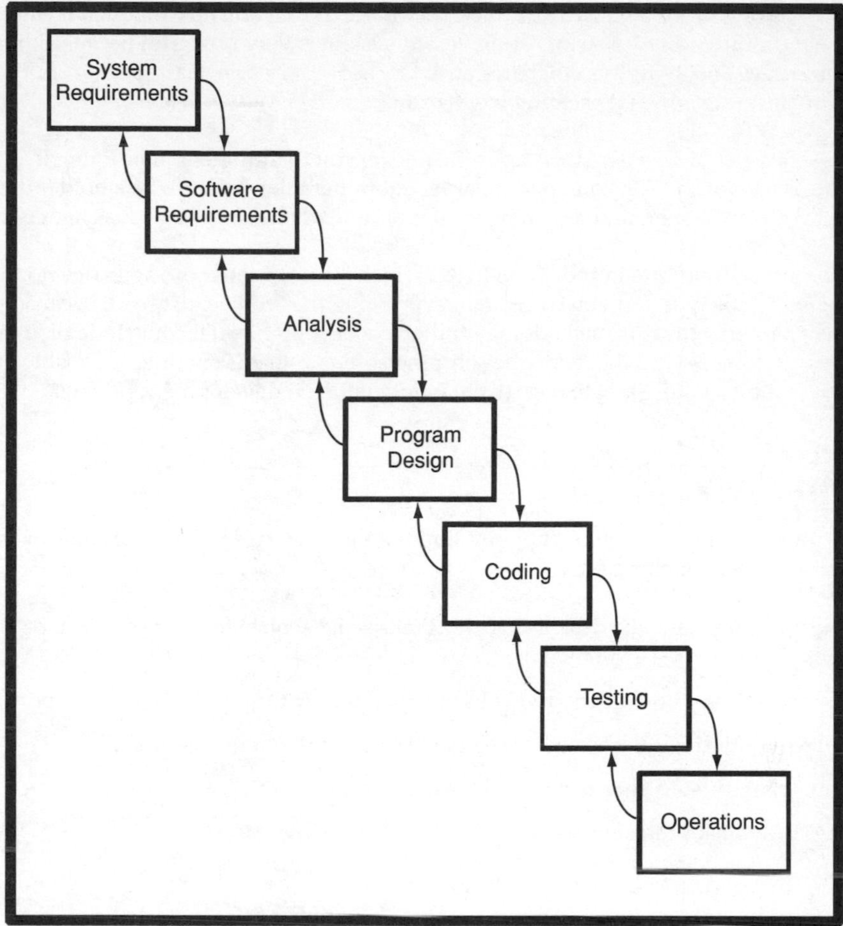

Figure 18-4

- It lacks flexibility and assumes that design will be done correctly the first time. With a span of weeks between phases, little or no time is available for a feedback loop, and, of course, hindsight is 20–20.
- It is hard to predict needed features because requirements are more than likely to change.

This certainly sounds almost like a setup for failure, which is why you're going to follow Kent Beck's principles (listed previously) in order to create a small, flexible system that is thoroughly tested as you write the code. You will work closely with your WW-SFAT Manager and get all required questions answered. Your WW-SFAT Manager has a wide breadth of Widget World business experience and will use the system on a daily basis.

It also means that you'll fix problems that you see and remove functionality that is no longer required. You'll stick to the "once and only once rule," which means that you'll consolidate duplicate logic and you'll be ruthless about it. Refactoring mercilessly keeps your entire system lean and powerful.

Finally, you'll have your unit tests. By testing every piece of functionality that you create, you'll constantly have a fully tested system. A fully tested system is very powerful because it makes you keenly aware of breakages and symptoms that are caused by secondary or tertiary bugs. A fully tested system lets you know instantly when something went wrong.

Having the safety net of a well-written test suite allows you to indulge in modifying features drastically. The test suite does not shackle you unnecessarily, but rather allows you to be a bolder developer by letting you take your system in different directions as and when business needs change.

This is really just a 10-minute introduction to XP, which is one of the more agile development methodologies. It's okay if you don't quite buy everything that you've just read, because you'll explore in the next few chapters how this methodology truly pays off. Soon, you'll come to realize that by using the practices described here, you'll not only be shipping software that is small, fast, flexible but adapting a process which allows your client to be actively involved in the development process.

The Technology

Although you've been warned about not building too much up front, these are some of the technological features that you'll be touching upon:

- Where appropriate, the design snapshots (class and sequence diagrams) will be shown in UML; a quick cheat-sheet is available.
- Design patterns, how to effectively use them and how to spot them in your code.
- Collections and iterators, where they make sense and where they don't.
- Dispatchers, just to get a taste of event-driven programming.
- SOAP, for one of the data-feeds.

Summary

Now that you understand the background of Widget World and its business needs, you can soon get to work utilizing the development techniques that were briefly outlined here.

Rather than follow the regimented waterfall development approach, you can make use of a more flexible approach that highlights quick releases, simple design, a well-tested code-base, a dedication to continuous code improvement, and a means of having constant feedback with access to the customer.

By utilizing this approach, you can produce an application that is capable of delivering business value in the first release, measurable in days and weeks rather than in months and years.

Project Management Methodologies

As a Web development professional, you might be curious to know whether a software architect can effectively manage projects. The answer is, "Yes! Provided that you have a bit of training under your belt."

Even if you are never confronted with your own project to manage, you will find it immensely useful to understand what the project manager, who is running the show, has to contend with on a daily basis. It will make you stronger as a software architect and as an individual to understand and be sympathetic to the skills required to run a successful development project from start to finish.

And in the event that you do find yourself in charge of a team of bright-eyed young developers one day, you'll find that the skills gleaned from this chapter and the next will serve you well.

This chapter discusses how to collate business requirements into a coherent brief and how to respond appropriately with a rock-solid specification and project plan. You'll learn how to identify and select the key personnel you need to work underneath you, as well as how to guide and manage them throughout the project life cycle. You'll also look at a couple of programming paradigms, discover how to evaluate their usefulness for your own project, and look at the two key approaches to tackling the development work on the shop floor. Finally, you'll discover how to effectively manage your working relationship with your clients.

Admittedly, this chapter doesn't have a whole lot to do with PHP. Nonetheless, the material covered is very relevant to any PHP project you might work on, even though the techniques demonstrated apply just as much to ASP, Java—any language. We decided to include them in this book nonetheless because they might well revolutionize the way you tackle big projects.

Do Your Homework

Generally, the most common, visible first step for a project occurs when a project manager tells a senior member of his development staff that he has something new for the team to work on; this often happens as nothing more than an informal chat around the office's water cooler. In practice, of course, the idea starts much further back. Tracing the roots of any given project is essential. A project management methodology can be successful only if it is applied from the very start of the project.

Before you take steps to receive the formal brief for the project, there are a few key questions to ask—your homework, if you will. These questions taken together will form the foundation of the strategy you adapt when receiving the formal brief. The first question to ask is "Why?"

Why Is the Project Happening?

This simple question has an enormous influence on everything you do from here on in because the way in which you build your project, from start to finish, must be determined by its intended function.

Typical reasons for a new Web project might include:

- Starting a new business for which "the business is the application."
- Replacing an existing application that is failing or no longer adequate.
- Taking over where an existing supplier has failed to deliver either on time, on budget, or what is required (or in some cases, all three).

There are, of course, other reasons that may require a new project to be taken on and not all of them are as critical as the three listed here. For example, you may simply find yourself having to implement the pet project of a VP or executive. Whatever it is, determining the *raison d'être* of the project is a number-one priority.

Who Is the Project For?

This is sometimes not as easy a question to answer as you might think. At the simplest level, the project is for another department within your own company or organization, a new customer, or an existing customer. Remember that you must identify the recipient of the project in the sense of who has actually commissioned the work. If a man goes to the store to buy his wife nail polish, he's not the real customer—he's simply responding to the real customer's request.

Similarly, your client may be commissioning this work only to satisfy some requirement of a third party to whom he or she is responsible. These ultimate end users of the product are known as domain experts, and you ignore them at your peril.

The end user for your product will often be the most hands-on people in your client's organization and, as such, their needs for the project will often be immensely different from the requisitioning individual who approaches you as a potential supplier.

Identifying Roles and Agenda

By way of example, say that you are the CTO of a medium-sized organization and have been commissioned by the Human Resources director to build an intranet for your whole company. You have both permanent and contract staff at your disposal. What do you think the various agendas of each role (you, the client, and the domain experts) are?

To take a slightly cynical perspective on things, the scenario most likely looks something like this:

- You want to deliver a high-quality, effective, efficient, and satisfactory solution as quickly as possible and with as little investment as possible so that you look good.
- The HR Director wants you to deliver a high-quality, effective, efficient, and satisfactory solution that makes him or her look good.
- Daily users of the intranet (the domain experts) want you to deliver a high-quality, effective, efficient, and satisfactory solution that does what they want it to do.

Notice that the only pure agenda here is held by the domain experts. The secret is to ensure that all three agendas are met. The first two are incredibly easy to meet, but by concentrating on the third, the first two will generally drop into place.

Manipulating Roles to Your Advantage

Consider this. Your client is merely a conduit to the domain experts on a project, no matter what else they might tell you. Although it is a lot easier for your client to express immense pleasure with what you've built at the point of delivery and walk away, if the domain experts don't like it, the axe will fall on the client's head and so, in turn, it will fall on yours. It is very much in the client's interest to represent the needs of the domain experts from the outset.

A good client will be able to sympathize with the true needs and requirements of his or her domain experts and assemble them into a single, harmonious voice for you to listen to. However, in practice, you will need to prod, probe, and cajole your client into representing the realistic and reasonable requirements of his or her domain experts properly.

If you feel that your client is not representing his or her domain experts sufficiently, it is vitally important that you suggest that he or she re-implements the consultative process. This can be accomplished through:

- A brainstorming session
- An anonymous suggestion box approach
- Appointing a working party to represent the needs of the domain experts

It is vitally important that if the roles aren't clearly carved out from the start, you must help carve them out. That way, when you do receive the formal brief for the project, you'll be able to respond to it, safe in the knowledge that what you're responding to is in fact what is really required.

What Is the History of the Project?

It is also vitally important to establish whether this project has any baggage attached to it. A fresh project is always exciting, but it may not actually be as fresh on the inside as it appears on the outside. Having a good handle on the history of the project allows you to tweak certain aspects of your approach accordingly.

Generally speaking, a project has serious baggage only if another attempt has been made to get it off the ground previously. If you know this to be the case, then you should immediately make yourself aware of the following potential baggage, no matter how long ago that previous attempt was made.

- **Departed staff**: If this project was previously handled by a member of staff who has since resigned, been fired, or been moved to other duties in the organization, beware. It is almost inevitable that the client considers the former staff member to have failed in his or her appointed task. The trick here is to gain a good idea of the strengths and weaknesses of the new representative, which the client puts forward to work with you. We talk a little more about this later in the chapter.
- **Departed supplier**: If you are undertaking the project as a replacement for another supplier (either commercial or internal), it is worth sizing up the reasons that the client dropped that supplier in the first place. If necessary, dig around with other former clients of that supplier to examine their experiences, and shape your approach according to any useful information you acquire. The client will want to trust you, so give him or her good reason to.
- **Difficulties in working with in-house staff:** If a project has been outsourced by a company to you, you may experience difficulties working with the client company's IT department. Sometimes this situation can arise even when no attempt to start the project has ever been made internally but there has been an expectation that one would have been made. The best advice is to get that IT department involved from the start. Give that department a call while you're writing the technical specification—it will be caught well and truly off guard and may even prove to be a great help as a result.

What Are the Anticipated Prerequisites of the Project?

You should be aware of these as early in the project life cycle as possible because they may even influence your decision as to whether you wish to proceed. Some typical prerequisites might include:

- Platform—does the client require the project to be built in ASP, ColdFusion, or some other development language not overly favored by you as a PHP professional?
- Deployment—does the client need this application to be deployed onto existing servers? If so, is the client happy for you to reconfigure those servers if necessary?
- Timescales—does the client have any specific expectations on delivery from the outset, possibly to meet some internal target or deadline?
- Budget—does the client have a specific budget? Is it realistic?

It is very important to get these prerequisites established before you embark upon the process of receiving the brief. After all, if you can't fulfill the prerequisites, there's little point in moving to the next step.

Receiving the Formal Brief

Having done your homework, you should receive the formal brief. The most important part of any brief is to get it in writing. By this stage you've probably already received a fair bit of information about the project, but getting the brief in writing ensures that you and your team are able to respond to it in the most effective manner possible.

Quite rarely, however, will the initial brief be in a satisfactory form—whether verbal or in note form. As a result, it's often up to you to turn the client's wishes into a coherent, written brief. Rather than make this a separate document in its own right, it is often best to incorporate this as part of your pitch, which we'll look at later.

Getting a client to articulate his or her requirements is one of the toughest things you'll ever have to do as a project manager. Worse still, clients rarely differentiate between incorrect assumptions you've made based on the absence of information, and assumptions you've made that are simply plain wrong. The way around this problem is to ensure that all the assumptions and guesses you're making in your pitch are based on the best and most exhaustive information available to you. As a result, you must be thorough in extracting the minutiae of the client's business requirements at this early stage.

Wherever possible, try to glean a phone conversation or, ideally, a meeting with the client before writing the brief and responding to it.

If you are fortunate enough to get a phone conversation or meeting with the client from which to construct the formal brief, it's important, therefore, to ask the right questions. You need to focus on a number of key areas that are covered here. After you have gone over these, you will be in a position to write your brief.

Business Requirements

Establish exactly what the broad requirements of the system or application you are building are at this stage. Focus on asking questions about the goals of the domain experts rather than the anticipated solution the client has in mind.

It doesn't matter if the solution you recommend is nothing like what the client is expecting, as long as you can precisely map your decisions to the goals of the domain experts. These mappings form the basis of your overall solution's rationale and are a key component of your pitch.

Ask leading questions. Try to listen rather than talk. The unprompted musings of the client can be immensely useful in optimizing your proposal to best suit his or her needs, even at a subconscious level. Try to effect a strong mix of commercial and logistical probing. For example, the following generic questions may be useful:

- What other solutions have you looked at?
- Why have you rejected them?
- Who will the end users of this system be?
- How are you currently handling this process without a system in place?
- What benefits do you think the system might bring?
- What kind of return on investment are you looking for?
- How will you measure that return?
- What are the three most important requirements you have of a supplier looking to provide this solution to you?
- How many other suppliers have you looked at?
- How satisfied have you been with the proposals you have received to date?
- Do you have a time frame for choosing a supplier, and what is driving this time frame?
- What people are likely to be involved in the decision-making process, and what are their roles?
- What are the biggest concerns you have about this project moving forward?
- Have other suppliers addressed those concerns to your satisfaction?

Again, don't be afraid to let the client do most of the talking. Try to avoid letting individual points drop as you scribble down notes; instead, ask probing questions to extract that "extra ten percent" from the client.

Here's an example dialogue between supplier and client:

SUPPLIER: Do you have a time frame for choosing a supplier?

CLIENT: Absolutely. We'll have made our decision by the 30th.

SUPPLIER: The 30th of this month, really. You guys are keen to get this off the ground, then?

CLIENT: Definitely. We've got a big marketing drive starting next month.

SUPPLIER: Oh, right; is this system likely to be a big part of that marketing drive?

CLIENT: Yes. If we have the build under way by then, it will definitely be a big selling point.

Compare the same dialogue without the additional probing:

SUPPLIER: Do you have a time frame for choosing a supplier?

CLIENT: Absolutely. We'll have made our decision by the 30th.

SUPPLIER: Great, thanks.

Notice the extra information gleaned from the probing:

- ❑ The client has a marketing drive taking place next month.
- ❑ The client would like to be able to show the unfinished system to prospective clients as part of his or her sales pitch.

This information is no secret, and the client isn't holding back deliberately—it just hasn't occurred to him to mention it. But make no mistake about it: This extra information should be very useful to you, indeed. The moral of the story is don't be afraid to take an interest in what your client is saying and ask the extra questions that might get you that extra nugget of information. It might just give you an edge on your competition.

Scope

We have established the broader business requirements of the system and worked out exactly what problem or need the client is trying to solve or fulfill. However, it's worth probing the client some more about the scope of requirements. Let's be clear about what we mean by the term *scope* here. By establishing scope, we're looking at how *far* we are going to go to solve that problem or fulfill that need.

People often speak of scope-creep, which refers to the magnitude of what's required growing in the middle of the project without regard to commercial impact. By establishing the scope now, you can prevent this from happening as much as possible. The specifications you produce allow you to enforce this chosen scope by mapping it to the specific components of functionality that will be included in the build process.

Scope is almost always artificially throttled by time and money. However, it can be a useful exercise to help manage expectations even at this early stage by drawing phase boundaries. Nine times out of ten, suggesting a two-phase approach to the client can help you immensely because the client will instantly illustrate for you the kind of functionality that might drop into a second phase of development and the kind of functionality that is required now. Commit to just the latter of these, and you have your initial scope well and truly defined.

If the client is reluctant to look at phases, a more direct approach is needed. Explain to the client that the only limitations in meeting his or her requirements are those of time and money, and that understanding what the absolutely essential components of the project are now can make life easier for the client, in so much as he or she will be able interpret proposals on delivery time and cost on a more equal footing. If no other suppliers are pitching for the work, explain to the client that establishing scope now will save huge amounts of time later and allow the project to progress more quickly with fewer revisions to specifications.

Timelines

Establishing timelines is about much more than just figuring out when the client needs the system to be delivered. It's vitally important to set milestones and agree to them with the client even at this early stage. You should try to gauge milestones for the date by which:

- the proposal is required
- a decision will be made on a chosen supplier (if appropriate)
- any written specifications are required from the supplier
- any written specifications will be signed off by the client or, if amendments will be required, those amendments will be tabled
- the specification process, including all amendments, must be finished
- any designs produced by the supplier must be put forward for initial approval
- any designs, including all amendments, must be finished
- the build must commence
- the build must be completed to beta standard
- the build must be completed to finished standard
- testing must take place
- the handover of the finished product must take place

Of course, asking for all these dates from the client may well overwhelm or even irritate him or her. To avoid this side effect, pick what you consider to be the key milestones and fill in the blanks yourself. You can even have a positive effect on the client's view of your processes at this early stage by announcing where the dates will fit together. Consider the following snippet of dialogue:

SUPPLIER: When do you need the completed system to be handed over?

CLIENT: We need to be up and running with the staff by the 1st of June.

SUPPLIER: In that case, we should aim to have the system handed over to you by the 22nd of May, to allow a few days for any last minute tweaks and changes that might need to be taken care of.

Don't forget to note all milestones carefully throughout the briefing process and, when necessary, guide the client away from any unrealistic expectations, as shown in the following example:

SUPPLIER: When do you need the completed system to be handed over?

CLIENT: We need to be up and running with the staff by the 1st of May.

SUPPLIER: I think that given the kind of scope we've agreed on, that is going to be a difficult date to meet. I would suggest a delivery date of 22nd of May is probably closer to the mark, which should have you up and running shortly afterward. I think we have two options: We can either reduce the scope of the system at this stage, or we have to look at a slightly later delivery date.

CLIENT: Well, in all honesty, we could live with the 22nd. Rather get it right first time.

Notice how we use passive language in explaining to the client that his or her date is unrealistic. We do not "tell" the client, because he or she may well think we are attempting a "we know best" tactic, which might offend. Rather, we "suggest," and in many cases, as in the preceding example, you'll often find that there is a little more room for maneuver than originally stated.

Always be sure to point out unrealistic dates; never let them slip. The client will expect anything unattainable to be pointed out now. If it is not mentioned until your written proposal comes through, you may risk alienating the client, especially if the client has already told others involved in the project of the anticipated dates. Essentially, anything not contradicted will be taken as tacit agreement, so beware.

Budget

Budget can be a thorny issue. Even if you are delivering a solution internally, you still have your direct costs to think about. Many larger companies bill each other's cost centers for internal activity, so budgeting and negotiations can be just as intense for internal work as they for an external commission.

Don't ask the budget question too early. It is immensely off-putting. The client expects to be asked it, but may quickly judge what he or she deems to be your own priorities as a supplier based on the order in which you ask questions. The right time is probably close to when the subject of scope is raised, because you have already established that scope is more than likely going to be limited by time and money.

A good way to phrase the cost question would be: "When I've looked at implementing similar solutions to this for companies like Acme in the past, they have typically been expecting to invest between $25,000 and $45,000. Does that sound like the kind of ballpark you had in mind for this project?"

Note that, first of all, you haven't asked what the budget is. Rather, you have suggested that:

- You have worked on similar projects in the past—*positive*
- You have worked with companies like Acme in the past—*positive*
- These companies have invested anywhere between $25,000 and $45,000—*neutral*

The emphasis on the positives in your interrogation means that the negative thoughts associated with determining budget will not kick in quite as automatically as they would if you were to ask the question directly.

Note that, second, you have offered a ballpark range. This range is, in fact, quite broad. Always do this; to be too specific at this stage suggests arrogance with respect to an understanding of the client's requirements, which you don't have yet. By suggesting a broad price range, you suggest subconsciously to the client that you still have yet to zero in on exactly what is required. Make sure that the minimum you suggest is the absolute minimum you're prepared to do the work for, and the maximum is about 40 to 50 percent more than that figure. That way, if the client agrees, you know for sure that you will have a profitable job on your hands. By how much remains to be seen, true; but you've negated the chances of a loss-maker.

Note, finally that we have used the phrase "they have typically been expecting to spend." We have used this in preference to "we have typically quoted them" for a good reason; namely, that you are suggesting that these companies actually anticipated spending this amount *before* they spoke to you, *not* that this is the amount you quoted them.

This does not, of course, answer the eternal question of "what is your budget?" What it does, generally speaking, is implant a firm idea in the head of the client as to what the project is actually worth in market terms.

If, upon becoming aware of this knowledge, the client realizes that there simply isn't the budget to proceed, he or she will usually tell you. This obviously isn't a good thing in itself, but it does allow you to judge very quickly whether your time put in receiving the brief is time well spent. Consider the following two approaches. In both dialogues, the supplier needs to charge around $15,000 just to break even on the application; the client's budget is only $5,000. Here is our first scenario:

SUPPLIER: Did you have a budget in mind?

CLIENT: I'd rather not give you a budget. When we've done that with suppliers in the past, they've simply come back and quoted what I told them my budget was. I'd rather you just went away, came up with a quote, and I'll tell you if it's doable or not.

SUPPLIER: OK, no problem.

Contrast this with:

SUPPLIER: John, I wanted to broach with you the issue of budget. When I've looked at implementing similar solutions like this in the past, they have typically been expecting to invest between $15,000 and $22,000. Does that sound like the kind of ballpark you had in mind for this project?"

CLIENT: Oh . . . no, it really isn't. I'm afraid the maximum we can afford to part with is $5,000; maybe $7,000 at a push.

SUPPLIER: Okay, John. I'm afraid I don't think we're going to be able to do business on this occasion, but thank you very much for your time.

In neither situation does the supplier get the business. But, in the second situation, the supplier knows straight away that there's no sale in sight, whereas in the first situation, days would be lost creating a comprehensive pitch, only to be turned down later.

Don't get embarrassed about asking about money. Be up front, and pick your language and your timing carefully.

Commercial Terms

It can be worth talking about commercial terms, even at this early stage. If you've established that the client is happy to pay approximately $50,000 to have his or her project developed to completion, this is certainly a good start—but certain technicalities that often don't get mentioned can pour cold water on this head start very quickly.

As with budgetary concerns, it's far better to get the issue of commercial terms out of the way early, so that if they prove to be stumbling blocks, you can be aware of them now and back out if necessary. The following questions are probably more relevant to smaller businesses rather than enormous technology agencies, but are still worth asking if you have any payment-related concerns:

- "We normally like to ask our clients for an up-front percentage contribution so that we can cover any incidental costs during the build process. Would this be a problem?"
- "Because we're a small company, we have to be quite strict with our payment terms. All our invoices are strictly 30 days. Do you think this would be all right with your accounts guys?"

Again, phrasing is very important here. For example, the use of the friendly interrogative statement, "Would this be a problem?" is highly recommended. You are far more likely to solicit a sympathetic "Oh, no, I wouldn't think so" response, rather than something more aggressive or perfunctory.

Another stock phrase is "Do you think this would be the kind of thing that could stop us doing business together?" It sounds incredibly emotive, but it suggests "no" as an appropriate answer in its tone, and so is much more likely to solicit that kind of answer. Positive responses are useful not just because they're what you want to hear, but also because they're what the client wants to say.

> **Hint: Research suggests that a meeting in which parties have used positive words and body gestures leaves a far better impression than one littered with "no's" and shakes of the head.**

By leaving your client with a positive impression of the meeting, you're leaving him or her with a positive impression of you as an individual.

Future Plans

As far as is reasonably possible, you should endeavor to press the client for his or her future plans for the system. You may well have determined what is "in-scope," but it is equally important to know what is both "out-of-scope" and equally likely to become a requirement in future.

As a software architect, you may be more than familiar with the concept of "coding yourself into a corner." The best project managers are aware of these concepts, too, which is one of the reasons that many of the best project managers tend to have backgrounds in architecture.

Determine as early as possible what is likely to become a requirement at a later date, even if it is conceivable or likely that another supplier will be taking the work on. Showing interest in what is clearly not going to be paid for or carried out at this stage demonstrates a commitment to avoiding "hit and run" programming, and shows that you are the kind of supplier with whom the client can forge a long-term relationship.

Look and Feel

There is no excuse these days for even the simplest of Web applications not to look good. Design needs to be an integral part of your process, not just an afterthought, and this should be emphasized to the client whenever possible.

Determine at this stage whether any requirements or specific requests exist on the part of the client with respect to the look and feel of what is being produced. Is there an expectation, for example, that a particular corporate branding is followed? Does the system need to closely resemble an existing system? How likely is it that the branding will change, and how often?

Technology

There's a good chance that the individual you are dealing with from the client company is not a technical person. For most projects, this is understandable because the goals of the required system, for which you are receiving the brief, are unlikely to be technical in nature. Even with this in mind, it is an immensely good idea at this stage to ask probing questions about technology.

Essentially, you need to gauge how much of a free reign you have on making these decisions. In your written proposal, you need at the very least to outline the platform and infrastructure choices you have made and be able to justify them if necessary. Aim to ask the kinds of questions that will determine whether the client is happy for you to code with PHP, what deployment issues there may be, and also what security issues might arise.

If any restrictions you discover look to be onerous, this may be another red flag—a sign that you need to cut your losses and pull out. As a PHP professional, if the client insists on ASP and SQL Server, you would be wise to think about declining the work or, alternatively, trying to convince the client that PHP is the way to go.

Either way, it is a conversation you must have early, to prevent any fruitless pitching.

Support

If there's one thing you should always try to raise with the client, it's the issue of after-production support. It may not have even crossed a client's mind, but it's extremely useful to establish what the client's expectations are and how they tally with your own.

Determining who will create user-orientated documentation (if required), who is to provide support after the system is deployed, and what kind of service the client expects during handover are all important issues to address. If the client appears at a loss, attempt to suggest suitable answers to your own questions, and gain client's tacit approval for inclusion in your pitch.

What Now?

Now that you have a formal brief, it's time to proceed with winning the business. If you're in the fortunate position of developing a project for another department in your own organization, you can probably skip the next section.

If, however, you need to actually convince the client of your worthiness as a supplier and provide a fully costed proposal in the process, read on.

Constructing the Pitch

The pitch itself could take many forms. It could be a presentation, a mock-up, a sample system, or even a demo of a similar solution you've worked on in the past. There does tend to be a written component to every pitch, however, and this is what we concentrate on in this section.

The first question, of course, is whether you need a pitch at all—or whether a mere quotation is what's needed.

Pitches versus Quotes

It goes without saying that you need to provide at the very least a quote for the work you've been briefed for. When to expand that quote so that it becomes a pitch, however, can be a tricky decision.

Consider the last time that you, as a consumer, were actively "sold to." It was probably the last time you bought a car, or a TV at the showroom, or a new kitchen. You expected to be sold to when you bought your $300 television, didn't you? So why is it that when you went to the store to buy $300 worth of groceries for the whole family in the holiday season, you didn't get sold to in the supermarket?

The difference is pretty clear. The television was a long-term investment; the groceries would be gone in a few weeks.

Think along the same lines with the work you're quoting for. Try not to get too hung up on the cash value. Think instead about what the work you're proposing means to the client. If it will have a long-term impact, you need to sell it, so you need to produce a pitch. If it's simply a short-term requirement—a consumable—then more than likely all you need is a quote.

Examples of work that may require only a quote would include specific changes to an existing application, provided that they are relatively simple, or the installation and configuration of PHP on a rackful of servers. In both cases, there isn't a great deal to say—so don't say it.

If you are providing only a quote, it may be useful to have a few pages of stock library propaganda about your business—perhaps outlining some your key skills, experience, past clients, and so on. This can be handed over with your quote in case anybody at the client company needs to see some traditional sales material.

For the rest of this section, we assume that you've gone the whole hog and opted for a pitch rather than a quote.

Pitches versus Specifications

If you're serious about winning the business, you'll be putting some serious effort into your pitch. This is no bad thing in itself, but you do need to be very careful not to fall into a very serious trap; that is, actually producing a specification rather than a pitch.

We'll meet up with specifications later in this chapter. Essentially, they are detailed blueprints for the system you'll build. You must be careful not to get into this level of detail at your pitch stage. Not only will you be doing more work than necessary, you may be giving away free advice if you do not eventually win the pitch.

Think carefully what you are trying to accomplish with your pitch. You are trying to convince the client company that:

- You have fully understood its brief.
- You have devised an efficient, effective, and innovative response to its brief.
- You are able to deliver the solution you are recommending within its required time frame.
- You are able to deliver the solution at price X and have arrived at that price in a methodical manner.
- You are the kind of supplier it should do business with.

Going into intense detail on the functionality or technology behind the system does not contribute to accomplishing these aims and therefore should be omitted.

Sometimes, a degree of upward management of the client is required to justify the absence of full functionality in the pitch document. Be totally candid; explain to the client that you have adopted a rigorous specification process to ensure that the system is delivered exactly to the client's requirements; at this stage, you are a high-quality solution provider who has fully understood the requirements rather than the specifics of the system. If the client accepts these assertions, then he or she must, by inference, accept that you are able to fully provide the required system.

If you're still pressed for more detail, proceed with caution. Don't sell yourself short by giving away free advice at the drop of a hat.

Who to Involve When Pitching

By now you probably have a good idea of who you want to involve on the project, should you win the business. We go into more detail about this later in the chapter, but for now it's worth considering who you should be involving in putting together the pitch. Because the pitch is your responsibility, ultimately any editorial decisions about its content lie with you.

That said, be aware that there is an element of creativity involved in the pitch process! You need to clearly demonstrate an edge over other suppliers competing for the business, as well as the competence to deliver the required solution within the budgetary constraints of your client. With this in mind, it's definitely worthwhile getting people who may be able to contribute to the creative process involved at this early stage.

Because you are not getting bogged down in specifics, however, it is not necessary to have more than maybe one senior technologist and one senior designer on board, assuming that you have such people at your disposal. How the three of you arrive at the content of the pitch is very much up to you. Producing the entire document in a brainstorming environment, with the project manager in the driving seat, has proven to be a lot more effective than simply dividing the pitch into assignable chunks and gluing it together later.

When to Go the Extra Mile

Some clients will really make you work to win the business. In many cases, it's well worth it. At other times, it can be too much of a risk. Knowing when and when not to go the extra mile is an essential skill. Don't think of this as being lazy; your time may be far better served chasing down other potential business leads instead of pouring effort into an unlikely candidate.

The extra steps sometimes requested by clients will include on-site presentations, demonstrations of similar systems you have developed in the past, and even references and testimonials from past clients. The questions you should ask yourself at this point are as follows:

- How likely are you to win the business?
- What are the costs involved in taking these extra steps?
- What are other suppliers doing?

If you're getting strong signals from the client that you are close to closing the deal, you should most certainly consider proceeding. If, however, the client isn't making the right noises, the decision may already have been made in someone else's favor, and you should decline the invitation to provide more information.

Always assess the cash cost (travel, consumables) and effective costs (time expressed as potential lost revenue) of taking these extra steps. As a rule, if the costs appear to be approaching anything more than 5 percent of the value of the project, definitely consider taking a step back.

If you can, try to dig around to see what other suppliers are up to. Having a friendly insider at the client can be hugely useful here. A receptionist, for example, is clearly not a decision maker but probably keeps his or her ear quite close to the ground. Try to glean what knowledge you can; if your competitors are going the extra mile, then so do you.

When to Say No

Curiously, few professionals consider when it is appropriate to decline to pitch on a particular piece of business, and yet it is just as important to know when to walk away as it is to know when to grab a brief with both hands and give it everything you've got.

Aside from the obvious, such as you lacking the necessary skills or personnel or the client lacking the necessary budget, you should always keep a close eye out for:

- "Just curious" briefs—the client has no real authority to commission you to carry out the project but has read about it in a trade journal and is curious to know how much it would cost. Typical warning signs include being briefed by a junior-level member of staff who makes frequent references to needing to talk to the boss.

- "Driving down a quote" briefs—the client has already picked a supplier but wants to drive that supplier's quote down by obtaining quotes from other suppliers to use as leverage.
- Pet projects—typically the brief is given by a relatively senior player in the company but nobody else seems to be involved or have any interest. Although the money can certainly be there for such projects, in the event that said senior player disappears, it's quite likely that your project will, too.

Always keep the dollar in mind; if the project seems like more trouble than it's worth, then don't be afraid to take a step backward. The client may even respect you for it.

Structuring the Pitch

The written aspect of your pitch can follow almost any structure you wish, as long as it is consistent from pitch to pitch. This is particularly important if you are likely to be producing multiple proposals for a single client; consistency from document to document is crucial.

A few key points are worth following:

- **Present an introduction:** Always date the pitch, title it with the name of the client (not your name), and add the line "prepared for XXX," where XXX is the name of your principle contact at the company—it's an instant points-winner.
- **Always reproduce the brief's key points as your first section:** If the client has provided a written brief, do not reproduce it verbatim but summarize in approximately half a page. Many clients will make their decision based on just the first page of your proposal, and the price—so use the space wisely.
- **Propose your solution:** Include simple Visio diagrams or illustrations if necessary, and describe in full in not more than two or three pages. Again, don't get bogged down in detail; this is a ten-mile-high top-down overview of the system—your own creative interpretation of the brief you have just described. Make bullet points of "neat features" and ideas you've had, rather than simply list components.
- **Always provide a clear "investment summary":** Call it this rather than your quote; *investment* has a much more positive note to it. Don't try to hide the price from the client. Show clearly how you have arrived at the price, and include details about any commercial terms you are proposing.

  If you have quoted for this client before, ensure that your quote is consistent with previous quotes; for example, if you have worked at a flat rate of $800/day on previous quotations, don't be tempted to show a daily rate of more than $800/day on this occasion without being fully prepared to justify it when the client picks it up.
- **Go into some detail:** Talk about your process (if you have one), your company, and its history and background. Name-drop previous clients if possible.
- **Be candid with dates:** Explain to the client both how long it will take you to do the work when you expect to hand over, and when you expect the client to be able to start using the system. Explain that you are fastidious when it comes to keeping deadlines.
- **Set objectives and expectations:** Include a what-to-do-next' line advising the client how to contact you with questions, and how to proceed if client wants to get started right away.

If you had a face-to-face meeting or telephone call when receiving the pitch, try to make reference to some of the leading questions you asked and the answers given. Remind the client of the answers he or she gave, and show how you have used these answers to drive the decisions you have made to date. (For example, "You told us when we met that you required the system to be accessible as an XML Web service. We have therefore included in our proposed solution the ability to. . . .")

If you're sending the document electronically, try to use PDFs rather than MS Word documents or any other proprietary format. Always follow up with a phone call to check whether the client has received the document, but resist the temptation to chase the client after this; let at least a week go by before any follow-up phone call.

Most important, if you've promised the client the pitch document by a certain time and date, don't miss the deadline. First impressions count, and you get to make only one.

Remember; you won't win them all, no matter how good you are.

Unless your strike rate is proving disastrous, however, don't dwell on any missed pitches. Move on, and try to get some friendly feedback from the client as to what you could do to improve your approach next time around. Assuming you get the go-ahead from the client, you're going to have to assemble a project team pretty quickly. Let's look at that now.

Choosing Your People

Before you can get started moving the project forward, you need to assemble a team to work on delivery. You should set aside a full day for this process, if possible—and make it clear to the client what you're doing. How big this team ends up being is obviously governed by the resources available to you and the requirements of the project. Let's look at the different roles in the project, and how they all fit together.

Project Manager

If you're reading this chapter, this is a role that you will probably occupy. The Project Manager has responsibility for the day-to-day running of the project, from the pitch right through to delivery and handover. Generally speaking, the project manager works directly with the senior members of the build team and, if there is no Account Manager handling the relationship with the client, with the client directly.

The Project Manager sets internal deadlines and objectives that are compatible with the broader goals for delivery of the project, manages progress, and identifies and resolves any conflicts or difficulties encountered by the build team throughout the project.

It is not a technical role in itself, but having a thorough understanding of the work undertaken by software architects, software engineers, and others is all but essential to be an effective Project Manager. The ideal Project Manager, therefore, is an approachable, technically aware, highly organized and efficient individual, with a proven track record in delivering projects on time and on budget. Any given project should need only one Project Manager unless a specific requirement to the contrary exists.

Account Manager

If available, an Account Manager is a valuable addition to your project team. The Account Manager provides the sole point of contact between you (the supplier) and your client. All communications in either direction are channeled through the Account Manager.

Should the client have a particular request of the build team, they would put it to the Account Manager, who would in turn pass the request on to the Project Manager. The Project Manager would then handle the request internally, working with the build team as appropriate.

The Account Manager does not get involved in the day-to-day running of the project itself, but is instead concerned with managing the relationship between client and supplier. However, it is important that the Account Manager and Project Manager communicate on a regular basis so that the Account Manager may keep the Project Manager abreast of the expectations of and feedback from the client, and that the Project Manager may make the Account Manager aware of the progress and attainment (or otherwise) of key project milestones.

An Account Manager is not essential but does often provide a closer, more fruitful relationship with the client, because the role does not have the team-focused responsibilities of that of the Project Manager. By the same token, however, this can sometimes lead to Account Managers being rather too quick to agree to demands of clients, because the burden of the actual implementation of such demands does not fall on their shoulders.

The ideal Account Manager is a gregarious and warm individual, the kind of person who can easily strike up and maintain a rapport with everyone he or she meets. In addition, the Account Manager must be sympathetic to the limitations of what can and cannot be accomplished by the rest of the project team, and able to communicate these limitations to the client when necessary.

As with the Project Manager, only one Account Manager should be assigned to any given project.

Lead Architect

The Lead Architect for the project is the technical decision maker for the entire project lifecycle. It is his or her responsibility to translate the immediate requirements of the project, on a day-to-day basis, into decisions on how those requirements should be realized through technology.

The Lead Architect on any given project will always be a software architect rather than an engineer, and hence considerably more experienced. However, the Lead Architect will also need to have some degree of project management experience to ensure that his or her decisions are client led; the Lead Architect should also possess exceptional team-management abilities, as more junior technologists will report directly into him or her.

In addition to possessing thorough competence as a software architect, the Lead Architect must have a thorough understanding of systems and networks, such that he or she may suitably devise any deployment infrastructures that the project may require.

Typical software architecture duties undertaken by the Lead Architect include creation, ratification, or both of the database schema and object model for the project, maintaining coding standards and holding regular code reviews. Given the scope of this position's duties, only one Lead Architect should be assigned to any given project.

Software Architects and Engineers

Any given project requires a number of software architects and engineers to work on the back-end technology behind the application (in the case of this book, PHP).

The difference between the two roles is one of seniority. A software architect has a degree of autonomy, within the confines and standards set by the Lead Architect, to make decisions on architecture, layout, structure, infrastructure, and coding standards. By contrast, a software engineer must follow the edicts and standards set out by the software architects.

If resources do not allow for the use of client-side developers (see the following section), software engineers may also be assigned the task of developing templates and HTML for use on the site.

Of course, there need be no limit to the number of Architects and Engineers which can be assigned to a project.

Client Side Developers

The responsibility of client-side developers is solely to produce the HTML, CSS, and JavaScript that provide the user interface to the application being developed. Generally, they will work in a template-driven environment using, for example, Smarty Templates. There is not generally any requirement for them to know PHP or any other server-side scripting language.

They work with the senior designers and studio artists on any given project to receive the designs for preparation in HTML, but will report directly to the Lead Architect. There is no limit to the number of client-side developers who may be deployed on any given project.

Senior Designers

The design process is headed up by senior designers, who are responsible for the overall conceptual design of the application being produced. They will produce initial designs for approval by the client and make broader decisions on fonts, colors, and imagery. They will work with the Lead Architect in making such decisions to ensure that the concepts being created are within the technical constraints of the project Usually, a project has no more than two senior designers.

Studio Artists

Senior Designers have a more junior resource at their disposal, too—that of studio artists. Not assigned creative concepts per se, studio artists are still skilled in Photoshop, Illustrator, and other design packages and typically respond systematically to requests for particular components; for example, the production of a navigation bar with a certain set of captions would normally fall under the responsibility of a studio artist.

Studio artists will typically work only with existing templates, styles, and colors set out by the senior designers on a project, and any number of studio artists may be deployed on a given project.

Doubling Up of Roles

Resourcing can often be a problem, even for the biggest of agencies. With this in mind, the following pointers may be helpful should you be forced to double up roles:

- Project Managers often make effective Account Managers, provided that they are client-facing by nature.
- The Lead Architect can, obviously, perform all the roles normally performed by software architects and software engineers.
- Software engineers can usually do the development work assigned to client-side developers.
- Senior designers can, of course, perform all the duties normally assigned to more junior studio artists.

Working Practices

As far as possible, it's a very good idea to try to have your project team work in one room together. That way, the often talked about and largely theoretical concept of synergy becomes one step closer. That is to say, that extra competitive edge derived from having a workforce whose strength is greater than the sum of its individuals. Perhaps more important, having your whole team under roof makes your job as Project Manager that much easier.

Your Client's Role

It is just as important that your client defines distinct roles for the project and assigns personnel to those roles as it is that you have your own team structured correctly. This is obviously something over which you have considerably less control than you have over the allocation of roles in your own project team.

However, if at all possible, you should ensure that your client assigns a relationship manager to act as your first point of contact with the client, to handle, raise, and address any queries regarding the project, as well as any commercial queries. The client should also assign an internal project manager should the client be required to provide any regular input into the project—typically, providing content. This individual is responsible for managing or carrying out any work at the client's end needed to provide you with this content.

Summary

In this chapter, you learned in some detail the basics of successful management of a software application project. You saw the importance of receiving a brief, including the key questions you should be asking to gain a competitive edge over other suppliers, as well as how to respond to that brief, including how and when to construct a suitable proposal.

In the next chapter, you'll learn about different software development processes and methodologies, how they apply to your team, and how to determine which is the best for you.

Planning the System

Developing complex, dynamic PHP business applications with a team of technical and business professionals is not a simple prospect. You'll be faced with many challenges, some of which won't be entirely technical in nature.

The business-planning framework that you choose to work with will certainly affect the direction in which your software project grows. Choosing a process that offers a strict yet comfortable structure will place limits on how dynamically your project can change, but conversely reward you with a paper trail and a detailed road map to follow. Taking a more dynamic approach to planning may, however, mitigate the risk associated with technical or business unknowns.

The choice of which approach to system planning best fits your project is not one to take lightly, and you should be familiar with all planning options before making your decision, regardless of your personal or professional preferences.

Choosing a Process

Now that you've got your project team together, no doubt you're eager to get started delivering the solution your client is so eagerly awaiting. Before you begin, however, you need to determine which *process* to adapt for building the finished product.

There are a few to choose from, but the two fundamental processes are known as the *Waterfall Process* and the *Spiral Process*. Both these processes have the same basic stages and elements in common. The difference lies in the order and manner in which they are approached.

The Waterfall Process

In the Waterfall Process, the entire project is treated as a single solution to be delivered. The approximate process that is followed is shown in Figure 20-1.

The key principle of the Waterfall Process is that none of the phases may begin until its predecessor has been completed in full. In other words, the specification for the entire project must be completed and approved in full before the design and architecture phase for the project is completed. Only

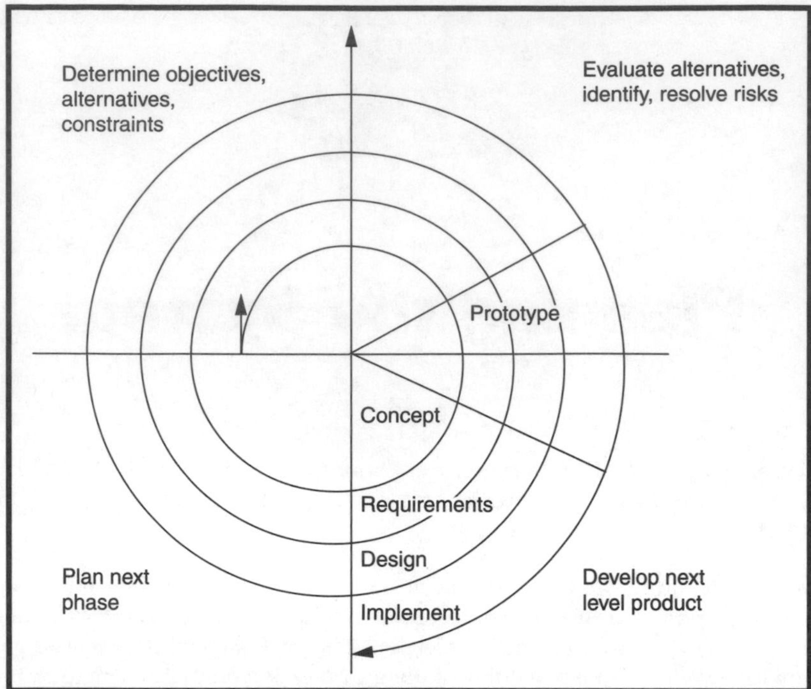

Figure 20-1

then can the build process of the project be completed and approved. Finally, the test phase of the project may take place.

This traditional process is fine in principle but has some latent problems in practice. For example, if an error is made during a particular phase that is not detected until later, that phase and all phases thereafter need to be repeated, which is immensely time consuming and expensive. An error at specification stage not picked up by the client until delivery will require respecification, redesign, rebuild, and retesting.

Another potential problem arises because the solution is built in one fell swoop, making it very difficult to offer the client anything partly finished to play with early on in the development process. If the client wants to provide early demos, or just needs reassurance as to progress, these can be very difficult to accomplish until very late in the project life cycle.

The Spiral Process

The Spiral Process has the same core components as those of the Waterfall Process—specification, design and architecture, build and test. However, rather than approach the entire solution as a single entity to which these four steps are applied, the system is divided into individual components, and the process is then applied to each component.

A component may either be a discrete piece of functionality or a partial evolution or layer of a piece of functionality. For each component, the four phases are applied: the specification of that component, followed by the design and architecture of that component, followed by the build of that component, followed by the testing of that component, in isolation.

The process is called the Spiral Process because you follow the path of a spiral—ever progressing down the path, but passing the same four compass points (each of the four phases) again and again (Figure 20-2).

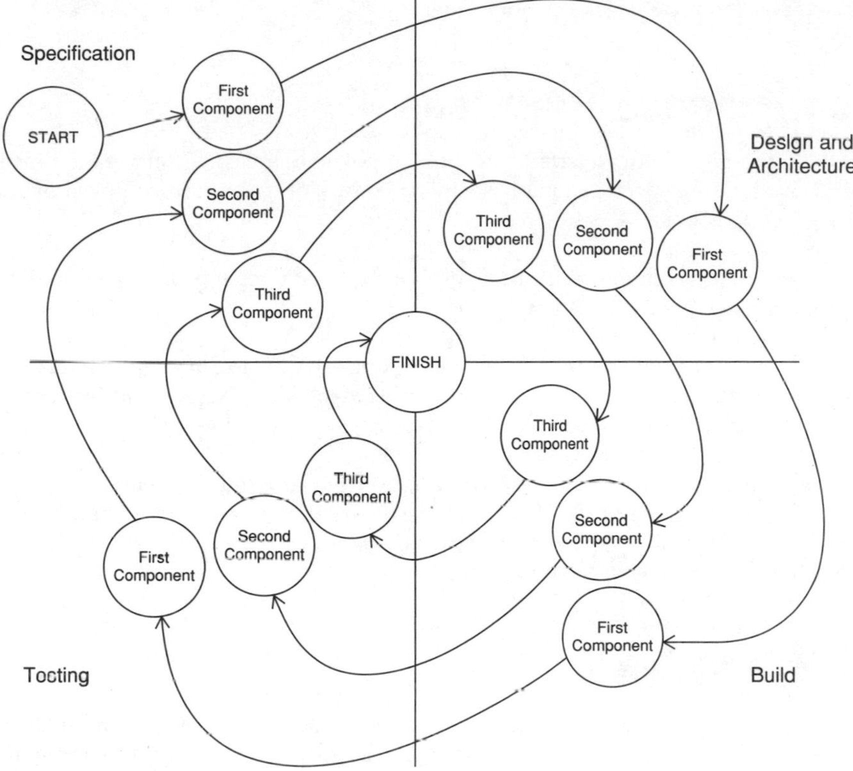

Figure 20-2

The big advantage of this process is that should an error be spotted at any stage during the four phases, the steps backward that have to be taken are much smaller because you are dealing with only one discrete component rather than with the entire application. In addition, the client is able to play with the first components of your application much sooner, which can have huge political benefits.

It's worth pointing out that the testing phase deviates from the Spiral Process slightly, in that the tests applied with each new component should ideally include all the previous tests from previous components, too, to ensure that no new piece of functionality is causing a previously tested and signed-off piece of functionality to fail.

Making the Decision

This chapter does not advocate either process over the other. In the next chapter, you'll see one of the processes again in the context of our Sales Force Automation application, but for now we will leave the door wide open. Which method you choose depends very much on the project at hand.

Although the Spiral Process certainly has huge advantages from a change request and exception handling perspective, the additional paperwork and administrative involvement has a cost to it, too, which must be weighed equally.

Your own experience will let you get a feel for both processes; much of the time the decision comes down to personal preference as much as anything else. Whichever way you go, there are common steps and a best practice for each one, which we examine next.

Common Process Practices

As mentioned previously, both waterfall and spiral approaches are consistent in their insistence that all development must have a specification phase, followed by a design phase, followed by a build phase, followed by a testing phase.

The difference lies in how much specification, design, build, and testing is done with each iteration, and the size of the chunks in which it is done.

However, the words *specification*, *design*, *build*, and testing are very much open to interpretation. Let's examine a little more closely now how you might implement each phase, regardless of whether you have chosen a waterfall or spiral approach to your project.

For the sake of clarity of language, we assume that you have adopted a waterfall approach for your project and hence describe the phases in application to an entire project rather than an individual component; however, if a spiral approach has been adopted, you can apply exactly the same methodology to each component in your spiral.

Specification Phase

The specification phase is, in many respects, the hardest part of any project; often much trickier than the build process itself. This is particularly true if you are assigned to build a slightly mundane system—a front-end to a simple database, for example. The task of development is not exactly challenging; the task of getting it right for the client the first time is a lot harder.

This phase is about ensuring that you know what you're planning to build and, more important, that the client knows what it is you're planning to build and that it matches the client's original business requirements as closely as possible. The easiest approach to adopt here is to produce paper specifications for the project—a functional specification and a technical specification.

Functional Specification

The Functional Specification for a project describes in detail the functionality of the system at a predesign level. It should be written in plain English and not place too much emphasis on or provide a rationale behind technology-led decisions. As a rule, you should roughly follow your pitch document, if you wrote one, and reproduce the brief in some detail here. It provides an excellent starting point for seeking affirmation from the client that the terms of reference for the project remain the same.

This is where the similarities with your pitch end, however. All the detail that we earlier implored you not to include in your pitch document should be included here. Remove any ambiguity from areas you would rather not repeat in case you get it wrong. Getting the level of detail right is a fine balancing act. Too much, and the document becomes unreadable; too little, and there is too much scope for interpretation or later disagreement over functionality.

With this in mind, try to be clear in any areas you think may be open to interpretation. For example, if you use the phrase "the user will be able to upload photographs to associate with his or her profile," the client is unlikely to latch onto the fact that you have omitted the number of photographs, or what format they may be in. When a scenario crops up of a user's wishing to upload eight hundred.PCX files but your application cannot support it, you may be in trouble. Instead, try to use phrases such as "the user will be able to upload a maximum of eight photographs in JPEG format to associate with his or her profile."

By the same token, however, mind-numbing detail should be avoided because that kind of level of detail could cause temporary paralysis in even the most patient of clients. If you find yourself using the sentence "The page will have a home button which, when pressed, will take the user to the home page," you're guilty.

The litmus test for whether a specification is on the money is whether you could give it to five different teams of competent development and design staff and in each five cases have roughly the same thing built. At the same time, though, you should leave open to interpretation any decisions that may best be left to a later phase or to others on the project; "The page will have a home button positioned at 124 pixels from the left side of the screen" should be avoided, because this decision should be left to a senior designer during the design phase.

In your functional specification, try to lay out the document as clearly as possible. The following is a suggested layout from start to finish:

- ❑ Replication of the client's brief, in not more than half a page, in your own words.
- ❑ An explanation as to what this document provides, what is expected of the client, and what other documents you will deliver as part of the specification process. Be clear at this stage that this is a document you expect the client to physically sign off on before you move forward.
- ❑ Explain in not more than half a page a top-line summary of your proposed solution, and list the components it is likely to entail.
- ❑ For each component, provide a detailed explanation of its functionality, including typical usage walkthroughs for dummy users.
- ❑ Provide diagrams if you genuinely feel it will improve clarity; otherwise, avoid them. No matter how hard you stress that they are only diagrams, clients invariably interpret them as completed designs, with predictable consequences. The same pitfall is equally true with page maps, which we will meet later in the next section.
- ❑ Complete the document with an explanation as to what the client needs to do next if they want to ask questions or make changes, or want to sign off the document. Explain the next stages after the document has been signed off, and gently advise that previously agreed delivery milestones are all subject to timely agreement to this document.

In practice, you will require at least two or three iterations of the specification before the client is happy. Indeed, you should be wary of any client who signs off a specification on the first attempt; nine times out of ten it implies the client hasn't read it.

Technical Specification

If the Functional Specification describes what you plan to do, the Technical Specification describes how you plan to do it.

The level of detail you need to include here will vary dramatically from client to client. Generally, if the client themselves has an IT department taking a keen interest in the project, you will need to provide an exhaustive level of detail right down to your coding practices. Otherwise, you can normally get away with providing:

- Suggested language for build, with rationale and explanations, and comparisons and rejections of other, rival languages
- Suggested database platform, with rationale and explanations, and comparisons and rejections of other database platforms
- Suggested operating system for Web and database servers, again, with comparisons to other platforms and reasons for their rejection
- Explaining the hosting and deployment plans for the project (if any), going into detail on bandwidth requirements, and so on, where appropriate.
- An explanation as to what this document provides, what is expected of the client, and what other documents you will deliver as part of the specification process. Be clear that this technical specification relates directly to the functionality the client has already signed off on in the functional specification.

If you have chosen to adopt a spiral process for your project, it is not necessary to provide a technical specification for every traversal of your spiral. Instead, provide a single technical specification at the start of the project, and explain to the client that this specification relates to the implementation of all individual components to follow.

With many clients, especially those not equipped with their own technology department, this document may prove to be quite alien. You have two choices: go to great lengths to explain the document in detail with them to ensure that they are happy with the decisions you've made, or let them sign it blindly, which they may be more than happy to do. Sometimes the latter decision is easiest; after all, clients will feel they are paying you to tell them what is technically sound, not ask their permission.

Design Phase

The word *design* may prove to be misleading here. It relates both to graphic design and to software design but, of course, the two are very different disciplines and you should be aware of the distinction. Yet it is almost inevitable that the client will want to see some individual graphic designs for the key components of the project as soon as possible.

It is absolutely fine for the senior designer on a project to take responsibility for and produce these designs, as long as it is done closely in consultation with the lead architect to ensure the technical feasibility of what is being proposed. Skilled senior designers will be aware of technical limitations and hence require less guidance when designing for the Web.

Once again, expect to produce a few iterations of the designs before you get it exactly right. This can be immensely tricky, too; the client will have his or her own unique vision of what is desirable and may struggle to articulate it to you as a supplier. All the client will know is that what you have produced is not what is wanted, and he or she will not hesitate to make this clear to you.

Sometimes it can be useful when presenting designs to a client to allow the senior designer to present the designs themselves, possibly, even, with a laptop loaded with graphics and RAD software so that suggested changes can be made in front of the client; the reaction "that's it, that's how I want it" can be most gratifying as well as commercially useful.

Creative Specification

With the key designs signed off on, it is a very useful exercise to produce what is known as a Creative Specification, or style guide. This document is not normally presented to the client for inspection, although if the client is very protective of branding or has in-house graphics staff, it may not be a bad idea.

The traditional purpose of this document is to communicate the artistic vision of the senior designer to more junior studio artists, and to ensure that any future design work carried out on the project is consistent with that vision, too.

Its likely content will include details of fonts, colors, layout, logos, backgrounds—all the components that make up the broader artistic vision, such that if a request such as "produce me a button that says Add to Basket" is made, the button that is made will look exactly as the senior designer would want.

Page Maps

Possibly the most controversial component of the design phase is the Page Map. Essentially a wire-frame, black-and-white model of a given page in the user's Web browser, it attempts to articulate the user interface without communicating any facets of the design. It allows the UI to be approved separately from the graphic design, when commercial or political pressures mean this could be useful, or when no specific graphic design has been produced for this page.

In addition, it can be given to the development team, alongside the Creative Specification, such that they can directly commission studio artists and client-side developers to produce designs and HTML needed to deliver some particular component.

In practice, however, page maps have two major pitfalls. First, it is often difficult to separate the concepts of user interface and design in the client's head. This can mean that presenting page maps to a client can be a tiresome and stress-inducing task, because they will perceive your wire-frame diagrams to be the finished look and feel and will balk at the prospect. Obviously, you need to make it clear exactly what you are presenting.

Second, the remit for actually producing page maps is hard to define. Graphic designers are rarely experts at producing "interfaces" per se and are often loathe to use Visio and other packages required to produce these deliverables. Project managers are usually far too busy. The result is that the task often falls on the shoulders of the lead architect. Given that the role of imparting a vision for the production of particular components to software architects and engineers is at the heart of the remit of the lead architect anyway, the arguments for documenting this vision are weakened.

Software Architecture: Ten-Point Plan

Again, another piece of documentation that you may or may not want to present to the client for approval is the Software Architecture plan. This is often called a *ten-point plan* because it is generally a series of short, punchy bullet points outlining the best approach to the actual project or component in hand, instead of being a prose-heavy document.

The production of this document is very much the remit of the lead architect, who will normally produce it well after the Technical Specification has been approved and signed off on. As such, it will not concern itself with technology choices, hardware, hosting, and so forth. Rather, it will concentrate on issues such as database schema, object models, and implementation of design patterns such as MVC.

He or she will communicate the document to his or her software architects, who will in turn interpret it as they see fit. In theory, the "architectural vision" should cascade down to software engineers working beneath them, too.

Build Phase

With all design parameters agreed upon, the build process itself can commence. There is no written documentation to accompany this phase, but a few points are worth keeping in mind:

- Always maintain both development servers and a staging server, as well as the production server. These do not necessarily have to be separate physical servers, but it is vitally important that you can release partly completed stages of development to the client so that the client can witness the progress you are making.
- Try to adapt a programming methodology, if one is appropriate to your project. These are discussed in more detail in the next major section of this chapter, "Programming Methodologies and Practices."
- It is the responsibility of the lead architect to manage the build process and ensure that his or her team delivers all components on time and at the required standard so that he or she can deliver the entire system to the project manager as a completed package, rather than piecemeal.
- Always maintain fastidious version control. Later in this book you'll learn about CVS, a free solution to this often problematic issue.

Testing Phase

Having built the solution, it is vital for you to conduct suitable testing, both to assure yourself of the quality of what you have produced, and to reassure the client that he or she doesn't have to perform exhaustive testing.

The testing you conduct should always be accompanied with written reports detailing your findings. For obvious reasons, you should not release these reports until you are 100 percent happy that the testing has been a complete success.

Functional Testing

Functional testing ensures that the product works exactly as expected, both that it fulfills the specification exactly and that it is free from errors or malfunction. Be systematic; test each area of functionality relentlessly, using a number of different data sets and/or input parameters. Record your findings systematically, too, to in effect demonstrate a check in the box next to each distinct feature.

Of course, you should always stress to your development team that it is vital to "test as they go" as far as possible, and never turn in code they know to be seriously buggy. You may consider using a bug-tracking system such as Mantis (`www.mantisbt.org`) to maintain a centralized repository of bugs as each is discovered, assign the bugs to developers, and annotate them appropriately.

Load Testing

If the application you are building is likely to be high traffic either now or at some point in the future, it makes sense to know how much it can take before it falls over.

Load testing can be conducted only if you can deploy the application onto a realistic environment, usually the production server. There is no point in testing your application on your Xeon-driven Linux development server if you know you'll be forced to deploy onto a Sun box running Solaris. A number of packages are available, the most popular of which is probably LoadRunner, from Mercury Interactive. Similar results, however, can be achieved using a suite of custom-built test scripts.

The key to load testing is to never be afraid to turn the volume up as high as it will go until the speakers explode. Simply knowing that the client's traffic expectations can be handled is good, but knowing exactly how much more they can handle beyond that is even better. The client will be gratified if you can provide an exact figure, such as "the site will handle one thousand simultaneous users with no problems."

Handover

Having produced a thoroughly documented, well-designed, fully tested piece of software, it is vital to arrange a proper handover meeting with the client. This is the client's final sign-off—either for the whole project or for this component, depending on the process you adapted in the previous section.

During the handover process, you should endeavor to ensure that the client is fully comfortable with the inner workings of the finished product. An element of training may be required as a result. Also, remember what you're there to do—hand over the project. Presenting the client with a CD containing a copy of the source code can have a symbolism that is hard to measure.

It is almost inevitable that small change requests will crop up during the handover process. Later in the chapter we look at how to handle them.

Programming Methodologies and Practices

Let's look briefly at the build process itself. There are a couple of best practice methodologies you may wish to adapt during the build process, regardless of the overall project process you have opted for.

Test-Driven Development

In the previous section of this book, you met PHPUnit, and with it you learned how to build Unit Testing frameworks. This knowledge can be applied, of course, only if you have built your application in a unit-driven fashion.

Test-driven development requires that you write the test before the code. The act of writing the test for the class in which you intend to code forces you to think about exactly how you mean to use a particular class, what it needs to do, and what its interface should be. PHP Unit (available through PEAR at `http://pear.php.net`) is a good framework for testing.

You will want to check that your unit test works before attempting to write the class itself. This may require using a dummy class with the same interface as that of your real class to make the test run and naturally fail.

The unit tests for that class, after being constructed, will probe the interface of your PHP class and analyze in detail the data it gets back. As a developer, your responsibility is to code the class in order to satisfy your unit tests.

Try to keep your unit tests as generic as possible; if you have numerous classes with similar interfaces, you can combine your unit tests into a single PHPUnit instance.

Using unit testing has numerous advantages, which are explored in more detail in Chapter 22, "Assembling the Sales Force Automation Toolkit." Whether it's right for your project is, once again, a judgment call. It is a testing methodology arguably much better suited to larger projects with more distinct components than to simple traditional "database applications."

eXtreme Programming

The concept of eXtreme Programming, or XP, is perhaps the truest example of a programming paradigm. It is a paradigm in the sense that is perhaps more aspirational than it is practical in every development case. However, as a working model, it has many facets from which to pick and choose as required.

What Is XP?

The description of XP is realized through a number of distinct working practices. They are too numerous to list in full, but we look at a few in detail.

The main goal of XP is to deliver quality software driven by the needs of the client. It achieves this goal by managing complexity. As a system grows more and more complex, the cost of adding and modifying features increases. But the reverse is also true: If the system does not get unnecessarily complex, then the cost of adding features later is roughly the same as adding features now.

This is a very powerful weapon, because traditional methodologies tend to follow the curve where the software modification cost increases significantly as more time is spent with all the phases of development.

For instance, it is more cost effective to add features in the requirements phase rather than during implementation, when it costs significantly more.

But, suppose your project development followed a curve where the costs of change grow more slowly and level off more quickly.

If you had the freedom to add, remove, and modify features whenever you'd like, then there would be pressure or reason to try to predetermine the entire feature set during the initial phases of the project.

The act of extreme programming is that of following a set of practices, best said by Kent Beck in *Extreme Programming Explained*:

- ❑ Planning—Determine the scope of the project by combining business priorities and technical estimates, continually updated.
- ❑ Small releases—Get the system used by the people to be using it and release new versions on a very short schedule.
- ❑ Simple Design—Keep the design as simple as possible at all times. Complexity is removed on an ongoing basis.
- ❑ Testing—Developers continually write unit-tests to ensure that the system runs flawlessly all the time. Customers write tests to demonstrate that features work as required.
- ❑ Refactoring—Restructuring the code without modifying the behavior in order to keep it easy to read, to remove duplication, or to simplify.
- ❑ On-site customer—The client should always be available to answer questions at all times throughout the development process.

The client, always being available throughout the build process, is in effect made *part of* the development process instead of simply driving it forward through his or her requirements. If at all possible, this is best accomplished by having the client, preferably some reasonably technical representative with domain expertise, on site at key stages during the development process. Don't worry about clients unnecessarily harassing your team; as long as they are suitably involved, your team will upward-manage the clients. This tenet of XP is particularly important in the attainment of elevated customer satisfaction; there can be no cries of "this isn't what I wanted" if the customer has been involved from day one.

By creating unit tests for your classes before the classes themselves, you save time should your code not work the first time. Across a larger project with a number of distinct classes, this time saving can easily amount to days.

Using unit testing brings with it other benefits. Psychologically, it conditions software architects and engineers into considering more fully and thoroughly the requirements of a given component, meaning that the finished product is often a closer fit to the true requirements than a non-unit–driven approach would have permitted. In addition, there is a positive, direct impact on coding style that is highly beneficial to all those involved in the development process.

Second, it ensures that coding standards are determined early on in the project, and that the entirety of the development team sticks to them. There is no "code ownership," and as such any developer is allowed to modify any piece of code as long as the unit tests continue to work.

Perhaps the most famous aspect of XP is its permitting two software engineers, or perhaps a software architect and engineer, to code at a single workstation simultaneously. Generally, the best configuration is for both individuals to sit side by side but with one driving—that is, controlling keyboard and mouse—and another guiding the code-authoring process. With two people actively involved in the development of each piece of code, the business and technical expertise is not stuck inside any single developer's head, which makes for a more even distribution of information and avoids the project's being dependent on any specific developer. Besides, two heads are almost always better than one, and pair programming doesn't just affect the quality of code but also results in the reduction of bugs.

Finally, the most controversial of XP's tenets is that overtime—that is, working programmers until they collapse—is frowned upon. The argument is that if a project is properly specified, budgeted, and managed, there should be no need for overtime in the first place, and when overtime is generally needed, the project is doomed to late completion anyway.

When to Use XP?

XP is most at home when the project in question has a high element of risk attached to it. Perhaps there is a tight deadline to be met. Maybe some unknown quantity or dynamic requirement means that the proposed solution is not cast-iron guaranteed to meet the eventual needs of the client. Conceivably, the solution being proposed is so cutting edge that it carries the risk of simply not working.

The actual development team should be small—not fewer than two and not more than ten or eleven, and all members of the project team, not just the development team, are free to take ownership of the build process.

The desired results of XP are as follows:

- The productivity of those in the development team is greatly increased.
- Client satisfaction is more easily attained.
- High standards of quality are attained and maintained.
- The client's requirements are met more precisely.
- Deadlines are met with greater accuracy and consistency.

There is a huge amount of debate over both the relative success and the feasibility of XP among the programming community. Often, enormous commercial pressures mean that it is simply an impossible paradigm to follow. As with any paradigm, however, it is simply a model—something to aim at. You can find a great deal more detail on the practices and recommendations of XP at `http://www.extremeprogramming.org/`.

Change Management

In almost every project of any scale, there are going to be change requests made by the client. Managing these changes is enormously important. You need not only to assess the commercial impact of any changes you make but also understand the enormous disruption that can occur through major changes to a well-entrenched software or systems architecture.

In this section, we look at some of the most common varieties of change requested by clients and the best way to handle each of them.

Specification Revisions

These are not only inevitable but should be actively encouraged. Your client will want to make changes to the specification you have produced, because it is almost certain that you will not quite have managed to hit the nail on the head first time around.

Collate any change requests together into 48-hour periods. Use a change management package such as Microsoft Project or MrProject (`http://mrproject.codefactory.se`) if necessary. Every 48 hours, incorporate the previous two days' changes into a new release of the specification and offer it back to the client.

Be sure to make the client aware of any requests that will for one reason or another prove unfeasible as soon as they are put forward.

Specification Changes That Arise after Sign-Off

If the client requests changes after signing off on the specification, you may have a problem on your hands. First, don't panic. You have the moral high ground. The client's signature on your specification is an affirmation that he or she was 100 percent happy with what has been produced. Should you feel the need to bill them for the change, you are, strictly speaking, within your rights to do so.

Before you make a decision, however, consult the rest of your team. Try to determine how far into the design and/or build phases your team has gone. Try to quantify in terms of work hours the kind of disruption that is involved in rewinding the process back to specification stage so that the requested change can be made.

If you can put a price tag on this work, it is worth making a judgment call as to whether it is worth passing this cost onto the client. It is normally considered to be in the interest of good client relations to show some grace and flexibility in these situations, unless they become a regular occurrence.

If you decide to proceed with the change, be sure to make it very clear to the client the time impact it will have, and come to an agreement concerning any revised milestones that the change may necessitate. Ensure that these your project team concurs and that the new timelines include a contingency margin.

Disputes Arising from Differences in Interpretation

Sometimes, a client can query the interpretation of a specification and request changes as a result. These queries are always difficult to manage. After all, you cannot accuse the client outright of simply being wrong. The best approach with these situations is to try hard to avoid them altogether in the first place by being as fastidious and specific as possible in your specification, avoiding ambiguity wherever possible.

When they do crop up, however, be prepared to negotiate with the client. Listen carefully to the client's concerns and endeavor to understand his or her point of view. Discuss with your team the time required to make the changes in question and then put them to a simple commercial test: in terms of cold, hard cash, is it worth arguing the point?

Bugs Reported by the Client

Be careful to determine whether the client is concerned about a bug or a change to the system. At this stage, any post-handover changes requested by the client are almost certainly outside the scope of the specification, and as such should be considered additional, billable work.

Always respond to bugs reported by the client as a priority, even if they appear to be nonbugs (for example, the client has made an error). Use a bug tracking system such as Mantis to keep track of all bugs reported, and give clients access so that they may report their own. Encourage clients to use this system in preference to immediately calling you about it.

Clients are generally sympathetic to bugs; most people these days are enlightened enough to accept that "these things happen." Being seen to respond quickly, efficiently, and systematically, even after the system has gone live, is often the difference between being on the receiving end of sympathy versus angry telephone calls.

Summary

You now know that the value of ensuring that a tight methodology is maintained even after you've won the business, right through to the completion of the project. You've met the various people who might play a part in your project and seen two different methodologies for running the show itself. You've also examined couple of theoretical paradigms, which you might want to apply during the build process itself.

Finally, in this chapter you encountered the concepts of change management and how to best deal with the situations that can arise as a result.

Systems Architecture

By now, you probably can't wait to get started and build your application. You've planned the system, chosen your people, selected an appropriate methodology, and gleaned specifications detailing exactly what it is you're going to build. There is, however, one final step you need to consider.

As a software architect or project manager, you may well be tempted to overlook the systems side of things. After all, you only build the thing. It's somebody else's problem as to how it gets deployed, right?

Well, that may be true, but having the moral high ground doesn't get Web sites launched. At the end of the day, if it's your application that's not running up to snuff (or worse, not at all), the blame is going to rest squarely on your shoulders.

In this short chapter, you'll learn the basis of systems architecture—what it is, why it's important, and how to effectively design one appropriate for your project based on the decisions you've already made about the architecture of the application itself.

What Is Systems Architecture?

At its simplest, systems architecture refers to the infrastructure supporting the application you're planning on building.

However, this doesn't just limit its scope to the specifications of your server hardware. You're looking at the servers, network, Internet connectivity, firewall, load balancing, and software running on each server.

This is, as you might have guessed, a big topic. We only scratch the surface over the next few pages, but we can at least point you in the right direction.

Why Is It Important?

Getting the right infrastructure for your application is vitally important. As an application developer, it's highly plausible that you have just one development server in your studio. This may double up as both a Web server and a database server, maybe running both MySQL and PostgreSQL. If you develop in more than just PHP, you may have the Java SDK installed, too, along with Jakarta or some other application server. If you've been in the business for a while, you may still have a PHP4 installation to support legacy applications.

This setup probably suits you just fine. Although your development server is clearly under a lot of strain, with only a handful of users ever connecting to it, it's rarely going to show that strain outwardly. And, with little or no outward access to or from the Internet at large, the server could probably quite happily connect to the Web using a treehouse phone.

Of course, when you go live, you go to an environment in which your application can be hit by literally hundreds of simultaneous users, some of whom will be on high-bandwidth connections. Your application must perform under such conditions.

In a later chapter we look a little more at the principles of Quality Assurance (QA), but you can save yourself a lot of time and hassle now by designing an effective systems architecture to complement and support the software architecture you've already developed.

What Needs Doing?

Your systems architecture is effectively a battle plan for your live environment. You may well wish to draw up a document to support it, or incorporate its contents into your existing technical specification. This is yet another decision-making process that is mainly up to you, but for which you should also endeavor to obtain client ratification and approval, just in case it goes wrong and you need some leverage.

That's not to say it will go wrong, of course—just that if you have a signed piece of paper saying "the application will have not more than X simultaneous users, hence we have specified Y," then if your application falls down under X + 1 simultaneous users, you can sit there looking smug while your client writes out the purchase order.

Assumptions or prerequisites like these form the heart of your systems architecture. This knowledge developed between you and your client needs translating into effective systems decisions.

The key decisions to be made are the following:

- Hosting—where is the application to be physically housed? Is it a suitable environment, that is, air conditioned and equipped with uninterruptible power supplies?
- Internet connectivity—what kind of link to the Internet is required? Who will provide it? How much is it likely to cost?
- Servers—what number and specification of servers are required to support the application?
- Network—what kind of topology is best to support those servers?
- Redundancy and resilience—what kind of guaranteed availability is required? Can there be a single point of failure?
- Maintenance—who will be responsible for maintaining each server and its software?
- Security—how will the infrastructure be secured from the outside world?

We consider each of these in more detail in a little while, but first let's look at how best to translate your client's commercial objectives when designing a systems architecture.

Effectively Translating Requirements

Let's face it—the rhetorical questions we've just posed will rarely be questions you can put directly to your client.

Although you may be confronted from time to time with projects for which the client takes full ownership of systems architecture and simply wants you to build the application (in which case, you can skip to the next chapter), far more likely is that you're expected to make the big decisions based on what the client has told you or the answers to questions you've asked him or her.

Far more likely, therefore, is that you're the one who will have to ask the questions. These questions should be designed to fill a veritable stockpile of information, which you can then use to design your environment. But what questions should you ask?

Hosting, Connectivity, Servers, and Network

The first question is "Do you have an Internet service provider?"

Unfortunately, the answer to this question is almost always yes and is also almost always followed by "And we'd like to use it to host this Web site, because Doug there is always so helpful; why, just last week he helped me get this virus off my laptop. . . . ."

If you then ask, "And who might they be?" and are told, "BudgetISP—just $300 a year for unlimited disk space," you could be forgiven for having a slight sinking feeling in your stomach.

You know as a PHP professional that getting budget or even expensive third-party ISPs to host PHP applications is a bit like asking your local mechanic to tune up a Formula One race car. On the other hand, being dismissive at this early stage of the project and trying to push the client toward your preferred ISP could well prove counter-productive.

Our preferred approach is a diplomatic one; "OK, I'll call BudgetISP tomorrow and explain our requirements to them." When you return to your client a few days later, you can truthfully say, "Well, I spoke to BudgetISP, and I'm afraid they don't think they're going to be able to host our application." Your client will inevitably respond, "What do you recommend?" At this time, you can launch into your spiel about how good Acme Hosting is, and your client will actually listen to you. Works every time.

In terms of asking questions to determine hosting requirements, the only question that needs to be asked is "What kind of traffic are you expecting, and at what times of day?" The answer to such a question will allow you to determine not only bandwidth requirements but also the approximate number and configuration of servers you're likely to need.

Should your client not be able to easily provide you with an answer, coax it out of him or her. Ask how big the client's customer base is and how often the client will be using the platform. The figure you are trying to arrive at is the approximate number of simultaneous users likely to be in-session at any given time.

It's also worth finding out whether your client knows whether the users are likely to be on broadband or dialup, and in what rough slices; we discuss why a bit later.

Redundancy and Resilience

Rather than ask your client "Do you need redundancy?" (which often solicits a stony look and a silent room), you should aim to get to the heart of the matter.

"Let's say the worst happened and a server blew up, taking this site down for a few hours. How bad would that be?"

You'd be amazed by the number of clients who say it wouldn't be a big deal. If this is the case, you don't need to worry too much about redundant power supplies, failover database servers, and so forth. However, you may want to then rephrase the question slightly: "What if when we got the site back up again, some of the database were lost?" You'll find very quickly that the client's attitude changes and that loss of data would be a big deal. Keep this in mind. Redundancy to handle temporary outages is very different from redundancy of data, as the next section explains.

Maintenance

What you should attempt to establish here is this: Who will take ownership of these servers? Not legal ownership, of course. We assume that legal ownership remains with your client unless you're providing the hosting, too.

Instead, think responsibility. Whose responsibility will it be to upgrade the kernel? Reboot the server if it goes down? Resist the temptation to go into sales mode here. Instead of saying "Would you be interested in a support package?" (which sounds suspiciously like "Can I interest you in an extended warranty?"), ask the question and then let the client decide:

"From time to time the software running on these servers might need an upgrade. Did you have any ideas about who you might like to be responsible for carrying those out?"

From the client's response, you have a place to start for discussing the benefits of taking out a support and maintenance contract with you, without appearing pushy.

> **The best sales technique you'll ever learn is not to sell; instead, you should delve, dig, probe, find pains, and help your client find them, too. Present obvious solutions to those pains and you'll have a sale.**

Security

This will often be a matter close to your client's heart. From friends and colleagues, the client will have heard horror stories of being hacked, and maybe even experienced it themselves. He or she will almost certainly have seen features on CNN.

An unexpected rant can be quite beneficial sometimes. The client may find it therapeutic in some manner or other. Try to solicit one with, "Would I be right in thinking it's important to you that this application and infrastructure is very secure against intruders?"

Listen and sympathize with the answer that follows, and propose a reassuring solution. There is no real question needed here, if we're honest; the answer is always "Yes, of course"—but it's worth asking for the political benefits it can bring. Shows you're on the ball. Clients like that.

Designing the Environment

With the dossier of information required from your client, you should be able to come up with a solid proposal for your systems architecture.

Let's take a look at each of the building blocks of systems architecture we've identified, and see how one can best design an environment to fit these requirements.

Hosting and Connectivity

Unless you're designing a totally closed system, there will almost certainly be a requirement for Internet connectivity and a secure environment for the hosting of your client's servers.

Without a doubt, the best approach here is a data center. The sole purpose of such facilities is to provide a secure, air-conditioned, controlled environment for servers and other equipment and, frequently, provide some kind of network connectivity to them.

Because these facilities house servers designed solely for remote access, they are often rather inhospitable environments for human beings. The use of carcinogenic fire retardants has been made unlawful in most states and countries, but the intense air conditioning can provide even the fittest and healthiest software architect with a wheeze upon exit. However, this environment is perfect for servers.

There are two types of data center—carrier-specific and carrier-neutral. A *carrier-specific* data center is typically owned by the ISP providing bandwidth and connectivity there, and, therefore, only that particular ISP is available for connectivity. A *carrier-neutral* center concerns itself only with housing equipment and allows you to connect with any number of ISPs providing connectivity there.

Both have their advantages and disadvantages. Carrier-specific centers tend to have a more integrated support and billing approach, which can certainly cut down on the hassle. With a carrier-neutral center, however, should one ISP prove unreliable or inappropriate, or you just fancy a change, you can move your equipment without physically moving it at all. Either way, you will typically be presented with a product that consists of a certain amount of rack space, a suite of IP addresses (or, in some cases, a range of addresses and a single IP on their network, requiring you to fit a router of your own), and a handoff—a physical Ethernet link into your ISP's network. Your ISP will, of course, give you a decent helping of support and assistance in getting up and running, but it's important that you actually order the right product in the first place.

Calculating CIR

Your ISP will sell you either a quantity of bandwidth measured as a Committed Information Rate (CIR) in megabits, or a quantity of monthly transfer, measured in gigabytes. A CIR will almost always be the more expensive option but is essential for bigger sites. It allows you to push as much traffic as possible within a given bandwidth. To calculate a CIR, consider the number of simultaneous sessions your application is likely to support.

Say that your Webmail Web application needs to support a total of one thousand simultaneous sessions. This represents one thousand people all using the application at any given point in time. It does not represent one thousand simultaneous connections. This distinction is cataclysmically important. When using any given application, each session will consist of a flurry of HTTP requests (page plus images), followed by a pause while content is read, followed by another flurry of HTTP requests, and so on. With this in mind, connectivity is being made only a given percentage of the time.

It is also important to understand the likely dwell time on each page. This is something only user testing can determine accurately, but you could estimate it to be something like 30 seconds for a typical Web page on a consumer Web site, or 60 seconds on a Web application (such as a Webmail application).

If you assume that each page takes approximately 10 seconds to load, then on a Web application there will be a pattern-per-session of 10 seconds of traffic followed by 60 seconds of no traffic, followed by 10 seconds of traffic . . . and so on.

One quick and slightly crude calculation later, this means that at any given moment in time, there is a 15 percent possibility that any given session is transferring data. The number of simultaneous connections is therefore likely to be equal to 15 percent of your simultaneous sessions for a Web application, or 2 percent for a Web site.

In the preceding example of 1,000 simultaneous sessions, we can tell that this represents 150 simultaneous connections. But with some users on T1 lines, and others on 56K dial-ups, how do we know what bandwidth requirement this represents?

This is where the data mined from your client comes in handy. The client may well have some figures on his or her projected demographic. People in offices, for example, are all likely to have E1 lines, but these are likely to be shared among other people in each office. For home users, you can use national figures on broadband penetration to figure out the likely percentage on broadband and the likely percentage on dial-up.

Even better, if you as a PHP professional have access to some server logs for similar past projects, dig them out and do the math yourself.

Assume that this application targets home users only. Broadband penetration in the United States is approximately 30 percent of all home Internet connections at the time of writing. This is all almost exclusively at 512 Kbps. The rest we can assume is at just 56 Kbps, which in reality always connects at 48K or less.

With this in mind, the math is simply 30 percent of 200 at 512K and 70 percent of 200 at 48K. Total requirement? About 37 Mbit to ensure that everybody gets full speed—let's say 40 Mbit after leeway—which is not cheap.

Thankfully, 1,000 simultaneous sessions is very rare. That would be a huge Web application. To help your client calculate simultaneous sessions, ascertain the total regular users of the application. If, for example, your Web application has 5,000 regular users, each of whom uses the platform once a day for a total of twenty minutes, and that usage follows an approximately normal distribution centered around 6 p.m., college calculus shows us that the likely maximum (at 6 p.m.) number of simultaneous sessions will be around 2 percent of your regular user base, or just 100 simultaneous sessions—a much more reasonable 4 Mbit.

Essentially, the integral of a graph showing sessions on the Y axis and time on the X axis, divided into intervals equal to the average length of a session, will equal the total number of user sessions per day. From this, you can determine the approximate formula that describes the curve and use that formula to calculate the peak number of sessions (the Y-value) at the known peak X-value.

For further information, pick up any college calculus textbook and hunt details on the "normal distribution."

Calculating Monthly Transfer

The other option available to you is a monthly transfer limit, an "all you can eat" of the ISP's bandwidth within that limit. Depending on the type of site, this may work out to be less expensive. For example, if you have a huge surge of users at 6 p.m. but a lot of dead time elsewhere, this option could be for you.

To calculate your monthly transfer requirement, simply multiply the number of monthly user sessions you expect to receive by the amount of data each will transfer.

If a typical session consists of 10 requests and each request has a page weight of 50K, each user session will consume about a half-megabyte of transfer. In the earlier example of 5,000 regular users each using the system once a day, this represents 5,000 sessions per day, or 2.5 gigabytes of transfer. During a month, this works out to 75 GB/month.

Ask your ISP which is likely to be cheaper—75 GB/month or 4 Mbit CIR.

Rack Space

How much rack space you require is obviously determined by the number of servers you'll be using. Keep in mind, though, that any network appliances such as switches and routers also take up space.

In planning for future expansion, you may wish to allow a certain amount of free rack space beyond your immediate requirements. If you buy only 5U in a shared rack, for example, it is almost inevitable that space either side of you will be sold by your ISP more or less right away and that future equipment may have to be cited elsewhere as a result.

Servers

Assessing your server requirements is a little more tricky than figuring out how much bandwidth you'll need. After all, every server is different and is capable of handling highly different numbers of simultaneous users.

You can be sure, though, that you will need at least one Web server and at least one database server to host your application. On much smaller sites you can probably get away with using a single shared server, but both MySQL and PostgreSQL are not friendly to other processes on the same machine. Your site will suffer as a result.

The real question is, then, how many of each? Only guesswork or load testing will establish this, but if you do find yourself needing more than one server, the following section may help you.

Using Multiple Web Servers

Deploying multiple Web servers is a very simple way to handle traffic beyond the capabilities and capacity of a single server.

There are a couple of techniques for load balancing Web servers: DNS load balancing and appliance load balancing.

Using DNS load balancing is easy. Simply assign (through your firewall) a separate external IP address to each Web server on your network and then create an A record pointing to not one address but the pool of addresses you wish to make available.

For example, if you normally have a DNS entry that looks like this:

```
$ORIGIN example.com.
www                         IN      A       192.168.111.222
```

you could instead specify a pool of addresses for that same record:

```
$ORIGIN example.com.
www                         IN      A       192.168.111.222
www                         IN      A       192.168.111.223
www                         IN      A       192.168.111.224
```

When clients attempt to resolve the address of your Web server, their computer will be presented with an address at random from the pool of addresses you have specified. Accordingly, different clients will use different Web servers.

The fault with this technique, of course, is that after a Web browser has resolved the address, it doesn't resolve it again—or at least, in most operating systems, it won't. It will cache it. This means one session equals one Web server. This isn't bad in itself. It isn't true load balancing, though, in that you could easily end up with a situation in which one Web server has to take the brunt of a truly intensive single session, whereas the other two servers sit there doing nothing.

A better approach is for every single request to be assigned to a different server; either in a round-robin fashion (that is, first server A, then B, then C, then back to A, then B . . .) or by using more sophisticated techniques, such as actually analyzing how much traffic each server is handling at any given point.

Unfortunately, the downside of this technique is its further hardware requirement—a *load balancer*. This appliance is responsible for accepting *all* HTTP requests and, instead of responding to them itself, passing them on by proxy to a Web server of its choosing and relaying the response back to the client on the Web server's behalf.

This works incredibly well and means that the full range of servers will be used on any given session, without the client machine's even being aware of it. Such load balancers are, however, often expensive—as much as $20,000 at the time of this writing.

Free alternatives are available, though, and you may wish to experiment with OpenBSD, which can be configured to perform a degree of load balancing in this manner.

If you do deploy multiple Web servers, it's worth adopting a strategy for keeping any disk-based data store they might have in sync. Chapter 24, "Deployment," deals with such a strategy in more detail.

Using Multiple Database Servers

Deploying multiple database servers seems like an obvious idea, at first. Not only can you configure your Web servers to use more than one source for their data, you also eliminate a single point of failure. Should one database server go down, your Web site stays up.

The problem, however, is that databases are not a read-only device, as are Web servers. Requests made to them are frequently to update, delete, or insert data, not just query it.

All is not lost, however. As long as whatever appliance you are using is "conscious" of this fact and can examine each request to determine whether it is a read or a write, load-balancing database servers can indeed be achieved.

This packet examination is crucial, however; a write request must be relayed to all servers, not just one. Should any server be unable to receive that write request, it must be buffered and replayed to that server as soon as it comes back online, lest each server's database get out of sync.

Bigger-name databases such as Oracle and SQL Server have had a solution for some years now. Thankfully, PostgreSQL and MySQL have caught up, too. Getting replication set up is a huge topic, but these Web sites have the detail you need: `http://gborg.postgresql.org/project/slony1/projdisplay.php` for PostgreSQL, and `http://dev.mysql.com/doc/mysql/en/Replication.html` for MySQL.

Network

Hooking all this equipment up might seem to be the simple part, but a bit of planning in this department can save you grief and heartache later.

Consider the traffic going across each interface and try to plan around that; for example, a database-heavy Web application will have enormous amounts of traffic going to and from the database server, traffic that is completely unrelated to the Web request being made by the client Web browser. With this in mind, you may wish to consider having a separate interface on each Web server linking into the database server.

Such a configuration is common; you have a core switch into which all your Web servers link and into which your firewall's internal interface will link, too. Your database switch is linked to the secondary NIC of each Web server and to the NIC of each database server you use.

As a result, traffic between Web servers and database servers doesn't interfere with true Web traffic—a performance increase. If you are using a high-end switch, you can even use a VLAN to separate, say, all 24 ports into two virtual switches of 12 ports each—one for the Web servers and firewall; one for the database servers and secondary Web server NICs.

A side-effect of this configuration is yet another layer of protection for your databases; with no exposed interface to the Internet, they are yet another step away from being compromised.

Redundant Storage

Having redundant Web servers and database servers in place is a good idea to ensure a high-availability application. But using redundancy in other areas can actually prevent the loss of data—perhaps even more important from a commercial point of view.

With this in mind, if you are given the option when specifying servers, always request a RAID configuration of SCSI disks or, in a pinch, IDE RAID.

Furthermore, do not be tempted to opt for maximum disk space with a RAID 0 stripe. Instead, go for RAID 5, which gives you as much disk space as you have disks, less the capacity of one disk. This gives you redundancy in that if one disk fails, the others should kick in and your server will stay up. Simply take out the faulty disk, replace it, and the RAID controller will bring it up to speed. There's also a big performance increase to be had from using RAID—highly recommended.

RAID is an enormous topic; for further reading, check out `http://www.uni-mainz.de/~neuffer/scsi/what_is_raid.html`.

While the data resilience theme is still in mind, you'd be wisely counseled to devise a coherent backup policy for your database servers and any data directories used by your Web servers. A tape backup is sufficient, but ensure that your data center is briefed to rotate the tapes on a daily basis. Talk to your data center about the various tape rotation services and other backup facilities they can provide, and choose one most appropriate to your project and budget.

Maintenance

Often, your ISP will offer to perform basic maintenance on your servers. It is very much up to you and the relationship with your client as to whether you opt for this or decide to take care of it yourself.

If you do decide to bear the burden, then you should devise a weekly action plan for server maintenance. This should be a list of tasks to perform weekly to ensure that your servers are clean, efficient, and up-to-date. Tasks for your action plan will include:

- Kernel version—is each server running the latest version?
- Apache and PHP versions—is each server running the latest version?
- PHP dependencies—libxml, libxslt, expat—are they all up-to-date?
- Disk space—does each server have enough space on each partition? Are any log files growing out of control and needing trimming? Apache, in particular, will not allow you to exceed 2GB in size for any given log file and will crash quite spectacularly if you do.

Security

Finally, you should include in your systems architecture a coherent plan for securing your entire network against unwanted intruders and attackers.

A firewall is absolutely essential. There is absolutely no excuse whatsoever for directly exposing servers on the Internet, no matter how secure or up-to-date they may be. You are simply asking for trouble.

Opt for an appliance firewall, if possible, rather than simply a Linux or BSD box with firewall software loaded. The less sophisticated its inner workings, the less chance it has to be compromised. A good choice would be one of the Cisco PIX series of firewalls. For a small site, the $300 PIX-501 will be more than adequate.

Don't be tempted to simply enable some kind of on-installation firewall on each server. This is inadequate for proper protection. A separate appliance is required.

One final hint: don't forget to enable outbound Internet access via NAT for your Web servers. If your application needs to send e-mail, your Web servers will need to be able to make outbound SMTP connections on port 25.

Summary

In this chapter, you learned about the importance of a robust systems architecture for your application. With systems architecture defined, , you then went on to learn the right questions to ask of your client to determine, in plain English, their exact requirements.

Next we discussed how to take that information and translate it into justifiable technical decisions. This way, when your project goes live, you won't encounter nasty surprises.

How you present this information is largely up to you. A three- or four-page guide for your client's reference might be enough, or you may wish to incorporate it into your technical specification. The important thing is to do the planning now, well ahead of application development. Load testing later on will ensure that your theories are correct. Better to have slightly wrong predictions now than have no predictions at all.

In the next chapter, following the project management methodologies and design patterns covered so far, we'll use the toolkit components and knowledge acquired so far and put the sales force automation project together, at long last.

Assembling the Sales Force Automation Toolkit

Now that you understand how the technology works, this is your chance to put it together as a cohesive whole. This chapter is about developing software from the ground up, and because it is a small project, you'll be utilizing many of the techniques of eXtreme Programming.

With all the fanfare and drama of starting on a new important project, it's easy to mentally jump ahead and start thinking about how to do stuff when you should be trying your best to consider what should be done.

So put your computer away, forget about your logins, passwords, databases, and just for now you won't need PHP, either. Instead you'll be using a technology that humans have spent the last few millennia refining—paper.

Yes, paper is technology. It's ubiquitous, inexpensive, readable even if wet, requires no batteries unless you're in the dark. The same media type supports both write-only, rewriteable, and color and black and white inks. When paper is cut into small index-sized cards they can be used quite nicely for representing your PHP classes, they are moveable, and they can be mounted on a wall, traded, stapled, clipped, sorted and stored.

In short, your design and development process depends just as much on social interaction, wits, and thousand-year-old technology as it does on computer hardware and software.

Starting the Project: Monday

You arrive at work well rested and happy. Although the Widget World IT Department is busily setting up your computer for your first day of work, fortunately your office-supply closet contains what you need for today's work:

- pens
- 3-x-5 index cards
- 4-x-6 index cards

Bridget, the Widget World Sales force Automation Tool Manager, sits near you and is ready to work with you on your first day.

Bridget mentions that since Edwina, the Widget World Eastern Regional Sales Manager, is in the office today, she has scheduled a meeting. Harold is a salesperson who happens to be working in the office because of conflicts; he will be available for the next two weeks. Wade, the Widget World Accountant, will be there; additionally, he is available for you 100 percent between 9:30 a.m. and lunchtime, every day if needed.

Off to the meeting, and don't forget your cards.

Getting an Earful

At the beginning of the meeting, after everybody has been introduced, you tell them that you're here to collect *stories* of what they'd like from the new system and how they'd like to use it.

Using your thousand-year-old technology of pen and paper, document the stories. Put each one on a separate card and insist that Wendy, Wade, and Edwina all partake in the fun. Of course, they may have questions of what is and is not technically possible, who has to sign off on what, and how the workflow goes.

Keep in mind that each story or feature should be broken down so that each is about the same size. This is probably the hardest part as you the developer is needed to keep everything in perspective. Size is about the amount of effort that it would take you to implement the story.

Determining the correct size as a unit of time for each story is not a trivial task, but try to keep the unit of time somewhere from a minimum of half a day, to a maximum of up to a week or two. Again, each story should be roughly the same size. The story size and time estimates will be used later to help you determine the amount of work you're doing and how to better estimate future tasks.

For instance, if one of the features is "Build a rocket ship," break it down into smaller, more manageable chunks such as "The escape pod should be launched within 10 seconds after the escape hatch is closed."

Your nearly all-day session results in the stories shown below. Although documenting the person who suggested it or insisted on it is not mandatory, a method of doing so is displayed here to give you an idea of how the process is often worked out. Starting with physical forms (Figure 22-1) is often a good starting point as it fits with the current workflow and structure.

- Story 1: Edwina: "We track the sales person's contacts using this faxable form" (Figure 22-1) "which is how we determine where to send them next depending on the feedback. Having access to this information in some sort of electronic format would be great."
- Story 2: Wade: "Collecting all the daily travel expenses and receipts of the salespeople is time consuming and error prone. We'd like to collect them on a weekly basis, subtotaled by day and category."
- Story 3: Harold: "Sometimes I need to explain a certain expense. For instance, I'll put $30.00 under 'postage' for a special FedEx delivery. I'd like a way to add comments at the bottom of the expense report."

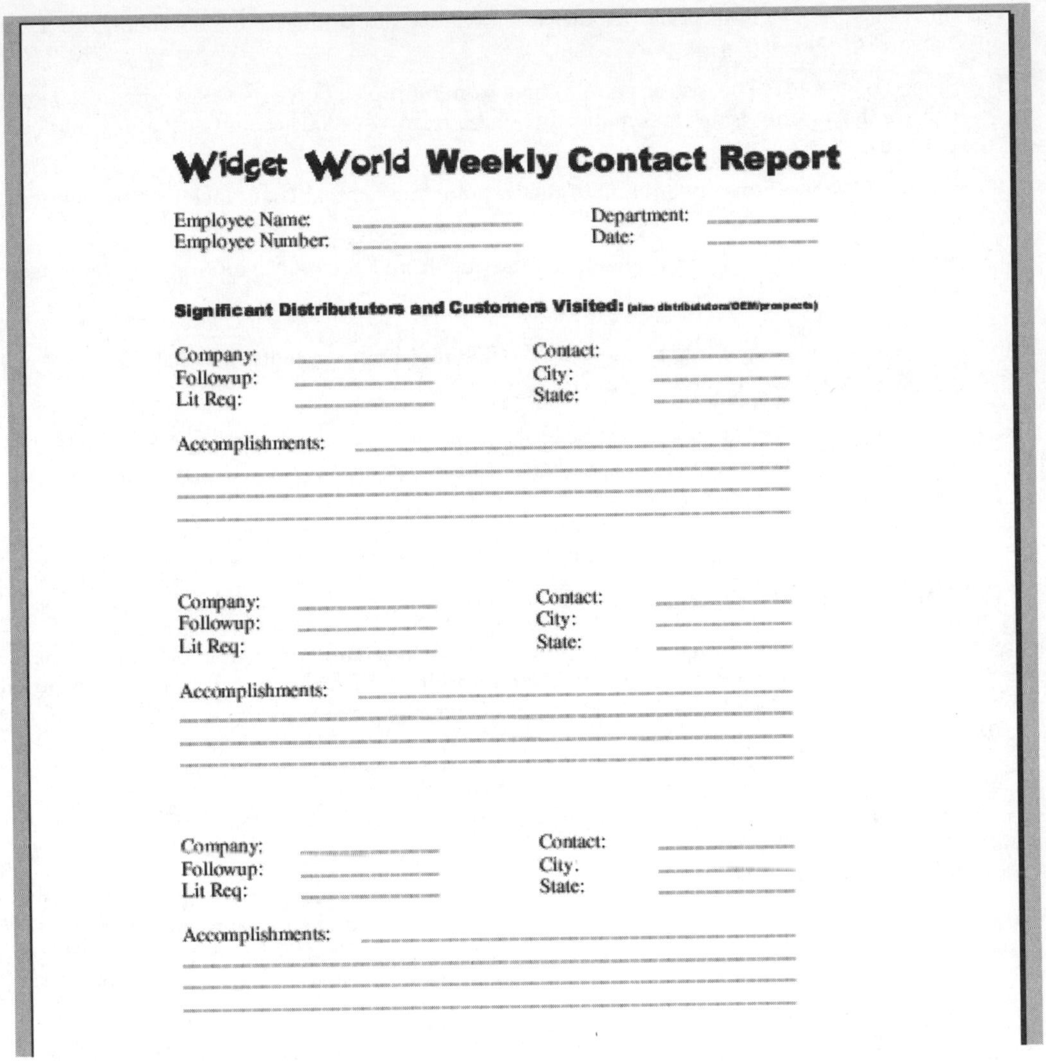

Widget World Weekly Contact Report

Employee Name: ____________ Department: ____________
Employee Number: ____________ Date: ____________

Significant Distribututors and Customers Visited: (also distributors/OEM/prospects)

Company: ____________ Contact: ____________
Followup: ____________ City: ____________
Lit Req: ____________ State: ____________

Accomplishments: ____________

Company: ____________ Contact: ____________
Followup: ____________ City: ____________
Lit Req: ____________ State: ____________

Accomplishments: ____________

Company: ____________ Contact: ____________
Followup: ____________ City: ____________
Lit Req: ____________ State: ____________

Accomplishments: ____________

Figure 22-1

- Story 4: Wade and Harold: "The expense report should subtotal the items in a manner similar to a spreadsheet."
- Story 5: Wade: "I'd like to be notified (with a summary) when an expense report is submitted."
- Story 6: Edwina: "I'd like to be notified (with a summary) when a contact report is submitted."
- Story 7: Harold: "I'd like each salesperson to receive the same notifications, just so they have the option of double-checking."
- Story 8: Edwina: "The mailroom needs to be notified when a contact report contains a literature request."
- Story 9: Edwina and Harold: "Each salesperson needs to have his or her own private login."

- Story 10: Wade: "I don't authorize the cash advances but still need to track them; add 'Less Cash Advance' to the expense report."
- Story 11: Harold: "The cash advances come from multiple sources, so allow the salespeople to control the amount (don't automatically debit it from a special account; just allow it to be entered in the expense report)."
- Story 12: Wade: "Store the amount of the cash-advance so that I can track the total amount per salesperson."
- Story 13: Wade: "I'd like to be able to get the data from the expense reports in order to feed it into my special spreadsheets."

At this point you have a plan for implementing the first revision of the software that Widget World needs in order for its sales force to be more productive.

This should round out your first day at work. The client stories that you collected today are the seeds of a plan that is based on the needs of your clients. Of course, you're not going to start writing the software yet, because your plan is not yet complete.

Story Weight Estimation

Now that your story sizes are roughly in the same ballpark in relation to each other, you sit down and try to estimate how much effort it will take to implement each one. This is done by assigning a numerical value to each of your stories. A simple project might have only three values:

- 1 light
- 2 medium
- 3 heavy

Another option is to take a stab at guessing the relative weight of each story implementation by the number of perfect-engineering time units that it would take to implement the story. A *perfect-engineering time unit* is the number of hours, days, or weeks that you envision a task taking if absolutely nothing goes wrong and your performance is stellar.

For instance, take Story 9: "Each sales person needs to have his or her own private login." Think about it for a moment: Private login means that you shouldn't be dependent on something like Apache's built-in security, but it could run the gambit from PHP Sessions to URL rewriting, to something in between the two. But let's face it: Sessions are not that hard to do correctly if done early, so if you were using the simple point scale it would be rated as a "1 light." If your points are based on "perfect engineering half-days," it would probably still be rated as a "1." However, if your points are based on "perfect engineering weeks" and the particular story would be complete in a matter of hours, it's an indication that this particular story needs to be more uniform in size with your other stories, which are presumably based on "perfect engineering weeks" rather than days or half-days.

Walk through a couple more of them:

- Story 13: "I'd like to be able to get the data from the expense reports in order to feed it into my special spreadsheets."

So, Wade needs access to the expense-report data in a format that is importable by spreadsheet software.

Assuming that the point-system is "perfect engineering half-days," remember that "perfect" here has some liberal but not absolutely perfect presuppositions. For instance, this story was submitted by Wade, the Widget World accountant, and it may very well apply only to his role as an accountant. This means that in addition to using a login screen you'll need to classify the users of the system into Wade/not-Wade, or better yet, accountant/user. Write that information directly on the card.

Spreadsheets can readily import data from files using comma-separated values (CSV files), which technically isn't challenging because it's simply a different view of the dataset.

So, adding user classification system and outputting a dataset as CSV would probably collectively rate at about one perfect engineering day, or in your system of perfect engineering half-days, 2 points.

Take a look at Story 5: "Wade needs to be notified (with a summary) when an expense report is submitted."

This is directly dependent upon the expense report described in story 2: "Collecting all the travel expenses and receipts. . . ." Write that dependency on the card and estimate the story as being "slightly easier than story 2" and estimate the value after estimating story 2.

Story 6: "Edwina needs to be notified (with a summary) when a contact report is submitted." Note that the functionality is similar to that of Story 5, so write it on each card.

Now go through each one, estimating how long it will take, writing required features on each and noting dependencies between them. Feel free to break stories up if they are too big and conversely consolidate them if they are too small.

Here is the list you now have:

- ❑ Story 1: "Track the sales person's contacts using this faxable form."
- ❑ Basic employee information (1 point)
- ❑ Each distributor/customer can be unique
- ❑ One-to-many relationship between salesperson and customer (1 point)

Putting it all together, making sure that the Web form works and so on, would be another points for a total of 3 points or two perfect-engineering days.

- ❑ Story 2: "Collect the daily travel expenses and receipts of each sales person on a weekly basis, subtotaled by day and category."
  - ❑ This is the Travel Expense Report
  - ❑ One-to-many relationship between salesperson and customer
  - ❑ Wade says it should look sort of like a spreadsheet; this is a nontrivial matter: 4 points
  - ❑ Broken down by category: 1 point
  - ❑ Getting everything right: 2 points

  7 points total.

- ❑ Story 3: "Comments at the bottom of the expense report."
    - ❑ Should probably be rolled into Story 2.
    - ❑ Oh no, that makes the relationship more interesting, rather than just being employee to daily expense, we're now charged with employee to daily expense and employee to weekly comments of daily expenses. See Figure 22-2.
    - ❑ Keep as separate story but is dependent upon Story 2.

sales person					Week starting: 5 Jan 2004		
	sun	mon	tue	wed	thr	fri	sat
breakfast	1						
lunch	2						
dinner	3						
sub total	6						
Sales person comments: Blah blah...							

Figure 22-2

2 points total

- ❑ Story 4: "The expense report should subtotal the items in a manner similar to a spreadsheet."
    - ❑ Although just front-end work, it'll be time-consuming

4 points

- ❑ Story 5: "Notify accountant (with a summary) when an expense report is submitted."
    - ❑ via e-mail
    - ❑ e-mail configuration, management, and so on: 1 point
    - ❑ actual work: 1 point
    - ❑ dependent upon Story 2.

2 points total

- ❑ Story 6: "Notify sales-manager (with a summary) when a contact report is submitted."
    - ❑ each sales-manager has multiple sales people
    - ❑ one-to-many relationship: 2 points
    - ❑ dependent upon Story 5 but easy: 1 point

3 points total

- ❑ Story 7: "Notify sales-people with expense-report details."
    - ❑ if dependent upon Story 2: 2 points
    - ❑ if dependent upon Story 5: 1 point
- ❑ Story 8: "The mailroom needs to be notified when a contact report contains a literature request."
    - ❑ Conditional notification: 1 point

- ❑ If dependent upon Story 2 or Story 5, 1 or 2 points

  2 or 3 total points

- ❑ Story 9: "Each sales person needs to have his or her own private login."
  - ❑ Authentication: 2 points
  - ❑ Authorization: 2 points

  4 points total

- ❑ Story 10: "Add 'Less Cash Advance' to the expense report."
  - ❑ Same problem as Story 3 (comments on expense report)
  - ❑ Dependent on Story 2
  - ❑ Not debited, no account tracking needed
  - ❑ Persisted not calculated

  2 points total

- ❑ Story 11: "Allow the salespeople to control the amount of cash advances (don't automatically debit it from a special account; just allow it to be entered in the expense report)."
  - ❑ Dependent on Story 10.
  - ❑ This story is not really a story; it is a critique of the current system; remove this story and add note: "not debited" on Story 10.

  0 points

- ❑ Story 12: "Store the amount of the cash advance so that I can track the total amount per salesperson."
  - ❑ Dependent on Story 10.
  - ❑ This story is trivial; add note: persisted

  0 points

- ❑ Story 13: "Export expense report data for spreadsheets."
  - ❑ Accountant only: 1 point
  - ❑ Work, 2 points

  3 points total

You've now broken the stories down and made your first pass at estimation. This step may take several iterations and require going back to ask the clients such questions as:

- ❑ Can the notifications be done utilizing e-mail?
- ❑ Are there three types of users: managers, salespeople, and accountants?
- ❑ Can the accountant accept CSV for the expense report export?
- ❑ How does the accountant want to specify the export? It could be done by employee, by employee and date, or something different such as by salesmanager.

After you've had the questions answered, however, you still aren't out of the woods. After all, you don't actually know whether the system supports outgoing e-mail, and even if it does, do you know how to do it in PHP?

Refining Your Estimation

Talk with your clients and get the answers to your new questions. It's important that they be available because you don't want these issues to hold up your work. Also, each of your clients (Wendy your project manager, Wade the accountant, Edwina the sales manager, and Harold the salesperson) will be using the system in some respect, so it's really their project and you're the one who makes it go.

Meanwhile, your client questions have been answered:

Q: "Can the notifications be done utilizing e-mail?"

A: Yes, and any summaries associated with the e-mail should be included as attachments.

Q: "Are there indeed three types of users: managers, salespeople, and accountants?"

A: Yes.

Q: "Can the accountant accept CSV for the expense report export?"

A: Yes, he does it all the time.

Q: "How does the accountant want to specify the export: by employee, by employee and date, or by something different, such as sales manager?"

A: Just by employees and date.

So now you're left with only the technical questions:

Q: How do you e-mail something using PHP?

Q: What about e-mail attachments?

The Spike

Your clients do not have the technical answers to your technical questions; that's your area. In this case you don't have enough information to to give a complete estimate.

It's time to do some homework, called a *spike*. Although the work may seem tangential, it is required in order to find out whether your line of thought will pay off or, in this case, answer a technical question.

Set aside some time to determine the *if* or *how* questions that invariably show up. These things may take some time, possibly a day or two, but in this case the answer is arrived at in short order. A walk through the PHP API shows us:

```
mail("wade@widgetworld.com", "Email Spike Test", "One\nTwo\nThree");
```

So yes, PHP can send e-mail in an easy fashion, so you need to test it or talk to the admin in order to get it working.

Now, as for e-mail attachments—those are not so easy. PHP does not support attaching e-mail as an easy-to-use function, but that's because the MIME e-mail definition is well documented in RFCs such as

RFC 822 (message headers), 2045 (MIME), and 2046 (MIME types). So a lot of reading and a little bit of coding result in this tidbit:

```
$mime_boundary = "<<<--==+X[".md5(time())."]";
$headers .= "MIME-Version: 1.0\r\n";
$headers .= "Content-Type: multipart/mixed;\r\n";
$headers .= " boundary=\"".$mime_boundary."\"";

$message .= "This is a multi-part message in MIME format.\r\n";
$message .= "\r\n";
$message .= "--".$mime_boundary."\r\n";

$message .= "Content-Type: text/plain; charset=\"iso-8859-1\"\r\n";
$message .= "Content-Transfer-Encoding: 7bit\r\n";
$message .= "\r\n";
```

The preceding code adheres to the aforementioned RFCs, which define the MIME mail headers (the lines defined in `$headers`) and the message content before the message is finally put together and passed off to your Message Transfer Agent (MTA). Reading through RFCs can be tortuous work, so be sure to test it on a real mail system, using the same mail clients that your customers use, and get it working without error.

This will have easily burned off at least one point.

Estimation Tips

Now that all your remaining technical questions have been laid to rest, you can confidently go ahead and fill in your story estimates:

- ❑ Story 1: Customer Contact Report, 3 points
- ❑ Story 2: Travel Expense Report, 7 points
- ❑ Story 3: Expense Report Comments, 2 points
- ❑ Story 4: Expense Report as Spreadsheet, 4 points
- ❑ Story 5: Accountant Notification, 3 points
- ❑ Story 6: Sales Manager Notification, 3 points
- ❑ Story 7: Sales Person Notification, 1 point
- ❑ Story 8: Mail Room Notification, 2 points
- ❑ Story 9: Authentication and Authorization, 4 points
- ❑ Story 10: Persisted Expense Report Cash Advance, 2 points
- ❑ Story 11: 0 points
- ❑ Story 12: 0 points
- ❑ Story 13: Expense Report Export, 3 points
- ❑ Total points: 34

Don't fall into the trap of thinking "Oh, 34 points is only 17 perfect engineering days," because the keyword here is "perfect." You'll have meetings to attend, there will be fast and slow days, and you'll have to deal with changes in the plans and many more human and imperfect items.

Plus, this is really only your first estimate; after each story has been completed, you'll write down exactly how much real time it took, and after a week or two your estimates will grow more precise, as will your point-to-time estimates.

But for now, you're happy.

Release Planning

After speaking more with Wendy, Wade, Edwina, and Harold, you realize that the first "release" of this project falls into three distinct segments (you can think of them as buckets). All parties agree that the segments need to be released, roughly in this order:

Customer Contact Report:

- ❑ Story 9: Authentication and Authorization, 4 points
- ❑ Story 1: Customer Contact Report, 3 points
- ❑ Story 6: Sales Manager Notification, 3 points
- ❑ Story 8: Mail Room Notification, 2 points

Travel Expense Report:

- ❑ Story 2: Travel Expense Report, 7 points
- ❑ Story 3: Expense Report Comments, 2 points
- ❑ Story 10: Persisted Expense Report Cash Advance, 2 points
- ❑ Story 4: Expense Report as Spreadsheet, 4 points

Travel Expense Services:

- ❑ Story 5: Accountant Notification, 3 points
- ❑ Story 7: Sales Person Notification, 1 point
- ❑ Story 13: Expense Report Export, 3 points

The decision that they put fourth is that the Customer Contact Report is needed in a more timely manner than the Travel Expense Report. The Customer Contact Report is also a much "simpler" input form with less interaction than the Travel Expense Report, yet the Customer Contact Report would also represent nearly an end-to-end test of the system as a whole.

Each of the buckets in which the stories fall is called an *iteration*, and in this case each one should take no longer than three weeks to complete. For now, this is the overall plan, and the end of each iteration should produce something that your client can use.

So your first goal is to create the Customer Contact Report complete with logins and notifications for the sales people. After you complete the first iteration, you'll see how well your estimates worked out in several respects:

- In relation with each other
- In relation with your original estimates
- In relation with time or your points per week.

The end of each iteration is when you take a step back and measure the progress, get feedback from the client, and adjust the plan in accordance with the evolving needs and goals of your client. Don't sweat it too much; this process is designed to be flexible to the needs of both you and your clients.

In this section you learned how to break your problem space up into user-defined stories and how stories can be created and broken out into more stories or consolidated into fewer stories of roughly the same size. Story estimation is an ongoing process, and feedback such as a tangential spike will help to solve technical issues.

It is important to work with your clients to determine what is most important to them and to give them honest feedback regarding the difficulty of each requested feature. This allows you to make better and more timely estimates and allows your clients the flexibility to see the system in action and to make informed decisions regarding the current state of the system.

Starting the Work

Now you and your clients understand exactly what will be implemented in the first iteration, or the Customer Contact Report:

- Story 9: Authentication and Authorization, 4 points
- Story 1: Customer Contact Report, 3 points
- Story 6: Sales Manager Notification, 3 points
- Story 8: Mail Room Notification, 2 points

Outlining Details of Story 9

"Each sales person needs to have his or her own private login."

This presumes, for one thing, that "salesperson" exists as a logical entity (not necessarily a PHP class, yet) so let's outline its needs.

There exists the need for basic human-readable user information:

```
First Name
Last Name
```

Yes, you *are* a number as well as a name:

```
Employee ID
```

Because the person needs to log in to the system, we'll allow him or her to choose both a login name and password:

```
Login Name
Login Password
```

You also need to know the role in which the person accesses the system. Although a person's role may be related to a job title, titles tend to be ephemeral. In addition, you need to determine only one of three roles: salesperson, accountant, sales manager.

```
Company Role
```

This brings up a good question: Can someone be in more than one role at a time? Can someone both be an accountant and a sales manager? What about a sales person and a sales manager? Wendy answers your question with a "Probably not; Wade and Edwina's responsibilities don't overlap." Popping your head into Wade's tidy cubicle confirms your hypothesis, as does a phone call to Edwina. Roles, therefore, are exclusive.

Because you are taking care of authentication, let's decide how we'd like to use the system.

Writing Tests

Ask yourself a few questions:

- How do you want to log in?
- For what purposeshould the login be used? Simple authenication?
- Who should use the login feature?

You know what the user consists of:

```
Employee ID
First Name
Last Name
Company Role
```

And what is required for authentication:

```
Login Name
Login Password
```

Recall from Chapter 15 the `UserSession` class? This is a plausible situation to use with two yet-to-be-defined classes, `WidgetSession` and `WidgetUser`:

```
<?php

$session = new WidgetSession(); // inherited from UserSession
$session->impress();
```

```
// authentication
$session->login("ed","12345");
if ($session->isLoggedIn() == false) exit;

$user = $session->getUser(); // returns WidgetUser
print $user->first_name;
print $user->last_name;
print $user->email;

// authorization
print $user->role;
print $user->isSalesPerson();
print $user->isSalesManager();
print $user->isAccountant();

?>
```

Keep in mind that the preceding code snippet is only "a plausible scenario." It's not yet a formalized test or running code; it is what exists solely in your mind regarding the use of new classes. When you are happy with this "what if" scenario, you will formalize its use in a test. Let's continue and write some tests!

PhpUnit

The idea here is that you will write the test to simulate the way in which you plan on using the software associated with your current story.

It's called *test-driven development*, and in addition to its development strengths, you end up with a great suite of tests.

> **Testing the application in the same manner in which you will be using it forces you to look at the function or object and nail down the arguments and other elements. This avoids creating functionality that isn't used or is used in the wrong places.**

Far from "tying you down," having a testing suite allows you a great degree of freedom because you know instantly whether you happened to break distant parts of the system by adding new features or modifying existing code.

Here are some new tests that are designed to reflect the common usage scenario, `test.widgetsession.php`:

```
<?php

require_once ("widgetsession.phpm");
require_once ("lib/phpunit/phpunit.php");

class TestWidgetSession extends TestCase
{
    private $_session;
```

```
    function setUp() {
        $dsn = array ('phptype'  => "pgsql",
                      'hostspec' => "localhost",
                      'database' => "widgetworld",
                      'username' => "wuser",
                      'password' => "foobar");
        $this->_session = new WidgetSession($dsn, true);

    }

    function testValidLogin() {
        $this->_session->login("ed","12345");
        $this->assertEquals(true, $this->_session->isLoggedIn());
    }

    function testInvalidLogin() {
        $this->_session->login("ed","54321"); // fail
        $this->assertEquals(false, $this->_session->isLoggedIn());
    }

    function testUser() {
        $user = $this->_session->getUser();
        $this->assertEquals("Lecky-Thompson", $user->last_name);
        $this->assertEquals("Ed", $user->first_name);
        $this->assertEquals("ed@lecky-thompson.com", $user->email);
    }

    function testAuthorization () {
        $user = $this->_session->getUser();
        $this->assertEquals("Sales Person", $user->role);
        $this->assertEquals(true, $user->isSalesPerson());
        $this->assertEquals(false, $user->isSalesManager());
        $this->assertEquals(false, $user->isAccountant());
    }

}

$suite = new TestSuite;
$suite->addTest(new TestWidgetSession("testValidLogin"));
$suite->addTest(new TestWidgetSession("testInvalidLogin"));
$suite->addTest(new TestWidgetSession("testUser"));
$suite->addTest(new TestWidgetSession("testAuthorization"));

$testRunner = new TestRunner();
$testRunner->run( $suite );

?>
```

However, when it is run you get the following error:

```
Class 'WidgetSession' not found in test.widgetsession.php on line 16
```

For now, let's mock up appropriate dummy `WidgetSession` and `WidgetUser` classes so that our tests can at least run. Incorporate the following code at the top of the previous listing:

```
class WidgetSession {
    public function __construct ($one, $two) {}
    public function login() {}
    public function isLoggedIn()      { return null; }
    public function getUser() {
        return new WidgetUser();
    }
}

class WidgetUser {
    public $first_name = "";
    public $last_name = "";
    public $email = "";
    public function isSalesPerson()  { return null; }
    public function isSalesManager() { return null; }
    public function isAccountant()   { return null; }
}
```

Now run the tests again in `test.widgetsession.php`. Here is the corresponding output from PhpUnit:

```
TestWidgetSession - testValidLogin FAIL
TestWidgetSession - testInvalidLogin FAIL
TestWidgetSession - testUser FAIL
TestWidgetSession - testAuthorization FAIL

4 tests run.
9 failures.
0 errors.
Failures

    1. testValidLogin
          true   type:boolean
          null   type:NULL
    2. testInvalidLogin
          false   type:boolean
          null   type:NULL
    3. testUser
          Lecky-Thompson  type:string
          type:string
    4. testUser
          Ed   type:string
          type:string
    5. testUser
          ed@lecky-thompson.com  type:string
          type:string
    6. testAuthorization
          Sales Person  type:string
          type:string
    7. testAuthorization
          true   type:boolean
          null   type:NULL
    8. testAuthorization
          false  type:boolean
          null  type:NULL
```

```
9. testAuthorization
     false   type:boolean
     null   type:NULL
```

At this point of the development process, every one of your tests should run without syntax error, but should be failing. This is because you haven't yet implemented any of the functionality for which the tests are designed! So yes, the first time you run the tests you should be happy that they all fail. Remember that the tests are based on the common usage scenario and that you should be testing all the features required by the scenario.

It is now your responsibility to implement the actual code that is required to pass the tests. The login and session process can be fixed quite easily because that behavior is found in `UserSession`.

Take care of the low-hanging fruit in regard to the `WidgetSession`. Because `WidgetSession` is adding functionality to `UserSession`, it makes sense to extend `UserSession`. So start with your spoofed `WidgetSession` class and extend `UserSession`:

```
class WidgetSession extends UserSession {
    public function getUser() {
        return new WidgetUser();
    }
}
```

Now rerun the `test.widgetsession.php` tests:

```
TestWidgetSession - testValidLogin ok
TestWidgetSession - testInvalidLogin ok
TestWidgetSession - testUser FAIL
TestWidgetSession - testAuthorization FAIL

4 tests run.
7 failures.
0 errors.
```

By utilizing the functionality inherent in `UserSession`, you've already passed half the tests.

Next, start work on the `WidgetUser` objects by first overriding `UserSession`'s `getUserObject()` function to return a `WidgetUser` class:

```
class WidgetSession extends UserSession {

    public function getUserObject() {
        $uid = $this->GetUserID(); // calling up from UserSession
        if ($uid == false) return null;

        // pull ourselves out of the database
        $stmt = "select * FROM \"user\" WHERE id = ".$uid;
        $result = $this->getDatabaseHandle()->query($stmt);
        return new WidgetUser($result->fetchRow());
    }
}
```

Your `WidgetUser` class needs to hold its state. However, the `WidgetUser` class is getting pumped out from a database which can return data in an associative array, so just go ahead and store `WidgetUser`'s state in an associative array.

Of course, `__set` and `__get` both need to be redefined.

```
class WidgetUser {

    protected $contentBase = array();

    function __construct($initdict) {
        $this->contentBase = $initdict; // copy
    }

    function __get ($key) {
        if (array_key_exists ($key, $this->contentBase)) {
            return $this->contentBase[$key];
        }
        return null;
    }

    function __set ($key, $value) {
        if (array_key_exists ($key, $this->contentBase)) {
            $this->contentBase[$key]=$value;
        }
    }

    public function isSalesPerson()  { return null; }
    public function isSalesManager() { return null; }
    public function isAccountant()   { return null; }
}
```

Once again, rerunning `test.widgetsession.php` results in most of the user tests passing, with one notable exception:

```
1. testUser
   ed@lecky-thompson.com   type:string
   null   type:NULL
```

Hmmm, looking closer at the MySQL version of the user table

```
CREATE TABLE "user" (
  id serial PRIMARY KEY,
  username varchar(32) default NULL,
  md5_pw varchar(32) default NULL,
  first_name varchar(64) default NULL,
  last_name varchar(64) default NULL
);
```

reveals that the `user` table is missing e-mail, so you need to add it to make the table look like this:

```
CREATE TABLE "user" (
  id serial PRIMARY KEY,
```

```
    username varchar(32) default NULL,
    md5_pw varchar(32) default NULL,
    first_name varchar(64) default NULL,
    last_name varchar(64) default NULL,
    email varchar(255) default NULL
  );
```

Run the `test.widgetsession.php` tests:

```
TestWidgetSession - testValidLogin ok
TestWidgetSession - testInvalidLogin ok
TestWidgetSession - testUser ok
TestWidgetSession - testAuthorization FAIL

4 tests run.
4 failures.
```

Zero errors.

Now that the `testUser` passes, pay attention to the `testAuthorization`. Because "role" is not included in the database yet, add that as well. The default value of `'s'` is short for "salesperson":

```
CREATE TABLE "user" (
  id serial PRIMARY KEY,
  username varchar(32) default NULL,
  md5_pw varchar(32) default NULL,
  first_name varchar(64) default NULL,
  last_name varchar(64) default NULL,
  email varchar(255) default NULL,
  role char(1) NOT NULL default 's'
);
```

Putting some state-retrieval accessor methods into `WidgetUser` solves most of the remaining issues:

```
public function isSalesPerson()  {
    if ($this->role == "s") return true;
    return false;
}

public function isSalesManager() {
    if ($this->role == "m") return true;
    return false;
}

public function isAccountant()   {
    if ($this->role == "a") return true;
    return false;
}
```

However, the test still fails on "role" because it expects a human-readable string and instead is limited to the single digits of `s`, `m`, and `a`:

```
1. testAuthorization
   Sales Person   type:string
   s   type:string
```

Recall from earlier what is being tested for:

```
function testAuthorization () {
    $user = $this->_session->getUser();
    $this->assertEquals("Sales Person", $user->role);
    $this->assertEquals(true, $user->isSalesPerson());
    $this->assertEquals(false, $user->isSalesManager());
    $this->assertEquals(false, $user->isAccountant());
}
```

Note that because of the nature of the next problem, when `$user->role` is called the expectation is to get "Sales Person." Keep in mind that that role is directly from the database, so either change the database or change your software instead.

How about this idea: Because you'd like to continue to directly access `$user->role` in the `__get` function, you can determine which role is being queried for and dispatch it to a `getRole()` function.

Here it is:

```
class WidgetUser {

    protected $contentBase = array();
    protected $dispatchFunctions = array ("role" => "getrole");

    function __construct($initdict) {
        $this->contentBase = $initdict; // copy
    }

    function __get ($key) {

        // dispatch by function first
        if (array_key_exists ($key, $this->dispatchFunctions)) {
            $funcname = $this->dispatchFunctions[$key];
            return $this->$funcname();
        }

        // otherwise return based on state
        if (array_key_exists ($key, $this->contentBase)) {
            return $this->contentBase[$key];
        }
        return null;

    }

    function __set ($key, $value) {
        if (array_key_exists ($key, $this->contentBase)) {
            $this->contentBase[$key]=$value;
        }
```

```
    }

    public function getRole() {
        switch ($this->contentBase["role"]) {
            case "s": return ("Sales Person");
            case "m": return ("Sales Manager");
            case "a": return ("Accountant");
            default: return ("");
        }
    }

    public function isSalesPerson()   {
        if ($this->contentBase["role"] == "s") return true;
        return false;
    }

    public function isSalesManager() {
        if ($this->contentBase["role"] == "m") return true;
        return false;
    }

    public function isAccountant()    {
        if ($this->contentBase["role"] == "a") return true;
        return false;
    }
}
```

Note that `isSalesPerson()`, `isSalesManager()`, and `isAccountant()` all access `contentBase` rather than call `$this->role`. Otherwise it would get dispatched through the `getRole()` function, which returns human-readable results such as "Sales Manager." It is not a good idea to try to return Boolean values based on human-readable results as they could change at whim.

Creating the login screen

Now that your `WidgetUser` and `WidgetSession` objects are working, it's time to use them with a real login.

Although the login screen is not terribly complicated, you'll continue to use Smarty as the templating system simply for its convenience.

Here's your initial `index.php` file:

```
<?php

require_once ("Smarty.class.php");
require_once ("widgetsession.phpm");

$session = new WidgetSession(array ('phptype'  => "pgsql",
                                    'hostspec' => "localhost",
```

```
                                    'database' => "widgetworld",
                                    'username' => "wuser",
                                    'password' => "foobar"));
$session->Impress();

$smarty = new Smarty;

if ($_REQUEST["action"] == "login") {
    $session->login($_REQUEST["login_name"],$_REQUEST["login_pass"]);
    if ($session->isLoggedIn()) {
        $smarty->assign_by_ref("user", $session->getUserObject());
        $smarty->display ("main.tpl");
        exit;
    } else {
        $smarty->assign('error', "Invalid login, try again.");
        $smarty->display ("login.tpl");
        exit;
    }
} else {
    if ($session->isLoggedIn() == true) {
        $smarty->assign_by_ref("user", $session->getUserObject());
        $smarty->display ("main.tpl");
        exit;
    }
}

$smarty->display ("login.tpl");

?>
```

The logic for the screen is as follows: If the action variable of the form is `login`, it indicates that a login attempt is trying to be made, so an attempt to log in is made by calling `$session->login()`. A positive result is dealt with by rendering the main menu. A negative result causes an error variable to be set, and the login screen again presented to the user.

Of course, if you're not trying to log in, the `$session->isLoggedIn()` is checked to confirm the login status with the session. If the user is logged in, the main menu screen is displayed. Otherwise, the login screen is again redisplayed.

The two screens, `login` and `main`, along with the header and footer, are all simple:

`login.tpl:`

```
{include file="header.tpl" title="Widget World Login"}

<h3>Please Login:</h3>
<p>
{section name=one loop=$error}{sectionelse}
  <font color="#FF0000">{$error}</font><p>
{/section}
```

```
<form action="index.php" method="post">
<table border="0">
<tr><td width="20"></td><td>User:</td>
    <td><input name="login_name" type="text" size="20" maxsize="50"></td></tr>
<tr><td width="20"></td><td>Password:</td>
    <td><input name="login_pass" type="password" size="20"
maxsize="50"></td></tr>
<tr><td width="20"></td><td></td>
    <td><input type="submit" value=" Login "></td></tr>
</table>
<input type="hidden" name="action" value="login">
</form>

{include file="footer.tpl"}
```

header.tpl:

```
<!DOCTYPE HTML PUBLIC "-//W3C//DTD HTML 4.01 Transitional//EN">
<html>
<head>
<meta HTTP-EQUIV="content-type" CONTENT="text/html; charset=ISO-8859-1">
<title>{$title|default:"no title"}</title>
</head>
<h1>Widget World</h1>
<hr><p>
```

footer.tpl:

```
<br/><br/>
<hr/>
For Widget World use only - testing environment.
</body>
</html>
```

main.tpl:

```
{include file="header.tpl" title="Widget World Menu"}

Welcome {$user->first_name} the {$user->role}!

<table border="0" cellspacing="8" cellpadding="8">
{strip}
{section name=security show=$user->isAccountant()}
  <tr><td><h3>Accountant functionality goes here.</h3></td></tr>
{/section}

  <tr><td valign="top"><h3><a href="travel-expenses.php">New Travel
Expenses</a></h3></td></tr>
```

```
  <tr><td valign="top"><h3><a href="customer-contacts.php">New Customer
Contacts</a></h3></td></tr>

{/strip}
</table>

{include file="footer.tpl"}
```

Figure 22-3 shows what this looks like.

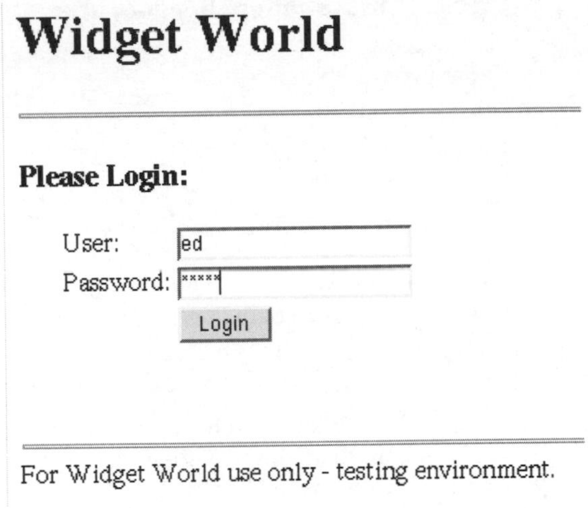

Figure 22-3

After you are logged in, you get the menu shown in Figure 22-4.

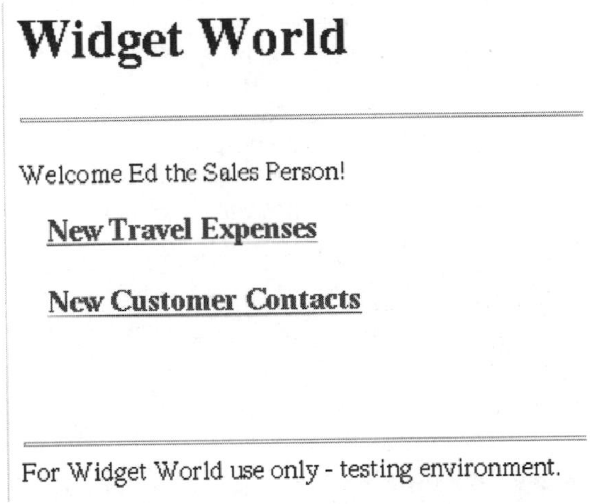

Figure 22-4

If you change ed to be an accountant by changing his role to be a, then ed would have a slightly different view, as displayed in Figure 22-5.

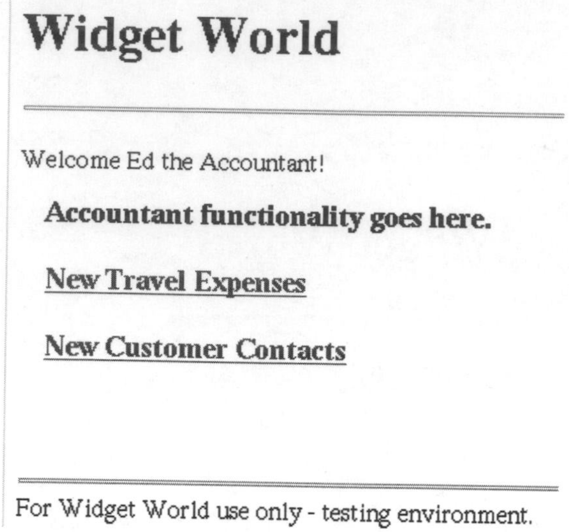

Widget World

Welcome Ed the Accountant!

Accountant functionality goes here.

New Travel Expenses

New Customer Contacts

For Widget World use only - testing environment.

Figure 22-5

Congratulations—your first story is now complete. You have done a lot of work with PHP sessions, database lookups, PEAR::DB, and PhpUnit to accomplish the functionality required to determine who is logging in and what they should be able to do, which is not at all a trivial feat.

Take a nice little break and enjoy munching on a biscuit; there is a lot more work coming up.

The Next Story

Your previous story (Story 9: "Authentication and Authorization") was worth 4 points. Write down how long in days or half days it took you to accomplish this 4-point task.

Recall that this iteration of the Customer Contact Report comprises:

- Story 9: Authentication and Authorization, 4 points (done)
- Story 1: Customer Contact Report, 3 points
- Story 6: Sales Manager Notification, 3 points
- Story 8: Mail Room Notification, 2 points

Time to get back to work.

Customer Contact Requirements

Recall from earlier (refer to Figure 22-1) what the Weekly Contact Report requires. The data requirements for this look something like this:

```
CREATE TABLE contact_visits (
  emp_id integer NOT NULL,
  week_start date NOT NULL,
  seq integer NOT NULL,
  company_name varchar(40) default NULL,
  contact_name varchar(40) default NULL,
  city varchar(40) default NULL,
  state varchar(40) default NULL,
  accomplishments text,
  followup text,
  literature_request text
);
CREATE UNIQUE INDEX cv_pk on contact_visits (emp_id,week_start,seq);
CREATE INDEX cv_emp_id ON contact_visits (emp_id);
CREATE INDEX cv_week_start ON contact_visits (week_start);
CREATE INDEX cv_seq ON contact_visits (seq);
```

The data is per week, is associated with the employee, and is unique when completed with the SEQuence column; there may be a lot.

Note that `state` is 40 chars long in order to accommodate non-U.S. states and provinces in Canada and Mexico.

Also note that the customer contact report has the employee's department that currently doesn't exist in the `USER` table. Go ahead and add it:

```
CREATE TABLE "user" (
  id serial PRIMARY KEY,
  username varchar(32) default NULL,
  md5_pw varchar(32) default NULL,
  first_name varchar(64) default NULL,
  last_name varchar(64) default NULL,
  email varchar(255) default NULL,
  role char(1) NOT NULL default 's',
  department varchar(40) NOT NULL default ''
);
```

Customer Contact Tests

Think about how you intend to use the customer contacts. From this input screen, nearly all the form data is provided to you via the Web server, which means that when you prepare to persist it you'll need the employee ID available from `WidgetSession`.

Also consider what minimum information you'll require before dumping into the table: `id`, `week_start`, and `sequence` with this PhpUnit test.

```
function testValidContactVisit() {
    $cv = new ContactVisit (
        array ('emp_id'             => "1",
               'seq'                => "1",
               'week_start'         => "1980-01-01",
               'company_name'       => "test one",
```

```
                    'contact_name'          => "Big One",
                    'city'                  => "Columbus",
                    'state'                 => "OH",
                    'accomplishments'       => "phone call",
                    'followup'              => "",
                    'literature_request' => ""));
        $this->assertEquals(true, $cv->isValid(), "valid log");
    }
```

This testing is the minimum information required by `ContactVisit`, thus if `emp_id`, `seq`, and `week_start` contain any values then `isValid()` will return true. Conversely, the opposite should also be tested:

```
    function testInvalidContactVisit() {
        $cv = new ContactVisit (
            array ('emp_id'                => "1",
                    'week_start'            => "", // date required
                    'company_name'          => "test one",
                    'contact_name'          => "Big One",
                    'city'                  => "Columbus",
                    'state'                 => "OH",
                    'accomplishments'       => "phone call",
                    'followup'              => "",
                    'literature_request' => ""));
        $this->assertEquals(false, $cv->isValid(), "invalid visit");
    }
```

Because the visits each require a unique sequence value, they might as well determine their order themselves:

```
    function testSequence() {
        $cv1 = new ContactVisit(array());
        $this->assertEquals(1, $cv1->seq);
        $cv2 = new ContactVisit(array());
        $this->assertEquals(2, $cv2->seq);
    }
```

Note that by creating `ContactVisits`, the sequence (`seq`) of each new `ContactVisit` is automatically incremented, which eliminates the need to require the container to assign each a unique sequence number.

Persistence is still in a state of flux, but this will certainly work:

```
        function testPersistence() {
            $this->_session->getDatabaseHandle()->query("delete FROM contact_visits
    WHERE emp_id = 1 and week_start = '1980-01-01'"); // remove multiples
            $cv = new ContactVisit (
                array ('emp_id'                => "1",
                        'week_start'            => "1980-01-01",
                        'seq'                   => 1,
                        'company_name'          => "test one",
                        'contact_name'          => "Big One",
                        'city'                  => "Columbus",
```

```
                    'state'                 => "OH",
                    'accomplishments'       => "phone call",
                    'followup'              => "",
                    'literature_request' => ""));
        $result = $this->_session->getDatabaseHandle()->query("select * FROM
contact_visits WHERE emp_id = 1 and week_start = '1980-01-01'");
        $this->assertEquals(0, $result->numRows());
        $cv->persist();
        $result = $this->_session->getDatabaseHandle()->query("select * FROM
contact_visits WHERE emp_id = 1 and week_start = '1980-01-01'");
        $this->assertEquals(1, $result->numRows());
    }
```

Also note that `week_start`'s value of New Year's day, 1980, was chosen for a reason:

- It is not the start of a normal week, which for Americans is normally Sunday.
- It stands out in your head, so if something goes horribly wrong and it ends up in the production database, it's easily recognized as not being a real contact.

Before running the tests, don't forget to stub out `ContactVisit` to make sure that the tests successfully FAIL (yet syntactically execute) before correctly satisfying the tests. Here are the contents of `contact.phpm`:

```
class ContactVisit {

    function __construct ($results) { }

    public function isValid() { return null; }
    public function persist() { }
    public function getSequence() { return null; }
}
```

Satisifying the Tests

Because the visits are going to be in sequence, utilize a static variable so that the sequence count is shared across all instances of the class. Incrementing it in the constructor also ensures that all your bases are covered without requiring any more plumbing. Go ahead and implement the constructor of `ContactVisit` in `contact.phpm`:

```
class ContactVisit {

    function __construct ($results, $dbh = null) {
        static $sequence = 0;
        $this->dbh = $dbh;
        $this->contentBase = $results; // copy
        $sequence = $sequence + 1; // increment across class
        $this->contentBase["seq"] = $sequence;
    }
```

```
    public function isValid() { return null; }
    public function persist() { }
    public function getSequence() { return null; }
}
```

Also note that `ContactVisit` needs to store a reference to the database; this is in addition to the normal data (company name, city, state, and so on) so return `ContactVisit`'s state in the last `return` of `ContactVisit`'s `__get()` function. Here it is in `contact.phpm`:

```
function __get ($key) {
    if (array_key_exists ($key, $this->contentBase)) {
        return $this->contentBase[$key];
    }
    return $this->$key;
}
```

Put it all together, add some functions for generating its required SQL, and you're set. The file `contact.phpm` follows:

```
class ContactVisit {

    protected $contentBase = array();
    protected $dbh = null; // database handle

    function __get ($key) {
        if (array_key_exists ($key, $this->contentBase)) {
            return $this->contentBase[$key];
        }
        return $this->$key;
    }

    function __construct ($results, $dbh = null) {
        static $sequence = 0;
        $this->dbh = $dbh;
        $this->contentBase = $results; // copy
        $sequence = $sequence + 1; // increment across class
        $this->contentBase["seq"] = $sequence;
    }

    private function isEmpty($key) {
        if (array_key_exists($key, $this->contentBase) == false) return true;
        if ($this->contentBase[$key] == null) return true;
        if ($this->contentBase[$key] == "") return true;
        return false;
    }

    public function isValid() {
        if ($this->isEmpty("emp_id") == true) return false;
        if ($this->isEmpty("week_start") == true) return false;
        if ($this->isEmpty("company_name") == true) return false;
        return true;
    }
```

```
    private function implodeQuoted (&$values, $delimiter) {
        $sql = "";
        $flagIsFirst = true;
        foreach ($values as $value) {
            if ($flagIsFirst) {
                $flagIsFirst = false;
            } else {
                $sql .= $delimiter;
            }

            if (gettype ($value) == "string") {
                $sql .= "'".$value."'";
            } else {
                $sql .= $value;
            }
        }
        return $sql;
    }

    private function generateSqlInsert ($tableName, &$metas, &$values) {
        return "insert into ".$tableName.
            "        ( ".implode              ($metas,  ", ")." ) ".
            " values ( ".$this->implodeQuoted ($values, ", ")." ) ";
    }

    public function persist() {
        if ($this->isValid() == false) return false;
        $sql = $this->generateSqlInsert ("contact_visits",
                                         array ( "emp_id",
                                                 "week_start",
                                                 "seq",
                                                 "company_name",
                                                 "contact_name",
                                                 "city",
                                                 "state",
                                                 "accomplishments",
                                                 "followup",
                                                 "literature_request" ),
                                         array ( $this->emp_id,
                                                 $this->week_start,
                                                 $this->seq,
                                                 $this->company_name,
                                                 $this->contact_name,
                                                 $this->city,
                                                 $this->state,
                                                 $this->accomplishments,
                                                 $this->followup,
                                                 $this->literature_request ));

        if (DB::isError ($this->dbh->query($sql))) return false;
        return true;
    }
}
```

Briefly, the methods implemented are as follows:

- `isValid()` satisfies both of your validity tests. `isValid()` relies upon `isEmpty()`, which is simply a convenience function.
- `persist()` satisfies your persistence test. `persist()` calls `generateSqlInsert()`, which generates a SQL `INSERT` statement based on the table name, table meta-information, and the values you'd like to insert. `generateSqlInsert()` in turn calls `implodeQuoted()`, which adds SQL quotes to values that are strings.

It may be noted that `implodeQuoted()` and `generateSqlInsert()` both insist that the arrays are passed by reference rather than by value. Of course, the default behavior of PHP5 is to pass objects by reference, but arrays are passed by value in the default case.

Creating the Screen

Consider this form, called `customer-contacts.tpl`:

```
{include file="header.tpl" title="Widget World - Customer Contact"}

<h3>Customer Contact Report</h3>

<form action="customer-contacts.php" method="post">
<table border="0" width="100%">
<tr><td><b>Employee Name:</b></td><td>{$user->first_name}
{$user->last_name}</td>
<td><b>Department:</b></td><td>{$user->department}</td></tr>
<tr><td><b>Number:</b></td><td>{$user->id}</td><td><b>Start Week:</b></td>
<td><SELECT NAME="week_start">{html_options values=$start_weeks
output=$start_weeks selected=$current_start_week}</SELECT></td></tr>
</table>

<br><br><hr>

<p><font size="+1"><b>Significant Distributors and Customers
Visited:</b></font><br>
(also distributors/OEM/prospects)<p>
<table border="0">
{section name=idx loop=$max_weekly_contacts}{strip}
<tr><td
width="20"></td><td><b>Company</b></td><td><b>Contact</b></td><td><b>City</b>
</td><td><b>State</b></td><td><b>FollowUp</b></td><td><b>Literature
Request</b></td></tr>
<tr>
<td width="20"></td>
<td><input name="company_name_{$smarty.section.idx.index}"        size="20"
maxlength="50"></td>
<td><input name="contact_name_{$smarty.section.idx.index}"        size="20"
maxlength="50"></td>
<td><input name="city_{$smarty.section.idx.index}"                size="20"
maxlength="50"></td>
<td><input name="state_{$smarty.section.idx.index}"               size="10"
maxlength="50"></td>
```

```
<td><input name="followup_{$smarty.section.idx.index}"          size="20"
maxlength="2000"></td>
<td><input name="literature_request_{$smarty.section.idx.index}" size="20"
maxlength="2000"></td>
</tr>
<tr>
<td width="20"></td>
<td colspan="7"><b>Accomplishments:</b></td>
</tr>
<tr>
<td width="20"></td>
<td colspan="7"><TEXTAREA NAME="accomplishments_{$smarty.section.idx.index}"
ROWS=4 COLS=95></TEXTAREA><br><br>
</td>
</tr>

{/strip}{/section}

</table>

<br><hr>

<input type="hidden" name="action" value="persist_contact">
<br><br>

<center>
<input type="submit" name="submit" value=" Save " onclick="return
checkInputs(this.form);">
</center>

</form>

{include file="footer.tpl"}
```

Note that the main loop, `{section name=idx loop=$max_weekly_contacts}`, iterates and creates unique names of inputs: `company_name_{$smarty.section.idx.index}`, which are then operated on.

Smarty offers the handy feature of populating drop-down boxes based on an array of dates for the current week:

```
<SELECT NAME="week_start">{html_options values=$start_weeks output=$start_weeks
selected=$current_start_week}</SELECT>
```

You may have noticed that the input screen is rather Spartan in appearance because it uses regular HTML rather than something stricter with better cross-platform browser compatibility such as XHTML and CSS. This is because at this point in the process you're more interested in getting the system to work, because the definition may change slightly in the near future. Later in the process, the display can be spruced up.

Feeding the Beast

Even though `ContactVisits` know how to persist themselves, it takes a surprising amount of work to gather together several weeks' worth of drop-down information and then save all contacts to the database. Here is the required functionality, simply placed in functions in `customer-contacts.php`:

```
<?php

require_once ("Smarty.class.php");
require_once ("widgetsession.phpm");

$session = new WidgetSession(array ('phptype'  => "pgsql",
                                    'hostspec' => "localhost",
                                    'database' => "widgetworld",
                                    'username' => "uwuser",
                                    'password' => "foobar"));
$session->Impress();

$smarty = new Smarty;

$GLOBALS["max-weekly-contacts"] = 5;

function getStartDateOffset ($i) {
    if ($i < 0) $i = 5;
    $dates = array("Sunday" => 0, "Monday" => -1, "Tuesday" => -2,
"Wednesday" => -3, "Thursday" => -4, "Friday" => -5, "Saturday" => -6);
    return date("Y-m-d", mktime (0,0,0,date("m"), date("d")+$dates[date("l")]-
(($i-5)*7),date("Y")));
}

function getCurrentStartWeek () {
    if (strlen($_REQUEST["week_start"]) >= 8) return $_REQUEST["week_start"];
    return getStartDateOffset(-1); // this sunday
}

function getStartWeeks () {
    $sudayArray = array();
    for ($i=20; $i > 0; $i--) {
        array_push($sudayArray, getStartDateOffset($i));
    }
    return ($sudayArray);
}

function persistContactVisits (&$dbh, $emp_id) {
    $dbh->query("delete from contact_visits where emp_id = ".$emp_id." and
week_start = '".getCurrentStartWeek()."'");
    $seq = 0;
    for ($i = 0; $i < $GLOBALS["max-weekly-contacts"]; $i++) {
        $cv = new ContactVisit (
            array ("emp_id"              => $emp_id,
                   "week_start"          => getCurrentStartWeek(),
                   "company_name"        => $_REQUEST["company_name_".$i],
                   "contact_name"        => $_REQUEST["contact_name_".$i],
                   "city"                => $_REQUEST["city_".$i],
                   "state"               => $_REQUEST["state_".$i],
                   "accomplishments"     => $_REQUEST["accomplishments_".$i],
                   "followup"            => $_REQUEST["followup_".$i],
```

```
                "literature_request"=> $_REQUEST["literature_request_".$i]),
            $dbh);
        $cv->persist();
    }
}

$user = $session->getUserObject();

// display
if ($_REQUEST["action"] != "persist_contact") {
    $smarty->assign_by_ref ("user", $user);
    $smarty->assign('start_weeks', getStartWeeks());
    $smarty->assign('current_start_week', getCurrentStartWeek());
    $smarty->assign("max_weekly_contacts", $GLOBALS["max-weekly-contacts"]);
    $smarty->display('customer-contacts.tpl');
    exit();
}

// persist contact visits
require_once ("contact.phpm");
persistContactVisits ($session->getDatabaseHandle(), $user->id);

$smarty->display('thankyou.tpl');
?>
```

The interesting features of this begin with `getStartDateOffset()`, which populates the date drop-down by returning the day of the start week based on an integer offset passed in.

```
function getStartDateOffset ($i) {
    if ($i < 0) $i = 5;
    $dates = array("Sunday" => 0, "Monday" => -1, "Tuesday" => -2,
"Wednesday" => -3, "Thursday" => -4, "Friday" => -5, "Saturday" => -6);
    return date("Y-m-d", mktime (0,0,0,date("m"), date("d")+$dates[date("l")]
(($i-5)*7),date("Y")));
}
```

It works by associating the weekday (say, "Tuesday"), retrieved by the use of `date("l")` to access the `$dates` array, which gets you an integer representing the number of days away from the target day of Sunday. When you know the date of the closest Sunday, the Sunday + week offset is calculated by multiplying the closest Sunday date by 7 and then adding those days to the current Sunday. Thus, regardless of the current day of the week, a Sunday +/– `$i` weeks is returned.

But because `getStartWeeks()` returns an array of 20 Sundays by counting from 20 to 0, `getStarteDateOffset()` also automatically adds 5 weeks to the default. This results in the week drop-down selection box's having 15 past weeks, the current Sunday and 4 weeks in the future.

The heavy lifting is done by `persistContactVisits()`, which removes the old contacts, creates new `ContactVisits`, and calls `persist()` on each one in order to save the results in the database.

Figure 22-6 shows the features in action.

So now, with two stories under your belt, you can take a decadent 10-minute break before heading off to get Wendy, Wade, Edwina, and Harold using the application. You'll need the rest.

Widget World

Customer Contact Report

Employee Name: Ed Lecky-Thompson
Number: 1
Department: sales
Start Week: 2004-06-13

2004-02-29
2004-03-07
2004-03-14
2004-03-21
2004-03-28
2004-04-04
2004-04-11
2004-04-18
2004-04-25
2004-05-02
2004-05-09
2004-05-16
2004-05-23
2004-05-30
2004-06-06
2004-06-13
2004-06-20
2004-06-27
2004-07-04
2004-07-11

Significant Distributors and Customers Visited:
(also distributors/OEM/prospects)

Company Contact City State FollowUp Lite… …st

Accomplishments:

Company Contact City State FollowUp Literature Request

Accomplishments:

Figure 22-6

Re-Estimation

The good news is that Wendy, Wade, Harold, and Edwina love the application. But keep in mind that they are human and have brought up some quite reasonable requests:

- Include a Logout button.
- Don't allow access to `customer-contacts.php` without first logging in.
- Changing the week should bring up a previously saved week.
- In the Customer Contact screen, also track the following: Number of Shop Calls, Number of Engineer Calls, Number of Distributor Calls, Approximate Mileage, Territory Worked, Territory Comments on a PER WEEK basis.
- The number of contacts may occasionally change; can that be configurable?

Doing some quick estimations, you figure the new tasks as:

- Include a logout button. (1/2 point)
- Don't allow access to `customer-contacts.php` without first logging in. (bug, 1/2 point)

- ❑ Changing the week should bring up a previously saved week. (1 point)
- ❑ In the Customer Contact screen, also track: Number of Shop Calls, Number of Engineer Calls, Number of Distributor Calls, Approximate Mileage, Territory Worked, Territory Comments on a PER WEEK basis. (1 point)
- ❑ The number of contacts may occasionally change; can that be configurable? (1/2 point)

The original plan:

- ❑ Story 9: Authentication and Authorization, 4 points (done)
- ❑ Story 1: Customer Contact Report, 3 points (done-ish)
- ❑ Story 6: Sales Manager Notification, 3 points
- ❑ Story 8: Mail Room Notification, 2 points

Considering that the half-pointers don't really count but the new ones do, you discuss it with your clients and determine that they'd like prefer it in this order:

- ❑ Story 9: Authentication and Authorization, 4 points (done)
- ❑ Story 1: Customer Contact Report, 3 points (done-ish)
- ❑ Story 14: Changing the week recalls a previous week. (new)
- ❑ Story 15: Per-week items on the customer contact report. (new)

They'd also prefer to get the spreadsheet in the next iteration before requiring the notifications, so these can be dropped for now:

- ❑ Story 6: Sales Manager Notification, 3 points
- ❑ Story 8: Mail Room Notification, 2 points

Now back to work.

Cleaning Up

Before taking off and completing your new stories, consider the state of your current corpus of code.

Yes, some bits are a ugly, but it's completely functional. Some bits are obviously copied and pasted from other places, but it works. It does, however, come with a great testing suite.

Don't knock yourself for a few warts on a fully tested working product. It happens and it's called "code debt." Just as in real life, when you're in a hurry or circumstances require, you can go beyond your means monetarily by going into debt.

Now that you have a bit of time to clean things up, it's time to work off the debt. It's easy and is best if you follow good development guidelines as you code in order to be as productive as you can without going into debt.

What is this referring to? Take a look at your current working files:

```
index.php
customer-contacts.php
contact.phpm
test.contact.php
widgetsession.phpm
test.widgetsession.php
templates/customer-contacts.tpl
templates/footer.tpl
templates/header.tpl
templates/login.tpl
templates/main.tpl
templates/thankyou.tpl
```

. . .and think: "Are all these files required to be in the root directory?" How about if you keep only client "landing points" in there?

Follow that lead and get rid of those PHP-modules (`.phpm`) files and tests. These are certainly things that a regular Web browser shouldn't accidentally land on. Move them into the following hierarchy:

```
index.php
customer-contacts.php
lib/contact.phpm
lib/test.contact.php
lib/widgetsession.phpm
lib/test.widgetsession.php
templates/customer-contacts.tpl
templates/footer.tpl
templates/header.tpl
templates/login.tpl
templates/main.tpl
templates/thankyou.tpl
```

This is now much better because your root directory has only two files, and they're both landed upon by the Web browser. You also might consider moving your testing files (test.*) into another separate directory, but the creation of a directory doesn't pay off if it contains only one or two files. Go ahead and do it when you have at least four testing files to drop in.

After you've moved the files, go through and make sure that you update your includes and requires, and ensure that your tests continue to run. Cleaning your house/apartment is slightly less fun, but you end up with the same nice feeling afterward.

Refactoring Code

There are some simple tasks to keep in mind when developing your code:

- Keep it simple.
- Don't create things you won't use.
- Remove duplication, an idea also known as Once and Only Once.
- Remove unused functionality, including classes and functions.

The last item is especially hard to do because writing code is hard, so why throw away "good work"? For the same reason that you prune your plants, getting rid of the dead wood leads to a healthier overall system.

Besides, your code *is* in a source code repository, right? Use CVS, Subversion, SourceSafe, or whatever you have at hand, but put all your files into your source code repository.

Just keep the coding guidelines in mind when knocking out your simple half-point tasks, such as the Logout button, because the `footer.tpl` is used everywhere.

```
<br><br>
<a href="index.php?action=logout">Logout</a><br>
<hr>
For Widget World use only - testing environment.
</body>
</html>
```

Now, before you modify the index, look at the copy-and-paste at the top of `customer-contacts.php` and `index.php`; both of those files start with:

```
require_once ("Smarty.class.php");
require_once ("widgetsession.phpm");

$session = new WidgetSession(array ('phptype'  => "pgsql",
                                    'hostspec' => "localhost",
                                    'database' => "widgetworld",
                                    'username' => "wuser",
                                    'password' => "foobar"));

$session->Impress();

$smarty = new Smarty;
```

It violates the "Once and Only Once" rule, so remove it—just cut it out and put it in another file. For now, put it in `lib/common.php`.

Also, you really shouldn't have logins and passwords in your Web space, so pull the content out and put it another file that is accessible by PHP but well outside the Web root where Apache can serve it up to the curious and/or malicious.

Remember that because we're dealing with settings, per request, add a setting for the maximum weekly contacts. All this should be placed in a new file `../../../../settings.php`, placed inconveniently outside of the Web root so that someone cannot use your own Web server to read the configuration file and consequently gain access to your database.

```
<?php

/*
 * database setup
 */
$GLOBALS["db-type"]        = "pgsql";
```

```
$GLOBALS["db-hostname"] = "localhost";
$GLOBALS["db-username"] = "wuser";
$GLOBALS["db-password"] = "foobar";
$GLOBALS["db-name"]     = "widgetworld";

/*
 * 3rd party environment
 */
$GLOBALS["smarty-path"] = "/usr/lib/php/smarty/";

/*
 * system settings
 */
$GLOBALS["max-weekly-contacts"] = 5;

?>
```

Your `lib/common.php` file should contain:

```
<?php

require_once ("../../../../settings.php");
require_once ("./lib/widgetsession.phpm");

require_once ($GLOBALS["smarty-path"].'Smarty.class.php');
$smarty = new Smarty;

$session = new WidgetSession(array ('phptype'  => $GLOBALS["db-type"],
                                    'hostspec' => $GLOBALS["db-hostname"],
                                    'database' => $GLOBALS["db-name"],
                                    'username' => $GLOBALS["db-username"],
                                    'password' => $GLOBALS["db-password"]));
$session->Impress();

?>
```

While you're at it, you might as well require a login for every page other than `index.php`, which is currently the only page utilizing the login feature. Append this to your `common.php`:

```
/*
 * require login
 */
$scriptname = end(explode("/", $_SERVER["REQUEST_URI"]));
if ($scriptname <> "index.php") {
    if ($session->isLoggedIn() == false) {
        Header ("Location: index.php");
    }
}
```

Now turn your attention to `index.php`, which, after you've added the logic to handle the logout, now looks like this (yes it handles *all* cases):

```
<?php

require_once ("lib/common.php");

if (array_key_exists("action", $_REQUEST)) {
    switch ($_REQUEST["action"]) {
        case "login":
            $session->login($_REQUEST["login_name"],$_REQUEST["login_pass"]);
            if ($session->isLoggedIn()) {
                $smarty->assign_by_ref("user", $session->getUserObject());
                $smarty->display ("main.tpl");
                exit;
            } else {
                $smarty->assign('error', "Invalid login, try again.");
                $smarty->display ("login.tpl");
                exit;
            }
            break;
        case "logout":
            $session->logout();
            $smarty->display ("login.tpl");
            exit;
            break;
        default:
            $smarty->display ("login.tpl");
            exit;
    }
} else {
    if ($session->isLoggedIn() == true) {
        $smarty->assign_by_ref("user", $session->getUserObject());
        $smarty->display ("main.tpl");
        exit;
    }
}

$smarty->display ("login.tpl");

?>
```

When you're trying to log in, you succeed and go to `main.tpl` or fail and go back to the `login.tpl`, and when logging out, you want to log out and go to `login.tpl`. If there is no action assigned, then you check the login status with `$session->isLoggedIn()` and finally the last line displays `login.tpl` even though it's a logical impossibility, currently, for your code to ever reach that point in execution. It may be in the future, however, so it's wise to use this as a "catch-all" in case you ever slip up.

Even though the preceding code technically works, there is something just not quite right about it. What the code needs to do is determine which screen to display, but it is dependent on both the login status and the request variables that represent state. The code ends up looking too verbose, so you need to take a few minutes to see what can be done to make it a bit more readable; in other words, it's time to refactor.

Refactoring is an ongoing process that may at first seem to be a subjective process, but you'll still objectively end up with a better-looking code base because of it.

Now back to the matter at hand. There is a technique for refactoring out similarities by creating similarities. It seems a little weird at first, but if your code smells as though it is a candidate for the removal of duplication, (also known as a "Once and Only Once" refactoring), then this technique is probably worth looking into.

Examine the code and consider how you can logically create similarities with what is already there. For instance, the following continues to be perfectly legal PHP—it passes the tests and continues to work on the browser side:

```
<?php

require_once ("lib/common.php");

if (array_key_exists("action", $_REQUEST)) {
    switch ($_REQUEST["action"]) {
        case "login":
            $session->login($_REQUEST["login_name"],$_REQUEST["login_pass"]);
            if ($session->isLoggedIn()) {
                $smarty->assign_by_ref("user", $session->getUserObject());
                $smarty->display ("main.tpl");
                exit;
            } else {
                if (array_key_exists("login_name", $_REQUEST)) {
                    $smarty->assign('error', "Invalid login, try again.");
                }
                $smarty->display ("login.tpl");
                exit;
            }
            break;
        case "logout":
            $session->logout();
            if ($session->isLoggedIn()) {
                $smarty->assign_by_ref("user", $session->getUserObject());
                $smarty->display ("main.tpl");
                exit;
        } else {
            if (array_key_exists("login_name", $_REQUEST)) {
                $smarty->assign('error', "Invalid login, try again.");
            }
            $smarty->display ("login.tpl");
            exit;
        }
        exit;
        break;
    default:
        if ($session->isLoggedIn()) {
            $smarty->assign_by_ref("user", $session->getUserObject());
            $smarty->display ("main.tpl");
            exit;
        } else {
            if (array_key_exists("login_name", $_REQUEST)) {
                $smarty->assign('error', "Invalid login, try again.");
            }
```

```
                $smarty->display ("login.tpl");
                exit;
            }
            exit;
        }
    } else {
        if ($session->isLoggedIn()) {
            $smarty->assign_by_ref("user", $session->getUserObject());
            $smarty->display ("main.tpl");
            exit;
        } else {
            if (array_key_exists("login_name", $_REQUEST)) {
                $smarty->assign('error', "Invalid login, try again.");
            }
            $smarty->display ("login.tpl");
            exit;
        }
    }

    $smarty->display ("login.tpl");

    ?>
```

What you just did was intentionally create similarities by adding the highlighted conditional within your current logical structure. It's copy-and-paste programming at its worst, but for a good reason.

Next, copy the similarities verbatim and create a function passing in any local state that is required. This particular refactoring is called "Extract Method" (see *Refactoring* by Martin Fowler, Addison-Wesley, 1999, p. 110.):

```
function displaySmartyPage (&$smarty, &$session, $pageToDisplay) {
    if ($session->isLoggedIn()) {
        $smarty->assign_by_ref("user", $session->getUserObject());
        $smarty->display ($pageToDisplay);
        exit;
    } else {
        if (array_key_exists("login_name", $_REQUEST)) {
            $smarty->assign('error', "Invalid login, try again.");
        }
        $smarty->display ("login.tpl");
        exit;
    }
}
```

Now with the new function `displaySmartyPage()` at your disposal, what remains with `index.php` is the following:

```
if (array_key_exists("action", $_REQUEST)) {
    switch ($_REQUEST["action"]) {
        case "login":
            $session->login($_REQUEST["login_name"],$_REQUEST["login_pass"]);
            displaySmartyPage ($smarty, $session, "main.tpl");
            break;
```

```
        case "logout":
            $session->logout();
            displaySmartyPage ($smarty, $session, "main.tpl");
            break;
        default:
            displaySmartyPage ($smarty, $session, "main.tpl");
    }
} else {
    displaySmartyPage ($smarty, $session, "main.tpl");
}

displaySmartyPage ($smarty, $session, "main.tpl");
```

The best part is that now that the code is clearer to read, it's obvious that your logic can be refactored to:

```
if (array_key_exists("action", $_REQUEST)) {
    switch ($_REQUEST["action"]) {
        case "login":
            $session->login($_REQUEST["login_name"],$_REQUEST["login_pass"]);
            break;
        case "logout":
            $session->logout();
            break;
    }
}

displaySmartyPage ($smarty, $session, "main.tpl");
```

Because the `displaySmartyPage()` function is being called only once, you probably can now see why you refactored out the code into the `displaySmartyPage()` function.

Now that the `displaySmartyPage()` function code is unnecessary, you reverse your previous refactoring of "Extract Method" and refactor it back using the "Inline Method" (*Refactoring*, p. 117) technique. It's exactly the opposite:

```
<?php

require_once ("lib/common.php");

if (array_key_exists("action", $_REQUEST)) {
    switch ($_REQUEST["action"]) {
        case "login":
            $session->login($_REQUEST["login_name"],$_REQUEST["login_pass"]);
            break;
        case "logout":
           $session->logout();
           break;
    }
}

if ($session->isLoggedIn()) {
    $smarty->assign_by_ref("user", $session->getUserObject());
```

```
        $smarty->display ("main.tpl");
    } else {
        if (array_key_exists("login_name", $_REQUEST)) {
            $smarty->assign('error', "Invalid login, try again.");
        }
        $smarty->display ("login.tpl");
    }

    ?>
```

With just a little bit of effort you significantly reduced the complexity, removed extraneous Smarty calls, and reduced the total line count by more than one third.

As you've seen, reducing complexity can lead to some surprising savings, and the code is easier to read and understand to boot.

Just remember to try to stay out of code debt by exercising the "Once and Only Once" rule. If given a choice, keep the solution simple and don't be afraid to remove unneeded functionality.

Finishing the Iteration

Keeping in mind your newfound skills in refactoring, tackle the remaining stories with an eye toward removing duplication and making the code simpler.

Story 14: Changing the Week Recalls a Previous Week

Recalling state is not hard because the `ContactVisit` state practically begs it. We quickly get halfway there by adding the following function to `customer-contacts.php`:

```
function gatherContactVisits ($dbh, $emp_id) {
    $result = $dbh->query ("select * from contact_visits where
emp_id = ".$emp_id." and week_start = '".getCurrentStartWeek()."' order
by seq");
    if (DB::isError($result)) {
        return array();
    }
    $visits = array();
    while ($row =& $result->fetchRow()) {
        array_push ($visits, new ContactVisit($row));
    }
    return $visits;
}
```

You should be lazy about calling the `gatherContactVisits()` function because the act of recalling `ContactVisits()` from the database might not be required each time; for instance, when `ContactVisits()` are being saved.

Now assign the contact visit data by reference to `ContactVisits` and recall it for display like so in the `customer-contacts.tpl`:

```
<input name="company_name_{$smarty.section.idx.index}" size="20" maxlength="50"
value="{$contactVisits[idx]->company_name}">
```

You've got everything except for the reload if the week is changed in the drop-down. Here is a cute trick; drop-downs don't normally cause submits to happen but in this case you need to force it.

In order to force a submit, you create a hidden form with the `week_start` value defined in it. When the date is changed, call the JavaScript function `reload`, which in turn populates the `week_start` with whatever was selected. Then, "submit" it with a new action.

```
{literal}
<SCRIPT TYPE="text/javascript">
<!--

function reload () {
    window.document.forms[0].week_start.value =
window.document.forms[1].week_start.value // hidden form
    window.document.forms[0].submit(); // hidden form
}

// -->
</SCRIPT>
{/literal}

<h3>Customer Contact Report</h3>

<form action="customer-contacts.php" method="post">
<input type="hidden" name="action" value="reload_contact">
<input type="hidden" name="week_start" value="">
</form>

<form action="customer-contacts.php" method="post">
<table border="0" width="100%">
<tr><td><b>Employee Name:</b></td><td>{$user->first_name}
{$user->last_name}</td>
<td><b>Department:</b></td><td>{$user->department}</td></tr>
<tr><td><b>Number:</b></td><td>{$user->id}</td>
<td><b>Start Week:</b></td>
<td><SELECT NAME="week_start" onchange="reload()">{html_options
values=$start_weeks
output=$start_weeks selected=$current_start_week}</SELECT></td></tr>
</table>

<br><br><hr>
```

Story 15: Per-Week Items on the Customer Contact Report

Remember, the elements of concern are Number of Shop Calls, Number of Engineer Calls, Number of Distributor Calls, Approximate Mileage, Territory Worked, and Territory Comments. All these occur on a per-week basis.

Realize that you're looking at a many-to-one ratio of contact visits to the new structure: `Contact`.

```
CREATE TABLE contact (
  emp_id integer NOT NULL default '0',
  week_start date NOT NULL,
  shop_calls integer default NULL,
  distributor_calls integer default NULL,
  engineer_calls integer default NULL,
  mileage decimal(9,2) default NULL,
  territory_worked varchar(60) default NULL,
  territory_comments text
);
CREATE UNIQUE INDEX co_pk on contact (emp_id,week_start);
CREATE INDEX co_emp_id ON contact (emp_id);
CREATE INDEX co_week_start ON contact (week_start);
```

Not a problem, because `Contact` is used in much the same way as `ContactVisits`. Create a test for contact persistence:

```
    function testContactPersistence() {
        $this->_session->getDatabaseHandle()->query("delete FROM contact WHERE
emp_id = 1 and week_start = '1980-01-01'"); // remove multiples
        $c = new Contact (
            array ("emp_id"              => "1",
                   "week_start"          => "1980-01-01",
                   "shop_calls"          => 2,
                   "distributor_calls"   => 3,
                   "engineer_calls"      => 4,
                   "mileage"             => 50,
                   "territory_worked"    => "Central Ohio",
                   "territory_comments"  => "Buckeyes are great. " ),
            $this->_session->getDatabaseHandle());
        $result = $this->_session->getDatabaseHandle()->query("select * FROM
contact WHERE emp_id = 1 and week_start = '1980-01-01'");
        $this->assertEquals(0, $result->numRows());
        $c->persist();
        $result = $this->_session->getDatabaseHandle()->query("select * FROM
contact WHERE emp_id = 1 and week_start = '1980-01-01'");
        $this->assertEquals(1, $result->numRows());
    }
```

`Contact` also shares the same scope as `ContactVisits`. This is a big hint because the two classes do pretty much the same thing and share the same scope; they're typically an easy refactoring target. Looking deeper into the classes, you see that your hunch is correct and that the new `Contact` class, and the existing `ContactVisit` and `WidgetUser` classes, all contain common functionality.

As you may recall from earlier, the footprint of `ContactVisit` and `WidgetUser` is

```
class ContactVisit {
    protected $contentBase = array();
    protected $dbh = null; // database handle
    function __get ($key) {}
    function __construct ($results, $dbh = null) {}
    private function isEmpty($key) {}
    public function isValid() {}
```

```
    private function implodeQuoted ()
    private function generateSqlInsert ($tableName, &$metas, &$values) {}
    public function persist() {}
}

class WidgetUser {
    protected $contentBase = array();
    protected $dispatchFunctions = array ("role" => "getrole");
    function __construct($initdict) {}
    function __get ($key) {}
    function __set ($key, $value) {}
    public function getRole() {}
    public function isSalesPerson()  {}
    public function isSalesManager() {}
    public function isAccountant()   {}
}
```

This is a great use of the "Extract Class" (*Refactoring*, p. 149) refactoring in order to consolidate the code. The consolidation moves a lot of persistence functionality up into a new class called `PersistableObject`.

```
class PersistableObject {
    protected $contentBase = array();
    protected $dbh = null; // database handle
    protected $dispatchFunctions = array ("role" => "getrole");

    function __get ($key) {
        // dispatch by function first
        if (array_key_exists ($key, $this->dispatchFunctions)) {
            $funcname = $this->dispatchFunctions[$key];
            return $this->$funcname();
        }

         // then state
         if (array_key_exists ($key, $this->contentBase)) {
             return $this->contentBase[$key];
        }

        // then self
        return $this->$key;
    }

    function __construct ($results, $dbh = null) {
        $this->dbh = $dbh;
        if ($results <> null) {
            $this->contentBase = $results; // copy
        }
    }

    public function implodeQuoted (&$values, $delimiter) {
         $sql = "";
        $flagIsFirst = true;
        foreach ($values as $value) {
```

```
            if ($flagIsFirst) {
                $flagIsFirst = false;
            } else {
                $sql .= $delimiter;
            }

            if (gettype ($value) == "string") {
                $sql.= "'".$value."'";
            } else {
                $sql .= $value;
            }
        }
        return $sql;
    }

    public function generateSqlInsert ($tableName, &$metas, &$values) {
        return " insert into ".$tableName.
            "       ( ".implode             ($metas, ", ")." ) ".
            " values ( ".$this->implodeQuoted ($values, ", ")." ) ";
    }

    public function generateSqlUpdate ($tableName, &$metas, &$values) {
        $sql = " update ".$tableName." set ";
        for ($i=0; $i<count($metas); $i++) {
            $sql .= $metas[$i]." = ".$vaules[$i].", ";
        }
        return $sql;
    }

    public function generateSqlDelete ($tableName) {
        return " delete from \"".$tableName."\" where ".$this->getSqlWhere();
    }

    // note: should be implemented by concrete classes
    public function getSqlWhere() {
        return "";
    }

    public function isValid() {
        return true;
    }
    public function persistWork ($tablename, $meta) {
        if ($this->isValid() == false) return false;
        $values = array();
        foreach ($meta as $mvalue) {
            array_push ($values, $this->$mvalue);
        }

        if (strlen($this->getSqlWhere()) > 0) {
            $sql = $this->generateSqlDelete ($tablename);
            $this->dbh->query($sql);
        }

        $sql = $this->generateSqlInsert ($tablename, $meta, $values);
```

```
        if (DB::isError ($this->dbh->query($sql))) return false;
        return true;
    }
}
```

You may have noticed that the addition of `generateSqlUpdate` and `generateSqlDelete` allows `PersistableObject` to respectively update and delete itself in the database. Of course, both of these functions require a `SQL WHERE` clause so that not every record in the table gets updated and deleted. This is why child classes (such as `ContactVisit`) have the responsibility of defining what makes them unique; they do this by implementing the `getSqlWhere` function.

By moving the persistence functions (`implodeQuoted`, `generateSqlInsert`, `isValid`, `persistWork`) and persistence state (`contentBase`, `dispatchFunctions`) up into `PersistableObject`, then `Contact`, `ContactVisit` and `WidgetUser` can all be implemented in a much shorter form:

```
class Contact extends PersistableObject {
    function __construct ($results, $dbh = null) {
        parent::__construct ($results, $dbh);
    }

    public function persist() {
        return $this->persistWork ("contact",
                                array ( "emp_id",
                                        "week_start",
                                        "shop_calls",
                                        "distributor_calls",
                                        "engineer_calls",
                                        "mileage",
                                        "territory_worked",
                                        "territory_comments"));
    }

    public function getSqlWhere() {
         return " emp_id = ".$this->emp_id." and week_start = '".$this-
>week_start."'";
    }
}
```

```
class ContactVisit extends PersistableObject {

    function __construct ($results, $dbh = null) {
        parent::__construct ($results, $dbh);
        static $sequence = 0;
        $sequence = $sequence + 1; // increment across class
        $this->contentBase["seq"] = $sequence;
    }

    private function isEmpty($key) {
        if (array_key_exists($key, $this->contentBase) == false) return true;
        if ($this->contentBase[$key] == null) return true;
```

```
        if ($this->contentBase[$key] == "") return true;
        return false;
    }

    public function isValid() {
        if ($this->isEmpty("emp_id") == true) return false;
        if ($this->isEmpty("week_start") == true) return false;
        if ($this->isEmpty("company_name") == true) return false;
        return true;
    }

    public function persist() {
        return $this->persistWork ("contact_visits",
                                   array ( "emp_id",
                                           "week_start",
                                           "seq",
                                           "company_name",
                                           "contact_name",
                                           "city",
                                           "state",
                                           "accomplishments",
                                           "followup",
                                           "literature_request" ));
    }
}

class WidgetUser extends PersistableObject {

    function __construct($initdict) {
        parent::__construct ($initdict);
        $this->dispatchFunctions = array ("role" => "getrole");
        $this->contentBase = $initdict; // copy
    }

    public function getRole() {
        switch ($this->contentBase["role"]) {
            case "s": return ("Sales Person");
            case "m": return ("Sales Manager");
            case "a": return ("Accountant");
            default: return ("");
        }
    }

    public function isSalesPerson() {
        if ($this->contentBase["role"] == "s") return true;
        return false;
    }

    public function isSalesManager() {
        if ($this->contentBase["role"] == "m") return true;
        return false;
    }

    public function isAccountant() {
```

```
        if ($this->contentBase["role"] == "a") return true;
        return false;
    }
}
```

Boy, it sure is great to have all those unit tests to indicate when something goes wrong. One obstacle you'll face is deciding how your target classes are used and how they differ from one another. For instance, `Contact` and `ContactVisit` have subtle differences in that you persist only valid `ContactVisits`, but there is always a possibly empty but still instantiated `Contact`.

Also notice that `Contact` implements the `getSqlWhere` function so that it can be deleted and updated; however, remember that `ContactVisit` gets deleted before insertions take place and `WidgetUser` is only persisted to the database, thus not requiring it to implement the `getSqlWhere` function.

However, the differences between `Contact` and `ContactVisits` have less to do with the classes themselves than with the business rules and the environment they exist in. Therefore, even though your classes are starting to consolidate and share code, their respective unit tests should continue to test individual class diversity.

Okay, `customer-contacts.tpl` now needs a new section in order to display the new `Contact` information:

```
<table border="0">
<tr>
<td>Number of Shop Calls:</td><td><input name="shop_calls" size="7"
maxlength="17" value="{$contact->shop_calls}"></td><td width="20"></td>
<td>Number of Engineer Calls:</td><td><input name="engineer_calls" size="7"
maxlength="17" value="{$contact->engineer_calls}"></td>
</tr>

<tr>
<td>Number of Distributor Calls:</td><td><input name="distributor_calls"
size="7" maxlength="17" value="{$contact->distributor_calls}"></td>
<td width="20"></td>
<td>Approximate Mileage:</td><td><input name="mileage" size="7" maxlength="17"
value="{$contact->mileage}"></td>
</tr>

<tr>
<td>Territory Worked:</td><td colspan="2"><input name="territory_worked"
value="{$contact->territory_worked}"></td>
</tr>

<tr>
<td colspan="7">Territory Comments:<br><TEXTAREA NAME="territory_comments"
ROWS=4 COLS=95>{$contact->territory_comments}</TEXTAREA></td>
</tr>
</table>
```

Add these new support functions to `customer-contacts.php` in order to read and save the `Contact` information:

```
function persistContact (&$dbh, $emp_id) {
    $c = new Contact (
        array ("emp_id"                 => $emp_id,
               "week_start"             => getCurrentStartWeek(),
               "shop_calls"             => $_REQUEST["shop_calls"],
               "distributor_calls"      => $_REQUEST["distributor_calls"],
               "engineer_calls"         => $_REQUEST["engineer_calls"],
               "mileage"                => $_REQUEST["mileage"],
               "territory_worked"       => $_REQUEST["territory_worked"],
               "territory_comments"     => $_REQUEST["territory_comments"]),
        $dbh);
    $c->persist();
}

function gatherContact (&$dbh, $emp_id) {
    $result = $dbh->query ("select * from contact where emp_id = ".$emp_id."
and week_start = '".getCurrentStartWeek()."'");
    if (DB::isError($result)) return array();
    return new Contact ($result->fetchRow());
}

$user = $session->getUserObject();

// display
if ($_REQUEST["action"] != "persist_contact") {
    $smarty->assign_by_ref ("user", $user);
    $smarty->assign_by_ref ("contact", gatherContact($session->
getDatabaseHandle(), $user->id));
    $smarty->assign_by_ref ("contactVisits", gatherContactVisits($session-
>getDatabaseHandle(), $user->id));
    $smarty->assign('start_weeks', getStartWeeks());
    $smarty->assign('current_start_week', getCurrentStartWeek());
    $smarty->assign("max_weekly_contacts", $GLOBALS["max-weekly-contacts"]);
    $smarty->display('customer-contacts.tpl');
    exit;
}

// persist contact visits
require_once ("lib/contact.phpm");
persistContact ($session->getDatabaseHandle(), $user->id);
persistContactVisits ($session->getDatabaseHandle(), $user->id);
```

See Figure 22-7 to view results of your hard work.

The speed at which the last story was accomplished indicates that if you keep your code base clean by not going into code debt, your forward momentum will not necessarily fall by the wayside.

Refactoring is something that you should strive for and in a way is never complete. There are sections that could still have a critical eye applied to them, notably those with striking similarities in the support functions for `Contact` and `ContactVisits`. The reason the support functions exist at all, as opposed to having the objects take care of everything themselves, is an indication of how their shared scope will probably lead to more consolidation.

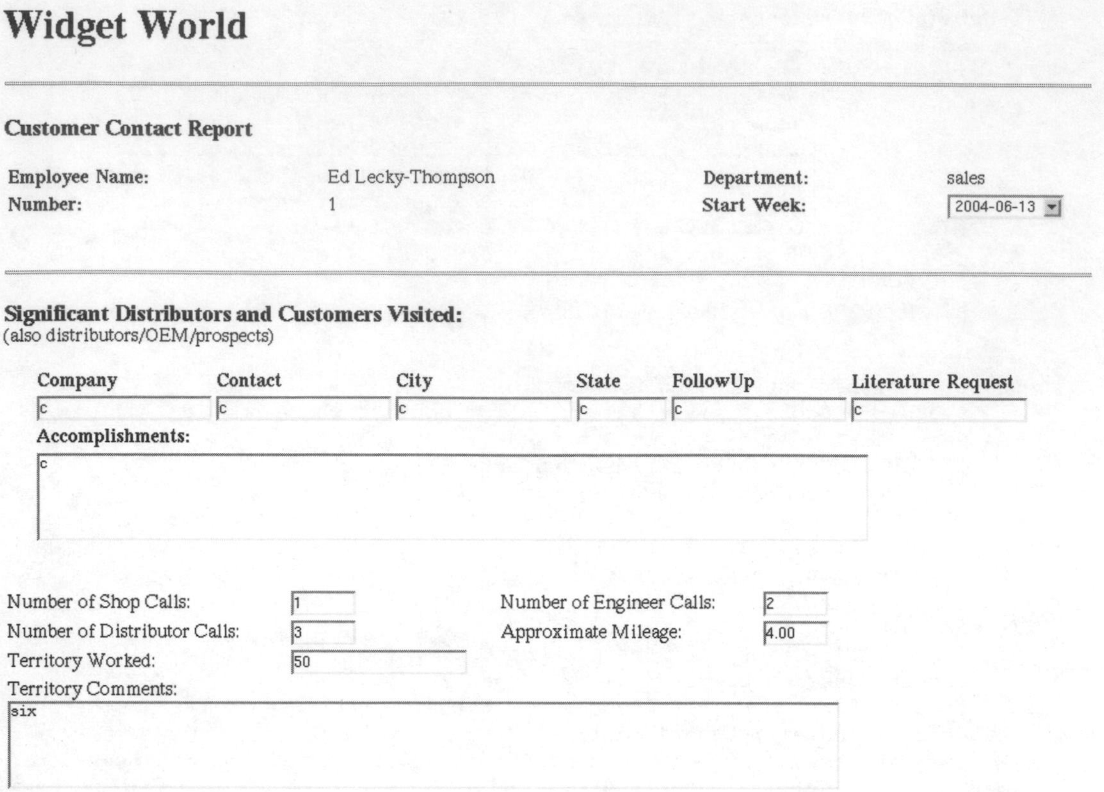

Widget World

Customer Contact Report

Employee Name:	Ed Lecky-Thompson	**Department:**	sales
Number:	1	**Start Week:**	2004-06-13

Significant Distributors and Customers Visited:
(also distributors/OEM/prospects)

Company	Contact	City	State	FollowUp	Literature Request
c	c	c	c	c	c

Accomplishments:

c

Number of Shop Calls:	1	Number of Engineer Calls:	2
Number of Distributor Calls:	3	Approximate Mileage:	4.00
Territory Worked:	50		

Territory Comments:

six

Figure 22-7

Regardless, that is still something that could go in a different direction, and you have to remember that in order for a particular refactoring to be successful, the resulting code should be easier to read and understand. If you find yourself spending more time writing excessive support plumbing or a framework, take that as an indication that maybe you should stop for a moment. Although large refactorings are sometimes needed, they should definitely be the exception.

Travel Expense Report

The outstanding road map that we have now is the following:

Travel Expense Report:

- ❑ Story 2: Travel Expense Report, 7 points
- ❑ Story 3: Expense Report Comments, 2 points
- ❑ Story 10: Persisted Expense Report Cash Advance, 2 points
- ❑ Story 4: Expense Report as Spreadsheet, 4 points

Travel Expense Services:

- ❑ Story 5: Accountant Notification, 3 points
- ❑ Story 7: Sales Person Notification, 1 point
- ❑ Story 13: Expense Report Export, 3 points

outstanding stories:

- ❑ Story 6: Sales Manager Notification, 3 points
- ❑ Story 8: Mail Room Notification, 2 points

By the sheer number of points, the Travel Expense Report will not be just an easy knockoff.

As seen previously in Figure 22-2, the expense report is pretty slim regarding details. Time to get to work talking. From conversations with Wendy and Edwina, you learn that what they really want is something that looks more like Figure 22-8.

Although it took the better part of the day to order and modify the categories (Lodging, Meals, and so on), what you now have is a close approximation to the appearance of the original Widget World faxable form. But now that your clients realize that things can change, then, well, they just may. Because even though a certain amount of flexibility and unknowns plague just about any project, you're going to roll with the punches and not overengineer every "just in case" feature that comes to mind.

Oh yeah, and the XXX in "Miles at XXX / mile" heading is a dollar amount based on federal tax law. Thankfully, it is a constant, so you don't need to track it for every state/province and you need to deal with only one country, *but* the rate changes from year to year, so you need to record the amount at the time of submission.

The all-important cash advance also needs to be part of the calculation and if the advance is enough, it might spill over into money owed to the company, represented by "Due Employee" and its Boolean counterpart "Due Company."

Ignoring for now the complexity, just start with the simple bits. The core of this sheet is a dollar amount associated with a date and a descriptor.

A quick scribble gets you the following data item:

```
CREATE TABLE travel_expense_item (
  emp_id            integer       NOT NULL,
  expense_date      date          NOT NULL,
  description       varchar(40)   NOT NULL,
  amount            decimal(9,2)  NOT NULL );
```

Add the weekly information that needs to be captured:

```
CREATE TABLE travel_expense_week (
  emp_id            integer NOT NULL,
  week_start        date    NOT NULL,
  comments          text,
```

```
territory_worked varchar(60),
cash_advance     decimal(9,2),
mileage_rate     decimal(3,2) NOT NULL );
```

As a technical note, you still need to add defaults, indexes, and so on to the database and, on the business side, note that you're tracking the `cash_advance` and `mileage_rate`. With each travel expense submitted on a weekly basis, the weekly subtotals sections of the form can be easily calculated, so storage of the subtotals is not required.

B / C	D	E	F	G	H	I	J	K
Employee Name:	XXXXX XXXXXXX			Department:		XXXXXX		
Number:	X			Starting Week:		YYYY-MM-DD (drop down)		
Territory Worked:	XXXXXXXXXXXX							
	Sun	**Mon**	**Tue**	**Wed**	**Thr**	**Fri**	**Sat**	**Total**
Lodging								
Lodging and Hotel	1	1	1	1	1	1	1	7
Other	1	1	1	1	1	1	1	7
Tips	1	1	1	1	1	1	1	7
Lodging Total	3	3	3	3	3	3	3	21
Meals								
Breakfast	1	1	1	1	1	1	1	7
Lunch & Snacks	1	1	1	1	1	1	1	7
Dinner	1	1	1	1	1	1	1	7
Tips	1	1	1	1	1	1	1	7
Entertainment	1	1	1	1	1	1	1	7
Meals Total	6	6	6	6	6	6	6	42
Transportation								
Airfare	1	1	1	1	1	1	1	7
Auto Rental	1	1	1	1	1	1	1	7
Auto Maint./Gas	1	1	1	1	1	1	1	7
Tolls / Parking	1	1	1	1	1	1	1	7
Trans. Sub Total	4	4	4	4	4	4	4	28
Num miles traveled	1	1	1	1	1	1	1	7
Miles at XXX / mile	1	1	1	1	1	1	1	7
Trans. Total	6	6	6	6	6	6	6	42
Misc								
Gifts	1	1	1	1	1	1	1	7
Telephone & Fax	1	1	1	1	1	1	1	7
Supplies	1	1	1	1	1	1	1	7
Postage	1	1	1	1	1	1	1	7
Other	1	1	1	1	1	1	1	7
Misc Total	5	5	5	5	5	5	5	35
Comments:					**Subtotal**			147
XXXXXXXXXXXXXXXXXXXXXXXXXXXXXXXXXX					**Less Cash Advance**			47
XXXXXXXXXXXXXXXXXXXXXXXXXXXXXXXXXX					**Due Employee**			100
XXXXXXXXXXXXXXXXXXXXXXXXXXXXXXXXXX					**Due Company**			

Figure 22-8

Travel Expense Item

Let's get to work on the tests. The simple case is simply validating the minimum required information, like this:

```
    function testValidTravelExpenseItem() {
        $tvi = new TravelExpenseItem (
            array ('emp_id'                  => "1",
                   'expense_date'            => "1980-01-01",
                   'description'             => "one",
                   'amount'                  => "1.0" ));
        $this->assertEquals(true, $tvi->isValid(), "valid expense");
    }

    function testInvalidTravelExpenseItem() {
        $tvi = new TravelExpenseItem (
            array ('emp_id'                  => "1",
                   'expense_date'            => "", // date required
                   'description'             => "one",
                   'amount'                  => "1.0" ));
        $this->assertEquals(false, $tvi->isValid(), "valid expense");
    }
```

What else does it need to do? If given an array, it can populate itself, so the travel expense item needs to persist itself accordingly. Add another test to the travel expense item:

```
    function testTravelExpenseItemPersistence() {
        $this->_session->getDatabaseHandle()->query("delete FROM
travel_expense_item WHERE emp_id = 1 and expense_date = '1980-01-01'"); //
remove multiples
        $tvi = new TravelExpenseItem (
            array ('emp_id'                 => "1",
                   'expense_date'           => "1980-01-01",
                   'description'            => "one",
                   'amount'                 => "1.0" ),
            $this->_session->getDatabaseHandle());
        $result = $this->_session->getDatabaseHandle()->query("select * FROM
travel_expense_item WHERE emp_id = 1 and expense_date = '1980-01-01'");
        $this->assertEquals(0, $result->numRows());
        $tvi->persist();
        $result = $this->_session->getDatabaseHandle()->query("select * FROM
travel_expense_item WHERE emp_id = 1 and expense_date = '1980-01-01'");
        $this->assertEquals(1, $result->numRows());
    }
```

Remember to connect to your testing database when running these tests. The last thing you want is to accidentally torch production data with an errant `DELETE` statement.

Stub out your travel expense item in the new file, `lib/expense.phpm`:

```
class TravelExpenseItem {
    public function isValid() { }
```

```
    public function persist() { }
}
```

Make sure that the tests run (and fail) and then get to work satisfying them.

Using ContactVisit as a template, it's surprisingly easy:

```
class TravelExpenseItem extends PersistableObject {
    function __construct ($results, $dbh = null) {
        parent::__construct ($results, $dbh);
    }

    private function isEmpty($key) {
        if (array_key_exists($key, $this->contentBase) == false) return true;
        if ($this->contentBase[$key] == null) return true;
        if ($this->contentBase[$key] == "") return true;
        return false;
    }

    public function isValid() {
        if ($this->isEmpty("emp_id") == true) return false;
        if ($this->isEmpty("expense_date") == true) return false;
        if ($this->isEmpty("description") == true) return false;
        if ($this->isEmpty("amount") == true) return false;
        return true;
    }

    public function persist() {
        return $this->persistWork (
            "travel_expense_item",
            array ( "emp_id",
                    "expense_date",
                    "description",
                    "amount" ));
    }

    public function getSqlWhere() {
        return " emp_id = ".$this->emp_id." and expense_date = '".$this-
>expense_date."' and description = '".$this->description."'";
    }
}
```

Recalling the definition of ContactVisit:

```
class ContactVisit extends PersistableObject {
    function __construct ($results, $dbh = null) {}
    private function isEmpty($key) {}
    public function isValid() {}
    public function persist() {}
}
```

Of course, the function `isEmpty()` is now redundant between the two classes, which share a common parent. What does that say to you? It screams "move `IsEmpty()` up into `PersistableObject`"! Don't forget to make `isEmpty()` protected, or subclasses can't call it.

When you're done with that, make sure that the `ContactVisit`'s test continues to pass. The respective classes should now look like this:

```
class PersistableObject {
    protected $contentBase = array();
    protected $dbh = null; // database handle
    protected $dispatchFunctions = array ("role" => "getrole");
    function __get ($key) {}
    function __construct ($results, $dbh = null) {}
    public function implodeQuoted (&$values, $delimiter) {}
    public function generateSqlInsert ($tableName, &$metas, &$values) {}
    public function generateSqlUpdate ($tableName, &$metas, &$values) {}
    public function generateSqlDelete ($tableName) {}
    public function getSqlWhere() {}
    public function isValid() {}
    protected function isEmpty($key) {}
    public function persistWork ($tablename, $meta) {}
}

class ContactVisit extends PersistableObject {
    function __construct ($results, $dbh = null) {}
    public function isValid() {}
    public function persist() {}
}

class TravelExpenseItem extends PersistableObject {
    function __construct ($results, $dbh = null) {}
    public function isValid() {}
    public function persist() {}
    public function getSqlWhere() {}
}
```

Now go and eat a cookie before taking on the Travel Expense Week class.

Travel Expense Week

By now you can easily knock out the simple test cases for travel expense week:

```
function testValidTravelExpenseWeek() {
    $tvi = new TravelExpenseWeek (
        array ('emp_id'              => "1",
               'week_start'          => "1980-01-01",
               'comments'            => "comment",
               'mileage_rate'        => "0.31",
               'territory_worked'    => "Midwest" ));
    $this->assertEquals(true, $tvi->isValid(), "valid expense");
}
```

```
    function testInvalidTravelExpenseWeek() {
        $tvi = new TravelExpenseWeek (
            array ('emp_id'                => "1",
                   'week_start'            => "", // date required
                   'comments'              => "comment",
                   'mileage_rate'          => "0.31",
                   'territory_worked'      => "Midwest" ));
        $this->assertEquals(false, $tvi->isValid(), "valid expense");
    }

    function testTravelExpenseWeekPersistence() {
         $this->_session->getDatabaseHandle()->query("delete FROM
travel_expense_week WHERE emp_id = 1 and week_start = '1980-01-01'"); //
remove multiples
        $tvi = new TravelExpenseWeek (
            array ('emp_id'                => "1",
                   'week_start'            => "1980-01-01",
                   'comments'              => "comment",
                   'territory_worked'      => "Midwest",
                   'mileage_rate'          => "0.31",
                   'cash_advance'          => "0"),
            $this->_session->getDatabaseHandle());
        $result = $this->_session->getDatabaseHandle()->query("select * FROM
travel_expense_week WHERE emp_id = 1 and week_start = '1980-01-01'");
        $this->assertEquals(0, $result->numRows(), "pre check");
        $tvi->persist();
        $result = $this->_session->getDatabaseHandle()->query("select * FROM
travel_expense_week WHERE emp_id = 1 and week_start = '1980-01-01'");
        $this->assertEquals(1, $result->numRows(), "persist");
    }
```

Also consider the fact that something has to be in charge of the lifecycle of all your `TravelExpenseItems`. `TravelExpenseWeek`? `TraveExpenseItem`? Does one of the two choices sound as though it would make a good container?

An (extremely explicit) test of `TravelExpenseWeek` as a container would look like the following:

```
    function testTravelExpenseWeekContainerRead() {

        // clear out the test database
        $this->_session->getDatabaseHandle()->query("delete FROM
travel_expense_item WHERE emp_id = 1 and expense_date >= '1980-01-06' and
expense_date <= '2001-09-15'");

        $dbh = $this->_session->getDatabaseHandle();

        // monday
        $item1 = new TravelExpenseItem (
            array ('emp_id' => "1", 'expense_date' => "1980-01-06",
                   'description' => "lodging_and_hotel", 'amount' => "1.1"),
            $dbh);
        $item2 = new TravelExpenseItem (
            array ('emp_id' => "1", 'expense_date' => "1980-01-06",
                   'description' => "meals_breakfast", 'amount' => "2.2" ),
            $dbh);
```

```
        $item3 = new TravelExpenseItem (
            array ('emp_id' => "1", 'expense_date' => "1980-01-06",
                    'description' => "misc_supplies", 'amount' => "3.3" ),
            $dbh);

        // tuesday
        $item4 = new TravelExpenseItem (
            array ('emp_id' => "1", 'expense_date' => "2001-09-10",
                    'description' => "lodging_and_hotel", 'amount' => "4.4" ),
            $dbh);
        $item5 = new TravelExpenseItem (
            array ('emp_id' => "1", 'expense_date' => "2001-09-10",
                    'description' => "meals_breakfast", 'amount' => "5.5" ),
            $dbh);
        $item6 = new TravelExpenseItem (
            array ('emp_id' => "1", 'expense_date' => "2001-09-10",
                    'description' => "misc_supplies", 'amount' => "6.6" ),
            $dbh);

        // wednesday
        $item7 = new TravelExpenseItem (
            array ('emp_id' => "1", 'expense_date' => "1980-01-01",
                    'description' => "lodging_and_hotel", 'amount' => "7.7" ),
            $dbh);
        $item8 = new TravelExpenseItem (
            array ('emp_id' => "1", 'expense_date' => "1980-01-01",
                    'description' => "meals_breakfast", 'amount' => "8.8" ),
            $dbh);
        $item9 = new TravelExpenseItem (
            array ('emp_id' => "1", 'expense_date' => "1980-01-01",
                    'description' => "misc_supplies", 'amount' => "9.9" ),
            $dbh);
```

The `TravelExpenseItems` populate the first three days of the week and are each a different type of item: `meals_breakfast`, `misc_supplies`, and `lodging_and_hotel`.

```
    $item1->persist();
    $item2->persist();
    $item3->persist();
    $item4->persist();
    $item5->persist();
    $item6->persist();
    $item7->persist();
    $item8->persist();
    $item9->persist();

    $week = new TravelExpenseWeek (
        array ('emp_id'              => "1",
               'week_start'          => "1980-01-06"),
```

```
        $this->_session->getDatabaseHandle());

    $week->readWeek();

    // monday
    $this->assertEquals(1.1, (float)
                         $week->getExpenseAmount(0, 'lodging_and_hotel'));
    $this->assertEquals(2.2, (float)
                         $week->getExpenseAmount(0, 'meals_breakfast'));
    $this->assertEquals(3.3, (float)
                         $week->getExpenseAmount(0, 'misc_supplies'));

    // tuesday
    $this->assertEquals(4.4, (float)
                         $week->getExpenseAmount(1, 'lodging_and_hotel'));
    $this->assertEquals(5.5, (float)
                         $week->getExpenseAmount(1, 'meals_breakfast'));
    $this->assertEquals(6.6, (float)
                         $week->getExpenseAmount(1, 'misc_supplies'));

    // wednesday
    $this->assertEquals(7.7, (float)
                         $week->getExpenseAmount(2, 'lodging_and_hotel'));
    $this->assertEquals(8.8, (float)
                         $week->getExpenseAmount(2, 'meals_breakfast'));
    $this->assertEquals(9.9, (float)
                         $week->getExpenseAmount(2, 'misc_supplies'));
    }
```

After the `TravelExpenseItems` have been persisted, this test shows that the new `TravelExpenseWeek` class will be able to retrieve a week of `TraveExpenseItems`, given the employee ID and starting week.

This is an important test in other respects, because here is where you are defining the interface of your Web page. Recall that `TravelExpenseItem` is day-based and the Web page is week-based, necessitating `TravelExpenseWeek`. Thus, the ability to iterate over the `TravelExpenseItems` in a weekly manner should be paramount.

Note that because `TravelExpenseWeek` knows which day is the first of the week (for Americans, Sunday), you don't need to explicitly spell out your target day; instead you can use an offset. Use 0 for Sunday, 1 for Monday, and so on.

The Spike

Before going on, consider how you'll display what you need to display on the screen.

Go back and eyeball Figure 22-8 again. Note that something will have to take care of the subtotaling, not to mention the order.

Something has to associate human names with what exists in the database.

Also remember that "something" ultimately stops with you and that anything that makes your life easier can't be a bad thing. Clearly, hard-coding the HTML will be a maintenance nightmare.

To avoid a hard-coded HTML maintenance nightmare, consider using a data structure like this following, which can be used to generate what you need to display as well as mapping it to your data fields:

```
array(
    array('name' => 'Lodging',
          'code' => 'lodging',
          'data' => array('Lodging &amp; Hotel','Other','Tips'),
          'persist' => array('lodging_and_hotel', 'lodging_other,
                            'lodging_tips')),
    array('name' => 'Meals',
          'code' => 'meals',
          'data' => array('Breakfast', 'Lunch &amp; Snacks',
                         'Dinner', 'Tips', 'Entertainment'),
          'persist' => array('meals_breakfast', 'meals_lunch',
                            'meals_dinner', 'meals_tips',
                            'meals_entertainment')),
    array('name' => 'Transportation',
          'code' => 'trans',
          'data' => array('Airfare', 'Auto Rental', 'Auto Maint./Gas',
                         'Local Transportation', 'Tolls/Parking'),
          'persist' => array ('trans_airfare', 'trans_auto_rental',
                             'trans_auto_maint', 'trans_local',
                             'trans_tolls', 'trans_miles_traveled')),
     array('name' => 'Miscellaneous',
           'code' => 'misc',
           'data' => array('Gifts', 'Telephone &amp; Fax', 'Supplies',
                          'Postage', 'Other'),
           'persist' => array('misc_gifts','misc_phone',
                             'misc_supplies', 'misc_postage',
                             'misc_other')));
```

The first level is an array of sections, which means that each section gets a subtotal and each section contains line items.

Each section has a `data` array, simply the human-viewable description as well as its computerized counterpart `persist`, which will presumably be the name of each item in the database. The `code` item in the associated array exists in order to automate the creation of semi-meaningful JavaScript variables that must be calculated per section, for example, one for Meals, Lodging, and Transportation. This data structure will be a some of the glue that holds the HTML, JavaScript math, database, and PHP objects together; it's your roadmap.

More Travel Expense Week Tests

Going from PHP's travel expense form response to the database is an important step. This is where you'll be defining what you expect to receive from the page. Remember that you need a way to take the entire response and easily create `TravelExpenseItems` from that. Sounds like a good job for the `TravelExpenseWeek` container.

Recall that the naming convention for determining the unique values of each individual cell is `lodging_sun_0`, which represents "section" + "day" + "line item". Because there is a nearly infinite number of ways to describe the same column/row, vertical/horizontal, spreadsheet-cell relationship, this naming convention is quite adequate.

Additionally, you can easily determine which horizontal row you happen to be working with as a result of its section offset (the "0" in `lodging_sun_0`). Day and line item are different types for a reason: your sanity. Manipulating data in different dimensions is hard enough; tracking which way against which one is harder and remembering what they are based on is asking for trouble. With all things being equal, there is more semantic information contained with `lodging_sun_0` than with `lodging_0_0`.

Here is the test for parsing the request:

```
function testTravelExpenseWeekContainerParseRequest() {

    $response = array ( 'lodging_sun_0' => "1.1",
                        'meals_sun_0'   => "2.2",
                        'misc_sun_2'    => "3.3",
                        'lodging_mon_0' => "4.4",
                        'meals_mon_0'   => "5.5",
                        'misc_mon_2'    => "6.6",
                        'lodging_tue_0' => "7.7",
                        'meals_tue_0'   => "8.8",
                        'misc_tue_2'    => "9.9" );

    $week = new TravelExpenseWeek (
        array ('emp_id'             => "1",
               'week_start'         => "1980-01-06"));

    $week->parse($response);

    $this->assertEquals(1.1,
                        $week->getExpenseAmount(0, 'lodging_and_hotel'));
    $this->assertEquals(2.2,
                        $week->getExpenseAmount(0, 'meals_breakfast'));
    $this->assertEquals(3.3,
                        $week->getExpenseAmount(0, 'misc_supplies'));

    $this->assertEquals(4.4,
                        $week->getExpenseAmount(1, 'lodging_and_hotel'));
    $this->assertEquals(5.5,
                        $week->getExpenseAmount(1, 'meals_breakfast'));
    $this->assertEquals(6.6,
                        $week->getExpenseAmount(1, 'misc_supplies'));

    $this->assertEquals(7.7,
                       $week->getExpenseAmount(2, 'lodging_and_hotel'));
    $this->assertEquals(8.8,
                       $week->getExpenseAmount(2, 'meals_breakfast'));
    $this->assertEquals(9.9,
                       $week->getExpenseAmount(2, 'misc_supplies'));
}
```

The `$response` array is simulating what you'll receive from your form input, and remember that the `$response` values and the `persist` meta-values are reflected in your road-map data structure.

Create one more test for persisting the container. It is very similar to the travel expense items test:

```
    function testTravelExpenseWeekContainerWrite() {

        $this->_session->getDatabaseHandle()->query("delete FROM
travel_expense_item WHERE emp_id = 1 and expense_date >= '1980-01-06' and
expense_date <= '2001-09-15'");

        $response = array (
            'lodging_sun_0'=>"1.1",'meals_sun_0'=>"2.2",'misc_sun_2'=>"3.3",
            'lodging_mon_0'=>"4.4",'meals_mon_0'=>"5.5",'misc_mon_2'=>"6.6",
            'lodging_tue_0'=>"7.7",'meals_tue_0'=>"8.8",'misc_tue_2'=>"9.9" );

        $week = new TravelExpenseWeek (
            array ('emp_id'              => "1",
                   'week_start'          => "1980-01-06",
                   'territory_worked'    => "Midwest",
                   'comments'            => "comment",
                   'cash_advance'        => "0",
                   'mileage_rate'        => "0.31"),
            $this->_session->getDatabaseHandle());

        $week->parse($response);
        $this->assertEquals(true, $week->persist());

        $week = new TravelExpenseWeek (
            array ('emp_id'              => "1",
                   'week_start'          => "1980-01-06",
                   'territory_worked'    => "Midwest",
                   'comments'            => "comment",
                   'cash_advance'        => "0",
                   'mileage_rate'        => "0.31"),
            $this->_session->getDatabaseHandle());

        $week->readWeek();

        $this->assertEquals(1.1, (float)
                             $week->getExpenseAmount(0, 'lodging_and_hotel'));
        $this->assertEquals(2.2, (float)
                             $week->getExpenseAmount(0, 'meals_breakfast'));
        $this->assertEquals(3.3, (float)
                             $week->getExpenseAmount(0, 'misc_supplies'));

        $this->assertEquals(4.4, (float)
                             $week->getExpenseAmount(1, 'lodging_and_hotel'));
        $this->assertEquals(5.5, (float)
                             $week->getExpenseAmount(1, 'meals_breakfast'));
        $this->assertEquals(6.6, (float)
                             $week->getExpenseAmount(1, 'misc_supplies'));

        $this->assertEquals(7.7, (float)
```

```
                                $week->getExpenseAmount(2, 'lodging_and_hotel'));
        $this->assertEquals(8.8, (float)
                                $week->getExpenseAmount(2, 'meals_breakfast'));
        $this->assertEquals(9.9, (float)
                                $week->getExpenseAmount(2, 'misc_supplies'));
    }
```

In this test, `TravelExpenseWeek` parses the `$response`, persists the `TravelExpenseItems` in `$week->persist()`, rereads them from the database `$week->readWeek()`, and finally validates what was read.

Note that these tests make heavy use of copy-and-paste programming. Keeping things tidy is a general rule, so if a majority of the tests require the same setup, put it in the setup but don't prematurely refactor your tests. Your tests are the first stop to where change happens, so they should be easy to read and easy to modify.

Satisifying the Travel Expense Week Tests

Satisifying `TravelExpenseWeek`'s validity and persistence tests should be predictably easy by now:

```
class TravelExpenseWeek extends PersistableObject {

    public $items = array();

    function __construct ($results, $dbh = null) {
        parent::__construct ($results, $dbh);
    }

    public function isValid() {
        if ($this->isEmpty("emp_id") == true) return false;
        if ($this->isEmpty("week_start") == true) return false;
        if ($this->isEmpty("territory_worked") == true) return false;
        if ($this->isEmpty("mileage_rate") == true) return false;
        return true;
    }

    public function persist() {
        return $this->persistWork ("travel_expense_week",
                                   array ( "emp_id",
                                           "week_start",
                                           "comments",
                                           "territory_worked",
                                           "cash_advance",
                                           "mileage_rate"));
    }

    public function getSqlWhere() {
    return " emp_id = ".$this->emp_id." and week_start = '".$this-
>week_start."'";
    }
```

```
    public function parse(&$request) { }
    public function readWeek() { }
    public function getExpenseAmount($offset, $description) { }
}
```

The functions `parse`, `readWeek`, and `getExpenseAmount` are required by the `TravelExpenseWeekContainerParseRequest` and `TravelExpenseWeekContainerWrite` tests and thus are simply syntactic stubs.

Satisifying the Parse Request Test

The `TravelExpenseWeekContainerParseRequest` test may be a bit tricky because it involves data manipulation. Your first order of business is to take care of the dependencies, which is part of your meta-array road map that you were thinking about earlier. Adding this function to the `TravelExpenseWeek` class in `lib/expense.phpm` will take care of the job:

```
public function getExpensesMetaArray () {
    return array(
        array('name' => 'Lodging',
              'code' => 'lodging',
              'data' => array('Lodging &amp; Hotel','Other','Tips'),
              'persist' => array('lodging_and_hotel', 'lodging_laundry',
                                 'lodging_tips')),
        array('name' => 'Meals',
              'code' => 'meals',
              'data' => array('Breakfast', 'Lunch &amp; Snacks',
                              'Dinner', 'Tips', 'Entertainment'),
              'persist' => array('meals_breakfast', 'meals_lunch',
                                 'meals_dinner', 'meals_tips',
                                 'meals_entertainment')),
        array('name' => 'Transportation',
              'code' => 'trans',
              'data' => array('Airfare', 'Auto Rental', 'Auto Maint./Gas',
                              'Local Transportation', 'Tolls/Parking'),
              'persist' => array ('trans_airfare', 'trans_auto_rental',
                                  'trans_auto_maint', 'trans_local',
                                  'trans_tolls', 'trans_miles_traveled')),
        array('name' => 'Miscellaneous',
              'code' => 'misc',
              'data' => array('Gifts', 'Telephone &amp; Fax', 'Supplies',
                              'Postage', 'Other'),
              'persist' => array('misc_gifts','misc_phone',
                                 'misc_supplies', 'misc_postage',
                                 'misc_other')));
}
```

Along with the meta-array, you also need a way to retrieve each `TravelExpenseItem`. Recall from your `TravelExpenseWeekContainerParseRequest` test that your tests require the `TravelExpenseWeek->getExpenseAmount()` function:

```
$this->assertEquals(8.8, $week->getExpenseAmount(2, 'meals_breakfast'));
```

For now, the function is simply implemented by iterating through `TravelExpenseWeek->item`. Make a note to yourself about the ugliness by adding this to the `TravelExpenseWeek` in `lib/expense.phpm`:

```
/**
* todo: put into an associative array
*/
public function getExpenseAmount($offset, $description) {
    $targetDate = $this->addDays($this->week_start, $offset);
    foreach ($this->items as $item) {
        if ($item->expense_date == $targetDate &&
            $item->description == $description) {
            return $item->amount;
        }
    }
 return "";
}
```

Note that you're calling an `addDays()` function with an offset to get the current string-based representation of the date.

Better make an `addDays()` method, then—a quick three-minute hack for adding the number of seconds in a day (86400 is 60*60*24). `TravelExpenseWeek` now contains:

```
/**
 * todo: will this fail on daylight savings time?
 */
public function addDays($start, $days) {
    return date("Y-m-d", strtotime($start)+$days*86400);
}
```

But this may come with a catch. When you think about it, during the jump to and from daylight-savings time in America, there is a difference of one hour's worth of seconds.for that particular day. How does PHP return the day? Is it local time or GMT? You'd better figure it out or in a mere six months you'll be sweating it out flipping burgers at your local fast-food chain. For now, note the ugliness and continue satisfying your `TravelExpenseWeekContainerParseRequest` test.

The killer function of the `TravelExpenseWeek` object is parsing the PHP's travel expense form response in order to create individual `TravelExpenseItems`, or an associative array of the data.

Recall that you are mapping the following data structure:

```
array(
    array('name' => 'Lodging',
          'code' => 'lodging',
          'data' => array('Lodging &amp; Hotel','Other','Tips'),
          'persist' => array('lodging_and_hotel', 'lodging_other,
                             'lodging_tips'))
```

with the following naming convention contained in PHP's response object:

```
lodging_sun_0
```

After you've got that figured out, it's just a matter of creating TravelExpenseItems and storing them in the TravelExpenseWeeks->items array. Add the parse function to TravelExpenseWeek in lib/expense.phpm:

```
/**
 * This function bridges the gap between the day-based DB and the
 * week-based view
 */
public function getWeekArray() {
    return array ('sun', 'mon', 'tue', 'wed', 'thr', 'fri', 'sat');
}

public function parse (&$request) {
    // section loop
    foreach ($this->getExpensesMetaArray() as $sectionlist) {

        // row loop
        for ($i=0; $i < count ($sectionlist['persist']); $i++) {
            $daynum = 0;

            // day loop
            foreach ($this->getWeekArray() as $day) {
                $index = $sectionlist['code']."_".$day."_".$i;

                if (array_key_exists($index, $request) and
                    $request[$index] <> null and
                    $request[$index] <> "") {
                   // create new item and store in $this->items
                    array_push (
                        $this->items,
                        new TravelExpenseItem (
                            array ('emp_id' => $this->emp_id,
                                   'expense_date' =>
                                   $this->addDays($this->week_start,
                                                  $daynum),
                                   'description' =>
                                      $sectionlist['persist'][$i],
                                   'amount' => (float) $request[$index]),
                            $this->dbh));
                }

                $daynum++;
            }
        }
    }
}
```

Together these five functions constitute the majority of the functionality implemented in TravelExpenseWeek. The class takes on the not-so-trivial task of modifying a web-based data-structure with a database centric one.

Satisfying the Travel Expense Week Container Read and Write Tests

Given the minimum amount of data, the employee ID, and the starting week, your test should populate the `TravelExpenseWeek` with `TravelExpenseItems` to and from the database. Recall that the test roughly does the following:

```
$week = new TravelExpenseWeek (
    array ('emp_id'              => "1",
           'week_start'          => "1980-01-061980-01-06",
           'territory_worked'    => "Midwest",
           'comments'            => "comment",
           'cash_advance'        => "0",
           'mileage_rate'        => "0.31"),
    $this->_session->getDatabaseHandle());

$week->readWeek();
```

This should do the job nicely. Add the `readWeek()` function to `TravelExpenseWeek` in `lib/expense.phpm`:

```
public function readWeek() {
    $sql = "select * from travel_expense_week where";
    $sql .= " emp_id = ".$this->emp_id." and ";
    $sql .= " week_start = '".$this->week_start."'";
    $result = $this->dbh->query($sql);
    if (DB::isError($result) <> true and $result->numRows() > 0) {
        $row = $result->fetchRow();
        $this->contentBase['comments'] = $row['comments'];
        $this->contentBase['territory_worked'] = $row['territory_worked'];
        $this->contentBase['cash_advance'] = $row['cash_advance'];
        $this->contentBase['mileage_rate'] = $row['mileage_rate'];
    }

    $sql = "select * from travel_expense_item where";
    $sql .= " emp_id = ".$this->emp_id." and ";
    $sql .= " expense_date >= '".$this->week_start."' and";
    $sql .= " expense_date <= '".$this->addDays($this->week_start, 6)."'";
    $this->items = array();
    $result = $this->dbh->query($sql);
    if (DB::isError($result) or $result->numRows() == 0) return;
    while ($row = $result->fetchRow()) {
        array_push ($this->items, new TravelExpenseItem ($row));
    }
}
```

Note that there are really two halves to this. The first database lookup returns the state of the `TraveExpenseWeek`; the second half returns the associated `TravelExpenseItems`, adding them to the `TraveExpeneWeek->items` array.

But do you notice a subtle problem? See how we're lazily passing the entire `$row` to `TravelExpenseItem` in its constructor? Recall that the constructor of `PersistableObject`, `TravelExpenseItem`'s parent, is

```
function __construct ($results, $dbh = null) {
    $this->dbh = $dbh;
    if ($results <> null) {
        $this->contentBase = $results; // copy
    }
}
```

Thus, `TravelExpenseItem` blindly stores whatever we give it? Regardless of *what* data it is? Hmmm, this is definitely wasteful, and although the database contains nothing that isn't found in the `TraveExpenseItem`, the object gets its behavior from `PersistableObject`, of which `TravelExpenseWeek`, `Contact`, and `ContactVisit` are all children. Passing any of those objects PHP's `$_REQUEST` would result in a criminal waste of resources.

To change `PersistableObject`'s default behavior from "store everything" to "store what you expect to find," take a step back and create a new test, one that tests the undesired behavior. Because `TravelExpenseItem` is simple, it's an ideal candidate:

```
function testIgnoreExtra() {
    $response = array ('emp_id'              => "1",
                       'expense_date'        => "1980-01-01",
                       'description'         => "one",
                       'amount'              => "1.0",
                       'extra'               => "extra bits");
    $tvi = new TravelExpenseItem($response);
    $this->assertEquals(null, $tvi->extra);
}
```

Sure enough, this test fails. It also means that `TravelExpenseWeek`, which is expected to parse out PHP's `$_RESPONSE` object, will be hugely bloated if we do something silly such as pass in the response during construction.

One way to get around the problem is to know ahead of time what is required by the object in order to ignore anything else. So, rather than have the `TravelExpenseItem->persist()` function looking like:

```
public function persist() {
    return $this->persistWork (
        "travel_expense_item",
        array ( "emp_id",
                "expense_date",
                "description",
                "amount"));
}
```

the `persist` function would be made more concise by passing in some internal state:

```
public function persist() {
    return $this->persistWork (
        $this->contentMetaTable,
        $this->contentMetaOnly);
}
```

Put it all together and you end up with the rewritten class. It's not that different; things are just moved around a bit:

```
class TravelExpenseItem extends PersistableObject {

    protected $contentMetaTable = null;
    protected $contentMetaOnly = null;

    function __construct ($results, $dbh = null) {
        $this->contentMetaTable = "travel_expense_item";
        $this->contentMetaOnly = array ( "emp_id",
                                         "expense_date",
                                         "description",
                                         "amount");
        $content = array();
        foreach ($this->contentMetaOnly as $key) {
            if (array_key_exists($key, $results))
                $content[$key] = $results[$key];
        }
        parent::__construct ($content, $dbh);
    }

    public function isValid() {
        if ($this->isEmpty("emp_id") == true) return false;
        if ($this->isEmpty("expense_date") == true) return false;
        if ($this->isEmpty("description") == true) return false;
        if ($this->isEmpty("amount") == true) return false;
        return true;
    }

    public function getSqlWhere() {
        return " emp_id = ".$this->emp_id." and expense_date ='".$this-
>expense_date."' and description = '".$this->description."'";
    }

    public function persist() {
        return $this->persistWork (
            $this->contentMetaTable,
            $this->contentMetaOnly);
    }
}
```

In this case, you check to see whether what is being passed in via the constructor is what you're looking for. Repair the last remaining `TravelExpenseWeek` test and then refactor.

The `TravelExpenseWeek` write takes significantly less work, considering that each `TravelExpenseItem` already knows how to persist itself. All you need to do is call the `persist()` function of each one.

Simply add the small loop at the end of your persistence function of `TravelExpenseWeek` in `lib/expense.phpm`:

```
public function persist() {
    $this->persistWork ("travel_expense_week",
                        array ( "emp_id",
                                "week_start",
```

```
                                        "comments",
                                        "territory_worked",
                                        "cash_advance",
                                        "mileage_rate"));
        // persist each item to the database
        foreach ($this->items as $item) {
            $item->persist();
        }
        return true;
    }
```

Congratulations. All your unit tests now pass. However there are some remaining features you need to add, including a quick refactoring.

A Quick Refactoring

Having all your unit tests satisfied is an important matter, because during the next refactoring they'll tell you if you have accidentally broken a seemingly unrelated section of code.

Now that `TravelExpenseItem` and `TravelExpenseWeek` have more similar structures but with varying degrees of error checking, move that functionality up into the `PersistableObject`.

Essentially, you want to add this to `PersistableObject`:

```
protected $contentMetaTable = null;
protected $contentMetaOnly = null;

public function persist() {
    return $this->persistWork (
        $this->contentMetaTable,
        $this->contentMetaOnly);
}
```

There is also the same loop in both constructors that can be moved up also:

```
foreach ($this->content as $key) {
    if (array_key_exists($key, $results))
        $this->content[$key] = $results[$key];
}
```

Here's a snapshot of the resulting object:

```
class PersistableObject {
    protected $contentBase = array();
    protected $contentMetaTable = null;
    protected $contentMetaOnly = null;
    protected $dbh = null; // database handle
    protected $dispatchFunctions = array ("role" => "getrole");

    function __get ($key) {
        // content removed for brevity
```

```
}

function __construct ($results, $dbh = null) {
    $this->dbh = $dbh;

    if ($this->contentMetaOnly <> null) {
        foreach ($this->contentMetaOnly as $key) {
            if (array_key_exists($key, $results)) {
                $this->contentBase[$key] = $results[$key];
            }
        }
    } elseif ($results <> null) {
        $this->contentBase = $results; // copy
    }
}

public function implodeQuoted (&$values, $delimiter) {
    // content removed for brevity
}

public function generateSqlInsert ($tableName, $metas, $values) {
    // content removed for brevity
}

public function generateSqlInsert ($tableName, $metas, $values) {
    // content removed for brevity
}

public function generateSqlUpdate ($tableName, $metas, $values) {
    // content removed for brevity
}

public function generateSqlDelete ($tableName) {
    // content removed for brevity
}

public function getSqlWhere() {
    // content removed for brevity
}

protected function isEmpty($key) {
    // content removed for brevity
}

public function isValid() {
    // content removed for brevity
}

public function persistWork ($tablename, $meta) {
    // content removed for brevity
}

public function persist() {
    return $this->persistWork (
```

```
            $this->contentMetaTable,
            $this->contentMetaOnly);
    }

}
```

The constructor is responsible for determining whether data is keepable. Also, note that the behavior is backward compatible because if the `contentMetaOnly` array is null, then `PersistableObject` simply copies the `$results` into its `contentBase`.

Now your `TravelExpenseItem` can be squeezed down ever smaller:

```
class TravelExpenseItem extends PersistableObject {

    function __construct ($results, $dbh = null) {
        $this->contentMetaTable = "travel_expense_item";
        $this->contentMetaOnly = array ( "emp_id",
                                         "expense_date",
                                         "description",
                                         "amount");
        parent::__construct ($results, $dbh);
    }

    public function isValid() {
        if ($this->isEmpty("emp_id") == true) return false;
        if ($this->isEmpty("expense_date") == true) return false;
        if ($this->isEmpty("description") == true) return false;
        if ($this->isEmpty("amount") == true) return false;
        return true;
    }

    public function getSqlWhere() {
        return " emp_id = ".$this->emp_id." and expense_date = '".$this-
>expense_date."' and description = '".$this->description."'";
    }
}
```

Do you see how the `TraveExpenseItem`'s constructor sets up its `PersistableObject` state and then passes the arguments up to `PersistableObject`?

So although you are charged with making an explicit call to the constructor, it gives you the freedom to preliminarily set state in the parent object, `PersistableObject`.

Now make the same modifications to `TravelExpenseWeek`:

```
class TravelExpenseWeek extends PersistableObject {

    public $items = array();

    function __construct ($results, $dbh = null) {
        $this->contentMetaTable = "travel_expense_week";
        $this->contentMetaOnly = array ( "emp_id",
                                         "week_start",
```

```
                                        "comments",
                                        "territory_worked",
                                        "cash_advance",
                                        "mileage_rate");
        parent::__construct ($results, $dbh);
    }

    public function isValid() {
        // content removed for brevity
    }

    public function persist() {
        if (parent::persist() == false) return false;

        // persist each item to the database
        foreach ($this->items as $item) {
            if ($item->persist() == false) return false;
        }
        return true;
    }

    public function getSqlWhere() {
        return " emp_id = ".$this->emp_id." and week_start = '".$this-
>week_start."'";
    }

    public function getExpensesMetaArray () {
        // content removed for brevity
    }

    public function getWeekArray() {
        // content removed for brevity
    }

    public function addDays($start, $days) {
        // content removed for brevity
    }

    public function parse (&$request) {
        // content removed for brevity
    }

    public function readWeek() {
        // content removed for brevity
    }

    public function getExpenseAmount($offset, $description) {
        // content removed for brevity
    }
}
```

Note that `TravelExpenseWeek` overrides `PersistableObject->persist()` function. However, it first calls the `PersistableObject->persist()` and then persists every `TraveExpenseItem` that it's holding. Remember that because the logic behind an insert/update/delete is in

PersistableObject->persistWork(), it continues to work and all you need to do is remember to implement the getSqlWhere function in your concrete classes such as TravelExpenseWeek. The tests are still passing? Good job, but not so fast, considering that a cash advance is not required (as shown in the validity test):

```
function testValidTravelExpenseWeek() {
    $tvi = new TravelExpenseWeek (
        array ('emp_id'                 => "1",
               'week_start'             => "1980-01-01",
               'comments'               => "comment",
               'mileage_rate'           => "0.31",
               'territory_worked'       => "Midwest" ));
    $this->assertEquals(true, $tvi->isValid(), "valid expense");
}
```

But every other test sets cash_advance to zero. What happens if you remove cash_advance from the test? It breaks! This is because PersistableObject blindly creates SQL based on every field of database record.

Modify the persistence test to reflect that neither cash_advance nor comments are required:

```
    function testTravelExpenseWeekPersistence() {
        $this->_session->getDatabaseHandle()->query("delete FROM
travel_expense_week WHERE emp_id = 1 and week_start = '1980-01-01'");
// remove multiples
        $tvi = new TravelExpenseWeek (
            array ('emp_id'                 => "1",
                   'week_start'             => "1980-01-01",
                   'territory_worked'       => "Midwest",
                   'mileage_rate'           => "0.31"),
            $this->_session->getDatabaseHandle());
        $result = $this->_session->getDatabaseHandle()->query("select * FROM
travel_expense_week WHERE emp_id = 1 and week_start = '1980-01-01'");
        $this->assertEquals(0, $result->numRows(), "pre check");
        $this->assertEquals(true, $tvi->persist(), "save");
        $result = $this->_session->getDatabaseHandle()->query("select * FROM
travel_expense_week WHERE emp_id = 1 and week_start = '1980-01-01'");
        $this->assertEquals(1, $result->numRows(), "persisted ok");
        $row = $result->fetchRow();
        $this->assertEquals(0.0, (float) $row['cash_advance'], "cash advance
default");
    }
```

The default values of cash_advance are an easy fix, too; just modify the constructor of TravelExpenseWeek to set the default of zero and an empty string:

```
class TravelExpenseWeek extends PersistableObject {

    function __construct ($results, $dbh = null) {
        $this->contentMetaTable = "travel_expense_week";
        $this->contentMetaOnly = array ( "emp_id",
                                         "week_start",
                                         "comments",
```

```
                                         "territory_worked",
                                         "cash_advance",
                                         "mileage_rate");
        $this->contentBase['comments'] = "";
        $this->contentBase['cash_advance'] = "0.0";
        parent::__construct ($results, $dbh);
    }
```

The tests are again passing, and that means that you're done now, right? Doing a quick "grep todo" uncovers this nagging problem:

```
/**
* todo: will this fail on daylight savings time?
*/
public function addDays($start, $days) {
    return date("Y-m-d", strtotime($start)+$days*86400);
}
```

Reading up on it, you think there may indeed be an issue. Daylight Saving Time ends on the last Sunday in October in most places of America, which means that the clocks are set back and there are more than 86400 seconds during that day. Write up a test to confirm that it fails:

```
function testDaylightSavingTime() {
    $tvw = new TravelExpenseWeek (array());
    $this->assertEquals("2004-10-30", $tvw->addDays("2004-10-29", 1));
    $this->assertEquals("2004-10-31", $tvw->addDays("2004-10-29", 2));
    $this->assertEquals("2004-11-01", $tvw->addDays("2004-10-29", 3),
    "no DST");
}
```

Sure enough, there is a problem. Adding three days to October 29th should land in November rather than October 31, twice. Reading up on your functions, `strtotime()` can do the date math for you by accepting date offsets. Recode the `addDays()` function of `PersistableObject` without the presumption of seconds per day:

```
public function addDays($start, $days) {
    return date("Y-m-d", strtotime($start." +".$days." days"));
}
```

Because your remaining "to do" of modifying the `getExpenseAmount` function is really an optimization, it can wait until later. There is no need for preoptimization, and it's important that you keep the momentum going.

Although that was indeed a lot of work, you now have reasonably well-written persistable objects that are completely backward compatible, your system is growing in stages, and you'll update `Contact` and `ContactVisit` the next time you touch them, so continue along with the current task of the travel expense report.

The Finalized Travel Expense Report

A few hours of work, and you've got what you see in Figure 22-9.

Widget World

Travel Expense Report

Employee Name:	Ed Lecky-Thompson	**Department:**	sales
Number:	1	**Start Week:**	2004-07-04
Territory Worked:	worked		

	Sun	Mon	Tues	Wed	Thur	Fri	Sat	Total
Lodging								
Lodging & Hotel	1.00	2.00	3.00					
Other	2.00							
Tips	3.00							
Lodging Total								
Meals								
Breakfast	4.00							
Lunch & Snacks	5.00							
Dinner	6.00							
Tips	7.00							
Entertainment	8.00							
Meals Total								
Transportation								
Airfare	9.00							
Auto Rental	10.00							
Auto Maint./Gas	11.00							
Local Transportation	12.00							
Tolls/Parking	13.00							
Transportation Subtotal								
Nbr of miles traveled	19.00							
Miles at 0.36 / mile								
Transportation Total								
Miscellaneous								
Gifts	14.00							
Telephone & Fax	15.00							
Supplies	16.00							
Postage	17.00							
Other	18.00							
Miscellaneous Total								
					Subtotal			
					Less Cash Advance			20.00
					Due Employee			
					Due Company			

Comments:

comment

Submit Report

Logout

For Widget World use only - testing environment.

Figure 22-9

It's a first pass, so start with how to feed the Smarty template in file `travel-expenses.php`, which is the user's landing point if coming in from the main menu:

```
<?php

require_once ("lib/common.php");
require_once ("lib/expense.phpm");

// is the user logged in?
if (!$session->isLoggedIn()) {
    redirect ("index.php");
}

$user = $session->getUserObject();

$week = new TravelExpenseWeek (
    array ('emp_id'              => $user->id,
           'week_start'          => getCurrentStartWeek(),
           'territory_worked'    => $_REQUEST["territory_worked"],
           'comments'            => $_REQUEST["comments"],
           'cash_advance'        => $_REQUEST["cash_advance"],
           'mileage_rate'        => $GLOBALS["expense-mileage-travelrate"]),
    $session->getDatabaseHandle());

// display
if ($_REQUEST["action"] != "persist_expense") {

    $week->readWeek();

    $smarty->assign_by_ref ("user",        $user);
    $smarty->assign_by_ref ("week",        $week);
    $smarty->assign('start_weeks',         getStartWeeks());
    $smarty->assign('current_start_week', getCurrentStartWeek());
    $smarty->assign_by_ref ('expenses',    $week->getExpensesMetaArray());
    $smarty->assign('travelrate',
    $GLOBALS["expense-mileage-travelrate"]);
    $smarty->display('travel-expenses.tpl');
    exit();
}

// gather and persist week
$week->parse($_REQUEST);
$week->persist();

print "saved, thanks";

?>
```

Being the user-accessible landing-spot, this script has two modes of operation: one is displaying the travel expenses by reading them from the database (`readWeek`); the other is saving the form data (`persist`) based on whether the action is set to `persist_expense`.

As usual, your very interesting `getExpensesMetaArray()` is the cornerstone of the screen and is passed in as the Smarty variable `expenses`. Also note that all heavy-weight objects are passed to Smarty by reference, so copies aren't automatically created.

Now for the basic Smarty template that displays the travel expense page, which is in `templates/travel-expenses.tpl`:

```
{include file="header.tpl" title="Widget World - Travel Expenses"}
{literal}
<SCRIPT TYPE="text/javascript">
<!--

function reloadCalc () {
    window.document.forms[0].week_start.value =
window.document.forms[1].week_start.value // hidden form
    window.document.forms[0].submit(); // hidden form
}

// -->
</SCRIPT>
{/literal}

<h3>Travel Expense Report</h3>

<form method="post">
<input type="hidden" name="action" value="reload_expense">
<input type="hidden" name="week_start" value="">
</form>

<form id="calc" name="calc" action="travel-expenses.php" method="post">

<table border="0" width="100%">
<tr>
<td><b>Employee Name:</b></td>
<td>{$user->first_name} {$user->last_name}</td>
<td><b>Department:</b></td><td>{$user->department}</td>
</tr>

<tr>
<td><b>Number:</b></td>
<td>{$user->id}</td>
<td><b>Start Week:</b></td>
<td><SELECT NAME="week_start" onchange="reloadCalc()">{html_options
values=$start_weeks output=$start_weeks selected=$current_start_week}
</SELECT></td>
</tr>

<tr>
<td><b>Territory Worked:</b></td>
<td colspan=3><input name="territory_worked" size=20 maxsize=60
value="{$week->territory_worked}"></td>
</tr>
</table>

<br><br>
```

The first form on the page is similar to that of the Customer Contact Report, in which you utilized a special "hidden" form that was populated (by JavaScript) with the value for your starting week. The form was then automatically submitted when a new week was selected.

The start of the second form simply contains some of the basic information that you are collecting, including the `territory_worked`.

The next section begins the spreadsheet part of the display. Code is simply replicated between Sunday and Saturday. Remember that this screen *is* your first attempt and you may have to change items, thus the neglect of a final "week" loop is understandable. For now it's just a basic input form without error-checking or spreadsheet-like activity:

```
<table border="0">
<tr><td></td><td>Sun</td><td>Mon</td><td>Tues</td><td>Wed</td><td>Thur</td>
<td>Fri</td><td>Sat</td><td>Total</td></tr>

{section name=idx loop=$expenses}{strip}
<tr><td><b>{$expenses[idx].name}</b></td><td></td><td></td><td></td><td></td>
<td></td><td></td><td></td><td></td></tr>
   {section name=idx2 loop=$expenses[idx].data}{strip}
   {assign var="p" value=$expenses[idx].persist[idx2]}
   <tr bgcolor="{cycle values="#eeeee,#dddddd"}">
   <td>{$expenses[idx].data[idx2]}</td>

<td><input name="{$expenses[idx].code}_sun_{$smarty.section.idx2.index}"
type="text" size="7" maxsize="17" value="{$week->getExpenseAmount(0, $p)}"></td>
```

Remember that you're building up HTML output that looks like:

```
<input name="lodging_sun_0" type="text" size="7" maxsize="17" value="1.00">
```

The two main loops here iterate through your expense array:

```
return array(
    array('name' => 'Lodging',
          'code' => 'lodging',
          'data' => array('Lodging &amp; Hotel','Other','Tips'),
          'persist' => array('lodging_and_hotel', 'lodging_laundry',
                             'lodging_tips'))
```

The Smarty variable `$p` is dynamically created as a convenience in order that the Smarty code not get too unwieldy: `getExpenseAmount(0, $p)` is more readable than `getExpenseAmount(0, $expenses[idx].persist[idx2])`. Finally, the last two lines representing Sunday are copied six more times to represent each day of the week; they are, thankfully, not displayed.

```
<td><input readonly
name="{$expenses[idx].code}_week_sub_{$smarty.section.idx2.index}"
type="text" size="7" maxsize="17"></td>
   </tr>
   {/strip}{/section}
```

This works well, but there is always an exception. Your clients have requested that transportation subtotal before accepting the "number of miles traveled," which then totals that section.

Smarty can handle its own conditionals, so put that in next. But the number of miles traveled is not in your expenses meta-array, so it must be accounted for:

```
{if $expenses[idx].code == 'trans'}
        <tr><td>{$expenses[idx].name} Subtotal</td>
<td><input readonly name="{$expenses[idx].code}_sun_sub" type="text" size="7"
maxsize="17"></td>
```

Again, the code is duplicated six more times (not displayed) before the subtotal:

```
<td><input readonly name="{$expenses[idx].code}_week_sub" type="text" size="7"
maxsize="17"></td></tr>

        <tr><td>Nbr of miles traveled</td>
            <td><input name="mitr_sun" type="text" size="7" maxsize="17"
value="{$week->getExpenseAmount(0, 'trans_miles_traveled')}"></td>
```

The rest of the week is not shown, for brevity.

```
        <td><input readonly name="mitr_tot" type="text" size="7"
maxsize="17"></td></tr>
        <tr><td>Miles at {$travelrate} / mile </td><td><input readonly
name="mitot_sun" type="text" size="7" maxsize="17"></td>
```

. . . as are the duplicated mileage (mitrs).

```
<td><input readonly name="mitot_tot" type="text" size="7"
maxsize="17"></td></tr>
        <tr><td>{$expenses[idx].name} Total</td><td><input readonly
name="{$expenses[idx].code}_sun_sub2" type="text" size="7" maxsize="17"></td>
    {else}
        <tr><td>{$expenses[idx].name} Total</td><td><input readonly
name="{$expenses[idx].code}_sun_sub" type="text" size="7" maxsize="17"></td>
```

This completes the transportation exception and continues with the standard processing. Essentially it's avoiding adding an extra line to the bottom of transportation for mileage.

```
<td><input readonly name="{$expenses[idx].code}_week_sub" type="text" size="7"
maxsize="17"></td></tr>
    {/if}

{/strip}{/section}
```

The rest of the screen is the subtotals, amounts due, and weekly comments:

```
<tr><td></td><td></td><td></td><td></td><td></td><td
colspan="3">Subtotal</td><td><input readonly name="subtotal"
type="text" size="7" maxsize="17"></td></tr>
<tr><td></td><td></td><td></td><td></td><td></td><td colspan="3">Less Cash
Advance</td><td><input name="cash_advance" type="text" size="7" maxsize="17"
value="{$week->cash_advance}"></td></tr>
<tr><td></td><td></td><td></td><td></td><td></td><td colspan="3">Due
Employee</td><td><input readonly name="totaldueemployee" type="text" size="7"
maxsize="17"></td></tr>
<tr><td></td><td></td><td></td><td></td><td></td><td colspan="3">Due
```

```
Company</td><td><input readonly name="totalduecompany" type="text" size="7"
maxsize="17"></td></tr>
</table>

<br><br>
Comments:<br><TEXTAREA NAME="comments" COLS=80 ROWS=6>{$week->comments}
</TEXTAREA>
<br><br><center>

<input type="submit" name="submit" value=" Submit Report " >

</center>

<input type="hidden" name="action" value="persist_expense">
</form>

{include file="footer.tpl"}
```

Even though the screen lacks even basic error-checking or any spreadsheet-like features, you're still at a very pivotal point in the project. This screen, as is, could technically be used in production.

Unadvisable, yes, but this is the point where you are delivering business value! Get this into the hands of your clients and start getting their feedback.

This big gulp has just taken care of stories 2, 3, and 10.

Travel Expense Report As Spreadsheet

Your clients are enjoying the travel expense report; they're using it and giving you valuable feedback regarding how, what, and why.

Fortunately for you, all the additional functionality they want is to get it to act like a spreadsheet. So, what's that going to take?

JavaScript offers one event that you're interested in, `onkeyup`; it can be applied to your input boxes in order to recalculate on the fly when new information is entered.

But it turns out that simulating a spread-sheet is not as easy as it sounds. Here is the new `template/travel-expenses.tpl`:

```
{include file="header.tpl" title="Widget World - Travel Expenses"}
{literal}
<SCRIPT TYPE="text/javascript">
<!--
function subtotal(thisForm, totalcell, cellArray) {
    var subtot = 0;
    for (var i=0; i < cellArray.length; i++) {
        if(isNaN(thisForm[cellArray[i]].value))
            thisForm[totalcell].value = 0;
        else
            subtot = Math.round(subtot*100 +
                                thisForm[cellArray[i]].value*100)/100;
    }
```

```
        thisForm[totalcell].value = subtot;
        return subtot;
    }
```

Starting from the top, the JavaScript function `subtotal()` takes a form, which is a place to put the answer and an array of numbers to add.

Although JavaScript supports decimals, it doesn't support arbitrary precision. So because we'd like dollars down to the penny (as in $9.99), we need to multiply everything by 100. Do the math, round the result, and then divide by 100.

So by adding 0.01 to 9.98, multiply everything by 100: 1.0 and 998.0; do the addition: 999.0; round the result: 999; and divide by 100: 9.99. Yes, it looks as though it'll be a pain.

The next few functions deal with totaling up columns in each section (Lodging, Meals, Transportation, and so on), vertically totaling each amount per day. Finally, `daycalc()` is called by each of the "cells":

```
    function subday (thisForm, totalcell, prefix, maxindex) {
        var cellArray = new Array (maxindex);
        for (var i=0; i < maxindex; i++) {
            cellArray[i] = thisForm[prefix+i].name;
        }
        return subtotal(thisForm, totalcell, cellArray);
    }

    function subweek (thisForm, totalcell, prefix, postfix) {
        return subtotal (thisForm, totalcell,
                        new Array (prefix+'sun'+postfix, prefix+'mon'+postfix,
                                   prefix+'tue'+postfix, prefix+'wed'+postfix,
                                   prefix+'thr'+postfix, prefix+'fri'+postfix,
                                   prefix+'sat'+postfix));
    }

    function daycalc (thisForm, day, code, thisindex, maxindex) {
        subday (thisForm, code+"_"+day+"_sub", code+"_"+day+"_", maxindex);
        subweek(thisForm, code+"_week_sub_"+thisindex, code+"_", '_'+thisindex);
        subday (thisForm, code+"_week_sub", code+"_week_sub_", maxindex);
        totalcalc (thisForm);
        return true;
    }
```

The function `daycalc()` is called from each cell that accepts user-input in the HTML form in such a manner:

```
    onkeyup="return daycalc(this.form, 'sun', 'lodging', '0', 3)"
```

Remember that the screen is generated from your expense meta-array:

```
    array('meals_breakfast', 'meals_lunch',
                             'meals_dinner', 'meals_tips',
                             'meals_entertainment')
```

But JavaScript has no knowledge of PHP or Smarty or whatever else you're using in the backend. So you need to be explicit and tell JavaScript which cell you are working with and how many cells need to be subtotaled. These, respectively, are the last two arguments in the `daycalc()` function call: `'0'` is the current row and `'3'` signifies the maximum number of rows that need to be vertically subtotaled in the `subday` function.

The number of miles, an exception, needs to be calculated separately. The cells for the mileage input are named `mitr_sun`, `mitr_mon`, and so on. Their subtotal, which is the number of miles multiplied by the mileage rate, is represented by `mitot_sun`, `mitot_mon`, and so on. After the horizontal weekly totals are calculated with `subweek`, the total mileage is updated based on the current vertical day. Finally, the grand total of the transportation section is updated.

```
function micalc (thisForm, day, travelrate) {
    var totalcell = 'mitot_'+day;
    var sourcecell = 'mitr_'+day;

    // mileage input and mileage total
    thisForm[totalcell].value = Math.round(
        thisForm[sourcecell].value * 100 * travelrate)/100;
    subweek (thisForm, 'mitr_tot', 'mitr_', '');
    subweek (thisForm, 'mitot_tot', 'mitot_', '');

    // trans total by day
    thisForm["trans_"+day+"_sub2"].value = Math.round(
       (thisForm[totalcell].value * 100) +
       (thisForm["trans_"+day+"_sub"].value * 100))/100;

    // grand total of week
    subweek (thisForm, "trans_week_sub2", "trans_", "_sub2");
    totalcalc (thisForm);
}
```

Next, some basic error-checking:

```
function checkTransInput (thisForm, day) {
    if (thisForm["trans_"+day+"_sub"].value > 0 &&
        thisForm["mitr_"+day].value == "" ) {
        alert( "Please enter your mileage for "+day);
        return false;
    }
    return true;
}

function checkInputs(thisForm) {
    if ( checkTransInput (thisForm, "sun") == false) { return false; }
    if ( checkTransInput (thisForm, "mon") == false) { return false; }
    if ( checkTransInput (thisForm, "tue") == false) { return false; }
    if ( checkTransInput (thisForm, "wed") == false) { return false; }
    if ( checkTransInput (thisForm, "thr") == false) { return false; }
    if ( checkTransInput (thisForm, "fri") == false) { return false; }
    if ( checkTransInput (thisForm, "sat") == false) { return false; }
    if (  thisForm["subtotal"].value == 0) {
        alert ("Please enter data.");
```

```
            return false;
        }
        if (thisForm["territory_worked"].value == "") {
            alert ("Please enter your territory worked.");
            return false;
        }
        return true;
    }
```

Now comes the monster function totalcalc(), which makes sure that the entire form is recalculated:

```
    //
    // No easy way to pass a php array to JS unless we generate it by hand.
    //
    function totalcalc (thisForm) {
        var sectionArray = new Array ('lodging', 'meals', 'trans', 'misc');
        var subtotal = 0;
        for (var i=0; i < sectionArray.length; i++) {
            subtotal = subtotal +
                Math.round(thisForm[sectionArray[i]+"_week_sub"].value*100)/100;
        }
        subtotal = subtotal + Math.round(thisForm["mitot_tot"].value*100)/100;
        thisForm["subtotal"].value = subtotal;
        var total = subtotal - Math.round(thisForm["cash_advance"].value*100)/100;
        total = Math.round(total*100)/100;
        if (total >= 0) {
            thisForm["totaldueemployee"].value = total;
            thisForm["totalduecompany"].value = "";
        }  else {
             thisForm["totaldueemployee"].value = "";
             thisForm["totalduecompany"].value = Math.round(total * 100)/100 *(-1);
        }

    }
```

In the event of an error, the recalculate() function will be attached to a "recalculate" button. This function "touches" every row and every column in order to cause the screen to be initially calculated. Remember that columns are represented by days, and rows are the first layer of your expense meta-array. Although the recalculate function is not the epitome of good programming, it is easier to read when it is laid out by brute force rather than by relying on another layer of looping.

```
    // don't knock it; looping is less readable
    function recalculate (thisForm, mileage) {

        daycalc(thisForm, 'sun', 'lodging', '0', 3);
```

Monday through Friday are removed for brevity.

```
        daycalc(thisForm, 'sat', 'lodging', '0', 3);
        daycalc(thisForm, 'sat', 'lodging', '1', 3);
        daycalc(thisForm, 'sat', 'lodging', '2', 3);

        daycalc(thisForm, 'sun', 'meals', '0', 5);
```

Monday through Friday are removed for brevity.

```
        daycalc(thisForm, 'sat', 'meals', '0', 5);
        daycalc(thisForm, 'sat', 'meals', '1', 5);
        daycalc(thisForm, 'sat', 'meals', '2', 5);
        daycalc(thisForm, 'sat', 'meals', '3', 5);
        daycalc(thisForm, 'sat', 'meals', '4', 5);

        daycalc(thisForm, 'sun', 'trans', '0', 5);
```

Monday through Friday are removed for brevity.

```
        daycalc(thisForm, 'sat', 'trans', '0', 5);
        daycalc(thisForm, 'sat', 'trans', '1', 5);
        daycalc(thisForm, 'sat', 'trans', '2', 5);
        daycalc(thisForm, 'sat', 'trans', '3', 5);
        daycalc(thisForm, 'sat', 'trans', '4', 5);

        daycalc(thisForm, 'sun', 'misc', '0', 5);
```

Monday through Friday are removed for brevity.

```
        daycalc(thisForm, 'sat', 'misc', '0', 5);
        daycalc(thisForm, 'sat', 'misc', '1', 5);
        daycalc(thisForm, 'sat', 'misc', '2', 5);
        daycalc(thisForm, 'sat', 'misc', '3', 5);
        daycalc(thisForm, 'sat', 'misc', '4', 5);

        micalc(thisForm, 'sun', mileage);
```

Monday through Friday are removed for brevity.

```
        micalc(thisForm, 'sat', mileage);
        return (totalcalc(thisForm));
    }

    function reloadCalc () {
        window.document.forms[0].week_start.value =
    window.document.forms[1].week_start.value // hidden form
        window.document.forms[0].submit(); // hidden form
    }

    // -->
    </SCRIPT>
    {/literal}
```

Now that there is code to calculate the row and column totals, every cell needs to responds to the `onkeyup` event by calling `daycalc()`. Modify the seven daily inputs in your `templates/travel-expenses.tpl`:

```
<input name="{$expenses[idx].code}_sun_{$smarty.section.idx2.index}"
onkeyup="return daycalc(this.form, 'sun', '{$expenses[idx].code}',
'{$smarty.section.idx2.index}', {$smarty.section.idx2.total})"
type="text" size="7" maxsize="17" value="{$week->getExpenseAmount(0, $p)}">
```

The mileage input functions also need to have their keyup function:

```
<input name="mitr_sun" onkeyup="return micalc(this.form, 'sun',
{$travel_rate})" ...
```

A recalculate button should be added; it will aid in debugging the JavaScript in the event that everything doesn't work perfectly.

```
<br><br>
<center>
<input type="button" value=" Recalculate " onclick="return recalculate
(this.form, {$travelrate})">
</center>
<br><br>
Comments:<br><TEXTAREA NAME="comments" COLS=80 ROWS=6>{$week->comments}
</TEXTAREA>
<br><br><center>
```

The main Submit button now checks for basic input errors by running `checkInputs()` from the `onclick` event:

```
<input type="submit" name="submit" value=" Submit Report " onclick="return
checkInputs(this.form);">
```

Almost done.

There are just a few outstanding issues. For instance, if the drop-down start week is changed, the form will reload and recalculate itself, but unfortunately that event won't be fired when the form initially loads itself.

You need to do make sure that the form runs your JavaScript `recalculate()` function when the form is loaded. This is accomplished from the onload event of the <body> tag. But the <body> tag is defined in your `header.tpl`, so here is what you do: In your `travel-expenses.php` file, modify the display section:

```
// display
if ($_REQUEST["action"] != "persist_expense") {

    $week->readWeek();

    $smarty->assign_by_ref ("user",          $user);
    $smarty->assign_by_ref ("week",          $week);
    $smarty->assign('start_weeks',           getStartWeeks());
    $smarty->assign('current_start_week',    getCurrentStartWeek());
    $smarty->assign_by_ref ('expenses',      $week->getExpensesMetaArray());
    $smarty->assign('travelrate',            $GLOBALS["expense-mileage-
                                             travelrate"]);
    $smarty->assign('formfunc',
        "recalculate(window.document.forms[1],".
        $GLOBALS["expense-mileage-travelrate"].")");
    $smarty->display('travel-expenses.tpl');
    exit();
}
```

You're assigning a function to the variable `formfunc`. Now change the `header.tpl` so that it reads accordingly:

```
<!DOCTYPE HTML PUBLIC "-//W3C//DTD HTML 4.01 Transitional//EN">
<html>
<head>
<meta HTTP-EQUIV="content-type" CONTENT="text/html; charset=ISO-8859-1">
<title>{$title|default:"no title"}</title>
</head>
<body onload="{$formfunc|default:""}">
<h1>Widget World</h1>
<hr><p>
```

The `$formfunc` Smarty variable holds the name of a JavaScript function that is executed when the HTML form is loaded, `$formfunc`. The `onload` form property is set to `$formfunc` or empty string if `$formfunc` is not defined. This allows you to selectively recalculate your entire spreadsheet during the loading process. By your doing so, `daycalc()` has to be concerned only with its column, row, and the totals rather than with recalculating every cell during every keystroke.

Anything Else

Feedback from your clients has told you that the "Number of Miles" doesn't appear to be persisted correctly from the screen. Being the exception to your meta-array, it's not taken care of in the `parse()` function.

By now you should know the drill. Whip up a test:

```
    function testParsingNbrMiles() {

        $this->_session->getDatabaseHandle()->query("delete FROM
travel_expense_item WHERE emp_id = 1 and expense_date >= '1980-01-06' and
expense_date <= '2001-09-15'");

        $response = array ('mitr_sun' => "1.1",
                           'mitr_mon' => "2.2");

        $week = new TravelExpenseWeek (
            array ('emp_id'              => "1",
                   'week_start'          => "1980-01-06",
                   'territory_worked'    => "Midwest",
                   'comments'            => "comment",
                   'cash_advance'        => "0",
                   'mileage_rate'        => "0.31"),
            $this->_session->getDatabaseHandle());

        $week->parse($response);
        $this->assertEquals(true, $week->persist());

        $week = new TravelExpenseWeek (
            array ('emp_id'              => "1",
                   'week_start'          => "1980-01-06",
```

```
                'territory_worked'    => "Midwest",
                'comments'            => "comment",
                'cash_advance'        => "0",
                'mileage_rate'        => "0.31"),
            $this->_session->getDatabaseHandle());

        $week->readWeek();

        $this->assertEquals(1.1, (float) $week->getExpenseAmount(0,
'trans_miles_traveled'));
        $this->assertEquals(2.2, (float) $week->getExpenseAmount(1,
'trans_miles_traveled'));
    }
```

Make it succeed accordingly with changes to `TravelExpenseWeek lib/expense.phpm`:

```
    private function createByRequest ($description, $daynum,
                                     $index, &$request) {
        if (array_key_exists($index, $request) and
            $request[$index] <> null and
            $request[$index] <> "") {
            array_push (
                $this->items,
                new TravelExpenseItem (
                    array ('emp_id' => $this->emp_id,
                           'expense_date' =>
                           $this->addDays($this->week_start, $daynum),
                           'description' => $description,
                           'amount' => (float) $request[$index]),
                    $this->dbh));
        }
    }

    /**
     * This function bridges the gap between the day-based DB and the
     * week-based view
     */
     public function parse(&$request) {
        foreach ($this->getExpensesMetaArray() as $sectionlist) {
            for ($i=0; $i < count ($sectionlist['persist']); $i++) {
                $daynum = 0;
                foreach ($this->getWeekArray() as $day) {
                    $index = $sectionlist['code']."_".$day."_".$i;
                    $this->createByRequest (
                        $sectionlist['persist'][$i], $daynum,
                        $index, $request);
                    $daynum++;
                }
            }
        }
        // arg, mitr is an exception
        $daynum = 0;
```

```
        foreach ($this->getWeekArray() as $day) {
            $this->createByRequest ("trans_miles_traveled", $daynum,
                                    "mitr_".$day, $request);
            $daynum++;
        }
    }
```

A new function, `TravelExpenseWeek->createByRequest()`, rids you of code duplication because it's called during normal processing and for the mileage.

All the tests pass, your clients are happy, the screen works. Now you're done with Story 4: "Expense Report as Spreadsheet," as shown in Figure 22-10.

So, other than "simply working," you've got a well-tested system and the beginning of a framework which is capable of evolution.

You've seen how PHP, JavaScript, and browsers do (and do not) interact, how each one is responsible for its layers, and how to move information among all of them. Creating complex spreadsheet-like behavior, although not easy, can be done with relatively little code.

So, where do you go from here? Just plod through the rest of the stories? Keep on reading, because there is another important lesson in the final section.

Mock Objects

Sometimes during testing you need to interact with a deterministic object that for various reasons you do not have access to in your testing environment. For instance:

- The real object is nondeterministic, such as a real-time stock or weather-feed.
- The real object is too slow for your test suites, such as an overloaded transactional production database.
- You need to test exceptional situations, such as an intrusion alarm or systems outage.
- The real object does not exist. This can be anything from not having access to the required object to required intra-object functionality.

Essentially, a mock object is an object that feigns enough functionality or required functionality for you to fully test your system.

For instance, if you wanted to test for session timeouts, errors, or just malicious cracking you might import `mock-widgetsession.phpm`, which consists of:

```
class MockWidgetSession extends WidgetSession {
    public function getUserObject() {
        return new WidgetUser(
            array (
                'id' => 1,
```

Widget World

Travel Expense Report

Employee Name:	Ed Lecky-Thompson	**Department:**	sales
Number:	1	**Start Week:**	2004-07-04
Territory Worked:	worked		

	Sun	Mon	Tues	Wed	Thur	Fri	Sat	Total
Lodging								
Lodging & Hotel	1.00	2.00	3.00					6
Other	2.00							2
Tips	3.00							3
Lodging Total	6	2	3	0	0	0	0	11
Meals								
Breakfast	4.00							4
Lunch & Snacks	5.00							5
Dinner	6.00							6
Tips	7.00							7
Entertainment	8.00							8
Meals Total	30	0	0	0	0	0	0	30
Transportation								
Airfare	9.00							9
Auto Rental	10.00							10
Auto Maint./Gas	11.00							11
Local Transportation	12.00							12
Tolls/Parking	13.00							13
Transportation Subtotal	55	0	0	0	0	0	0	55
Nbr of miles traveled	19.00							19
Miles at 0.36 / mile	6.84	0	0	0	0	0	0	6.84
Transportation Total	61.84	0	0	0	0	0	0	61.84
Miscellaneous								
Gifts	14.00							14
Telephone & Fax	15.00							15
Supplies	16.00							16
Postage	17.00							17
Other	18.00							18
Miscellaneous Total	80	0	0	0	0	0	0	80
					Subtotal			182.84
					Less Cash Advance			20.00
					Due Employee			162.84
					Due Company			

Recalculate

Comments:

comments

Save Report

Logout

For Widget World use only - testing environment.

Figure 22-10

```
                        'username' => 'ed',
                        'md5_pw' => "827ccb0eea8a706c4c34a16891f84e7b",
                        'first_name' => "Ed",
                        'last_name' => "Lecky-Thompson",
                        'email' => "ed@lecky-thompson.com",
                        'role' => "s",
                        'department' => "sales"));
        }

    }
```

Coding details aside, this `MockWidgetSession` example would allow your testing environment to simulate a login for whatever reason you require.

Smarty can also be used to mock up HTML screens. Other than displaying the HTML to the screen, you can save the HTML in a variable and do with it as you please.

For instance, Story 6 requires sales manager notification, so you merely need to send an e-mail to the managers when the contacts are saved. Sounds pretty simple, but you're faced with an issue of how intensively you'd like to test, especially since they'd like the content of the e-mail to include the HTML from the input screen.

Getting the screen HTML is not an issue. Essentially, you need to test the browser output, which is nice because up until now, you haven't been testing what the browser sees. For end-to-end completeness, the following test will reference the HTML output using a regular expression.

```
function testContactEmail () {
    $u = new WidgetUser(
        array ('id'          => 1,
               'username'    => "ed",
               'first_name' => "Ed",
               'last_name'  => "Lecky-Thompson",
               'email'       => "ed@lecky-thompson.com",
               'role'        => "s",
               'department' => "sales"));
    $cv = new ContactVisit (
        array ('emp_id'              => "1",
               'week_start'          => "1980-01-01",
               'company_name'        => "test one",
               'contact_name'        => "Big One",
               'city'                => "Columbus",
               'state'               => "OH",
               'accomplishments'     => "phone call",
               'followup'            => "",
               'literature_request' => ""));
    $c = new Contact (
        array ("emp_id"              => "1",
               "week_start"          => "1980-01-01",
               "shop_calls"          => 2,
               "distributor_calls"  => 3,
               "engineer_calls"      => 4,
               "mileage"             => 50,
               "territory_worked"    => "Central Ohio",
```

```
                "territory_comments" => "Buckeyes are great." ),
            $this->_session->getDatabaseHandle());

        list ($email,_$from, $subject, $message, $headers) =
            generateContactEmail($u, $c, array ($cv), false);

        // test screen capture, requires 7bit ascii encoding (read: none)
        $this->assertEquals(1, preg_match ("/Employee Name..............Ed
Lecky-Thompson/", $message), "employee name");
        $this->assertEquals(1, preg_match
 ("/company_name_0........................................test one/",
$message), "company name");
        $this->assertEquals(1, preg_match
 ("/shop_calls..................................2/", $message),"shop calls");
        $this->assertEquals(1, preg_match ("/To: ed@lecky-thompson.com/",
 $headers),"email");

        // test base64 encoding
        list ($email_from, $subject, $message, $headers) =
            generateContactEmail($u, $c, array ($cv));
        $this->assertEquals(0, preg_match ("/Employee Name..............Ed
Lecky-Thompson/", $message), "employee name");
        $this->assertEquals(1, preg_match ("/To: ed@lecky-thompson.com/",
 $headers),"email");
    }
```

The `generateContactEmail()` function is designed to return what is required by the PHP `mail()` function: `mail($email_address, $subject, $message, $headers);`.

Also note that in this example you're testing what the browser sees. Instead of testing 100 percent of the HTML output, you're making sure that the form contains the information you expect. Thus, the simple regular expression of:

```
"/Employee Name..............Ed Lecky-Thompson/"
```

will perfectly match the generated HTML of:

```
<tr><td><b>Employee Name:</b></td><td>Ed Lecky-Thompson</td>
<td><b>Department:</b></td><td>sales</td></tr>
```

Also note that because the base64 encoding is unreadable by humans, the tests of base64 encoding check only for the existence of the e-mail address in the e-mail header, and not the `Employee Name` because `Employee Name`, being in the message and base64 encoded, can't be normally read.

Here are the functions that might be placed in your `lib/common-functions.phpm`:

```
function mimeifyContent ($content, $mime_boundary,
                         $filename, $flagBase64=true) {
    $message = "";

    $message .= " \r\n";
    $message .= "--".$mime_boundary."\r\n";
```

```
    $message .= "Content-Type: text/html;\r\n";
    $message .= " name=\"".$filename.".html\"\r\n";

    // default is 7bit ascii
    if ($flagBase64) {
        $message .= "Content-Transfer-Encoding: base64\r\n";
    }

    $message .= "Content-Disposition: attachment;\r\n";
    $message .= " filename=\"".$filename.".html\"\r\n";
    $message .= "\r\n";

    if ($flagBase64) {
        $message .= base64_encode($content);
    } else {
        $message .= $content;
    }

    $message .= "\r\n";

    return ($message);
}

function generateContactEmail (&$user, &$contact,
                               $contactVisits, $flagBase64=true) {
    global $GLOBALS;
    require_once ($GLOBALS["smarty-path"].'Smarty.class.php');
    $smarty = new Smarty;
    $smarty->assign_by_ref ("user", $user);
    $smarty->assign_by_ref ("contact", $contact);
    $smarty->assign_by_ref ("contactVisits", $contactVisits);
    $smarty->assign('start_weeks', getStartWeeks());
    $smarty->assign('current_start_week', $contact->week_start);
    $smarty->assign("max_weekly_contacts", $GLOBALS["max-weekly-contacts"]);

    $email_body = @$smarty->fetch('customer-contacts.tpl');

    $headers = "";
    $headers .= "From: ".$GLOBALS["email-from"]."\n";
    $headers .= "To: ".$user->email."\n";
    if (strlen ($GLOBALS["email-contact-cc"]) > 0)
        $headers .= "Cc: ";
        $headers .= $GLOBALS["email-contact-cc"];
    $headers .= "\n";
    if (strlen ($GLOBALS["email-contact-bcc"]) > 0)
        $headers .= "Bcc: ".$GLOBALS["email-contact-bcc"]."\n";

    $mime_boundary = "<<<--==+X[".md5(time())."]";
    $headers .= "MIME-Version: 1.0\r\n";
    $headers .= "Content-Type: multipart/mixed;\r\n";
    $headers .= " boundary=\"".$mime_boundary."\"";

    $message = "";
    $message .= "This is a multi-part message in MIME format.\r\n";
```

```
        $message .= "\r\n";
        $message .= "--".$mime_boundary."\r\n";

        $message .= "Content-Type: text/plain; charset=\"iso-8859-1\"\r\n";
        $message .= "Content-Transfer-Encoding: 7bit\r\n";
        $message .= "\r\n";

        $message .= $GLOBALS["email-contact-message"]."\n\n";

        $nextEnding = "\r\n";

        $message.=mimeifyContent($email_body,$mime_boundary,
                              "customer-contact", $flagBase64);

        $message.="--".$mime_boundary."".$nextEnding;

        $subject = $user->emp_id." ".$user->last_name." : ".$user->email_subject;

        return array ($user->email, $subject, $message, $headers);
    }
```

Two things should be noted here. You're calling `$smarty->fetch()` instead of `$smarty->display()`. The `fetch` function places the HTML output into a variable rather than to the screen, as does the `display` function.

Also, for technical reasons, it's safer to base64-encode HTML output if there is any chance of its using non-7bit ASCII, for instance, if you're using Unicode or non-English characters. However, base64 encoding the HTML in the e-mail makes it practically untestable, which is why the `$flagBase64` argument exists.

If this function contained the function to physically mail the e-mail instead of simply creating the content, you'd most certainly create and utilize a mock object that simulated the e-mailing API and didn't base64 encode the content.

Summary

We're concluding this Widget World software development effort at this point. You would be correct in pointing out that not all the stories and features have been completed, but the authors have no desire to be a historical revisionist of this real-world example or force you through another one hundred redundant pages of the same procedure; by now you have the tools and know-how to complete it yourself.

Testing is one aspect of software development that has historically been considered little more than "busy work," but you've experienced how test-driven development can help you not only develop your code but also find bugs and continue to test even when you're working on distant parts of the system.

Refactoring is not just a technical word for "code cleanup." Ideally, it shouldn't even be considered a distinct task from software development. Refactoring is simply a coding priority, much in the same way that developing system objects is a coding priority, too. Plus, you've seen how constant refactoring can help to develop a complex framework without the need for excessive analysis and unused features.

These are just a few of the principles of eXtreme Programming, which is designed to reduce complexity in order to sustain development by keeping your code base nimble and flexible. Although not every project is a candidate for the complete methodology of XP, that does not mean that your methodology of Spiral, Waterfall, or RUP cannot benefit from some of the practices such as testing and constant refactoring. Additionally, due to lack of peer programmers (for you the reader), as well as space and focus on code, there are many aspects of XP that we haven't formally delved into, such as planning for a release and measuring the project metrics. XP is quite a disciplined approach and we encourage you to learn more about it, because its strengths and payoffs are solidly concerned with the subtleties of software development as a team.

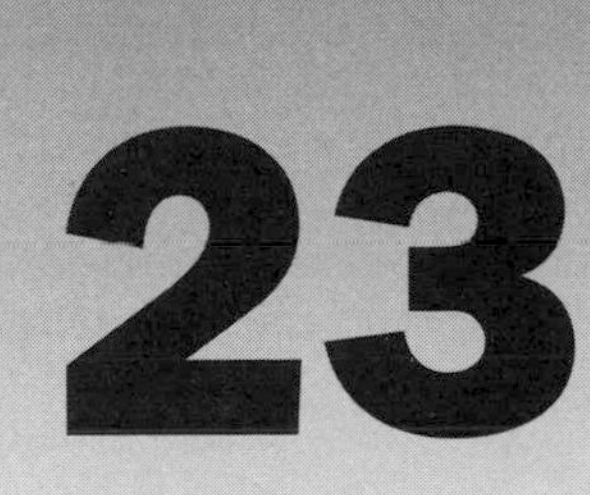

Quality Assurance

Your Sales Force Automation project is looking pretty good. You're on schedule and on budget, and the client is, thus far, happy with the beta version running on your development environment. Furthermore, by employing rigorous unit testing throughout the build process in the previous chapter, you can be sure that the individual components that comprise the application all function more or less correctly independently, and hence there shouldn't be any deep-rooted problems in the code itself.

At this time, you might well be tempted to let your guard down. In fact, you have now reached one of the most critical stages in the entire project. The application is more or less complete and the client is urging you to let him or her use it. You must resist, however.

Quality assurance, usually abbreviated to QA, is a term you might be familiar with. Indeed, it is borrowed from traditional manufacturing and engineering processes and is the kind of procedure you expect to be carried out on your new DVD player or luxury family sedan. Why would you not, therefore, want to apply it to something as complex and crucial as your application?

In this short but crucial chapter, you're introduced to the process of quality assurance in large-scale PHP projects. You'll learn about why quality is of great importance and what it means in terms of your expectations and those of your client. You'll learn about the kinds of testing you need to do to confidently be able to give your application a seal of approval, and how to get your team on board to help you when things go wrong.

Introduction to QA

Somewhat understandably, expectations of the reliability of the Web and the Internet at large are still rock-bottom among its everyday users. Chances are you've had a client call you recently to say that her e-mail was down and so she might not have received anything you've sent her. Maybe you've tried to order something online recently, only to get kicked off while your credit card was being processed. Maybe your friend's ISP has been down for a couple of days and nobody in tech support seems to be able to tell him when he'll be back online again.

Scenarios like this are all too common. What is truly terrifying is that they accepted. Your client didn't sound surprised when she told you her e-mail was down. You probably didn't even curse under your breath when your online order went wrong. And your friend shrugged his shoulders and found an Internet café downtown.

This is unique to the Internet. If you bought a new car, and it stalled on the highway just weeks later, you'd be pretty mad at your dealer. If you ordered a mocha latte before work and your barista gave you a cappuccino, you'd get mad at her and make her fix it. And if your DVD player went wrong, you'd take it back.

There are two reasons people don't get mad when the Internet doesn't work right. The first is that they reason that there's something innately complicated about the Internet, and that it must go wrong as a result. This is a non sequitur, of course; yes, the Internet is complicated, but so is your DVD player. In practice, too, the underlying infrastructure (that is, the servers, routers and so forth) of the Internet is pretty much rock solid; it's bad programmers who make things break.

The second and more crucial reason applies to those who have had previous experience with Internet application developers. Frequently, their past experiences with these agencies and individuals have been such that their expectations with present vendors have hit rock bottom. The fact of the matter is that there are few other industries in which such an explosion of dangerously underskilled labor has occurred in the past few years. This has manifested itself in both appalling freelance Web "professionals" and some truly appalling Web agencies. Excellence is the exception rather than the rule. In effect, there are literally thousands of vendors who talk the talk but don't walk the walk.

The more cynical inference from this observation is that because your client's expectations will be low, you should aim low, too, because they're not likely to get mad at you if things go wrong. This approach, however, is not only cynical but also not commercially sensible.

Why You Should Aim High

Aiming to have a high-quality product before handing over to the client is not just about keeping the client happy; it's about maintaining your own sanity, too.

It is inevitable that your assembled system will, initially at least, be functionally defective in some way. This does not necessarily mean that it will malfunction in the traditional sense; it could be slow when real-world data is applied, or have some unforeseen business logic error. A systematic approach to quality assurance prior to handover ensures that:

- Developer time and, hence, cost spent on resolving defects is minimized through a thorough, structured approach
- The team's timely transition onto other projects can be closely adhered to
- Problems encountered during deployment can be isolated as being unrelated to the application itself

Quite apart from that, it is perhaps a question of attitude. Compare the following with one another:

- "The client's expectations are low, therefore I can underdeliver without fear of reprisal."
- "The client's expectations are low, therefore when I overdeliver I will be seen to excel."

It goes without saying that being seen to excel will quickly set you apart from the competition. The client's previous experience with other suppliers may have been lackluster and their expectations low as a result, but have you noticed how they have not used those other suppliers again?

Aiming high means striving for high quality. The difference between striving and achieving starts with knowing what quality means in the first place.

What Is Quality?

There is some confusion over what constitutes quality in a software application. Let us return to our analogy of a family sedan. When a motoring journalist speaks of a high-quality car, he or she is probably not referring explicitly to reliability or performance per se but rather to less tangible and quantifiable factors, such as:

- The durability of the interior
- The use of expensive, solid materials such as brushed chrome
- Purely aesthetic touches, such as blue-illuminated readouts
- The firm clunk noise made when the driver slams the door shut

Quality here is not so much a single deciding factor or even anything positive; rather, it is a function of all the areas in which something *could* go wrong, but doesn't.

This view is supported in the approach often taken by motoring journalists when reviewing a car or inspecting it for the first time at a trade show. The repeated activation of the cup-holder mechanism, the pressing of switches, the caressing of upholstery—these are the quick-and-dirty litmus tests used to assess quality. Yet none of these tests tells us anything about the car's handling, gas mileage, reliability, or annual depreciation. So why are they important?

The truth of the matter is that although you can't judge a book by its cover, you can more often than not judge a car by its interior. A car with a smoothly ejecting cup holder, tactile, chrome-tipped switches, and seamless mechanisms is almost certainly also going to enjoy superb reliability going forward. The highest-quality brands in these exterior facets—BMW, Audi, Mercedes—are all consistently rated among the most reliable on the road, too.

This same rule can be applied to your Web applications. Quality is not just about whether the site stays up and does what the functional specification said it would do. It's more about the little things and, inevitably, when the little things on the surface are right, the big things underneath are right, too.

Enough about cars! What makes a Web application high quality, and how is it measured?

Measurable and Quantifiable Quality

There are a number of core areas of quality that need to be assessed when conducting quality assurance on your application. Inevitably, the importance you apportion to each one depends very much on the nature of your product and its target audience.

Functional Compliance

At the most simple and basic level, your application should provide functionality exactly as detailed in your project's original functional specification.

This goes beyond simply ensuring that no PHP warnings or errors appear, of course. The behavior of your application must be correct, under an exhaustive set of test conditions. This includes:

- When an update button is pressed, the database is actually updated.
- When a welcome e-mail should be sent to a new user, the e-mail is sent and is correct.
- When a user conducts a search, the data returned is accurate against the database and the search criteria specified.

Such compliance may seem obvious, but often the most obvious points are overlooked in quality assurance programs.

Real-World Tolerance

Real World Tolerance (or RWT) means that your application should be able to cope with environments and conditions closer to its real-world, live operation than those it may run under during development.

This does not just refer to quantities of users or data on the system. It also refers to the requirement that the system be able to cope properly when a user, for example, does not enter data in an expected format. The correct behavior in such a situation should be, of course, to provide the user with an error message. It is hugely important to simulate such conditions because it is all but inevitable that users will not only themselves do bad things from time to time, but that the data they supply shall from time to time be bad, too.

Grace During Failure

There is a temptation when developing to not account for every possible scenario; certain scenarios might seem unlikely.

However, this temptation should be resisted. The only thing worse than the failure of a user's credit card to be processed successfully, for example, is failing to inform the user that his or her credit card was not processed successfully.

At any stage at which a failure could occur, however unlikely it may be, your application must cope gracefully. Consider, for example, an unreachable database server. Clearly, this is an undesirable situation and the application will not function correctly when this occurs; with luck, it is a problem that will be resolved correctly by your systems administrators. However, if not accounted for, your application may simply return zero search results on searches or tell people their login is incorrect. Both these pieces of information arise because your application does not account for the condition of the database being completely inaccessible, and your user will be severely misled as a result. Providing a simple "Sorry, the site is unavailable at present" page offers an obvious and immediate workaround.

Load Tolerance

During functional testing, your application will have been hit by a combined audience probably not much bigger than your development team; ten, maybe eleven people simultaneously using the system.

But in practice, of course, your audience may be much bigger than this, with a requirement for a hundred, a thousand, maybe even ten thousand simultaneous users to be supported.

You will know this figure from your technical specification and will have drafted an architecture to suit. What may have worked on paper will not necessary translate to the real world, however. It is vital, of course, that it does.

If the application's response under heavy load is an unacceptable response time or, worse still, outright failure, then clearly the client will not be in a position to accept the product as satisfactory.

Usability

The latest buzzword in interface architecture these days is that of usability. Championed by leading experts such as Jakob Nielsen (see his excellent Web site at `www.useit.com`), it refers to the inherent intuitiveness and logic of a user interface. It can apply to not only the Web but also traditional client-side software applications, and even the control panel of a washing machine.

It is typically measured by the ease and speed with which a user new to the application can perform certain tasks. These tasks are expressed as objectives, and no specific instructions on their completion are issued. For example, users of a Web mail application might be asked to compose a new message to `foo@example.com`. They would not be asked to click the Compose button in the top-left corner of the screen, or enter `foo@example.com` in the recipient box, and so forth.

The observation of the user's effectiveness in carrying out these tasks is the cornerstone of usability testing, discussed shortly.

Veneer

Just one step removed from usability is the veneer or finish of the product. Remember the earlier analogy involving chrome switches and cup holders in the sedan? The veneer of your application is the direct equivalent, and, because it is the first real experience users will have of your application, it provides a telling insight into the underlying quality of the application beneath.

What do we mean by veneer, however? Consider the quick-and-dirty examples throughout this book, outside the realm of our larger Sales Force Automation project. We have constructed them to demonstrate a concept, with no other purpose in mind. As a result, they've never looked or felt that great—a bit rough around the edges, perhaps. That's never really mattered, however, because we've merely been demonstrating a technical concept. A finished product should never adapt this approach, of course.

The chrome switches in the driver's cabin are the properly rendered Previous and Next buttons on your pagination. The cup holders' smooth eject mechanism is the manner in which the navigation refreshes updates with each section of your application selected. This is the veneer or finish of your application and, although not a showstopper if poorly implemented, it can speak volumes about the overall quality of your application.

Many software architects and engineers are less gifted with designing the aesthetics of a user interface than you might think. As part of your own project management methodology, it is important to ensure that an experienced senior designer with interface architecture skills is on hand to ensure that the polish on your finished product stays well and truly intact.

When a small change is requested late in the project, the temptation is to cut corners and allow a software engineer to take ownership of the new feature. Do this only if you have a rock-solid style guide in place, as discussed in the chapter on project management methodologies earlier in this book. Otherwise, you may find your beautiful application blighted by the appearance of a grey rectangular Submit button just where you least expect it.

Testing

It goes without saying that the single most effective way to ensure that the core qualities alluded to previously pervade throughout your project is to test, test and test some more.

Testing can, however, take many forms. Each of the previous qualities has one or more testing methodologies associated with them. Let's look at them in turn.

Unit Testing

Good news; you've already done this at least once before, or at least you have if you followed the previous chapter in detail.

We discussed the concepts of unit programming and testing framework earlier in the book, including the theory of why these are good practices to employ in large projects. In the previous chapter, you put that theory into practice in building the application.

Let's recap briefly, however. Unit-driven programming involves constructing your application in neatly packaged, distinct components that have an interface yielding human-predictable results from a given set of a data. A testing framework is then constructed for each component that asserts a series of human-determined theoretical results based on a series of theoretical inputs, and then tests the validity of those assertions by comparing those theoretical results against the actual results derived from the execution of that component's methods.

These frameworks become black boxes that allow you to continuously test the functionality of your components throughout their evolution. You can construct such frameworks, therefore, early in your project, and regression test your components as they evolve and become more sophisticated to ensure that they still produce the results expected. Put crudely, you can test to ensure that your changes have not broken something that used to work!

Unit testing picks up coding errors. Such errors are typically oversights on the part of the programmer. It does not pick up any other form of problem, and hence it is only part of the testing required to ensure high levels of quality with respect to functional compliance. As an example; consider a Web mail application. You may have built a user class, a mailbox class, and a message class. All three may pass your unit tests.

However, consider the Reply button on a message being viewed. It would instantiate a new message object and copy the sender property of the original message object to the recipient object of the message object. This action may not be performed by any specific method in any class and hence may not be the subject of any unit test.

Should the recipient for the e-mail not be set correctly when Reply is clicked, this is very clearly a functional error that needs resolving. It is not, however, one that a unit testing framework would pick up in any three of the tests being performed. You can see, therefore, that unit testing is not the ultimate test of functional compliance; in effect, it tests the model in your model, view, controller (MVC) design pattern.

Functional Testing

Functional testing is the other half of ensuring functional compliance quality on your project. It is normally conducted with due deference to the original functional specification of the project.

There are a number of possible approaches to formalizing functional testing. The most important rule to follow is that it is in fact formalized in the first place. Merely having a developer perform a quick run-through of key functionality isn't enough on a large-scale project.

One approach to consider is to assemble a team of test personnel, ideally relatively intelligent individuals typical of your target audience, and issue them formal paperwork for completion. Consider assigning each test team member a specific area of the site to test.

The Functional Test Paper

Considering our Web mail example, you may devise a form that looks something like the table that follows. The Action and Expected Result columns should be completed by you in your role as project manager. Your test team will complete the actual result, which you can then use to score each test as either a FAIL or a PASS.

Action	Expected Result	Actual Result	Score
Open the login page by clicking the login link on the navigation.	Login page is displayed, featuring username and password text boxes, and the Submit button.	Expected result	PASS
Enter the login **joet1301f** and password **ixrsh0z1** and press Login.	The form submits and the page reloads, stating that your login is successful. After five seconds, you are automatically transferred to the home page.	Expected result	PASS
Click the Inbox link in the navigation.	You will be taken to your inbox. You will see a number of messages listed. For each message, subject, date received, and sender should be listed. The total number of pages comprising this mailbox will be shown. Previous and Next buttons will be visible if more than one page exists.	Expected result EXCEPT that no Next button displayed despite showing page 1 of 18.	FAIL

It is, of course, extremely important that any FAIL marks are followed up. As project manager, it is worth assuming a role whereby any failures are first double-checked by yourself and, if found to be genuine, entered into a fault management system, the likes of which we discuss later.

The actions you place on each functional testing paper will of course be derived directly from the functional specification in one form or another. Essentially, you are devising a user journey. Your test team will need to follow the actions sequentially; for example, it will obviously be important that any logins take place before any activity dependent on the user is logged in. Advise your test users that if they find themselves unable to execute subsequent actions due to a block failure, they should mark their paper accordingly and move on.

Functional Testing Considerations

You must make sure that each branch of the user journey is covered in testing, or at least to the extent at which you can be reasonably confident that the system is functionally correct. A branch occurs every time a decision is made. For example, if logins to your system come in three flavors (say, a normal user, super user, and administrator), you will need to have three initial branches. If for each of these logins a user may choose one of three mailboxes to view, an additional three branches per initial branch will be created.

It may be helpful to draw all the possible user journeys using a tree diagram of some sort, which you can then translate into the previous testing paperwork.

This method of functional testing is not infallible but far more effective than simply asking the development team to "test thoroughly." The resulting paperwork also forms a sort of affidavit that can be presented to the client as documented proof that the system has been thoroughly tested prior to handover.

Load Testing

The general principle of load testing is to determine exactly what kind of extreme environmental conditions your application can cope with before it falls over.

The traditional belief is, of course, that it is sufficient to simply ascertain whether the application can support the number of simultaneous users specified in the technical specification, and whether the response times under such a usage level are within a reasonable limit.

A more bullish approach is to keep turning up the amp until the speakers blow. Clients much prefer to be told that "your site can, under its present infrastructure, support 530 simultaneous users" than simply "yes, it supports the 500 simultaneous users you need it to." Knowing that the system has support for only 30 additional users may not be the news that clients want to hear, but it is better that they hear it sooner rather than later.

The principles of load testing are detailed further in Appendix C, "Performance Tuning PHP."

Usability Testing

Cast your mind back to the sample functional testing worksheet discussed earlier in the chapter. We allocated tasks to our testers such as: "Open the login page by clicking the login link on the navigation."

A similar task in Usability Testing would be simply phrased: "Log in to the system."

The purpose is quite different, of course, hence the very different phrasing. Usability testing does not concern itself with whether things work; this is taken as read from the functional testing. Rather, it asks how effectively or how easily the user can perform the task in question.

Perhaps uniquely in software testing, usability testing rarely involves questions put directly to the test subjects. Rather, observation is key.

When instructed to, say, "log in to the system," the user will be observed, either in person or remotely. Their actions in achieving (or not achieving) the task required of them, which are only in part quantifiable in figures, are of a great deal of interest.

For example, you may want to attempt to answer the following questions:

- Where does the user physically look for the login link? Is it where you placed it, or somewhere else? (Note: the position of a user's cursor on-screen is often a clue to where the user is looking.)
- What sort of delay is there between when the login screen loads and the user starts typing his or her username?
- Does the user visit any other pages in error prior to finding the login page?

The answers to these questions will allow you to formulate a good idea as to the usability of your application. It can, admittedly, be difficult to quantify such research into figures, however.

Usability testing and useful metrics thereof is a huge topic in and of itself and outside the scope of this chapter. More information on the various approaches available can be found on the excellent site `www.useit.com`, run by Jakob Nielsen himself.

Fault Tracking

The testing you carry out using the previous techniques will inevitably lead to observations, such as:

- Functional testing has shown that the recipient address is not correctly copied into the new message when replying to an existing message.
- Load testing has shown that the system does not respond in a sufficiently timely manner to requests made at 530 simultaneous sessions.
- Usability testing has shown that people expect the Previous and Next buttons in the Mailbox view to be at the top of the page, not the bottom.

These observations are relatively useless without the tabulation of corresponding action points. For the issues outlined previously, you may raise action points as follows:

- Please ensure that the recipient, when replying to a message, is automatically set to be the sender of the message being replied to.
- When 530 sessions are active, divert users to a "service unavailable" page explaining that the server is not able to process their request at this time.
- Move the Previous and Next buttons in the Mailbox view to the top of the page.

These actions are all simple enough. But on a larger project, you may have hundreds, even thousands of action points: bugs that need fixing and tweaks for fine tuning. How do you keep track?

Effective Fault Management Using Mantis

In the last part of this chapter, you'll encounter a fault management system known as Mantis, a freely available package currently available from `http://mantisbt.sourceforge.net`.

The purpose of Mantis is to allow you to effectively keep tabs on all faults and defects in your projects, assign them to developers for resolution, and allow developers to pass comment on them where appropriate.

Mantis is a Web-based application written in PHP (what else?) that would typically function as an extranet. Whether you choose to open it up for access to your clients is entirely up to you. When working with smaller clients this can often be beneficial because it allows them to feel part of the QA process. Mantis supports multiple users, each with his or her own access levels and rights, so you can offer different access to yourself and, say, your developers.

Many other fault management systems exist, of course. We have chosen to look at Mantis specifically because it is freely available, easy to use, and written in PHP. This means that you could, in theory, modify and extend it to better suit your needs if so required.

Installing Mantis

Download the Mantis installation archive from its Web site and unpack it in the usual manner:

```
# tar -xzvf mantis-0.18.2.tar.gz
```

This will create a directory called `mantis-0.18.2` containing all the source and configuration files for Mantis. You should have a Virtual Host in Apache's `httpd.conf` configuration file pointing to this location as follows:

```
<VirtualHost 192.168.168.2>
        ServerAdmin you@example.com
        ServerName mantis.example.com
        CustomLog /home/ed/logfile_mantis common
        ErrorLog /home/ed/errlog_mantis
        DocumentRoot /home/ed/public_html/mantis-0.18.2
</VirtualHost>
```

If you are using some Web server other than Apache, you should set up a virtual server to support Mantis in the manner in which you are accustomed.

Configuring Mantis for the First Time

Mantis is dependent on MySQL, so you need to have this installed to be able to go any further. We have thus far in this book advocated almost exclusively the use of PostgreSQL in preference to MySQL, but as Mantis is an off-the-shelf product we don't have a lot of choice. If you feel strongly, Mantis is rather well written in that it uses a database abstraction layer of sorts, found as `core/database_api.php` in the installation. You could, in theory, adapt it to function with PostgreSQL instead.

Assuming that you have better things to do with your time, Mantis includes a wizard to get MySQL set up with the necessary database tables for you automatically. Simply create a database called Mantis, and pipe `sql/db_generate.sql` into that database as follows:

```
# /usr/local/mysql/bin/mysqladmin -uroot -p<your root password> create
mantis
# /usr/local/mysql/bin/mysql -uroot -p<your root password> mantis <
sql/db_generate.sql
```

If your MySQL server is not running on the same server as your Web server, you will of course need to include the `-h` directive, for example:

```
# /usr/local/mysql/bin/mysqladmin -hservername -uroot -p<your root
password> create mantis
# /usr/local/mysql/bin/mysql -hservername -uroot -p<your root password>
mantis < sql/db_generate.sql
```

This will create a blank database. All future database changes can be done using Mantis itself.

All that remains now is to tell Mantis where to find the database. Copy the file `config_inc.php.sample` to `config_inc.php` in the installation directory; then open it in your text editor of choice.

There is a huge number of options for you to adjust, but the most important of them are the name and location of your database. Amend the lines in question so that they match your setup:

```
# set these values to match your setup
$g_hostname      = "db";
$g_port          = 3306;         # 3306 is default
$g_db_username   = "root";
$g_db_password   = "myrootpassword";
$g_database_name = "mantis";
```

Note that in the previous example we are using root as the user to connect to MySQL. This is probably a bad idea on a production system, and you may want to use `mysqladmin` to create a less privileged user with access only to your Mantis database, and specify this as the connecting user in your configuration.

You are now ready to log in to Mantis for the first time.

Logging in As Administrator

Fire up your Web browser and point it at the virtual host you created earlier. You should see a login screen similar to Figure 23-1.

Now, log in as administrator. By default, the password has been set in the MySQL database generation script to be `root`.

After you've logged in, you should first lock down your Mantis installation. The best way to do this is to create another account, not named administrator, and with a more secure password that you can use for day-to-day administration. This is particularly important if you are able to access your Mantis installation over the public Internet.

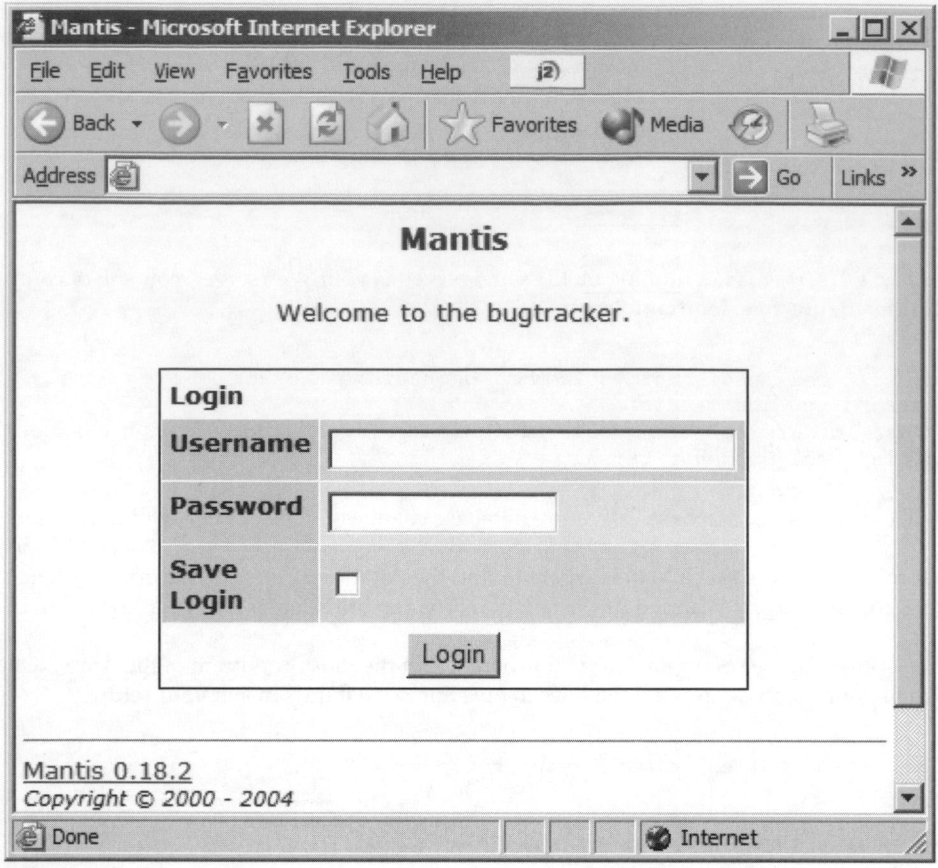

Figure 23-1

Creating and Editing Users

Everybody who will have access to Mantis—that is, yourself, your development team, and maybe your client's representatives—will require a user account.

To create an account, click the `manage` link when logged in as an administrator. Manage users is selected by default, and accordingly you will see a list of user accounts on the system. Creating a new account is as simple as clicking Create New Account. Don't forget to set the access level to an appropriate level; anyone whose only task is to report bugs or defects need be only a reporter, whereas you want your own account to be administrator.

After you have created all necessary user accounts (including at least one with administrative privileges), you can completely remove the administrator account.

After you have created a user, you can modify even more properties of that user's account by clicking his or her username. Figure 23-2 shows a typical user editing session in Mantis.

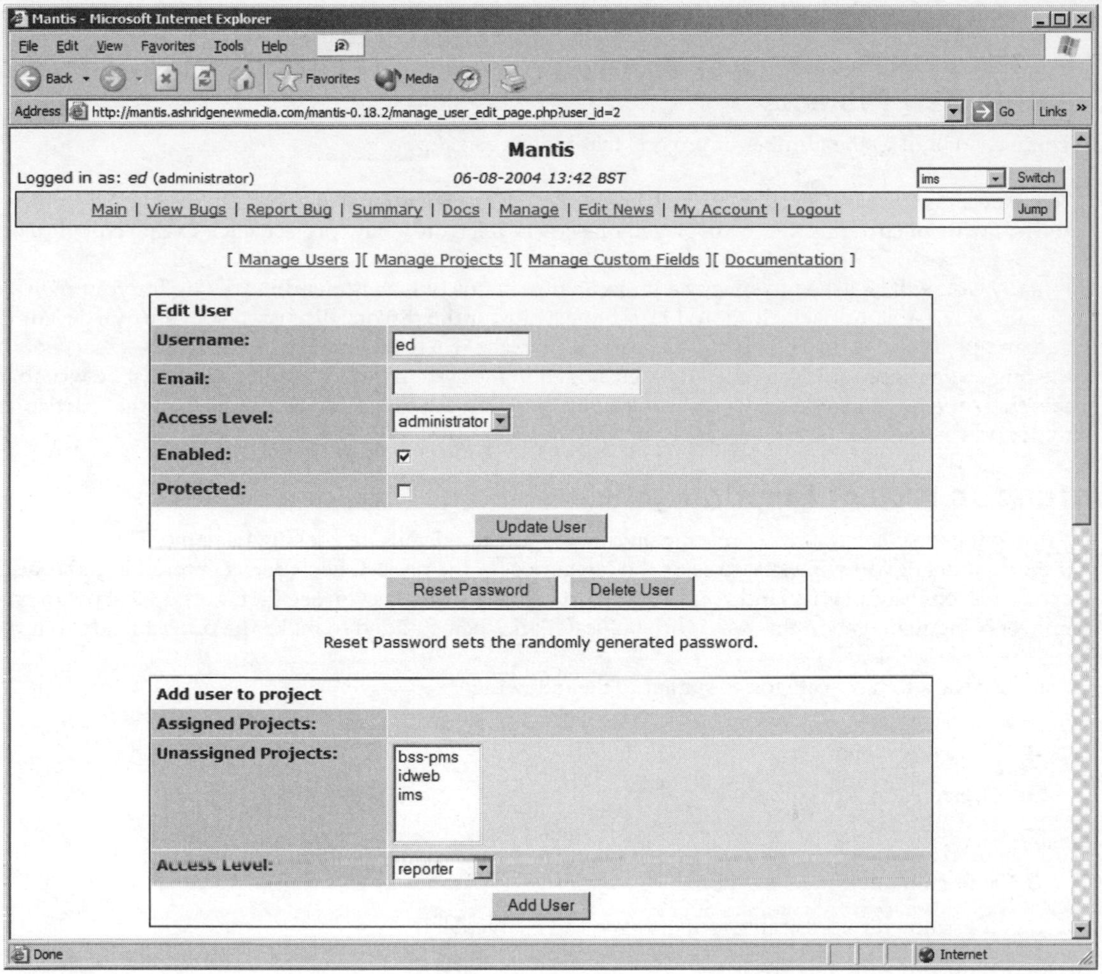

Figure 23-2

Adding a User to a Project

Crucially, you can use the Edit User screen not only to edit the user's details but also to add that user to a project. By default, a user does not have access to any projects, which means that even if he or she has a reporter status, that user can't report any bugs.

To add the user you are editing to a project, select the project in question (if this is your first time using Mantis, you won't have any yet) and click Add. If a project is marked as public, you can skip this step because all users will have access. This is very rarely desirable, especially if you have clients using the system.

It is worth pointing out that when creating an account your new users will automatically be sent an e-mail containing their username and password, and the URL for accessing this installation of Mantis. If this behavior is not desirable, you can disable it in the Mantis configuration file you were editing a few moments ago.

Creating New Projects

There is no limit to the number of projects that Mantis can support.

To create a new project, select Manage Projects. A similar view to that shown in Manage Users will be shown, with all current projects displayed on-screen. To create a new project, click Create New Project.

Initially, you will be asked to specify a project name, status (which is an arbitrary flag for your own reference), view status (which should be set to private for the reasons discussed previously), description, and an upload file path. The upload file path is the place where any binary files (such as screenshots of the bugs being replicated) attached to bugs lodged in the system will be stored. This must be writable by the Web server, which you may need to effect by manually changing the permissions of that particular folder on your server.

Setting up Project Bug Categories

After you have created a new project, you can edit its finer details by clicking its name. The most important detail you will want to set is the categories for the project. Each defect entered into the system can be placed in a category, and you will want to define as many as you see fit. Figure 23-3 shows a typical project being managed in this way, with bug categories being added to make the project ready to use.

You may want to have categories similar to the following:

- Copy/text change
- Design and Appearance
- Usability
- Functionality: Business Logic
- Functionality: Desirable (out of scope and chargeable)
- Functionality: Incorrect
- Functionality: Malfunction
- Functionality: Missing (but detailed in specification)
- Functionality: User Interface
- Project Management and Administration
- Database Schema
- Systems and Infrastructure

After you have created a set of categories, you can easily reuse these on future projects by using the Copy From and Copy To buttons judiciously.

With your project set up, you may need to select it whenever you log into Mantis in future, especially if you have more than one project on the system. The small drop-down list box in the top-right corner of the screen allows you to flip among projects by name.

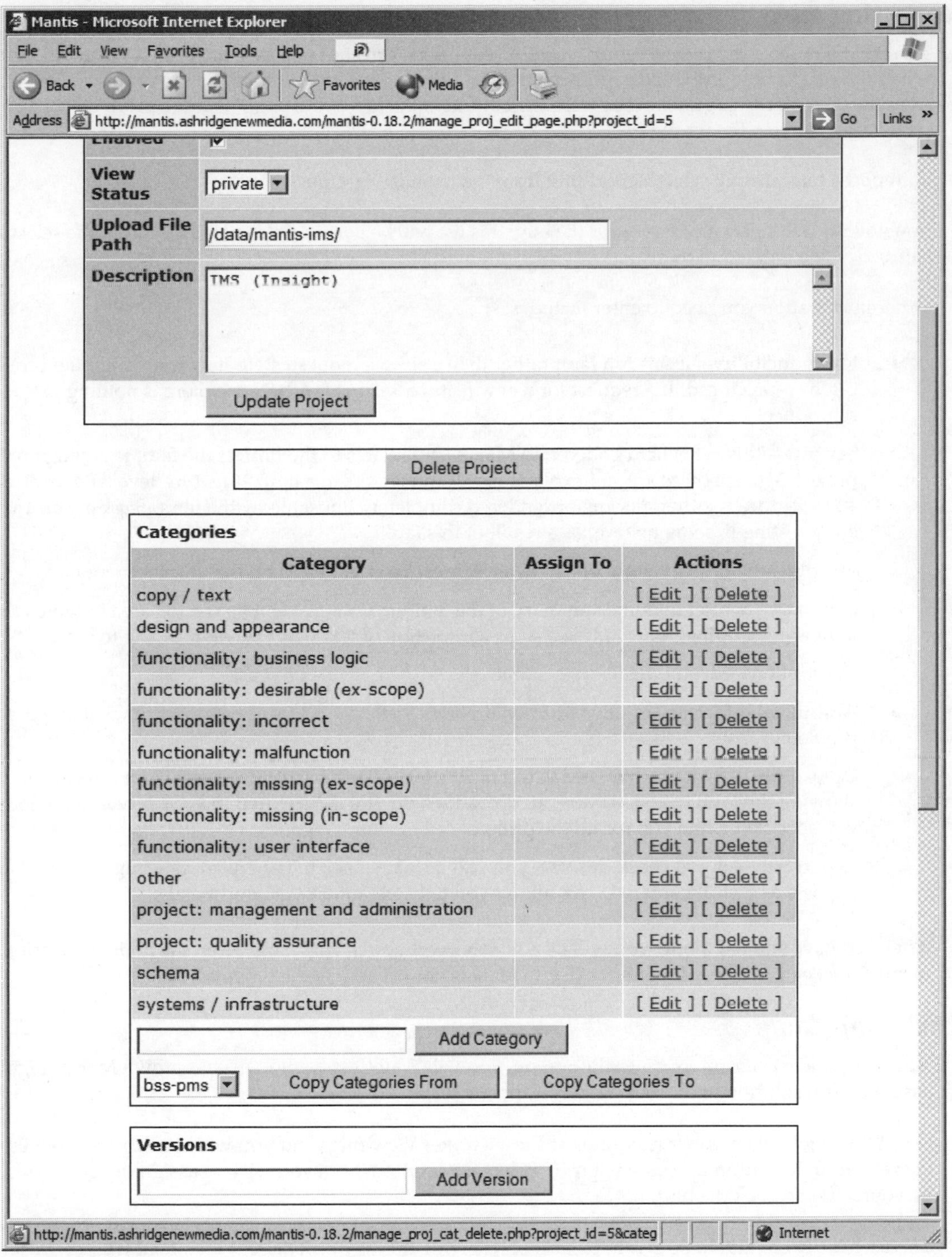
Mantis - Microsoft Internet Explorer
File Edit View Favorites Tools Help
Back Favorites Media
Address http://mantis.ashridgenewmedia.com/mantis-0.18.2/manage_proj_edit_page.php?project_id=5
Go Links
View Status
private
Upload File Path
/data/mantis-ims/
Description
IMS (Insight)
Update Project
Delete Project
Categories
Category
Assign To
Actions
copy / text
design and appearance
functionality: business logic
functionality: desirable (ex-scope)
functionality: incorrect
functionality: malfunction
functionality: missing (ex-scope)
functionality: missing (in-scope)
functionality: user interface
other
project: management and administration
project: quality assurance
schema
systems / infrastructure
[Edit] [Delete]
Add Category
bss-pms
Copy Categories From
Copy Categories To
Versions
Add Version
http://mantis.ashridgenewmedia.com/mantis-0.18.2/manage_proj_cat_delete.php?project_id=5&categ
Internet

Figure 23-3

Reporting Bugs

Now that you have the project set up, you and your team can start entering bugs. Don't forget to translate the faults you have found into more specific tasks rather than simply announce the problem. For example, "Move the pagination bar from the bottom to the top of the page" is more productive than "The pagination bar is in the wrong place."

To report a bug, simply select Report Bug from the main navigation.

You will need to select a category for the bug; this list will be generated dynamically from the selection of categories you entered earlier.

Other information you need to enter includes:

- Reproducibility—if this is a fault rather than a simple request, state how frequently the problem can be reproduced. If a request for a new feature, select N/A because there is nothing to reproduce!
- Severity—this list is hard-coded into Mantis and relates to the impact the fault is having on the project. Most of these are self-explanatory. *Feature* refers to a fault at feature-level and implies that a key feature is either missing or rendered completely unusable by the fault. *Block* means that other testing is being held up as a result of this fault!
- Priority—the priority with which the fault must be attended to by the development team.
- Summary—a brief one-line summary of the fault or, if insufficient space, the area in which the fault is developing, for example, "Auto-completion of text fields when replying to e-mails."
- Description—further detail on the fault.
- Additional Information—any additional points that may aid the developers in resolving the problem.
- Upload file—if you wish to associate a binary file with this fault (for example, a screenshot showing the fault in action) you can upload it here. It will be stored in your server in the location you specified when you set up the project.
- Report Stay—if you check this box, you will be taken back to the report new bug screen when the bug is successfully entered. This allows you to batch-enter bugs more easily.

After you have entered a bug, you will be able to view it under View Bugs from the main navigation menu. One key point worth noting is that the bug is not yet assigned to anyone. This is the next step!

Assigning Bugs

After bugs have been entered into the system, you will doubtless want to use your own Mantis login to assign their resolution to one of your development team.

Select the bug by its number from the list shown under View Bugs and you will see a drop-down list of users next to the button named Assign To. Select the user to whom you wish to assign the bug (which can be yourself) and click the button.

The user lucky enough to be given the task of resolving this bug will be sent an e-mail with a direct link to the bug.

You can also bulk-assign bugs from the View Bugs screen. This can be useful if you are working on a small project and you want to assign all open bugs to a given user. Place a check mark next to the bugs you want to assign, select Assign in the drop-down list box at the bottom of the list, and click Go. You will be invited to select a user, and the checked bugs will then be assigned to that user in the same way.

Annotating Bugs

Your developers may want to take issue with a bug you have raised or, alternatively, add their questions or comments.

They may do this by viewing the bug, entering text in the relevant text box, and clicking Add Bugnote. The comment will be recorded against the bug, and a copy is sent to the person who raised the bug in the first place. The bug raiser may then want to add their own comments (in reply if necessary), which will in turn be sent to the developer, and so on.

A developer may also want to make use of the resolution status of the bug to indicate his or her progress on the task at hand, or reaction to the bug overall. This includes such flags as "not a bug," "won't fix," "fixed," and so forth. Any changes in status also generate notification e-mails to the bug raiser.

Resolving Bugs

After a developer has fixed a bug, he or she simply marks it as resolved by clicking the Resolved button. This changes both the resolution status and the overall status of the bug to "resolved," firing e-mails to the bug raiser in the process.

If the project administrator agrees that the bug is resolved, he or she may set its overall status to "closed." If he or she disagrees that it is resolved, it can be set back to be assigned and the resolution status is set to "reopened." Again, the developer will be notified that the bug has been reopened.

Both status flags are of particular use in the View Bugs view, in which filters may be applied to see only bugs of specific statuses. Color coding is used to indicate the status of bugs at a glance.

Getting the Most Out of Mantis

Despite being quite straightforward to get started with, Mantis is a hugely powerful package that requires and deserves in-depth attention.

There is not the space here to touch on all its power, but the Mantis Web site at `http://mantisbt.sourceforge.net` features in-depth instructions, including a useful FAQ.

Summary

In this chapter, you were introduced to the basics of quality assurance. You first learned what quality really means in application development, and the six core concepts that constitute it.

You then learned how many of those concepts can be tested in the real world to determine and measure quality on any given project, and how best to record the results of those tests.

Finally, you were introduced to Mantis, a powerful bug tracking and fault management tool. You learned how to install and configure it, as well as how to use it from day to day for your own projects.

By now, you should have a quality product, free from defects. In the next chapter, you'll learn how to devise an effective deployment strategy for getting that product from your development and staging servers onto a live environment.

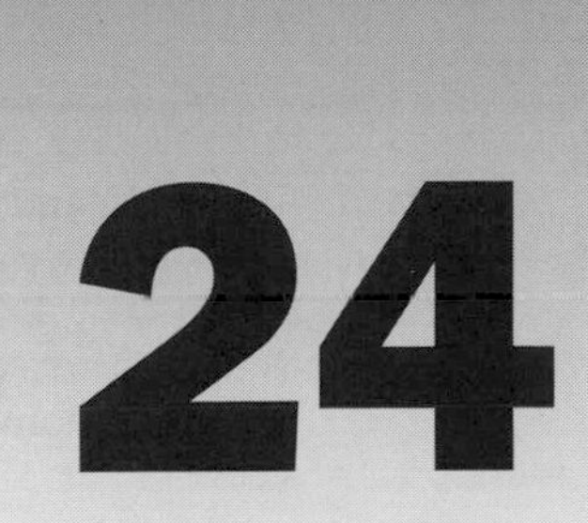

Deployment

Your Sales Force Automation application is now not only fully developed but also fully bug free , thanks to some thoroughgoing quality assurance in the previous chapter.

The process of getting your application uploaded onto a production server might have seemed simple enough when you first started out in Web development, but for a true professional there is, as ever, a best practice to be followed. This best practice is not just posturing. It is vital to version control and quality assurance—two subjects touched upon elsewhere in this book.

In this short chapter, you'll learn about structuring a server environment for a development team and managing the transition of source code between each server. You'll also examine how and when to apply each transition to match the immediate commercial objects of both your team and your client.

Devising Development Environments

When developing a large-scale PHP application, there is an inextricable requirement for multiple servers or development environments throughout the development process.

Of course, ultimately, your completed application, be it a public Web site or a closed intranet application, will reside on a server somewhere. This server may be in a dedicated data center or simply in the server cupboard of the client company.

This server is, however, the production server. It may not even have been purchased when you start the project. As a result, a series of interim environments are required to provide the chronological stepping stones for the deployment of your project.

The Studio Development Environment

You will need to equip your development team with a local development environment in which to develop.

In this example, we assume that your project is called Widgets. Your local development server will probably sit on your internal network only, with an IP address of 192.168.1.1 or similar, and not be exposed to the outside world. You may also have devised an internal domain name—maybe `mydevelopmentco.local`—which resolves using only your own internal DNS servers.

You may then establish a virtual server in Apache or your Web server of choice:

```
http://dev.widgets.mydevelopmentco.local
```

The corresponding entry in Apache's `httpd.conf` would be:

```
<VirtualHost 192.168.1.1:80>
 ServerName dev.widgets.mydevelopmentco.local
 ServerAdmin ed@example.com
 CustomLog /home/widgets/logfile_wid common
 ErrorLog /home/widgets/errlog_wid
 DocumentRoot /home/widgets/public_html/dev/php
</VirtualHost>
```

Obviously, you would amend the IP address, server name, e-mail addresses, and paths to match, and configuration syntax in other Web servers would of course be subtly different.

You would, obviously, need to expose the home directory of the user widgets to all of your development team, such that they may modify the code. In a typical setup, they may be using Windows workstations to modify code; in such a case, the use of Samba (`www.samba.org`) is highly recommended to create a network drive from which they can access the source base.

Modifications that your team then makes to the source base will be visible at the development URL only—`http://dev.widgets.mydevelopmentco.local`—and not on the live site.

If you are using any form of version control methodology as described in Appendix A, you need to provide virtual server instances for each of your developers, too—such as `http://johndoe.dev.widgets.mydevelopmentco.local`. More detail on this setup is provided in Appendix A. In such a setup, the master development server alluded to previously still exists but is a reflection of the source base as committed to the version control repository, rather than of any in-progress development.

> **Hint: It can be time-consuming in larger development studio environments to have to create DNS entries for every new project and, if using version control, every new developer, too. If you are using just one physical server for all your projects, you can simplify this process by using a Wildcard DNS setup. This means that `*.mydevelopmentco.local` will automatically resolve to 192.168.1.1. You can find information on how to do this on the Web. Just search for "Wildcard DNS."**

The Studio Staging Environment

As a development outfit, you will want a production server of your own—a place for you and your team to host your own ratified, finalized code prior to dispatch to the client.

If you're using version control, this will be a reflection of your repository, but not necessarily of the very latest versions in all cases. Rather, it will be the latest versions of each file that have been approved for submission to the client. In practice, this will represent the versions of each file that have been tagged as *release*. You can find more information on tagging in Appendix A.

The studio staging environment is of most use to project managers wishing to assess the true progress of a project, and for QA and testing where modifications to the live database cannot be risked.

In the previous example, our studio staging environment might be named:

```
http://studiostaging.widgets.mydevelopmentco.local
```

The corresponding Apache entry may read as follows:

```
<VirtualHost 192.168.1.1:80>
 ServerName dev.widgets.mydevelopmentco.local
 ServerAdmin ed@example.com
 CustomLog /home/widgets/logfile_wid-staging common
 ErrorLog /home/widgets/errlog_wid-staging
 DocumentRoot /home/widgets/public_html/staging/php
</VirtualHost>
```

The Live Staging Environment

The live staging environment provides a test bed for you to demonstrate new functionality to your client prior to release onto the live production environment.

The staging environment is typically hosted on the same server as the production environment, but with a subtly different URL. For example, if your live site was called `http://www.widgets.com`, you might use `http://staging.widgets.com` for your live staging environment.

A typical Apache configuration might read as follows:

```
<VirtualHost 192.168.2.1:80>
 ServerName staging.widgets.com
 ServerAdmin ed@example.com
 CustomLog /home/widgets/logfile_wid-staging common
 ErrorLog /home/widgets/errlog_wid-staging
 DocumentRoot /home/widgets/public_html/staging/php
</VirtualHost>
```

Note the different IP address—indeed, a different subnet—compared with your development server. It's worth using different private address ranges for each cluster of servers for which you are responsible. Because your live staging environment will likely reside in a data center and not on your local network, a second subnet has been introduced: 192.168.2.x instead of 192.168.1.x. Keeping subnets different will allow you to configure VPN (Virtual Private Network) access to your remote data center more easily should you ever wish to do so. It's also a lot less confusing.

If your live production environment uses multiple servers in a load-balanced configuration, you're wise to run your staging environment off a single server. After all, your staging environment is unlikely to attract the kinds of loads that warrant the use of multiple servers.

It may be prudent to protect your live staging environment with a username and password because it is, strictly speaking, publicly accessible. You should avoid using an `.htaccess` file to accomplish this, however, because that file risks being replicated onto your production environment during deployment, which would expose your live environment to that same password protection.

Instead, you can add this layer of security directly into your Apache configuration file:

```
<VirtualHost 192.168.2.1:80>
 ServerName staging.widgets.com
 ServerAdmin ed@example.com
 CustomLog /home/widgets/logfile_wid-staging common
 ErrorLog /home/widgets/errlog_wid-staging
 DocumentRoot /home/widgets/public_html/staging/php
 <Directory /home/widgets/public_html/staging/php>
  AuthType Basic
  AuthName Staging
  AuthUserFile /home/widgets/.htpasswd
  Satisfy All
  Require valid-user
 </Directory>
</VirtualHost>
```

The `.htpasswd` file is created in the normal manner; that is, using `/usr/local/apache/bin/htpasswd`.

The Live Production Environment

Finally, your live production environment provides the environment that the public sees. This may not be the general public if this is a closed system, but it is nonetheless the place for fully tested, fully approved, ratified code.

A typical Apache configuration might read as follows:

```
<VirtualHost 192.168.2.1:80>
 ServerName www.widgets.com
 ServerAdmin ed@example.com
 CustomLog /home/widgets/logfile_wid-live common
 ErrorLog /home/widgets/errlog_wid-live
 DocumentRoot /home/widgets/public_html/live/php
</VirtualHost>
```

Development Databases

Assuming that your application is database driven, you will need to make a conscious decision about what instance of the database (that is, which physical server and which database on that server) should be used for each of your environments.

This is particularly pertinent considering that certain evolutions of code may require modifications to database schema that, if made against a production database still being driven by an older release of code, would surely cause errors.

With this in mind, consider the following strategy:

- Individual development environments if used, should employ a locally hosted database, specific to that individual; for example, John Doe will use a database called widgets-johndoe.
- The master development environment should employ a locally hosted database (perhaps simply named widgets-dev), not specific to any individual developer but reflecting the latest database schema required to support the very latest versions from your version control platform.
- The studio staging environment should employ a locally hosted database (perhaps simply named widgets-stg), not specific to any individual developer but reflecting the latest database schema required to support the latest release-tagged versions from your version control platform.
- The live production environment should, naturally, use the live database server and the live database.
- The live staging environment should also use the live database so that when it's being used by the client for testing and approval purposes, it provides an accurate reflection of how the live environment will behave once the changes are deployed.

Of course, with at least four databases in existence at any one time, keeping track of necessary changes to the database schema itself can be tricky.

Version control software is of little use here. Yes, it is possible to maintain a dump of the database structure in your repository, but simply retrieving this dump will not physically update the database schema when it is downloaded. Simply dropping and recreating the database is an option, but this will lose any test data stored therein. It is also difficult to use such an SQL "dump" file to determine differences in database schema when you're working on larger projects.

The best approach, therefore, is one of good communications. Version control can play an important part here. Creating a folder called db-changes in your repository and instructing your developers to add text files containing a series of `ALTER` statements whenever they make changes to the database schema means that any developer performing "get latest versions" will also receive a series of changes to make to his or her own database.

Such files can, also, be tagged as *release* so that those responsible for maintaining the master development and studio staging environments can ensure that both databases are kept up-to- date to the appropriate degree.

> **Telling your application which database to use can result in awkward `switch` statements or, worse, hard-coded values that need changing by hand. There is another way, however. You doubtless have a file called `constants.phpm` or similar that dictates database IP address, database name, username, password, and so forth. By adapting this to consult the `$_SERVER["HTTP_HOST"]` property, the database IP, name, username, and password can be conditionally and dynamically determined and the correct database selected automatically, depending on the virtual server being used. Everybody can, therefore, share the same constants file.**

The Deployment Workflow

Simply having these development environments does not automatically facilitate best practice deployment strategy. The workflow of source code is important, too.

You may find the diagram shown in Figure 24-1 useful in illustrating the source code flow, from deployment to live.

The crux of the process is that:

- Individual developers develop against their own development environment, localized to their own database.
- This code is deployed to a master development environment. This may happen automatically or be initiated by the project manager on a semi-regular basis. Any changes that need to be made to the master environment's database schema are also made at this time.
- This code on the master development environment is tested, inspected, and approved by the project manager or, preferably, the project's lead architect. Certain files may be tagged as ready for the studio staging environment and, hence, release.
- This code then makes its way either in full or in part to the studio staging environment, where it undergoes a final review before submission to the client. The studio staging environment database is also amended if required.
- This code is then deployed to the live staging environment and the live database amended to support any schema changes. This is where the client approves or rejects the changes you have made.
- Finally, the code makes its way from the live staging environment to the live production environment. There is no need to change the database at this transition, because the same "live" database is used both for the live staging environment and the live production environment.

Let's now look at the technology behind these transitions.

Automated Version Control Repository Extraction

Many larger projects use a technique called *version control*, which is a technique for ensuring that the work done by different developers on a project does not conflict at any stage. It also keeps track of changes made to code as and when they are made, in case something goes wrong during the development process. More information on version control can be found in Appendix A.

When employing version control on a project, you may find it necessary from time to time to automate the retrieval of the latest versions from the repository. In the previous process, this is required for collating the efforts of your development team to assemble the snapshot master development environment.

Using CVS

Using CVS, this can be accomplished using syntax similar to the following. The following syntax is for UNIX implementations of CVS; using the Windows CVS client the process becomes a simple point and click.

```
cvs -d :pserver:username@cvsserver:/path checkout -r tag module
```

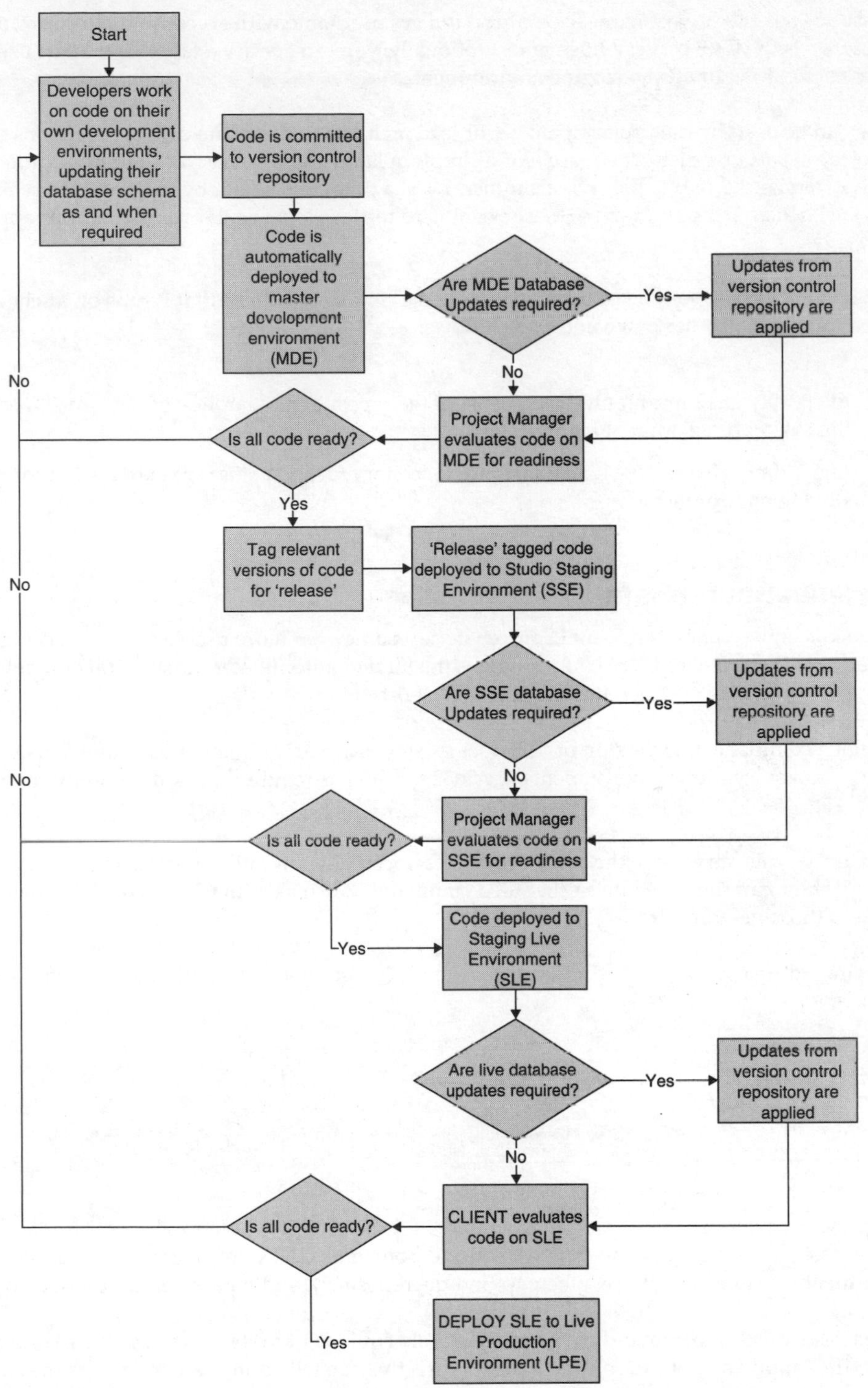
Start
Developers work on code on their own development environments, updating their database schema as and when required
Code is committed to version control repository
Code is automatically deployed to master development environment (MDE)
Are MDE Database Updates required?
Yes
Updates from version control repository are applied
No
Project Manager evaluates code on MDE for readiness
Is all code ready?
No
Yes
Tag relevant versions of code for 'release'
'Release' tagged code deployed to Studio Staging Environment (SSE)
Are SSE database Updates required?
Yes
Updates from version control repository are applied
No
Project Manager evaluates code on SSE for readiness
Is all code ready?
No
Yes
Code deployed to Staging Live Environment (SLE)
Are live database updates required?
Yes
Updates from version control repository are applied
No
CLIENT evaluates code on SLE
Is all code ready?
No
Yes
DEPLOY SLE to Live Production Environment (LPE)

Figure 24-1

Here, `module` is the project name, `username` is a cvs username with access to that project, and `cvsserver` is the CVS server's hostname. Optionally, you can specify a tag This may be useful if you want to extract to your studio staging environment.

The tag can be used by the project manager or lead architect to designate different versions of each file on the project as part of a distinct release. For example, a latest stable release of your application might consist of version 1.3 of one file, 1.5 of another, 1.4 of a third, and so on. By tagging each relevant version with a tag such as `lateststable`, those wishing to retrieve a particular release of your application can do so easily.

Such a command may well be committed to your server's `crontab` so that it runs on a scheduled basis. For example, you may have two entries as follows:

- Every day at 12 midnight, the contents of the repository, regardless of tag, are extracted to form the master development environment.
- Every day at 3 a.m., the contents of the repository tagged *release* are extracted to form the studio staging environment.

Using Visual SourceSafe

In Appendix A, we champion Visual SourceSafe as a somewhat more usable and practical (albeit commercial) alternative to CVS. Unfortunately, the kind of automated release extraction described previously is one area in which it falls somewhat short.

Although a command-line version of VSS does exist, it is a Win32 binary. Accordingly, to automate checkouts to your various environments, a Win32 machine is required even if your environments are UNIX based.

Using Samba, you can expose the source code directories of your environments as network drives. This Win32 machine can then execute a scheduled command, much as with CVS, to do a "get latest versions" straight to those network drives.

The command-line syntax for VSS is a complex topic, but the syntax you are likely to require most often is as follows:

```
SET SSDIR=\\sourcesafeserver\sourcesafe
SET SSUSER=ed
ss Workfold /$Widgets z:\public_html\live
ss Get /$Widgets -R
```

In the previous example, we set the working folder for the project Widgets to be `z:\public_html\live`, which we assume to be an exposed network drive from your UNIX development server. We also use environment variables to tell VSS where to find the repository, and what username to use to log in.

We then issue the `Get` command, which is effectively equivalent to `Get Latest Versions` in the SourceSafe Windows application. Using the `-R` directive, we tell SourceSafe to give us the contents of the repository in a recursive fashion.

Further information on the command-line syntax of SourceSafe can be found at:

```
http://msdn.microsoft.com/library/en-
us/guides/html/vstskuse_command_line_syntax.asp
```

Using rsync

It is not difficult to see that the most common deployment requirement is to upload the contents of folder A on server B, onto folder C on server D.

This is a simple operation in itself, but when the size of the source base of modern projects is taken into account, the task of shifting hundreds of megabytes across the Internet just to deploy a small change can rightly seem inefficient.

This is where `rsync` comes in. The `rsync` utility is a UNIX-only utility, although recently a number of authors have attempted to produce Windows ports. It provides a means to copy the contents of a given folder on a local server to another given folder on a remote server, while copying only the files that have changed. In other words, it synchronizes the two folders.

However, this is a synchronization in only one direction; from A to B. Files that have changed on A since the last deployment to B are copied, but anything that has changed on B in the meantime is not be copied back to A. This is not a problem, however, if the pattern of deployment discussed in this chapter is followed.

The most likely two occasions on for you to use `rsync` are as follows:

- For the deployment of the contents of the studio staging environment to the live staging environment
- For the deployment of the contents of the live staging environment, after being approved, to the live production environment

`rsync` even works across two folders on the same server; accordingly, even if your live production environment is the same physical server as your live staging environment, you can still use it to make your deployment. When copying from server to server, `rsync` makes use of the SSH (or, in a pinch, RSH) protocol. Hence, the only firewall rule required to allow the copy to take place is port 22 to be opened for TCP traffic. There is an `rsync`-specific protocol, too, but unless for some reason you cannot use SSH, you will not need to use it.

Basic rsync Usage

You will normally use `rsync` as part of a shell script; for example, you might create a script called `deploy-studio-staging-to-live-staging` and another called `deploy-live-staging-to-live-production`. They all work in much the same way, however, and call `rsync` using syntax as follows:

```
rsync -avrz -e ssh /local/directory/* username@remotehost:/remote/directory
```

The relevant directives are as follows:

- The `-a` flag causes directory permissions and symbolic links to be left intact when the transfer is initiated.
- The `-v` flag causes verbose output; you will see a detailed list of which files are in fact being chosen to be copied.
- The `-r` flag causes the copy to take place recursively.
- The `-z` flag causes data being transferred to be compressed before transfer; on a same-server copy, this should be omitted.
- The `-e` ssh directive tells `rsync` to use SSH to transfer files, rather than RSH.
- The source directory is specified as `/local/directory/*` (the * simply meaning that all files within that directory should be copied).
- The remote directory is specified as `username@remotehost:/remote/directory`, but if you're copying to another folder on the same server, the `username@remotehost` directive should be omitted.

Upon executing an `rsync` command, you may be prompted for a password. This is the login password associated with the username on the remote server specified, as if you were ssh'ing into that server in the normal fashion.

Let's look at some examples of this syntax at work.

rsync Syntax Examples

Let's first see how we might deploy the contents of our studio staging environment to our live staging environment at our client's data center. We would use the following syntax:

```
rsync -avrz -e ssh /home/widgets/staging/*
widgets@staging.widgets.com:/home/widgets/staging
```

If the client then approves the changes on the staging server, we can put them live. In this example, say that we put live simply to another folder on the same server. We would use the following syntax:

```
rsync -avr /home/widgets/staging/* /home/widgets/live
```

Note now we omit the protocol directive because this is a local-only synchronization; also, we do not enable compression because we assume that the speed increase will be minimal.

If our client's live production server were a physically different server, we might use the following syntax:

```
rsync -avrz -e ssh /home/widgets/staging/* widgets@live:/home/widgets/live
```

Alternatively, if our client used load balancing across three servers, we would have to execute the deployment three times, once for each target server:

```
rsync -avrz -e ssh /home/widgets/staging/* widgets@web01:/home/widgets/live
rsync -avrz -e ssh /home/widgets/staging/* widgets@web02:/home/widgets/live
rsync -avrz -e ssh /home/widgets/staging/* widgets@web03:/home/widgets/live
```

Keeping Servers in Sync with rsync

If your live production environment does involve multiple Web servers, there's another phenomenally useful role for rsync, too.

Many sites involve the use of server-writable data folders. These are containers for large binary files and other data that is not appropriate for a database such as PostgreSQL or MySQL. Often included are user-uploaded documents. For example, a user may have uploaded a photograph for a "my profile" page.

In setups with multiple live Web servers, a dilemma arises: How does one make newly uploaded data accessible to all the Web servers in the cluster?

One way is to use a centralized file server, much as a centralized database server is used, perhaps exporting its contents via NFS. This can be very slow, however, and is an additional overhead that must be considered.

The alternative is to use rsync between the servers in the cluster on a very frequently scheduled basis, so that when a new binary is uploaded, it is leaked into the other servers in the cluster within just a few minutes.

This approach can be accomplished quite effectively using rsync, but the password prompt discussed previously could prove to be a barrier if we try to schedule any such commands; after all, crontab can't type passwords for us.

There is a workaround, mercifully; it is the use of what is known as passwordless SSH and involves the placement of a key file on both client and server prior to connection. Because rsync depends on SSH in an environment with passwordless SSH setup, rsync is also passwordless, hence the scheduling or such tasks is made much easier.

Setting up key-driven SSH is slightly challenging and outside the scope of this chapter, but further information can be found on the Web; check out the following excellent "How To" document for all the configuration details you'll need:

```
http://www.massey.ac.nz/~jriden/passwordless-ssh.html
```

One word of warning: If you do adopt this approach, make sure that your PHP is aware of the fact that binary data may not necessarily be available in the minutes immediately following an upload. For example, if you know that your cron job is set to run every five minutes, you should suppress the display of any user profile photograph until five minutes after the upload has completed in favor of displaying a "photo coming soon" message. After the five minutes have elapsed, you can be sure that the photo exists on all Web servers in the cluster, and you can safely attempt to display the photo normally. Accomplish this by simply adding a time_photo_uploaded property to the user's database record and measuring the time elapsed since.

If for some reason you simply must allow instant access to such uploaded photographs, you can consider implementing a system whereby the first time that photograph is requested on a Web server that does not have that photograph (for example, web01), that Web server immediately initiates an rsync for that file in isolation with other Web servers until it finds one that does (for example, web04) and then displays the newly copied photograph to the user. This may sound long winded, but in practice the user will experience a very short delay while the file is copied; subsequent visitors requesting that photograph from that Web server will be served it in the normal way.

If you do adopt this approach, consider ensuring the uniqueness of filenames of uploaded data so that if they are replaced with a new version, you won't have some servers serving the old version and others serving the new. For example, if your user profile photographs are named using the user's ID from the database table user, for example, `/data/userpics/193913.JPG`, consider using a serial number suffix, so that the filename becomes `193913_1.JPG`, and the next version `193913_2.JPG`, and so forth. You would store which serial number was current against the user's record in the database, and hence display only the most recent version.

Summary

In this brief chapter, you learned about the principles of deployment in enterprise-level PHP applications. You learned about the effective structuring of development environments for your team and managing the transition of source code between each server using repository extraction and `rsync`.

In the next chapter, you'll learn how to extend the Sales Force Automation application with a robust reporting system.

Designing and Developing a Robust Reporting Platform

With your project deployed and the client thrilled to bits, you may be tempted to dust your hands off, walk away, and look for your next challenge in life, be it PHP related or not.

You would be wise to avoid leaving the country too quickly, however. In addition to the client's inevitable tirade of functional change requests—which will require at least discussion, if not implementation as well—you are also highly likely to be deluged with requests for data.

After your solution has been up and running in a production mode for a few weeks, a myriad of data will have been collated in the database. If your project was a simple e-commerce site there will, if you're lucky, have been sales made. In the case of our Sales Force Automation tool, data on the activity of our salespeople will have been recorded. How do you turn this raw data into something usable?

In this chapter, we look at this challenge and see how you can best rise to meet it. In the first section, you learn the basics of reporting, including the kind of requests that are typically made and how best to accommodate them. Then we examine an intelligent approach to the systems architecture of report generation and determine the best way to deliver reports to your clients.

Introduction to Working Data

The phrase "working data" refers to the data collected by your application in its day-to-day operation. Here are a few examples:

- In an e-commerce site, working data will be collected on orders placed by customers.
- In the Sales Force Automation application, working data will be collected on the communications made with clients by sales people.
- In a company Intranet featuring a time sheet facility, working data will be collected on the hours worked by employees on each account.

Not all data held and recorded in a database can be validly classified as working data. For example, information on user logins, access groups, sessions, and so forth relate solely to the administrative operation of the system and are not at the heart of it.

Understanding Your Client's Needs

A bold statement: It is highly unlikely you will be able to detail your application's reporting requirements at the specification stage (see Chapter 19, "Project Management Methodologies").

The first reason for this is that your client will not be able to see the wood for the trees, at this stage, and will be so caught up on what she wants the application to do that she may well struggle to take a step backward, approach the project from a different angle, and come up with details of the required reports.

The second reason is that in a high-pressure commercial environment, reports are needed only when they're needed. Think back to the days before computers. When a boss used to come over and ask a secretary for a report, the secretary didn't have the report already written and ready to be handed over to the boss right then and there. The same rule also applies nowadays. Reporting requirements are inextricably linked to commercial objectives and market conditions, which change rapidly and constantly. They are reactive.

With this in mind, it is perfectly reasonable to state in a functional specification that "this application will have a facility for producing reports, the exact nature of and implementation of which shall be determined in the weeks and months following the launch of the application." Of course, the onus remains on you or your project manager to ensure that this is a commercially viable promise.

Managing Your Client

The biggest challenge you will face in implementing any form of reporting system is ensuring that you are able to effectively manage the requests put forward by your client.

In practice, this means reading between the lines to allow you to stay one step ahead of your clients' requirements. They may struggle to articulate what they really need, irrespective of what they want. You can make life considerably easier for yourself if you attempt to side-step their own proposed solution (what they want) and get to their objectives instead (what they need). You'll meet an example of this dichotomy shortly.

The client instinctively tries to take ownership of designing the report. Often, they may see themselves as being helpful. In practice, their limited experience and narrow perspective on the task at hand can mean this is simply not true. Their own approach to the problem—what they want—will not accurately or completely solve the problem at hand—what they need. Even if it does, you may well find yourself hugely limiting report re-use possibilities should you blindly follow their proposed solution.

Consider the following dialogue between you and your client, for whom you have built an online bookstore:

CLIENT: I want to be able to see how my June sales figures compare to my May sales figures.

YOU: OK, that shouldn't be a problem.

CLIENT: I'm particularly interested in the figures for any titles published by Acme Publishing Inc, so I'd like you to build me a report showing the figures for Acme in May compared to the figures for Acme in June, and the percentage change between the two.

YOU: Sure. Give us a few hours and we'll have the report with you.

Allow this approach and you'll be at the beck and call of your client for months, as they repeatedly request the same report with slightly different criteria, and you have to respond accordingly.

Instead, convince them to let you take ownership of the report design process. Let them take ownership of defining their objectives; but you should design the report.

How you achieve this very much depends on the relationship you have with the client. Some clients will be happy to bow to your experience and let you take over; with others, proactive psychology and clever language skills will be required.

However you approach it, you are looking for dialogues similar to the following, whereby you combine your knowledge of the client's business objectives with pure common sense to propose an attractive solution on the spot:

CLIENT: I want to be able to see how my June sales figures compare to my May sales figures.

YOU: How about I build you a report showing sales volumes in dollars, whereby you select an author or group of authors, or publisher or group of publishers, and specify a couple of date ranges to compare?

CLIENT: That's fine. Can I also have it showing the percentage difference between the two date ranges?

YOU: Great idea. Okay, give us a day or two and we'll be good to go.

In the previous dialogue, you quickly got to the objective at hand by discarding the chaff offered by the client (the months in question) and then rapidly identified likely useful criteria (authors, publishers, and dates) and communicated them to the client. One thing you weren't able to know was that the client wanted the results shown as a percentage as well as in dollars, but this information was duly offered.

In fact, one tactic for dealing with difficult clients can be to deliberately withhold relatively minor nuggets of information such as this so that they may suggest them. Of course, you may well have known them to be requirements all along, but letting your client suggest them leaves them feeling involved in the design process. You, of course, know that the design process is firmly in your hands.

Report Deliverables

It's worth discussing with your clients how they want the report to be presented. There are a number of potential formats, with each suited to a slightly different scenario.

What you should always avoid, of course, is verbal delivery. In the previous dialogue, the need was immediate, and the client would have been content with the answers over the phone. The emphasis, however, should always be on the client requesting and viewing all reports from within the application itself. We demonstrate later in this section how to produce such an interface for your clients.

Assuming electronic delivery, therefore, the following formats are among those available to you:

- **HTML**—This has the obvious advantage of familiarity and ease of use, plus seamless display on-screen in your client's Web browser. Also has the disadvantage of being notoriously difficult to print with any degree of fidelity. Probably best suited for small outputs.
- **PDF**—Using packages such as the R&OS PDF generation class (`www.ros.co.nz/pdf`), it is technically quite simple to produce PDF output using PHP. Unfortunately, the concept of the page as a canvas is taken a little too literally here. A great deal of time can be spent (or wasted, depending on your perspective) drawing tables and manually word-wrapping text. The resulting PDF, however, will always print perfectly and is often be favored by the client for this reason.
- **Microsoft Excel**—Some clients may actually want their report generated as an Excel spreadsheet so that they can play with the results. Obviously, if they were to tell you what they plan to do in Excel, you could build that into the report yourself and simply produce a PDF, but that is often not practical in reality. Mercifully, it is possible to produce an Excel spreadsheet using PHP; a suitable package can be found in PEAR (see `http://pear.php.net/package/Spreadsheet_Excel_Writer` for more details).
- **XML**—You may actually wish to consider producing your reports in XML and then translating to one of the previous three formats (or some other format) using XSLT or some other translation mechanism (such as Apache FOP—see `http://xml.apache.org/fop/`). Although it takes a little longer to implement at the outset, this approach does have the benefit of allowing you to keep your results data extraction layers and presentation layers totally separate, thereby saving you time in the long run. This is the approach we adopt in this chapter.

Designing a Report

There are three key steps to designing a report for your application: designing the user interface for requesting the report, determining what the output data needs to be, and figuring out how to extract that output data from the database.

Designing the Interface

Using our chosen architecture, which we describe shortly, you do not have to concern yourself with the appearance of the user interface on a report-by-report basis. Rather, you concern yourself with the parameters that the user may specify to produce the report.

For each report you are commissioned to write, you need to draw up a list of input criteria. For each criterion, you need to determine the following:

- If a number, is this a minimum value, a maximum value, or an exact value?
- If a string, is this an exact string or a partial match?
- If a partial match, is this left-biased, right-biased, or not biased at all?
- If a string, is it case sensitive?
- If a maximum value parameter, is it inclusive or exclusive?
- Is this parameter optional or mandatory?
- What default value should be presented in the interface, if any?
- What implicit value should be taken if optional and not specified?

In the previous book sales figures comparison example report, we might draw up a list of parameters to ask our user, as follows:

- First date range—start day, month, and year (exact, mandatory)
- First date range—end day, month, and year (exact, inclusive, mandatory)
- Second date range—start day, month, and year (exact, mandatory)
- Second date range—end day, month, and year (exact, inclusive, mandatory)
- Publisher(s) to include (optional, implicit value any)
- Author(s) to include (optional, implicit value any)

The preceding is an exhaustive list of our input parameters into our report. Next, we must decide what output information we want to see.

Designing the Output

For the purposes of your sample report, don't concern yourself too much with appearance. Instead, assume that the output will be in XML so it can be presented in whatever format suits best, be it PDF, HTML, or another format.

The key data that needs to be displayed, however, is as follows:

- A summary of the input criteria used to generate the results, to aid in making sense of the results
- The sales in dollars in the first date range
- The sales in dollars in the second date range
- The difference in dollars between the two date ranges
- The percentage difference (positive or negative) between the two date ranges

With this information in mind, we can now concern ourselves with how we arrive at the previous output from the input parameters upon which we have already decided.

Extracting the Data

The process of extracting the data in this report is relatively simple. In any report, though, this will almost always be achieved by means of SQL queries made against the database.

Throughout this book, you have been coached to make use of the `GenericObject` class to minimize your use of SQL queries, hence maximizing the portability of your application and the cleanliness of your code.

This counsel does not apply here, however.

There is little point in adapting your carefully crafted object hierarchy to arbitrarily support some obscure query you need to perform solely for the purpose of producing a report. You will find it makes your core application more difficult to support and maintain.

In addition, you should not consider your application and its database to be so inextricably linked. It is not beyond the realms of possibility that you might at some stage in the future introduce a Web service connector to your application written in some language other than PHP, which may read and write directly from the database.

Accordingly, you should extract the data directly from the database and concern yourself with optimizing your SQL queries to produce the desired output as quickly as possible, rather than somewhat awkwardly adjusting your SQL to fit snugly with your object model, as you did in Chapter 7.

The data set or sets you are producing will be constructed using the output of one or more SQL queries. Each SQL query may have to be adapted or built dynamically depending on the input criteria the user has specified.

For example, consider our book sales scenario; if the requesting user simply wants to know the volumes for two periods, you can use the following queries:

```
SELECT COUNT(id) FROM order WHERE date_placed >= '2004-05-01' AND date_placed
<= '2004-05-31';
SELECT COUNT(id) FROM order WHERE date_placed >= '2004-03-01' AND date_placed
<= '2004-03-31';
```

If, however, the report is a little more involved and further criteria have been specified, you need to amend the query slightly. Say, for example, that a particular author has been specified:

```
SELECT COUNT(id) FROM order WHERE date_placed >= '2004-05-01' AND date_placed
<= '2004-05-31' AND book_id IN (SELECT id FROM book WHERE author_id=1295);

SELECT COUNT(id) FROM order WHERE date_placed >= '2004-03-01' AND date_placed
<= '2004-03-31' AND book_id IN (SELECT id FROM book WHERE author_id=1295);
```

The previous queries rely on a heavily simplified schema for the purposes of clarity, of course. In practice, support for more than one book will likely be allowed in any given order.

For any given report, it is very likely that there will be a number of possible query formats, depending on the verbosity or otherwise of criteria provided. Using a `switch` statement to account for each combination of criteria would be unwise because this could quickly run to hundreds of permutations for a complex criteria set.

Instead, it's best to use standard conditional logic to build the SQL query as a string, based on the criteria supplied.

Consider the following code snippet:

```
$strSQL = "SELECT COUNT(id) FROM order WHERE date_placed >= '$from_date'
AND date_placed <= '$until_date'";
if ($author_id) {
  $strSQL .= "AND book_id IN (SELECT id FROM book WHERE author_id=$author_id)";
};
if ($publish_id) {
  $strSQL .= "AND book_id IN (SELECT id FROM book WHERE
publisher_id = $publish_id)";
};
```

As demonstrated, you have dynamically constructed the SQL query based on the criteria supplied; using conditionals, you have appended to a base SQL query and increased its complexity depending on the number of criteria actually supplied.

This theory can be applied to the nth degree when designing your report. Consider the input criteria which must be supplied and compare with the input criteria which might be supplied. Hard code the query where you can be sure input criteria will be supplied; use conditionals where it can be supplied.

Report Generation Architecture

You've learnt now the basics of reporting in PHP against a typical database. How do you put this theory into practice, however, and build a reporting platform for your application?

You may be tempted to follow an approach similar to the following:

- A page called `salesreport.php` renders a form requesting input criteria.
- When submitted, this page performs an HTTP POST to `salesreport-results.php`, which performs the SQL queries necessary to retrieve the report results, and renders the data on screen.

Quick, yes, but dirty, too; there a number of drawbacks to this approach:

- It's not a good example of using the MVC design pattern that, for reasons discussed in Chapter 13, is to be encouraged and employed wherever possible.
- There is little scope for code reuse (except through the copy-and-paste approach) when developing different reports in the future.
- If the user wants to view the report's output again at some point in the future, the report has to be generated once more. This results in not only a waste of processing time but also the possibility of different results. What if the database has changed since then? A report is a snapshot in time; users will expect it to be the same next time they view it.
- Users may be kept waiting for a long time while the report generates. On more complex reports, this could be up to a minute or more; what if the request times out at their end, that is, in their Web browser? What if they click the Stop button? It's generally accepted that a Web page should load pretty quickly to keep the user happy, and this includes a report that's been generated.

The last of these drawbacks is potentially the most serious, of course. Our book sales example won't take more than a few seconds on even the slowest of database servers, but many reports run to considerably more complex output than that and can even comprise hundreds, if not thousands, of queries.

As a rule, and given the nature of HTTP as a stateless protocol, if the rendering of a subsequent page on your application is dependent on some external, potentially slow process, you should attempt to take that process *offline*.

To cite another example, consider how many e-commerce sites ask their users for credit card numbers to make online purchases. It's a fair number, isn't it? Consider, however, how many of those sport almost comical messages declaring "don't click the Submit button more than once" or something similar. Furthermore, even the most credit-worthy of you will have been made to wait as many as forty seconds to have your card authorized. If your request times out, how do you know whether you've been charged?

The approach adopted by Amazon is very different, and certainly far more highly recommended. Why do you need to authorize there and then? Why not do it offline and let the user know in due course whether the purchase went through successfully?

Of course, since Amazon's delivery is physical rather than electronic, it can afford to notify its user of success or otherwise by e-mail some minutes, or even hours, later. But the same principle can be applied to real-time scenarios, too, such as when allowing access to online content requiring credit card payment.

Consider the traditional approach to authorizing credit cards:

- First page requests card number in HTML form; offers data via SSL HTTP POST.
- Second page accepts HTTP POST from first page, authorizes card in real time, and returns result to user thirty seconds later.

Compare this to a more intelligent approach, which is an extension of that adopted by Amazon and provides pseudo real-time processing:

- First page requests card number in HTML form; offers data via SSL HTTP POST.
- Second page accepts HTTP POST from first page, puts card data into to-be-processed database, and returns user to authorization-pending page a split second later.
- The authorization-pending page refreshes on the client side every couple of seconds until consultation with the database shows that the card transaction has been processed and a result has been determined.
- An entirely separate process on the server that runs independently of the Web servers periodically (or constantly) checks the database for pending card transactions and, if it finds them, processes them, updating the database with the result when finished.

The benefits are obvious:

- There is virtually no scope for the user to click the Stop button, because there is virtually no delay in returning the page to him/her.
- If the user clicks the Submit button more than once, it's no big deal because a UNIQUE key on the database can prevent duplicate entries.
- If the user clicks Refresh on the authorization-pending page, there's no problem because it isn't changing any data—it simply refreshes.

We can apply this same logic to generating reports, as discussed next.

The Offline Approach

Using the offline approach to generating reports has huge benefits from both a user experience and an application performance perspective. Admittedly, the report itself doesn't generate any more quickly, since exactly the same database queries are being executed. But the user experience is far better, and many of the practical and technical pitfalls discussed previously are avoided altogether.

The basic principles are as follows:

- A database table called `report` contains template information for every distinct report available on the system.
- A generic page called `reporting.php` lists the available reports by consulting said table (and, of course, uses a Smarty template so as to be MVC-compliant). A link is also provided to the My Reports page (more on that shortly).
- The user can select a given report from the table, which links to another page called `newreport.php`, with the report identifier passed as an HTTP `GET` parameter (for example, `newreport.php?report_id=14`). This page uses an XML template associated with that report to render a page specific to that report, which is then used by the users to specify the criteria for this instance of the report.
- When the user submits the report, it is entered into a table called `report_instance` and flagged as PENDING. The supplied criteria are entered into a table called `report_instance_criteria`. The user is then redirected to the My Reports page.
- The My Reports page shows a list of all reports held in the database for that user, along with their status; PENDING, PROCESSING, or COMPLETED. The COMPLETED ones can be viewed in one of a number of formats (for example, HTML, PDF, Excel). Which formats are available depends on the "translator" scripts available for that report.
- A single PHP script called `reportprocessor.phpx` (with the extension `.phpx` signifying this is a command line executable rather than a Web page) runs constantly on a machine attached to the application's database server, constantly scanning for reports in the `report_instance` table with their status set to PENDING. It immediately sets them to PROCESSING and then forks a new handler process appropriate to that script, with each script having its own dedicated handler, which is also a PHP script. It then recommences the loop, again looking for reports marked as PENDING.
- The handler script consults the `report_instance_criteria` to determine the criteria for this report and then builds SQL queries as needed to extract the relevant data. This data is written to an XML file and the instance marked as COMPLETED.
- Should the user then look at the My Reports page, the report in question will be seen to be COMPLETED rather than PROCESSING. The user can then view the results of the report.
- The "translator" scripts for a given report take the raw XML output of the handler scripts and translate them into the output format in question. In the case of HTML, this might be accomplished using XSLT. In the case of a PDF, this might be accomplished using an XSLT followed by a pass of Apache FOP to translate that XML into a PDF document, as discussed in the first section of this chapter.

Let's look at this approach in more detail now. We don't give you the source code verbatim because it would run to many hundreds of pages; however, if you follow the architectural outline detailed in this section, you should easily be able to construct a reporting platform to fit your application's requirements perfectly. Alternatively, the full source code for an example implementation of this methodology can be found on the Wrox Web site at `www.wrox.com`.

Later in the chapter, you'll meet a real-world example of using this methodology to process a user's request for a report.

The Reports Interface

The main Reports interface is the home page of the reporting component of your application. Should you add reporting as an option to your navigation, this is inevitably the first page to be rendered.

The page will comprise two files—`reporting.php` and `reporting.tpl`, a Smarty template.

The purpose of the interface is as follows:

- ❑ Welcome the user to the reporting component of the application.
- ❑ Provide a link to the My Reports page so that the user may view any requested reports and see their status.
- ❑ Provide a list of the types of report on the system and allow the user to create a new instance of that report.

Note that "instance" has nothing to do with OOP. It is simply an incarnation of a particular report. For example, you may have a generic report that generates sales comparison figures; an instance of that report would be that generated by Joe Bloggs on the 3rd of August to compare figures from April and June, for example. A report is not associated with particular input criteria, whereas an instance of it *is* associated with a very particular set of input criteria.

The list of types of report available on the system would be achieved through the consultation of the report table. You may wish to provide some administrative interface to allow new reports to be added to this table, but keep in mind that in the architecture we are presenting there is a requirement for some fairly sophisticated files to be constructed for each new report. With this in mind, you may see limited value in providing an interface to create brand-new reports. Indeed, it is probably commercially preferable that your client is dependent on you for creating new report templates.

The `report` database table, which contains the list of available report types and is used by the Reports interface to generate the list of available report types, is structured as shown in the following table.

Column	Data Type	Description
`Id`	SERIAL	The identifier and primary key of the table
`report_code`	character varying(8) NOT NULL	Another unique identifier, but more human readable, such as `salesrep`
`report_name`	character varying(64) NOT NULL	The name of the report, such as "sales comparison"
`report_desc`	character varying(256)	A description for the report

Note that the preceding is tailored for PostgreSQL in keeping with the rest of this book. It would be a trivial matter to adapt this table structure for MySQL or another database platform, however.

As you can see, we don't store much data about the report in the `report` table. We don't need to; almost everything else will be stored on disk, as you'll see.

The data about available reports is extracted from the preceding table. Unless a huge number of reports are available, you probably don't need to concern yourself with pagination. You simply provide the name of each report type and a link to create a new instance of a report of this type, using the interface discussed in the next section.

This should be passed as an HTTP GET parameter to newreport.php, discussed next. The preceding information should be presented using a Smarty template (see Chapter 13), perhaps named reporting.tpl.

The New Report Interface

This page will be called exclusively from the master Reports interface of the previous section. It will be passed as an HTTP GET parameter the database identifier of the report required. The purpose of this page, which will also be comprised of two files (a .php model and Smarty template as view and controller) is to render a criteria entry form for the given report.

Essentially, the user must be presented with a form showing the available criteria for that form, including showing clearly which are mandatory and which are optional.

You could, of course, use a Smarty template for each report, (for example, report salesrep uses /templates/salesrep.tpl) but if you have to construct tens or even hundreds of reports, the prospect of hand-coding HTML forms for each one will doubtless be an unpleasant one. After all, you are a PHP professional; there are plenty of high school kids just itching to do some HTML for you.

Instead, you can use XML templates, one for each report.

The Report Interface XML Templates

Each report will have an XML template detailing which criteria are available for data entry. In the case of our rolling sales comparison report example, it is permissible to specify two start dates, two end dates, and, optionally, a publisher, an author, or both. These permissible criteria are detailed in an XML template associated with this report.

Each XML document should live somewhere central and be named to correspond with the code used in the database. Don't use the id column of the report table as a naming mechanism; this may change if you move the database from one server to another, or upgrade PostgreSQL. Consider it for internal use only; instead, name your XML templates /templates/salesrep.xml or similar.

The exact format of this XML is of course entirely down to you, but consider something similar to the following. This file might well be named /templates/salesrep.xml:

```
<report id="salesrep">
 <criterion type="date" name="datefrom1" mandatory="true" caption="Date
From (1)"/>
 <criterion type="date" name="dateto1" mandatory="true" caption="Date
To (1)"/>
 <criterion type="date" name="datefrom2" mandatory="true" caption="Date
From (2)"/>
 <criterion type="date" name="dateto2" mandatory="true" caption="Date
To (2)"/>
```

```
 <criterion type="fkmultiple:author/id/author_name" name="authors"
caption="Select Author(s)"/>
 <criterion type="fkmultiple:publisher/id/publisher_name" name="publishers"
caption="Select Publisher(s)"/>
</report>
```

As demonstrated, we list each criterion made available for use when you generate the report by using several instances of the `criterion` tag.

Each tag has a name used when storing the input, a caption (displayed on screen), and a `type`.

The `type` is crucial. It determines how the field is presented when rendered in the Web browser. You might want to consider supporting types as follows:

Type	Description
`freetext`	A free text entry box, stored as entered
`date`	A date, represented as three form components (day, month, year) but stored as a single ISO date (YYYY-MM-DD)
`time`	A time, represented as three form components (hour, minute, seconds) but stored as a single ISO time (HH:MM:SS)
`datetime`	A date and time, represented as six form components (day, month, year, hours, minutes, seconds) but stored as a single ISO date (YYYY-MM-DD HH:MM:SS)
`fkmultiple`	A list box showing entries from a foreign key table. The format for this type is fkmultiple:tablename/storecolumn/displaycolumn, where tablename is the table containing the foreign entity, storecolumn is the column containing the values to be stored, and displaycolumn is the column to display in the list box. This is used in our preceding example to allow the selection of a publisher or author (from the `publisher` and `author` tables respectively).
`fksingle`	As described previously, but allowing only a single entity from the foreign table to be selected

Of the types in the preceding table, probably only the `fkmultiple` and `fksingle` criterion types require further explanation.

The purpose of these types is to easily allow the user to select from either a drop-down list or static list box of values from a foreign table. In the previous example, we allow the user to select author(s) or publisher(s) to which to restrict the report. Rather than require the requesting user to enter author IDs or publisher IDs, we allow the user to select from a list box that is automatically generated for that user.

This is another example of why the XML approach is preferred; there is no need to write code to generate such list boxes for every report. A single piece of code can be used for every report.

In our example XML, your new report interface would likely parse it and render an HTML form that resembles Figure 25-1.

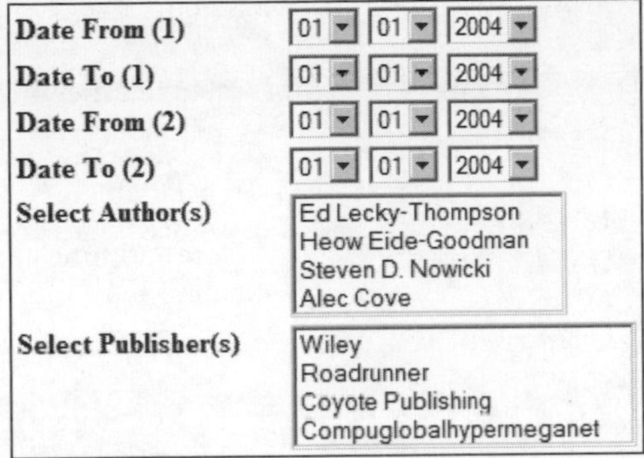

Figure 25-1

You can, of course, jazz up this simple form to match the styling and design of the interface of your particular application.

Your page searches for the XML template that corresponds to the report being requested and then traverses it to render an appropriate HTML form in the user's Web browser.

Each form element is named so that when the data is posted, the criterion name can be easily decoded. For example, for a criterion called `date_from1`, the form element name `CRITERION_date_from1` may be used. Using the `CRITERION_` prefix means that you can differentiate between the value of criteria being submitted and other, unrelated form parameters.

You may wish to extend the previous architecture slightly to suit your needs. For example, you may want to prepopulate form elements with default values, such as by setting any date elements to today's date.

The target for the form should always be `newreport.php`. The page should be adapted so that a separate block of logic is executed if it is receiving `POST` data as opposed to `GET` data, because this implies that a report is being submitted with populated criteria rather than a request for a new form being made, as described previously.

Storing Requests for Reports

When `newreport.php` does receive `POST` data, it's important that it handle that data correctly. The task at hand, of course, is to lodge a new instance of the report in question so that the report processor script, discussed shortly, can start processing it.

Instances of reports are effectively requests for a given report with a given set of criteria and made at a given point in time. Each instance is generated only once and stored in its generated state, so if the user does need to refer back to it later, it won't be regenerated needlessly. However, the user also has the opportunity to create a whole new instance to reflect the most up-to-date data available to the Reports engine.

With this in mind, you should store such requests in a database table called `report_instance` or similar, structured as follows:

Column	Data Type	Description
Id	SERIAL	The identifier and primary key of the table
report_id	int4	The report in question, a foreign key from the report table
submitted	datetime	Date and time at which the report was submitted for processing
submitting_user_id	int4	The ID of the user submitting the report, used for matching on the My Reports page
status_flag	character(1)	The status of the report for the processor; P is pending, I is in progress, and C is completed

You will also need a table to store the criteria that you are associating with the instance of the report. A separate table ensures that some degree of normalization is maintained, necessary because you will undoubtedly have more than one criterion specified per report. Without using a separate table, you would be forced to comma-separate that data when storing it in the table. Yuck!

Call this table `report_instance_criterion` or similar:

Column	Data Type	Description
Id	SERIAL	The identifier and primary key of the table
instance_id	int4	The report instance in question, a foreign key from the `report_instance` table
criterion_name	character varying(128)	The name of the criterion in question, such as `datefrom1`
criterion_value	character varying(128)	The value of the criterion in question, such as `2004-01-01`

This table structure allows you to support multiple criteria for a given report instance; there would simply exist more than one row in the `report_instance_criterion` table for the `report_instance` in question.

Your script should read input parameters from the `POST` data and record them into the database as appropriate. You should use the P (Pending) status for the report so that the processor knows to start processing it. Ideally, it should also consult the XML template for the report in question to determine which fields are mandatory and which are not; if the user has not supplied mandatory fields, he or she should be returned to the criteria entry screen (and be suitably castigated).

When storing criterion values, you may have to suffer a degree of poor database normalization. The previous example invited users to provide lists of authors and publishers. This can result in having more than one author or publisher provided for a given report request. If you apply the rules of Boyce-Codd normalization (or 3rd Normal Form), you should separate this into two tables rather than one:

`report_instance_criterion` and `report_instance_criterion_value` instead of just `report_instance_criterion`. You may well consider this to be overkill, however, and resort to storing lists as comma-separated values in the `criterion_value` field. If so, you will be forgiven for this, on this occasion.

If you are likely to encounter occasions when a `criterion_value` entry can contain, say, many hundreds of different values, you may need to increase the length of the `criterion_value` column in your table from 128 characters to, say, 1024 characters. Because PostgreSQL allows up to 8192 for character fields, this wouldn't pose a problem.

Having recorded the relevant information into both `report_instance` and `report_instance_criterion`, your front-end PHP has really done its work; the back-end takes over from here. To aid the user experience, you should use a 302 redirect to transport the user to the My Reports page, like this:

```
header("Location: /myreports.php");
exit(0);
```

The user will be able to see the report just submitted with a Pending status against it or, if the processor gets to it in time, an "In progress" status against it.

The Report Processor Script

The report processor script (which might be named/scripts/reportprocessor.phpx—note the .phpx extension to signify a server executable rather than a Web page) is an example of an off-line or back-end PHP script. It is not invoked by the user's Web browser. Rather, it runs on the server independently of Apache.

Its purpose is to run continuously, seeking out report instances that are set to PENDING, update them to IN PROGRESS and then invoke an appropriate script (a handler) to actually generate the report results.

There are a couple of approaches for this. You can simply have a single instance script that runs continuously from server boot in an infinite loop, or you can use the server's `crontab` to schedule the script to run every few seconds.

The first approach is possibly a better bet, though. Simply invoking the procedure every *n* seconds would be fine if you knew how long the procedure would take. You don't, however, and you could end up with multiple instances of the processor launching, with unpredictable results. Far better to have the script run in perpetuity from the moment the server boots up, and maybe have a `cron` job to ensure that it is still running at any given time, relaunching it if it has stopped or failed for some reason.

The Process

The pseudo-code for your script will probably look something like this:

- ❑ Begin Loop.
- ❑ Look for any reports set as status P (Pending).

- For each report set as status I (In Progress), determine the report code, such as `salesrep`, and then look for a handler script with that name, such as `/scripts/handlers/salesrep.phpx`.
- Launch the handler, if found, into the background to generate the script results.
- For any handlers that appear to have finished, mark the corresponding report as C for Completed.
- Sleep for 5 seconds.
- Repeat loop.

Setting the report to status I, In Progress, not only allows users to be informed that their report request is being processed but also prevents the processor from attempting to process the report request again on the next pass.

The five-second delay with each loop is at your discretion; keep in mind, however, that each pass of the script requires at least one SQL query to be made, so you will almost certainly want some kind of delay to prevent your database from becoming saturated with connections.

It is important that you launch the appropriate handler script into the background rather than simply launch it and wait for it to execute. Do not be tempted to execute it using `require()` or `include()`. You should launch it as though it were any other system executable. This way, the execution of the report processor script is not impeded by the launch of your handler script, and it can proceed to process any other reports that might be pending.

You may want to consider using the syntax provided by `proc_open()` to effect this. See `http://www.php.net/manual/en/function.proc-open.php` for more details. This allows you to launch a process and then have some control over it from within your code rather than simply be a slave to its execution. This allows you to have handlers with read-only rights on your database. You pass the handler the name of the output file (for the results) as a command-line parameter and the criteria for the report as standard input parameters.

The output file in question should be associable with the report instance in question. For example, for instance ID 19039, name your output file `/generated/output19039.xml` or similar.

Keep track of the process you have invoked during subsequent iterations, and when it has terminated, update the database to reflect this by marking that report request as C for completed.

Having your handlers separate from the reporting system itself is an excellent approach; it means that they can be truly dumb scripts, concerning themselves only with querying the database, and be highly efficient as a result. Redundant code duplication is also minimized.

The Report Handler Scripts

In the previous section, we mention that each type of report supported by your architecture will require its own "handler" script, such as `/scripts/handlers/salesrep.phpx` in the case of a report called `salesrep`.

This handler script will be invoked by the report processor script and will accept as a single command-line argument the name of an output document in which its results are stored. As mentioned previously, this output filename is determined exclusively by the `request_instance` ID.

More important, of course, the handler needs to be presented with key/value pairs of criteria as set by the user originally requesting the report.

These, too, will be provided by the processor script, but it would obviously be impractical to allow such criteria to be passed using the command line.

Instead, the processor script should pass such parameters as key/pair values directly through standard input—that is, as though they were being typed at the keyboard. A terminating double newline (that is, a blank line) indicates the end of such criteria and allows the script to start.

If the handler script were run at the command line, the following would be valid input:

```
# /scripts/handlers/salesrep.php /generated/output19039.xml
datefrom1=2004-03-01
dateto1=2004-03-31
datefrom2=2004-05-01
dateto2=2004-05-31
authors=31,14,12,11,15
publishers=
[blank line]
[script executes here]
```

Of course, all the previous data entry is actually provided by the processor script. The handler script therefore has the following tasks upon launch:

- Determine output filename using `argv` array. Create this file.
- Loop through STDIN input receiving key/value pairs until a newline character is encountered. Push such key/value pairs into an associative array.
- After a newline character is received, ignore any further input and execute whatever SQL queries are necessary to produce suitable output.
- Push this output into a suitably formatted XML document and save it into the output file determined and opened in the first step.

Simple. The handler script doesn't even need to update the database—it's a read-only process. The process of terminating will allow the processor script to determine that the report is completed.

The format of the output XML is unimportant. At least one translator script is needed for every report on the system, and each translator script will be unique to that report. Accordingly, the output XML is up to you.

In our recurring example, however, it may look something like this:

```
<results>
 <rangeonesales>31319</rangeonesales>
 <rangetwosales>33153</rangetwosales>
 <percentuplift>5.856</percentuplift>
</results>
```

The output XML is short and simple, as you can see. Even though the input criteria specified were quite complex, including two date ranges and a list of five authors, the results from the report are still simple: the sales for these five authors in the first date range, the sales for the five authors in the second date range, and the percentage difference between the two.

Regardless of the specificity or vagueness of the input criteria for this report instance, the output data will always be of the same format. This is very useful because it allows the translator scripts, which are covered shortly, to be completely generic—that is, it doesn't matter in the slightest what input criteria were originally specified.

Very shortly, we discuss these translator scripts and how they can turn this XML data into something more readable.

The My Reports Page

Back to online pages now. This page, as the name suggests, will show requesting users a paginated summary list of all reports they have requested on the system, along with the reports' status (pending, in progress or completed).

Options to view completed reports will be shown. The user may view in native format (XML) or, more usefully, and depending on which translator scripts are available, a number of translated formats, such as HTML or PDF.

You may also wish to provide an option for users to remove reports, or to e-mail the results to an address of their choice.

How the system determines which output formats are available is based on the translator scripts available. The next section shows how this works.

The Report Translator Scripts

The report translator scripts take the XML output results of a given script as produced by the handler scripts discussed earlier and present it in a more user-readable format.

These are online scripts in the sense that they are executed in real time and viewed using the Web browser. However, they will almost always be linked to the My Reports page and not called explicitly by the user.

In practice, you will want to name them in a convention that allows the My Reports page to see instantly which translators are available for each report:

```
/translators/html/salesrep.php
/translators/pdf/salesrep.php
/translators/excel/salesrep.php
```

. . . and so forth.

We recommend that you adopt a consistent input and output approach for each script. The input is simply the name of the input XML to parse; the output is the parsed data itself. For example, to render our recurring example in PDF format, use

```
/translators/pdf/salesrep.php?filename=output19039.xml
```

as the URL. This link will, of course, be directly generated by the My Reports page, which checks for the existence of the appropriately named script to determine whether it's available. If not, it would respond with an error; however, this situation should never crop up, given that the My Reports page will only ever display links to view report instances that have been successfully generated.

How you perform the translation is very much up to you and depends on the report in question and how much data is likely to be rendered, as well as the XML schema you have adopted to produce the report output.

You may find the following hints useful, however.

Producing HTML

HTML in its purest form is just another form of XML—albeit with a very precise, defined DTD (document type definition). With this in mind, it is relatively simple to use an XSL style sheet to convert your input XML to well-formatted output HTML.

In PHP4, this was accomplished using the Sablotron package and was tricky at best, horrendous at worst. In PHP5, DOM (Document Object Model) XML has taken over, so XSL translation has become simply a function of the interaction of two DOM objects:

```
$objDomXML = new DomDocument;
$objDomXML->loadXML($strXML);

$objDomXSL = new DomDocument;
$objDomXSL->loadXML($strXSL);

$proc = new XSLTProcessor;
$proc->importStyleSheet($objDomXSL);
$strHTML = $proc->transformToXML($objDomXML);
```

As you can see, the trick is to instantiate two DOM classes and load the XML and XSL into each. Because XSL is just another form of XML, it's perfectly allowable to load it straight into a DOM Document object as if it were a piece of XML.

You can then create an instance of the `XSLTProcessor` utility class. This is the class that actually performs the XSL transformation, but it cannot work with XSL in a raw string form. You therefore must tell it about the XSL style sheet by making reference to the DOM Document object you just created for that style sheet.

Having done this, you can use the `transformToXML` method, passing in your original XML DOM Document object, to perform the translation of your original XML against this XSL. The result is pure HTML, which is easily captured into a string.

Producing PDFs

There are a number of ways to produce PDFs. If you are insistent on using PHP, you can put together a solution for your particular DTD using the R&OS PDF class (`http://www.ros.co.nz/pdf/`). This has the huge advantage over PHP's recommended PDF methodology, in that it is completely free of any third-party library dependencies and, hence, any commercial licensing restrictions.

Producing PDFs in this way is harder than you think, though, because you're the one responsible for line wrapping, getting table borders and cell interiors drawn, and so on. It is akin to producing a magazine page in Visio instead of Publisher.

An easier route may well be using Apache FOP—see `http://xml.apache.org/fop/` for more details. This provides a standard DTD for representing PDF documents. Using a simple XSL translation followed by processing in FOP, you can easily produce PDFs of your work without having to worry about the finer points of Cartesian geometry.

The downside of FOP is that it is Java based. It therefore requires the Java SDK to run, and hence is slightly trickier to get up and running than a native PHP application.

However, the architecture you have adopted so far (of keeping translator scripts away from your database and reporting infrastructure) means that this isn't such a big deal—you can even run a separate Java application server (such as Jakarta) on another port, and keep the PDF translator on there. As long as it can see the same output XML documents as an equivalent PHP page, you'll be fine.

Producing Excel Spreadsheets

You can produce Microsoft Excel spreadsheets using the `Spreadsheet_Excel_Writer` package from PEAR (see `http://pear.php.net/package/Spreadsheet_Excel_Writer` for more information). It is a native mechanism for writing Excel documents and hence needs no external libraries or COM objects to function, and will happily run on UNIX-based servers.

Example Usage of the Reports Engine

It may be difficult to visualize all the previous in practice. Here we work through an example from start to finish, examining what happens in the background throughout.

The user journey starts on the Reports home page, where a list of reports available to be generated appears. Our user picks the sales comparison report (known as `salesrep` internally) and clicks through to generate a new instance of that report.

The `newreport.php` page loads the corresponding XML template file and renders the criteria fields silently and transparently. The user then populates these with the criteria in question and submits the form. The same page then records the user's criteria in the database and creates a new report instance with the status set to `P` for pending. Meanwhile, the user is transported back to the My Reports page, where he will see the status of the new report as "pending processing" (hence why it can't be viewed at this stage).

The processor script, already running in the background, then almost immediately picks up on that new entry in the database and sets its status to In Progress. It then locates the appropriate handler script and launches it as a new process. This may take a while, so it gets on with its subsequent iterations until the script finishes executing. Meanwhile, the handler script parses the input parameters it has been passed and uses them to query the database and generate useful output in XML, using the filename passed to it by the processor to stores its output. When it finishes, the processor script takes over and marks the report as status `C` for Completed.

When users next visit the My Reports page, they notice that their report are marked C for Completed. Options to view the report in XML, PDF and HTML are presented to them and they choose to view it in PDF. The link to do so is in fact a link to a translator script, which takes the report's XML as input and produces a neatly formatted PDF as output, which users then print.

Visualizations

You may often find, particularly when producing HTML output, that it is easier to show some or all of your report's results in a graphical format. You may have a long string of value pairs in your report's raw XML. It would be far easier to show these on a line graph, for example.

When producing Excel output, users theoretically can easily implement such graphs themselves. When producing HTML output, however, no such facility exists, and you must embed appropriate graphics directly into the HTML.

Thankfully, producing graphs and charts in PHP is relatively straightforward.

The `Image_Graph` package to be found in PEAR (see `http://pear.php.net/package/Image_Graph/` for more information) allows you to easily convert raw data sets into line and bar charts, and myriad unsupported third-party packages for producing pie charts can be found on Google.

The principle is that you use your translator script to generate output PNGs, which are saved on disk in a path accessible to the Web server; the output HTML generated then includes references to these PNGs so that they can be displayed in-line.

Summary

In this chapter you learned how to build a sophisticated reporting structure for your application. First, you learned how to translate the sometimes incoherent requests of your client into a clear set of objectives, and how to design an appropriate report to cope with those objectives and their likely future derivatives.

Then you looked at a robust, reliable, and extensible architecture for integrating a suitable reporting platform into your application, a platform capable of handling any number of diverse and distinct reports, and of delivering output in a variety of formats.

In the next and final chapter, we look to the future. Where can you go from here in your career as a PHP professional?

Where Do You Go from Here?

If you somehow managed to make it this far without touching a computer, please refer to at least a few of the previous 25 chapters. Humans tend to learn very well by physically doing what they've learned. Go back and pick up a chapter or two that pique your interest and feel free to experiment with the code. The adage "You get out what you put in" has never been more appropriate.

This should ring true even if you've scrupulously read every paragraph and run every application. After all, you're sure to have experienced a thought that starts with: "What happens if . . . ?" Don't know the answer? Can't find it in the documentation? Experiment. There is no shame in breaking code by exploring boundaries, and by now your PHP skills should be up to a critical point. You can dig yourself out of any hole that you've managed to get yourself into.

This is an important distinction. Digging yourself out of a hole by using your technical skills, leveraging unit tests, and pondering the how's and why's means that your education can continue and, we hope, extend itself beyond the technical realm.

Motivation

Regardless of why you've purchased this book, the work involved to get here is certainly nontrivial, and you deserve a pat on the back. Getting here probably involved sacrificing at least some time that you'd rather have spent playing video games, attending social gatherings, interacting with your family, or just getting enough sleep.

We hope you can now appreciate some of the features and ubiquity of PHP. Go out and apply what you've learned, using baby steps if need be, but apply the lessons you've learned. Install PHP Unit. Cruise through the PEAR archives, and don't just install and run third-party PHP applications, but look at them, read them, figure out what they're doing, and fix them if need be.

Even though your skill set may be both deep and wide, you really never stop learning. Contrary to the belief that Wrox is attempting to torture you, every chapter exists for a reason and none is purely academic. PHP professionals (in the field) have created this book, and everything that was presented to you is used in a professional environment.

That also means that everything has a history. Neither this book nor PHP5 was created out of ether, so these functions and practices are worth further exploration. Entire books, even entire companies and some subindustries, support the concepts that have been presented to you. Please continue reading because some great resources are coming right up.

Your Career As a Developer

Assuming that you are serious about being a software developer, you really should make a conscious effort to further your skills. The shelf life of technical skills is growing ever shorter, and no effort put forth in keeping up-to-date in trends and developments can be considered wasted.

But how should you spend your precious time? You can't possibly learn everything about everything, and well-rounded technical individuals are considered quite valuable commodities.

More Than Web Development Skills

PHP is more than the details of session management, file-downloads, and configuration variables. PHP is a language that grows and changes over time to suit the needs of developers like you who need to have it done by yesterday.

Although the design and implementation of PHP is geared toward Web site development, PHP can be used for more than interacting with a browser. Consider what you can do if you have a tool that had the ability to run seamlessly across Windows and Linux as well as communicate with file systems and nearly every popular database. What else can you do with it? How about:

- Translate databases
- Process XML
- Gather RSS/Atom feeds
- Test forms/sites from alternate Web development technologies
- Use Perl-like text processing
- Run generic utilities

Even if you don't create Web sites every day, you can still find opportunities to leverage your hard-earned and valuable PHP skills.

Soft Skills

Yes, these are also known as the dreaded "people skills." Even PHP geeks need to interact with real physical people, even if they are other PHP geeks. Plus, not all code is considered equal, and unused code is even considered a liability, so scoping your problem and creating the right product is paramount for success.

Predictably, these abilities are not thought of as standard technical skills, even though you may spend a significant amount of time interacting with clients and co-workers; even though an unsuccessful project may threaten your project, company, and very livelihood; and even though months of work might be wasted solving the wrong problem or adding useless features.

Time invested in enhancing your nontechnical technical skills goes far. You may consider beefing up your agile development techniques, such as in those used in eXtreme Programming. Lessons can be learned about how *not* to write software, so knowing at least a bit of how previously popular development methodologies work will help your understanding of where you are going.

Academic Skills

Writing software isn't exactly magic, and more of what was considered art is slowly falling into the category labeled science. Here are a few resources that are academic in nature yet offer a short-term payback.

Well-written, concise code will tend to have a high degree of design patterns even if unintentional. *Design Patterns* by Gamma, Helm, Johnson, and Vlissides (Addison-Wesley) is a classic and comes in easy-to-swallow chapters. Learning just one per week will make half a year fly by in no time. With *Writing Compilers and Interpreters* by Ronald Mak (Wiley), knowing how PHP and similar languages do their magic goes a long way when the going gets tough. *Refactoring* (Addison-Wesley) by Martin Fowler examines the techniques for achieving well-written concise code. *Agile Modeling: Effective Practices for eXtreme Programming and the Unified Process* by Scott Ambler (Wiley) goes into detail regarding the integration of agile development practices and standard modeling techniques.

Community Skills

PHP exists because it was developed as a community effort. Scores of developers have been involved in the process, even if in the capacity of testing, which, by the way, should probably carry more weight as they seriously influence the development process.

The day will arrive when you find when a PHP utility or application that needs to be repaired, or someone might offer a patch for something that you wrote. Either way, a dose of humility goes a great distance in the political process, and this is no exception because a reputation for being foul-mouthed and short-tempered will not help any project.

On the other hand, actively contributing to community projects such as PEAR increases your personal PHP skills, and the value of the effort is multiplied by the time saved by similar developers using your tools. Even if you're not as technically astute as the project may initially require, the act of creating a How-To or developer-targeted tutorial is often a great help in learning a new technology. Unfortunately, good documentation is often lacking in the best of projects.

Summary

The technical concepts presented in this book are considered best practices, and you should be prepared to know what they are. As a software developer, you'll most certainly be presented with both good and bad examples of MVCs, refactorings, UML, design patterns, and collections.

Therefore, utilizing your new skills is as important as learning them in the first place. Try to leverage what you know in other areas and be on constant lookout for interesting tools, development techniques, designs, and projects.

After all, you do share planet earth with us, the authors, who welcome any help in creating a place where poorly written software is not shockingly easy to find.

Remember then, young Jedi: "Always in motion is the future" (Yoda).

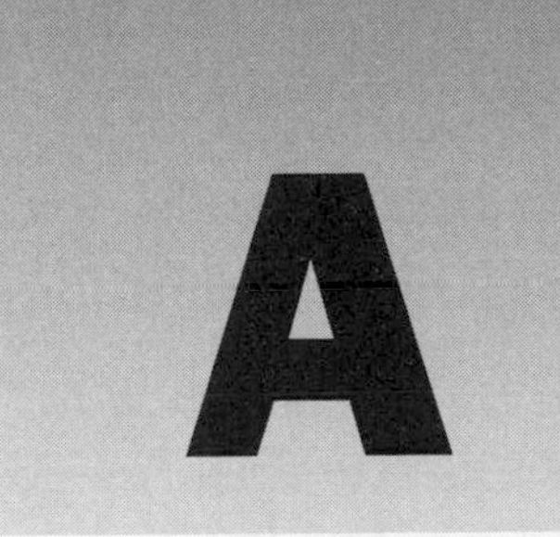

Why Version Control Is a Good Thing

Many programmers dread big projects, often for a whole host of reasons. However, one particular aspect to big projects can sometimes seem more unappealing than any other—code organization. Six or seven software developers, two software architects, a lead architect, and client-side developers all working on the same project often represent a recipe for disaster.

Mercifully, code organization on big projects has been made much easier in recent years with the advent of readily available, straightforward version control software.

In this short appendix, you'll encounter the basic principles of version control and see how to organize a version control strategy for your project. Then, you'll learn how these principles are applied in the most popular version control software and how to choose which (if either) suits your project best.

Principles of Version Control

The purpose of version control is twofold. The first is to avoid the version conflicts in development that can arise when multiple programmers work on the same set of files on a project. The second is to automatically journal changes to key files on a project.

By requiring programmers to check out a file from a central repository when they wish to work on it, a version control platform can keep a record of who is working on which files and at what times. Depending on the approach taken, this method can either wholly exclude other developers from working on that file at the same time, or allow other developers to also work on the file and then merge their changes together when they both check the file back in again.

Journaling of files in a project involves the retention of previous versions of each file. Whenever a file is checked in to a repository, the version control platform marks it as current so that anybody retrieving that file from the repository does retrieve that latest version by default. However, a copy is taken of the file in its previous state. Not only does this allow the project administrator or lead architect to roll back a file should a new version prove problematic, it also allows the changes between versions to be easily listed, which, from a project management perspective, is a major boon.

All version control systems use some variety of repository for storing a copy (usually verbatim on disk, but sometimes as part of a more complex and often proprietary database format) of the file and directory structure of the project. How this repository is accessed varies from system to system. We examine a typical topology later in this appendix.

Concurrent vs. Exclusive Versioning

Version control platforms differ immensely in their implementation of the principles discussed earlier, not least in their means of checking out a file.

In any version control platform, when a file is being checked out by a programmer the latest version is always retrieved from the repository, and the user's local version is replaced with that latest version.

However, in a platform employing Exclusive Versioning, a lock is then placed on that file with immediate effect. While the file is checked out, other developers may still retrieve the latest version of that file, but they themselves will not be able to check it out to work on it. This Exclusive Versioning is usually enforced by marking the developer's local copy of the file as read-only. Of course, this is only notional enforcement and does require the developer's cooperation to work well in practice. The lock is removed after the developer working on it checks in the file in question. The repository is then updated to reflect the latest version.

Concurrent Versioning adopts quite a different approach. The acts of retrieving the latest version of a file and checking it out to work on are combined so that they are essentially one and the same. In other words, to work on a file, all a developer must do is ensure that he or she has the latest version of that file and then start working on it. When each developer has finished making changes to the file, he or she will check it in. This is where the magic happens. If the developer in question checked out the file after another developer had checked it out, and is attempting to check it in after that other developer has checked in a changed version, the two newly submitted versions will be merged.

A Concurrent Versioning Example

To try to make things a little clearer, consider the following example. This is an imaginary file called `helloworld.php` that prints "hello world" in the Web browser. You will see that line numbers have been included. Of course, these would not be included in the code as it is saved.

```
1: <?php
2:    $strToPrint = "Hello World";
3: ?>
4: <html>
5:    <body>
6:       <?=$strToPrint?>
7:       <br /><br />
8:    </body>
9: </html>
```

You can call this snippet of code version 1.0 of the file.

Imagine that Jane Doe and John Doe are both working on the project. Assume that John works out of New York and Jane out of Los Angeles.

A meeting has been called with the client. They wish to change the code of this particular file so that instead of printing "Hello World," it would print "Goodbye World." John Doe's manager has given John the task of modifying the code to reflect this requirement.

In that meeting, the client also requested that a horizontal rule be drawn underneath the text where printed. Jane Doe's manager has given her the task of modifying the code to include that extra line.

In an Exclusive Versioning setup, it would be impossible for John and Jane to make their changes at the same time. John would have to check out the file, make the change, and check it in again. Jane could then check out the file, make her change, and check it in again.

In a Concurrent Versioning setup, no such requirement exists. Say that at 12:00 p.m. (Eastern Time) John does a check out to get the latest version of the file, currently version 1.0. He then starts work on making his change. At 12:01 p.m. (Eastern Time), Jane does a check out as well, also to get the latest version of the file. This is still version 1.0; John hasn't checked anything in yet. Jane starts work on her change.

At 12:05, John is done. The code works fine, so he decides to check in his work. He does so, and the repository saves his newly submitted version as the latest version—version 1.1. Version 1.1. now looks like this:

```
<?
  $strToPrint = "Goodbye World";
?>
<html>
  <body>
    <?=$strToPrint?>
    <br /><br />
  </body>
</html>
```

At 12:09, Jane is done, too. The code works fine for her, so she now wants to check in her work. Her code now looks like this:

```
<?
  $strToPrint = "Hello World";
?>
<html>
  <body>
    <?=$strToPrint?>
    <br /><br />
    <hr />
  </body>
</html>
```

When she checks in, the repository notices that she is checking in a changed edition of version 1.0—not 1.1, which is now the latest. This recognition of which working version has been modified by the developer is usually facilitated by a tag line (a line automatically included in all source code files, usually held in comment tags to avoid upsetting compilers and interpreters). This line is created and updated by the repository and normally is not touched by the developer.

The repository now must merge the changes made by John between version 1.0 and 1.1 with the changes made by Jane between 1.0 and her new proposed version.

The repository determines that the change John made was as follows:

Change line 2 from:

```
2:   $strToPrint = "Hello World";
```

to:

```
2:   $strToPrint = "Goodbye World";
```

The repository determines that the change Jane made was as follows:

Insert after line 7 a new line reading:

```
8:     <hr />
```

The repository then simply takes the last version (1.0) and systematically applies both John's and Jane's changes. The merged code now looks likes this:

```
1: <?
2:   $strToPrint = "Goodbye World";
3: ?>
4: <html>
5:   <body>
6:     <?=$strToPrint?>
7:     <br /><br />
8:     <hr />
9:   </body>
10: </html>
```

As you can see, both developers' changes have been successfully included. The repository now labels this version 1.2, and any subsequent requests for the latest version will yield this version. Neither developer is likely to be any the wiser of the merge that just took place.

Concurrent Versioning Conflicts

There will be scenarios when two or more developers working on the same version of a file make changes that are not compatible with each other—in other words, a conflict has occurred.

Suppose that a further client meeting takes place and two further requests are made: to include the time of day when saying goodbye to the world, and to include the date. The project manager assigns John the task of implementing the time-of-day requirement and Jane with implementing the date requirement.

John checks out version 1.2 and amends it to read as follows:

```
1: <?
2:   $strTime = time("H:i:s");
3:   $strToPrint = "Goodbye World, it's $strTime";
4: ?>
5: <html>
6:   <body>
```

```
7:      <?=$strToPrint?>
8:      <br /><br />
9:      <hr />
10:    </body>
11: </html>
```

Jane also checks out version 1.2 and amends it to read as follows:

```
1: <?
2:    $strTime = time("Y-m-d");
3:    $strToPrint = "Goodbye World, it's $strDate";
4: ?>
5: <html>
6:    <body>
7:      <?=$strToPrint?>
8:      <br /><br />
9:      <hr />
10:    </body>
11: </html>
```

The first check in (whoever gets there first) will cause a version 1.3 to be created. Can you picture what will happen when the slower of the two developers checks his or her code in? A new line has been inserted in each case and an existing line modified. Although the version control platform may well be able to combine the two new lines (by simply incorporating both), it will not know how to combine the changes made to the single line (line 3 in both cases). As PHP developers, you can see the resolution that is required—it's common sense:

```
3: $strToPrint = "Goodbye World, it's $strTime on $strDate";
```

The version control platform, however, isn't that smart and so will simply throw a conflict. It is then up to the developer whose recent check-in has thrown the conflict to resolve it. In practice, the version control system will create a temporary new version, 1.4, which will actually contain details of the conflict. This temporary version will not be issued until the conflict is resolved and that version is made live. The last developer to check the file in will be notified of the conflict by the version control platform and invited to edit the temporary version to resolve the conflict him- or herself. It is the responsibility of the latter of the two developers checking in to resolve the conflict, because the version control platform will view that developer to have caused the conflict.

The temporary version 1.4 created by the repository might look something like this:

```
1: <?
2:    $strTime = time("Y-m-d");
<<<<<<< helloworld.php
3:    $strToPrint = "Goodbye World, it's $strTime";
=======
3:    $strToPrint = "Goodbye World, it's $strDate";
>>>>>>> 1.3
4: ?>
5: <html>
6:    <body>
7:      <?=$strToPrint?>
```

```
8:      <br /><br />
9:      <hr />
10:    </body>
11: </html>
```

You can see the mark-up the version control platform has introduced to show the two different alternatives for line 3.

The previous example is a very simple conflict to resolve. The conflict mark-up is removed and the line in question modified to incorporate both developers' changes with the finished version and then activated in the repository.

Obviously, in more realistic examples, the resolution of conflicts can be tedious, time consuming, and costly. This is the double-edged sword of Concurrent Versioning. It is useful that two developers can concurrently work on the same file, but they must be prepared to take the responsibility to resolve conflicts when they do arise.

Making the Choice

In practice, Concurrent Versioning may be of limited use in a well-designed PHP project. As strongly encouraged throughout this book, dividing your project into multiple components and expressing each of those components as a single file is considered best practice.

Accordingly, the requirement for two developers to work on a single file rarely crops up. If it does, it may be wise to consider whether that file is not best broken down into two smaller files, or even two smaller components.

Furthermore, consider the previous example. How likely is it that Jane and John would both be given the task of implementing these two incredibly similar requirements? One programmer could handle both requirements in this very simple example, but even in more complex examples this is almost always the case. Often a single developer will be assigned ownership of a single component and will be responsible for all changes that might be required in that component.

Finally, the principles of Concurrent Versioning seem to suggest that developers can co-participate in a development project without ever communicating. A short dialogue between two developers when a file is checked out and locked in an Exclusive Versioning environment ("Hey, Jane, are you working on `helloworld.php` right now? I need to make a small change") actually aids communication. Concurrent Versioning negates that requirement to communicate, and hence developers will actually talk to each other less. This is not a good thing. It is no surprise that Concurrent Versioning is used so frequently in open source development—which involves thousands of developers, many of whom have never even met but all of whom are working on the same project. Although open source development is viewed by and large to be an excellent philosophy, some of the side effects of thousands of disconnected contributors working on a single project can be seen in the incredible complexity of configuring PHP on UNIXplatforms.

The alternative is Exclusive Versioning, which prohibits two developers from working on the same file at the same time. After a file is checked out, it is physically locked from other developers until such a time as the first developer checks it back in. Accordingly, it is not possible for check-in conflicts to arise as described previously.

Of course, Exclusive Versioning has its downsides, too, even if your project is designed so that there will never be any chance of two people ever needing to work on a file at the same time. One particular bugbear that crops up time and time again is the on-vacation syndrome. That is, a developer has gone on vacation and accidentally left a file checked out, and another developer now needs to work on it. Sure, you could go into that developer's workstation and check it in, but what if it's a work in progress that isn't ready? If you undo check-out, you risk losing changes that, for all you know, may be 90 percent complete! This is, naturally, a procedural issue as much as anything else, and suitable policies for your development team can avoid this scenario.

The choice is very much up to you. A well-designed PHP5 project with maybe four or five developers all working in the same office is an obvious candidate for Exclusive Versioning of some ilk. A legacy PHP3 project with thousands of developers from all over the world is an obvious candidate for Concurrent Versioning.

Version Control Topology

Very shortly you'll encounter a few software packages that provide a version control platform. Before that, it's worth understanding a bit better how a version control topology works in a real-world setup.

A topology like this will normally apply regardless of the software you decide to use, and irrespective of whether you opt for Concurrent or Exclusive Versioning for your project. Consider Figure A-1, in which John, Jane, and David are all developers working on the same project—project `foo`. They all have access to a workstation of their own, which is for their use only.

Obviously, they do not run PHP on each of their workstations, so they all share a powerful central development server. Each developer has his or her own instance of a virtual server representing that developer's own copy of project `foo`, based on source code stored in his or her own home directory on the development server.

For example, John uses `http://john.projectfoo.example.com`, which points to source held in his own home directory on the development server, in `/home/jon/public_html/projectfoo`. Similar setups exist for each developer working on the project.

There is also a staging server that is used by the lead architect as a base for testing and examining the latest version of the project, and possibly for internal demonstrations. An external staging server likely is maintained off-site for external client demonstrations.

When John, Jane, or David wants to work on the code for the project, they work on the copies of code in their own home directories, to which nobody else has access. These home directories reside on the server, so they use Samba (see `www.samba.org` for more information) to map a network drive on their workstation to the home directory on the server. They then edit files in their own copy of the project directly. This is their working area. No project files are ever stored on their own workstation, but because the files are exposed through the network drive, developers edit them on the workstation as though they were local.

However, John, Jane, and David must use version control software on this project. This means that whenever they wish to work on a file, they must perform a check-out action using their version control software running on their workstation (for the sake of argument, say it's Microsoft Visual SourceSafe, which we describe shortly). This downloads the latest version of the file in question from the repository

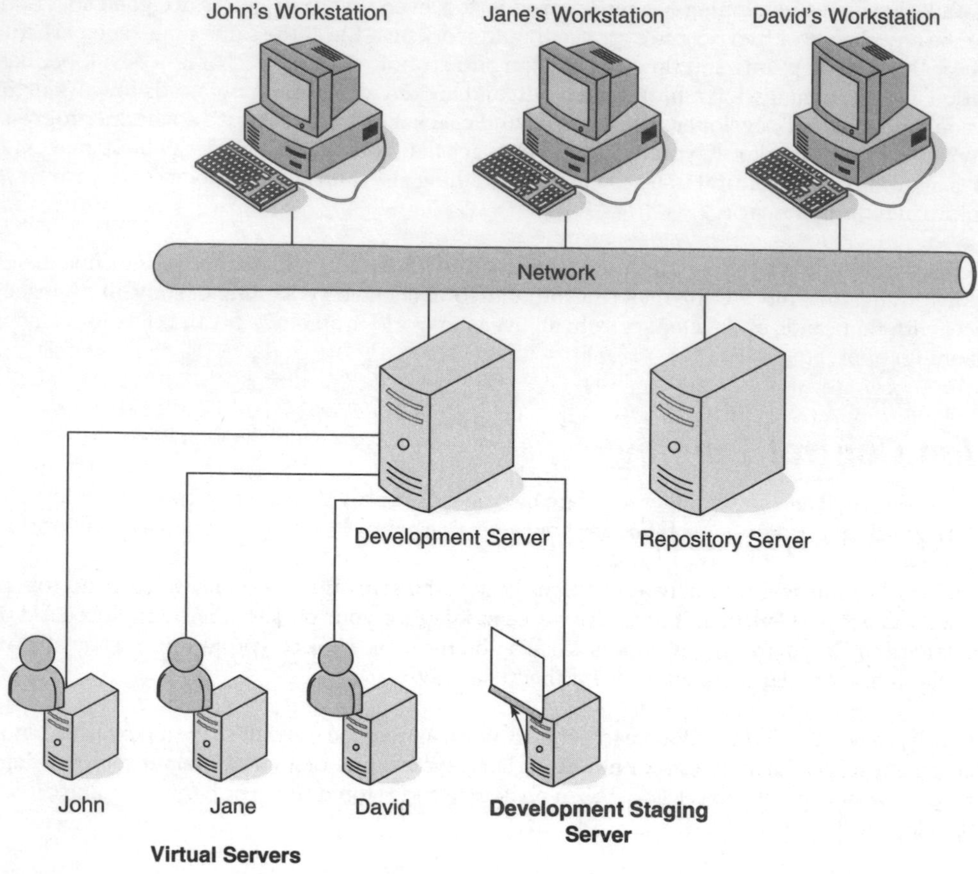

Figure A-1

server to the home directory on the development server. This copy of the file is set to writable so that they may freely work on it. If John, Jane, or David forgets to check out a file before opening it in their IDE of choice, they will find that it is set to read-only and they are unable to save their changes. While the file is checked out, nobody else may check it out to work on it.

When they have finished working on the file, they simply check in the file, which records the latest version in the repository. Others who check out the file in the future will then be presented with the latest version incorporating the changes just made. The process is similar should one of them wish to add a new file to the repository—a quick push of the Add File button and the file is incorporated permanently.

Because John, Jane, and David are working on the project simultaneously, they need to periodically perform a "get latest versions" operation. This means that the latest versions of all files from the repository will be copied to their local copy in their home directory on the development server, even if they have no intention of ever checking those files out. This is an important practice for two reasons. It be necessary to have some extra functionality that somebody has recently added to the project to make some other component you wish to work on function correctly. Also, this practice allows developers to quickly see what their colleagues have been working on and, if necessary, point out any errors or provide constructive criticism.

Now and again, Paul, lead architect, may choose to perform a "get latest versions" into a directory (not his own) on the server marked as staging. Doing so allows him to see a snapshot of the project as it exists in the repository so that he, too, may provide constructive criticism of his team's work.

If one is using another version control package, minor variations in this topology and process may exist. For example, with CVS, the developers would be unlikely to use any client software on their workstation. Rather, they would simply create some kind of terminal connection (such as an SSH connection) to the development server and run the CVS client directly on the server.

It is worth pointing out that the exact role of the repository server varies, too. CVS supports a genuine client-server protocol for the exchange of data, called pserver. Visual SourceSafe, however, simply uses a shared data volume on a network drive. As a result, a separate physical repository server may not be necessary, and the development server could quite easily double up in a repository role.

Version Control Software

A number of software titles exist for handling version control. In this short section, you'll explore three of them, examine the pros and cons, and see how they implement the common functionality and principles of version control.

There isn't space in this appendix to go into much detail regarding the setup, installation, and maintenance of each one. Plenty of documentation exists on the Web detailing the ins and outs of each. But this section should at least allow you to make an informed choice as to which version control platform is most appropriate for your project.

Microsoft Visual SourceSafe

SourceSafe has been around for a long time and now comes bundled with copies of Visual Studio .NET. It may seem an unusual package to use in a PHP environment, but it is definitely worth a look.

Although not free, its Windows-based client is particularly pleasant and easy to use. Although PHP development folk never shy away from a challenge, there is little point expending energy on figuring out how to use your version control client when you could be using it to figure out a neat way to approach an algorithm or object model. SourceSafe is so straightforward to use, you can do just that. Figure A-2 shows a typical view from SourceSafe. As you no doubt can see, it appears to be very similar to Windows Explorer and hence is very easy to pick up.

On the flip side, SourceSafe uses shared disk space rather than a proper client server protocol for its repository. This has the usual problems associated with shared Access databases, and accordingly can be horrifyingly slow to use on larger files with many revisions. There are also a few irritating facets that boil largely down to differences between Windows and UNIX, such as filename case-sensitivity.

SourceSafe uses solely Exclusive Versioning—that is, when a file is checked out, nobody else may check it out. As with many packages that use Exclusive Versioning, this is enforced using the read-only attribute of the local copy of the file. Because this is a Windows-based client, developers will almost certainly be

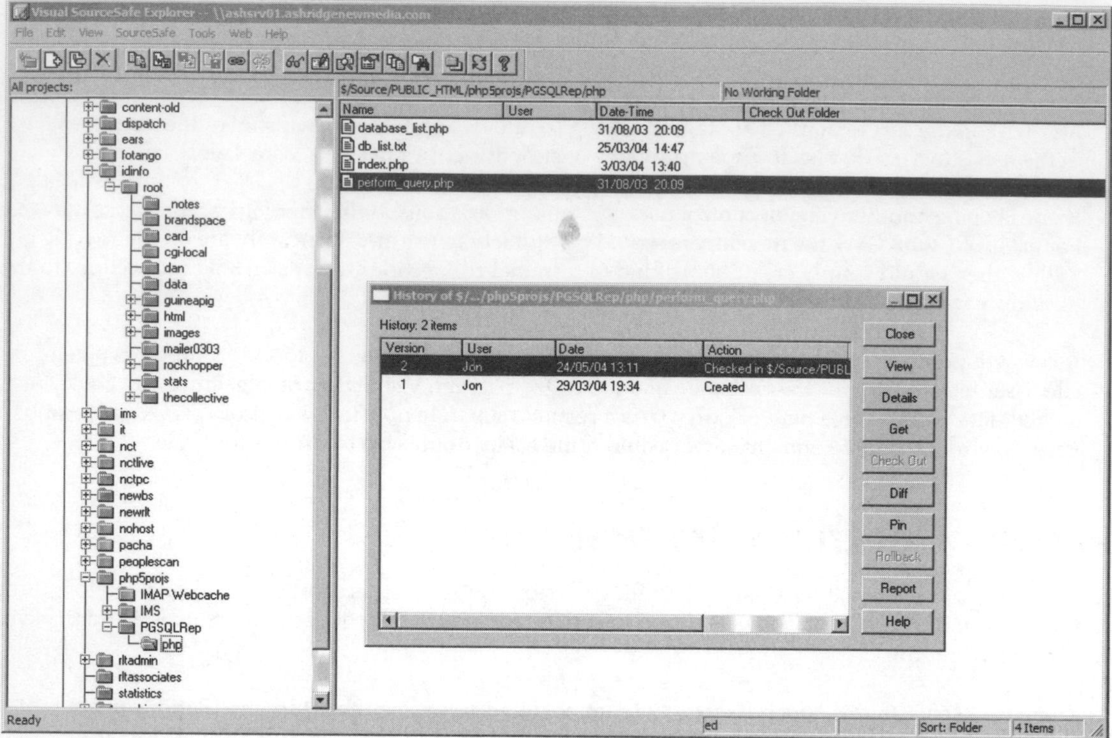

Figure A-2

checking out to a network drive. Strictly speaking, this is slightly inefficient. The workstation is acting as a conduit for the downloaded data rather unnecessarily.

SourceSafe stores its database in a completely arbitrary format, so you can't use its repository storage area as a form of automatic staging server. There is a fairly comprehensive command-line syntax, however, which you could use to build automated scripts for downloading latest versions for a staging server. Such a script, of course, would need to run from a Windows environment because there is no UNIX client of any description.

Well worth a look, but keep in mind that the licensing costs may be prohibitive for small projects. You need to pay only for copies of SourceSafe, however. Because it relies on shared disk space, there is no server as such, and you could even use a network drive presented by Samba running on Linux.

CVS

CVS stands for Concurrent Versioning System and, as the name suggests, is one of the better-known examples of a version control platform that implements Concurrent Versioning for developer check-outs. CVS has the great advantage of being released under the GNU Public License, which means that it is essentially free to download and use.

It stores its repository in a folder largely mirroring the real directory structure of the project in question, and uses small tag lines in files, hidden files in directories, and minor filename concatenations to store auxiliary data beyond the latest versions of the files themselves. This is in stark contrast to the manner in which SourceSafe stores its files.

CVS clients can connect to CVS in one of two ways: by simply looking at the repository directly (if it resides on the local machine) or by connecting using the pserver protocol. It would, in theory, be possible to share a network drive (à la SourceSafe) to allow the former connection method, but using the pserver protocol is by far the best way to implement CVS over a client/server environment.

CVS is generally run underUNIX, and typically on the same machine on which the local copies of the files are to live. In the previous topology example, CVS was run by each user via a shell connection to the development server. For the more UNIX-savvy, this is probably the preferred route. For the not-so UNIX-savvy, a SourceSafe-like Windows client called WinCVS exists that replicates most of the UNIX client's own functionality. Figure A-3 shows a typical view from the Windows client. As you can see, the WinCVS client shares an interface remarkably similar to that of SourceSafe.

Resolving conflicts in CVS is usually relatively straightforward. CVS takes the merger as far as it possibly can and then presents the user with a new version, annotated to demonstrate the conflict. The user then

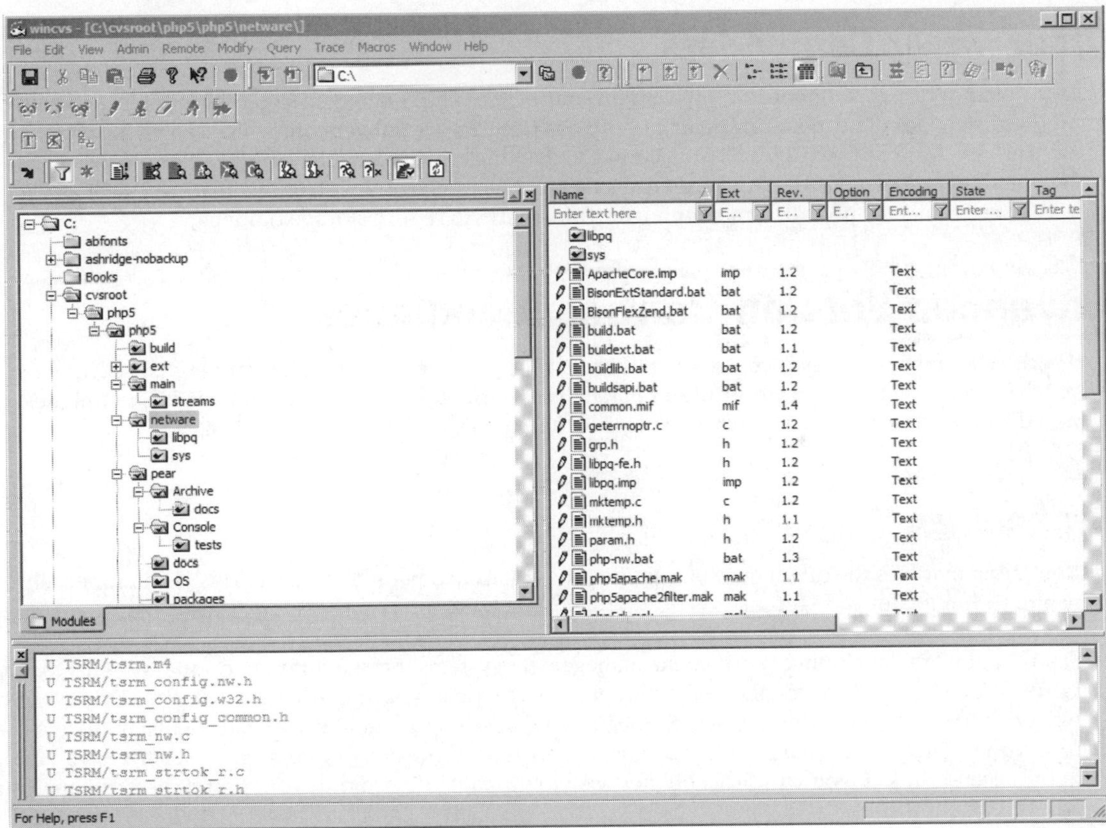

Figure A-3

modifies this new version to resolve the conflict, saves it, and recommits it. CVS then stores this as the latest version. Difficulties do, of course, arise when the conflict is more serious.

CVS can be a good choice, but its Concurrent Versioning may not be to everybody's taste, for the reasons outlined earlier in this appendix. Consider carefully whether this is appropriate for the project, and if not, whether its presence could encourage poor working practices among your developers.

RCS

The ancestor of and indeed still the underlying basis of CVS, RCS is a nonconcurrent Exclusive Versioning platform that has been around going on twenty-five years now. Concerning projects for which SourceSafe is too expensive, too slow, or too cumbersome, it provides an attractive alternative, although it is arguably less well supported than CVS these days.

In addition, many useful features of CVS are not related to Concurrent Versioning, such as the grouping of files into a single collection (treated as one object, in effect) and automatic determination of file states. In effect, RCS is a more raw version of CVS. This may suit some developers, but for many it will prove just a little too fussy to live with on a daily basis.

Other Minor Contenders

A number of minor contenders in the version control arena have emerged in recent months, and some are well worth a look. The most compelling of these is Greg Stein's Subversion, which can be found at `http://subversion.tigris.org`. Unlike CVS, which is based on the aging RCS protocol, Subversion has been written from the ground up and has some quite intriguing features, such as using HTTP as a transport protocol, and supporting binary diff to reduce storage burdens.

Advanced Version Control Techniques

There's a lot more to version control than there is space to cover it in this short appendix. As with so much in PHP, the topic can constitute a book in its own right. There are a few interesting techniques, however, that you may wish to employ in your chosen version control environment.

Branching

Branching involves the divergence of a single project into two parallel projects. This is an immensely useful technique for code reuse.

Say that you are developing two content-management systems for two different clients, systems that are virtually identical in functionality—the only differences are minor or aesthetic in nature. Obviously, you will wish to reuse code from one in the other, but doing so has a pitfall. If you make a major change in the first, you will want that change to propagate to your second project. Conversely, any changes you make in the second project, you will probably not wish to propagate upward to your first project, because these will be customizations.

Branching is the solution. By branching the first project to form a second, your version control software will automatically propagate any changes made to the first project into the second project as and when they happen, while retaining changes made in the second project as customizations unique to that second project.

Branching can also be used to maintain two different directions for a project. For example, you may wish to have one set of developers work on a maintenance release of your product while another set works on the next big major release. Branching allows you to take a snapshot of your product in time and then branch off into two distinct development paths, safe in the knowledge that any major changes in the prebranch product will be propagated into both paths.

Tagging

Not to be confused with the tags CVS places in individual files as mnemonics for its own use, tagging involves applying an arbitrary attribute to a given version of each file to create release versions.

For example, you may wish to create a beta version of your project. This will involve more or less every file in your project being packaged together, but you may wish to use different versions of each file—version 1.3 of this file, 1.5 of that file, and so on. By tagging the right version of each file, you can then easily tell your version control software to deliver a particular version on demand. Individual developers can move tags as and when they feel confident, so that at any given time when requesting a particular version—be it beta, release candidate 1, or whatever, you can be sure that you will be getting the latest stable version.

Comments

One often overlooked facility of all version control systems is the application of comments at check in. When checking in a file, the developer will be asked to supply a comment. It is a good idea to ensure that your developers do take advantage of this facility and supply a brief description, even if it is something as simple as "fixed bug 21301." When showing the history of a particular file, this information can be immensely useful.

Binary Files

Care should always be taken when adding binary files, such as images, to a repository,. Although it is generally a good idea to keep the entire project in one place, many version control packages are immensely inefficient at handling binary files and can slow to a crawl when faced with a few dozen JPEGs.

Consider whether there is a third way. For example, consider all those .GIF files containing page titles. Could they be replaced by a single PHP script, which uses `imagefttext` to render a caption as and when required? Such an "outside the box" approach can be of critical importance, because binary files represent one of a small number examples of when version control can prove inappropriate or cumbersome.

Summary

In this appendix, you encountered the principles and methodology of version control and its usefulness in larger projects. You learned about the difference between Concurrent and Exclusive Versioning. You looked briefly at the topology of a typical version control infrastructure and took a look at how this infrastructure is implemented in a number of popular version control packages. Finally, you looked at some of the more advanced techniques possible with version control and how they could be useful on your own projects.

PHP IDEs

Many developers still tend to program PHP with their favorite editor and have developed their own preferred methods of debugging their code. But, with millions of developers using PHP, the fact that Integrated Development Environments (IDEs, sometimes abbreviated to Development Environment, or DE) are not as widely used as, say, Visual Studio .NET is for ASP .NET is a bit of a mystery. This may be down to the fact that many people still don't view PHP5 as a full-fledged programming language in its own right (we hope that from what you have seen in this book, you believe otherwise).

At any rate, PHP5 *is* a full-fledged programming language, and IDEs for it do exist. If you haven't been developing using an IDE that supports PHP5, this appendix is for you. There are a host of useful features packed into the IDEs that might make the investment worthwhile to you. One of their biggest uses, of course, is the sophisticated debugging facilities that most IDEs provide.

Although this appendix won't give you a fully comprehensive rundown of each IDE out there, it will give you an idea of what you can expect from some of the main ones, and an idea of what else is available. For the most part, you should be able to get a deeper understanding of the functionality of each of the DEs from their documentation. We cover the Zend Studio Client first, and in more detail, because this is the largest PHP-centric DE on the market. Following this, alternatives such as Komodo will briefly be explored.

Choosing an IDE

The aim of an IDE is to give you, the developer, all the support and help you could possibly need to develop robust applications efficiently and accurately. The number of different ways to do this varies wildly from product to product, but there is one thing which you should look for in all of them. As with any software you use, one of the first things to decide before forever developing in one environment is whether that environment benefits you. In other words, does the IDE make it easier for you to develop your applications? If so, then it stands to reason that you should really be using that product as your development environment of choice. Simple as that.

Having simplified the argument to whether you think the DE of your choice is performing its job ignores one important fact, which you should bear in mind. As would be true with any other software, it may take some time to fully utilize the power inherent in these IDEs, so it is worth investing the hours finding your way around them. To that end, the following few sections should give you an idea of what to expect.

Zend Studio Client

Zend's offering should arguably be your first stop when looking for an IDE to use—assuming that you are happy to fork out the $249 or so that it will set you back. Of course, before purchasing anything, you should really take a close look at it, and you can download a free trial version from the Web site `http://www.zend.com/store/products/zend-studio.php`.

As of this writing, the current release version of Zend Studio is 3.5.0, which now includes full support for PHP 5. It is available for the Windows, Linux, and Mac OS X platforms.

If you are not familiar with IDEs, they can appear a little daunting at first. Keep in mind that they are here to help, not to confuse things. In this case, the Zend Studio is more than an IDE; it also provides you with features apart from the Development Environment. The server version comes with a precompiled version of PHP and Apache, for example. For the purposes of this appendix, we concentrate mainly on the Zend Development Environment (ZDE), which is the tool that allows you to manage and develop your code. With that in mind, the first screen you are presented with in the ZDE, after you have downloaded and installed it, is much like Figure B-1.

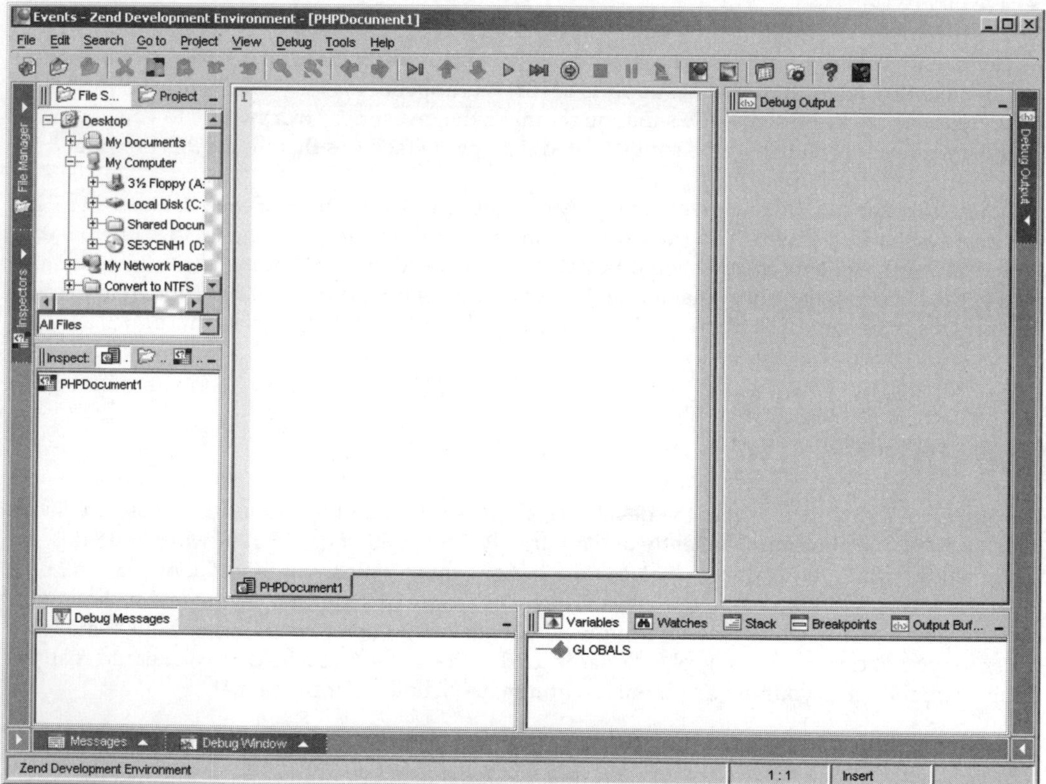

Figure B-1

Before doing anything else, click Tools ➪ Preferences ➪ Debug and then click the PHP5 option. You will run into all sorts of problems if the debugger is using PHP4. With that done, you are more or less ready to begin using the development environment. Plenty of documentation covers all the functionality in ZDE, so we won't cover everything exhaustively. Instead, we go through the most important features to give you a broad idea of what the ZDE is all about. We leave it to you to play around with the ZDE and make your mind up about whether to adopt it.

Managing Files and Projects

At the highest level, the DE has two tabs that allow you to manage your file system and your PHP projects. Looking at Figure B-1, toward the top left of the screen, you will notice that the File System window is the one with focus. You can use this to search for files using the drop-down list immediately below it to filter your results.

The Project window allows you to navigate any given project you are working on and perform various actions such as adding and removing files from a particular project. It is probably prudent for us to mention that the Project menu item on the ZDE's main menu allows you to create, open, save, and close projects.

Use projects to define a common working environment for files in any given project. For example, you may wish to have a specific debugging setup while working on a new site for a client, and placing the site's files into a project allows you to do this in an efficient manner.

Editing Code

Obviously, you would expect certain editing abilities to come with a full DE like this, and certainly, it has some neat features. The editing window is the large, central one shown in Figure B-1 earlier, and it contains a host of tools that are designed to make coding easier. One of the major features is code completion, which is available for both PHP and HTML. This allows you to display pop-ups of function parameters, declared functions, keywords, and constants. Figure B-2 shows an example of the pop-up displayed when you begin typing in a PHP5 array function.

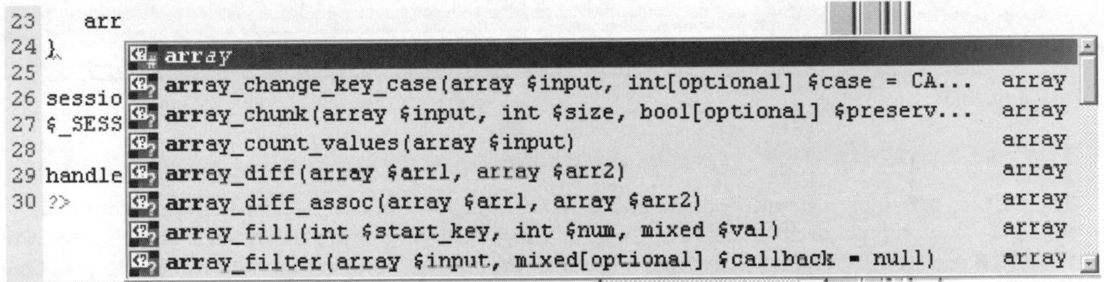

Figure B-2

As with most aspects of this DE, code completion is configurable, and you can check out the options by choosing Tools ➪ Preferences ➪ Code Completion. Figure B-3 shows you the screen presenting your options.

The Preferences window provides you with many other configurable settings, such as editing and debugging options.

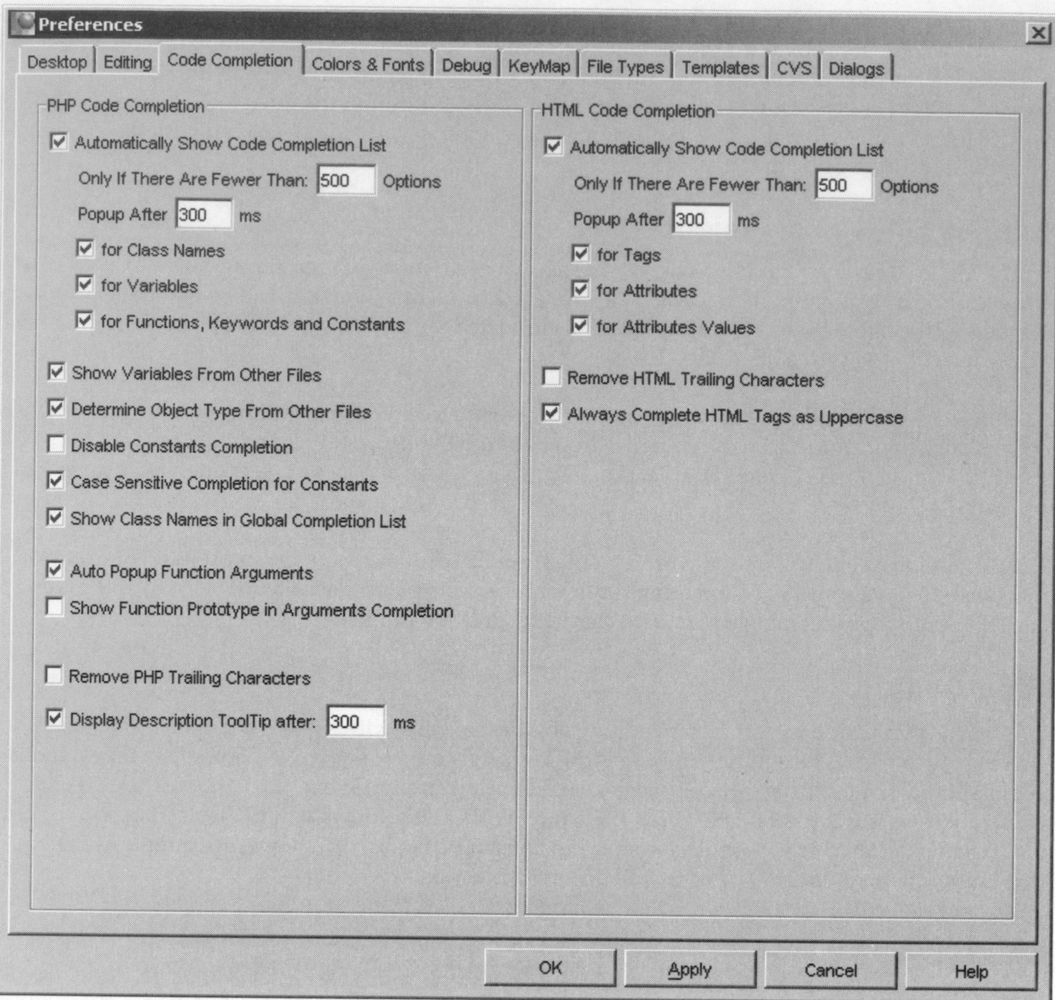

Figure B-3

The DE also provides you with code indentation facilities. You can either chose to indent your code manually, as you type, or all at one time—a nice feature that makes life a bit easier. If you click the editing tab of the Preferences menu, you will see a list of all the editing features that are available to you. One of the more useful ones is the matching brackets feature, shown in action in Figure B-4.

Placing the cursor immediately before the beginning elements or immediately after the closing elements causes the editor to highlight the matching element. A useful trick here is to press Ctrl+M to jump between matching elements to avoid tiresome scrolling. See the Go To Main Menu option for more navigation shortcuts.

Templates are also available to help speed up otherwise repetitive tasks. There are plenty provided as standard, but you can also add your own or even modify the ones that are already there. You can view

```
function secure_handler(){
   if ($_SESSION['name'] == "David"){
      $this->handled_event();
   }else{
      echo "Sorry $_SESSION[name] you are not
   }
}
```

Figure B-4

the available templates by going to the Template tab of the Preferences window. Each template has a given key that denotes its specific template. For example, Figure B-5 shows the results of typing **my** into the Editor window.

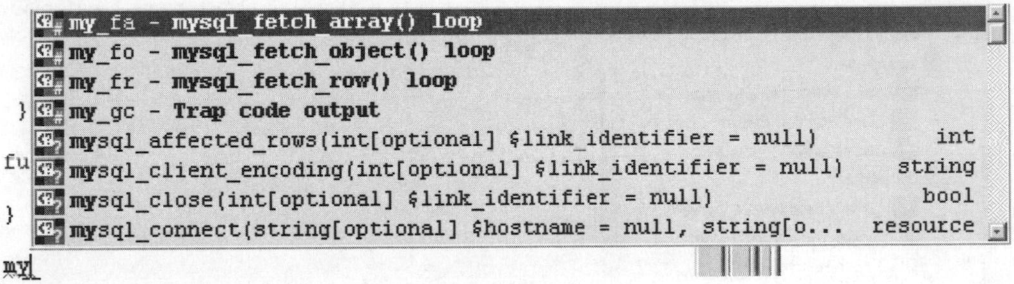

```
my_fa - mysql fetch array() loop
my_fo - mysql_fetch_object() loop
my_fr - mysql_fetch_row() loop
my_gc - Trap code output
mysql_affected_rows(int[optional] $link_identifier = null)             int
mysql_client_encoding(int[optional] $link_identifier = null)        string
mysql_close(int[optional] $link_identifier = null)                    bool
mysql_connect(string[optional] $hostname = null, string[o...      resource
my
```

Figure B-5

The top four options are all templates that come with the DE. If you click one of them, the template code assigned to that key is automatically added to the Editor window. Figure B-6 shows the results of clicking the second option.

```
while ($row = mysql_fetch_object($query)) {

}
```

Figure B-6

A bunch of other useful editing features are available, ranging from HTML tag shortcuts to syntax error highlighting. The only way to really learn your way around these is to play with them. The help files do a good job of outlining all the DE's features, so use this to find your way around. Let's move on and look at another useful feature of the ZDE.

Inspecting Code

Recall from Figure B-1 the window on the bottom left of the ZDE, called Inspect. This comes with three options: File, Project, and PHP. The first option gives you a collapsible list of all the elements of the file, which has focus in the Editor window. Figure B-7 shows an example of this in action:

You can use this for navigation if you wish. Double-clicking any of the elements listed in the Inspect window will take the cursor directly to that piece of code in the source file.

You can look at things from one level up by clicking the Project tab. This gives you an overview of everything in the current project. It acts pretty much in the same way as the File window in that you can

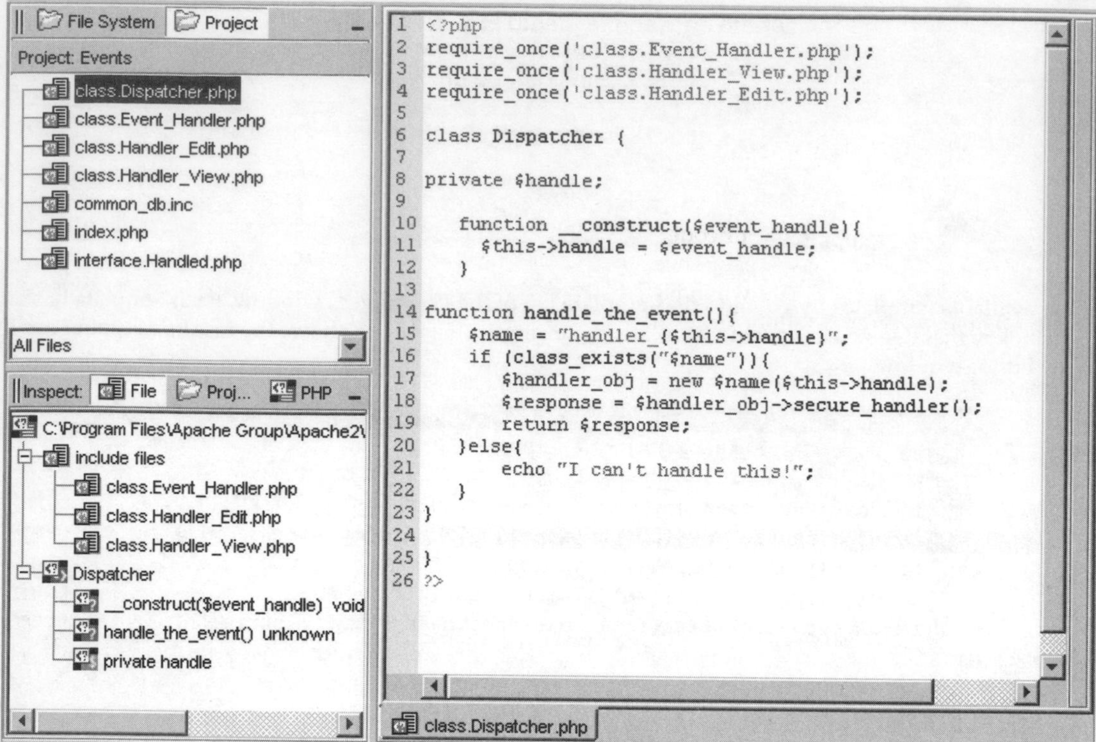

Figure B-7

click any file or displayed element of that file in the Project window and it will be opened for editing in the main window.

The final option—PHP—gives you a list of all the PHP functions and their syntax. Of course, you may wish to know a little more than just their usage, so if you highlight the function in the Inspect window and press F1, a slightly more in-depth information file will pop up in a browser window. Incidentally, this also works for PHP functions within your Editor window—simply highlight the function you wish to learn about and press F1.

Debugging with the ZDE

For brevity's sake, we assume that you have everything running on one machine (in other words, you have downloaded and installed the Zend Studio Client) so that you can debug your applications locally. It is possible to set up a multiuser debugging environment by installing the Studio Server package on a central, nonlocal server, and you should consult the documentation for more information on this.

One of the biggest advantages you can derive from using a development environment is making use of the innovative debugging features they provide. Plowing through error log files is one way to do it, but that can be quite clumsy in comparison to the more sophisticated methods available. The internal debugger has a list of features designed to help you keep tabs on exactly what is happening in your code. Specifically, its main function is to provide you with:

- Program flow monitoring
- A debug window
- A debug messages window
- Output rendering

Let's look at these in some detail. One of the first things with which you need to familiarize yourself is how to go about debugging your code. The ZDE provides several methods for moving from place to place. Some involve setting breakpoints; others simply trace the flow of the program step by step. You will notice a set of arrows (shown in Figure B-8) that can be used for stepping over, moving between breakpoints, or simply running your code.

Figure B-8

Note that the final icon you see in Figure B-8 runs the code analyzer. The analyzer's main job is to help determine where errors may be located in the code open on the Editor screen. Add a syntax error to your code and run the analyzer on it to see how it works.

After you have the hang of stepping over your code or following a script's execution, you can use these to find out valuable information on the state of your code. For this, though, you need the Debug window. The Debug window, located by default on the bottom right of the ZDE, provides you with five options to monitor and manage your project's debugging. From here you will be able to view the value of variables, the position of watches, the stack trace, the position of breakpoints, and the buffer. All these come in handy depending on what it is you are trying to determine about your code.

For example, we have stepped over the execution of a very simple PHP script to demonstrate how the Variables tab shows you information on all the variables associated with your code (including the global ones). This is shown in Figure B-9.

Notice that the fifth line in the Editor window is highlighted. This is because, at present, the debugger is stopped at this point in the script's execution. The values you see in the Variables window are the values at this particular point in the program's execution. If you know the piece of code you want to inspect, you can forgo stepping over it line by line and place the cursor on the line you wish the debugger to go to. Clicking the Go to Cursor (fifth, from left to right in Figure B-9) button will take you straight there.

The next tab along is the Watches tab. You might find that you want the debugger to keep an eye out on a number of different pieces of code. If this is the case, then set watches for the code elements you wish to trace. We highlighted the `$answer` variable in our code example shown previously and clicked Debug ⇨ Add Watch. This time, stepping over the program's execution using the debugger gives the following, not entirely unexpected, results (Figure B-10).

Tracking the execution stack is also a useful way of determining where you are in your code. The Stack tab allows you to view where you are in the program's stack. This can be helpful because if one part of your code calls a function, the program's execution leaves the current place to go off and run the called function. If the function itself makes use of other functions, then the program's execution heads off again to go execute those. Being able to determine exactly where you are in all this is where the Stack tracking capability of the debugger comes in.

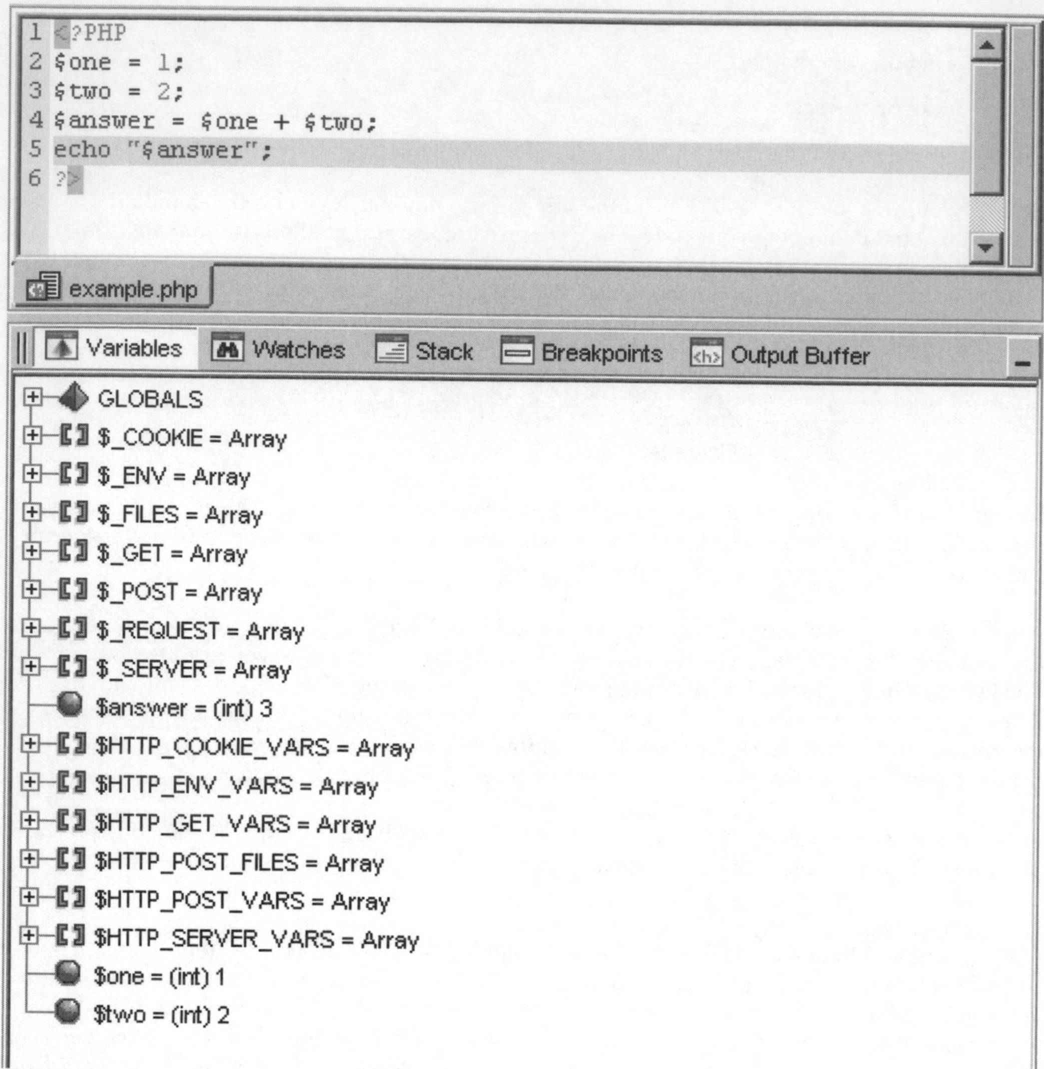

Figure B-9

Figure B-11 shows an example of the Stack window being used to track a simple script that has two functions.

To get the debugger to stop where we want, we need to set breakpoints. Breakpoints are simply delimiters that tell the debugger to freeze execution as is so that you can look over whatever you need to. In Figure B-11, two breakpoints have been set by clicking the line number in the Editor window. This causes the selected line to be highlighted in pink (although you won't see color in the screenshot, you can see which lines are highlighted) and means that this is now a set breakpoint. Clicking the Breakpoint tab will verify this for you (see Figure B-12).

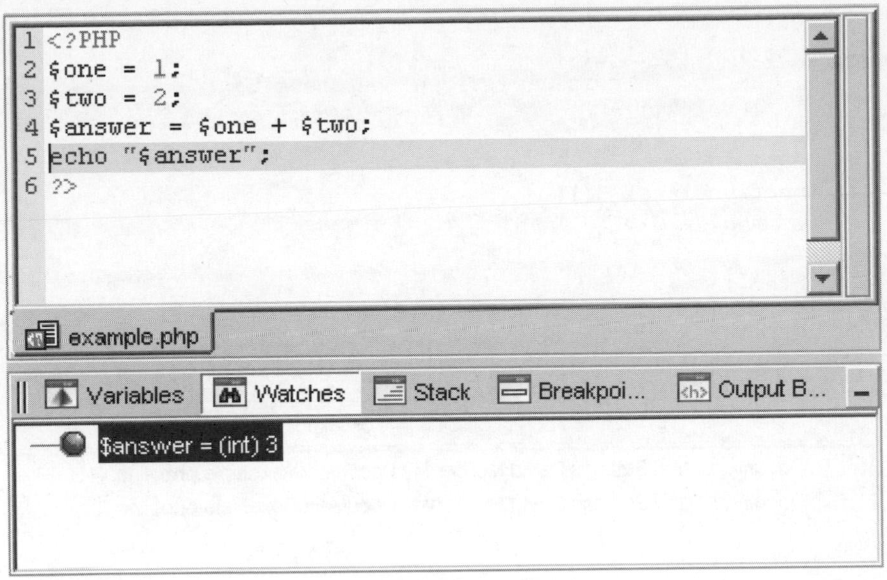

```
<?PHP
$one = 1;
$two = 2;
$answer = $one + $two;
echo "$answer";
?>
```

example.php

Variables | Watches | Stack | Breakpoi... | Output B...

$answer = (int) 3

Figure B-10

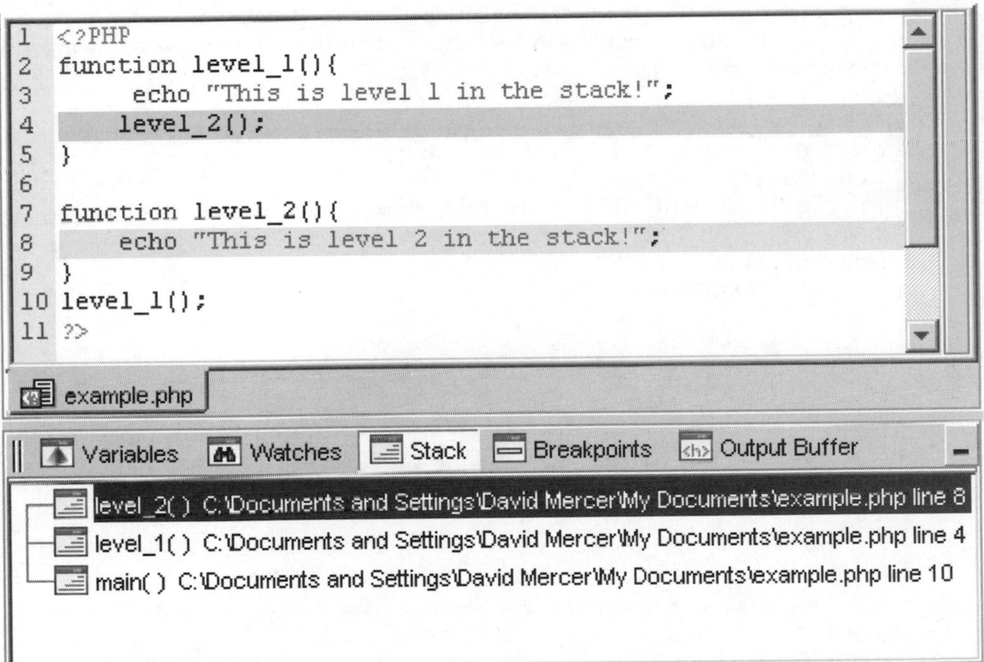

Figure B-11

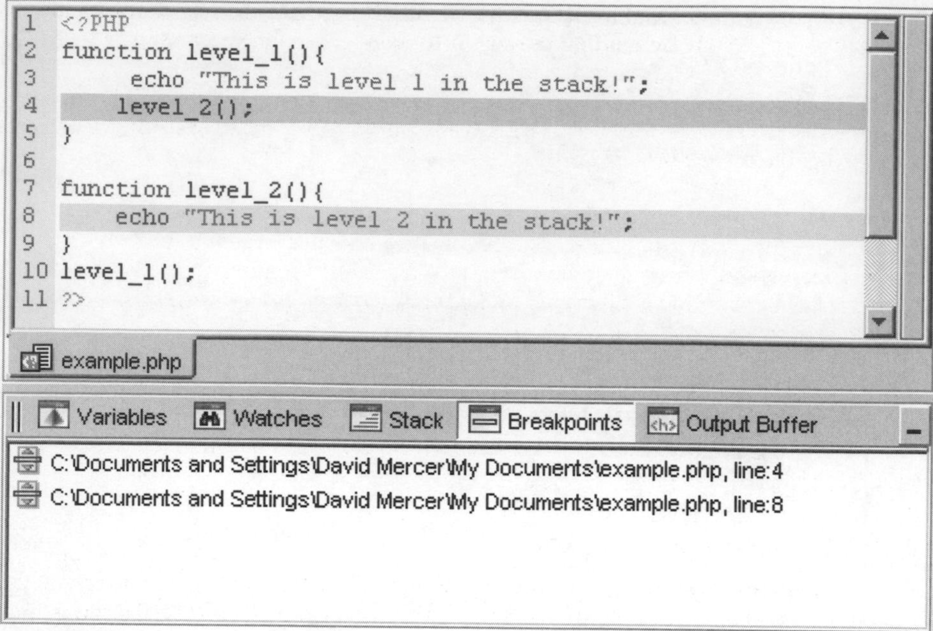

Figure B-12

Finally, if you are making use of PHP's output buffering functions, then the final tab, Output Buffer, is just for you. Basically, it shows whatever is in the buffer, and we tested it with the following script (Figure B-13) to demonstrate.

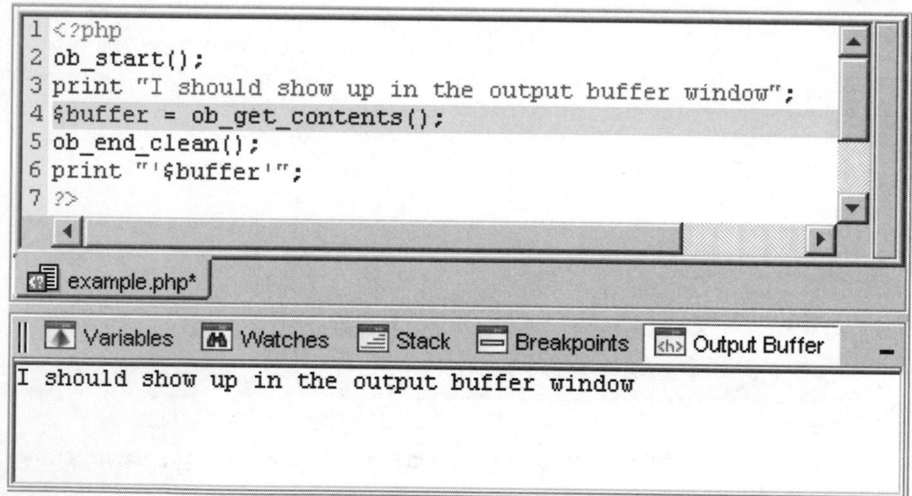

Figure B-13

With that done, two things are left to mention. The first is the Debug Messages window, which is located, by default, to the left of the Debug window. It displays notices, warnings, and errors that crop up during the debugging of your scripts. Double-clicking the messages in the Messages window allows you to locate their source quite easily by sending the cursor to them in the Editor window.

Finally, the ZDE also renders your script's output in the Debug Output window. This pops up on the right side of the ZDE as soon as your script creates any output. Use this to keep an eye on whether your scripts are creating the correct browser code.

Zend provides still other debugging facilities. For example, using remote debugging, you can actually debug your application as it works on the site. This has several advantages in that you can track your application working with input as it would normally. This is often quite hard to do otherwise. Further, the output from the Debug window is displayed in the browser. This all requires Zend Server to be running on the Web server, but we won't go into that here.

With all the debugging and editing functionality provided, we say it once again: Download a demo copy and play around with it. You never know: you might find that this is the answer to your programming dreams. Before we finish our whirlwind tour of Zend's development offering, several other important tools should get a mention.

More Zend Studio tools

Zend has also provided developers with a profiler (found within the Tools menu option on the ZDE) to help analyze the performance of their applications. This profiler can be used to determine how to improve an application's performance by identifying problem areas. Several tabs provide you with different types of information, ranging from pie charts showing the amounts of time consumed by scripts, tables, and diagrams displaying statistics for various functions to a call trace to monitor the linear consumption of time from call to call.

Also, Zend can integrate with CVS version control, and you should consult the documentation to see how to get this up and running.

Finally, you can also install the safeguard suite. This gives you the option to electronically license your software. The suite comes in two sections: the Encoder and the License Manager. The encoder simply creates encoded binary files which are then distributed. This helps to prevent intellectual property from being copied or modified. The License Manager creates license keys that allow you to impose the license restriction you want, based on the criteria you supply.

That brings us to the end of the tour of Zend Studio Client and the ZDE. Now we take a look at other development environment offerings.

Komodo

A trial version of Active State's Komodo can be downloaded at its site: `http://www.activestate.com/Products/Komodo/`. The professional version, used for commercial purposes, will set you back $295, so it is certainly a good idea to give the demo version a try before buying. Historically, it has been available for both Linux and Windows, but as of the latest release, 2.5, it is now also available on the Solaris platform.

Komodo is an open source development environment, as opposed to being PHP specific, and it supports, among other things, Perl, Python, Tcl, and XSLT. As of this writing, however, the PHP5 debugger extension is not yet available, so debug support in Komodo is restricted to earlier versions. You should consult the Komodo Web site for any updates on this.

Managing Projects

Komodo provides you with a Project Manager that can be used to perform a large number of actions. By default, it appears down the left side of the DE window, and project-related functionality can be accessed through the Project main menu item. Among other things, you can:

- Create and open projects
- Add files and folders
- Add commands, templates, URLs, Web services, and dialog boxes
- Organize, save, and close projects

Additionally, you can access pop-up context menus, as shown in Figure B-14, by right-clicking the project members.

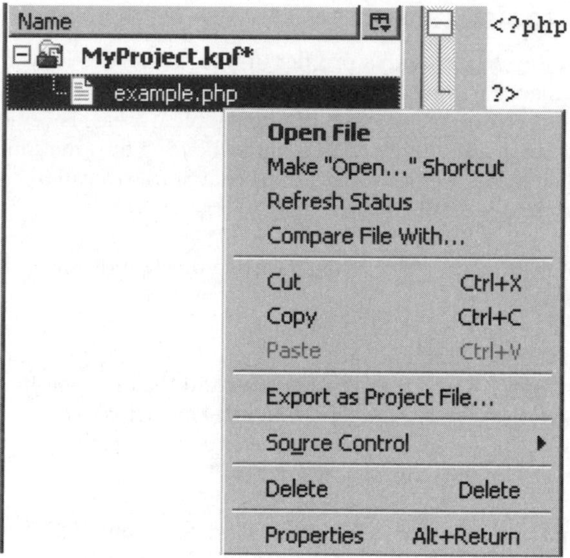

Figure B-14

The context menu you get depends on the type of element you have chosen.

Editing Code

Komodo's code editor has some interesting features, as well as the more standard ones such as coloring and indentation. For example, code folding is provided to collapse sections of code, allowing you to look at abstracted, or skeleton, versions of your code to get an overview of what is happening. Figure B-15 shows the Editor window with collapsed code.

The editor also provides autocomplete functionality for PHP—specifically, for classes, functions and variables. Classes in the current and included files are displayed when the word *new* is typed in, and class

```
<?php
Function one(){
Function two(){
Function three(){
  echo "I am the third function in my script!";
}
?>
```

Figure B-15

methods are displayed when the -> operator is used. Similarly, all user-defined functions and PHP functions will be displayed after four matching characters are typed in.

Another nice feature of the editor is called *tips* (tips tell you what parameters you can use with a function), which display after you have typed in the opening brace for a given function—either user defined, or PHP. Figure B-16 shows the call tip for a user-defined function.

```
<?php
Function one($param_1, $param_2 = 0){
one(
?>  ($param_1, $param_2 = 0)
```

Figure B-16

There are plenty of other features in the editor, but most of them are pretty intuitive to use and need not be covered here in any detail. A brief list follows:

- Most Recently Used List
- Detect Changed Files
- Preview in Browser
- Background Syntax Checking
- Code Commenting

Debugging with Komodo

We won't look into the debugger in too much detail here because the PHP5 extension has not yet been released. There are some configuration requirements to get Komodo's PHP debugger working, and you should consult the documentation for instructions. Apart from this, Komodo provides you with a full-fledged debugger, which includes:

- Breakpoint control
- Stepping

- Watching variables
- Viewing the call stack
- Sending input
- Adding command-line arguments

Of course, Komodo comes with a host of other tools to supplement their editor and debugger. Let's take a quick look through those here.

More Komodo Tools

Because Komodo allows a host of items to be added to projects, such as shortcuts, folders, files, commands, and templates, it also provides a toolbox in which to store all these for easy access. You can work with the toolbox either through the tab in the left pane (shared with the Project tab), or the Toolbox main menu item. Figure B-17 shows the sample items available in the toolbox. In this case, the snippet was added to the code window simply by double-clicking it.

Figure B-17

Komodo can also be integrated with CVS and Perforce (Perforce is SCM, or Software Configuration Management software). To get this up and running, you need to go to the main menu and click Edit ➪ Preferences ➪ Source Code Control ➪ CVS. This will bring up the dialog box shown in Figure B-18 (assuming that you haven't installed CVS yet), and from there you can download CVS if you require, or search for the relevant executable. Notice that the configuration settings for Perforce are directly below those for CVS in the navigation tree.

With that, we leave Komodo and urge you once more to download the demo version to play around with. One caveat in terms of cost here is that you might find that you are paying extra for functionality that is not really useful to you. For example, some tools that come with Komodo are specifically for Perl, such as the Perl Dev Kit. This adds to the development costs of Komodo without providing much value to PHP developers.

Other IDEs and Editors

A host of other development environments is available for the professional PHP developer. Some are more useful than others, depending on what you want to use them for. For example, PHPEdit, for Windows, offers a bunch of useful editing tools as well as a debugger. It is available for download free of charge at `http://www.waterproof.fr/products/PHPEdit`. Very briefly, some of its main features are as follows:

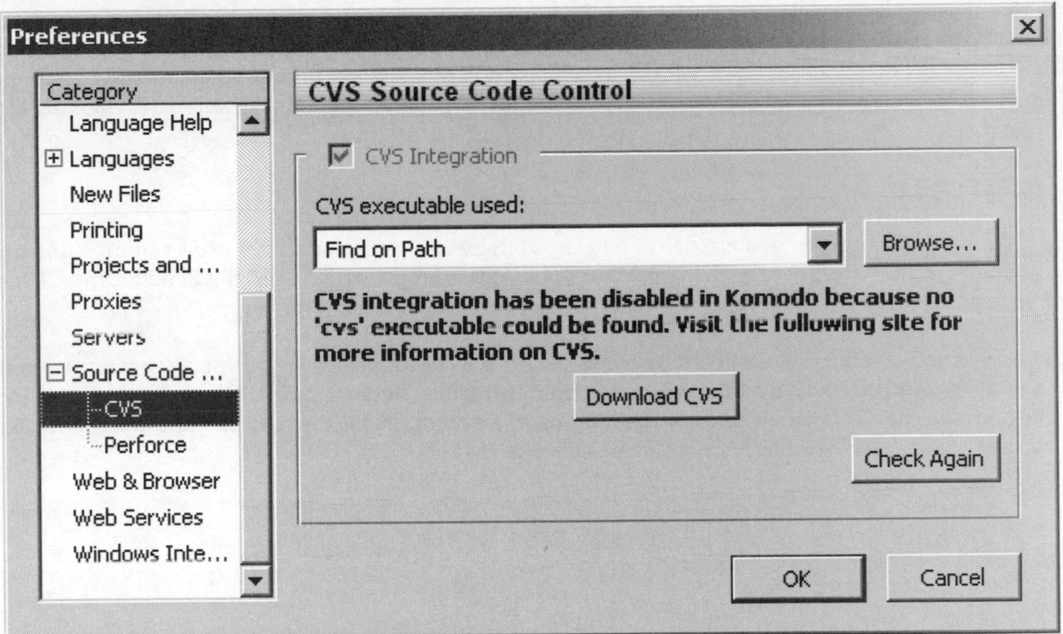

Figure B-18

- Syntax Highlighting
- Code Hint, Code Insight
- Integrated PHP debugger
- Help Generator
- Customizable shortcuts
- More than 100 scriptable commands
- Keyboard templates
- To-do report generator
- QuickMarks
- Plug-ins

Here are some other IDEs and editors you may want to take a look at:

- PHPEclipse: `http://www.phpeclipse.de/tiki-view_articles.php`
- EditPlus: `http://www.editplus.com/`
- NuSpherePHPEd: `http://www.nusphere.com/products/index.htm`
- PHPCode: `http://www.phpide.de/`

This ends our brief discourse on PHP-based IDEs. Of course, simply because we haven't covered all the options available doesn't mean that they aren't worth looking at. For example, NuSphere's PHPEd provides tons of advanced features such as code completion, debugging, profiling, and deployment facilities, among other things. As an IDE, it has received some acclaim and is well worth looking over.

Summary

This appendix has given you an idea of what's out there and what you might expect from an Integrated Development Environment with support for PHP. To this end, we discussed the Zend Studio Client as a PHP-specific platform, and Komodo as an open source environment with support for PHP5.

Discovering the advantages offered by using an IDE is a rewarding process, especially from the point of view that your productivity should increase from using one. Because purchasing a development tool like the aforementioned IDEs represents an investment, we recommend that you spend some time looking at the features of each one carefully before you choose.

Performance Tuning PHP

PHP is extremely quick. In fact, for many applications, both simple and complex, PHP can beat the likes of Java, ASP, ColdFusion, and ASP.NET with very little work.

Sometimes, however, the need for speed will be of fundamental importance to the overall success of your project. At these times, gaining that last drop of performance can mean the difference between success and failure, so planning your application with speed in mind is vital from the outset.

But there are other reasons for using PHP. For example, you may have inherited a poorly written application from another party and need to increase performance without spending money on new hardware. Although it's rarely pleasant working with other people's code, especially those who have not been lucky enough to read this book, you'd be surprised how easy it is to squeeze seconds off.

In this appendix, you'll learn to identify the different types of performance bottleneck and how to track down their culprits. Then, you'll look at how to design and code for optimum efficiency and speed, as well as how to retroactively repair bad code you've been unfortunate enough to inherit.

Introduction to Performance Problems

The first time you'll hear about an application running slowly is probably from a user report. Unfortunately, users are rarely particularly useful in this respect; the cry of "this thing is so slow" across the office tells you virtually nothing. It's important, therefore, to do a little digging.

Types of Performance Bottlenecks

Let's go back to basics for a minute and look at the structure of an HTTP `GET` or `POST` request. When the user's Web browser makes a request, it makes a socket connection to the Web server, usually on port 80 or, for SSL connections, 443. This is a blocking activity in the Web browser, so called because the browser cannot do anything else until the connection is successfully made. In practice, however, most modern Web browsers will allow the user to cancel while the connection attempt is being made, and on faster connections the connection is made in literally fractions of a second. But if the server is heavily loaded the connection may take a while to establish. If this is the case, it points to other applications or processes on that server slowing things down (not necessarily the application in question).

After achieving connection, the Web browser does not wait for any response because the HTTP protocol does not dictate there should be any. Immediately, it sends a very small request packet, usually not more than a few bytes in size. This request contains, among other data, the document that the Web browser requires, and any `GET` or `POST` parameters the user has offered as part of the request.

This request is, in itself, small. The time between the socket connection's being established and the request's being sent to the Web server is likely to be minimal.

The time between when the Web server has received the request and when it starts to return data is known as the processing time for your script. In most cases, PHP will not attempt to send any output to the Web browser until the entire script has finished executing, unless the volume of your output exceeds the value of `output_buffering` in `php.ini`. This means that the processing time is roughly equal to the time between when PHP starts executing your script and the time it finishes executing. This is the most likely place for a delay. The time between when data starts to be returned to the Web browser and when that data is finished transferring is the delivery time and is not likely to be related to PHP in any way. The time for this data to be transferred is much more likely to be tied to network performance, either at the server side (for example, an overloaded connection) or client side (a horrifyingly slow modem). Unless your page weight exceeds 55K, which is generally regarded as the limit for sensible Web pages, this is unlikely to be a cause of delays.

The easiest way to identify where a performance bottleneck is occurring is to use some manual tool, rather than a bona fide Web browser, to make the HTTP request, and analyze the results yourself.

Differentiating Between Different Types of Bottleneck

Suppose you want to analyze where poor performance might be occurring in requests for the page `/example.php`, on the server `www.example.com`, with `GET` parameter `foo` equaling `bar`. This is, of course, equivalent to `http://www.example.com/example.php?foo=bar`. Start a console session and use telnet as follows:

```
ed@genesis:~$ telnet www.example.com 80
Trying 192.168.1.2...
Connected to www.example.com
Escape character is '^ ]'.

GET /example.php?foo=bar HTTP/1.1
Host: www.example.com


<HTML>
 <BODY>
  Hello, World!
 </BODY>
</HTML>
```

In Windows, the same approach applies—start a command prompt and use telnet in exactly the same manner.

To get real-life output, you will need to substitute the hostname and URL for real-life examples. You need to press Enter where you see a blank line, and enter spaces exactly as above. You may find it easier to write it all out in Notepad and paste it into telnet.

Have a stopwatch handy when you do this. Observe where the delay lies, and infer as follows:

- A delay between pressing Enter and observing `Trying 192.168.1.2` indicates a delay in resolving the IP address of the server against a name server. This is unusual. It could indicate unresponsive name servers, either those you are using yourself (typically those of your own ISP) or those serving the domain of the server in question (typically the ISP hosting the server). Why this unresponsiveness exists is outside the scope of this book, but you can at least reassure yourself PHP is not to blame. To a real-world user, this delay would be experienced only once, when first accessing the site, because most Web browsers (and, indeed, operating systems) cache the results of name server lookups.
- A delay between the `Trying...` line and the `Connected` line indicates that the server itself took a while to successfully respond to your requests to connect. A delay here is massively damaging, because a page with several images could easily consist of twenty or thirty HTTP requests. If each one has a delay attached, the page could appear dramatically sluggish even if script execution time is markedly quick. Unfortunately, the delay could exist in one of two places—either the network to/from the server or in the server's ability to respond to connections in a timely manner. The latter of these could be caused by server load, which could be caused by poorly optimized PHP (not necessarily this script) or other processes bringing the server to its knees. A quick check of memory and CPU utilization on the server can reveal the truth here. If it's the former, then it's outside the scope of this book; if it's the latter, then you should try to track down which script is causing the problem and, if it's PHP, apply the same methods seen here to that script.
- A delay between pressing Enter twice after having entered your HTTP request and seeing the HTML of your response almost certainly indicates poor performance at processing time. This can be validated and verified by adding watches in code.

Assuming that the delay appears to be down to script processing time, you can now determine what in the script is causing the delay (or delays).

Causes of Poor Performance

Forgetting the wider edicts on good PHP architecture for just a moment, we must remember that PHP is a scripting language. Its scripts have a start, a middle, and an end, just like any scripting language. The truth of the matter is that at the most basic, simplified level, the pattern of execution of any PHP script looks something like this:

- Read input parameters, be they `GET`, `POST`, or `COOKIE`
- Use those input parameters to make decisions, consulting external data sources in the process
- Produce output

The first and last of these three steps are not likely to cause performance bottlenecks because they are integral to PHP and your Web server. In other words, it's not your code. Only the real processing of data could be causing delays.

These delays will boil down to one of three things:

- Poor algorithms—inefficient code resulting in high execution time
- Poor hardware—the code's not unreasonable, but the hardware it's running on is elderly or overworked
- External bottlenecks—a database causing holdups

We should point out that hardware is rarely the problem. Except in extreme cases such as intense usage of `Gd` for graphics rendering, PHP does not require the latest or greatest in server hardware.

Tracking Down the Bottleneck

There are straightforward steps to resolving each different variety of identifiable bottleneck, as we discuss in the remainder of this appendix.

However, the first step is to determine where the bottleneck can be found and which of the three categories described previously it falls into.

Database Queries

The easiest offenders to track down are slow database queries. Almost all enterprise-class PHP applications depend on a database of some kind. In this book we have heavily advocated PostgreSQL, but many applications, particularly those you will encounter that are written by third parties, will make use of the more popular MySQL.

You must eliminate database bottlenecks before attempting to optimize code. Because most code is dependent on the database in some respect, even if only for the supply of data, to look at code before its data source is optimized is not time well spent.

The simplest way to determine whether database bottlenecks exist in a script is to temporarily adapt your database abstraction layer (first described in Chapter 8) to add a timer method.

Consider the query method of your abstraction layer for PostgreSQL. By adding error log stamps before and after each query, you can show how long each query took and easily produce an analyzable log for your page. The following excerpt shows an example, demonstrating how you might measure the time taken to perform a query in the database abstraction layer by sandwiching the `execute query` statement as follows:

```
$intTimeNow = microtime();
$q_handle = pg_exec($this->link_ident, $sql);
$intTimeTaken = microtime() - $intTimeNow;
error_log("DEBUG: QUERY: $sql\n");
error_log("DEBUG: TIME TAKEN: $intTimeTaken\n");
```

This will yield error log output similar to the following:

```
[Sun May 16 22:10:19 2004] [error] DEBUG: QUERY: SELECT id,logged_in,user_id
FROM "user_sessions" WHERE session_id='98ce552be0a2ea6b6f69fbebcd14997c' AND
```

```
user_agent='Mozilla/4.0 (compatible; MSIE 6.0; Windows NT 5.1)' AND
ip_address='192.168.4.3'
[Sun May 16 22:10:19 2004] [error] DEBUG: TIME TAKEN: 0.003752
```

Executing a typical PHP script with your database abstraction layer doctored as shown in the preceding example will then yield a series of `DEBUG: QUERY` *xx* and `DEBUG: TIME TAKEN` statements as above.

The pattern of queries will be easier to analyze whether you can ensure that no other warnings, error messages, or code-initiated debug statements are writing to the error log and that the analysis of the time being taken by your query has exclusivity for now.

You should easily be able to spot the slow performers. In typical setups, anything lasting more than half a second should raise a red flag. Also note the sum total of the duration of queries for a page. Anything totaling more than three seconds is considered incredibly bad form and will drive your user nuts.

Algorithms

After any database bottlenecks have been addressed, you may safely look at the code itself. PHP is very fast, so algorithmic holdups are certainly less likely to be a factor than is poor database performance.

However, by enseeding your script with similar time stamp output as those used in tracking down database problems, you can determine where bottlenecks might lie.

You cannot do this in one fell swoop, for obvious reasons. The burden is on you to place "start the clock" and "stop the clock" statements at either side of blocks of code you feel might be troublesome. If you do find one, you can always drill down and add more start/stop statements within that block of code to find the precise culprit. Don't be afraid to output variable values in your `error_log` statement, too, to give a clue as to progress in `for` loops, for example.

This approach can be automated to some extent by using a package such as APD, the Advanced PHP Debugger (`http://pecl.php.net/package/apd`), though for smaller applications, and those built in a "best practice" modular fashion, its immense functionality may well prove to be overkill.

Progress between steps should be nearly instantaneous in PHP, as long as an external data source is not involved. Delays of more than fractions of a second between logical blocks point to serious problems in your code.

Patching for Performance

Now that you know what's to blame and where it is, you can concentrate on patching your code to improve performance.

Mercifully, there is one thing of which you can be certain: You won't be the only PHP developer who's ever encountered bottlenecks like yours. As a result, there are some tried and tested techniques you can follow to try to patch them.

Fixing Database Holdups

Earlier, you saw how to identify which queries were holding up execution of your script. But why a query is running badly could be a result of any number of factors. Optimizing SQL statements is a massive topic, and there simply isn't the space to go into much detail here. There are numerous excellent volumes on PostgreSQL, MySQL, and other databases that deal with query optimization. However, the following headline points are worth bearing in mind:

- Primary keys that are numbers will always be faster as a primary index than primary keys that are alphanumeric, even if there are unique alphanumeric values that would ordinarily be an obvious candidate for primary key. In general, an "id" column is what is required.
- Ensure that columns and, perhaps more important, combinations of columns by which you will filter or order in `SELECT` statements have corresponding indices defined.
- Scheduled scripts to clean up tables (using, for example, the `VACUUM` statement in PostgreSQL) whose contents are updated frequently may well prove to be sound investments.
- Never use `SELECT *`. If you know the names of the columns you want, specify them. This will improve performance.
- Try to minimize the number of queries you are performing to achieve your desired result. Selecting a string of matching `id` values and then using a brace of queries to retrieve their contents may fit better with your object model, but it is very inefficient. Is there a way to find a middle ground? In Chapter 7, for example, you met the `GenericObjectCollection` class, which let you do just that—adopt an OOP-compliant approach to development while minimizing the number of SQL queries necessary to effect that approach.
- Subselects are easier to put together than `INNER` or `OUTER` joins, but nowhere near as efficient. Avoid them if possible (this will also, as a side effect, increase RDBMS portability). If you suspect that subselects may be slowing your application down, try replacing them with either `INNER` or `OUTER` joins as appropriate. Consult the documentation of your preferred flavor of database for more information.

Most tips such as the preceding increase speed by only fractions of a second. But this really is a case of every little bit helping, especially when you are dealing with pages with a large number of queries.

Don't forget that you will almost certainly need to look outside the PHP script itself to track down the offending SQL query, particularly if you are following the best practice principles as set out in this book. If you have devised an object model that is heavily dependent on a database backend, you may find that performance tweaks in queries used in that model have unexpected performance gains elsewhere. By the same token, however, when changes are being made to such high-level classes, care should be taken to thoroughly test all components that depend on them to ensure that functionality and behavior remain consistent with expectations.

Fixing Code Holdups

Ultimately, the same principles as those for optimizing database queries apply here. It's not good enough to know simply which block of code is causing a holdup; you need to work out which PHP statement is being slow and under what circumstances.

Logic Errors

However, it is sometimes the case that simple errors in application logic are to blame. In such cases, the application does function as expected, so ordinary QA techniques have not registered a bug. However, some human error in the code has caused performance to be adversely affected. These are the easiest to fix.

Consider the following example:

```
switch ($i) {
 case 0:
  array_pop($arMediumArray);
  break;
 case 1:
  array_reverse($arAnotherHugeArray);
 case 2:
  $arHugeArray = array_unique($arHugeArray);
  break;
};
```

As you can probably spot, we are missing a `break` statement under the case where `$i` is equal to 1. This means that the case where `$i` is equal to 2 will also be executed when `$i` is equal to 1. In that case, all that is necessary is for `$arAnotherHugeArray` to be reversed. But, in fact, `$arHugeArray` is also being made unique, as a side effect. It is quite possibly the case that `$arHugeArray` will never be used again after this `switch` statement should `$i` equal 1, so this method being erroneously called may not cause a malfunction per se. What it likely does, however, is double the execution time for the block. Adding the `break` statement stops the redundant method call and speeds execution as a result.

The methods alluded to previously should still allow you to track down such problems. By printing the execution time for the entire block, and the execution time for the statements you think should be getting executed, you will often see a discrepancy between the two. Although this discrepancy may be the result of any number of problems, it is entirely possible that a logic error is to blame. Accordingly, it is worthwhile checking for such problems, particularly when using prone constructs such as the `switch` statement, before getting too in-depth with query optimization and other more intense performance tuning.

Bottleneck Avoidance

At all other times, judicious use of the techniques met earlier should allow you to narrow your bottleneck down to a single offender, or at least, a collection of offenders.

The most common methods built into PHP, which can be very slow for one reason or another, include:

- Any method that relies on an external source for data. We have looked at databases as a bottleneck separately, but consider, for example, disk access to a busy disk or network drive, HTTP and FTP requests, IP address resolution, and communication with other objects via Web services protocols such as SOAP and RPC.
- Anything memory intensive may have no problems when called in isolation, but when fighting for physical memory with other instances of the script, and forced to use virtual memory (that is, disk) as a result, such methods can grind to a halt. Typically, anything to do with the built-in graphics library `Gd` is likely to be an offender, especially when having to work with large images. Consider whether implementing caching techniques, or performing offline generation using scheduled tasks, is feasible.
- Anything involving sockets is heavily dependent on network performance. Again, an approach whereby socket conversations are made offline and the user is advised as to his or her status when a request is made, rather than a socket conversation's being initiated as a direct

consequence of a request's being made, is a better approach. Consider, therefore, maintaining an e-mail queue database table, which is processed every five minutes, and inserting into that queue from within your script instead of sending mail directly from within a script.

- Exercise extreme caution when using shared network drives (over NFS in particular) as sources for large binary files. For example, a community Web site may allow users to upload a JPEG photograph of themselves for use in their profiles. In a multiple-server environment, this JPEG needs to be accessible by all Web servers. It makes sense to use disk rather than the database (databases are still awful at storing binary data), but shared network disk protocols are notoriously slow. Consider, instead, replicating binary data across each server using rsync or similar tools. A sync script might run as a background process every five minutes, redistributing data between servers, so a local copy is always available within five minutes of the initial upload.

There are many more examples of methods that can cause bottlenecks. The PHP online documentation often refers to potential performance problems in its entries for particular methods and classes.

When you're relying on PEAR classes, it is also worth checking that your server is installed with the latest supported versions. As with all distributed components, bugs do crop up, and it's worth ensuring that you have the latest versions to rule out any performance problems that might arise from those bugs.

Testing

Any changes you make to your code or SQL queries as a result of the discoveries discussed previously need to be tested thoroughly. Make sure that you apply the same basic first principles of QA as those discussed in Chapter 23, "Quality Assurance," when testing the scripts and components you have changed as you would when testing the application as a whole.

This includes testing not just the input parameters and usage scenarios you used while making your changes, but all conceivable parameters and scenarios where it is conceivably possible that your changes could have an impact. Err on the side of overtesting rather than undertesting.

If you have made changes on a development environment rather than a live environment, try to snatch a copy of your live database or data store and test locally. If this is not possible, try to set up a Virtual Server in Apache (or your preferred Web server) to use as a temporary staging environment, using your new code base against the live database but running distinctly from the live environment.

Either way, be sure that when you go live, you are confident not only that your changes will have the desired effect in improving performance but also that they will not adversely affect functionality in any way.

Preemptive Avoidance

Everything we have discussed so far refers to fixing an existing application. This is all well and good, but it relies on having the end users of your product pointing out the poor performance they are experiencing, which can have quite serious commercial ramifications.

A more productive as well as professional approach is to design with performance in mind from the outset. This is, of course, a whole book in its own right. Generally speaking, the principles set out in this book have had performance as a priority, so with luck, none of them will adversely affect your application if used appropriately and with reasonable volumes of data. It is in your own architecture that you need to be careful.

Tips for High-Performance Architecture

Here are a few useful tips you can employ when architecting your application, which may be useful in ensuring fast, efficient design from the outset:

- **Get the hardware right.** The fastest PHP in the world will still run like a dog on the wrong hardware. Serving Web pages is relatively simple, so put your weaker hardware to work as Apache workhorses. Keep the big guns for running databases. Also, try to equip all servers with high-performance SCSI disks in a RAID configuration where possible.
- **Use caching at the lowest level possible.** If some of your more intensive scripts are producing the same output time and time again, should you really hit the database every time? True, the database will cache the responses to queries at some level, but if the HTML remains the same each time, why not cache the HTML itself? Various third-party caching packages of variable quality are available in PECL, but you can easily write your own using the serialization of `GET`, `POST`, and `COOKIE` parameters passed to your script. By comparing that serialization to those made on previous requests, you can determine the "uniqueness" of each request; requests that are identical to those made previously can be satisfied using cached data, rather than having to hit the database again.
- **Perform unpredictable processes offline.** If some process in one of your scripts is dependent on some unpredictable third party, strongly consider taking it offline. The most obvious example is processing credit cards through a payment service provider. If you must have real-time authorization (for example, if you are allowing customers to purchase access to online content), then use a simple, automatically refreshing page that diverts to a success page after the database has been updated to indicate authorization. Assign an external script, run as a scheduled task, even if once every 60 seconds, the task of batch-processing requests to authorize cards, and update the database to reflect the successful authorization, or otherwise, of those requests.
- **Use databases judiciously.** Not all data needs to be stored using a database. For example, a content-management system that stores its content in XML may be better off storing that data on disk than in a database. Databases are not good at storing large chunks of text.
- **Optimize database queries.** Learn what does and doesn't run quickly in your particular flavor of database, and err toward the quicker techniques. PostgreSQL, for example, is noticeably slow when handling subselects, and INNER joins are likely to prove a more efficient choice. In addition, make sure that all necessary indices are in place and, equally important, remove any unnecessary indices, because these will actually slow the database down.
- **Load test.** Load test individual components using realistic traffic levels and data sets to ensure that real-world performance will match performance at development time. We discuss this in more detail shortly.

Load Testing

Functional testing is an important part of QA, but load testing is of equal importance in ensuring the overall quality of your finished project.

In a nutshell, load testing entails simulating a number of simultaneous connections to the Web server and carrying out typical user flow scenarios in each case. At the same time, the performance of the scripts should be measured as load increases, as well as the overall impact on the server as a whole.

A table of data can then be produced that, properly analyzed, can advise that at a given number of simultaneous users, response time will be *n*. *n* will obviously tend toward infinity as the number of simultaneous users increases, but at what stage does it reach an unacceptable value and, hence, what is the maximum number of simultaneous users that can be supported on the setup in question?

Excellent packages such as ApacheBench (`http://codeflux.com/ab/`) can simulate the very simplest of scenarios, but more sophisticated commercial software such as LoadRunner can recreate more realistic scenarios by randomly deviating the interval between the requests of each user, and requesting randomly altering sequences of pages to more realistically match the behaviour of a real human user.

When load testing, you should endeavor to use another server—or, ideally, servers—to act as clients connecting to the live Web server(s). This ensures that the load test software itself is not a burden on your Web server. In addition, you should always try to use the live server running in a staging mode or, if not feasible, an accurate recreation of the live environment and configuration on another server, to ensure that the results are representative.

It can often be helpful to present the results of your tests (assuming that they are positive) in a nontechnical manner to your client. It will help the client plan for future expansion against his or her own commercial or operational objectives.

Summary

In this appendix, you learned how to spot the different types of bottlenecks that may occur in your code, how to pinpoint them one by one, and how to quickly amend them.

You also learned how to avoid performance bottlenecks in the first place by avoiding some common pitfalls of software and systems architecture.

Finally, you were introduced to load testing, and some of the factors that must be considered when it is carried out on your own projects.

Best Practice PHP Installation

These days it seems anybody can handle a simple installation. Even your mom and dad could probably handle popping the latest version of Windows on their PC.

The exception to this rule seems to be server applications such as PHP. Although the PHP Web site and supplied documentation do touch on how to get it up and running, they really go as far as telling you exactly that—getting it up and running. Having a usable installation is quite a different matter and requires some inside knowledge.

In this short appendix, you'll learn the ins and outs of getting PHP properly set up in a configuration best suited to the kind of enterprise development detailed in this book. We also look at the differences between PHP on Windows and PHP on UNIX, and examine which is better suited for enterprise development.

If you haven't yet got PHP up and running, start here before you attempt the rest of this book.

Introduction to PHP Installation

PHP is an application language. It is not a server in its own right, nor is it a piece of software in the traditional sense. Nor is it a compiler like Pascal or C++. It needs to be installed—wrapped, if you like—in a Web server. With this in mind, for every installation of PHP, you will need some kind of Web server, such as Apache.

The phrase "installing PHP," therefore, is perhaps not quite accurate. The phrase "installing PHP and Apache" would be better, but that misses the fact that PHP is heavily dependent on third-party libraries and applications for any of its more sophisticated functionality, such as `libxml` for XML parsing.

To make things worse, most applications that this book introduces you to, as well as anything useful you'll write yourself, require some kind of a backend database. In this book, we use PostgreSQL in preference to MySQL, but they are much the same in practice.

In fact, therefore, the actual steps for a PHP installation look something more like this:

- Install and configure the various external libraries
- Install and configure your database platform
- Install and configure your Web server
- Install and configure PHP

As you can see, it's far from child's play. To make matters a lot worse, the exact manner in which the preceding steps are accomplished varies, depending on your chosen operating system (UNIX or Windows), your chosen Web server (Apache, IIS, Zeus, and so forth) and your chosen database platform (MySQL, PostgreSQL, MS SQL Server, Oracle, IBM DB2, Informix).

To present the lowdown on every possible permutation in this appendix would not just have a huge impact on the number of trees required to produce this book, it would be madness, because there's a very convincing argument for one particular combination over all others.

The Winning Platform

Let's be clear about something—this book is not about operating system wars. Those of you interested in the great Windows versus UNIX debate can find literally thousands of pages of well-thought-out, informed dialogue among the ever rational and well-spoken denizens of *Slashdot* (`slashdot.org`).

It is, however, worth our making the following bold statement: "Windows is bad at being an Internet application server, just as UNIX is bad at being a workstation operating system."

This is somewhat of a sweeping generalization, and there are exceptions to the rule. But the fact is that tens of thousands of ISPs and big businesses in the United States alone can't be wrong. Although Windows will frequently be found in the corporate environment as an Exchange server or domain controller, it is UNIX that hosts Web sites and DNS, and routes mail at SMTP-level across the whole of the Internet. Similarly, although there are those who choose to use Linux with X window managers such as Enlightenment, Gnome, and KDE on their laptops, they are in a minority. Most people recognize that Windows excels on the desktop while UNIX excels as a server environment.

The reasons for this distinction are really quite simple. The Windows interface is optimized for the desktop because it has undergone year after year of development. Many thousands of hours have gone into researching and evolving the Windows user interface to make it intuitive and efficient. It's not perfect, but it is better than the equivalents offered by its UNIX counterparts.

Similarly, Windows isn't very good at being an Internet services server. As of this writing, Microsoft's Internet Information Services (IIS) is the default and most popular choice for hosting Web sites on the Windows platform. Although it is vastly better than it used to be, IIS is still suffering from the ongoing discovery of major and widely publicized security flaws on a fairly regular basis as well as often being regarded as unstable and unreliable by systems administrators. In addition, the massive overhead of the Windows environment means that dedicated Windows servers on the Internet still carry enormous amounts of unnecessary baggage. A server with 2 GB of RAM could easily have 512 MB chewed up by the operating system and its various services, with only 64 MB of that being used to actually power the Web server running on it. By contrast, UNIX is smooth, sleek, and streamlined. Admittedly, it's not quite as easy to configure, but it's infinitely quicker, more stable and reliable, and a greater respecter of resources.

You can probably see where this is going. There is an argument for using IIS/Windows–based Web servers for ASP-based Web sites, of course, because ASP on UNIX is incredibly difficult to get working successfully. But this is a PHP book, and it is fair to say that PHP on Windows is every bit as bad an idea as is ASP on UNIX.

Even if you are passionately committed to using Windows in the server, you will find that you are fighting a losing battle. The ISPs that will ultimately host your application simply won't run PHP on Windows, for all the reasons we've just discussed. They will run PHP on UNIX—period. If you want to develop for PHP on Windows, do so, but you're only going to be deploying onto a UNIX environment in the end, and it must be fairly obvious that it is always preferable to replicate your ultimate production environment as closely as possible when you develop.

There may be legitimate times when, for example, you are developing an Intranet platform for a client whose setup is entirely Windows based, and insists you deploy onto the client's Windows-based environment. With this in mind, there are notes at the end of this appendix to help you out with the differences. This will be the exception, however, not the rule. You will almost always deploy onto an ISP's servers.

With this in mind, this book assumes that your PHP installation is on UNIX, not Windows. This assumption will be applied uniformly throughout and is evident in all examples demonstrated, without exception. PHP on UNIX is the choice of the professional, and this is a professional's book.

Don't panic. This does not mean that you need to use UNIX yourself. Indeed, the earlier appendix on the various development environments such as Zend Studio suggests that Windows is the best platform to use on your desktop, and indeed it is. The development server you will use, which could be situated just a couple of inches away from your own PC, will need to run UNIX—but your workstation won't.

The Winning Web Server

By choosing the operating system at this stage, you have eliminated a number of Web server choices—in particular, IIS, which has never made it to the UNIX platform (perhaps unsurprisingly). You are left with a number of choices on UNIX—Apache, Zeus, AOL Server, and Pi3Web.

There are two main manners in which PHP can be compiled and installed: as a CGI executable or as an integral part of the Web server, known as a SAPI module. The latter of these is a great deal faster and can handle many more concurrent connections. A CGI binary requires an instance of the PHP interpreter to load with every single HTTP request, which is very inefficient. All the previous choices stated support PHP as a SAPI module.

The previous choices are all perfectly valid, but so prevalent is the Apache server that it is practically unavoidable. It is running on something like 70 percent of the world's Web servers. Picking up from our earlier argument, the ISPs to whom you will be deploying will almost certainly be running Apache in preference to any of the other alternatives. You will make your life considerably easier if you stick to Apache.

It's a good choice in its own right, too. Apache has proven to be stable, secure and very well supported; also, it is constantly being further developed.

Also interesting to note is that at the time of this writing, AOL Server's own Web site at `www.aolserver.com` isn't running AOL Server; it's running Apache.

With all this in mind, the instructions in this section relate to getting PHP up and running on Apache on UNIX. Thankfully, the Web server in use, in contrast to the operating system, doesn't really affect PHP syntax at all, so the examples in this book, although they may be specific to UNIX, aren't specific to any particular Web server.

The Winning Database

Although you've restricted your PHP/Web server to the UNIX platform, there's nothing to stop your database server from being a completely different physical machine. In fact, many of the more high-traffic sites and applications you build will almost certainly require a separate database server or, in some cases, two or three.

With this in mind, therefore, the doors are flung wide open. You have to choose between PostgreSQL, MySQL, Oracle, Informix, DB2, Microsoft SQL Server, SAP DB, and many more.

Indeed, all the previous suggestions would be excellent choices. They are all highly accomplished and frequently updated. Because database servers are not exposed to the Internet, any security flaws discovered are of little importance. As long as a proper firewall is in place, they are all as secure as each other.

There are minor discrepancies in their notional reliability, but in all honesty, for every champion of, say, SQL Server, there is also a champion of MySQL, Oracle, DB2, and so on.

They're all fast, too. Any real difference in performance often comes down to the way in which you have structured your database rather than having anything to do with the database server itself.

With this in mind, you might struggle to choose. So have we, but in this book we have encouraged the use of PostgreSQL. Why? A number of reasons.

First, we wanted to stick to free software as much as possible, because Apache and PHP are both free of charge to download and use. MySQL isn't, strictly speaking, free. PostgreSQL is, and this means it passes the first test.

Second, PostgreSQL is about as close to industry standard heavyweights such as Oracle as you can get without actually being Oracle. Its syntax is largely ANSI compliant, meaning that porting an application away from PostgreSQL to another database is a relatively straightforward job.

Finally, it's great all around. In addition to being free and standards compliant, it's also extremely fast, extremely stable, and pretty easy to get set up and installed. It's also very well supported by PHP, which is a huge bonus given the title of this book.

The Installation Itself

Now that you understand the background, it's time to start the installation. The following assumes that you have a working UNIX machine, installed and ready to go.

If you don't already have a UNIX machine and want a good place to start, Linux is the ideal UNIX-based operating system for PC-based hardware. Just make sure to tell it to install all the developer utilities during installation, because you'll need these to get PHP up and running.

We assume that your UNIX machine is networked, has a private IP address assigned, and can be pinged from your workstation (and your workstation from it). We also assume that you are familiar with basic UNIX commands and utilities.

If all this looks good to you, then you can get started. Log in to your UNIX machine as `root` (or become `root` from a normal user account using `su`), and you can begin.

Downloading and Installing PostgreSQL

Because your development environment is for your own use only, you don't need to worry about putting PostgreSQL on a separate machine. You can use the same machine to run Apache, PHP, and your database without any real performance implications.

Make sure that you get the complete archive of PostgreSQL from `www.postgresql.org` and that you download the source code—not any binaries. You'll compile it yourself for maximum speed and resilience. The filename of your downloaded file will look something like `postgresql-7.4.3.tar.gz`.

You can download the file using lynx or ftp if you must, but our preferred route is wget:

```
# wget ftp://ftp.postgresql.org/pub/latest/postgresql-7.4.3.tar.gz
```

After you've downloaded it, unpack PostgreSQL in the normal way:

```
# tar -xzvf postgresql-7.4.3.tar.gz
```

This will create a directory called `postgresql-7.4.3` that contains the source files for PostgreSQL. Change into that directory:

```
# cd postgresql-7.4.3
```

Now, run the configure script to generate a Makefile appropriate to your particular UNIX environment.

```
# ./configure
```

With luck, you won't see any errors and you'll get a string of checks passed, with the last line reading:

```
config.status: linking ./src/makefiles/Makefile.linux to src/Makefile.port
```

or something very similar to this line. If this all looks good, you can start the compilation process by simply typing:

```
# make
```

It may take quite a while for PostgreSQL to compile, so go have a cup of coffee at this point. When you return, PostgreSQL will have compiled without incident, we hope, and you can install it as follows:

```
# make install
```

Strictly speaking, PostgreSQL is now installed. But a certain amount of configuration is still required. Follow these steps to get your database working directory set up (where all your data will be stored):

```
# adduser postgres
# mkdir /usr/local/pgsql/data
# chown postgres /usr/local/pgsql/data
# su - postgres
# /usr/local/pgsql/bin/initdb -D /usr/local/pgsql/data
```

You're almost ready to start the PostgreSQL daemon (server) now. One final step: You have to tell PostgreSQL where to allow connections from. Normally, this will just be from the same server or, in a pinch, from other machines on the same network.

Say that your server's IP address in this case is 192.168.1.1, and you want to allow access from that IP address only. Edit the file `/usr/local/pgsql/data/pg_hba.conf` using your favorite editor, and add this line to the very bottom of the file:

```
Host  all  all  192.168.1.1  255.255.255.255  trust
```

Save the file and quit the editor. You can now start PostgreSQL using the following syntax:

```
# su - postgres
# /usr/local/pgsql/bin/postmaster -i -D /usr/local/pgsql/data &
```

The first line is very important. The postmaster process must run as your new `postgres` user and not as `root` or whoever you may have been logged in as. The `-i` directive when starting is important, too, because it tells PostgreSQL to allow TCP/IP connections—something it disallows by default.

That's it. You can create a database as follows, again as the user `postgres`:

```
# /usr/local/pgsql/bin/createdb databasename
```

Then you can manipulate it using the PostgreSQL console as follows:

```
# /usr/local/pgsql/bin/psql databasename
```

Finally, you can create new users as follows:

```
# /usr/local/pgsql/bin/createuser username
```

This concludes your crash course in PostgreSQL installation. Anything else you might need to know is in the PostgreSQL documentation or explained throughout the course of this book.

Installing the Various Support Libraries

In an ideal world, you could now press on and install PHP and Apache. Unfortunately, life isn't fair and, as a result, you're now presented with the unenviable task of installing a number of support libraries for PHP.

Which libraries you need depends on exactly what functionality you require. For example, if you need to parse XML and XSL (which you do), you'll need the XML and XSL support libraries.

You'll need the following libraries for the examples in this book:

- ZLib v1.1.3 or later—see `http://www.gzip.org/zlib/`
- libJPEG v6b or later—see `http://www.ijg.org/`
- libPNG v1.0.8 or later—see `http://www.libpng.org/pub/png/libpng.html`
- Expat XML Parser 1.95.5 (1.95.6 has issues)—see `http://sourceforge.net/projects/expat/`
- Freetype 2.1.4—see `http://www.freetype.org`
- LibXML 2.6.4 or later—see `http://www.xmlsoft.org`
- LibXSLT 1.1.4 or later—see `http://www.xmlsoft.org`

Mercifully, all the preceding libraries are free, too.

The process for downloading and installing each of the these packages is much the same in each case. Just follow these simple steps:

1. Visit the Web sites in the preceding list to locate a download URL for each package.
2. Download the relevant `.tar.gz` source file using `wget`.
3. Unpack the archive using `tar -xzvf filename.tar.gz`.
4. Change to the directory just created, usually named `filename` (that is, the same as what you just downloaded, but without the `.tar.gz` suffix).
5. Run `./configure` with the `--enable-shared` suffix (that is, `./configure --enable-shared`).
6. Run `make`.
7. Run `make install`.
8. Change back to your original directory (`cd..`) and go to the next package.

There are a couple of exceptions and additions, however:

- Before configuring the Freetype library, modify `include/freetype/config/ftoption.h` using a text editor to uncomment the line reading `#define TT_CONFIG_OPTION_BYTECODE_INTERPRETER`. This is important if you want to be able to render TrueType font strings correctly in PHP. Then, compile as normal.

- libPNG has no configure script. Instead, you must copy the correct Makefile from the script's directory, for example: `cp scripts/makefile.lnx ./Makefile`, and then install as normal.

With all the previous packages installed, you're ready to get onto PHP and Apache themselves.

Installing PHP and Apache

PHP and Apache must be installed in tandem, so we've put them together in one section here. It'll become clear exactly why very shortly.

First, download the latest versions of Apache and PHP from their respective Web sites—`www.apache.org` and `www.php.net`. It's worth pointing out that Apache v2 and PHP are not yet the best of friends. We strongly recommend at this writing that you stick with the latest 1.3.*x* version of Apache, currently 1.3.31.

The two files you'll download will be named something like `apache-1.3.31.tar.gz` and `php-5.0.0.tar.gz`. Uncompress them in the normal manner:

```
# tar -xzvf apache-1.3.31.tar.gz
# tar -xzvf php-5.0.0.tar.gz
```

The first step is to do an initial configure on Apache. Change into the Apache directory (probably `apache-1.3.31`) and run the configure script with no parameters. It will complain, but ignore it:

```
# ./configure
Configuring for Apache, Version 1.3.31
 + Warning: Configuring Apache with default settings.
 + This is probably not what you really want.
```

When it's done, you can go ahead and configure PHP. Change back out of the Apache directory and into the PHP directory:

```
# cd ..
# cd php-5.0.0
```

You now configure PHP using a fairly long configure statement. This should be entered on a single line:

```
./configure --with-apache=../apache_1.3.31 --with-libxml-dir=/usr/local/lib
--with-gd --with-gettext --without-mysql --with-pgsql --enable-sockets
--with-jpeg-dir=/usr/local/lib --with-png-dir=/usr/local/lib --with-zlib-dir=
/usr/local/lib --enable-gd-native-ttf --with-freetype-dir=/usr/local/lib
--with-xmlrpc --with-dom -enable-xslt --with-expat-dir=/usr/local/lib
--with-xsl
```

Note that if you are using a newer version of Apache than 1.3.31, you will need to amend the `--with-apache` directive accordingly to reflect the unpack path.

It may well take a few minutes to configure, but assuming that you've followed this appendix correctly up until now, you shouldn't receive any error messages and all should configure okay.

You can then go ahead and build PHP:

```
# make
# make install
```

Note that the make may well take a few minutes, depending on the speed of your server. The make install will probably not take too long at all. If it fails, you may need to retrace your steps. Check, in particular, that all the support packages mentioned in the previous section have been configured correctly.

PHP has now created a module in your Apache unpack directory; you can now configure and install Apache making use of that module:

```
# cd ..
# cd apache-1.3.31
# ./configure --prefix=/usr/local/apache --activate-
module=src/modules/php5/libphp5.a
```

Once again, the `configure` statement must be on a single line when entered. You should see Apache configure, and advise that it is activating the module you just told it to. This is a good thing and implies everything is working okay to this point.

You can now go ahead and compile Apache:

```
# make
# make install
```

There's just one final step: You need to tell the Apache configuration file how to handle the .php extension. Modify the file `/usr/local/apache/conf/httpd.conf` and add the following lines:

```
AddType application/x-httpd-php .php .php4 .php3 .php5
AddType application/x-httpd-php-source .phps
```

These lines can be added virtually anywhere but should be placed near all the other `AddType` and `AddHandler` directives in the file to keep things clean.

Testing Your Installation

All that remains is to test your installation. Start Apache using the following syntax:

```
# /usr/local/apache/bin/apachectl start
```

Now create a file in `/usr/local/apache/htdocs` called `test.php` containing the following code:

```
<?php
phpinfo();
?>
```

Save it and, in your workstation's Web browser, point it to the IP address of your UNIX machine, followed by `/phpinfo.php`. For example, if your server was 192.168.1.1, point it to `http://192.168.1.1/phpinfo.php`. You should see a screen similar to Figure D-1.

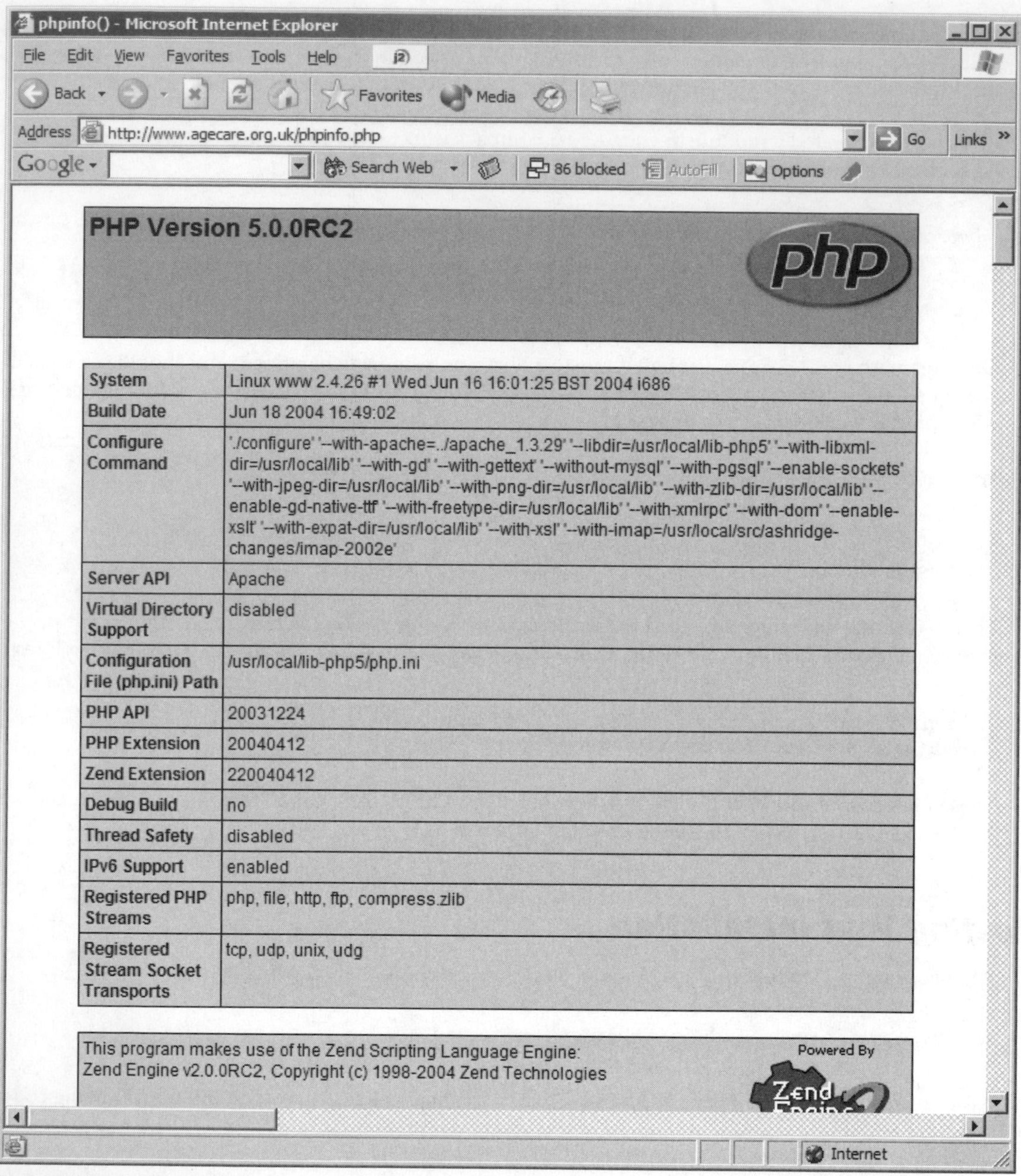

Figure D-1

If so, congratulations. Your PHP installation has been successful! You will probably want to create Virtual Server entries for each project that you work on, however. Much more information on this can be found in Chapter 24, "Deployment."

When Windows Is Needed

Scenarios do crop up when you will simply have to use Windows. The most classic example is for the installation of a closed system onto a large company's IT infrastructure, which is already Windows based, and there is a resolute refusal to install a UNIX server.

With some adaptation, the examples in this book will all still work just fine. The following pointers may help you transfer your PHP from UNIX to Windows.

Changing Paths

Don't forget that paths on Windows look very different from paths on UNIX. References to paths such as `/data/res/1230.jpg` on disk will need to be changed to a Windows equivalent, such as `C:\data\res\1230.jpg`.

PHP is kind and allows you to keep the slashes oblique (/). If you avoid drive letters by using relative paths, you may be able to keep your application more portable.

Weird Differences

Some differences between PHP on UNIX and Windows are truly bizarre. One notable example is that in Windows you cannot use a class named `Variant`, whereas in UNIX this is perfectly allowable. Other such differences must surely exist. There is not a lot you can do to avoid them given their officially undocumented nature, however; when faced with a bizarre, head-scratching problem, go ahead and hit Google to see whether others have encountered the same difficulty.

External Libraries

Because Windows does not come with a built-in and highly pervasive C/C++ compiler in the same way UNIX does, PHP does not require a myriad of external libraries to work under Windows. Instead, PHP supplies with its Windows installations a huge set of precompiled DLLs for the various extensions discussed in this appendix—libxml, libxslt, and so forth.

To enable such extensions, copy the relevant DLLs into both your PHP directory (such as `C:\PHP`) and your `windows\system32` directory, and restart your Web server. You should find that the relevant functionality becomes available to PHP right away.

Using PEAR

Using the PEAR repository to install library packages in Windows is a little different from how it is accomplished under UNIX.

Before you can use PEAR, you need to set it up using the following bundled script:

```
C:\php\PEAR>..\php go-pear.php
Welcome to go-pear!
Go-pear will install the 'pear' command and all the files needed by
it. This command is your tool for PEAR installation and maintenance.
```

This script will ask you various questions about proxy servers and so forth, but will create a single `pear` command as a batch file, which you can then use in exactly the same manner as its UNIX counterpart.

Summary

In this short appendix, you learned the key reasons that this book has opted for UNIX, Apache, and PostgreSQL in its examples, and why you might wish to consider doing the same in your own PHP enterprise development.

You then learned the fundamental steps involved in setting up a working, practical installation of Apache, PHP and PostgreSQL on a UNIX platform from start to finish.

Finally, you learned some of the key differences between PHP on Windows and UNIX, and how to circumnavigate them effectively in your own development.

Index

SYMBOLS AND NUMERICS

-> operator, method invocation, 8

A

abstract classes
- Contact Manager, 56
- support, 29

abstract functions, 25
abstraction, factory method design pattern and, 179
- database abstraction and, 182

`AbstractWidget` class, observer pattern and, 81
academic skills, career as developer, 567
accessor methods, 10–11
account manager (Widget World project), selecting, 387
activation, objects, 45
activity diagrams (UML), 42
actors, case diagrams, 33
`addItem( )` method
- `Collection` class, 104–105
- `obj` parameter, 103

agenda, project recipient (Widget World), 372–373
algorithms, bottleneck location, 603
Apache installation, 616–617
- testing, 617–619

`Application` class
- Builder pattern, 96–97
- Facade pattern and, 93

applications
- event-driven, designing, 189–191
- Web, MVC and, 243

arrays, Smarty templates
- associative, 269–270
- linear, 269
- multidimensional, 273–274

artificial intelligence, FSMs and, 354
associations, relationships, class diagrams (UML), 37
associative arrays, Smarty templates, 269–270
attributes of class diagrams (UML), 35
authentication class sessions, session management connection to database, 316–317

B

`BeginBuildNumber( )` method, 351–352
bi-directional navigability, associations (UML class diagrams), 37
binary files, version control and, 581
bindings/operation in WSDL documents, 230
bottlenecks, 599–600
- avoiding, 605–606
- locating
  - algorithms, 603
  - database queries, 602–603
- types, differences, 600–601

branching, version control and, 580–581
budget (Widget World project), 378–379
bugs (Widget World project), change management and, 403–404
build phase (Widget World project), 398
`Builder` pattern, 93–97
- implementation, 94–96

`BuildNumber( )` method, 352
business requirements (Widget World), 375–376

C

callbacks, lazy instantiation, 108
- implementation, 110–112

`call_user_func`, `Collection` class, 108–110
capturing output, Smarty templates, 274–275
career as developer
- academic skills, 567
- community skills, 567
- soft skills, 566–567
- Web development skills, 566

case diagrams, UML, 32–35
CGI (Common Gateway Interface), 301

change management (Widget World project) bugs reported, 403–404
disputes, difference in interpretation and, 403
specification revisions, 402–403
after sign-off, 403
CIR (Committed Information Rate), systems architecture design, 409–411
monthly transfer calculation, 411
rack space, 411
class diagrams, UML
attributes, 35
domain modeling, 35–36
implementation, 39–42
operations, 35
relationships, 36–42
associations, 37
composites, 38–39
generalizations, 37–38
realizations, 37–38
class keyword, 7
class.Dispatcher.php class, 191–193
classes. *See also* **subclasses**
abstract support, 29
AbstractWidget observer pattern and, 81
Collection, 101
design, 102–103
CollectionIterator, 101, 127–129
Communication, 285–286
Contact Manager, 50
contact type classes, Contact Manager, 56–60
creating, 7
database class, 162–164
DataManager, Contact Manager, 60–62
Debugger, 217–220
declaration, object instantiation and, 7
definition, 5
EmailRecipient, 285–286
Entity, Contact Manager, 62–70
FSM, 348–350
GenericObject, 133, 134–156
GenericObjectCollection, 146–156
hierarchy, communication as, 281–286
Individual, Contact Manager, 62–70
inheritance and, 15–19
InterbaseConnection, 185
KeyInUseException, 104
Logger, 203–207
LoggerBackend, 211–212
subclassing, 212–213
methods, 6
adding, 7–8
modularity, 4
Organization, Contact Manager, 62–70
overview, 6
properties, 6
adding, 8–10
PropertyObject, Contact Manager, 54–56
Recipient, 281–282
Request, 249–256
unit testing and
implementation, 332
interfaces, 330
test suite, 331
UserSession, 317
class.Event_Handler.php, 193–194
class.Handler_Edit.php, 195
class.Handler_View.php, 194–195
client interviews, UML requirements gathering, 32
client side designers (Widget World project), selecting, 388
clients
management, reporting and (Widget World project), 544–545
reporting and, 544
role (Widget World project), 389
SOAP
creating, 227–235
exception handling, 234–235
request and response envelopes, 232–234
clone operator, Iterator interface, 130–132
close( ) function, 25–26
session management, 316–317
code
editing
Komodo, 594–595
Zend Studio Client, 585–587
inspection, Zend Studio Client, 587–588
reusing, 4
inheritance and, 16
Collection class
addItem( ) method, 104–105
basics, 103–107

call_user_func, 108–110
design, 102–103
getItem( ) method, 105
improvements, 122
introduction, 101
Iterator interface, clone operator, 130–132
lazy instantiation, 107–116
purpose, 101–102
removeItem( ) method, 105
setLoadCallback( ) function, 112–116
uses, 106–107, 116–122
CollectionIterator class, 101, 125, 127–129
comments, version control and, 581
commercial terms (Widget World), 380
communication, 277
characteristics of communications, 280
as class hierarchy, 281
Communication class, 285–286
EmailRecipient class, 282–285
Recipient class, 281–282
e-mail, 286–298
EmailCommunication class, 287–290
Smarty templates, 296–298
e-mail-to-fax gateways, 299
reasons
information, 279
notification, 278
validation, 279–280
recipients, 281
SMS text messaging, 298–299
subclasses, 298
types, 280–281
Communication class, 285–286
community skills, career as developer, 567
Component abstract class, composite pattern and, 74
component diagrams, 46–47
Composite objects, 74
composite pattern, 73–74
considerations, 79–80
implementation, 75–79
composites, UML, 38–39
concurrent versioning, 570–572
conflicts, 572–574
exclusive versioning comparison, 570–572
conditionals in Smarty templates, 270
Config class, PEAR, 357–358
writing configuration files, 358
XML file parsing, 358
configuration
database abstraction layers, 158
Mantis, 522–523
runtime, Smarty templates, 273
configuration files
best practices, 358–359
custom
INI files, 355–356
INI files, parsing, 356–357
PHP, 354–355
XML, 355
FSMs, 353–354
writing, Config class (PEAR), 358
connection string, Logger class
parsing, 208–209
using, 209–211
connections, PEAR DB class, 164–166
constants
increments, 248
MVC mini toolkit, 246–249
Constraint class, MVC mini toolkit, 256–257
ConstraintFailure class, MVC mini toolkit, 257–258
constructors, 11–12
unified, 28
UserSession class, 326–327
Contact Manager, 49–50
abstract classes, 56
contact type classes, 56–60
DataManager class, 60–62
diagrams, 50–54
Entity class, 62–70
Individual class, 62–70
Organization class, 62–70
PropertyObject class, 54–56
relationships, symbols, 52
contact type classes Contact Manager, 56–60
controller (MVC), 243
cookies, session perpetuation, 306–307
creative specification (Widget World project), 397
current( ) function, 126
customer contacts (Widget World project)
per-week items, 460–468
requirements, 440–441
screen creation, 446–447
tests, 441–446
CVS (Concurrent Versioning System) version control, 578–580
Widget World project, 536–538

D

data extraction, reporting (Widget World project), 547–549
data handling, PEAR DB class, 167–168
database abstraction layers
building, PEAR DB class and, 170–177
connection, 159
implementation
configuration file, 158
connection, 159
information selection, 159–160
introduction, 157
overview, 158
syntax, 158
`Database` class
exceptions, 171
instance( ) method, 176
uses, 177
database class, 162–164
database tables, logging, 214–217
`database_fields` property, `GenericObject` **class, 143**
databases
abstraction, factory interface and, 182
connections
DSN syntax, 164
PEAR DB and, 165–166
`delete( )` method, 160–162
development databases (Widget World project), 534–535
holdups, patching, 603–604
information selection, 159–160
`insert( )` method, 160–162
PEAR DB and, 164
PHP installation, 612
queries, bottleneck location, 602–603
servers, multiple, systems architecture and, 413
session management and, 316–317
database schema, 317–318
Singleton design pattern, 175–177
transactions, 174–175
factory interface and, 184–185
type strings, 165
`update( )` method, 160–162
`DataManager` class, Contact Manager, 60–62
`DataSource` object, observer pattern, 83–85
`DB::connect( )` method, 166
`Debugger` class, 217–220
debugging
bug annotation, Mantis, 529
bug assignment, Mantis, 528–529
bug categories, Mantis, 526–527
bug reporting, Mantis, 528
Komodo and, 595–596
mechanism creation, 217–220
Zend Studio Client and, 588–593
`debugPrint( )` function, 219
decision point, activity diagrams (UML), 42
declaring classes, 7
object instantiation and, 7
Decorator pattern, 86–91
combining, 89–91
considerations, 91
definitions, WSDL documents, 230
`delete( )` method, databases, 160–162
`DELETE` statement, transactions and, 174
dependencies, component diagrams, 46
deployment diagrams, 46–47
deployment (Widget World project)
development environments
development databases, 534–535
live production environment, 534
live staging environment, 533–534
studio development environment, 531–532
studio staging environment, 532–533
version control
CVS, 536–538
rsync, 539–542
Visual SourceSafe, 538–539
dereferencing, support, 28
design
`Collection` class, 102–103
event-driven applications, 189–191
reports (Widget World project)
data extraction, 547–549
interface, 546–547
output, 547
systems architecture
CIR, 409–411
connectivity, 409
hosting, 409
maintenance, 414
network, 413
redundancy and resilience, 414

security, 414–415
servers, 411–413
Widget World project, 367
design patterns
Builder, 93–97
composite pattern, 73–80
implementation, 75–79
Decorator pattern, 86–91
Facade, 92–93
factory interface and, 179
factory method, 179
introduction, 73
MVC, 242
observer pattern, 80–86
design phase (Widget World project), 396–397
creative specification, 397
page maps, 397
software architecture, 397–398
`destroy( )` function, session management, 317
`Destroy` method, `GenericObject` class, 144
destroying objects, 12–15
`_destruct` function, 12–15
destructor support, 29
development environments (Widget World project)
development databases, 534–535
live production environment, 534
live staging environment, 533–534
studio development environment, 531–532
studio staging environment, 532–533
diagrams (UML)
activity diagrams, 42
case diagrams, 32–35
class diagrams, 35
component, 46–47
Contact Manager, 50–54
deployment, 46–47
sequence diagrams, 42–45
state diagrams, 45–46
dispatcher classes, event handling, 189
documentation, WSDL documents, 230
documents, WSDL, 230–232
`DoEqual( )` method, 353
domain expert, UML, 32
domain modeling, UML class diagrams, 35–36
`DoOperator( )` method, 352–353
`draw( )` method, 86
DSN (data source name) syntax, database connections and, 164

E

e-mail
e-mail-to-fax gateways, 299
`EmailCommunication` class
sending message, 290–296
Smarty templates, 296–298
test version, 287–290
recipients, 281
edit events, 189
editing code, Zend Studio Client, 585–587
`EditPlus`, 597
`EmailCommunication` class
sending message, 290–296
test version, 287–290
`EmailRecipient` class, 282–285
encapsulation, 5, 27–28
`EndBuildNumber( )` method, 352
`Entity` class (Contact Manager), 62–70
event-driven applications
designing, 189–191
implementation
`class.Dispatcher.php`, 191–193
`class.Event_Handler.php`, 193–194
`class.Handler_Edit.php`, 195
`class.Handler_View.php`, 194–195
`interface.Handled.php`, 193
security, 195–198
event handlers
`Handler_Edit`, 192–193
`Handler_View`, 192–193
event handling, 188–189
events
edit events, 189
introduction, 187
exception handling, SOAP clients, 234–235
exceptional notification, 278
expiry times, sessions, 310–311
`extends` keyword, 16

F

`Facade` pattern, 92–93
`factory` interface, 179
example, 180–184
transactions and, 184–185

factory method design pattern, 179
abstraction and, 179
database abstraction, 182
runtime flexibility and, 179
fault tracking, QA
introduction, 521–522
Mantis
administrator log in, 523–524
bug annotation, 529
bug assignment, 528–529
bug reporting, 528
bug resolution, 529
configuration, 522–523
installation, 522
new projects, 526
project bug categories, 526–527
users, adding, 525–526
users, creating/editing, 524–525
fetch*( ) methods, PEAR DB, 167–168
file logging, 201–202
file system layout example, 202
files
binary, version control and, 581
configuration
best practices, 358–359
FSMs, 353–354
INI files, 355–356
INI files, parsing, 356–357
PHP, 354–355
XML, 355
management, Zend Studio Client, 585
splitting, MVC and, 244
writing to, 202
financial layer, Widget World project, 366
fopen( ) method, 202
ForceLoaded method, GenericObject class, 144
framework, PHPUnit testing and, 337
FSM class
installation, 348–349
syntax, 349
default transition, 349–350
instantiation, 349
transitions, setting, 350
FSM (Finite State Machine), 345
artificial intelligence and, 354
configuration files, 353–354
implementation
FSM class, 348–350
theoretical, 348
introduction, 346
RPN (Reverse Polish Notation) Calculator, 346–348
transition tables, 348
functional specification (Widget World project), 394–395
functional testing (Widget World project), 398–399
Functional Test Paper, 519–520
functions
abstract, 25
current( ), 126
debugPrint( ), 219
_destruct, 12–15
get functions, 10–11
getConnection( ), 61
GetUserID( ), 327–328
GetUserObject( ), 327–328
impress( ), 327
IsLoggedIn( ), 327
key( ), 126
next( ), 126
PEAR DB class
nextID( ), 168–169
query( ), 168
quoteSmart( ), 170
PHP5 SOAP extension, 226–227
rewind( ), 126
set functions, 10–11
Smarty templates, 274
SoapClient object, 225–226
SoapServer object, 226
fwrite( ) method, 202

G

gc( ) function, session management, 317
generalizations, UML, 37–38
GenericObject class
benefits of, 146
capabilities, 134–135
database connectivity, 141–143
implementation
suitability, 135–136
typical, 136–138

introduction, 133
methods, 144
parent class, 138–141
properties, 143
Save method, 145–146
when to use, 134

GenericObjectCollection class, 146–147
id values, 149
implementation
traditional, 147–148
typical, 152–153

_get( ) overload method, UserSession class, 328

get functions, 10–11

getAll( ) method, 166

GetAllFields method, GenericObject class, 144

getConnection( ) function, 61

GetField method, GenericObject class, 144

GetID method, GenericObject class, 144

getInstance( ) method, 205

getItem( ) method, 103
Collection class, 105

getIterator( ) method, 129

getName( ) accessor method, 11

getOne( ) method, 166

GetSessionIdentifier( ) function, 328

GetUserID( ) function, UserSession class, 327–328

GetUserObject( ) function, UserSession class, 327–328

grace during failure, QA, 516

H

Handler_Edit event handler, 192–193

Handler_View event handler, 192–193

handling events. See event handling

handling exceptions. See exception handling

handover (Widget World project), 399

hierarchy, communication as, 281
Communication class, 285–286
EmailRecipient class, 282–285
Recipient class, 281–282

hosting, system architecture and, 406

HTML (Hypertext Markup Language)
.php (control page) and, 245
.phpm (classes) and, 245
report translator scripts and, 561
reporting format (Widget World project), 546

HTTP (Hypertext Transfer Protocol), 302–304

I

id property, GenericObject class, 143

IDEs (Integrated Development Environments)
EditPlus, 597
Komodo, 593–596
NuSpherePHPEd, 597
PHPCode, 597
PHPEclipse, 597
PHPEdit, 596–597
selection tips, 583–596
Zend Studio Client, 584–593

implementation
callbacks, 110–112
class diagrams (UML), 39–42
classes, unit testing and, 332
composite pattern, 75–79
database abstraction layers
configuration file, 158
connection, 159
event-driven applications
class.Dispatcher.php, 191–193
class.Event_Handler.php, 193–194
class.Handler_Edit.php, 195
class.Handler_View.php, 194–195
interface.Handled.php, 193
FSMs
FSM class, 348–350
theoretical, 348
GenericObject class and, 135–136
typical, 136–138
GenericObjectCollection class
traditional, 147–148
typical, 152–153
lazy instantiation, 107–116
security, 195–198
sessions, basic PHP sessions, 312–315
Widget object, 88–89

importing WSDL documents, 230

impress( ) function, UserSession class, 327

increments, constants, 248

Individual class (Contact Manager), 62–70
information, user communication and, 279
infrastructure (MVC), 243
inheritance, 15–19
- code reuse and, 16
- definition, 5
- how it works, 23–24
- `InterbaseConnection` class, 185
- methods, overriding, 20–22
- parent class, functionality, 22–23

INI files
- configuration files, custom, 355–356
- parsing, 356–357
  - `Config` class (PEAR), 358

initialization, objects, 11–12
`Initialize` method, `GenericObject` class, 144
`insert( )` method, databases, 160–162
`INSERT` statement, transactions and, 174
installation
- FSM class, 348–349
- PHP, 609–610
  - Apache, 616–619
  - database, 612
  - libraries, 615–616
  - platform, 610–611
  - PostgreSQL download, 613–614
  - PostgreSQL installation, 613–614
  - Web server, 611–612
  - Windows and, 619–620
- PHPUnit, 333
- Smarty, 267–268

`instance( )` method, `Database` class, 176
instantiation
- FSM class, 349
- lazy, 102
  - implementation, 107–116
- objects, 7

`Interbase` database, factory interfaces, 184
`InterbaseConnection` class, inheritance, 185
`interface.Handled.php` class, 193
interfaces
- abstract classes, 29
- definition, 5
- factory interface, 179
- how they work, 25–27
- `Iterator`, 125–129
- `IteratorAggregate`, 129–130
- overview, 24–25
- `Recipient` class and, 282
- reports (Widget World project), 546–547
- Traversable, 126
- unit testing and, 330

internal member variables, 10
internal operators, variables and, 9
Internet connectivity, system architecture and, 406
invoking methods, 8
IP addresses, variance, session security and, 311
`IsLoggedIn( )` function, `UserSession` class, 327
`Iterator` interface, 125–129
- clone operator and, 130–132

`IteratorAggregate` interface, 125, 129–130

K

`key( )` function, 126
`KeyInUseException` class, 104
keywords
- class, 7
- extends, 16
- public, 9

Komodo, 593–594
- code editing, 594–595
- debugging, 595–596
- project management, 594

L

lazy instantiation, 102
- callbacks, 108
  - implementation, 110–112
- implementation, 107–116

lead architect (Widget World project), selecting, 387–388
libraries
- PHP installation, 615–616
- SOAP implementation, 224

lifelines, 45
linear arrays, Smart templates, 269
live production environment (Widget World project), 534
live staging environment (Widget World project), 533–534
`Load` method, `GenericObject` class, 144
load testing (Widget World project), 399
- QA and, 520

load tolerance, QA, 516–517
loaded property, GenericObject class, 143
Logger class
connection string
parsing, 208–209
using, 209–211
extending, 207–217
introduction, 203–207
methods
getInstance( ), 205
logMessage( ), 205–206
LoggerBackend class, 211–212
subclassing, 212–213
logging
database tables, 214–217
file logging, 201–202
system layout example, 202
logic errors, patching, 604–605
logins
PhpUnit, 429–436
screen, creating, 436–440
session security, 311
writing tests, 428–429
logMessage( ) method, 205–206

M

maintenance, system architecture and, 406
design, 414
Mantis fault tracking (QA)
administrator log in, 523–524
configuration, 522–523
installation, 522
projects
bug annotation, 529
bug assignment, 528–529
bug categories, 526–527
bug reporting, 528
bug resolution, 529
new, 526
users
adding, 525–526
creating, 524–525
editing, 524–525
measurable quality, 515–518
member variables
access protection, 10–11
internal, 10
Request class, MVC mini toolkit, 254
static, 28
messages, WSDL documents, 230
methods, 6
accessor methods, 10–11
adding, 7–8
addItem( ), 103
BeginBuildNumber( ), 351–352
BuildNumber( ), 352
close( ), 25–26
DB::connect( ), 166
delete( ), 160–162
DoEqual( ), 353
DoOperator( ), 352–353
draw( ), 86
EndBuildNumber( ), 352
fopen( ), 202
fwrite( ), 202
GenericObject class, 144
getInstance( ), 205
getItem( ), 103
getIterator( ), 129
INI file parsing, 356–357
insert( ), 160–162
invoking, 8
logMessage( ), 205–206
open( ), 25–26
overload methods
_get( ), UserSession class, 328
_set( ), UserSession class, 328
overriding, 20–22
PEAR DB
fetch*( ), 167–168
getAll( ), 166
getOne( ), 166
removeItem( ), 103
request object, 255–256
Save, GenericObject class, 145–146
select( ), 159–160
_toString( ), 118
update( ), 160–162
Microsoft SQL Server. See SQL Server databases
MIME, e-mail and, 298
mock objects (Widget World project), 506–511
model (MVC), 242
modified property, GenericObject class, 143
modified_fields property, GenericObject class, 143
modularity of classes, 4

modules, 4
monthly transfer calculation, CIR, 411
multidimensional arrays, Smarty templates, 273–274
MVC (model, view, controller)
ConstraintFailure class, 257–258
controller, 243
file splitting, 244
infrastructure, 243
introduction, 241–242
mini toolkit, 245–246
constants, 246–249
Constraint class, 256–257
Request class, 249–256
request object methods, 255–256
search.phtml, 260–261
searchresults.php, 261–263
uses, 258–265
model, 242
native templating, 245
PHP and, 243–245
searchresults.phtml, 263
view, 242–243
Web applications and, 243
My Reports page (Widget World project), 560
MySQL databases, 157

N

native templating, 245, 266
navigability, associations, relationships (UML class diagrams), 37
network, system architecture and, 406
design, 413
next( ) function, 126
nextID( ) function, PEAR DB class, 168–169
nodes, 46
notifications, 278
NuSpherePHPEd, 597

O

object diagram, 78
objects, 6–7
activation, 45
children, 74
classes, creating, 7
Composite, 74
definition, 5
destroying, 12–15
initializing, 11–12
instantiation, 7
interfaces and, 24–25
lifeline, 45
mock objects (Widget World project), 506–511
object composition, 73
Observable interface, 80
Observer interface, 80
Observable interface connection, 85–86
observer pattern, 80–86
DataSource object, 83–85
widgets, 80–81
design, 81–83
on-site customs, Widget World project development, 367
OOP (Object-Oriented Programming)
advantages, 4
overview, 3–5
PHP5 and, 28–29
open( ) function, session management, 316
open( ) method, 25–26
operations, class diagrams (UML), 35
operators, internal, variables and, 9
Oracle databases, 157
Organization class (Contact Manager), 62–70
output capture, Smarty templates, 274–275
overriding methods, 20–22

P

page maps (Widget World project), 397
parameter types, hints, 29
parent classes
functionality, inheritance and, 22–23
GenericObject class, 138–141
parsing
connection string, Logger class, 208–209
INI files, 356–357
Config class (PEAR), 358
parse request test, travel expense report, 481–483
XML files, Config class (PEAR), 358
patching
code holdups, logic errors, 604–605
database holdups, 603–604
testing, 606

patterns. See design patterns
PDF files
- report translator scripts, 562
- reporting format (Widget World project), 546

PEAR
- Config class, 357–358
  - INI file parsing, 358
  - writing configuration files, 358
  - XML file parsing, 358
- data handling, 167–168
- database abstraction layer, building, 170–177
- database connections, 165–166
- `DB::connect( )` method, 166
- functions
  - `DB_Error`, 166
  - `nextID( )`, 168–169
  - `query( )`, 168
  - `quoteSmart( )`, 170
- information retrieval, 166–168
- introduction, 164–165
- type strings, 165

performance tuning
- bottlenecks and, 599–601
  - avoiding, 605–606
  - locating, 602–603
- patching and
  - code holdups, 604–606
  - database holdups, 603–604
  - testing, 606
- poor performance causes, 601–602
- preemptive avoidance
  - high-performance architecture, 607
  - load testing, 607–608

`PersistentInterbaseConnection`, 185
PHP, MVC and, 243–245
`.php` (control page) files
- HTML and, 245
- `require( )` statements, 245
- SQL queries and, 245

PHP installation, 609–610
- Apache, 616–619
- database, 612
- libraries, 615–616
- platform, 610–611
- PostgreSQL downlod, 613–614
- PostgreSQL installation, 613–614
- Web server, 611–612
- Windows and, 619–620

PHP5 SOAP extension, 224–227
- functions, miscenallaneous, 226–227
- `SoapClient` object, 225–226
- `SoapServer` object, 226

PHPCode, 597
PHPEclipse, 597
PHPEdit, 596–597
`.phpm` (classes) files, HTML and, 245
PHPUnit, 329
- framework and, 337
- functional testing, 338
- installation, 333
- introduction, 332–333
- quality assurance, 338
- regression testing and, 337
- test cases, 333–336
- test suite, 336
- xDir example, 338–343

PhpUnit, login tests, 429–436
`.phtml` (templates) files, SQL queries and, 245
pitch (Widget World project)
- involved parties, 383–384
- *versus* quotes, 382
- *versus* specifications, 383
- structure, 385–386

planning, Widget World project development, 367
platform, installation and, 610–611
political layer, Widget World project, 366
polymorphism
- basic description, 79
- definition, 5

portType, WSDL documents, 230
PostgreSQL databases, 157
- downloading, 613–614
- installation, 613–614

prerequisites of project (Widget World), 374
private member variables, visibility, 27
process (Widget World project)
- build phase, 398
- design phase, 396–397
  - creative specification, 397
  - page maps, 397
  - software architecture, 397–398
- handover, 399
- specification phase, 394
  - functional specification, 394–395
  - technical specification, 396

process (Widget World project) (*Continued*)
Spiral Process, 392–393
testing phase
functional testing, 398–399
load testing, 399
Waterfall Process, 391–392
project, Widget World. *See* **Widget World project**
project management (Widget World project), methodologies, 371–389
project manager (Widget World project), selecting, 386
properties, 6
classes, adding, 8–10
`GenericObject` class, 143
`GenericObject` class and, 134
methods, accessor methods, 11
`PropertyObject` class, 58
variables and, 8
`PropertyObject` class
Contact Manager, 54–56
properties, 58
protected member variables, visibility, 27
public keyword, 9
public member variables, visibility, 27

Q

QA (Quality Assurance)
definition of quality, 515
fault tracking
introduction, 521–522
Mantis, 522–529
functional compliance, 516
grace during failure, 516
high standards, 514–515
introduction, 513–514
load tolerance, 516–517
measurable quality, 515–518
quantifiable quality, 515–518
RWT (Real World Tolerance), 516
testing
functional testing, 519–520
load testing, 520
unit testing, 518–519
usability testing, 520–521
usability, 517
veneer, 517–518
quantifiable quality, 515–518
`query( )` function, PEAR DB class, 168
`quoteSmart( )` function, PEAR DB class, 170

R

rack space, systems architecture design, 411
RCS version control software, 580
re-estimation (Widget World project), 450–451
`read( )` function, session management, 317
realizations, UML, 37–38
recalling state (Widget World project), 459–460
`Recipient` class, 281–282
interfaces, 282
redundancy, system architecture and, 406
refactoring, Widget World project development, 367
tips, 452–459
travel expense report week tests, 487–492
regression testing, PHPUnit, 337
relationships, class diagrams (UML), 36–42
associations, 37
composites, 38–39
generalizations, 37–38
realizations, 37–38
symbols, 52
release planning, sales force automation toolkit, 426–427
`Reload` method, `GenericObject` class, 144
`removeItem( )` method, 103
`Collection` class, 105
reporting (Widget World project)
deliverables, 545–546
design
data extraction, 547–549
interface, 546–547
output, 547
generation, 549–557
My Reports Page, 560
offline approach, 550–551
process, 557–558
report handler scripts, 558–560
report processor script, 557
report translator scripts, 560–562
reports engine example, 562–563
Reports interface, 552–557
HTML format, 546

Microsoft Excel format, 546
PDF format, 546
working data, 543–544
client management, 544–545
client needs, 544
XML format, 546
Reports interface (Widget World project), 552–557
requests storage, 555–557
XML templates, 553–555
request and response envelopes, SOAP client, 232–234
Request class, MVC mini toolkit, 249–256
request object, methods, 255–256
requirements gathering, UML
case diagrams, 32–35
client interviews, 32
resilience, system architecture and, 406
reusing code, 4
inheritance and, 16
rewind( ) function, 126
roles, project recipient (Widget World), 372–373
RPN (Reverse Polish Notation) Calculator, 346–348, 350–351
BeginBuildNumber( ) method, 351–352
BuildNumber( ) method, 352
DoEqual( ) method, 353
DoOperator( ), 352–353
EndBuildNumber( ) method, 352
rsync version control, 539–540
servers and, 541–542
syntax, 540
runtime configuration, Smarty templates, 273
runtime flexibility, factory method design pattern and, 179
RWT (Real World Tolerance), quality, 516

S

Save method, GenericObject class, 144, 145–146
scenarios, case diagrams, 33
scope, (Widget World), 376–377
search.php (MVC mini toolkit), 259–260
Smarty template rewrite, 271–273
search.phtml (MVC mini toolkit), 260–261
searchresults.php (MVC mini toolkit), 261–263
searchresults.phtml (MVC mini toolkit), 263
security
implementation, 195–198
sessions
expiry times, 310–311
good practice, 310–312
IP address variance, 311
logins, 311
timeouts, 310
traffic levels, 311
user agent consistency, 311
valid, 307–308
valid, discovery, 308
variable storage, 312
system architecture and, 406
design, 414–415
select( ) method, 159–160
sequence diagrams (UML), 42–45
servers
databases, multiple, system architecture and, 413
rsync version control and, 541–542
system architecture and, 406
design, 411–413
multiple database servers, 413
multiple Web servers, 412–413
Web, PHP installation, 611–612
service WSDL documents, 230
session management
authentication class, 316–317
close( ) function, 316–317
database schema, 317–318
destroy( ) function, 317
gc( ) function, 317
open( ) function, 316
read( ) function, 317
UserSession class, 317
GetSessionIdentifier( ) function, 328
GetUserID( ) function, 327–328
GetUserObject( ) function, 327–328
impress( ) function, 327
IsLoggedIn( ) function, 327
_session_read_method( ) handler, 327

session management (*Continued*)
testing, 322–326
variables, 326
usersession.phpm file, 318–322
write( ) function, 317
_session_read_method( ) handler, UserSession class, 327
sessions, 301
authentication class, 316–317
definition, 304
expiry times, 310–311
identifiers, 304
implementation, basic sessions, 312–315
limitations, 315–316
perpetuation
cookies, 306–307
URL rewriting, 304–305
security
good session practice, 310–312
IP address variance, 311
logins, 311
obliterating session guessing, 308
traffic levels, 311
user agent consistency, 311
valid sessions, 307–308
valid sessions, discovery, 308
variable storage, 312
timeout, 304, 310
user agent consistency, 311
_set( ) overload method, UserSession class, 328
set functions, 10–11
SetField method, GenericObject class, 144
setLoadCallback( ) function, Collection class, 112–116
setName( ) accessor method, 11
Simple Design, Widget World project development, 367
Singleton design pattern, databases, 175–177
small releases, Widget World project development, 367
Smarty templates, 266–267
arrays
associative, 269–270
linear, 269
multidimensional, 273–274
conditionals, 270
EmailCommunication class, 296–298
functions, 274
installing Smarty, 267–268
output capture, 274–275
runtime configuration, 273
search.php rewrite, 271–273
smartytest.php, 268
smartytest.tpl, 268–269
traditional templating comparison, 275
variable modifiers, 274
SMS text messaging, 298–299
SOAP (Simple Object Access Protocol)
clients
creating, 227–235
exception handling, 234–235
request and response envelopes, 232–234
introduction, 223
libraries, 224
PHP5 SOAP extension, 224–227
server, creation, 235–237
SoapClient object, functions, 225–226
SoapServer object, 226
SoapClient object, functions, 225–226
SoapServer object, functions, 226
soft skills, career as developer, 566–567
software, version control
CVS, 578–580
RCS, 580
Visual SourceSafe, 577–578
software architects (Widget World project)
design phase and, 397–398
selecting, 388
software engineers (Widget World project), selecting, 388
SourceSafe. *See* Visual SourceSafe version control
specification phase (Widget World project), 394
after sign-off, 403
functional specification, 394–395
technical specification, 396
specification revisions (Widget World project), 402–403
Spiral Process (Widget World project), 392–393
spreadsheets, travel expense report as, 498–504
SQL Server databases, 157
SQL (Structured Query Language) queries
.php (control page) and, 245
.phtml (templates), 245

staging environment (Widget World project), 532–534
starting point, activity diagrams (UML), 42
`startTransaction( )` method, databases, 174
state diagrams (UML), 45–46
stateless, 301
static member variables, 28
stories, sales force automation toolkit, 417–420
spike, 424–425
weight estimation, 420–424
studio artists (Widget World project), selecting, 388–389
studio development environment (Widget World project), 531–532
studio staging environment (Widget World project), 532–533
subclasses. *See also* classes
communication, 298
`LoggerBackend` class, 212–213
methods, overriding, 20
syntax
database abstraction layers and, 158
FSM class, 349
default transition, 349–350
instantiation, 349
transitions, setting, 350
rsync version control, 540
systems architecture
connectivity, 406
design, 409
requirements, 407–408
design
CIR, 409–411
connectivity and, 409
hosting and, 409
maintenance, 414
network, 413
redundancy and resilience, 414
servers, 411–413
hosting, 406
design, 409
requirements, 407–408
importance of, 405–406
key decisions, 406–407
maintenance, 406
requirements, 408
network, 406
design, 413
requirements, 407–408
overview, 405
redundancy and resilience, 406
design, 414
requirements, 408
requirements
connectivity, 407–408
hosting, 407–408
maintenance, 408
network, 407–408
redundancy and resilience, 408
security, 408–409
servers, 407–408
security, 406
design, 414–415
requirements, 408–409
servers, 406
design, 411–413
multiple database servers, 413
multiple Web servers, 412–413
requirements, 407–408

T

`table_name` property, `GenericObject` class, 143
tables, database tables, 214–217
tagging, version control and, 581
technical layer, Widget World project, 365
technical specification (Widget World project), 396
templating
native templating, 245, 266
disadvantages, 266
true templating, 265
Smarty templates, 266–274
test-driven development (Widget World project), 399–400
PhpUnit, 429–436
testing
Apache installation, 617–619
customer contacts (Widget World project), 441–446
logins, 428–429
patching, 606

testing (*Continued*)
QA
functional testing, 519–520
load testing, 520
unit testing, 518–519
usability testing, 520–521
Widget World project development, 367
testing phase (Widget World project)
functional testing, 398–399
load testing, 399
test.php code, 70–71
text messaging, SMS, 298–299
timelines, Widget World project, 377–378
timeouts, sessions, 310
_toString( ) method, 118
traffic levels, session security and, 311
transactions (databases), 174–175
DELETE statement, 174
factory interface and, 184–185
INSERT statement, 174
UPDATE statement, 174
transition tables, FSM, 348
transitions
activity diagrams (UML), 42
FSM class
default, 349–350
setting, 350
travel expense report (Widget World project), 468–470
finalized, 492–506
spike, 476–477
as spreadsheet, 498–504
test cases for week, 473–476
validation, 471–473
week tests, 480–481
container read and write tests, 484–487
parse request test, 481–483
refactoring, 487–492
Traversable interface, 126
true templating, 265
native templating, 266
Smarty templates, 266–267
associative arrays, 269–270
conditionals, 270
functions, 274
installation, 267–268
linear arrays, 269
multidimensional arrays, 273–274
output capture, 274–275
runtime configuration, 273
search.php rewrite, 271–273
smartytest.php, 268
smartytest.tpl, 268–269
traditional templating comparison, 275
variable modifiers, 274
types, WSDL documents, 230

U

UML (Unified Modeling Language)
activity diagrams, 42
class diagrams
attributes, 35
domain modeling, 35–36
implementation, 39–42
operations, 35
relationships, 36–42
diagrams, Contact Manager, 50–54
domain expert, 32
introduction, 31
requirements gathering, 31–32
case diagrams, 32–35
client interviews, 32
sequence diagrams, 42–45
state diagrams, 45–46
unidirectional navigability, associations (UML class diagrams), 37
unified constructors, 28
unit testing, QA, 518–519
Unit Testing frameworks, 329. *See also* **PHPUnit**
classes
implementation, 332
interfaces, 330
test suite, 331
framework and, 337
functional testing, 338
overview, 329–332
quality assurance, 338
regression testing, 337
xDir example, 338–343
update( ) method, databases, 160–162
UPDATE statement, transactions and, 174
URL rewriting, session perpetuation, 304–305
usability testing, QA, 520–521
user agent consistency, sessions, 311

users
communication, 277
e-mail, 286–298
e-mail-to-fax gateways, 299
reasons, 278–280
SMS text messaging, 298–299
Mantis
creating, 524–525
editing, 524–525
UserSession class, 317
constructor, 326–327
_get( ) overload method, 328
GetSessionIdentifier( ) function, 328
GetUserID( ) function, 327–328
GetUserObject( ) function, 327–328
impress( ) function, 327
IsLoggedIn( ) function, 327
session management
testing, 322–326
_session_read_method( ) handler, 327
_set( ) overload method, 328
variables, 326
usersession.phpm file, 318–322

V

valid sessions, 307–308
validation
travel expense report (Widget World project), 471–473
user communication and, 279–280
variables
internal member variables, 10
member
internal, 10
Request class, 254
modifiers, Smarty templates, 274
operators, internal, 9
properties and, 8
visibility, 27
veneer, QA, 517–518
version control
binary files and, 581
branching, 580–581
comments, 581
concurrent versioning, 570–572
conflicts, 572–574
exclusive versioning, 574–575
exclusive versioning comparison, 570–574
overview, 569–577
software
CVS (Concurrent Versioning System), 578–580
RCS, 580
Visual SourceSafe, 577–578
tagging, 581
topology, 575–577
version control (Widget World project)
CVS, 536–538
rsync, 539–542
Visual SourceSafe, 538–539
view (MVC), 242–243
visibility, variables, 27
Visual SourceSafe version control, 538–539, 577–578

W

Waterfall Process (Widget World project), 391–392
Web applications, MVC and, 243
Web development skills, 566
Web servers, PHP installation, 611–612
Widget object, implementation, 88–89
Widget World project
account manager selection, 387
automation toolkit
cleanup, 451–459
customer contacts, 440–450
customer contacts per-week items, 460–468
login (story 9), 427–429
mock objects, 506–511
re-estimation, 450–451
recalling state, 459–460
release planning, 426–427
stories, 417–425
travel expense report, 468–506
change management
bugs reported, 403–404
disputes, difference in interpretation and, 403
specification revisions, 402–403
client side developers selection, 388
clients, role, 389

Widget World project (*Continued*)
customer contacts
per-week items on report, 460–468
requirements, 440–441
screen creation, 446–447
tests, 441–446
deployment
development environments, 531–535
workflow, 536–542
development approach, 367–369
financial layer, 366
formal brief, 374–375
budget, 378–379
business requirements, 375–376
commercial terms, 380
future plans, 380–381
look and feel, 381
scope, 376–377
support, 381
technology, 381
timelines, 377–378
lead architect selection, 387–388
logins, screen creation, 436–440
methodologies for project management, 371–389
mock objects, 506–511
overview, 363–364
pitch
involved parties, 383–384
versus quotes, 382
versus specifications, 383
structure, 385–386
political layer, 366
process planning
build phase, 398
design phase, 396–397
handover, 399
specification phase, 394–396
Spiral Process, 392–393
testing phase, 398–399
Waterfall Process, 391–392
project history, 373–374
project management methodologies, 371–389
project manager selection, 386
project prerequisites, 374
project purposes, 372
project recipient, 372–373
agenda, 372–373
roles, 372–373
QA (Quality Assurance)
definition of quality, 515
fault tracking, 521–529
functional compliance, 516
grace during failure, 516
introduction, 513–518
load tolerance, 516–517
RWT (Real World Tolerance), 516
testing, 518–521
re-estimation, 450–451
reporting
deliverables, 545–546
design, 546–549
generation, 549–563
working data, 543–549
roles, doubling up, 389
software architects selection, 388
software engineers selection, 388
studio artists selection, 388–389
technical layer, 365
technology, 366, 370
test-driven development, 399–400
travel expense report, 468–470
finalized, 492–506
spike, 476–477
test cases for week, 473–476
validation, 471–473
week tests, 480–492
Weekly Contact Report, 365
working practices, 389
XP (eXtreme Programming), 400–402
widgets, observer pattern, 80–81
design, 81–83
Windows, PHP installation and, 619–620
working data, reporting and, 543–544
client management, 544–545
client needs, 544
working practices (Widget World project), 389
`write( )` function, session management, 317
writing to files, 202
WSDL (Web Service Description Language), 224
documents, 230–232
SOAP servers and, 235
WW-SFAT Manager (Widget World), 367

X

xDir, unit testing example, 338–343
XMethods, SOAP-based Web server, 228
XML (eXtensible Markup Language)
configuration files, custom, 355
file parsing, `Config` class (PEAR), 358
reporting format (Widget World project), 546
`Reports` interface (Widget World project), 553–555
XP (eXtreme Programming), 367
Widget World project, 400–402

Z

Zend Studio Client, 584–585
code editing, 585–587
code inspection, 587–588
debugging and, 588–593
file management, 585
project management, 585